CliffsNotes®

GMAT® with CD-ROM

by
BTPS Testing

Contributing Authors

Ed Kohn, M.S.

Joy Mondragon-Gilmore, Ph.D.

Karen Elizabeth Lafferty, Ph.D.

Jerry Bobrow, Ph.D.

Kyle Marion, B.A.

Mark Zegarelli, B.A.

Consultants

Ron Podrasky, M.S.

Pitt Gilmore, B.A.

Peter Z. Orton, Ph.D.

Mary Ellen Lepionka, M.A.

Andrea Markowitz, Ph.D.

Barbara Swovelin, M.A.

David A. Kay, M.S.

WILEY

John Wiley & Sons, Inc.

About the Author

BTPS Testing has presented test preparation workshops at the California State Universities for over 35 years. The faculty at BTPS Testing have authored more than 30 national best-selling test preparation books including CliffsNotes preparation guides for the GRE, CSET, SAT, CBEST, PPST, RICA and ACT. Each year the authors of this study guide conduct lectures to thousands of students preparing for the GMAT and many other graduate-level exams.

Author's Acknowledgment

We would like to thank Christina Stambaugh for her many hours of editing the original manuscript and her careful attention to the production process.

Editorial

Acquisition Editor: Greg Tubach

Project Editor: Christina Stambaugh

Copy Editor: Cate Schwenk

Technical Editors: Jane Burstein, Mary Jane Sterling, Tom Page

Composition

Proofreader: Kathy Simpson

John Wiley & Sons, Inc., Composition Services

CliffsNotes® GMAT® with CD-ROM

Published by:
John Wiley & Sons, Inc.
111 River Street
Hoboken, NJ 07030-5774
www.wiley.com

Copyright © 2013 John Wiley & Sons, Inc., Hoboken, NJ

Published by John Wiley & Sons, Inc., Hoboken, NJ
Published simultaneously in Canada

Library of Congress Control Number: 2012942056
ISBN: 978-1-118-07752-8 (pbk)
ISBN: 978-1-118-22269-0; 978-1-118-26156-9; 978-1-118-23656-7 (ebk)

Printed in the United States of America

10 9 8 7 6 5 4 3 2 1

This book is dedicated to the memory of

Jerry Bobrow, Ph.D.

Educator and Author

His wisdom, insight, and humor continue to give strength to those who knew him.

Table of Contents

PART III: ANALYTICAL WRITING ASSESSMENT SECTION

PART IV: VERBAL SECTION

PART V: QUANTITATIVE SECTION

PART VI: FULL-LENGTH PRACTICE TEST

Preface

CliffsNotes GMAT with CD-ROM is a comprehensive and easy to follow study guide that provides you with a positive, systematic learning experience to maximize your GMAT score. Exam-oriented approaches and practice material help you evaluate and analyze your strengths while providing you with valuable instructional tools to overcome your weaknesses. If you follow the lessons and strategies in this book and study regularly, you will deepen your understanding of GMAT analytical thinking concepts and question types to do well on the exam.

In keeping with the fine tradition of *CliffsNotes,* this guide was developed by leading experts in the field of test preparation and graduate school college entrance preparation. The authors of this text have been successfully teaching thousands of graduate business students to prepare for the GMAT for many years. The material, strategies, and techniques presented in this guide have been researched, tested, and evaluated in GMAT preparation classes at leading California universities. BTPS Testing is a leader in the field of graduate test preparation and continues to offer classes at many universities. This test-preparation guide uses materials developed for and practiced in these programs.

Navigating This Book

This study guide is designed to provide you with important information and the tools necessary for comprehensive and successful preparation. For optimal results, try to follow the recommended sequence of topics within each chapter and take detailed notes on the pages of the book to highlight important facts and concepts. Each chapter presents a review of subject matter material, and sample questions that are arranged by level of difficulty. Start in sequence with the easy questions first, and then work your way up through the difficult questions as you progress through the book.

After reading the introductory material, begin with the diagnostic test to assess your strengths and weaknesses. The diagnostic test will help you pinpoint any areas that may require more concentration and preparation time. Focus on specific areas to further develop your skills and awareness of GMAT test questions. Then continue to work through subsequent chapters, examining and reviewing each exam area, including question types, step-by-step instructions for solving problems, and up-to-date examples.

Once you have taken the diagnostic test and studied the exam areas, this guide provides you with extensive practice, including four full-length model practice tests (one practice test in the book and three additional practice tests on the accompanying CD-ROM). All four practice tests include answers with thorough explanations and sample essay responses. Finally, the last part of this book includes a checklist on page 512 as a reminder of "things to do" before you take your exam.

How This Book Is Organized

- **Introduction: An Overview of the GMAT:** This is a general description of the GMAT, test format, scoring, frequently asked questions, general strategies, and general tips.
- **Part I—Diagnostic Test:** An introductory diagnostic test acquaints you with GMAT question types, evaluates your areas of improvement, and provides you with a baseline starting point.
- **Parts II through V—Review of Exam Areas:** Review chapters focus on the abilities tested in the Integrated Reasoning, Analytical Writing, Verbal, and Quantitative sections, along with the basic skills and concepts you will need, directions, suggested strategies with samples, and additional tips.

  An intensive math skills review is at the end of Part V. It covers the basics of arithmetic, algebra, geometry, data analysis, data interpretation, and word problems. Each math review content area offers a diagnostic test, illustrated sample questions, and practice questions. Important symbols, terminology, and equivalents are also included.

  The review chapters are broken out by test section:

  - **Part II: Integrated Reasoning Section**—multi-source reasoning, table analysis, graphics interpretation, and two-part analysis
  - **Part III: Analytical Writing Assessment Section**—analysis of an argument

- **Part IV: Verbal Section**—sentence correction, reading comprehension, and critical reasoning
- **Part V: Quantitative Section**—problem solving and data sufficiency, along with the math skills review chapter
- **Part VI: Full-Length Practice Test**—One full-length practice test with answers and in-depth explanations. The practice test is followed by analysis worksheets to assist you in evaluating your progress.
- **CD-ROM:** The CD-ROM contains Practice Test 1 from the book, plus three additional full-length practice tests with answers and in-depth explanations. PDFs of the Introduction and the review chapters are also included on the CD.

Getting Started

Start your preparation by identifying question types, assessing your skills, reviewing test content material, understanding strategies, and practicing what you have learned. For optimal results, take detailed notes on the pages of this book to highlight important information.

Step 1—Awareness

Become familiar with the test—the test format, test directions, question types, test material, and scoring outlined in the Introduction or visit the GMAT website at www.mba.com.

Step 2—Assess Your Strengths and Weaknesses

Take the diagnostic test in Chapter 1 to assess your current level of understanding so that you can develop a study plan unique to your individual needs.

Step 3—Review Test Content and Question Types

Review the content and basic skills required for each section of the GMAT, and become familiar with the question types outlined in Parts II–V.

- The **Integrated Reasoning Section** (pages 57–96) tests your ability to interpret multiple sources of data (numeric and text) that represent real-life problems in business. You will be asked to solve four different question types: multi-source reasoning, table analysis, graphics interpretation, and two-part analysis.
- The **Analytical Writing Assessment** (pages 99–113) measures your ability to think critically, reason, and analyze an argument, and then to convincingly articulate and support complex ideas in a well-written essay. There is one writing task that appears on the exam—analysis of an argument.
- The **Verbal Section** tests your ability to read, evaluate, comprehend, and identify relationships in written material. Question types include sentence correction (pages 117–145), reading comprehension (pages 147–170), and critical reasoning (pages 171–197).
- The **Quantitative Section** tests your knowledge and application of math skills and concepts, and tests your ability to reason and solve problems in arithmetic, algebra, geometry, data analysis, data interpretation, and word problems. Questions may appear as math problem solving (pages 203–243) or data sufficiency (pages 244–284). Chapter 9, "Math Skills Review" (pages 285–439) is a comprehensive math review with practice questions that will help you to sharpen your quantitative skills.

Step 4—Learn Strategies and Techniques

Study the strategies outlined in the Introduction (pages 7–10) and decide which strategies work best for you. Remember that if it takes you longer to recall a strategy than to solve the problem, it's probably not a good strategy for you to adopt. The goal in offering strategies is for you to be able to work easily, quickly, and efficiently. Don't get stuck on any one question. Taking time to answer the most difficult question on the test correctly but losing valuable test time will not get you the score you deserve. Most important, remember that you must answer *every* question—even if you answer with only an educated guess.

Step 5—Practice, Practice, Practice

Research shows that repeated practice is one of the keys to your success on the GMAT. In addition to the sample practice problems in chapters 2 through 8, there is one full-length practice test starting on page 441. The accompanying CD-ROM includes the practice test from this book, plus three additional practice tests to help you benefit from a "computer-based practice experience." Be sure to practice in the format of the actual test as often as possible. To get a realistic sense of the actual test, take the online practice test using the GMAT software published by the Graduate Management Admission Council (GMAC) and Pearson VUE. This online simulated practice test is available for free at www.mba.com.

Introduction

An Overview of the GMAT

The Graduate Management Admission Test (GMAT) is a standardized computer-adaptive exam that is commonly administered and evaluated as part of the assessment process for admission to graduate business school. The GMAT is designed to evaluate skills that are important for the changing demands of the twenty-first century business student. The weighted degree of importance of the GMAT for admission varies widely by colleges and universities. In general, most graduate business programs use GMAT test results to assess readiness for graduate-level academic coursework and to predict academic performance.

The GMAT requires that you critically analyze, interpret, and apply your general abilities in four subject areas: Analytical Writing, Integrated Reasoning, Quantitative, and Verbal. Effective preparation begins with strategic learning. This is why you should begin your preparation immediately by contacting the university admissions office for more information about specific minimum score standards, application requirements, and admission deadlines.

Test Structure

Structure of the GMAT		
Content	**Question Type**	**Number of Questions**
Analytical Writing Assessment	Analysis of an Argument	One single essay **Time: 30 minutes**
Quantitative Section	Problem Solving Data Sufficiency *(questions intermingled)*	37 questions **Time: 75 minutes**
Verbal Section	Sentence Correction Reading Comprehension Critical Reasoning *(questions intermingled)*	41 questions **Time: 75 minutes**
Integrated Reasoning Section	Multi-Source Reasoning Table Analysis Graphics Interpretation Two-Part Analysis *(questions intermingled)*	12 questions **Time: 30 minutes**
Total Questions		**78 Multiple-Choice Questions 12 Integrated Reasoning Questions 1 Essay Writing Task**
Total Testing Time		**Approximately 3½ hours***

*Note: There are two optional five-minute breaks during the 3½-hour exam. Structure, scoring, and the order of sections are subject to change. Visit www.mba.com for updated exam information.

Scoring

The total GMAT *scaled score* report ranges from **200 to 800** (with 10-point increments) and is computed from separate subscores. The total scaled score reflects your overall performance on the combined equally weighted multiple-choice sections: Quantitative and Verbal. The Analytical Writing Assessment and Integrated Reasoning sections are scored independently.

Scaled scores determine your **percentile ranking** that business schools use to compare your score with other applicants. Percentiles are used to establish your "ranking" and determine how many test-takers scored higher, lower, or at the same level of your ability. The global GMAT average scale score is about 550 and is equivalent to approximately a 50th percentile ranking. The nation's top-ranked business schools have higher admission average scores that equate to a score greater than 700, or the 93rd percentile ranking. This example explains how a score of 700 can show that students who are accepted to the top-ranked business schools scored 93 percent higher than other candidates who took the GMAT. Since the range of admission score averages can vary depending upon the business school, it is best to start your preparation by contacting individual graduate programs to know the estimated score (and percentile) you will need for admission when combined with your GPA, work experience, letters of recommendation, and other admission criteria.

Conditions that determine GMAT scores are:

- the number of questions answered.
- the number of questions answered correctly.
- the difficulty of the questions answered.

Measure	Type of Questions	Score Range
Quantitative	Multiple-Choice	0 to 60 converted to a scaled score combined with the Verbal Section ranging from 200–800
Verbal	Multiple-Choice	0 to 60 converted to a scaled score combined with the Quantitative Section ranging from 200–800
Integrated Reasoning	Multiple-Choice	Score 1 to 8 (in single-digit intervals)
Analytical Writing Assessment	Essay: Analysis of an Argument	Score 0 to 6 averaged by two readers. The two final scores are totaled, averaged, and then rounded up to the nearest half-point to report one score from 0 to 6.

Multiple-Choice Adaptive Scoring

In the multiple-choice section, the Quantitative and Verbal questions are *computer adaptive*. The computer simulated multiple-choice questions appear one at a time and subsequent questions are produced based upon your performance of correct or incorrect responses. The first question is entirely random and has a difficulty level of "average." Each question that follows is matched to an ability level that is based on a computerized algorithm and adjusts based on the responses to previous questions. Test-takers are not necessarily presented with identical questions; rather questions are drawn from a large pool of master questions that have been categorized and calculated by content and level of difficulty. As the level of difficulty adjusts to your performance level, you will see more questions that are within your range of ability. This means that the computer adaptive system ultimately determines the selected questions.

Your final score is based upon the number of questions you answer correctly, so just try to do your best and answer every question to achieve your best possible overall results.

Analytical Writing Scoring

In the **Analytical Writing section,** one essay is scored holistically and receives a score from two independent readers. To be scored holistically means that readers look at the *overall quality* of the essay. One of the two readers may be an "automated electronic scoring engine" that analyzes your essay based upon structure, syntax, organization, language, and topic. Scores range from 0 to 6 (zero for off-topic or not in English), and the overall mean score is approximately between 4.0 and 4.5.

After each reader assigns a score to the essay, scores are added together, averaged, and then rounded up to the nearest half-point to produce a single final score. If there is a discrepancy of more than one point in the assigned scores from the two readers, a third (human) reader will read and evaluate your essay. The general scoring guidelines in the following table provide you with a brief analysis of criteria for your Analytical Writing essay score. For more information about scoring criteria read Chapter 3, "Introduction to Analytical Writing Assessment."

Analytical Writing Scoring Guide

Score 6 – Excellent Analysis

You will receive a score of 6 if your response . . .
- identifies specific aspects of the argument relevant to the task and examines them in an insightful way.
- reflects superior organization and logically develops ideas using clear transitions.
- provides relevant and thorough support from the argument.
- shows mastery of well-chosen vocabulary and varied sentences to convey complex ideas.
- demonstrates superior usage of the conventions of standard written English.

Score 5 – Strong Analysis

You will receive a score of 5 if your response . . .
- identifies the aspects of the argument relevant to the specific question and examines them in a thoughtful way.
- develops logical and organized ideas and connects them with suitable transitions.
- provides mostly relevant and complete support from the argument.
- uses appropriate vocabulary and sentence variety to convey ideas.
- demonstrates correct usage of the conventions of standard written English with occasional flaws.

Score 4 – Competent Analysis

You will receive a score of 4 if your response . . .
- identifies relevant and generally acceptable aspects of the required argument but also addresses some unrelated points.
- adequately develops the ideas clearly but may not connect them with transitions.
- provides some support from the argument but with uneven development.
- uses language to convey ideas in a generally clear way.
- demonstrates general control of the conventions of standard written English, but with some minor errors.

Score 3 – Flawed

You will receive a score of 3 if your response . . .
- shows some competence in examining the issue, but is generally flawed.
- fails to identify most of the relevant aspects of the argument.
- discusses unrelated points or presents poor reasoning.
- develops ideas in a limited or less logical way.
- provides support that is less relevant to the argument.
- uses language in an unclear way.
- demonstrates major errors or frequent minor errors in conventions of standard written English.

Score 2 – Weak

You will receive a score of 2 if your response . . .
- fails to respond to the directions for the task and/or shows weakness in examining the issue.
- does not identify the relevant aspects of the argument but instead presents your opinion on the issue.
- fails to develop ideas or organize them logically.
- provides little or no support.
- contains serious flaws in the conventions of standard written English that make the meaning unclear.

Score 1 – Deficient

You will receive a score of 1 if your response . . .
- reveals basic deficiencies in analytical writing.
- shows little or no understanding of the argument.
- is short, disorganized, and incoherent.
- uses language in a way that prevents understanding.
- is incoherent and contains serious, frequent errors in conventions of standard written English.

continued

Score 0

You will receive a score of 0 if your response . . .

❏ is completely off topic and does not respond to the writing task.

❏ is written in a foreign language.

❏ consists of random keystrokes.

No Score

You will receive a score of NR if your response . . .

❏ is blank.

Essay Originality

Analytical Writing Assessment essays must clearly express your original thoughts, ideas, and perspectives, not those of others. If GMAT readers detect that your essay is not original work, or if the written assignment has been taken from another source, and does not reflect independent intellectual thinking, GMAC reserves the right to cancel your score.

Integrated Reasoning Scoring

The Integrated Reasoning section, just like the Analytical Writing section, is not computer-adaptive and is scored independently from your overall score on the multiple-choice sections. This section computes a *raw score* that is based on the number of questions you answer correctly to a *scaled score*. Scores range from 1 to 8 with 1-point intervals and the overall mean is approximately 4.5 to 5.0. The scaled score is equated and converted into a percentile rank that many graduate programs use to compare your score results with those of other applicants. A score of 1.0 reflects difficulty in performing reasoning tasks that require analysis and manipulation of multiple sources of data. A score of 8.0, on the other hand, demonstrates a depth of understanding in analyzing and responding to complex sources of data. Integrated Reasoning questions contain "multiple parts." You must answer all parts of each question correctly to receive credit for a correct response. No partial credit is given.

Taking the Computer-Based GMAT

The GMAT is offered by computer in the United States, Canada, and many other countries. If you live outside the United States, check the official GMAT website at www.mba.com to see if the computer-based test is used in your area.

Computer-adaptive testing means that the Verbal and Quantitative sections each begin with an average difficulty question. Each subsequent question varies in difficulty based on the response from the previous question. The questions that you will receive are chosen from a large pool of questions that have been categorized by level of difficulty and content. As the level of questions adjusts to your ability level, you will receive more questions that are within your ability range. This "adaptive" system ultimately determines your questions. After you have answered a question and moved to the next screen, you cannot return to a previous question.

Because the GMAT is a computer-adaptive test, once you have worked through the review chapters of this book, it is important to practice test questions that simulate a computerized exam. This is why we have provided you with computer practice on the accompanying CD-ROM at the end of this book. You can also download free official practice tests at http://www.mba.com/the-gmat/download-free-test-preparation-software.aspx.

Advantages of Computer Testing

- Numerous test dates are available each week because appointments can be scheduled year-round.
- Your scores are available immediately for the multiple-choice sections: Verbal and Quantitative.
- Answers recorded electronically can reduce the chance of human error in posting written responses.

- Computer-friendly functions—a word processing program to write your Analytical Writing essay that has the ability to edit material (cut, paste, undo); use of an on-screen calculator for the Integrated Reasoning section; and the ability to answer multiple-choice questions with the click of your mouse.

Using a Calculator on the GMAT Integrated Reasoning Section

A simple four-function on-screen calculator is available to help you perform simple computations on the Integrated Reasoning section. (Remember: No calculator is available for the Quantitative section.) The calculator will look something like this:

```
Calculator                                            x
 ┌───────────────────────────────────────────────────┐
 │                                                     │
 ├────────┬─────────────┬────────────┬────────────────┤
 │        │  Backspace  │     CE     │       C        │
 ├────────┼───┬───┬───┬───┬──────┤
 │  MC    │ 7 │ 8 │ 9 │ / │ sqrt │
 │  MR    │ 4 │ 5 │ 6 │ * │  %   │
 │  MS    │ 1 │ 2 │ 3 │ - │ 1/x  │
 │  M+    │ 0 │+/-│ . │ + │  =   │
 └────────┴───┴───┴───┴───┴──────┘
 Click on buttons, or click in answer window to use keyboard
```

Here are a few on-screen calculator tips:

Time-Consuming Problems—Although the calculator will help you save time performing lengthy handwritten calculations, you must have a basic knowledge of math problem solving to be able to determine if your calculation results make logical sense. The general rule of thumb is that you should only use the on-screen calculator for time-consuming computations (i.e., problems with several digits). Use your time wisely to quickly determine if a problem appears to be easy to solve mentally. Keep in mind that if you use the on-screen calculator for every Integrated Reasoning question, you may not be able to complete the Integrated Reasoning section in the allotted time.

Basic Functions—Using your keyboard and mouse, you will be able to move the image of the on-screen calculator to any location on the screen. The on-screen calculator can perform the basic functions of addition, subtraction, multiplication, division, parentheses, and square roots.

Practice Before the Exam Date—To help you become familiar with the on-screen calculator, use a calculator similar to the on-screen computerized calculator while practicing sample problems from this book. The TI-108 (Texas Instruments 108) calculator has functions that are similar to the on-screen calculator. Familiarize yourself with the best keystrokes to accomplish certain math tasks as you work through sample problems.

Frequently Asked Questions

Q. Where do I apply to take the GMAT?

A. Under the direction of the Graduate Management Admission Council (GMAC), the GMAT is administered by Pearson VUE, www.mba.com, P.O. Box 581907, Minneapolis, MN 55458-1907.

Americas: phone (toll-free within the United States): (800) 717-GMAT (4628) or (952) 681-3680; toll-free for Canadian test sites: +1 (866) 442-GMAT (4628)

Asia Pacific: phone 603 8318 9961, India: phone +91 120 439 7830

China: phone +86-10-82345675

Europe/Middle East/Africa: phone +44 (0) 161 855 7219

Q. When is the computer-adaptive GMAT exam given?

A. The computer-adaptive GMAT is offered weekdays and year-round throughout the world, but testing hours may vary depending on the location. You should schedule your GMAT appointment early to get your preferred time, date, and location. During the peak season (September–December), it is suggested that you call at least two months in advance to reserve your preferred test date. Walk-in appointments are *not* available. You must call to reserve you appointment at least 24 hours in advance. To find a location near you, visit www.mba.com/testcenterlist.

Q. How is my GMAT score used?

A. Your GMAT score is used as part of an assessment of your probable academic success in graduate business school. Other factors, such as undergraduate grades (GPA), work experience, your interview, essays, and letters of recommendation, also figure into the admission application process. The importance of GMAT scores varies from school to school.

Q. Which test should I take (GMAT or GRE)?

A. The GMAT is a widely recognized standardized test for graduate business school programs. The school(s) you apply to will influence which exam to take. Start by calling the graduate business department where you would like to complete your coursework. Although the GRE is now accepted by many MBA programs, it is wise to check with the graduate department for specific requirements because some graduate business school advisors believe that the GMAT may hold more weight with the admission committee.

Q. What are the additional requirements for international students?

A. Many international students from Europe, the Middle East, Asia, and the Americas study in graduate business programs in the United States. In general, if your native language is not English or if you hold a degree from a university that did not provide instruction in English, most schools require a minimum TOEFL (Test of English as a Foreign Language) passing score to show proficiency in verbal and written English. For example, TOEFL Internet-based format (score of 80 to 100), TOEFL paper-and-pencil format (score of 550 to 600), and TOEFL computer-based format (score of 213 to 250). Some universities may accept the International English Language Testing System (IELTS) test results in lieu of the TOEFL, but it is important to check with individual schools regarding minimum score requirements.

Another general requirement is that you must complete a Certificate of Eligibility (I-20) from the school you would like to attend after you have proof of financial support, and apply for a Student Visa (F-1) to continue your graduate education in the United States.

An excellent English resource for additional GMAT review and practice is *CliffsNotes Verbal Review for Standardized Tests* by Dr. Deborah Covino.

Q. What computer skills are necessary to take the GMAT?

A. The GMAT requires limited computer skills that include the use of a mouse, keyboard, and an elementary word processing program. The Analytical Writing Assessment section uses a word processing program that includes basic functions: insert, delete, cut and paste, and undo (previous action). Be sure to take the online practice test at www.mba.com to have the experience of using these computer skills.

Q. When will I receive my scores?

A. You can view your unofficial score report for the multiple-choice sections immediately after you finish the exam. Your complete official score report can be retrieved online or mailed approximately 20 days after the testing date.

Q. What is the process for taking the test?

A. You should arrive at the testing center with valid, original photo identification at least 30 minutes prior to your exam. When you check in, you will be asked to have your photograph taken and a to supply a "palm vein pattern" (except where prohibited). You must store any personal items in a locker, including your purse, cell phone, watch, drinks, and food. A noteboard (erasable writing board) will be provided. You will sign an agreement and be directed to a private computer workstation.

The test is approximately $3\frac{1}{2}$ hours, including two scheduled, but optional, 5-minute breaks. Expect to be at the test center about $4\frac{1}{2}$ hours total to allow for early arrival and documentation validation. If you need additional breaks, raise your hand and time will be deducted from the test time allowed.

Q. Should I guess on the GMAT?

A. Yes. If you get stuck on a question or simply don't know the answer, guess. It is in your best interest to take an educated guess on each question since the computer-adaptive GMAT requires that you answer every question. Questions that are left blank will be scored as incorrect responses.

Q. How long is a GMAT score valid?

A. A GMAT score is valid for five years after the test date.

Q. Can I take the GMAT more than one time?

A. Yes. You may take the exam once per calendar month (31 days), but no more than five times per year (12 calendar months). Contact the school(s) to which you are applying for individual admission regulations regarding retaking the GMAT.

Q. Can I cancel my GMAT scores?

A. Yes. You can only cancel your scores on the day of your exam at the test center, but you cannot view your scores before canceling them. Note that score cancellations are permanent and will appear on future score reporting records. If you choose to cancel your scores, you will *not* receive a refund.

General Tips and Strategies

Test-taking strategies can give you the edge you may need to complete the GMAT with greater ease and confidence. The multiple-choice questions cover a broad range of topics while considering a variety of question types. To be successful on the exam, you need to recall basic facts and major concepts in math and English. The facts and concepts on the GMAT are often presented in subtle variations of selected answer choices that make it difficult for test-takers to narrow down the correct answer. Additionally, subtle variations in answer choices can distract you from choosing the correct answer.

This section was developed as a guide to introduce general test-taking guidelines, approaches, and strategies that are useful on the GMAT and many other standardized exams. Although this section is limited to general tips and strategies, specific strategies related to *specific subject area question types* are included in the seven review chapters.

As you practice problems using the strategies outlined in this section, determine if the strategies are compatible with your individual learning style. What may work for some people, may not work for others. If it takes you longer to recall a strategy than to solve the problem, it's probably not a good strategy for you to adopt. The goal in offering you strategies is for you to be able to work through problems quickly, accurately, and efficiently. And remember, don't get stuck on any one question—keep moving. Taking time to answer the most difficult question on the test correctly, but losing valuable test time won't get you the score you deserve. More important, remember to answer *every* question on the test.

Consider the following guidelines when taking the exam:

- **Manage your time wisely.** When you begin the exam, keep track of the time indicated on the computer screen. Try to spend no more than $1\frac{3}{4}$ minutes on any one question. Remember there are 37 Quantitative questions (75 minutes) and 41 Verbal questions (75 minutes). The Integrated Reasoning section has 12 questions (30 minutes), but the questions contain multiple parts so try to limit your time to less than 1 minute for each part of the question because you must read, analyze, and respond to 2, 3, or 4 parts in each question. With sufficient practice, you will almost automatically know when a question is taking you too long to answer.

- **Don't get stuck.** In the first five questions within each section, it is worth taking the time (within reason) to do your very best to answer the questions correctly. If time is tight later in the section, you can narrow down your choices and take an educated guess rather than spending an inordinate amount of time on a question. Many people who take standardized tests don't get the score they could achieve because they spend too much time dwelling on a single question, leaving insufficient time to answer other questions they could get right. Keep in mind that the GMAT requires that you answer every question, and time is limited so it is helpful to have a strategy that drives you forward *before* the day of your exam.

- **Read each question carefully.** Do not make a hasty assumption that you know the correct answer without reading the whole question and all the possible answers. The hurried test-taker commonly selects an incorrect answer when jumping to a conclusion after reading only one or two of the answer choices. Note that some of the answer choices only show a "part" of the correct answer. You must look at the entire list of answer choices in order to select the *best* answer.

- **Click (or fill in) the correct answer.** Be very careful that your responses match your intended response. When answering questions quickly, it is common to click the wrong answer choice by mistake.

- **Be on alert for the "attractive distractor" answer choice.** Watch out for answers that look good, but are not the best answer choice. Attractive distractor answer choices are carefully crafted to be *close to the best* answer, but there is never more than one right answer. When you narrow down your choice to two answers, one is probably the attractive distractor. If this happens, read the question again and take an educated guess.

- **Be on alert for "negative questions."** Another common mistake is misreading a question that includes negative words such as *except* and *not*. *A negative question* reverses the meaning of the question and asks for the opposite to be true in order to select the correct answer. Negative questions can initially be confusing and challenge your thinking. It is helpful to write down brief notes to avoid misreading a question (and therefore answering it incorrectly). Simply *write down* what you must answer in the question. To help answer a negative question, treat the answer choices as *true* or *false* statements, searching for the answer that is *false.*

General Approaches to the Multiple-Choice Questions

The Elimination Approach

For the computer-adaptive GMAT, when you can eliminate one or more choices, the statistical odds of answering the question correctly will significantly increase. Try to eliminate answer choices from consideration and make an educated guess on the remaining answer choices whenever possible. Use the erasable noteboard provided to keep track of the choices you have eliminated. Quickly write down the position of the wrong answer choices (with a diagonal line through them) to prevent you from spending too much time mulling over the possible choices. Keep in mind that the answer choices on the actual computer exam are not numbered or lettered, but you can number or letter the position on your noteboard to keep track of incorrect answer choices.

For example, if you know that answer choices A, C, and D (or positions 1, 3, and 4 on the list) are incorrect, write down the letters A, C, and D with diagonal lines through them. It should only take a few seconds to use this strategy to narrow down your choices.

In the example below, notice that some choices are crossed out with diagonal lines and some choices are marked with question marks, signifying that they may be possible answers. Using question marks will help signify that these choices are possible answers. Either of these methods will help you narrow down your possible answers. Remember to keep this marking system very simple because your time is limited.

A̶.

? B.

C̶.

D̶.

? E.

The Multiple-Multiple-Choice Approach

Some questions use a "multiple-multiple-choice" format. This type of question gives you answers marked with Roman numbers (I, II, III) and the task is to determine if one, two, or possibly all three of the choices are correct statements. At first glance, these questions appear more confusing and more difficult than normal five-choice, multiple-choice questions. Actually, once you understand the "multiple-multiple-choice" question type, these questions are often *easier* than comparable standard multiple-choice questions. "Multiple-multiple choice" questions can appear in these question types:

Quantitative: Problem solving questions

Verbal: Reading comprehension questions

Verbal: Critical reasoning questions

Multiple-Multiple Question Format

I.   Statement
II. Statement } Consider each statement as true or false.
III. Statement

○ I and II only
○ II and III only
○ II only } Answer choices vary with each question.
○ III only
○ I, II, and III

Follow these steps to solve multiple-multiple choice problems.

1. Consider each statement (I, II, or II) as a *true* or *false* statement.

2. Write I, II, and III on your noteboard. Look at all of the statements and eliminate (cross out with a diagonal line) statements that are *false*. If you prefer, write an F next to *false* statements, or a T next to *true* statements.

   I̶. or   I. F
   II. or   II. T
   III̶. or   III. F

3. Look at the remaining statements in the answer choices to determine the correct answer. In the example above, only statement II is true. Therefore, the second choice is the only possible correct answer.

○ I only
○ II only
○ III only
○ I and II only
○ I, II, and III

In the following example, look for the statement(s) that are *true* to solve the problem, following the steps detailed above.

If x is a positive integer, then which of the following must be true?

  I. $x > 0$
  II. $x = 0$
 III. $x < 1$

○ I only
○ II only
○ III only
○ I and II only
○ I and III only

---

1. You may immediately recognize that x is a positive integer, so it must be a counting number. Note that possible values of x could be 1, 2, 3, or 4, and so on. Therefore, statement I, $x > 0$, is always *true*. Knowing that the final answer *must* contain statement I, $x > 0$, you can eliminate (cross out) the second and third choices.

○ I only
∅ II only
∅ III only
○ I and II only
○ I and III only

2. Now that you have determined that statement I is true, look at statement II to determine if it is true or false. Statement II is incorrect, and therefore *false*. If x is positive, x cannot equal 0. Knowing that statement II is false allows you to eliminate the fourth choice. Only the second and fifth choices are left as possible correct answers.

3. Finally, determine if statement III is true or false. Statement III is also false, as x must be 1 or greater, therefore, you can cross out statement III, thus eliminating the fifth choice. The correct answer is the first choice, because only statement I is *true*.

PART I

DIAGNOSTIC TEST

Answers and explanations for the Diagnostic Test can be found on pages 37–54.

This section contains a shortened GMAT diagnostic test designed to introduce you to the question types. While this diagnostic test does not adapt (as the computer-adaptive test does) based upon your right or wrong answers, you will gain valuable insight into your strengths and weaknesses. The diagnostic test is followed by answers, complete explanations, and analysis techniques to help you to pinpoint any areas that may require more preparation time.

The actual GMAT is copyrighted and may not be duplicated; these questions are not taken directly from actual tests. When taking this diagnostic test, try to simulate the test conditions. Budget your time effectively, and if you need a break, stop the clock and take a 10-minute break after the second section.

After you have completed the diagnostic test, work through subsequent chapters, examining the comprehensive analysis and review chapters of each exam area including question types, step-by-step instructions, and practice questions.

> Section 1: Analytical Writing Assessment – Analysis of an Argument
> Section 2: Quantitative
> Section 3: Verbal
> Section 4: Integrated Reasoning

Chapter 1

Diagnostic Test

Section 1: Analytical Writing Assessment—Analysis of an Argument

Time: 30 minutes
1 Essay

Directions: This section will require you to critique the argument given. Note that you are NOT being asked to present your own viewpoint. Questioning the underlying assumptions, finding alternative explanations or counterexamples, and delineating evidence to strengthen or weaken an argument are some possible approaches.

Your response will be evaluated for its overall quality, based on how well you:

- respond to the specific instructions.
- organize, develop, and communicate your ideas.
- support your evaluation with relevant reasons and/or examples.
- use standard written English.

It is important to simulate the actual computer-adaptive exam; therefore, it is recommended that you type your response on your home computer. Before you begin writing, you may want to think for a few minutes about the passage and instructions, and then plan your response by prewriting on scratch paper. Be sure to develop your evaluation fully and organize it coherently, but leave time to reread what you have written and make any revisions you think are necessary.

Argument Topic

The following appeared in a magazine article on career development:

> "When describing their ideal next position, many employment seekers try to balance a variety of personal and professional factors. Personal factors are varied and often include considerations such as 'how well I'll fit in with the work environment' and 'whether my new workmates might make good friends.' This concern is a fundamental error that severely distracts from the task at hand: finding a job that pays well and advances your career. I tell all my clients: Look for a job that pays you what you're worth—or more, if possible—then show up, work hard, and be professional. Save personal considerations for your family and friends—that's where they're appropriate."

Write a critique of the argument. Your essay should consider its line of reasoning and how well it uses evidence. You should consider what doubtful assumptions undermine the reasoning, and consider what other evidence might support or weaken the argument. Your essay may also consider how the argument could be made more persuasive and its conclusion more convincing.

IF YOU FINISH BEFORE TIME IS CALLED, CHECK YOUR WORK ON THIS SECTION ONLY. DO NOT WORK ON ANY OTHER SECTION IN THE TEST.

Section 2: Quantitative

The answer choices for multiple-choice questions on the actual computer version of the GMAT are not labeled with letters. Answer choices in this study guide have lettered choices A, B, C, D, and E for clarity. On the actual exam, you will be required to click on the appropriate oval to select your answer.

Time: 35 Minutes
20 Questions

General Directions: Your score on the Quantitative section will be based on how well you do on the questions presented and on the number of questions you answer. You should try to pace yourself so that you have sufficient time to consider every question. If possible, answer all 20 questions in this section and guess if necessary. Select the best answer choice for each question. Use a blank sheet of paper to record your answers. Use scratch paper for any necessary calculations.

Note: Some problems may be accompanied by figures or diagrams. These figures are drawn as accurately as possible except when it is stated in a specific problem that the *figure is not drawn to scale.* The figure is meant to provide information useful in solving the problem. Unless otherwise stated or indicated, all figures lie in a plane and angle measures are greater than zero. All numbers used are real numbers.

Data Sufficiency Directions: Each of the data sufficiency questions below consists of a question and two statements, labeled (1) and (2), in which certain data are given. You must decide whether the data given in the statements are *sufficient* to answer the question. Using the data given in the statements plus your knowledge of mathematics and everyday facts (such as the number of days in July or the meaning of *counterclockwise*), choose the best answer choice.

    Ⓐ Statement (1) ALONE is sufficient, but statement (2) alone is not sufficient to answer the question asked.

    Ⓑ Statement (2) ALONE is sufficient, but statement (1) alone is not sufficient to answer the question asked.

    Ⓒ BOTH statements (1) and (2) TOGETHER are sufficient to answer the question asked, but NEITHER statement ALONE is sufficient.

    Ⓓ EACH statement ALONE is sufficient to answer the question asked.

    Ⓔ Statements (1) and (2) TOGETHER are NOT sufficient to answer the question asked, and additional data specific to the problem are needed.

Problem Solving Directions: Answer each problem-solving question in this section by using the information given and your own mathematical calculations. Then select the correct answer of the five choices given.

---

1. Bob weighs 183 pounds. Maria weighs 110 pounds. Approximately what percent of Bob's weight is Maria's weight?

    Ⓐ 50%
    Ⓑ 60%
    Ⓒ 70%
    Ⓓ 80%
    Ⓔ 90%

2. In the $\triangle ABC$ figure below, $AC = 16$, $AB = 34$, and $\overline{AC} \perp \overline{BC}$. What is the area of $\triangle ABC$ in square units?

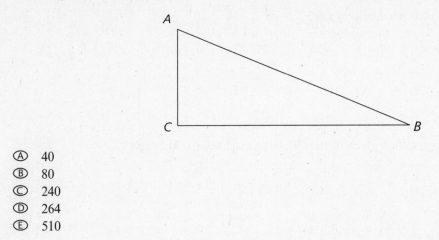

   Ⓐ   40
   Ⓑ   80
   Ⓒ   240
   Ⓓ   264
   Ⓔ   510

3. Is $a > b$?

(1) $a^2 > b^2$
(2) $a < 0$ and $b < 0$

   Ⓐ   Statement (1) ALONE is sufficient, but statement (2) alone is not sufficient to answer the question asked.
   Ⓑ   Statement (2) ALONE is sufficient, but statement (1) alone is not sufficient to answer the question asked.
   Ⓒ   BOTH statements (1) and (2) TOGETHER are sufficient to answer the question asked, but NEITHER statement ALONE is sufficient.
   Ⓓ   EACH statement ALONE is sufficient to answer the question asked.
   Ⓔ   Statements (1) and (2) TOGETHER are NOT sufficient to answer the question asked, and additional data specific to the problem are needed.

4. What is the area of trapezoid $ABCD$ below if $\angle A = 45°$ and $\angle D = 30°$?

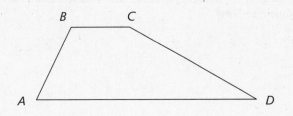

(1) $BC = 8$ and $CD = 12$
(2) $AB = 6\sqrt{2}$ and $CD = 12$

   Ⓐ   Statement (1) ALONE is sufficient, but statement (2) alone is not sufficient to answer the question asked.
   Ⓑ   Statement (2) ALONE is sufficient, but statement (1) alone is not sufficient to answer the question asked.
   Ⓒ   BOTH statements (1) and (2) TOGETHER are sufficient to answer the question asked, but NEITHER statement ALONE is sufficient.
   Ⓓ   EACH statement ALONE is sufficient to answer the question asked.
   Ⓔ   Statements (1) and (2) TOGETHER are NOT sufficient to answer the question asked, and additional data specific to the problem are needed.

5. A 6-quart saltwater mixture that is $\frac{2}{3}$ water is mixed with an 8-quart saltwater mixture that is $\frac{3}{4}$ water. The final mixture is approximately what percent salt?

- Ⓐ 30%
- Ⓑ 40%
- Ⓒ 50%
- Ⓓ 60%
- Ⓔ 70%

6. If a, b, and c are odd integers, then which of the following must be an odd integer?

- Ⓐ $4a + 5b + 6c$
- Ⓑ $3a - 4b - 5c$
- Ⓒ $a^2 + 2b^2 + 3c^2$
- Ⓓ $2a^2 + 4b^2 + 6c^2$
- Ⓔ $(a + 1)^2 + (2b)^2 + (a + 3)^2$

7. What is the probability of selecting a red ball out of 20 balls?

   (1)   12 balls are not red.
   (2)   There are 3 green balls and 9 yellow balls.

- Ⓐ Statement (1) ALONE is sufficient, but statement (2) alone is not sufficient to answer the question asked.
- Ⓑ Statement (2) ALONE is sufficient, but statement (1) alone is not sufficient to answer the question asked.
- Ⓒ BOTH statements (1) and (2) TOGETHER are sufficient to answer the question asked, but NEITHER statement ALONE is sufficient.
- Ⓓ EACH statement ALONE is sufficient to answer the question asked.
- Ⓔ Statements (1) and (2) TOGETHER are NOT sufficient to answer the question asked, and additional data specific to the problem are needed.

8. The average (arithmetic mean) of six numbers is 20. If the average of two of those numbers is 26, what is the average of the other four numbers?

- Ⓐ 14
- Ⓑ 17
- Ⓒ 30
- Ⓓ 52
- Ⓔ 68

9. If x and y are integers, is $(x + 2y)^2 - (2x + y)^2$ divisible by 6?

   (1) $x - y$ is an even integer
   (2) xy is an odd integer

- Ⓐ Statement (1) ALONE is sufficient, but statement (2) alone is not sufficient to answer the question asked.
- Ⓑ Statement (2) ALONE is sufficient, but statement (1) alone is not sufficient to answer the question asked.
- Ⓒ BOTH statements (1) and (2) TOGETHER are sufficient to answer the question asked, but NEITHER statement ALONE is sufficient.
- Ⓓ EACH statement ALONE is sufficient to answer the question asked.
- Ⓔ Statements (1) and (2) TOGETHER are NOT sufficient to answer the question asked, and additional data specific to the problem are needed.

10. In the figure below, points A, B, C, and D are points on the circle. Point E is the intersection of $\overline{AC}$ and $\overline{BD}$. $\overset{\frown}{AB} = 112°$. What is the measure of $\angle ACD$?

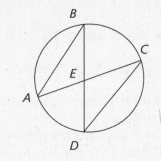

   Ⓐ   34°

   Ⓑ   36°

   Ⓒ   56°

   Ⓓ   68°

   Ⓔ   Cannot be determined from the given information.

11. In the equation $5w - 10v + z = 25$, what is the value of z?

   (1) $w + z = 7$

   (2) $w - 2v = 6$

   Ⓐ   Statement (1) ALONE is sufficient, but statement (2) alone is not sufficient to answer the question asked.

   Ⓑ   Statement (2) ALONE is sufficient, but statement (1) alone is not sufficient to answer the question asked.

   Ⓒ   BOTH statements (1) and (2) TOGETHER are sufficient to answer the question asked, but NEITHER statement ALONE is sufficient.

   Ⓓ   EACH statement ALONE is sufficient to answer the question asked.

   Ⓔ   Statements (1) and (2) TOGETHER are NOT sufficient to answer the question asked, and additional data specific to the problem are needed.

12. Is $x > y$?

   (1) x is the standard deviation of a set of six different integers, each of which is between 0 and 10.

   (2) y is the standard deviation of a set of six different integers, each of which is between 10 and 20.

   Ⓐ   Statement (1) ALONE is sufficient, but statement (2) alone is not sufficient to answer the question asked.

   Ⓑ   Statement (2) ALONE is sufficient, but statement (1) alone is not sufficient to answer the question asked.

   Ⓒ   BOTH statements (1) and (2) TOGETHER are sufficient to answer the question asked, but NEITHER statement ALONE is sufficient.

   Ⓓ   EACH statement ALONE is sufficient to answer the question asked.

   Ⓔ   Statements (1) and (2) TOGETHER are NOT sufficient to answer the question asked, and additional data specific to the problem are needed.

13. Is $x + 2y > 12$?

    (1) $x > 12$

    (2) $4x + 8y < 30$

    Ⓐ   Statement (1) ALONE is sufficient, but statement (2) alone is not sufficient to answer the question asked.

    Ⓑ   Statement (2) ALONE is sufficient, but statement (1) alone is not sufficient to answer the question asked.

    Ⓒ   BOTH statements (1) and (2) TOGETHER are sufficient to answer the question asked, but NEITHER statement ALONE is sufficient.

    Ⓓ   EACH statement ALONE is sufficient to answer the question asked.

    Ⓔ   Statements (1) and (2) TOGETHER are NOT sufficient to answer the question asked, and additional data specific to the problem are needed.

14. The chart below has some information regarding employees at Harvest Factory.

	Young Adults	Mature Adults	TOTAL
Males			
Females			720
TOTAL	600		

If $\frac{3}{4}$ of the male employees and $\frac{1}{5}$ of the female employees are mature adults, what is the probability that an employee selected at random from this factory will be a mature adult male?

    Ⓐ   Less than 5%

    Ⓑ   More than 5% but less than 7%

    Ⓒ   More than 7% but less than 9%

    Ⓓ   More than 9%

    Ⓔ   Cannot be determined from the information given.

15. How much money did Paul invest in stocks?

    (1)   Paul invested only in stocks, bonds, and real estate in the ratio of 3:4:5, respectively.

    (2)   Paul's investments in bonds and real estate total $360,000.

    Ⓐ   Statement (1) ALONE is sufficient, but statement (2) alone is not sufficient to answer the question asked.

    Ⓑ   Statement (2) ALONE is sufficient, but statement (1) alone is not sufficient to answer the question asked.

    Ⓒ   BOTH statements (1) and (2) TOGETHER are sufficient to answer the question asked, but NEITHER statement ALONE is sufficient.

    Ⓓ   EACH statement ALONE is sufficient to answer the question asked.

    Ⓔ   Statements (1) and (2) TOGETHER are NOT sufficient to answer the question asked, and additional data specific to the problem are needed.

16. A person will drive from point A to point B at an average rate of x miles per hour, then walk from point B to point C at an average rate of y miles per hour. If a total of t hours was spent traveling, and $\frac{2}{3}$ of that time was spent walking, what was the person's average rate for the combined trips?

(A) $\dfrac{x+2y}{t} \dfrac{\text{mi}}{\text{hr}}$

(B) $\dfrac{2x+y}{t} \dfrac{\text{mi}}{\text{hr}}$

(C) $\dfrac{2x+y}{3t} \dfrac{\text{mi}}{\text{hr}}$

(D) $\dfrac{x+2y}{3t} \dfrac{\text{mi}}{\text{hr}}$

(E) $\dfrac{x+2y}{3} \dfrac{\text{mi}}{\text{hr}}$

17. According to the graph below, how many students received a grade of D in the class?

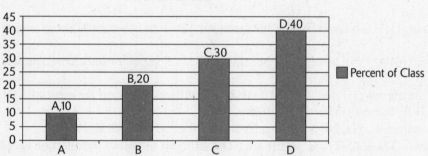

Percent of Class

(1) 60 students received a grade of A.

(2) 60 more people received a grade of C than received a grade of B.

(A) Statement (1) ALONE is sufficient, but statement (2) alone is not sufficient to answer the question asked.

(B) Statement (2) ALONE is sufficient, but statement (1) alone is not sufficient to answer the question asked.

(C) BOTH statements (1) and (2) TOGETHER are sufficient to answer the question asked, but NEITHER statement ALONE is sufficient.

(D) EACH statement ALONE is sufficient to answer the question asked.

(E) Statements (1) and (2) TOGETHER are NOT sufficient to answer the question asked, and additional data specific to the problem are needed.

18. If $x^{\#} = (x + 1)(x - 1)$, then what is $(5^{\#})^{\#}$?

(A) 20

(B) 24

(C) 575

(D) 576

(E) 600

19. All the integers 1 through 5 are written in a row on separate index cards, with each index card *containing* all 5 integers, but not necessarily in number order. The set of index cards *contains* every possible arrangement of the 5 integers. If one index card is randomly selected from this set of index cards, what is the probability it will *contain* the first two integers as consecutive integers when reading them from left to right?

(A) $\frac{1}{5}$

(B) $\frac{1}{4}$

(C) $\frac{1}{6}$

(D) $\frac{1}{24}$

(E) $\frac{1}{120}$

20. If x and y are integers, what is the value of $x + y$?

(1) $-3 \leq x \leq y \leq 0$
(2) $x = 2y$

(A) Statement (1) ALONE is sufficient, but statement (2) alone is not sufficient to answer the question asked.
(B) Statement (2) ALONE is sufficient, but statement (1) alone is not sufficient to answer the question asked.
(C) BOTH statements (1) and (2) TOGETHER are sufficient to answer the question asked, but NEITHER statement ALONE is sufficient.
(D) EACH statement ALONE is sufficient to answer the question asked.
(E) Statements (1) and (2) TOGETHER are NOT sufficient to answer the question asked, and additional data specific to the problem are needed.

IF YOU FINISH BEFORE TIME IS CALLED, CHECK YOUR WORK ON THIS SECTION ONLY. DO NOT WORK ON ANY OTHER SECTION IN THE TEST.

Section 3: Verbal

Time: 40 Minutes
20 Questions

General Directions: Your score on the Verbal section will be based on how well you do on the questions presented and also on the number of questions you answer. Try to pace yourself so that you have sufficient time to consider every question. If possible, answer all 20 questions in this section. Guess if you need to. Select the best answer choice for each question. Use a blank sheet of paper to record your answers. You will encounter three kinds of questions in this section: sentence correction, reading comprehension, and critical reasoning.

Sentence Correction Directions: For questions 1–7 (sentence correction questions), some part of each sentence is underlined; sometimes the whole sentence is underlined. Five choices for rephrasing the underlined part follow each sentence; the first choice repeats the original, and the other four are different. If the first choice seems better than the alternatives, choose that answer; if not, choose one of the others.

For each sentence, consider the requirements of standard written English. Your choice should be a correct and effective expression, not awkward or ambiguous. Focus on grammar, word choice, sentence construction, and punctuation. If a choice changes the meaning of the original sentence, do not select it.

1. Already having been detected in fabrications of the truth that could have warranted even more extreme consequences, <u>the judge gave the witness a stern warning that any similar behavior in the future would be charged with contempt of court</u>.

   Ⓐ the judge gave the witness a stern warning that any similar behavior in the future would be charged with contempt of court
   Ⓑ the judge gave the witness a stern warning that he would be charged with contempt of court for any similar behavior in the future
   Ⓒ the witness received a stern warning from the judge that any similar behavior in the future would be charged with contempt of court
   Ⓓ the witness received a stern warning from the judge that any similar behavior in the future would be treated as contempt of court
   Ⓔ charging the witness with contempt of court was the stern warning that the judge gave regarding any similar behavior in the future

2. The social worker, the physician on call, and, most important, both parents of the patient <u>has agreed upon the same course of treatment that the nurse was in suggestion of three days ago</u>.

   Ⓐ has agreed upon the same course of treatment that the nurse was in suggestion of three days ago
   Ⓑ have agreed upon the same course of treatment that the nurse suggested three days ago
   Ⓒ is in agreement as to the same course of treatment that the nurse had suggested three days ago
   Ⓓ are agreeing upon the same course of treatment suggested by the nurse three days ago
   Ⓔ agree upon the same course of treatment being suggested three days ago by the nurse

3. Neither of the senior partners at the law firm <u>was either impressed by his experience nor won over by his sense of humor</u>, though they did acknowledge that his numerous publications were notable.

  Ⓐ was either impressed by his experience nor won over by his sense of humor
  Ⓑ were impressed by his experience nor did his sense of humor win them over
  Ⓒ found his experience impressive and also his sense of humor didn't win them over
  Ⓓ was impressed by his experience or won over by his sense of humor
  Ⓔ were neither impressed by his experience nor won over by his sense of humor

4. The economic disadvantages of her proposed two-year plan already having been noted by the accounting department, <u>the owner of the company and her chief operations officer and the controller were obliged to withdraw their support</u> for the relocation of the company's headquarters to Chicago.

  Ⓐ the owner of the company and her chief operations officer and the controller were obliged to withdraw their support
  Ⓑ the owner of the company, her chief operations officer, and the controller, being obliged to withdraw their support
  Ⓒ the owner of the company, along with her chief operations officer and controller, were obliged to withdraw their support
  Ⓓ the owner of the company, along with her chief operations officer and controller, was obliged to withdraw her support
  Ⓔ the owner of the company, along with her chief operations officer and controller, obliged to withdraw her support

5. Because the authors were not properly credited with their contribution to the project, <u>they filed a civil claim, resulting in a cease-and-desist order promising to undermine the editorial process; ultimately, placed</u> the entire publication schedule in jeopardy.

  Ⓐ they filed a civil claim, resulting in a cease-and-desist order promising to undermine the editorial process; ultimately, placed
  Ⓑ they filed a civil claim, resulted in a cease-and-desist order that promised to undermine the editorial process and, ultimately, place
  Ⓒ they filed a civil claim; which resulted in a cease-and-desist order that promised to undermine the editorial process and, ultimately, placing
  Ⓓ they filed a civil claim; this action resulted in a cease-and-desist order, which promised to undermine the editorial process and, ultimately, place
  Ⓔ they filed a civil claim, that resulted in a cease-and-desist order, promising to undermine the editorial process and, ultimately, placing

6. Fundamentally different from most other periodicals, <u>which depends upon advertising revenue for its continued survival, our magazine is distinct among monthly news publications in that it is entirely subscriber supported; therefore, it remains</u> uninfluenced by corporatism.

  Ⓐ which depends upon advertising revenue for its continued survival, our magazine is distinct among monthly news publications in that it is entirely subscriber supported; therefore, it remains
  Ⓑ which depends upon advertising revenue for their continued survival, our magazine is distinct among monthly news publications in that it is entirely subscriber supported and, therefore, remains
  Ⓒ which depend upon advertising revenue for their continued survival, our magazine is distinct among monthly news publications in that it is entirely subscriber supported, thus remaining
  Ⓓ depending upon advertising revenue for their continued survival, our magazine is distinct among monthly news publications in that it is entirely subscriber supported and remain
  Ⓔ they are dependent upon advertising revenue for their continued survival, our magazine is distinct among monthly news publications in that it is entirely subscriber supported, so it remains

7. <u>An articulate Wellesley graduate, an attractive young professional, and the mother of a child under the age of two, Edie was naturally the first choice of the photojournalist's for the magazine's cover story on women in the modern workforce.</u>

Ⓐ An articulate Wellesley graduate, an attractive young professional, and the mother of a child under the age of two, Edie was naturally the first choice of the photojournalist's for the magazine's cover story on women in the modern workforce.

Ⓑ As an articulate Wellesley graduate, an attractive young professional, and the mother of a child under the age of two, the first choice of the photojournalist for the cover story on women in the workforce was naturally Edie.

Ⓒ As an articulate Wellesley graduate, an attractive young professional, and the mother of a child under the age of two, the photojournalist's first choice for the magazine's cover story on women in the modern workforce was naturally Edie.

Ⓓ As an articulate Wellesley graduate, an attractive young professional, and the mother of a child under the age of two, Edie was naturally the photojournalist's first choice for the magazine's cover story on women in the modern workforce.

Ⓔ An articulate Wellesley graduate, an attractive young professional, and the mother of a child under the age of two was Edie, naturally the first choice of the photojournalist for the magazine's cover story on women in the modern workforce.

Directions: For questions 8–15, a reading passage will be followed by questions based on its content. After reading the passage, choose the best answer to each question. Answer all questions about the passage on the basis of what is *stated* or *implied* in the passage. You may refer back to the passage.

Questions 8–12 are based on the following passage.

Scientists know how black bears are born white. They're just not sure why. The phenomenon, known as Kermodism, is triggered by a recessive mutation at the MC1R gene, the same gene associated with red hair and fair skin in humans. To be born white, a bear must inherit the mutation from both parents. The parents themselves don't have to be white. They just need to carry the recessive mutation. So it's not uncommon for
(5) white bears [also called spirit bears] to be born to black parents.

White fur occurs in only one of every 40 to 100 black bears on the British Columbia mainland coast, but the trait is especially pronounced on certain islands in the Great Bear Rainforest. On Princess Royal Island, one in ten black bears is white. On Gribbell Island, it's one in three.

It's unclear how the trait arose. One theory was the "glacial bear" hypothesis that Kermodism represented
(10) a remnant adaptation from the last great ice age, which ended here 11,000 years ago. At that time, most of modern-day British Columbia was still icebound, and a white coat may have offered camouflage. But the glacial bear theory raised a question: Why didn't the white fur trait die out when the glaciers receded?

Researchers have recently proved that the spirit bear's white coat gives it an advantage when fishing. Although white and black bears tend to have the same success after dark—when bears do a lot of their
(15) fishing—scientists Reimchen and Dan Klinka from the University of Victoria noticed a difference during the daytime. White bears catch salmon in one-third of their attempts. Black individuals are successful only one-quarter of the time. "The salmon are less concerned about a white object as seen from below the surface," Reimchen speculates. That may answer part of the question about why the white-fur trait continues to flourish today. If salmon are a coastal bear's primary fat and protein source, a successful female can feast on
(20) salmon to store more fat for winter, potentially increasing the number of cubs she can produce.

8. Which of the following titles best summarizes the contents of the passage as a whole?

Ⓐ "A Study in Contrast: White Bears, Kermode Bears, and Spirit Bears"
Ⓑ "Feeding and Hunting Habits of Spirit Bears in British Columbia"
Ⓒ "Why Do Black Bears Produce White Offspring?"
Ⓓ "The Glacial Bear Theory: Black Bears Before and After the Great Ice Age"
Ⓔ "Recessive Mutation Traits in Spirit Bears"

9. According to the passage, the author would agree with all of the following statements EXCEPT:

   Ⓐ   A white bear could be born to a black mother.

   Ⓑ   Salmon are a common food source for spirit bears.

   Ⓒ   During the last great ice age, white bears probably had the advantage of camouflage.

   Ⓓ   When fishing at night, black bears are more successful than white bears.

   Ⓔ   The glacial bear hypothesis is inadequate to explain the current prevalence of white bears.

10. It can be inferred from the passage that the purpose of the third paragraph is to

   Ⓐ   state a secondary theme of the passage that is implied but not directly stated in the first paragraph.

   Ⓑ   provide statistics that support claims made earlier in the passage and then end with a rhetorical question that spurs the reader to continue.

   Ⓒ   propose a solution to the central question that the passage addresses, but then raise a fundamental objection to that solution.

   Ⓓ   admit that the main theme of the passage includes a mystery that may never be adequately solved, and then posit a partial explanation.

   Ⓔ   indict the scientific orthodoxy for its heretofore shallow explanation of a natural process, setting up the heroic introduction of maverick scientists in the following paragraph.

11. Which of the following outlines for a detective novel most closely follows the rhetorical flow of the passage?

   Ⓐ   A crime occurs whose motive is unknown; one detective proposes a motive that is ultimately found to be inadequate; in the second half of the book, another detective produces a motive that better fits the facts of the case.

   Ⓑ   Two detectives each attempt to reconstruct a robbery by assuming two different points of entry to the crime scene; the plot thickens when they discover a third point of entry, which proves to be correct.

   Ⓒ   An heiress disappears and foul play is assumed; a private detective is hired to question several possible assailants and, in the process, one is arrested for another crime; in a surprise ending, the heiress is found to have staged her own disappearance.

   Ⓓ   A bank robbery occurs, but only a small amount of money appears to have been stolen; the novel ends when a detective proves that, in fact, the robbery was staged only to camouflage embezzlement by a bank manager.

   Ⓔ   A detective interviews two suspects who appear equally guilty; further facts are uncovered which point equally to both parties. Ultimately, both suspects turn out to be accomplices.

12. According to the author, the glacial bear hypothesis falls short because it explains the

   Ⓐ   behavior of white bears but not black bears.

   Ⓑ   percentages of white bears on the mainland coast of British Columbia but not on the nearby islands.

   Ⓒ   original emergence of white bears but not their continued survival.

   Ⓓ   advantage that white bears have in daytime fishing but not in reproduction.

   Ⓔ   presence of the MC1R gene in white bears born to white parents but not in those born to black parents.

Questions 13–15 are based on the following passage.

For many Americans, the traditional imagery of pre-Columbian North America is one of small- or medium-sized native tribes living in vast, primeval forests or on rolling plains largely untouched by human hands. The first part of this evocative description is relatively accurate, since settlers moving west often traveled through large swaths of unoccupied land, encountering native tribes only occasionally, if at all.

(5) However, evidence indicates the pre-Columbian population of North America was much larger and more advanced than popular myth has taught. As a result, the land in many regions was far from pristine. Native tribes engaged in large-scale agriculture; built towns, roads, and temples; and conducted far-ranging commerce. Thriving civilizations were found across the continent. Yet, by the time settlers arrived in significant numbers, many tribes had vanished, or were vastly reduced in number and power, through disease

(10) and warfare.

No accurate count is possible due to a dearth of written records, but estimates of pre-Columbian native populations in the Americas range between 20 and 100 million, with a "consensus estimate" of between 40 and 80 million. Geographer William Denevan has suggested a total of 53.9 million. He estimates only 5.6 million remained by 1650.

(15) An absence of major settlements and large tribes convinced many nineteenth century American scholars and settlers that the continent had been largely empty prior to the arrival of European explorers. They also seem to have been unaware of first-person accounts written by early explorers, such as Hernando De Soto, as well as letters and diaries kept by early colonists who described the size and complexity of the native societies they encountered.

(20) The decimation of native tribes by disease and the resulting impression that North America was home only to small, primitive settlements helped foster the "manifest destiny" belief that the newly formed American nation was destined to conquer and civilize a largely "empty" continent. Nineteenth century historians such as Frederick Jackson Turner popularized the latter, in conjunction with the related myth of the frontier as a steadily westward-moving line between civilization and primitive life.

13. The primary purpose of the passage is to

Ⓐ contrast the experience of Native Americans at the height of pre-Columbian civilization with that of their post-Columbian descendants.

Ⓑ explain the disappearance of Native Americans as a function of disease and intertribal warfare rather than as a result of colonization.

Ⓒ dispel the popular myth that the North American continent was unspoiled and virtually unpopulated before the arrival of Europeans.

Ⓓ provide a version of the story of North American colonization from the viewpoint of Native Americans.

Ⓔ estimate the population of North America at its pre-Columbian height, in its decline, and finally after colonization was firmly established.

14. According to the passage, which of the following statements would the author probably NOT agree with?

Ⓐ Disease and war in the early days of colonialism resulted in a sharp decline in the Native American population.

Ⓑ The impression that North America was largely undeveloped before Europeans arrived led to and supported the belief in manifest destiny.

Ⓒ Prior to colonization, Native American civilizations actively developed and cultivated the landscape around them in accordance with their own needs.

Ⓓ In the nineteenth century, virtually no written documentation existed to correct the scholarly misapprehension that North America had never been home to large and thriving civilizations.

Ⓔ Many European-American settlers moving west rarely, if ever, came into close contact with Native Americans.

15. It can be inferred from the second paragraph in the passage that the author primarily

- Ⓐ supports an assertion from the previous paragraph, countering a possible objection by the reader before it arises.
- Ⓑ makes a bold claim and then acknowledges its probable inaccuracy and retreats to a safer middle-ground position.
- Ⓒ refutes a popular false impression described in the previous paragraph and then alleges how this impression may originally have gained credibility.
- Ⓓ establishes a set of premises, that virtually any reader would be forced to agree with, in support of the troubling conclusion introduced in the following paragraph.
- Ⓔ pretends to concur with a mythical version of history while satirizing those who would, in fact, adopt this simplistic outlook.

Directions: For questions 16–20, you will read a brief passage and determine the author's line of reasoning using only commonsense standards of logic. No knowledge of formal logic is required. Then choose the best answer, realizing that several choices may be possible, but only one is best.

16. Employee: Several other employees in this department have recently received 3 percent merit raises in addition to the minimum cost-of-living increase that all employees receive. According to several reliable objective measurement scales, my productivity is greater than that of most of these employees. Additionally, I have received high marks from my supervisor on all of my employee reviews in the three years that I have worked here. Therefore, it's only fair that I receive a 3 percent raise in addition to my cost-of-living increase.

Which of the following additional pieces of information, if true, would most weaken the employee's argument?

- Ⓐ Cost-of-living increases were already in excess of 3 percent.
- Ⓑ The other employees who received merit raises work in a different department, where merit can be less reliably measured.
- Ⓒ The supervisor who gave this employee favorable reviews has been fired from the company for vandalism.
- Ⓓ The president of the company, who makes all decisions regarding merit pay, has often been accused of playing favorites in this regard.
- Ⓔ Only employees with five years or more of service are eligible for merit raises.

17. Many business owners are not in favor of government regulations. They argue that regulations raise the cost of their operations, which in turn require them to raise their prices or else lose revenue. (However, an increase in prices tends to negatively affect a company's ability to compete in the marketplace, because when a business is forced to raise its prices, it loses customers, which also lowers revenue.) The inevitable loss of revenue due to government regulation explains why so many companies are going out of business.

Which of the following most seriously undermines the above argument?

- Ⓐ A significant block of customers are business owners and, therefore, not in favor of government regulations.
- Ⓑ Regulations tend to apply to all businesses across a given industry.
- Ⓒ When a business loses customers, its costs proportionally drop.
- Ⓓ Compliance with certain regulations requires little or no expenditure.
- Ⓔ The penalties against persistent noncompliance with regulations tend to be so exorbitant that compliance turns out to be more cost-effective.

18. A study of the town of Freeport divides the population into two categories: adults and children. It further divides the adult population into two subcategories: seniors and nonseniors. The study finds that in the last 10 years, the overall population of the town has increased, while the population among seniors has remained constant.

Which of the following CANNOT be deduced from the above passage?

Ⓐ   If the population of adults has increased, then the population of nonsenior adults has also increased.

Ⓑ   If the population of children has decreased, then the population of nonsenior adults has increased.

Ⓒ   If the population of nonsenior adults has remained constant, then the population of children has increased.

Ⓓ   If the population of children has increased, then the population of adults has also increased.

Ⓔ   If the population of nonsenior adults has decreased, then the population of adults has also decreased.

19. Many species of male birds perform elaborate dances to attract a mate. Female birds who witness these performances tend to be drawn to these males because the dance demonstrates strength, agility, and other desirable genetic attributes. In one species of bird, a male of mating age enlists the assistance of a younger male bird for his performance. The presence of an assistant significantly raises the likelihood that the lead male's courtship will be successful. However, the assistant is not mature enough to mate and is usually not related to the lead male, so his participation in the performance seems paradoxical.

Which of the following statements, if true, best explains the apparent paradox above?

Ⓐ   A young male who assists is more likely to die of hunger before maturity than one who does not assist.

Ⓑ   In some cases, a female onlooker challenges the female who is being courted for the right to mate with the lead male.

Ⓒ   Once he matures, a young male assistant is more likely to find an assistant of his own than a young male who doesn't assist.

Ⓓ   By a variety of objective measurements, young males who later participate as assistants can be shown early on to be stronger and more agile than males who do not.

Ⓔ   Offspring of birds who mate as a result of a mating dance are no more likely to survive to maturity than offspring of birds who do not.

20. A major law firm has hired an advertising agency to improve the general standing of lawyers who are seen in the mind of the public as dishonest. The agency has identified the problem to be twofold: First, people who earn less are generally put off by the large hourly rates that lawyers typically command. Second, those who are not trained in the law tend to be suspicious of the incomprehensible jargon that lawyers typically employ in conjunction with their work. By addressing these two issues, the agency hopes to correct the problem.

Which of the following, if true, casts the most doubt on the hope that the advertising agency will improve the public perception of lawyers?

Ⓐ   Professionals who earn the same amount or more than lawyers tend to consider their ethics to be honest or at least neutral.

Ⓑ   Medical doctors and psychotherapists typically charge large hourly rates and employ jargon in the course of their work, but neither of these groups inspires the same negative perception.

Ⓒ   Generally, women tend to view lawyers significantly less negatively than men do.

Ⓓ   As a group, lawyers tend to volunteer their services for more hours each year than virtually any other group of professionals.

Ⓔ   Even though lawyers themselves claim to distrust other lawyers, in objective terms, their level of distrust tends to be lower than that of nonlawyers.

IF YOU FINISH BEFORE TIME IS CALLED, CHECK YOUR WORK ON THIS SECTION ONLY. DO NOT WORK ON ANY OTHER SECTION IN THE TEST.

Section 4: Integrated Reasoning

Time: 15 minutes

7 Questions

General Directions: Use a blank sheet of paper to record your answers.

Questions 1–2

Message #1

Phone Message from Mike Rivers, a plumber, to his client Anne Calloway

Hi, Anne, this is Mike. I had a chance to look over the problem while you were out today. As you said, the water in the two upstairs bathrooms is running very slowly. This is most likely the result of a blockage where your old iron pipes have rusted and collapsed from inside. The solution is to find and then route around this blockage.

The water in the house is connected into a single line where the water connects into the house. The blockage occurs somewhere on this line before the water reaches those bathrooms. The water is running normally in the kitchen but slowly in the bathrooms, so the blockage occurs someplace after the water leaves the kitchen and before it reaches the bathrooms.

A lot depends on where the blockage is located. Sooner or later, all of the iron pipes in the house need to be replaced. In the short term, though, if you could tell me what you need to get done and by when, I'll try to accommodate you.

Message #2

Phone message from Anne Calloway to Mike Rivers

Hi Mike, thanks for getting back to me so quickly. My main concern right now is to get my son's bathroom working before he comes home for the summer in about two weeks. The other upstairs bathroom is less important since we only use it when guests visit.

Our downstairs bathroom is working fine, so our son could use it if he needs to. But it would be best if we could get his bathroom working in the next couple of weeks.

Message #3

Phone message from Mike Rivers to Anne Calloway

Hi, Anne, this is Mike. Sorry for the phone tag. If your main concern is to get your son's bathroom working, I think this will be the easier of the two problems to fix because it's closer to the water source than the guest bathroom. If we get lucky, removing this blockage will also solve the problem in the guest bathroom. If not, it means that there's another blockage further along the pipe. But at the very least you'll have one more working bathroom in the house.

I'm available early next week, so call me to let me know how you'd like to proceed.

Directions: For each statement, determine if the information in the three messages above supports the stated conclusion. If it does, select *Yes.* Otherwise, select *No. Note: On the actual exam, you will click on the Yes or No oval to the left of the statement.*

Yes	No		
○	○	**1a.**	Water from the source must reach the kitchen before reaching the guest bathroom.
○	○	**1b.**	Water from the source must reach the downstairs bathroom before reaching the kitchen.
○	○	**1c.**	If there is more than one blockage, then there cannot be a blockage in the pipe between the downstairs bathroom and the son's bathroom.

Directions: In the question that follows select the *best* answer of the five choices given that best supports the stated conclusion from the three messages above. *Note: On the actual exam, you will click on the oval to the left of the correct answer choice.*

2. If there is only one blockage, then it must be

   Ⓐ   between the water source and the kitchen.
   Ⓑ   between the water source and the downstairs bathroom.
   Ⓒ   between the son's bathroom and the guest bathroom.
   Ⓓ   between the downstairs bathroom and the son's bathroom.
   Ⓔ   between the downstairs bathroom and the kitchen.

Question 3

The data in the table below provide information on the sales of hybrid cars in the United States from 2004 through 2008. *Note: On the actual exam, the table below can be sorted in ascending order by clicking on the drop-down menu for the column you want to sort.*

Total Reported U.S. Hybrid Sales					
	Number of Units Sold				
Month	**2004**	**2005**	**2006**	**2007**	**2008**
Jan	4,252	8,455	15,867	17,591	22,392
Feb	5,249	10,400	14,957	22,998	22,411
Mar	6,586	16,429	17,841	34,637	38,214
Apr	6,832	20,974	21,707	27,351	39,898
May	7,275	16,887	23,554	43,095	35,943
Jun	6,062	19,223	23,048	34,300	24,917
Jul	7,277	19,454	25,626	28,585	24,877
Aug	6,232	23,707	26,249	25,139	26,045
Sep	5,861	19,180	23,301	22,859	20,834
Oct	9,530	17,020	18,754	24,443	21,979
Nov	8,632	16,065	18,283	33,233	14,571
Dec	10,441	18,240	22,625	30,871	17,698

Source: http://www.greencarcongress.com/2009/11/hybrid-sales-20091105.html

Directions: Carefully review the data in the table above and read each of the following statements about the sales of hybrid cars. Based on the information in the table, determine whether each statement is *true* or *false* and fill in the corresponding oval. *Note: On the actual exam, you will click on the true or false oval to the left of the statement.*

Yes	No		
○	○	**3a.**	The range in the number of units sold per month from 2004 to 2008 was greater than the range in the number of units sold from 2004 to 2007.
○	○	**3b.**	From 2004 to 2008, the median number of units sold in March was greater than the mean number sold in March.
○	○	**3c.**	U.S. hybrid sales exceeded 25,000 units in exactly 13 months of the 36 months from January 2006 through December 2008.

Question 4

The graph below provides usage information about five computer languages for the years 2004 through 2008.

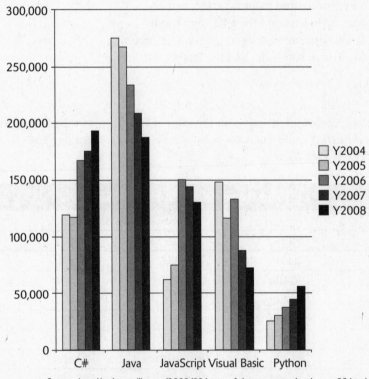

Source: http://radar.oreilly.com/2009/02/state-of-the-computer-book-mar-22.html

Directions: In each question you will be presented with a sentence that has one or two blanks indicating that something has been omitted, or left out of the sentence. Use the given data in the graph above to select the best answer that completes the following four statements. *Note: On the actual exam, the corresponding answer is selected from a drop-down menu.*

4a. Visual Basic was more popular than JavaScript in _____ (one, two, three, four, five) different years.

4b. In 2006, the mean number of usage units among the five languages was closest to _____ (120,000; 130,000; 140,000; 150,000).

Question 5

The bar graph below provides information on new passenger car registration in the European Union (EU). Each of the six months from October 2010 through March 2011 is compared with the same month one year earlier.

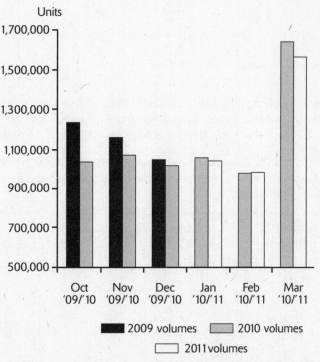

New Passenger Car Registrations in the EU – Last 12 months

Source: http://www.acea.be//news/news_detail/passenger_cars_registrations_down_27_over_january_april/

Directions: In the question below you will be presented with a sentence that has two blanks indicating that something has been omitted, or left out of the sentence. Use the given data in the graph above to select the best answers that complete the following statement. *Note: On the actual exam, the corresponding answers are selected from drop-down menus.*

---

5. In the first quarter of 2010, the total number of new car registrations _____ (increased, decreased) by approximately _____ (less than 10%, 10% to 20%, 20% to 30%) compared to the previous quarter.

Question 6

A building company is currently working on two development projects. At completion, Edwardian Villas will have 840 units, 30% of which are currently completed; and Sunnyvale Meadows will have 600 units, 10% of which are currently completed. The owner is requesting that the two projects be coordinated such that in exactly four weeks, the same number of units in both developments are still to be completed.

Directions: In the table below, identify the necessary number of units per week that will need to be built in each development. Make only one selection in each column by filling in the oval in the row that represents the correct answer. *Note: On the actual exam, you will click on the two ovals that represent the correct answer.*

Question 6a Edwardian Villas	Question 6b Sunnyvale Meadows	New Units Per Week
○	○	10
○	○	15
○	○	18
○	○	24
○	○	27
○	○	32

Question 7

A theater owner is designing a new seating plan for her theater. The width of the theater is 139 feet. Of this width, 23.5 feet is already allocated for aisle space. She wishes to use a combination of two types of seats. Each plush seat requires a width of 2.25 feet, and each velvet seat requires a width of 2.5 feet.

Directions: In the table below identify the necessary number of plush and velvet seats. Make only one selection in each column by filling in the oval in the row that represents the correct answer. *Note: On the actual exam, you will click on the two ovals that represent the correct answer.*

Question 7a Plush	Question 7b Velvet	Number of Seats
○	○	6
○	○	12
○	○	18
○	○	24
○	○	30
○	○	36

IF YOU FINISH BEFORE TIME IS CALLED, CHECK YOUR WORK ON THIS SECTION ONLY. DO NOT WORK ON ANY OTHER SECTION IN THE TEST.

Answer Key

Section 2: Quantitative

1. B	**8.** B	**15.** C
2. C	**9.** D	**16.** E
3. C	**10.** E	**17.** D
4. A	**11.** B	**18.** C
5. A	**12.** E	**19.** A
6. A	**13.** B	**20.** E
7. A	**14.** C	

Section 3: Verbal

1. D	**8.** C	**15.** C
2. B	**9.** D	**16.** E
3. D	**10.** C	**17.** B
4. D	**11.** A	**18.** D
5. D	**12.** C	**19.** C
6. C	**13.** C	**20.** B
7. D	**14.** D	

Section 4: Integrated Reasoning

1a. Yes	**3b.** No	**6a.** Edwardian Villas: 27 new units per week
1b. No	**3c.** No	
1c. No	**4a.** two	**6b.** Sunnyvale Meadows: 15 new units per week
2. D	**4b.** 140,000	
3a. No	**5.** increased, less than 10%	**7a.** Plush seats: 18
		7b. Velvet seats: 30

Charting and Analyzing Your Test Results

The first step in analyzing your results is to chart your answers. Use the charts on the following pages to identify your strengths and areas of improvement. Complete the process of evaluating your essay and analyzing questions in each area in the Diagnostic Test. Re-evaluate your results as you look for:

- Trends
- Types of errors (frequently repeated errors)
- Low scores in the results of *specific* topic areas

This assessment and analysis is a tremendous asset to help you maximize your best possible score. The answers and explanations following these charts will provide you clarification to help you solve these types of questions in the future.

Analytical Writing Assessment Worksheet

Analyze your responses using the following chart, and refer to the high-scoring sample response on page 37 as a reference guide. Then estimate your score using the "Analytical Writing Scoring Guide" on page 3 for characteristics of a high-scoring essay to rate your essay. Remember that when you take the actual GMAT, scores are averaged from two separate readers. Since we are trying only for a rough approximation, a strong, average, or weak overall evaluation will give you a general feeling for your score range.

Analysis of an Argument Essay			
Questions	Strong Response Score 6 – Excellent Score 5 – Good	Average Response Score 4 – Competent Score 3 – Limited	Weak Response Score 2 – Weak Score 1 – Poor
1. Does the essay response focus on the specific topic and cover all of the tasks?			
2. Does the essay response identify and analyze important features of the argument?			
3. Does the essay response show cogent reasoning and logical development?			
4. Does the essay response show sufficient supporting and relevant details and/or examples?			
5. Is the essay response well-organized?			
6. Does the essay response show a command of standard written English?			

Analysis Worksheets: Multiple-Choice Questions

One of the most important instructional tools for test preparation is to analyze WHY you answered a question incorrectly. Now that you have taken the Diagnostic Test and checked your answers against the answer key on the multiple-choice sections, carefully tally your mistakes by marking them in the proper column. As you review the data, you will be able to pinpoint specific areas of concentration.

First, review the answer explanations following these worksheets to help you understand how to solve these types of questions. Then, before you take any practice tests, take advantage of the information gathered in your analysis to help you focus on specific subject areas. The following subject review chapters for Quantitative, Verbal, and Integrated Reasoning will introduce you to the GMAT question types and fundamental skills necessary in each area to help you accomplish your goals.

Quantitative Worksheet

Types of Questions Missed					
			Number Incorrect		
Content Style Topic	**Total Possible**	**Number Correct**	**(A) Simple Mistake**	**(B) Misread Problem**	**(C) Lack of Knowledge**
Arithmetic Problem Solving – Questions 1, 5 Data Sufficiency – Question 15, 20	4				
Algebra Problem Solving – Questions 6, 18 Data Sufficiency – Questions 3, 9, 11, 13	6				
Geometry Problem Solving – Questions 2, 10 Data Sufficiency – Question 4	3				
Data Analysis Problem Solving – Questions 8, 19 Data Sufficiency – Questions 7, 12	4				
Word Problems Problem Solving – Question 16	1				
Data Interpretation Problem Solving – Question 14 Data Sufficiency – Question 17	2				
Total Possible Explanations for Incorrect Answers: Columns A, B, and C					
Total Number of Answers Correct and Incorrect	20	Add the total number of correct answers here: _____	Add columns A, B, and C: _____ Total number of incorrect answers		

Verbal Worksheet

Types of Questions Missed					
			Number Incorrect		
Question Type	Total Possible	Number Correct	(A) Simple Mistake	(B) Misread Problem	(C) Lack of Knowledge
Sentence Correction Questions 1, 2, 3, 4, 5, 6, 7	7				
Reading Comprehension Questions 8, 9, 10, 11, 12, 13, 14, 15	8				
Critical Reasoning Questions 16, 17, 18, 19, 20	5				
Total Possible Explanations for Incorrect Answers: Columns A, B, and C					
Total Number of Answers Correct and Incorrect	20	Add the total number of correct answers here: _____	Add columns A, B, and C: _____ Total number of incorrect answers		

Integrated Reasoning Worksheet

Types of Questions Missed					
			Number Incorrect		
Content Topic	Total Possible	Number Correct	(A) Simple Mistake	(B) Misread Problem	(C) Lack of Knowledge
Multi-Source Reasoning Questions 1, 2	2				
Table Analysis Question 3	1				
Graphics Interpretation Questions 4, 5	2				
Two-Part Analysis Questions 6, 7	2				
Total Possible Explanations for Incorrect Answers: Columns A, B, and C					
Total Number of Answers Correct and Incorrect	7	Add the total number of correct answers here: _____	Add columns A, B, and C: _____ Total number of incorrect answers		

Answers and Explanations

Section 1: Analytical Writing—Analysis of an Argument

A sample student response is provided below to help you evaluate your essay. Compare your essay to this sample essay. Use the checklist suggested earlier in the chapter to evaluate your essay and to help you take a closer look, as well as understand your scoring range.

Argument Topic

The following appeared in a magazine article on career development:

> "When describing their ideal next position, many employment seekers try to balance a variety of personal and professional factors. Personal factors are varied and often include considerations such as 'how well I'll fit in with the work environment' and 'whether my new workmates might make good friends.' This concern is a fundamental error that severely distracts from the task at hand: finding a job that pays well and advances your career. I tell all my clients: Look for a job that pays you what you're worth—or more, if possible—then show up, work hard, and be professional. Save personal considerations for your family and friends—that's where they're appropriate."

Write a critique of the argument. Your essay should consider its line of reasoning and how well it uses evidence. You should consider what doubtful assumptions undermine the reasoning, and consider what other evidence might support or weaken the argument. Your essay may also consider how the argument could be made more persuasive and its conclusion more convincing.

High-Scoring Sample Response

While the argument is grounded in the important and obvious truth that the personal and professional dimensions are distinct, thus requiring different responses, it overshoots the mark in its conclusion that professionalism is best served in the total exclusion of all personal considerations. At its core, the key flaw in this argument lies in its failure to address one fundamental question: What ultimate purpose does a career serve?

Certainly, as the author argues, we work to make money. We also work to advance our career so that we can make more money in the future. These two facts are beyond dispute. However, money is never an end in itself. The professional life is only superficially separate from the personal life; in fact, ultimately it must *support* the personal life. And when it fails to do so—or when professional life threatens to become a drain on the professional himself—the very purpose of a career path is undermined.

The author's advice to consider salary can be placed in question, but it's worth considering the other contention made about the purpose in choosing a job: to advance one's career. It seems rather shortsighted to discount the worth of personal relationships in the choice of a position. How often have we heard of the value of networking and the potential of finding worthwhile career paths through personal relationships cultivated at work? In a contemporary world where resumes are so easily discounted, pursuing professional friendships is an excellent tool for career development. The small investment in having dinner with co-workers from time to time may pay off in career advancement when one of them hears of a job opportunity and passes it along. Of course it's not advisable to locate all of one's friendships in the workplace, but creating bonds with colleagues may play a dual role: opening avenues for career advancement and precluding negative relationships.

We've all witnessed the deleterious effects of a toxic work environment on the people who work there. Similarly, most people have experienced job situations that seemed perfect on paper but, in reality, made them miserable simply because they didn't like or enjoy the company of people they worked with. This is where the writer's admonition to "be professional" can become quite a strain. And conversely, many of us have been happy to sacrifice a few dollars in pay for the opportunity to work with people whom we admire and respect. In these cases the advice to "show up" and "work hard" become much less difficult to follow. Each of these situations exemplifies the need to balance the personal with the professional in any job search.

Of course, no one would argue that all monetary and career considerations should be abandoned for the opportunity to work with friendly people. In reality, however, each job seeker must sift through a combination of professional and personal considerations in deciding what his or her ideal next job might be. This is commonly accepted wisdom; the author's argument simply fails in its attempt to persuade a careful reader otherwise.

Section 2: Quantitative

1. **B. Method 1.** Translate the English into an algebraic sentence, then solve.

"What percent of Bob's weight is Maria's weight?"

$$\frac{x}{100} \times 183 = 110$$

$$\frac{x}{100} = \frac{110}{183}$$

$$x = \frac{11,000}{183}$$

Divide 183 into 11,000 and stop as soon as you recognize which answer it is.

$$
\begin{array}{r}
60 \\
183\overline{)11000} \\
\underline{1098} \\
20 \\
\underline{0}
\end{array}
$$

The best answer is 60%.

Method 2. Trial and error. Use the percent values and multiply them with 183 to see which one produces the answer closest to 110. In this case, start with the middle value. If it's too big, there are only two other answers possible. Similarly, if it's too small, there are only two other answers possible.

Try 70%: 70% × 183 = 128.1 This is greater than 110. Try 60%: 60% × 183 = 109.8. This is very close to 110, but less than 110. Any percent less than 60% will produce an even smaller value. So the answer is between 60% and 70%. The 60% answer was closer to 110 than the 70% answer.

2. **C.** Insert the information in the diagram.

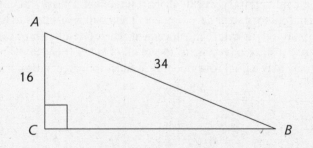

The formula for the area of a triangle $= \dfrac{(\text{base})(\text{height})}{2}$. Since $\overline{AC} \perp \overline{BC}$, you can use $\overline{BC}$ as a base and $\overline{AC}$ as a height in order to find the area of this triangle. In order to find $\overline{BC}$, use the Pythagorean theorem.

$$\left(BC\right)^2 + \left(AC\right)^2 = \left(AB\right)^2$$
$$\left(BC\right)^2 + \left(16\right)^2 = \left(34\right)^2$$
$$\left(BC\right)^2 + 256 = 1{,}156$$
$$\left(BC\right)^2 = 900$$
$$BC = 30$$

Therefore, the area of $\triangle ABC = \dfrac{(30)(16)}{2} = 240$.

Had you recognized this Pythagorean triple as a version of the 8-15-17 (each side doubled) you would have arrived at $BC = 30$ much faster. Here are some of the most frequently used Pythagorean triples: 3-4-5; 5-12-13; 7-24-25; and 8-15-17.

3. **C.** From statement (1) $a^2 > b^2$, you **cannot** conclude that $a > b$. What you can conclude is that $|a| > |b|$. For example $(-5)^2 > (-3)^2$, but -5 is not greater than -3. What is true is $|-5| > |-3|$. Therefore, statement (1) is not sufficient information to conclusively say whether $a > b$ or not.

From statement (2), you can only conclude that both a and b are negative values, but you cannot conclude which is the larger value.

Using statements (1) and (2) together, you can make the conclusion that a is more negative than b (both are negative and $a^2 > b^2$). Hence the answer to the question "is $a > b$?" is *no*. Be careful here. Don't let the fact that the answer to the question is *no* make you think you do not have sufficient information.

4. **A.** First, insert the original information into the diagram.

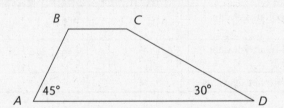

Then insert the information from each statement separately.

This problem requires knowledge of 45-45-90 right triangles and 30-60-90 right triangles. In 45-45-90 right triangles, the sides opposite the 45° angles are equal in length and the hypotenuse is that length times $\sqrt{2}$. In 30-60-90 right triangles, the side opposite the 30° angle is the smallest length, the hypotenuse is twice that size, and the side opposite the 60° angle is the small length times $\sqrt{3}$. What you need to notice is that in either special right triangle, knowing any one of its three sides provides sufficient information to find each of the other two sides. This is different than most right triangles where you would need to know two of its sides in order to find the third side.

Statement (1) says $BC = 8$ and $CD = 12$. Insert this information and draw perpendicular segments from B and C to segment $\overline{AD}$ at F and E, respectively.

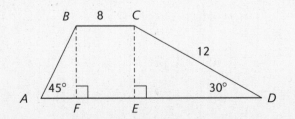

Notice that $\triangle ABF$ is a 45-45-90 right triangle and that $\triangle CDE$ is a 30-60-90 right triangle. Since $ABCD$ is a trapezoid, then $\overline{BC} \parallel \overline{AD}$, which would make $BF = CE$.

Finding the area of trapezoid $ABCD$ requires knowing BC, AD, and either BF or CE since the formula for the area of a trapezoid is $\text{Area} = \dfrac{(\text{height})(\text{base}_1 + \text{base}_2)}{2}$.

Using the 30-60-90 right triangle information with $CD = 12$, you can conclude that $CE = 6$ and $DE = 6\sqrt{3}$. With $CE = 6$, you can conclude that $BF = 6$, because $BF = CE$. Then using the 45-45-90 right triangle information, by knowing $BF = 6$, you can conclude $AF = 6$ and $AB = 6\sqrt{2}$. Since $BC = 8$, you can conclude that $EF = 8$. Therefore, statement (1) provides sufficient information to find the area of the trapezoid because $BC = 8$, $AD = 6 + 8 + 6\sqrt{3}$, and $BF = 6$.

Statement (2) says $AB = 6\sqrt{2}$ and $CD = 12$. Start with the original diagram and its initial information. Then insert the new information.

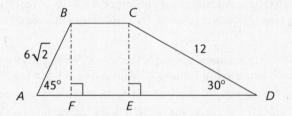

In $\triangle ABF$, you can find that $AF = 6$ and $BF = 6$. Then in $\triangle CDE$, $CE = 6$ and $DE = 6\sqrt{3}$. You do not have any information that allows you to find BC or FE. Hence, statement (2) alone is not sufficient.

5. **A.** If the 6-quart mixture is $\frac{2}{3}$ water, then it is $\frac{1}{3}$ salt. If the 8-quart mixture is $\frac{3}{4}$ water, then it is $\frac{1}{4}$ salt. This problem can be made easier to envision by using a chart.

	Amount of Salt	Amount of Water
6-quart saltwater	$\frac{1}{3}(6) = 2$	$\frac{2}{3}(6) = 4$
8-quart saltwater	$\frac{1}{4}(8) = 2$	$\frac{3}{4}(8) = 6$
14-quart saltwater	4	10

You can now see the final mixture has 14 quarts of salt and water of which 4 quarts are salt. $\frac{4}{14} = \frac{2}{7}$ and $\frac{2}{7} \approx 29\%$. The best answer is 30%.

6. A. This problem requires knowing the following.

odd ± odd = even	(odd)(odd) = odd
odd ± even = even ± odd = odd	(odd)(even) = (even)(odd) = even
even ± even = even	(even)(even) = even

Now analyze each choice.

(A) $\underset{\text{even + odd + even = odd}}{4a \ + \ 5b \ + \ 6c}$

(B) $\underset{\text{odd − even − odd = even}}{3a \ - \ 4b \ - \ 5c}$

(C) $\underset{\text{odd + even + odd = even}}{a^2 \ + \ 2b^2 \ + \ 3c^2}$

(D) $\underset{\text{even + even + even = even}}{2a^2 \ + \ 4b^2 \ + \ 6c^2}$

(E) $\underset{\text{even + even + even = even}}{\underset{(\text{even})^2 + (\text{even})^2 + (\text{even})^2}{(a+1)^2 + \ (2b)^2 \ + (a+3)^2}}$

Only choice A produced an odd result.

Another approach would be to replace a, b, and c with simple odd values and do the arithmetic.

7. A. Begin with how to calculate probability: probability $= \dfrac{\text{\# favorable outcomes}}{\text{\# total outcomes}}$.

From statement (1), you find that 12 balls of the 20 balls are not red. Hence, the remaining 8 balls are red. You can now answer the question; the probability would be $\dfrac{8}{20}$. Statement (1) alone is sufficient.

From statement (2), there are 3 green balls and 9 yellow balls. You can conclude that there are 8 balls remaining, but you do not know how many of them are red, since you do not know what colors are included with the 20 balls. Therefore statement (2) alone is not sufficient.

8. B. The mean of a set of numbers is found by taking the sum of the numbers and dividing by how many numbers there are. The mean of six numbers is 20 translates into $\dfrac{\text{sum of six numbers}}{6} = 20$. Therefore the sum of six numbers = 120.

The average of two of those numbers is 26 translates into $\dfrac{\text{sum of two numbers}}{2} = 26$. Therefore, the sum of two numbers = 52. The remaining four numbers have a sum of 68 since 120 − 52 = 68. The average of these four numbers is $\dfrac{68}{4} = 17$.

9. D. First multiply out the expression, combine like terms, and factor the remaining expression.

$$
\begin{aligned}
(x+2y)^2 -(2x+y)^2 &= \left(x^2+4xy+4y^2\right)-\left(4x^2+4xy+y^2\right) \\
&= x^2+4xy+4y^2-4x^2-4xy-y^2 \\
&= 3y^2-3x^2 \\
&= 3\left(y^2-x^2\right) \\
&= 3(y+x)(y-x)
\end{aligned}
$$

For a number to be divisible by 6, it must be divisible by 3 and be even. This last expression $3(y + x)(y - x)$ is divisible by 3 since it has a factor of 3. The expression will be even when the answer of $(y + x)(y - x)$ is even.

From statement (1), that $x - y$ is an even integer, you can conclude that $y - x$ must also be even, thus $(y + x)$ $(y - x)$ will be even since the product of two numbers is even when one of the numbers is even. Notice that (even)(odd) = even and (even)(even) = even. Thus you can answer the question. The expression is divisible by 6. Statement (1) is sufficient.

From statement (2), xy is an odd integer, you can conclude that both x and y are odd integers since only (odd)(odd) = odd. Notice that (odd)(even) = even, and (even)(even) = even. With x and y odd, then $y + x$ will be even and $y - x$ will be even. Therefore, $(y + x)(y - x)$ will be even. Again you can answer the question. Statement (2) is sufficient. Hence, each statement alone is sufficient.

10. E. Look at the diagram again.

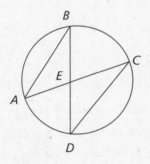

The most common error made here is assuming that the intersection of $\overline{AC}$ and $\overline{BD}$ at point E is the center of the circle. That is something you cannot assume. Knowing that $\overset{\frown}{AB}=112°$ does not provide sufficient information to find the measures of any of the remaining arcs. Inscribed $\angle ACD$ would have the measure of half $\overset{\frown}{AD}$, but there is not enough information to find the measure of $\overset{\frown}{AD}$.

11. B. The given equation $5w - 10v + z = 25$ can be rewritten as $5(w - 2v) + z = 25$.

Using statement (1), $w + z = 7$, together with $5w - 10v + z = 25$, you cannot determine the unique value for z. Statement (1) is not sufficient.

Using statement (2), $w - 2v = 6$, together with the rewritten form of the given equation, $5(w - 2v) + z = 25$, the unique value for z can be determined. You would replace the $(w - 2v)$ with 6 and get $5(6) + z = 25$ and eventually get $z = -5$. It is true that you cannot determine the values of w and v from this fact, but you were not asked to determine their values, only the value of z. Statement (2) alone is sufficient.

12. E. Neither statement alone is sufficient since each one makes reference to only x or y, not both. Now use the statements together. The error in thinking in this problem comes from assuming that since the y value came from integers between 10 and 20 and the x value came from integers between 0 and 10, y has to be more than x, and thus you can answer the question. To appreciate this better, you need to know how standard deviation is calculated.

The standard deviation for a set of data is found using the following five steps:

(1) Find the mean of your data values (sum of data values ÷ number of data values).

(2) For each data value, do the following: (data value – mean)^2.

(3) Add together all the answers from step 2.

(4) Take the answer from step 3 and divide by the number of data values.

(5) Take the square root of the answer in step 4. This is now the standard deviation value.

Consider the six different integers, each of which is between 0 and 10, and six other different integers between 10 and 20. After finding their mean and then doing the subtraction of (data value – mean), it is possible that the answers for the (data value – mean) could all be the same.

For example: x is the standard deviation for the integers 1, 2, 3, 4, 5, 6 and y is the standard deviation for the integers 11, 12, 13, 14, 15, 16.

To calculate x, first find the mean of 1, 2, 3, 4, 5, 6:

$$\frac{1+2+3+4+5+6}{6} = 3.5$$

Next you would find all the squares of the differences:

$$(1-3.5)^2 \quad + \quad (2-3.5)^2 \quad + \quad (3-3.5)^2 \quad + \quad (4-3.5)^2 \quad + \quad (5-3.5)^2 \quad + \quad (6-3.5)^2$$
$$=(-2.5)^2 \quad + \quad (-1.5)^2 \quad + \quad (-0.5)^2 \quad + \quad (0.5)^2 \quad + \quad (1.5)^2 \quad + \quad (2.5)^2$$

The remaining steps would be to add these together, divide that result by 6, and then take the square root of that answer.

To calculate y, first find the mean of 11, 12, 13, 14, 15, 16:

$$\frac{11+12+13+14+15+16}{6} = 13.5$$

Next find all the squares of the differences:

$$(11-13.5)^2 \quad + \quad (12-13.5)^2 \quad + \quad (13-13.5)^2 \quad + \quad (14-13.5)^2 \quad + \quad (15-13.5)^2 \quad + \quad (16-13.5)^2$$
$$=(-2.5)^2 \quad + \quad (-1.5)^2 \quad + \quad (-0.5)^2 \quad + \quad (0.5)^2 \quad + \quad (1.5)^2 \quad + \quad (2.5)^2$$

The remaining steps would be to add these together, divide that result by 6, and then take the square root of that answer.

Notice that at each point of the remaining steps, the results are the same. In this example, the x-value and the y-value will be the same. If different integers between 0 and 10, and between 10 and 20 are used to find the x and y values, it can be arranged that the x- and y-values will be different from one another. Hence, even using statements (1) and (2) together, there is not sufficient information to answer the question.

13. **B.** Statement (1) says that $x > 12$. Do not assume that y is a positive value. You were <u>not</u> given that as a fact. Only knowing that x is more than 12 is not sufficient to determine whether the expression $x + 2y$ is greater than 12 or not.

Statement (2) says that $4x + 8y < 30$. Notice the relationship between $4x + 8y$ and $x + 2y$ in the question. If you divide $4x + 8y$ by 4, you get $x + 2y$. Therefore, divide each side of the inequality $4x + 8y < 30$ by 4 and get $x + 2y < 7.5$. Now you can answer the question of whether $x + 2y$ is greater than 12 or not. In this case, the answer is *no*. Don't let the fact that the answer to the question is *no* make you think that there is not sufficient information.

14. C. According to the chart, there are a total of 720 females, of which $\frac{1}{5}$ are mature adults:

$$\left(\frac{1}{5} \times 720 = 144\right)$$

Thus there are 144 females that are mature adults and 576 females (720 − 144 = 576) that are young adults. Put this information in the chart.

	Young Adults	Mature Adults	TOTAL
Males			
Females	576	144	720
TOTAL	600		

Since there are 600 people who are young adults, and 576 of them are female, then 24 are male (600 − 576 = 24). Put that information in the chart.

	Young Adults	Mature Adults	TOTAL
Males	24		
Females	576	144	720
TOTAL	600		

The information in the question states that $\frac{3}{4}$ of the males are mature adults, which means $\frac{1}{4}$ of the males are young adults.

Thus, the 24 male young adults represents $\frac{1}{4}$ of the total males. Therefore, there are 96 males (4 × 24 = 96). Hence, there are 72 males that are mature adults (96 − 24 = 72).

Inserting this information into the chart and completing it, you get the following.

	Young Adults	Mature Adults	TOTAL
Males	24	72	96
Females	576	144	720
TOTAL	600	216	816

To find the probability that an employee selected at random from this factory will be a mature male, take the number of mature males and divide that by the total number of employees:

$$\frac{72}{816} = \frac{3}{34}$$

Now convert this fraction to a percent:

$$\frac{3}{34} \times 100\% = \frac{300}{34}\% \approx 8.8\%$$

15. **C.** Statement (1) lacks information regarding the amount of money invested. Statement (2) only makes reference to the money invested in bonds. If you take the statements together, you can find the total invested in stocks. Below is one method that could be used to find the actual amount invested in stocks.

Using statement (1):   Let $3x =$ amount invested in stocks

$4x =$ amount invested in bonds

$5x =$ amount invested in real estate

Using statement (2): $4x + 5x = 360,000$

$9x = 360,000$

$x = 40,000$

Therefore, the amount invested in stocks, $3x$, is 3($40,000) = $120,000. Statements (1) and (2) together are sufficient.

16. **E.** This problem requires knowing that (average rate) × (total time) = (total distance).

This can also be expressed as $\dfrac{\text{total distance}}{\text{total time}} = \text{average rate}$.

One method for doing this problem would be to first find the distance traveled for each part of the trip and then divide that result by the total time of the trip to get the average rate for the trip. Since the total time was given as t hours, and $\frac{2}{3}$ of it was spent walking, then $\frac{1}{3}$ of it was spent driving. The person went from A to B at x mi/hr for a total of $\frac{1}{3}t$ hours for a total distance of $x\left(\frac{t}{3}\right) = \frac{xt}{3}$ mi. The person went from B to C at y mi/hr for a total of $\frac{2}{3}t$ hours for a total distance of $y\left(\frac{2t}{3}\right) = \frac{2yt}{3}$ mi. The average rate for the trip is then expressed by

$$\frac{\left(\dfrac{xt}{3} + \dfrac{2yt}{3}\right)\text{mi}}{t\ \text{hr}} = \frac{xt + 2yt}{3} \times \frac{1}{t}$$

$$= \frac{(x + 2y)t}{3} \times \frac{1}{t}$$

$$= \frac{x + 2y}{3}\ \frac{\text{mi}}{\text{hr}}$$

17. **D.** From statement (1), 60 students received an A. Since this represents 10% of the class, you can determine that there are 600 students in the class. Since 40% of the class received a D, then 40% of 600, or 240, students received a D. Statement (1) is sufficient.

From statement (2) you find that the difference between 30% of the class and 20% of the class is 60 students. That is, 10% of the class is 60 students. With this you can find the number of students in the class, which allows you to find the number of students who received a D. Statement (2) is sufficient.

18. **C.** Use the given definition to evaluate the expression in parentheses first. Then use the definition to evaluate that result. We are given that $x^{\#} = (x + 1)(x - 1)$.

$$5^{\#} = (5 + 1)(5 - 1) = (6)(4) = 24 \text{ then } 24^{\#} = (24 + 1)(24 - 1) = (25)(23) = 575.$$

19. A.

Recall that probability $= \dfrac{\text{\# favorable outcomes}}{\text{\# total outcomes}}$.

The favorable outcomes look like this: 1, 2, _, _, _

2, 3, _, _, _

3, 4, _, _, _

4, 5, _, _, _

In each case, there are $(3)(2)(1) = 6$ ways to arrange the remaining three numbers for a total of 24 favorable outcomes. There are a total of $(5)(4)(3)(2)(1) = 120$ ways to arrange all five numbers, so the total number of outcomes is 120. The probability becomes $\dfrac{24}{120} = \dfrac{1}{5}$.

20. E. From statement (1), you can find that either x or y could be –3, –2, –1, or 0 since the comparisons included the "equals." That is, x and y could be the same value. From this you cannot get a unique value for $x + y$.

From statement (2), only knowing that $x = 2y$, you cannot determine a unique value for $x + y$.

Using the statements together, the fact that either x or y could be –3, –2, –1, or 0 and $x = 2y$, you find two possibilities: $x = –2$ and $y = –1$ or both x and y are zero. So either $x + y = –3$ or $x + y = 0$. So even together, the statements are not sufficient to get a unique solution.

The most common error made on this problem is assuming that x and y have different values and that $x < y$. With that assumption and using both statements together, $x = 2y$ only when $x = –2$ and $y = –1$. That means you can get a unique answer for $x + y$ (but only when you falsely assume x and y have different values).

Section 3: Verbal

Sentence Correction

1. D. This sentence begins with the dangling participle *having been detected,* which modifies *the witness.* This construction requires that *the witness* be introduced immediately after the comma as the subject of the sentence. Additionally, the subject of the final clause is *behavior,* which does not match with the verb *charged;* either *the witness* can be *charged with contempt of court* or his *behavior* can be *treated as contempt of court.* Choices A and B are incorrect because *the witness* (not *the judge*) must immediately follow the comma. Choice C is incorrect because *the witness* can be *charged with contempt of court,* but his *behavior* can only be *treated* as such. Choice E is incorrect because the gerund phrase *charging the witness* is incorrectly the subject of the sentence, rather than *the witness.* Choice D is correct because the subject *the witness* immediately follows the comma; in the final clause, the verb *treated* matches the subject *behavior.*

2. B. The subject of this sentence includes four people—*the social worker, the physician,* and *both parents*—so it requires a plural verb instead of *has.* Additionally, *in suggestion of* as an adjective to describe *the nurse* is awkward and ungrammatical. Choices A and C are incorrect because the subject of the sentence is plural, but the verbs *has* and *is* are singular. Choice D is incorrect because the progressive tense verb *are agreeing* is awkward and the passive construction *suggested by* is a weak word choice. *Being suggested,* choice E, is an incorrect verb tense in reference to an event that occurred *three days ago.* The plural verb *have,* choice B, is in agreement with the subject; the verb *suggested* is correctly in the past tense and active voice.

3. D. The use of *nor* with *either* is an incorrect pairing of correlative conjunctions. The proper forms would be *either . . . or* and *neither . . . nor.* However, because the sentence opens with the indefinite pronoun *neither,* further encumbering the sentence with correlative conjunctions is awkward and should be improved. Choice A is incorrect because the use of the pairing *either . . . nor* is incorrect; the pairing should be *either . . . or.* Choice B is incorrect because the subject of the sentence is *neither,* which is singular, but the verb *were* is plural. Choice C is incorrect because the construction beginning with *and also* is awkwardly worded. Choice E is incorrect because the subject is singular and the verb *were* is plural. In choice D, the singular verb *was* is in agreement with the subject *neither.* Parallel construction *impressed by . . . won over by* is strong. The use of passive construction is acceptable here, given that the subject of the sentence refers to *the senior partners.*

4. D. Eliminate choice A because the first part of the sentence mentions *her proposed two-year plan,* so the subject of the sentence is singular, not plural. Choice B is incorrect for the same reason and, additionally, because it has no verb. Choice C is incorrect because the subject of the sentence is singular and the verb *were* is plural. Rule out choice E because the word *obliged* cannot act as a verb in this context. Choice D provides a singular subject with a singular verb.

5. D. Choice A is incorrect because the use of a semicolon before *ultimately* requires the reintroduction of a subject. Rule out choice B because the verb *resulted* gives the inaccurate impression that the authors rather than their claim resulted in a cease-and-desist order. Choice C is incorrect because the use of a semicolon requires an independent clause and the word *which* subordinates the clause that follows. Eliminate choice E because the use of a comma before *that* in this context is ungrammatical. Choice D properly divides this sentence into two independent clauses, with *this action* clearly referring to the entire first clause.

6. C. Rule out choice A because the singular verb *depends* and the singular possessive pronoun *its* do not agree with the plural subject *periodicals.* Choice B is incorrect for the same reason. Eliminate choice D because the word *depending* is awkward and obscures whether the phrase that follows modifies *periodicals* or *magazine.* Choice E is incorrect because the context requires a dependent (or subordinate) clause and the word *they* begins an independent (or main) clause. Choice C correctly uses the plural verb *depend* and the plural possessive pronoun *their,* which both agree with the subject *periodicals.*

7. D. Choice A is incorrect because *photojournalist's* should not be possessive. Choice B is incorrect because after three phrases describing Edie, the additional modifying phrase "the first choice of the photojournalist" is awkward at best. Choice C also falls short for this reason. Rule out choice E because of the awkward passive phrasing. Choice D correctly places the subject *Edie* squarely at the center of the sentence, just after the three modifying phrases and just before the predicate.

Reading Comprehension

8. C. The main idea of the passage is to explore Kermodism, which is the production of white offspring (spirit bears) by black bears. Thus, choice C is the correct answer. Choice A is incorrect because white bears, Kermode bears, and spirit bears are all different names for the same animal, so there is no contrast among them. Rule out choice B because, while the feeding and hunting habits of black and white bears are explored, this study is in service of answering the large question of why Kermodism exists. Similarly, choice D is incorrect because the article mentions the glacial bear theory as one possible answer to Kermodism, but then dismisses it and seeks an alternate explanation. Finally, eliminate choice E because Kermodism is the only recessive mutation trait that the article explores.

9. D. Line 14 states that black bears and white bears tend to have the same success when fishing at night, so the correct answer is choice D. Rule out choice A because lines 4–5 state that white bears are commonly born to black parents. Eliminate choice B because line 19 discusses salmon as an important food source. Choice C is also incorrect because the glacial bear hypothesis rests upon plausible conjecture, discussed in lines 9–11, that white bears had the advantage of camouflage during the ice age. Choice E is incorrect because lines 11–12 point out that the glacial bear hypothesis fails to explain why white bears have continued to survive since the ice age ended.

10. C. In the third paragraph, the author introduces the glacial bear hypothesis as a possible theory to explain the existence of white bears, but then shoots it down because it fails to explain why white bears continue to flourish in the absence of constant snow and ice. Thus, the correct answer is choice C. Eliminate choice A because the glacial bear theory is not really a secondary theme and, in any case, no reference is made to it in the first paragraph. Choice B is incorrect because the third paragraph includes no statistics, and the question at the end of is it not rhetorical but is, in fact, intended to be answered. Choice D is incorrect because the third paragraph does not say that main theme of the passage—why black bears produce white offspring—is unanswerable. Choice E must be ruled out because the third paragraph includes no hint of indictment of the scientific orthodoxy, but simply an accounting of the pros and cons of the glacial bear theory.

11. A. The passage centers on the mystery of why black bears produce white offspring. It proposes the glacial bear theory as a possible explanation, but then finds that this explanation fails to explain the white bear's continued existence. Finally, the Klinkas propose the theory that white bears have an advantage in daytime fishing, which answers the objections that the glacial bear theory raises. This overall arc is most similar to a detective story with one motive ultimately displacing another, so the correct answer is choice A. Choice B is incorrect because the passage offers two explanations, not three. Choice C is incorrect because it implies willful duplicity that is nowhere present in the passage. Eliminate choice D because, again, duplicity is implied in this answer. Choice E is incorrect because the passage concludes with one explanation being preferable, rather than both being equally valid.

12. C. The glacial bear hypothesis falls short because it explains how white bears may have emerged during the ice age, but fails to account for how they have continued to survive since then. Thus, the correct answer is choice C. Choice A is incorrect because the glacial bear hypothesis relates directly to white bears and isn't intended to explain the existence of black bears. Choice B is incorrect because the hypothesis makes no distinction between coastal and island bears. Eliminate choice D because the hypothesis doesn't focus on fishing or reproduction. Finally, choice E can be ruled out because the hypothesis makes no reference to the presence of the MC1R gene.

13. C. The passage begins with the traditional story of North America as empty, untouched land before Europeans arrived. It discusses how this story gained traction, but does so in service to its main theme of exposing this story as a myth. Thus, the correct answer is choice C. Eliminate choice A because, while the passage does contrast pre-Columbian and post-Columbian Native American civilization, it does so in service to its larger theme of explaining how the myth of an empty continent gained a foothold. Rule out choice B because the passage does not distinguish the effects of colonization and effects that were not directly related to colonization. Choice D is incorrect because the passage is not attempting to provide a Native American viewpoint but simply to introduce additional facts. Choice E is incorrect because, although the passage includes estimates of population before and after colonization, these statistics are in service to a larger theme.

14. D. Lines 16–19 discuss letters and journal entries by early Europeans predating the nineteenth century, detailing the large and thriving Native American civilizations that they had encountered. Thus, the correct answer is choice D. Eliminate choice A because lines 8–10 discuss the sharp population decline among Native Americans due to disease and warfare. Choice B is incorrect because lines 20–22 link the myth of an undeveloped North America to manifest destiny. Choice C is incorrect because lines 5–8 describe pre-Columbian North America as containing agriculture, roads, and other earmarks of a developed landscape. Rule out choice E because lines 1–4 give the reasons why many settlers did not encounter Native Americans.

15. C. In the second paragraph, the author refutes the myth that the North American continent was largely empty prior to the arrival of Europeans, but explains that this myth may have arisen due to the attrition in Native American population during the early colonial period. The correct answer is choice C. Choice A is incorrect because the second paragraph doesn't support an assertion from the previous paragraph, but rather undercuts it. Rule out choice B because the claim made in the second paragraph is not excessively bold and, therefore, requires no retreat. Choice D is incorrect because the second paragraph is not concerned with establishing premises. Eliminate choice E because the tone of the second paragraph is not satirical.

Critical Reasoning

16. E. This argument can be weakened either by demonstrating that the employee's merit is questionable or by identifying an additional criterion that the employee doesn't meet. This employee has only three years of service, so a five-year requirement for a merit raise would be such a criterion (choice E). Rule out choice A because the amount of cost-of-living increases should not affect merit raises. Choice B is incorrect because if other employees received merit raises based on less reliable measurement of merit, this employee should certainly receive one. Choice C is incorrect because, by objective measurement, this employee performs well, and should not be held responsible for the conduct of a bad supervisor. Eliminate choice D because these allegations against the president should strengthen rather than weaken the employee's argument.

17. B. The argument hinges on the fact that when a company raises its prices in comparison with other companies, it tends to lose customers and, therefore, revenue. To undermine this argument, look for a statement that would mitigate this difficulty. If regulations tend to apply to all businesses across a given industry, a set of competing companies would all be affected by them, so all would have to raise their prices accordingly (choice B). Choice A is incorrect because whether customers are in favor of regulations is irrelevant. Eliminate choice C; a small drop in costs due to loss of customers cannot be considered a mitigating factor because the overall result is still loss of revenue. Choice D is incorrect because while compliance with some regulations may be low cost, the effect of the remaining regulations is not addressed. Choice E can be ruled out because a comparison is being made between the cost of compliance and noncompliance, without addressing the assertion that regulations reduce revenue.

18. D. The overall population of the town has increased, but this increase is not accounted for by a growth in the population of seniors. Thus, it is accounted for by an increase among either children or nonsenior adults, but not necessarily both. Therefore, an increase among children does not imply an increase in adults (choice D). Choice A is incorrect because the population of seniors has remained constant, so an increase among adults implies an increase among nonsenior adults. Choice B can be ruled out because if the population of children has decreased, then the only explanation for the overall increase in the town is that the population of nonsenior adults has increased. Similarly, choice C is incorrect because if the population of nonsenior adults has remained constant, then the population of children has increased. Rule out choice E because the population of seniors has remained constant, so a decrease among nonseniors implies a decrease among adults.

19. C. To explain the paradox, look for an incentive for a young male bird to assist in the mating dance. Being the lead bird in a mating dance significantly increases the likelihood that the courtship will lead to mating. Therefore, an incentive could be that assisting in the dance increases a young male bird's likelihood of finding his own assistant when the time comes (choice C). Choice A is incorrect because being more likely to die of hunger would be a disincentive to being an assistant rather than an incentive. Rule out choice B because the presence of a second female would be irrelevant because the assistant is not yet mature enough to mate. Choice D is incorrect because the greater strength and agility of a bird before becoming an assistant would not help to explain why it becomes an assistant. Eliminate choice E because, again, the young bird's participation in the dance provides no incentive.

20. B. The advertising agency's premises are that lawyers are generally disliked because they make a lot of money and because they use unfamiliar jargon. The fact that medical doctors and psychotherapists also make a lot of money and use unfamiliar jargon but are not generally disliked throws this whole argument into question (choice B). Choice A is incorrect because the argument is intended to explain why people who earn less than lawyers are hostile to them. Choice C is incorrect because the distinction between women's and men's perception doesn't come into the argument. Similarly, choice D is incorrect because the fact that lawyers volunteer their services more than other professionals is immaterial to the argument. Eliminate choice E because the argument focuses on the perception of lawyers by nonlawyers rather than by other lawyers.

Section 4: Integrated Reasoning

Multi-Source Reasoning

Questions 1–2

Message #1 states that water is running normally in the kitchen but slowly in the two upstairs bathrooms. This is because of a blockage in the pipes someplace between the water source and the first bathroom. But this blockage doesn't affect the kitchen, so you can set up the following table:

Source	Kitchen	Blockage	2 Upstairs Bathrooms
	(Normal)	X	(Slow)

According to Message #2, the two upstairs bathrooms are the son's bathroom and the guest bathroom. Message #3 states that the son's bathroom is closer to the water source than the guest bathroom, so you can improve this table as follows:

Source	Kitchen	Blockage	Son's Bathroom	Guest Bathroom
	(Normal)	X	(Slow)	(Slow)

Message #2 states that the water in the downstairs bathroom is running normally, so the downstairs bathroom is closer to the water source than the either of the other bathrooms. However, it cannot be determined whether the downstairs bathroom or the kitchen is closer to the water source, so this is left out of the diagram above.

1a. **Yes** The water in the kitchen is running normally and the water in the guest bathroom is running slowly, so the water reaches the kitchen before the blockage and the guest bathroom after the blockage. Therefore, the water must reach the kitchen before reaching the guest bathroom.

1b. **No** According to Message #2, the water in the downstairs bathroom is running normally, so the water reaches the downstairs bathroom before reaching the blockage. However, the downstairs bathroom could be on the line either before or after the kitchen, so water does not necessarily reach the downstairs bathroom before reaching the kitchen.

1c. **No** The water in the downstairs bathroom is running normally and the water in the son's bathroom is running slowly, so under all circumstances there must be a blockage between these two rooms.

2. **D** According to the table above, there must be a blockage between the kitchen and the son's bathroom. Thus, if there is only one blockage, then it must be between the downstairs bathroom and the son's bathroom. Choice D is correct.

Table Analysis

Question 3

3a. **No** From 2004 to 2008, the least number of units sold per month was 4,252 (in January 2004) and the greatest number was 43,095 (in May 2007). Thus, the range in the number of units sold from 2004 to 2007 was the same as the range from 2004 to 2008.

$$\begin{array}{r} 43,095 \\ -\,4,252 \\ \hline 38,843 \end{array}$$

3b. **No** The *median* number is the middle number in the set. Before the median can be determined, each number in the set of data should be ordered from smallest to largest, or from largest to smallest. Hence, from 2004 to 2008, the number of units sold in March were:

$$6,586, \quad 16,429, \quad \mathbf{17,841}, \quad 34,637, \quad 38,214$$

The median number is 17,841.

The *mean* is found by adding the numbers in the set of data and then dividing by the total number of items in the set. The mean is also called the average. Calculate the mean as follows:

$$\frac{6,586+16,429+17,841+34,637+38,214}{5} = 22,741.40$$

Thus, the median is 17,841, and the mean is 22,741.40. Therefore, the answer is *No* because the median is less than the mean.

3c. **No** Sorting the table by *2006* shows that two months (July and August) had sales over 25,000 units.

Month	Number of Units Sold				
	2004	2005	2006	2007	2008
Feb	5,249	10,400	14,957	22,998	22,411
Jan	4,252	8,455	15,867	17,591	22,392
Mar	6,586	16,429	17,841	34,637	38,214
Nov	8,632	16,065	18,283	33,233	14,571
Oct	9,530	17,020	18,754	24,443	21,979
Apr	6,832	20,974	21,707	27,351	39,898
Dec	10,441	18,240	22,625	30,871	17,698
Jun	6,062	19,223	23,048	34,300	24,917
Sep	5,861	19,180	23,301	22,859	20,834
May	7,275	16,887	23,554	43,095	35,943
Jul	7,277	19,454	**25,626**	28,585	24,877
Aug	6,232	23,707	**26,249**	25,139	26,045

Sorting the table by *2007* results in the following:

Month	Number of Units Sold				
	2004	2005	2006	2007	2008
Jan	4,252	8,455	15,867	17,591	22,392
Sep	5,861	19,180	23,301	22,859	20,834
Feb	5,249	10,400	14,957	22,998	22,411
Oct	9,530	17,020	18,754	24,443	21,979
Aug	6,232	23,707	26,249	**25,139**	26,045
Apr	6,832	20,974	21,707	**27,351**	39,898
Jul	7,277	19,454	25,626	**28,585**	24,877
Dec	10,441	18,240	22,625	**30,871**	17,698
Nov	8,632	16,065	18,283	**33,233**	14,571
Jun	6,062	19,223	23,048	**34,300**	24,917
Mar	6,586	16,429	17,841	**34,637**	38,214
May	7,275	16,887	23,554	**43,095**	35,943

The year 2007 accounts for eight more months (March, April, May, June, July, August, November, and December) of sales over 25,000. Finally, sorting the table by *2008* results in the following:

Month	Number of Units Sold				
	2004	2005	2006	2007	2008
Nov	8,632	16,065	18,283	33,233	14,571
Dec	10,441	18,240	22,625	30,871	17,698
Sep	5,861	19,180	23,301	22,859	20,834
Oct	9,530	17,020	18,754	24,443	21,979
Jan	4,252	8,455	15,867	17,591	22,392
Feb	5,249	10,400	14,957	22,998	22,411
Jul	7,277	19,454	25,626	28,585	24,877
Jun	6,062	19,223	23,048	34,300	24,917
Aug	6,232	23,707	26,249	25,139	**26,045**
May	7,275	16,887	23,554	43,095	**35,943**
Mar	6,586	16,429	17,841	34,637	**38,214**
Apr	6,832	20,974	21,707	27,351	**39,898**

This accounts for four more months (March, April, May, and August) of sales over 25,000 units. Thus, 14 of the 36 months from January of 2006 through December of 2008 showed numbers in excess of 25,000 units, not exactly 13 months as stated. This statement is false.

Graphics Interpretation

Question 4

4a. two Compare each of the five respective bars over JavaScript and Visual Basic. Note that for the first two bars, representing 2004 and 2005, Visual Basic was more popular than JavaScript. But for the last three bars, representing 2006 through 2008, JavaScript was more popular than Visual Basic. Thus, Visual Basic was more popular than JavaScript in two different years.

4b. 140,000 In 2006, the graph shows usage units of approximately 170,000 for C#, 230,000 for Java, 150,000 for JavaScript, 130,000 for Visual Basic, and 40,000 for Python. Calculate the mean as follows:

$$\frac{170,000 + 230,000 + 150,000 + 130,000 + 40,000}{5} = 144,000$$

Thus, the mean is nearest to 140,000.

Question 5

5. increased, less than 10% In the first quarter of 2010 (January through March), new car registrations totaled approximately 10.5 million + 10 million + 16.5 million = 37 million. In the previous quarter (October through December 2009), new car registrations totaled approximately 12.5 million + 11.5 million + 10.5 million = 34.5 million. Thus, new car registrations increased by 37 million – 34.5 million = 2.5 million. Calculate this percent increase as follows:

$$\frac{2,500,000}{34,000,000} \approx 0.074 = 7.4\%$$

Thus, new car registrations increased by less than 10%.

Two-Part Analysis

Question 6

6a. Edwardian Villas: 27 new units per week

6b. Sunnyvale Meadows: 15 new units per week

At 100%, Edwardian Villas will have 840 units. With 30% of these already complete (252 units), there are 588 units to go. Similarly, at 100%, Sunnyvale Meadows will have 600 units. With 10% of these already complete, (60 units), there are 540 units to go:

Edwardian Villas	30% of 840 = 252 complete	588 to go
Sunnyvale Meadows	10% of 600 = 60 complete	540 to go

The owner has requested that in four weeks, both projects should have the same number of units remaining to be built. Currently, Edwardian Villas requires 48 more units to be built than Sunnyvale Meadows (588 – 540 = 48). So, Edwardian Villas will need to catch up by 12 units per week (48 ÷ 4 = 12).

Use the following equation for your calculation:

Edwardian Villas units – 12 units = Sunnyvale Meadows units

Test the values for Edwardian Villas using the equation above, starting with the highest value in the New Units Per Week column (because you know that Edwardian Villas must exceed Sunnyvale Meadows by 12, using a higher number to start makes sense) until you find a combination that works:

$$32 - 12 = 20$$
$$27 - 12 = 15$$

Thus, the correct combination is as follows:

$$588 - 4(\textbf{27 new units / week for Edwardian Villas}) = 540 - 4(\textbf{15 new units / week for Sunnyvale Meadows})$$
$$588 - 108 = 540 - 60$$
$$480 = 480$$

Question 7

7a. **Plush seats: 18**

7b. **Velvet seats: 30**

The total width of the theater is exactly 139 feet. Of this, 23.5 feet are accounted for, so you can calculate the remaining width as follows: $139 - 23.5 = 115.5$ feet.

Thus, 115.5 feet must be accounted for as a combination of plush seats and velvet seats, so this is the target number.

Each plush seat has a width of 2.25 feet and each velvet seat has a width of 2.5 feet. The following table shows the number of feet of each possible number of seats:

Plush	Velvet	Number of Seats
13.5 feet	15 feet	6
27 feet	30 feet	12
40.5 feet	45 feet	18
54 feet	60 feet	24
67.5 feet	75 feet	30
81 feet	90 feet	36

Use the following equation for your calculation: 115.5 – plush seats = velvet seats

You can limit your calculations by noticing that every width in velvet column is a whole number of feet, but the target number is 115.5, which is not a whole number of feet. Thus, the correct width in the plush column cannot be a whole number of feet. Test the three possible values in the plush column using the equation above:

$$115.5 - 13.5 = 102$$
$$\mathbf{115.5 - 40.5 = 75}$$
$$115.5 - 67.5 = 48$$

30 velvet seats take up 75 feet. $115.5 - 75 = 40.5$, or 18 plush seats. Thus, the correct combination is as follows:

$$\textbf{18 plush seats} + \textbf{30 velvet seats} + \text{aisle space}$$
$$= 40.5 \text{ feet} + 75 \text{ feet} + 23.5 \text{ feet}$$
$$= 139 \text{ feet}$$

PART II

INTEGRATED REASONING
SECTION

Chapter 2

Introduction to Integrated Reasoning

The Integrated Reasoning section of the GMAT focuses on the key skills that will be required to excel in a twenty-first century MBA program. The Integrated Reasoning section acknowledges the importance of analytical thinking and technology-related skills. This section does not require a predisposition of business, but will require the test-taker to make sound decisions by interpreting, extrapolating, and assimilating data that are presented in text, graphs, spreadsheets, and tables.

Integrated Reasoning tests your ability to interpret multiple sources of data (numeric and text) that represent real-life problems in business by asking you to solve four different question types: *multi-source reasoning, table analysis, graphics interpretation,* and *two-part analysis.* Each question presents a word problem that requires you to use skills that manipulate, analyze, and interpret data. These analytical skills are important for students to be successful in graduate school and in the business world.

This chapter describes each question type and presents sample questions and strategies that show you how to approach and solve the problems, step by step. After you review the samples, be sure to sharpen your test-taking skills further with the practice questions that follow. As you review this material, it is very important to determine which types of questions challenge you the most by observing where you tend to make mistakes or take too much time. Then focus most of your practice time on improving your knowledge and understanding of how to solve these problems until you find that you can answer the questions with greater ease and efficiency. After you finish completing the practice questions, continue to improve your proficiency by completing the four full-length practice tests, one in the book and three on the accompanying CD-ROM.

Format

The Integrated Reasoning section is 30 minutes long and is comprised of 12 computer-generated problems. The structure of each problem contains four basic parts that make up a *data problem set.*

1. Statement: word problem
2. Data: graphic display or text
3. Questions: two to four
4. Answer choices

Consider each data problem set as a whole *unit* as you strategize to solve questions within the setup. For example, you may refer to the same word problem statement and data for two to four questions.

In the Integrated Reasoning section you will see similar data components in the problem setup, but questions can appear in four distinct question type categories: *multi-source reasoning, table analysis, graphics interpretation,* and *two-part analysis.*

Question Types	Answer Format
Multi-source reasoning questions ask you to decide whether statements are true or false based on a combination of two or three separate sources (charts, tables, or text).	Four questions in two different formats: Format 1: (3 questions) Respond *Yes* or *No* to three separate statements. Format 2: (1 question) Select one answer from among five choices in a multiple-choice format.
Table analysis questions ask you to decide whether statements are true or false based on data provided in a table.	Format: (3 questions) Respond *Yes* or *No* (true/false) to three separate statements.
Graphics interpretation questions ask you to answer questions based on information in a graph.	Format: (2 questions) Fill in each blank by selecting the correct answer from a list of choices in a drop-down menu.
Two-part analysis questions present you with a statement or scenario and ask you to select two choices from a two-column table that draw a parallel to the statement provided.	Format: (2 questions) Select one correct choice per column from the table provided.

Calculator

A simple four-function **on-screen calculator** is available to help you perform simple computations in this section only. You may not use your own calculator, and you will not be provided with a calculator for the Quantitative section of the GMAT. You can use a noteboard to work out the calculations and organize other tasks.

The calculator will look something like this:

Time-Consuming Problems   Although the calculator will allow you to forego time-consuming handwritten calculations, you must have a basic knowledge of problem solving to be able to determine if your calculation results make logical sense. Calculators do not replace your math skills, but can support your answer results. The general rule of thumb is that you should only use the on-screen calculator for time-consuming computations. Use your time wisely to quickly determine if a problem appears to be easy to solve mentally.

Basic Functions   The on-screen calculator can perform the basic functions of addition, subtraction, multiplication, square root, percent, and division. The on-screen calculator has basic functions keys: a *clear* [C] button to help you clear the display, a *memory clear* [CE] button that erases the last number or operation entered. Other basic function buttons include *memory clear* [MC], *memory recall* [MR], *memory sum* [MS], and *memory plus* [M+] buttons. Clicking on the [M+] button adds the number displayed to the contents of the memory.

Practice Before the Exam Date   To help you become familiar with the on-screen calculator, and to help you avoid clicking the wrong buttons, use a calculator similar to the on-screen computerized calculator while practicing sample problems from this book. The TI-108 (Texas Instruments 108) calculator has functions that are similar to the on-screen calculator. Familiarize yourself with the best keystrokes to accomplish certain math tasks as you work through sample problems.

Skills and Concepts Tested

The Integrated Reasoning section assesses your ability to draw upon your executive function thinking skills under time constraints. You are required to apply judgment as you analyze multiple sources of data, make interpretations, and draw conclusions about the material presented. Candidates who do well in this section understand how to solve technology-related problems by analyzing questions correctly, reading and interpreting data displays accurately, organizing information logically, and remembering details from information presented.

In order to do well on this portion of the test, you will need to combine your reading comprehension skills, analytical skills, and quantitative skills to recognize relationships, trends, and tradeoffs from tables, graphs, charts, spreadsheets, and word problems.

Directions

You will have 30 minutes to answer 12 questions—roughly 2½ minutes for each problem set.

Some questions require that you answer up to four questions per source (passage, table, graph, etc.). Keep this in mind as you practice so you get used to budgeting your allotted time. Your task is to respond to each question as you:

- select *True* or *False* buttons or *Yes* or *No* buttons
- select the correct answer from a drop-down list
- click on the correct row in two columns of a table
- click on the correct answer from among five answer choices

General Strategies

Read the following general strategies and tips that apply to all Integrated Reasoning questions before you study the suggested strategies, approaches, and exercises that follow.

As you read each question, determine how to approach it. What kind of graph or table is it? What does the information tell you? Do you need to make comparisons? Calculate percentages? Look for trends? You may find it helpful to read all of the statements that the question asks you to evaluate *prior* to beginning your calculations, so that you focus on the most relevant information and you do not waste time performing tasks or calculations that you assume are necessary but may not be.

1. **Practice strategies.** Memorize and practice the four possible types of questions *before* your exam date to save time the day of the test. Practice computer simulated practice problems at www.mba.com.
2. **Manage your time wisely.** Integrated Reasoning questions can be time-consuming, so do not let questions slow your pace. As mentioned earlier, you have about 2½ minutes per question to read and answer all parts of the question, but this does not include the time it takes you to read and interpret the data. Remember that each question may have several components. To allow time to read, analyze, and respond to the information, when practicing problems in this study guide, shorten your practice time to no more than 2 minutes per question.

3. **Analyze data from general to specific.** Examine the *general* scope of the data and graphic displays before answering *specific* questions. Briefly analyze the whole statement or graphic display (table, chart, spreadsheet, etc.) to see what it's all about before starting to solve each problem. By scanning the question data first, you will have a general picture of the topic and its content before you look at specific data. Look for obvious, dramatic trends (high points or low points) and look at the headings that clarify the data (legends, units of measurement, axes labels, or tabs) as you scan the graphic display. Do not try to memorize the data; just get a general sense of the overall picture.

4. **Write down key words (data, dates, times, numbers).** After you have a general sense of the topic, *write* down one or two key words from each question statement to provide you with *clues* about what to look for in the text, table, or chart. Because many of the graphics and questions contain multiple parts of data material, writing down key words will help your eyes to stay focused on the task at hand. Allow your eyes to move quickly over each statement as you make a mental note of the key points.

5. **Use reading skills.** Integrated Reasoning information statements are similar to reading comprehension brief passages, but the questions require you to apply logical relationships in addition to comprehending the author's meaning. As you read each passage, continue to practice the same skills that helped you with reading comprehension questions (read actively, draw inferences, clarify, etc.).

6. **Look for the logical relationship.** In most questions, you are asked to: (1) examine if the given information is in agreement; (2) evaluate how strongly two variables are correlated; and (3) identify pertinent facts that substantiate the line of reasoning. In all of these instances, you will need to look for a logical relationship and determine if the relationship is true or false (yes or no) based upon data provided. This usually involves examining each data statement individually to determine if the logical relationship supports or weakens the information. You will also notice that many of the statements may be interrelated. Looking for the logical relationship among the statements allows you to settle on the correct answer more quickly.

7. **Use only the information that is directly provided in the question data.** Answer all questions about the text, table, or chart on the basis of what is directly stated in that data. The data must support your final answer. Do not consider outside information, even if it seems more accurate than the given information.

8. **Use your knowledge of mathematics to help solve the problems.** You do not need to have strong math skills to answer Integrated Reasoning questions, but some knowledge of math will help you to determine if your answer makes logical sense.

9. **Utilize computer tools.** The whole question may not fit on the computer screen. Make sure you are comfortable with the method of clicking the **select** drop-down menu, and clicking multiple **tabs** to view the entire question on the computer screen (see simulated question types at www.mba.com).

10. **Do not skip questions, and answer all parts of the problem set.** Multiple parts of each question must be completed correctly to receive credit for a correct response. No partial credit is given.

Suggested Strategies with Samples

The most basic strategy for approaching Integrated Reasoning questions is to try to understand the question data's *general purpose* and to analyze the given data to determine a *specific outcome*. In other words, first you must read and analyze the data and then manipulate or apply the information to individual questions to find their specific solutions.

As you learn to identify the four types of questions, you should be more confident in your ability to answer questions with greater accuracy. Use the general strategies presented in this chapter to help direct your line of reasoning to the correct solution, and practice the specific strategies in the practice exercises in this chapter. Sample question types that follow are:

- Multi-source reasoning
- Table analysis
- Graphics interpretation
- Two-part analysis

Multi-Source Reasoning Question Type

A *multi-source reasoning* question asks you to decide whether statements are true or false, based on two or three separate sources of information that are each labeled with a tab. One question is a multiple-choice question based on your analysis of the information sources. At least one source of information appears as written text and the other source(s) may be text or text with a graphic reference (table or graph). Information may include e-mails, notes, letters, newspaper articles, presentations, statements, charts, and other sources.

Sample Questions

Message #1

E-mail sent on Monday afternoon from a paper supplier to the Mother Superior in charge of Dominican University:

Thank you for your e-mail of this morning. Here is a list of our current per-box prices for the five items you mentioned in your query:

Item	Contents per Box	Price per Box
Wide-ruled white paper	5 reams (2,500 sheets)	$30.00
Construction paper	10 reams (5,000 sheets)	$32.00
Computer paper	10 reams (5,000 sheets)	$42.00
3-by-5-inch index cards	30 packs (6,000 cards)	$16.00
Self-adhesive envelopes	24 packs (2,400 envelopes)	$36.00

I hope this is helpful. We would enjoy working with you, so please let me know how else I can assist you.

Message #2

E-mail sent on Tuesday morning from the Mother Superior to the supplier:

I appreciate your taking the time with this. Overall, your prices are fair. As you know, however, ours is a small parochial school and we must cut costs wherever we can. Having said that, let me add that we are loyal customers to those companies that are willing to work with us. (Unfortunately for us, our previous paper supplier closed its doors several months ago.) We will certainly need to start the school year with 60 reams of computer paper and 7,200 self-adhesive envelopes, for which I can spend a total of $300. Would this be a workable price for you?

Message #3

E-mail sent on Tuesday afternoon from the supplier to the Mother Superior:

Generally speaking, I cannot usually offer more than a 10% discount even to our best customers. However, as an introductory price, this one time I am willing to extend you a 15% discount on this order, in the hopes that you will consider taking us on as your new supplier. As always, this price includes delivery to your stockroom. Please let me know if you would like to take us up on this offer.

Directions: For each statement, determine if the information in the three e-mails above supports the stated conclusion. If it does, select *Yes*. Otherwise, select *No*. Note: *On the actual exam, you will click on the Yes or No oval to the left of the statement.*

Yes	No	
○	○	**1a.** If the Mother Superior's $300 limit on her order is non-negotiable, she must refuse the supplier's offer.
○	○	**1b.** If the Mother Superior accepts the supplier's offer, then she will pay less than $3.50 per ream for computer paper on this order.
○	○	**1c.** Assuming that the supplier is telling the truth, the Mother Superior might, as a regular customer, reasonably hope to pay less than $2.80 per ream for construction paper with this supplier.

Directions: In the question that follows, select the *best* answer of the five choices given that best supports the stated conclusion from the three messages above. Note: *On the actual exam, you will click on the oval to the left of the correct answer choice.*

2. With the standard discount, how much will the Mother Superior spend per sheet for wide-ruled white paper?

   Ⓐ   Less than $0.01 per sheet.
   Ⓑ   Between $0.01 and $0.02 per sheet.
   Ⓒ   Between $0.02 and $0.05 per sheet.
   Ⓓ   Between $0.05 and $0.10 per sheet.
   Ⓔ   More than $0.10 per sheet.

1a. Yes The order is for 60 reams of computer paper and 7,200 self-adhesive envelopes. This equals 6 boxes of computer paper (60 reams ÷ 10 reams per box = 6 boxes), and 3 packs of envelopes (7,200 envelopes ÷ 2,400 envelopes per pack = 3 packs). At the listed price, the computer paper would cost $42 × 6 = $252 and the envelopes would cost $36 × 3 = $108. Thus, the total would be $252 + $108 = $360 at the listed price. The supplier has offered a 15% discount, which would take $54 off of this price, leaving the total at $306. This offer exceeds the limit of $300, so if this limit is non-negotiable, the Mother Superior must refuse it.

1b. No The supplier has offered a 15% discount on each box of computer paper, whose listed price is $42. Thus, he is offering a price of $35.70 per box ($42 × .15 = $6.30 discount per box; $42 − 6.30 = $35.70). Each box contains 10 reams of paper, so this price equals $3.57 per ream ($35.70 ÷ 10 = $3.57). Thus, the Mother Superior will not pay less than $3.50 per ream.

1c. No Construction paper is listed at $32 for a box of 10 reams. This is $3.20 per ream, but with a 10% discount this would be reduced by $0.32 to $2.88 per ream ($3.20 × .10 = $0.32; $3.20 − $0.32 = $2.88). Assuming that the supplier is telling the truth, he can extend no more than a 10% discount, even to a regular customer, so the Mother Superior cannot reasonably hope to pay less than $2.80 per ream for construction paper.

2. **B.** The listed price for a box of wide-ruled paper is $30. With a standard 10% discount, which is $3 off, this price is $27.00 for 2,500 sheets, which is between $0.01 and $0.02 per sheet ($27.00 ÷ 2,500 sheets = $0.0108 cents per sheet). Therefore, choice B is correct.

Table Analysis Question Type

A *table analysis* question asks you to decide whether statements are *true* or *false* (*yes* or *no*) based on a set of data provided in a table. You will be able to sort the data in increasing order in each column by selecting a heading from a drop-down menu.

Each table contains headings for easy reference. In questions that mention specific headings, you will have the advantage of being able to quickly spot where the information is located. After you spot the location, be sure to read (and sort) the specific information within the column for easy reference. In addition, reading the other column headings can be very helpful in putting the information in the proper context and answering the question.

Sample Question

The table below gives demographic information about those who were saved and lost on the ship *Titanic*. For each passenger category, the table lists the percent saved and lost, the number in that category who were saved and lost, and the total number in that category. *Note: On the actual exam, the table below can be sorted in ascending order by clicking on the drop-down menu for the column you want to sort on.*

Titanic Disaster – Official Casualty Figures					
Passenger Category	**Percent Saved**	**Percent Lost**	**Number Saved**	**Number Lost**	**Number Aboard**
Children, First Class	100.00%	0.00%	6	0	6
Children, Second Class	100.00%	0.00%	24	0	24
Children, Third Class	34.18%	65.82%	27	52	79
Men, First Class	32.57%	67.43%	57	118	175
Men, Second Class	8.33%	91.67%	14	154	168
Men, Third Class	16.23%	83.77%	75	387	462
Men, Crew	21.69%	78.31%	192	693	885
Women, First Class	97.22%	2.78%	140	4	144
Women, Second Class	86.02%	13.98%	80	13	93
Women, Third Class	46.06%	53.94%	76	89	165
Women, Crew	86.96%	13.04%	20	3	23
Total	**31.97%**	**68.03%**	**711**	**1,513**	**2,224**

Source: http://www.anesi.com/titanic.htm

Directions: Carefully review the data in the table above and read each of the following statements about the *Titanic* disaster. Based on the information in the table, determine whether each statement is *true* or *false* and fill in the corresponding oval. If the statement is true, select *Yes;* otherwise select *No. Note: On the actual exam, you will click on the Yes or No oval to the left of the statement.*

Yes No

○ ○ **3a.** Children accounted for more than 8% of the total number of non-crew members on board.

○ ○ **3b.** The survival rate among male adults was less than 19.5%.

○ ○ **3c.** Among passengers who were saved, the two largest groups, in terms of numbers, were female first-class passengers and male crew members.

3a. Yes. First perform the following calculations:

The number of children on board was 6 + 24 + 79 = 109.

The total number of people on board was 2,224.

The total number of crew members on board was 885 + 23 = 908.

Thus, the number of non-crew members on board was 2,224 – 908 = 1,316.

Now calculate the percentage of children among non-crew members.

$$\frac{109}{1,316} \approx 0.083 = 8.3\%$$

Thus, children accounted for more than 8% of non-crew members and the statement is *true*.

3b. **No.** To determine the survival rate among male adults, remember to include "non-crew and crew" male passengers. Now perform the following calculations:

The number of male adults who were saved was 57 + 14 + 75 + 192 = 338.

The total number of male adults was 175 + 168 + 462 + 885 = 1,690.

To find your answer, calculate the survival rate as a percentage problem.

$$\frac{338}{1,690} = 0.2 = 20\%$$

Thus, the survival rate among male adults was greater than 19.5%. Therefore, the statement is *false* and the answer is No.

3c. **Yes.** Sorting the table by *Number Saved* results in the following:

Passenger Category	Percent Saved	Percent Lost	Number Saved	Number Lost	Number Aboard
Children, First Class	100.00%	0.00%	6	0	6
Men, Second Class	8.33%	91.67%	14	154	168
Women, Crew	86.96%	13.04%	20	3	23
Children, Second Class	100.00%	0.00%	24	0	24
Children, Third Class	34.18%	65.82%	27	52	79
Men, First Class	32.57%	67.43%	57	118	175
Men, Third Class	16.23%	83.77%	75	387	462
Women, Third Class	46.06%	53.94%	76	89	165
Women, Second Class	86.02%	13.98%	80	13	93
Women, First Class	97.22%	2.78%	**140**	4	144
Men, Crew	21.69%	78.31%	**192**	693	885
Total	**31.97%**	**68.03%**	**711**	**1,513**	**2,224**

Thus, female first-class passengers and male crew members were the two largest groups among those who were saved.

Graphics Interpretation Question Type

A *graphics interpretation* question asks you to analyze data based on information that is presented in a graph, chart, or scatter plot. Your task is to choose among three to five answer choices to complete each statement related to the data. Commonly, graphs fall into several categories:

- *Bar graph*—Shows comparisons among items in a two-variable data set.
- *Line graph*—Shows change in data over time in two variables.
- *Bubble graph*—Shows changes in data values for a third variable presented in graduating circles.
- *Pie chart*—Shows comparisons of data as percentages of a whole.
- *Scatter plot*—Shows where individual data points fall in relation to a pair of parameters.
- *Flow chart*—Shows a diagram of a step-by-step process.
- *Organizational chart*—Shows a chart of hierarchical relationships.

Sample Question

The gray and black bars in the bar graph below represent female and male visitors, respectively. All website visitor data were gathered during the four weeks ending July 19. Each website's share of female and male visitors is stated in percentages on the *x*-axis of the graph.

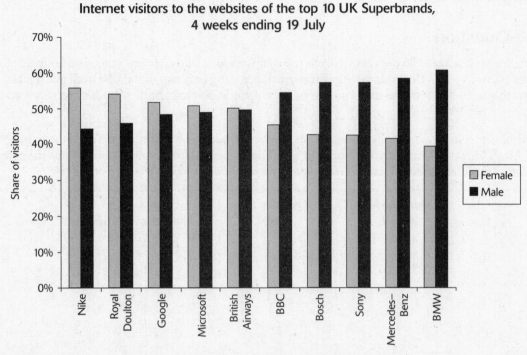

Source: http://weblogs.hitwise.com/robin-goad/2008/07/superbrands_demographics_and_lifestyle.html

Directions: In each question you will be presented with a sentence that has one or two blanks, indicating that something has been omitted, or left out of the sentence. Use the given data in the graph above to select the best answer that completes the following four statements. *Note: On the actual exam, the corresponding answer is selected from a drop-down menu.*

4a. The probability that two randomly chosen visitors to the BMW website will both be female is approximately _____ (0.16, 0.24, 0.36, 0.48).

4b. If the Microsoft website had 60,000 male visitors, then the total number of visitors during this time is _____ (from 0 to 60,000, from 60,000 to 120,000, from 120,000 to 180,000, more than 180,000).

4a. **0.16** Notice that 40% of the visitors to the BMW website are female, which is equivalent to a probability of 0.4. The probability that two randomly chosen visitors will be female is $0.4 \times 0.4 = 0.16$.

4b. **from 120,000 to 180,000** The Microsoft website shows slightly fewer than 50% male visitors and slightly more than 50% female visitors. Thus, if this website had 60,000 male visitors, then it had slightly more than 60,000 female visitors, so its total number of visitors was slightly more than 120,000.

Two-Part Analysis Question Type

A *two-part analysis* question requires you to read a short word problem and then to manage resources between two different, but related, components of the scenario. For example, "strengthen/weaken," "cause/effect," "increase/decrease." It is important to remember that in this type of problem you *must* allocate *all* available resources. Your task is to choose two answers, one per column, in a table format.

Resources to allocate may include:

- *money* in dollars or other currency
- *time* in days, hours, minutes, seconds, and so forth
- *distance* in miles, feet, inches, kilometers, meters, and so forth
- *quantity* in whole numbers, decimals, fractions, and so forth

Sample Question

A bartender needs exactly 2,000 ounces of cola to use as mixers for a party. He has exactly 464 ounces of cola left over from a previous party. He needs to supply the remainder using only two brands: Refresh and Tingle. Refresh is only available in 16-ounce bottles and Tingle is only available in 20-ounce bottles. Both drinks are sold only in quantities of 12 bottles.

Directions: In the table below, identify the necessary number of bottles of Refresh and Tingle the bartender must purchase. Make only one selection in each column by filling in the oval in the row that represents the correct answer. *Note: On the actual exam, you will click on the two ovals that represent the correct answer.*

Question 5a Refresh	Question 5b Tingle	Number of Bottles
○	○	12
○	○	24
○	○	36
○	○	48
○	○	60
○	○	72

5a. Refresh: 36 bottles

5b. Tingle: 48 bottles

In this two-part analysis question, the resource to be managed is *exactly* 2,000 ounces of cola. This must be supplied as a combination of bottles of Refresh and bottles of Tingle, plus other cola left over from a previous party.

A Step-by-Step Approach to Solving Two-Part Analysis Questions:

Solve the problem posed in the question by following these four steps:

Step 1: Find the target number. The *target number* is the number of units that must be reached *exactly* using the only two options in the columns (Refresh and Tingle). Often, this will involve subtracting the two numbers mentioned in the short passage.

Because the question tells you that you need 2,000 ounces of cola and that you already have 464 ounces of cola, you subtract 464 from 2,000 to find how many ounces you still need. This is the *target number*:

$$2,000 \text{ oz.} - 464 \text{ oz.} = 1,536 \text{ oz.}$$

Thus, the target number for this problem is 1,536 ounces.

Step 2: Multiply to fill in the table. Use scratch paper to create a simple table. Fill in the table by multiplying the unit value for each column by the number of units in each row. In this question, the unit value for Refresh is 16 ounces and the unit value for Tingle is 20 ounces:

Refresh	Tingle	Number of Bottles
192	240	12
384	480	24
576	720	36
768	960	48
960	1,200	60
1,152	1,440	72

The resulting table shows you the number of ounces for each possible answer choice in each column.

Step 3: Find the correct pair. The *correct pair* is a pair of numbers—one in each column—that adds up to the target number. You can typically do this in one of two ways: *eyeballing* and *calculating*.

Method	Level of Difficulty	Example
Eyeballing	Easy problems. In easier problems, you may be able to spot one number in the correct pair just by eyeballing the numbers in the two columns. When you can find one number this way, finding the other number is much easier.	For example, in this problem, notice that the last digit of the target number (1,536) is 6. Every number in the second column ends in 0, so the correct number in the first column must end in 6; therefore, it is 576. Now, to find the other number, subtract 576 from the target number: 1,536 oz. − 576 oz. = 960 oz. Therefore, the correct pair is 576 and 960.
Calculating	Difficult problems. In tougher problems, you will need to carry out calculations to find the right answer.	For example, if you could not use eyeballing to solve this problem, you could subtract every number in the first column from the target number (1,536) until you produce a number that is listed in the second column: 1,536 oz. − 192 oz. = 1,344 oz. 1,536 oz. − 384 oz. = 1,152 oz. 1,536 oz. − 576 oz. = 960 oz. Once you find a pair (one number from each column, that when totaled, equals your target number), there's no reason to continue calculating: The correct pair is 576 oz. and 960 oz.

Step 4: Fill in the right answer. When you find the correct pair, use the table that is provided with the question to fill in the correct answer by clicking on the circle in the corresponding column and line for each number in the pair. The correct answer in the table always corresponds to correct pair of numbers. In this case, the answers are 36 bottles of Refresh and 48 bottles of Tingle.

Practice Integrated Reasoning Questions

Now let's practice the approaches and strategies you have learned. Read the following data sets and answer the questions that follow. Questions are arranged by question type. Answers and explanations are provided at the end of the section.

Multi-Source Reasoning

Questions 1–2

Message #1

Note from the executive director of a nonprofit agency to a newly hired administrative coordinator.

Welcome aboard, and thanks for your inquiry on how our agency is funded. For your purposes, I'll focus on how our five main programs are funded. (I'll send along a breakdown of these programs separately.)

Most of our program funding is covered separately by a Catholic Charities grant. This amount varies from year to year, usually in an amount of around $300,000. Additionally, our agency is likely to receive two additional grants this year: one from the Marie Steiner Memorial Fund and the other from the Jewish Children's Youth Services Committee (JCYSC).

Any monies from the Steiner Fund can be spent entirely at our discretion. In accordance with a recent board decision, this will be evenly distributed among our five main programs—20% per program. In contrast, the JCYSC funding, assuming that it is forthcoming, must be spent entirely for youth programming.

Hope this is enough to get you started.

Message #2

Reply from the administrative coordinator to the executive director.

I found the following table on our website, noting our five programs and the percentage of Catholic Charities funding that it receives:

Program	Percentage of Catholic Charities Funding
Drug/Alcohol Rehabilitation	25%
Medical Assistance	25%
Women's Shelter	20%
Youth Services	20%
Food Bank	10%

Is this information accurate for the coming year? And could you let me know what dollar amount the grant will be, assuming it's been approved and announced?

Message #3

> *Follow-up from the executive director to the administrative coordinator.*
>
> Yes, the table on the website accurately reflects the breakdown of Catholic Charities funding for the coming year. This amount has received initial approval for an amount between $300,000 and $320,000. We'll know the final amount within a few weeks, and it will definitely be in that range.
>
> Happily, we have received approval from the Steiner Fund for a grant in the amount of $150,000. This is more generous than we had dared to hope, and we are still reeling from the good news.
>
> The Jewish Children's Youth Services Committee grant is still pending. If it arrives, it will be in the amount of $20,000. Let's cross our fingers.
>
> I hope that's enough basic financial information to help you to begin getting organized. Once again, welcome to the team!

Directions: For each statement, determine if the information in the three messages above supports the stated conclusion. If it does, select *Yes*. Otherwise, select *No*.

Yes	No	
○	○	**1a.** This year, the drug/alcohol rehabilitation program is guaranteed no less than $105,000.
○	○	**1b.** If the JCYSC grant is approved, youth services funding will be no less than $110,000 for the year.
○	○	**1c.** If the JCYSC grant is not approved, youth services funding will not exceed $92,000 for the year.

Directions: In the question that follows, select the *best* answer of the five choices given that best supports the stated conclusion from the three messages above.

2. If the Catholic Charities grant is approved for the maximum amount and the JCYSC grant is also approved, how much funding will the food bank receive?

    Ⓐ $30,000
    Ⓑ $32,000
    Ⓒ $60,000
    Ⓓ $62,000
    Ⓔ $82,000

Questions 3–4

Message #1

E-mail from an estate attorney Stephen Donaldson to Pamela Gordimer, personal assistant to antiques dealer Beth Marinaro:

Dear Ms. Gordimer:

Thank you for your inquiry into the estate of Ida Kendall. As of today, nine pieces have been appraised and their prices approved by the executrix, Mrs. Kendall's daughter Georgia Walker. (You can also view photos of them on Ms. Walker's Facebook page.) They are as follows:

Grandfather Clock	$2,400
Armoire	$2,000
Desk	$1,200
Bed	$1,000
Bureau	$750
Armchair	$700
Dresser	$600
Nightstand	$400
Desk Chair	$350

Individually, these prices are firm, and I respectfully ask that you do not make any lower offers. Having said that, I will add that for any block of items that exceeds $5,000, we will extend a 5% discount. Beyond this, pricing is non-negotiable.

Also, for sentimental reasons, please note that Ms. Walker has specified that the bed, dresser, and nightstand are to be sold as a single lot.

Please let me know if you are interested.

Thank you,
Stephen Donaldson
Legal counsel to Ms. Georgia Walker regarding the estate of Mrs. Ida Kendall

Message #2

E-mail from Beth Marinaro to Pamela Gordimer:

Thanks for sending me the prices. I looked at the website and all of the pieces look reasonably priced except for the armchair—way overpriced. If it's non-negotiable, leave it alone.

Also, the desk would be worthless without the matching desk chair—either grab both or don't buy either of them.

We've got a budget of $6,000 for this, and not a penny more. You know I trust your eagle eye. Go get 'em, Pam!

Thanks,
Beth

Directions: For each statement, determine if the information in the two messages above supports the stated conclusion. If it does, select *Yes*. Otherwise, select *No*.

Yes	No	
○	○	**3a.** Assuming all statements in both e-mails are true, Pamela's purchase might include the grandfather clock, armoire, and bed.
○	○	**3b.** Assuming all statements in both e-mails are true, Pamela's purchase might include the grandfather clock, desk chair, armchair, and nightstand.
○	○	**3c.** Assuming all statements in both e-mails are true, Pamela's purchase might include the armoire, desk, nightstand, and bureau.

Directions: In the question that follows, select the *best* answer of the five choices given that best supports the stated conclusion from the three messages above.

4. Assuming that the armchair is, in fact, negotiable down to $550 and that all other statements in the e-mails are true, what would be the total cost of the armoire, armchair, dresser, and desk chair?

Ⓐ Less than $5,700
Ⓑ Between $5,700 and $5,800
Ⓒ Between $5,800 and $5,900
Ⓓ Between $5,900 and $6,000
Ⓔ More than $6,000

Questions 5–8

Message #1

Letter from Dr. Iris Stone to Professor Kenneth Sterling:

Dear Professor Sterling,

You were right, of course. Throughout this archipelago, the currency is undervalued and, of course, subject to taxation (not to mention theft). It's useful for external trade, but since most of the people here are farmers and fishermen, barter is preferred.

The change of seasons has also brought one further observation to light. Now that the rain has started, non-food items (especially clothing) are at a premium.

And so forth. It makes for an interesting life. You can continue to send my grant money to my sister in Dallas. It's of little use to me here!

Any additional insights would be helpful.

Thank you,
Dr. Iris Stone

Message #2

Letter from Professor Kenneth Sterling to Dr. Iris Stone:

Dear Dr. Stone,

Yes, what you've observed is all true, as far as it goes. Now, here are the following equivalencies as I recall them:

2 mangos = 3 unblemished avocados

1 kilo of fish = 8 unblemished avocados

1 unblemished avocado = 10 large grapes

2 unblemished avocados = 3 blemished avocados

5 large grapes = 8 small grapes

Also, in the rainy season, there the premium on clothing is a 50% increase. Thus:

	Dry Season	Rainy Season
Pair of Boots	40 unblemished avocados	60 unblemished avocados
Raincoat	500 large grapes	750 large grapes

I hope this is useful information. Please keep us in the loop.

Thanks,
Ken Sterling

Directions: For each question, determine if the information in the messages above supports the stated conclusion. If it does, select *Yes*. Otherwise, select *No*.

Yes	No	
○	○	**5a.** If you have 80 small grapes, you can trade for 5 unblemished avocados.
○	○	**5b.** If you have 80 small grapes, you can trade for 1 kilo of fish.
○	○	**5c.** If you have 80 small grapes, you can trade for 2 mangos and 3 blemished avocados.

Yes	No	
○	○	**6a.** If you have 10 kilos of fish and 15 blemished avocados, you can trade for 50 mangos.
○	○	**6b.** If you have 10 kilos of fish and 15 blemished avocados, you can trade for 60 mangos.
○	○	**6c.** If you have 10 kilos of fish and 15 blemished avocados, you can trade for 70 mangos.

Yes	No	
○	○	**7a.** In the dry season, if you have a pair of boots and a raincoat, you can trade for 900 large grapes.
○	○	**7b.** In the dry season, if you have a pair of boots and a raincoat, you can trade for 1,000 large grapes.
○	○	**7c.** In the dry season, if you have a pair of boots and a raincoat, you can trade for 1,200 large grapes.

Directions: In the question that follows, select the *best* answer of the five choices given that best supports the stated conclusion from the three messages above.

8. If a shirt is worth 24 mangos during the rainy season, how many kilos of fish is it worth in the dry season?

(A) 1
(B) 2
(C) 3
(D) 4
(E) 5

Questions 9–10

Message #1

E-mail from Nadine Kaplan, head of Human Resources for Ballard Graphics, to Zachary Washington, a prospective hire:

Zach,

I've heard the good news that you are strongly considering accepting the position we are offering. In response to your query, I'll try to shed some light on the chain of command at our company.

Ballard Graphics is essentially an outsized family company, headed by Chuck Ballard, who founded it. It breaks down into three basic departments: Operations, Sales, and Finance.

Operations divisions are Design (headed by Lisa Calloway) and Site Ops (headed by Art Stormgren). They both report to Marion Ballard, Chuck's wife, who technically reports to Chuck.

Sales is subdivided into three regions: Metro East, Metro West, and Upstate. Currently, Upstate handles all Canadian accounts, and Matt Colaritola manages the region. But Canada is growing fast, and there's talk that it will become its own region starting in January, to be managed by Angela Carmichael, Matt's right hand.

Sorry—rushed! Did I leave anything out? Feel free to ask.

Nadine

Message #2

E-mail from Zachary Washington to Nadine Kaplan:

Hi Nadine,

Okay, that makes sense. Am I correct in my understanding that Jason Ballard is sales manager for Metro East and his brother Tom is sales manager for Metro West? And that all sales managers report directly to Chuck? And how, exactly, does Human Resources fit in?

Thanks for your time,
Zach

Message #3

E-mail from Nadine Kaplan to Zachary Washington:

Hi Zach,

Yes to all—sorry for the confusion. And technically, I'm the head of Human Resources, but it's a department of two (me and my assistant, Carrie Simpson—plus you, if you accept the position). She reports to me and I report to Derek Kramer, who heads Finance and reports directly to Chuck.

Chuck and Marion, and their sons Tom and Jason, plus Derek, are the core of the company. One way or another, all big decisions are vetted through them.

Take care,
Nadine

Directions: For each statement, determine if the information in the three messages above supports the stated conclusion. If it does, select *Yes*. Otherwise, select *No*.

Yes	No	
○	○	**9a.** Carrie Simpson is in Tom's chain of command.
○	○	**9b.** Lisa and Art both report directly to Jason's mother.
○	○	**9c.** If Zach accepts the position, he will be in Derek's chain of command.

Directions: In the question that follows, select the *best* answer of the five choices given that best supports the stated conclusion from the three messages above.

10. If Canada becomes a separate region, how many people will report directly to Chuck?

    Ⓐ Fewer than 5
    Ⓑ 5
    Ⓒ 6
    Ⓓ 7
    Ⓔ More than 7

Table Analysis

Question 11

	Applications and Awards for Benefits (Numbers in the Thousands)				
Year	Number of Applicants	Number of Awards	Awards as % of Applicants	% Increase/ Decrease	Awards per 1,000 Insured Workers
1970	869.8	350.4	40.3%	−7.2%	4.8
1971	923.9	415.9	45.0%	+4.7%	5.5
1972	947.5	455.4	48.1%	+3.1%	5.9
1973	1,067.5	491.6	46.1%	−2.0%	6.2
1974	1,330.2	536.0	40.3%	−5.8%	6.6
1975	1,285.3	592.0	46.1%	+5.8%	7.0
1976	1,232.2	551.5	44.8%	−1.3%	6.4
1977	1,235.2	568.9	46.1%	+1.3%	6.5
1978	1,184.7	490.8	41.4%	−4.7%	5.5
1979	1,187.8	440.5	37.1%	−4.3%	4.7
1980	1,262.3	420.3	33.3%	−3.8%	4.3
1981	1,161.2	381.0	32.8%	−0.5%	3.8
1982	1,019.8	336.1	33.0%	+0.2%	3.3
1983	1,019.3	428.5	42.0%	+9.0%	4.1
1984	1,036.7	410.0	39.5%	−2.5%	3.9
1985	1,066.2	416.1	39.0%	−0.5%	3.9
1986	1,118.4	424.9	38.0%	−1.0%	3.9
1987	1,118.9	420.3	37.6%	−0.4%	3.8
1988	1,108.9	415.3	37.5%	−0.1%	3.8
1989	984.9	430.7	43.7%	+6.2%	3.7
1990	1,067.7	472.1	44.2%	+0.5%	4.0

Source: http://www.ssa.gov/oact/STATS/table6c7.html

Directions: Carefully review the table above and read each of the following statements. Based on the information in the table, determine whether each statement about applications and awards for social security is *true* or *false* and fill in the corresponding oval. If the statement is true, select *Yes;* otherwise select *No.*

Yes	No	
○	○	**11a.** In 1969, the figure for *Awards as Percentage of Applicants* was less than in 1979.
○	○	**11b.** During the year in which the number of awards per 1,000 insured workers was the lowest, a little less than one-third of all applicants received the awards that they applied for.
○	○	**11c.** The three lowest years for awards as a percent of applicants were three consecutive years.

Question 12

New Passenger Car Sales (Thousands of Units)						
	New Passenger Car Sales (Thousands of Units)					
			Import Sales			
Year	Total Sales	Domestic	Total	Japan	Germany	Others
1990	9,303	6,919	2,384	1,719	263	402
1991	8,185	6,162	2,023	1,500	193	330
1992	8,214	6,286	1,928	1,452	201	275
1993	8,518	6,742	1,776	1,328	186	262
1994	8,989	7,255	1,734	1,239	192	303
1995	8,635	7,129	1,506	982	207	317
1996	8,527	7,255	1,272	727	237	308
1997	8,272	6,917	1,355	726	297	332
1998	8,142	6,762	1,380	691	367	322
1999	8,698	6,979	1,719	758	467	494
2000	8,848	6,831	2,017	863	517	637
2001	8,423	6,325	2,098	837	523	738
2002	8,103	5,878	2,226	930	547	749
2003	7,610	5,527	2,083	830	544	709
2004	7,545	5,396	2,149	810	542	797
2005	7,719	5,533	2,186	923	534	729
2006	7,821	5,476	2,345	1,154	561	630
2007	7,618	5,253	2,365	1,183	567	615
2008	6,814	4,535	2,279	1,142	507	630
2009	5,455	3,619	1,836	829	407	600

Source: RITA New Passenger Car Sales (Thousands of Units) – Table 1-16

Directions: Carefully review the table above and read each of the following statements. Based on the information in the table, determine whether each statement about new passenger car sales is *true* or *false* and fill in the corresponding oval. If the statement is true, select *Yes;* otherwise, select *No.*

Yes	No	
○	○	**12a.** In the highest year for total import sales, imports accounted for more than 25% of total sales.
○	○	**12b.** In the top year for German import sales, domestic sales dropped more than 4% from the previous year.
○	○	**12c.** The five lowest years for Japanese import sales were all consecutive years.

Question 13

U.S. Imports of Footwear by Country/Region						
Country/ Region	1998	2002	2006	2007	% Change 2006–2007	% Share of Total 2007
Brazil	83,294	101,627	66,714	51,726	–22.5%	2.2%
China	1,107,566	1,525,520	2,043,582	2,041,614	–0.1%	86.4%
Hong Kong	8,326	10,301	12,672	8,529	–32.7%	0.4%
India	1,985	6,566	10,383	10,252	–1.3%	0.4%
Indonesia	74,279	73,103	42,185	33,614	–20.3%	1.4%
Italy	48,683	43,550	25,490	24,409	–4.2%	1.0%
Mexico	42,782	26,247	11,095	11,029	–0.6%	0.5%
Taiwan	15,855	10,185	8,955	11,923	+33.1%	0.5%
Thailand	26,485	27,077	23,578	19,964	–15.3%	0.8%
Vietnam	7,175	17,537	86,115	89,503	+3.9%	3.8%
All Others	95,893	56,353	40,431	59,784	+47.9%	2.6%
Total	1,512,323	1,898,066	2,371,200	2,362,347	–0.4%	100.0%

Source: https://www.wewear.org/assets/1/7/ShoeStats2008.pdf

Directions: Carefully review the table above and read each of the following statements. Based on the information in the table, determine whether each statement about U.S. imports of footwear is *true* or *false* and fill in the corresponding oval. If the statement is true, select *Yes;* otherwise, select *No.*

Yes	No	
○	○	**13a.** The country or region that showed the greatest increase in U.S. imports from 2006 to 2007 showed a decrease in U.S. imports from 1998 to 2006.
○	○	**13b.** Of the four top countries or regions for U.S. imports in 1998, only two were still among the top four in 2007.
○	○	**13c.** Every country or region that showed an increase in U.S. imports from 2006 to 2007 also showed an increase from 2002 to 2006.

Graphics Interpretation

Question 14

The following bar graph compares the quarterly performance of a 401(k) with the stock performance index between 2008 and 2012. The bars and the left axis show the average amount of the 401(k) balance per quarter, and the line and the right axis show the stock index figure for each quarter.

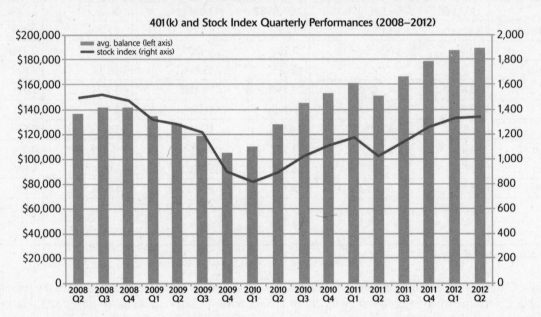

401(k) and Stock Index Quarterly Performances (2008–2012)

Directions: In the question below you will be presented with a sentence that has two blanks, indicating that something has been omitted, or left out of the sentence. Use the given data in the graph above to select the best answers that complete the following statement.

14. During the quarter when the stock index was at its lowest, 401(k) balances had already increased by approximately _____ ($140, $400, $2,200, $6,000), as compared with the previous quarter, representing a percentage increase of approximately _____ (4.8%, 5.2%, 5.5%, 5.8%).

Question 15

The pie chart below depicts a single family residential breakdown of sales, the percent of sales and the median sales price for eight dwelling types: detached, semi-detached, condo townhouse, condo apartment, link, attached/row house/townhouse, co-op apartment, and detached condo.

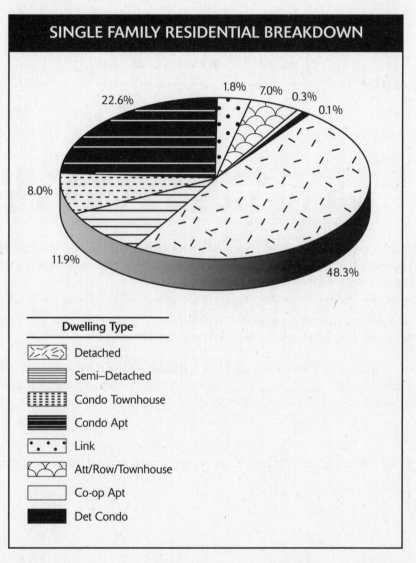

Directions: In each question below you will be presented with a sentence that has one or two blanks, indicating that something has been omitted, or left out of the sentence. Use the given data in the graph above to select the best answer that completes the following two statements.

15a. If the data set contains exactly 12,000 items, then the number of condo apartments in the set is _____ (from 0 to 1,500; from 1,500 to 3,000; from 3,000 to 4,500; more than 4,500).

15b. If the data set contains exactly 238 semi-detached residences, then the number of attached/row/townhouse residences is _____ (133, 140, 147, 154).

Question 16

The bar graph below shows the total U.S. annual pizza sales by the three leading companies: Vespucci (light gray), Carpini (dark gray), and Vincenza (black). The *y*-axis indicates the amount of sales in millions of dollars. The *x*-axis indicates the year in which the sales were made.

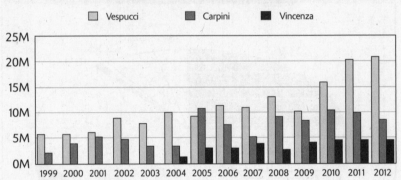

Directions: In each question below you will be presented with a sentence that has one or two blanks, indicating that something has been omitted, or left out of the sentence. Use the given data in the bar graph above to select the best answer that completes the following two statements.

16a. In the year that Vincenza entered the market, Carpini controlled approximately _____ (one-third, one-fourth, one-fifth, one-sixth) of the total pizza market sales.

16b. In the only year in which a new leader emerged as a top seller among the three brands, the other two brands upheld a combined share of _____ (between 30% and 40%, between 40% and 50%, between 50% and 60%, between 60% and 70%) of the market.

Question 17

The following graph is a scatter plot with 81 points, each representing the unemployment rate and the investment to GDP ratio.

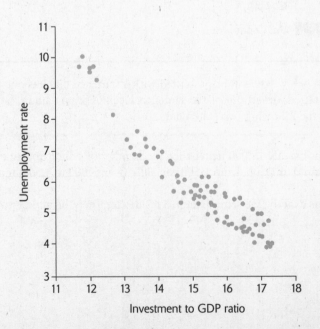

Directions: In each question below you will be presented with a sentence that has two blanks, indicating that something has been omitted, or left out of the sentence. Use the given data in the scatter plot graph above to select the best answer that completes the following statement.

17. An unemployment rate less than 7% indicates an investment-to-GDP ratio that could reasonably be any amount on the scatter plot that is _____ (greater than, less than), _____ (12, 13, 14, 15).

Two-Part Analysis

Question 18

A scientist has just cleared a width of 45 centimeters of shelf space, where he intends to store copies of two journals: Journal X and Journal Y. Journal X has a thickness of 0.8 cm and Journal Y has a thickness of 1 cm. Each journal is published 6 times per year, so the scientist wants to keep blocks of 6 journals on the shelf. Additionally, he intends to place a separator with a width of 5.4 cm between the journals, with all of the remaining width to be used for the journals themselves.

Directions: In the table below, identify the necessary number of each type of journal to be stored on this shelf. Make only one selection in each column by filling in the oval in the row that represents the correct answer.

Question 18a Journal X	Question 18b Journal Y	Number of Journals
O	O	6
O	O	12
O	O	18
O	O	24
O	O	30
O	O	36

Question 19

An IT department has a $30,000 budget to update its computers. The department wishes to spend its entire budget, and $4,500 has already been allocated for other purposes. The remaining funds are to be spent on two different computer models. Model A can be purchased at $600 each and Model B costs $700 each. Both of these models must be bought in sets of 5 to take advantage of these prices.

Directions: In the table below, identify the necessary number of each computer model to be purchased. Make only one selection in each column by filling in the oval in the row that represents the correct answer.

Question 19a Model A	Question 19b Model B	Number of Computers
O	O	5
O	O	10
O	O	15
O	O	20
O	O	25
O	O	30

Question 20

Specifications for a new office building state that its height must rise to the legally zoned maximum of exactly 440 feet. The design for a ground floor of exactly 36.25 feet in height has already been approved. Each of the remaining floors must be either office space or residential space. Each floor containing office space will be 8.75 feet in height, and each floor containing residential space will be 9.25 feet in height.

Directions: In the table below, identify the necessary number of floors containing office space and residential space. Make only one selection in each column by filling in the oval in the row that represents the correct answer.

Question 20a Office Space	Question 20b Residential Space	Number of Floors
○	○	10
○	○	15
○	○	20
○	○	25
○	○	30
○	○	35

Question 21

A 100-hour block of simulator time has been freed up for use by two flight teams: Team Blue and Team Green. Each Team Blue simulation requires exactly 3 hours and 15 minutes and each Team Green Simulation requires 3 hours and 30 minutes. Team Blue has already been approved for 4 simulations during this 100-hour block. The rest of the time must be divided between Team Blue and Team Green so that all of the time is utilized.

Directions: In the table below, identify the necessary number of simulations by Team Blue and Team Green. Make only one selection in each column by filling in the oval in the row that represents the correct answer.

Question 21a Team Blue	Question 21b Team Green	Number of Simulations
○	○	6
○	○	8
○	○	10
○	○	12
○	○	14
○	○	16

Answers and Explanations for Practice Integrated Reasoning Questions

Multi-Source Reasoning

Questions 1–2

The problem mentions three sources of funding: Catholic Charities, the Steiner Fund, and the Jewish Children's Youth Services Committee (JCYSC).

Perform the calculations as shown below to answer the questions posed in this multi-source reasoning word problem.

According to Message #3, the Catholic Charities grant is expected to be between $300,000 and $320,000, and it must be split according to the percentages outlined in the table in Message #2. Thus, excluding the JCYSC grant for the moment, you can outline the following minimum and maximum amounts:

	Minimum	Maximum
Drug/Alcohol Rehabilitation	$75,000	$80,000
Medical Assistance	$75,000	$80,000
Women's Shelter	$60,000	$64,000
Youth Services	$60,000	$64,000
Food Bank	$30,000	$32,000

Additionally, according to Message #3, the Steiner Fund grant has been approved for $150,000. According to Message #1, this money is to be split evenly among the five programs, so each program will receive at least $30,000 for the year, resulting in the following:

	Minimum	Maximum
Drug/Alcohol Rehabilitation	$105,000	$110,000
Medical Assistance	$105,000	$110,000
Women's Shelter	$90,000	$94,000
Youth Services	$90,000	$94,000
Food Bank	$60,000	$62,000

Finally, according to Message #3, if the JCYSC grant comes in, it will be for $20,000. According to Message #1, this grant must go exclusively to youth programming, which results in the following:

	Minimum	Maximum
Drug/Alcohol Rehabilitation	$105,000	$110,000
Medical Assistance	$105,000	$110,000
Women's Shelter	$90,000	$94,000
Youth Services	$90,000 or $110,000	$94,000 or $114,000
Food Bank	$60,000	$62,000

1a. **Yes** The drug/alcohol rehabilitation program will receive 20% of the $150,000 from the Steiner Fund, which is $30,000. It will also receive 25% of at least $300,000 from Catholic Charities, which is at least $75,000. Thus, it will receive at least $30,000 + $75,000 = $105,000.

1b. **Yes** If the JCYSC grant is approved, youth services funding will receive $20,000 in addition to $90,000 minimum funding from the other two sources. Thus, it will receive at least $90,000 + $20,000 = $110,000.

1c. **No** If the JCYSC grant is not approved, youth services funding will be in the range of $90,000 to $94,000, depending on the size of the Catholic Charities grant. Therefore, it could exceed $92,000.

2. **D.** The Steiner Fund will contribute $30,000 to the food bank. The maximum possible funding from Catholic Charities is $32,000, which brings the food bank total up to $62,000 for the year. The JCYSC funding is irrelevant, because it can be spent only on youth services. Therefore, the correct answer is choice D.

Questions 3–4

The prices are as follows:

Grandfather Clock	$2,400
Armoire	$2,000
Desk	$1,200
Bed	$1,000
Bureau	$750
Armchair	$700
Dresser	$600
Nightstand	$400
Desk Chair	$350

However, Message #1 states that the bed, dresser, and nightstand are to be sold only as a single unit. Similarly, Message #2 states that Pamela is to purchase the desk and desk chair only as a single unit. Finally, she is not to purchase the armchair at its stated price of $700.

Grandfather Clock	$2,400
Armoire	$2,000
Desk and Desk Chair	$1,550
Bed, Dresser, and Nightstand	$2,000
Bureau	$750
Arm Chair	$700 (not at this price)

Finally, Message #1 extends a 5% discount for a purchase exceeding $5,000. Pamela's budget is $6,000, but when you add the 5% discount to her $6,000 budget, the discount extends her purchasing power to $6,300 ($6000 × .05 = $300; $6000 + $300 = $6,300).

3a. **No** This purchase would result in the following total:

Grandfather clock	$2,400
Armoire	$2,000
Bed, dresser, and nightstand	$2,000
Total	$6,400
	× .05 discount
	$ 320

$6,400 – $320 = $6,080

Even with a 5% discount of $320, as mentioned in Message #1, the total price would be $6,080, which exceeds the budget of $6,000. Thus, Pamela cannot make this purchase.

3b. **No** Beth tells Pamela that she cannot buy the armchair at the stated price, and Message #1 states that it's non-negotiable. Thus, Pamela cannot make this purchase, even though it's within her $6,000 budget.

3c. **Yes** This purchase would result in the following total:

Armoire	$2,000
Desk and Desk Chair	$1,550
Bed, Dresser, and Nightstand	$2,000
Bureau	$750
Total	$6,300

The amount of $6,300 exceeds the budget, but Message #1 extends a 5% discount to all purchases over $5,000. The discount of $315 ($6,300 × .05 = $315) brings the price down to $5,985 ($6,300 – $315 = $5,985), which is within Pamela's budget, so she can make this purchase.

4. **B.** This purchase would result in the following total:

Armoire	$2,000
Arm chair	$ 550
Bed, dresser, and nightstand	$2,000
Desk and desk chair	$1,550
Total	$6,100
	× .05 discount
	$ 305

With the 5% discount mentioned in Message #1, the price is $5,795. This is between $5,700 and $5,800, so the correct answer is choice B.

Question 5

Message #2 provides five equivalencies, as follows:

2 mangos = 3 unblemished avocados

1 kilo of fish = 8 unblemished avocados

1 unblemished avocado = 10 large grapes

2 unblemished avocados = 3 blemished avocados

5 large grapes = 8 small grapes

Finally, remember the 50% markup for clothing items mentioned in Message #2.

5a. Yes 8 small grapes are worth 5 large grapes, so:

$$80 \text{ small grapes} = 50 \text{ large grapes}$$

10 large grapes are worth 1 unblemished avocados, so:

$$50 \text{ large grapes} = 5 \text{ unblemished avocados}$$

Therefore, you can trade 80 small grapes for 5 unblemished avocados, so the answer is Yes.

5b. No

$$1 \text{ kilo of fish} = 8 \text{ unblemished avocados}$$

Thus, you cannot trade 5 unblemished avocados for 1 kilo of fish, so the answer is No.

5c. Yes

$$2 \text{ mangos} = 3 \text{ unblemished avocados}$$

$$2 \text{ unblemished avocados} = 3 \text{ blemished avocados}$$

Thus, you can trade 5 unblemished avocados for 2 mangos and 3 blemished avocados, so the answer is Yes.

Question 6

One kilo of fish is worth 8 unblemished avocados. To find how many unblemished avocados = 10 kilos of fish, multiply 8 unblemished avocados times 10:

$$10 \text{ kilos of fish} = 80 \text{ unblemished avocados}$$

Every 3 blemished avocados = 2 unblemished avocados, so divide 15 blemished avocados by 1.5 to find the equivalent in unblemished avocados:

$$15 \text{ blemished avocados} = 10 \text{ unblemished avocados.}$$

Thus, 10 kilos of fish and 15 blemished avocados are worth a total of 90 unblemished avocados. Every 3 unblemished avocados are worth two mangos, so divide 90 by 1.5 to obtain the equivalent number of mangos:

$$90 \text{ unblemished avocados} = 60 \text{ mangos}$$

Therefore, 10 kilos of fish and 15 blemished avocados are worth 60 mangos, so you can get either 50 or 60 mangos, but not 70 mangos.

6a. Yes

6b. Yes

6c. No

Question 7

In the dry season, a pair of boots is worth 40 unblemished avocados, and an unblemished avocado is worth 10 large grapes, so:

One pair of boots = 40 unblemished avocados × 10 large grapes = 400 large grapes

Additionally, in the dry season, a raincoat is worth 500 large grapes. Thus, in the dry season, a pair of boots and a raincoat are worth a total of 900 large grapes, so you can get 900 large grapes, but you can't get 1,000 or 1,200 large grapes.

7a. Yes

7b. No

7c. No

Question 8

8. C. First, determine that if a shirt is worth 24 mangos during the rainy season, then it's worth 16 mangos during the dry season because of the 50% markup during the rainy season (16 × .50 = 8; 16 + 8 = 24). The information in the e-mail does not tell you how many mangos equal a kilo of fish, but it does tell you how many unblemished avocados equal a kilo of fish and the ratio of mangos to unblemished avocados. You first have to convert mangos to unblemished avocados. Every 2 mangos is worth 3 unblemished avocados, so multiply 16 mangos times 1.5 to obtain the equivalent in unblemished avocados:

16 mangos × 1.5 = 24 unblemished avocados

Since 1 kilo of fish equals 8 unblemished avocados, divide 24 by 8 to find the worth of a shirt in kilos of fish, or 24 ÷ 8 = 3.

Every 8 unblemished avocados is worth 1 kilo of fish. To obtain the equivalent of 3 kilos of fish in unblemished avocados, multiply the 8 unblemished avocados times 3, and the answer is:

24 unblemished avocados = 3 kilos of fish

Thus, if a shirt is worth 24 mangos during the rainy season, it is worth exactly 3 kilos of fish in the dry season, so the correct answer is C.

Questions 9–10

Message #1 states that Chuck is the head of the company, and that the company includes three departments: Operations, Sales, and Finance. Chuck's wife, Marion, runs Operations; Derek runs Finance; Jason, Tom, and Matt are sales managers. Thus, these five people report directly to Chuck.

Operations breaks down to Design, run by Lisa, and Site Ops, run by Art. They both report directly to Marion.

Finance includes Human Resources, run by Nadine. She reports directly to Derek. Carrie reports directly to Nadine, as will Zach if he accepts the position.

Finally, Angela reports directly to Matt.

Here is a chart that captures the chain of command:

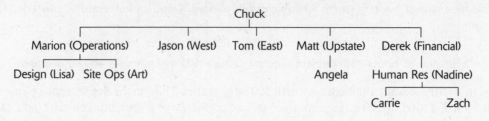

9a. **No** Carrie reports to Nadine, who reports to Derek, who reports to Chuck. Thus, Carrie is not in Tom's chain of command.

9b. **Yes** Lisa and Art both report to Marion (per Message #1), who is Jason's mother (per Message #3).

9c. **Yes** If Zach accepts the position, he will be in the Human Resources department, which is in Derek's chain of command.

10. **C.** Currently, five people report directly to Chuck (Marion, Jason, Tom, Matt, and Derek). If Canada becomes a separate region, Angela will manage it, and she will begin to report directly to Chuck. This accounts for six people, so the correct answer is choice C.

Table Analysis

Question 11

11a. **No** The statement requires that you compare two different years, 1969 and 1979, but notice that 1969 is not listed in the table. Start with datum that is available in the table. In 1979, the figure for *Awards as Percentage of Applicants* was 37.1%.

In 1970 (one year after 1969) the *Awards as Percentage of Applicants* was 40.3%, which was a *decrease* of 7.2% from the 1969. At this point, it is not necessary to perform arithmetic calculations because the data show that the figure in 1969 for the *Awards as a Percentage of Applicants* was greater than in 1979.

11b. **Yes** Sorting the table in ascending order by *Awards per 1,000 Insured Workers* moves the following row to the top of the table:

Year	Number of Applicants	Number of Awards	Awards as % of Applicants	% Increase/ Decrease	Awards per 1,000 Insured Workers
1982	1,019.8	336.1	33.0%	+0.2%	3.3

The lowest number of awards per 1,000 insured workers was in 1982, where awards were made to 33% of applicants, which is slightly less than one-third. Hence, the statement is *true*.

11c. **Yes** The three lowest years for awards as a percent of applicants were three consecutive years.

Sorting the table by *Awards as % of applicants* moves the following three rows to the top of the table:

Year	Number of Applicants	Number of Awards	Awards as % of Applicants	% Increase/ Decrease	Awards per 1,000 Insured Workers
1981	1,161.2	381.0	32.8%	−0.5%	3.8
1982	1,019.8	336.1	33.0%	+0.2%	3.3
1980	1,262.3	420.3	33.3%	−3.8%	4.3

Thus, three lowest years for awards as a percent of applicants were in 1980, 1981, and 1982, which were three consecutive years.

Question 12

12a. Yes Sorting the table by the *Total* column under *Import Sales* moves Year 1990 to the bottom of the table.

Year	New Passenger Car Sales (Thousands of Units)					
	Total Sales	Total Domestic Sales	Import Sales			
			Total	Japan	Germany	Others
1990	**9,303**	6,919	**2,384**	1,719	263	402

Thus, 1990 was the top year for total import sales. Calculate total import sales as a percentage of total sales:

$$\frac{2,384,000}{9,303,000} \approx 0.256 = 25.6\%$$

Thus, in 1990, the total import sales accounted for more than 25% of total sales.

12b. Yes Sorting the table by the *Germany* column under *Import Sales* moves the following two rows to the bottom of the table:

Year	New Passenger Car Sales (Thousands of Units)					
	Total Sales	Total Domestic Sales	Import Sales			
			Total	Japan	Germany	Others
2006	7,821	5,476	2,345	1,154	**561**	630
2007	7,618	5,253	2,365	1,183	**567**	615

Thus, the top year for German import sales was 2007. From 2006 to 2007, the decrease in domestic sales was 5,476,000 − 5,253,000 = 223,000. Calculate this percentage decrease as follows:

$$\frac{223,000}{5,476,000} \approx 0.041 = 4.1\%$$

Thus, the statement is *true* because the decrease in domestic sales from 2006 to 2007 was 4.1%, which is greater than 4%.

12c. No The five lowest years for Japanese import sales were all consecutive years.

The statement that the five lowest years for Japanese import sales were all consecutive years is not true. Sorting the table by the *Japan* column under *Import Sales* moves the following five rows to the top of the table:

Year	New Passenger Car Sales (Thousands of Units)					
	Total Sales	Total Domestic Sales	Import Sales			
			Total	Japan	Germany	Others
1998	8,142	6,762	1,380	691	367	322
1997	8,272	6,917	1,355	726	297	332
1996	8,527	7,255	1,272	727	237	308
1999	8,698	6,979	1,719	758	467	494
2004	7,545	5,396	2,149	810	542	797

Because 2004 is nonconsecutive with the years 1996 through 1999, the five lowest years for Japanese import sales were not all consecutive.

Question 13

13a. Yes The country or region that showed the greatest increase in U.S. imports from 2006 to 2007 showed a decrease in U.S. imports from 1998 to 2006.

Sorting the table by *% Change 2006–2007* moves All Others to the top of the table:

Country/ Region	1998	2002	2006	2007	% Change 2006–2007	% Share of Total 2007
All Others	95,893	56,353	40,431	59,784	**+47.9%**	2.6%

Thus, All Others had the greatest increase in U.S. imports from 2006 to 2007. In addition, you find when you compare All Others import numbers across the row from 1998 through 2006 (95,893; 56,353; and 40,431), that All Others experienced a decrease in U.S. imports during that period. Therefore the statement is true.

13b. No Of the four top countries or regions for U.S. imports in 1998, only two were still among the top four in 2007. This statement is not true.

Sorting the table by *1998* moves the following four rows to the bottom of the table:

Country/ Region	1998	2002	2006	2007	% Change 2006–2007	% Share of Total 2007
Indonesia	74,279	73,103	42,185	33,614	−20.3%	1.4%
Brazil	**83,294**	101,627	66,714	51,726	−22.5%	2.2%
All Others	**95,893**	56,353	40,431	59,784	+47.9%	2.6%
China	**1,107,566**	1,525,520	2,043,582	2,041,614	−0.1%	86.4%

And sorting the table by *2007* moves the following four rows to the bottom of the table:

Country/ Region	1998	2002	2006	2007	% Change 2006–2007	% Share of Total 2007
Brazil	83,294	101,627	66,714	**51,726**	−22.5%	2.2%
All Others	95,893	56,353	40,431	**59,784**	+47.9%	2.6%
Vietnam	7,175	17,537	86,115	89,503	+3.9%	3.8%
China	1,107,566	1,525,520	2,043,582	**2,041,614**	−0.1%	86.4%

This sort shows that China, All Others, and Brazil were among the four top countries or regions for U.S. imports in both 1998 and 2007. Therefore three, not two, of the top four countries or regions in 1998 were still among the top four in 2007.

13c. No Every country or region that showed an increase in U.S. imports from 2006 to 2007 also showed an increase from 2002 to 2006.

This statement is not true. Sorting the table by *% Change 2006–2007* moves Vietnam, Taiwan, and All Others to the bottom of the table. Note that they are the only three countries or regions that showed an increase in U.S. imports from 2006 to 2007:

Country/ Region	1998	2002	2006	2007	% Change 2006–2007	% Share of Total 2007
Vietnam	7,175	17,537	86,115	89,503	+3.9%	3.8%
Taiwan	15,855	10,185	8,955	11,923	+33.1%	0.5%
All Others	95,893	56,353	40,431	59,784	+47.9%	2.6%

Both Taiwan and All Others had an increase in U.S. imports from 2006 to 2007, but a *decrease* from 2002 to 2006. Therefore the answer is false.

Graphics Interpretation

Question 14

14. **$6,000; 5.8%** To answer the first part of the problem, the graph shows that the stock index was at its lowest in 2010 (first quarter). In that first quarter, the 401(k) was valued at approximately $110,000. During the previous quarter (2009 fourth quarter), the 401(k) was valued at approximately $104,000. Therefore, the gain between the fourth quarter of 2009 and the first quarter of 2010 was $110,000 – $104,000 = $6,000.

To answer the second part of the question, calculate the percentage as follows:

$$\frac{6,000}{104,000} \approx 0.058 = 5.8\%$$

Thus, 401(k) balances increased by approximately 5.8% during the quarter when the stock index was at its lowest.

Question 15

15a. **from 1,500 to 3,000** The condo apartment represents 22.6% of the total data set. Thus, if the data set contains exactly 12,000 items, 2,712 (22.6%) of them would be condo apartments, because 12,000 × 0.226 = 2,712.

15b. **140** Semi-detached residences represent 11.9% of the data set. If this percentage equals 238, then let x equal the number of residences in the entire data set and calculate as follows:

$$0.119x = 238$$
$$x = \frac{238}{0.119}$$
$$x = 2,000$$

Thus, the data set has 2,000 residences. Exactly 7.0% of these are attached/row/townhouse residences. Calculate as follows:

$$0.07 \times 2,000 = 140$$

Thus, the data set includes 140 attached/row/townhouse residences.

Question 16

16a. **one-fifth** Vincenza entered the market in 2004. In that year, Carpini's sales were a little more than 3 million, Vincenza's sales were a little under 2 million, and Vespucci's sales were approximately 10 million. Thus, the total market numbered 15 million pizzas, of which Carpini sold a little more than 3 million. Therefore, Carpini had slightly more than a one-fifth share of the market.

16b. between 50% and 60% Vespucci dominates the market as the consistent leader except for 2005, when Carpini was the top seller. In that year, Carpini sold approximately 11 million pizzas, Vespucci sold approximately 9 million, and Vincenza sold approximately 3 million. Thus, the total market was approximately 23 million pizzas. Of this number, the combined sales for Vespucci and Vincenza were approximately 12 million. Calculate this percentage as follows:

$$\frac{12,000,000}{23,000,000} \approx 0.522 = 52.2\%$$

Thus, the combined sales that year were between 50% and 60%.

Question 17

17. **greater than, 13** Every dot on the scatter plot that is below the 7% line represents an unemployment rate that is less than 7%. Follow the position of the data points straight downward to determine where they align with the investment to GDP ratio. All data points that are lower than the 7% unemployment rate align with investment to GDP ratios greater than 13. Thus the correct answer is that for an unemployment rate that is less than 7%, the investment-to-GDP ratio could reasonably be any amount on the scatter plot that is greater than 13.

Two-Part Analysis

Question 18

18a. Journal X: 12 copies

18b. Journal Y: 30 copies

The total width of the shelf is exactly 45 centimeters. Of this, 5.4 cm is needed for the separator, so you can calculate the remaining width as follows:

$$45 \text{ cm} - 5.4 \text{ cm} = 39.6 \text{ cm}$$

Thus, 39.6 cm must be accounted for as a combination of thicknesses of Journal X and Journal Y, so this is the *target number*.

Each copy of Journal X is 0.8 cm and each copy of Journal Y is 1 cm. To obtain the width of each possible block of journals, use the calculator provided on your computer to multiply the number of journals in each row of the Number of Journals column by 0.8 for Journal X and enter the product in the corresponding row in the Journal X column on a piece of scratch paper: then multiply the number of journals in each row of the Number of Journals column times 1 for Journal Y and enter the amount in the corresponding row in the Journal Y column. The following table shows the width of each possible block of journals:

Journal X	Journal Y	Number of Journals
4.8	6	6
9.6	12	12
14.4	18	18
19.2	24	24
24	30	30
28.8	36	36

Every number in the Journal Y column is a whole number, and the target number is 39.6, so the correct number in the Journal X column must account for the decimal; therefore, it is 9.6.

To find the number for Journal Y, subtract as follows:

$$39.6 \text{ cm} - 9.6 \text{ cm} = 30 \text{ cm}$$

Thus, the correct combination is as follows:

12 copies of Journal X + 30 copies of Journal Y

= 9.6 cm + 30 cm

= 39.6 cm (target number)

You can double-check your response by adding the following numbers:

12 copies of Journal X + 30 copies of Journal Y + Separator

= 9.6 cm + 30 cm + 5.4 cm

= 45 cm total width of the shelf

Question 19

19a. Model A Computers: 25

19b. Model B computers: 15

The total budget is exactly $30,000. Of this, $4,500 is otherwise allocated, so you can calculate the remaining budget as follows:

$$\$30,000 - \$4,500 = \$25,500$$

Thus, $25,500 must be accounted for as a combination of expenditures for Model A and Model B computers, so this is the *target number*.

Each Model A computer costs $600 and each Model B computer costs $700. Multiply the Number of Computers in each row by $600 for Model A and by $700 for Model B. The following table shows the cost of each possible block of computers:

Model A	Model B	Number of Computers
$3,000	$3,500	5
$6,000	$7,000	10
$9,000	$10,500	15
$12,000	$14,000	20
$15,000	$17,500	25
$18,000	$21,000	30

Use the following equation for your calculation:

$$\$25,500 - \text{Model A} = \text{Model B}$$

Plug each of the six values in the Model A column into this equation until you find a result that's in the Model B column:

$$\$25,500 - \$3,000 = \$22,500$$
$$\$25,500 - \$6,000 = \$19,500$$
$$\$25,500 - \$9,000 = \$16,500$$
$$\$25,500 - \$12,000 = \$13,500$$
$$\mathbf{\$25,500 - \$15,000 = \$10,500}$$

Or, because you know that the target number ends in 500, you can narrow your choices in the Model B column to $10,500 and $17,500, because there are no figures in the Model A column that end in $500. Subtract $10,500 from the target number ($25,500). The answer is $15,000. You know that you have the correct answer because $15,000 is one of the choices in the Model A column. (*Hint:* If $10,500 were not the right answer, then you would choose the remaining answer that ends in 500 in the Model B column, $17,500, because it would be your only other choice.)

Thus, the correct combination is as follows:

25 Model A computers + 15 Model B computers

You can double-check your response by adding the following numbers:

25 Model A computers + 15 Model B computers + Other Allocations

$$\$15,000 + \$10,500 + \$4,500$$
$$= \$30,000 \text{ total budget}$$

Question 20

20a. Office space: 25 floors

20b. Residential space: 20 floors

The total height of the building must be exactly 440 feet. Of this, 36.25 feet are accounted for in the ground floor, so you can calculate the remaining height as follows:

$$440 \text{ feet} - 36.25 \text{ feet} = 403.75 \text{ feet}$$

Thus, 403.75 feet must be accounted for as a combination of office and residential space, so this is the *target number*.

Each office floor is 8.75 feet in height and each residential floor is 9.25 feet in height. Multiply the number of floors in each row of the Number of Floors column by 8.75 for Office Space, and by 9.25 for Residential Space, and enter each answer in the corresponding column and row. The following table shows the height of each possible block of floors:

Office Space	Residential Space	Number of Floors
87.5	92.5	10
131.25	138.75	15
175	185	20
218.75	231.25	25
262.5	277.5	30
306.25	323.75	35

Use the following equation for your calculation of how many floors of each type of space the building can hold:

$$403.75 \text{ feet} - \text{Office Space} = \text{Residential Space}$$

Plug each of the six values in the Office Space column into this equation until you find a result that's in the Residential Space column:

$$403.75 - 87.5 = 316.25$$
$$403.75 - 131.25 = 272.5$$
$$403.75 - 175 = 228.75$$
$$\mathbf{403.75 - 218.75 = 185}$$

Thus, the correct combination is as follows:

25 Floors of Office Space + 20 Floors of Residential Space

You can double-check your response by adding the following numbers:

25 Floors of Office Space + 20 Floors of Residential Space + Ground Floor

$= 218.75 \text{ feet} + 185 \text{ feet} + 36.25 \text{ feet}$

$= 440 \text{ total building feet}$

Question 21

21a. Team Blue: 16 simulations

21b. Team Green: 10 simulations

The total simulator time available is exactly 100 hours. Some of this time is already allocated for 4 Team Blue simulations, each of which requires 3.25 hours. Thus, 13 hours is already allocated ($4 \times 3.25 = 13$), so calculate the remaining time as follows:

$$100 \text{ hours} - 13 \text{ hours} = 87 \text{ hours}$$

Thus, 87 hours must be accounted for as a combination of simulator time for Team Blue and Team Green, so this is the *target number.*

Each Team Blue simulation requires 3.25 hours and each Team Green simulation requires 3.5 hours. The following table shows the hours required for each possible block of simulations by each team:

Team Blue	Team Green	Number of Simulations
19.5	21.0	6
26.0	28.0	8
32.5	35.0	10
39.0	42.0	12
45.5	49.0	14
52.0	56.0	16

Use the following equation for your calculation:

$$87 \text{ hours} - \text{Team Blue} = \text{Team Green}$$

You can limit your calculations by noticing that every amount of time in the Team Green column is a whole number of hours, and the target number is 87 hours. Thus, the correct amount of time in the Team Blue column must also be a whole number of hours. Test these three values in the Team Blue column using the equation above:

$$87 \text{ hours} - 26 \text{ hours} = 61 \text{ hours}$$
$$87 \text{ hours} - 39 \text{ hours} = 48 \text{ hours}$$
$$\textbf{87 hours} - \textbf{52 hours} = \textbf{35 hours}$$

Thus, the correct combination is as follows:

16 simulations for Team Blue + 10 simulations for Team Green

You can double-check your response by adding the following numbers:

16 simulations for Team Blue + 10 simulations for Team Green + 4 additional simulations for Team Blue

$$= 52 \text{ hours} + 35 \text{ hours} + 13 \text{ hours}$$
$$= 100 \text{ total simulator hours}$$

PART III

ANALYTICAL WRITING ASSESSMENT SECTION

Chapter 3
Introduction to Analytical Writing Assessment

The Analytical Writing Assessment is the first section that appears on the GMAT. This section requires you to compose an original essay that critiques a persuasive argument. The purpose of this section is to see how well you can demonstrate the ability to reason critically under time constraints while you apply the rules and conventions of standard written English.

A good command of writing style and grammar conventions has been identified as one of the best predictors for advanced performance in graduate-level coursework. Although writing a critical essay can be intimidating to some students, anyone can learn the procedures for writing clearly and analytically. If you feel a little uneasy about this section, remember that you have already written many essays and research papers for your college classes, and that reviewing and practicing the writing guidelines presented in this chapter will give you an additional edge on the test. The pool of essay topics available on the GMAT website under the Analytical Writing Assessment section at www.mba.com also offers you additional opportunities to practice your analytical writing skills.

Skills and Concepts Tested

The Analytical Writing section of the GMAT consists of only one writing task: Analysis of an Argument. This task tests your ability to carefully read and develop a well-written essay that analyzes a short argument. You will apply reasoning skills to consider the evidence presented in the argument, evaluate and critique the argument's persuasiveness, and write a convincing essay that demonstrates your reasoning and writing skills.

Your ability to communicate and support your thoughts and ideas clearly will help you with this section.

To score well, your response should:

- express your ideas clearly.
- be organized and developed into a logical sequence of ideas.
- show unity within paragraphs and coherence from paragraph to paragraph.
- use the conventions of standard written English.
- provide supporting examples, evidence, and relevant reasons.

Directions and Scoring

You have 30 minutes to read one topic and respond directly to the argument provided. On-screen clock prompts will warn you how much time you have remaining on the test.

Each essay is scored on a scale from 1 to 6. Two different readers (one human and one electronic) score your essay. Your total score is an average of these two scores. For example, if the first reader gives your essay a score of 4 and the second gives it a score of 5, the two scores will be averaged to a 4.5. The electronic reader is an automated electronic system that analyzes more than fifty components of written expression, including sentence type, organization, and other structural aspects of language. If there is more than a 1-point discrepancy between the two scores, the essay goes to a third party (human reader) to settle the discrepancy. Official scores are reported in increments of 0.5 and are available approximately 20 calendar days after your exam date.

Because you must write your essay within a limited period of time, minor errors in mechanics will not affect your score. Scorers are also trained to be sensitive in assessing the responses of test-takers for whom English is not the first language. It is important, however, to use appropriate vocabulary and vary your sentence openings, length, and structure. Using smooth transitions will also help guide your readers through the logical development of your ideas.

Computer Word Processor

Although you can take notes to plan your essay, you must type your essay response on a computer keyboard that is connected to a very simple word processing software program. The word processor includes basic functions: cut, paste, copy, undo, and redo. You can use either a computer mouse or keyboard to use these functions. Remember that this basic word processor does *not* include a spellchecker or grammar tool, but minor errors will not affect your score. Since the software does not allow you to use tabs to indicate a new paragraph, you will need to use the Enter key to leave a space between paragraphs.

The essay prompt will appear in a box at the top of the screen and remain there as you prepare, compose, and edit your essay in a separate box below. The best way to prepare yourself for using the word processor is to download the free GMATPrep® software, which includes a tutorial for the word processor functions. It is available to registered test-takers at www.mba.com under the Free Test-Preparation Software section of the website. Another way to prepare to compose your essay using this type of word processor is to use the basic word processors available in Windows (Word Pad) and Mac OS (Text Edit).

Overview of Analysis of an Argument

Time: 30 minutes
1 Essay

The Analysis of an Argument task requires that you evaluate the reasoning of a short argument and then write a persuasive response. The argument's passage is often a topic of interest such as a letter to the editor of a newspaper, a company memo, or another type of short piece that seeks to persuade the reader. All of the arguments are deeply flawed. These flaws include assumptions, missing information, and the failure to consider alternative explanations for a given situation. Your task is to identify and analyze the flaws in the argument.

Note: Your task is not to agree or disagree. You are not being asked to provide your opinion or take a position on the argument presented. Instead, you must explain how the argument could be made more persuasive, what assumptions exist, and what missing information, if supplied, would improve its reasoning.

Following each argument is a basic set of directions. Your task is to:

- explain assumptions that the author makes or implies.
- suggest evidence that is needed to evaluate the argument or make it more persuasive.
- discuss alternative explanations for the situation.
- identify changes that would make the argument more persuasive.

Common Argument Flaws

As you read argument sample topics, you will begin to see the same flaws in logic repeated over and over. The table below does not contain every flaw, but will give you an idea of what to expect as you read a variety of sample tasks.

Theme	Common Flaw	Description
Extrapolation	Applying one instance to every situation	Extrapolation flaws take a narrow piece of evidence and then apply it broadly to all cases. For example, the argument may take a study done at one school and try to apply the results to all schools in a state. Because what is true for one school may not apply to others, this flaw is based on false assumptions and overgeneralization.
Apples to oranges	Making unfounded comparisons	Arguments that make unfounded comparisons try to compare two situations that are not alike, such as comparing a small town to a large city, or a private university to a public one. These arguments are flawed because the comparisons are not valid: the situations are not alike, so the argument is based on false assumptions and, usually, missing information.
Trends	Assuming a trend will continue	These arguments present a current trend—usually including numbers or other data—and assume that the trend will remain unchanged. A common example involves prices, say for housing. The argument may assume that home prices will continue to rise because historically real estate prices increase with economic inflation, but it ignores any other possible factors. These arguments fail to consider alternative explanations.
Sole factor	Identifying only one variable	Most of the arguments for this task involve complex cause-and-effect situations. The sole factor flaw singles out one reason for a given situation and ignores all others. An argument may cite the increase in the number of police officers as the sole factor for a drop in crime. It may ignore other possible reasons like an improved economy, changes in the weather, and longer prison sentences for offenders. These flaws allow you to offer and discuss other explanations for the cause-and-effect relationship.
Weasel words	Using deceptive language	Many arguments will use deceptive wording to hide missing information. For example, saying that the number of criminal arrests has dropped may sound good, but has the actual number of crimes decreased? These flaws try to hide missing information that would make the argument less convincing.

Scoring Rubric

Because you are writing your essay within a limited amount of time, even the highest scoring essay may contain minor errors. Scorers take this into consideration. Scores for this task are averaged in half-point (0.5) increments.

Score of 6: Excellent Analysis

The highest scoring essays present an insightful, well-articulated analysis. Test-takers:

- identify the aspects of the argument that are relevant to the prompt and examine them in an insightful way.
- develop the ideas that respond to the argument coherently.
- use clear transitions to connect ideas.
- provide relevant and thorough support from the argument.
- use well-chosen vocabulary and varied sentence openings, lengths, and structure to convey ideas.
- demonstrate correct usage of the conventions of standard written English.

Score of 5: Strong Analysis

Essays that receive this score present a thoughtful, organized examination of the argument. Test-takers:

- identify the aspects of the argument that are relevant to the prompt and examine them in a generally thoughtful way.
- develop the ideas logically and connect them with clear transitions.
- provide mostly relevant support from the argument.
- use appropriate vocabulary and varied sentence openings, lengths, and structure to convey ideas.
- demonstrate correct usage of the conventions of standard written English.

Score of 4: Competent

Essays that receive this score present a competent and generally clear examination of the argument. Test-takers:

- identify relevant aspects of the argument, but lose points by addressing some unrelated factors.
- develop the ideas clearly, but lose points by not always connecting them with clear transitions.
- provide some support from the argument, but lose points because development of the support is uneven.
- use language to convey ideas in a generally clear way.
- demonstrate mostly correct usage of the conventions of standard written English, but also make some errors.

Score of 3: Flawed

Essays that receive this score show some competence in examining the argument but have a number of flaws. Test-takers:

- fail to identify most of the relevant aspects of the argument.
- discuss unrelated aspects or present poor reasoning.
- develop the ideas in a limited or less logical way.
- provide support that is less relevant to the argument.
- use unclear language.
- make some major or frequent minor errors in standard written English language conventions that interfere with communicating their ideas clearly.

Score of 2: Weak

Essays that receive this score either fail to respond to the directions for the task and/or show weakness in the ability to examine the argument. Test-takers:

- do not identify the relevant aspects of the argument, and present their own opinion on the issue instead.
- do not follow the specific directions for the task.
- fail to develop their ideas.
- organize their ideas illogically.
- provide little to no support for the ideas they present.
- use language in a way that interferes with clear communication.
- make serious errors in conventions that cause the meaning to be unclear.

Score of 1: Deficient

Essays that receive this score reveal basic problems in analytical writing. Test-takers:

- demonstrate little or no understanding of the argument.
- write essays that are short and disorganized.
- use language in a way that makes the content difficult to understand.
- make serious, frequent errors in conventions that result in incoherence.

Score of 0

Essays that receive this score may be off-topic or written in a foreign language, they may not respond to the writing task, they may simply repeat the argument, or they may consist of random keystrokes.

Score of NR

If there is no response to the analytical writing prompt, this section of the GMAT receives a score of NR.

Sample Arguments with Responses

The Analysis of an Argument task requires you to read and evaluate a short passage. The passage appears with a standard set of directions. Below are two sample arguments; two sample responses are shown for each argument.

Sample Argument 1

The following recommendation appeared in a budget report:

> A recent series of blind taste tests conducted by Fizzio Bottling Company indicates that customers are not able to tell the difference between soft drinks made with more expensive cane sugar and those made with high fructose corn syrup. However, the majority of those surveyed stated a preference for buying soft drinks made with cane sugar. Despite the higher costs, Fizzio should change its recipe to include cane sugar and promote this ingredient in its advertising. This will enable Fizzio to maintain its market share and profits.

Write a response to explain how convincing you find this argument. You should consider its reasoning and how well it uses evidence. You should also discuss any doubtful assumptions and how counterexamples or alternative explanations might undermine the argument's persuasiveness. Consider as well any changes that would make the argument more convincing or what additional information would help you better assess its conclusion.

Sample Responses

A High-Scoring Model Essay Response

On the surface, this memo from Fizzio Bottling Company appears to make a good argument for switching to a cane sugar recipe. But when you look beneath the surface it becomes evident that the argument is deeply flawed in its assumptions, handling of evidence, and failure to consider alternative scenarios.

Much of the argument's weight rests on the taste tests and customer survey, however little information is given about them. We know it was a blind taste test, but how was it conducted? Did people sip from small cups or did they drink a full serving? For example, in the famous Pepsi Challenge, consumers preferred Pepsi to Coca-Cola in the initial small taste, but did not maintain that preference when drinking larger amounts of soda. If consumers only tasted a small amount of Fizzio sodas, the results may not prove valid. It would also be important to know how many people participated in the taste test and survey. Were the numbers significant enough to warrant changing the drink recipe? A very small sample size would not give as trustworthy a result as a larger one. Another consideration is whether the taste tests and survey were even given at the same time. People may respond differently when given a paper survey without being given the opportunity to taste the product. Also, while consumers may express a preference on a survey for sodas made with cane sugar, it's not guaranteed they will choose the more expensive soda when purchasing soft drinks in the grocery store.

The argument also fails to consider the costs associated with changing its recipe, suppliers, and advertising campaign. No information is provided on how much it will cost to retool the Fizzio drinks recipes for cane sugar as opposed to corn syrup. Development costs could be significant, especially on top of the added ingredient costs in production. The argument states that Fizzio will maintain market share and profits, but provides no numbers to support that contention. Even if market share were maintained, the company will still need to promote its new line of cane sugar sodas and require added funds for marketing. It is difficult to imagine a scenario where Fizzio is able to keep its profits at the same level, at least in the near term.

Finally, the argument relies on Fizzio's competitors staying on the sidelines and not developing their own lines of cane sugar sodas. If the other soft drink manufacturers follow suit, then it's unlikely Fizzio will see any benefit from changing its recipe. With taking all of these issues into consideration, it is difficult to find the plan convincing to any degree.

A Low-Scoring Model Essay Response

Fizzio's plan to change its soda recipes from high fructose corn syrup (HFCS) to cane sugar is a smart idea. Recent studies have shown that consumption of HFCS is linked to obesity, diabetes, and heart disease. Changing to a cane sugar formula is the right thing to do for both economic and health reasons.

Companies that use more expensive cane sugar may have higher production costs but they can also charge more for their products. Consumers desire more natural foods and cane sugar is viewed as an authentic agricultural product. It seems worth the cost to drink sodas made with ingredients that come from the farm rather than the laboratory.

Fizzio also has a responsibility to its customers with regard to their health. Study after study has cited the problems associated with consumption of HFCS and its detrimental effects, particularly on children. It may even come to be seen as negligent to market beverages containing HFCS to children. With one-third of kids now diagnosed as overweight, it is important that the foods they eat come from high-quality, natural sources.

Finally, Fizzio should consider changing to a cane sugar formula because of possible tax legislation. Some states are looking at charging a tax on drinks containing HFCS. This is the right response to a public health threat. If people have to pay a tax on sweetened drinks perhaps they will lower their intake of HFCS sweetened beverages and switch to a safer, more natural alternative.

Evaluation of Responses

The first response would score well because it addresses a wide variety of flaws present in the argument. In each paragraph the writer identifies issues and explains how each one undermines the persuasiveness of the argument. The writer also suggests ways in which the recommendation could be made more convincing by detailing alternative scenarios. Although it is a strong response, it likely would not earn the highest score due to its unimpressive writing style. The second response, while well written, would score as weak. The writer does not respond to the prompt, but offers opinions and evidence that are not stated in the argument regarding the use of cane sugar versus high fructose corn syrup. Because it fails to analyze the argument and instead presents the writer's viewpoint on the topic, it would be assigned a lower score.

Sample Argument 2

The following appeared in an email memo to company executives:

> The current lease for our office space is expiring soon. The terms of renewal include both a moderate increase in rent and the addition of fees for employee parking spaces. Management has opted out of paying for the parking spaces in the new lease. Employees will retain the option of paying for their own parking, but as there is adequate on-street parking within easy walking distance of the building, we anticipate people will choose the convenient, free spaces already available. This will mitigate the increase in rent, enabling us to remain competitive without imposing an undue burden on our workers.

Write a response to explain how convincing you find this argument. You should consider its reasoning and how well it uses evidence. You should also discuss any doubtful assumptions and how counterexamples or alternative explanations might undermine the argument's persuasiveness. Consider as well any changes that would make the argument more convincing or what additional information would help you better assess its conclusion.

Sample Responses

A High-Scoring Model Essay Response

The recommendation made in the email memo is short sighted and flawed in its assumptions about employee behavior. It is also missing specific information needed to make the argument convincing and fails to consider possible results of the changes to the parking situation.

First, the writer of the memo assumes that employees will accept the loss of on-site parking without complaint, saying the change will not result in an "undue burden" on them. It's difficult to assess the accuracy of that statement without knowing more specific information. How much street parking is actually available? How much is "adequate"? The memo states that the parking is "easy walking distance" but does not indicate a distance. Some people may think a five-minute walk is reasonable, while others may consider any distance over 100 yards a burden. Even if it is a reasonable distance, are employees willing to walk in order to save the company money on its rent? This change may breed resentment over time, resulting in lower morale.

The writer also fails to provide specific information about the costs involved. The memo states that there is a "modest" increase in rent and added fees for parking. How much of a percent increase does this represent over the current lease terms? How much are the fees and how much do they add up to per employee? Given more specific numbers it would be possible to assess the validity of claims that declining the parking spaces would have a significant impact on the ability of the company to remain competitive. Because employees will have the option to pay for their own parking, they will see the actual costs involved. If the fees are perceived as high, it will create an undue burden. If the fees are perceived as negligible, employees may feel that the company is pinching pennies and not looking out for the interests of its workers.

Finally, there may be some unintended consequences of declining the parking spaces. Employees may find it more challenging to find parking than anticipated and begin showing up late for work. There may be safety issues with pedestrian traffic and crossing busy intersections. Another unexamined issue concerns the company's client. Will they be expected to park on the street? What impression might they have of the company's finances if the firm is unable to provide parking for employees and clients? If a prospective client's first impression is negative due to parking hassles it could adversely affect business. Although it may seem like the best idea to minimize costs in the new lease, the memo does not provide enough relevant information and support to make a convincing case for declining the parking spaces and shifting any burden to employees.

An Average-Scoring Model Essay

The argument made in the company memo is weak for many reasons.
- It assumes employees are willing to walk.
- It doesn't tell how far the street parking is.
- It doesn't give the amount of the rent increase.
- It doesn't tell how much the parking fees will be.

The company executives think that employees will be fine with parking on the street without asking their opinion. Employees may not like having to walk from their cars. Also, the memo doesn't tell how far the parking is from the office. If it is a long distance, women may not feel comfortable working late, especially if it is in a neighborhood without good streetlights.

The memo also doesn't tell how much the rent increase and fees will be. Maybe it is just a small amount and the executives are being cheap. If the employees think that they have to lose parking spaces so that people at the top can have bigger bonuses it could make them upset and worsen productivity.

The argument needs to give more specific information about the situation with the street parking and not make as many assumptions about what employees want.

Evaluation of Responses

The first response would score well due to its identification of a wide range of problems in reasoning that are present in the memo and an explanation of why the reasoning is faulty. The use of questions to point out information that could help support the argument strengthens the analysis. The second response uses bullet points in a similar way, but does not develop the analysis in as much depth.

A Three-Step Writing Process

For any timed writing task, you should follow three steps from start to finish: *prewriting, writing,* and *proofreading.* One of the biggest mistakes a test-taker can make is to begin to write an essay without first taking the time to plan the response. You wouldn't get in the car to go to a new destination without consulting a map or plugging the address into your navigation system. Who knows where you would end up? Similarly, it is important to take the time to organize your ideas before you begin typing your essay. It is also essential to save a few minutes at the end to proofread, review the flow of your essay, and make sure that you have left spaces between paragraphs to indicate breaks.

Here is a sample Analysis of an Argument task with the suggested three-step approach:

> The following appeared as a recommendation from a city budget committee:
>
> A recent survey of public library patrons found that the majority of visitors are using the branch libraries from 3:00 in the afternoon until 8:00 in the evening. Most of those responding said they would prefer that the library hours be extended to 10:00 p.m. during the week. The extension of evening hours can be done by opening the library at 11:00 a.m. rather than the current 9:00 a.m. opening. This will cause the least inconvenience to patrons and allow a better use of library resources.

Write a response to explain how convincing you find this argument. You should consider its reasoning and how well it uses evidence. You should also discuss any doubtful assumptions and how counterexamples or alternative explanations might undermine the argument's persuasiveness. Consider as well any changes that would make the argument more convincing or what additional information would help you better assess its conclusion.

Step 1: Prewriting

Many students believe that good writers just sit down and miraculously produce an essay. On the contrary, most experienced writers know that effective writing requires an organization and planning process. This prewriting process helps you gather information and ideas as you prepare to compose a well-written essay.

You will have 30 minutes total for the writing task. For the first five minutes, use your scratch paper to brainstorm ideas, organize the logical development of your essay, and map out a strategy. This will also help you manage your time once you begin writing.

Brainstorming

The technique for creating and accumulating ideas and examples is called *brainstorming*. Brainstorming is an exploration process that allows you to imagine and generate ideas about your topic. Your "imaginings" will help you compile words and phrases about the essay topic by simply jotting down as many thoughts, ideas, and possibilities as you can bring to mind to address the topic. It is important to remember that *all ideas are acceptable* during the brainstorming process and that neatness, order, and spelling do not matter *at this point*.

After generating as many ideas or examples as you can, evaluate and organize your notes by looking for patterns or themes so you can group your ideas into categories. Read the sample argument and develop a brainstorming list of the types of evidence that may be missing from the recommendation or conclusion:

- Is there is a shortage of library resources?
- How many library patrons were surveyed?
- How was the survey conducted (handed out to everyone, left at the checkout counter)?
- How long was the survey conducted?
- Who uses the library in the morning (maybe young children, retired people)?
- Who uses the library in the afternoon (maybe students)?
- Will librarians want to work until 10:00 p.m.?
- How many people indicated that they wanted the library open until 10:00 p.m.?
- What activities are scheduled in the morning from 9:00 a.m. to 11:00 a.m.?

Organizing Your Brainstorming

The next step in prewriting is to organize the brainstorming. You will not have time to write an outline. Instead, use numbers to label the points in your brainstorming. In this case, we want to start with the broadest concept and then cluster similar ideas together:

Topic 1: Shortage of library resources?

Topic 2: How was the survey conducted?

Topic 3: Keep libraries open until 10:00 p.m.?

With these topics established, you can now organize your brainstorming list:

Topic 1: Is there is a shortage of library resources?

Topic 2: How many library patrons were surveyed?

Topic 2: How was the survey conducted (handed out to everyone, left at the checkout counter)?

Topic 2: How long was the survey conducted?

Topic 1: Who uses the library in the morning (maybe young children, retired people)?

Topic 1: Who uses the library in the afternoon (maybe students)?

Topic 3: Will librarians want to work until 10:00 p.m.?

Topic 3: How many people indicated they wanted the library open until 10:00 p.m.?

Topic 1: What activities are scheduled in the morning from 9:00 a.m. to 11:00 a.m.?

Mapping a Strategy

The final step in prewriting is to map out the strategy. After you have organized your ideas, it is time to strategize how to plan your essay. A typical argument essay will include four to five paragraphs:

Paragraph One—Start with a strong opening paragraph that presents an overview of the argument's conclusion. Try to avoid a long introduction, and try to keep it about the same length as the conclusion.

Paragraphs Two, Three, and Four—The body of your essay should provide detailed evidence to support the information introduced in the first paragraph. As you focus on the task, consider writing about invalid assumptions or inferences. You can also offer alternative explanations that challenge the argument's logical flow of reasoning. Whatever you choose to focus on, your writing should challenge the argument with clearly developed points and an insightful analysis.

You should spend more time on the body than on your introduction and conclusion, but keep your writing concise and to the point. Begin each paragraph with a unifying sentence and then provide supporting evidence with specific examples. Each paragraph should elaborate on and provide examples of the main argument from the first paragraph.

- Paragraph two: Most important point or argument
- Paragraph three: Second most important point or argument
- Paragraph four: Third most important point or argument

In the sample argument presented, the biggest missing piece of evidence is whether a shortage of library resources exists. It is most logical to begin there (Topic 1) and ask about the activities and usage schedule for both the morning and afternoon. The next set of missing evidence concerns the way in which the survey was conducted (Topic 2). The final area of evidence centers on the issue of keeping the libraries open until 10:00 p.m. (Topic 3) and whether there is enough information to support this conclusion.

Paragraph Five—Your concluding paragraph should be about the same length as your introduction and should summarize the main points of your argument. The fifth paragraph repeats the points (in the same order) that were presented in paragraph one. If you follow this order, you will be adding a sense of continuity and structural integrity to your writing. This is the time to briefly clarify any points that you presented that may need further illumination.

Step 2: Writing

The actual writing step of the essay should take approximately 20 minutes of the total 30-minute time limit for the Analysis of an Argument task. Begin by reviewing and organizing the bullet points generated during prewriting to focus your attention on one paragraph at a time. Then develop each topic as a paragraph, using the bullet points from the prewriting as a guide.

Explain how the missing evidence would either undermine or strengthen the argument for changing the library hours. Elaborate on the bullet points by providing examples and explanation. Manage your time so that within approximately 15 minutes you finish the paragraph about the survey and are ready to make your final set of points about changing the closing time to 10:00 p.m.

Step 3: Proofreading

You should use the last three to five minutes to read over your essay and correct errors. You will be able to insert text to add any transitions you may have left out and to use the Enter key to leave spaces between paragraphs. Look for words that you typed twice or may have left out. Watch the clock! Once the timer reaches zero, you will be unable to make any more changes.

Writing Tips and Strategies

The scoring for the writing task emphasizes three key elements of writing: organization, vocabulary, and variety of sentence length and structure. You can learn to address each element with the help of these few simple reminders as you practice writing sample essays in preparation for the exam.

Organization

The first step in logical organization is to take the time to brainstorm and then outline your response. It is best to develop two or three points in depth and aim for paragraphs of three to five sentences in length. Organize your ideas from the general to the specific. For example, in responding to a prompt about assumptions, you would begin with the major assumption that underlies the entire argument and then work toward the more specific elements.

Another aspect of organization is to provide transitions that guide the reader through your essay. Words and phrases like *first, initially,* and *a primary consideration* indicate the beginning of a chain of logic. Words and phrases like *another, also,* and *in addition* let the reader know you are continuing with the development of your reasoning. To show another point of view, say, in a concession, words and phrases such as *although* and *however* help provide contrast. While these short essays do not require a formal conclusion, a sentence near the end of the final paragraph with the words *finally* or *lastly* let the reader know you are drawing your essay to a close.

Vocabulary

The scorers are looking for effective, appropriate vocabulary that conveys a clear meaning. You should avoid slang, technical jargon, and informal spoken English. For example, in spoken English one might use the expression *on the flip side,* while in a written essay, *another viewpoint* would be more apt. If you want to use a word but are unsure of how to spell it, use your scratch paper to write the word with different spelling combinations to determine the correct spelling. If you are still unsure, consider using the word sparingly rather than throughout your response, or try to use a synonym. A single misspelling will not have an impact on your score, but multiple errors will have a greater effect.

Sentence Variety

Although scorers will be reading your essay quickly, they will get a sense of your overall style, mainly through sentence variety. Aim to vary the lengths of your sentences to create a rhythm and flow to your writing. Sentences that are all the same length can seem choppy when they are too short. Conversely, many long and complex sentences will deaden your style. Another way to vary your sentences is by checking the first word of each sentence. Highlight the first word and look for patterns. If each sentence begins with the same word or words (*The, This*), the resulting pattern can create monotony for the reader. Try changing the order of ideas in the sentence, but beware of obscuring their meaning. The primary criterion that scorers consider is clarity of expression.

Try out these tips by writing practice essays. In the following pages you will find a variety of Analysis of an Argument topics. You can also find the entire topic pool online at the GMAT website (www.mba.com). Another strategy as you select topics is to complete the prewriting exercises as practice for the reasoning required for the task. As you gain more confidence, use a timer to limit yourself to 30 minutes per response. It is highly recommended that you practice typing your essays on the special Analysis of an Argument word processer, too. The free GMATPrep software includes the basic word processor that you will use for the actual exam.

Response Scoring Checklists

Use the following checklist to assess your essays. You can either ask someone else to read and evaluate them, or put your essays aside for a few days and read them again yourself with a fresh eye.

Questions	Completely	Partially	No
1. Does the essay respond directly to the specific directions for the prompt?			
2. Does the essay identify the relevant aspects of the argument and develop an insightful analysis?			
3. Does the essay include support drawn from the argument?			
4. Is the essay well organized with clear transitions?			
5. Is the essay written using correct English, and does it use a variety of vocabulary words, and sentence openings, lengths, and structure?			

Extra Practice Topics

For the following topics use the set of directions below:

Write a response to explain how convincing you find this argument. You should consider its reasoning and how well it uses evidence. You should also discuss any doubtful assumptions and how counterexamples or alternative explanations might undermine the argument's persuasiveness. Consider as well any changes that would make the argument more convincing or what additional information would help you better assess its conclusion.

* * * * *

The following is from the minutes of a school board meeting:

> Last year Ortega High School began offering online classes for physical education, digital photography, and computer science. The pass rate for all of these classes was more than 95%, indicating a high level of engagement and achievement by students. As these online classes appeal to high school students—and are less expensive to offer—the school should consider expanding the online courses to English, math, and science.

* * * * *

The following is from a company memo:

> The last five years have seen explosive growth in gourmet grocery stores here in Rewand County. Of the four new markets opened near the city center, three are still in business and Expresso Foods plans to open another location in the next two months. To capitalize on this new demand for upscale markets, Thriftfoods should consider opening its own gourmet grocery store.

* * * * *

The following recommendation was made in an email to the dean of student affairs:

In the last ten years, the disparity between job offers tendered to Pilo University graduates and to Limnit University graduates has widened. Graduates with a Pilo diploma are three times more likely to find employment within six months of graduation as compared to nine months for those earning their degrees at Limnit. In order to make our graduates more marketable and to increase enrollment, Limnit should include free career counseling to all seniors.

* * * * *

The following comes from the minutes of a chamber of commerce meeting:

A recent study indicates that artichokes are an excellent source of dietary fiber, and they are low in fat and calories. Not surprisingly, residents of Burtonville, where a large percentage of the state's crop is grown, report a lower than average incidence of obesity, heart disease, and certain types of cancer. It stands to reason that a statewide promotion of artichoke products would improve the health of our citizens.

* * * * *

The following email was sent to directors of a retail company:

A recent study of workplace behaviors indicated that employees who know they are under video surveillance provide better customer service and spend less time on nonwork-related tasks during their shifts. In order to improve our company's reputation for being customer-focused and to increase worker productivity, we should consider adding cameras in all of our retail locations. The initial costs will be quickly repaid in the form of higher profits.

* * * * *

The following recommendation was made at a city council meeting:

Due to current high unemployment in Lowton, we ought to consider offering tax incentives to businesses that relocate here. When neighboring Westville offered similar tax incentives three years ago, the city attracted a large number of companies, and the unemployment rate dropped considerably. Any reduction in business tax revenue will surely be offset by personal income and sales tax revenue increases.

* * * * *

The following is a recommendation from a city planner:

Traffic congestion has become a major impediment to business in the Fretser City metropolitan area. A recent survey of companies indicated that commute times rank among the highest concerns for their employees and are cited as a reason for possibly leaving the area. For these reasons, it is imperative we consider adding carpool lanes along the major transportation routes in the city. This will result in less congestion, lower commute times, and more satisfied employees.

* * * * *

The following comes from the minutes of a city council budget committee meeting:

> Every year the city's libraries operate at a loss, requiring massive infusions of cash to stay open. Every year this situation strains the city's finances. It's clear that privatization would force libraries to run more efficiently and stay within budget. Shifting responsibility from the city government to a private company would save the taxpayer from having to support a poorly run system.

* * * * *

The following comes from a company memo:

> The recent introduction of our "Living Lite" mayonnaise has breathed new life into our grocery product line. In just two months its sales have lifted our bottom line considerably. For this reason we should consider adding reduced-sodium as well as flavored options like bacon and jalapeño to our lineup of mayonnaise products. They will be sure to build on the success of "Living Lite" and improve our profitability.

* * * * *

The following appeared as a recommendation in a quarterly report:

> Six weeks ago, our flagship restaurant in Los Angeles added whole-wheat buns to the menu as an alternative to regular buns and bread for patrons who order burgers and sandwiches. Sales of burgers have increased 10 percent during this time. In order to increase sales of both burgers and sandwiches, our restaurants across the nation should add whole-wheat buns to the menu despite the slight added cost of the buns.

* * * * *

The following appeared in a letter to the editor of the local newspaper:

> The spring migration of white-eared tortoises through Peterville creates traffic jams and other distractions, costing businesses time and money during the three-day period. In neighboring Dayton, the city has created a festival to celebrate the migration, which draws tourists from around the area. A similar festival in Peterville would be sure to increase tourism and offset current business losses.

* * * * *

The following appeared as a company memo:

> In our latest development of single-family homes, we offered one-story and two-story models while our competitor offered only models with a single floor. Our development took twice as long to sell out and our customers did not opt for as many upgrades, resulting in a lower profit margin. In order to remain competitive, and offer homebuyers the models they prefer, our next development should feature only one-story homes.

* * * * *

The following recommendation appeared in the minutes of the council:

> Last year the Greater Westfall Economics Council sponsored a scholarship contest for high school students. Despite an extension of the deadline, only 20 applications were received. Clearly, there is a lack of interest in the study of economics among the young people of Westfall. Our committee recommends that the prize monies be reallocated to students already enrolled in college.

*   *   *   *   *

The following appeared in a company memo:

> Each year the Perkins Firm faces large increases in its contribution to medical insurance benefits for employees. In order to cut costs and promote healthier habits, the firm should consider increasing the employee contribution for health care. When people share more of the burden for medical insurance, they will adopt better diet and exercise habits, which will result in lower costs for all.

*   *   *   *   *

The following appeared as a recommendation by a city council:

> Road repairs in Midville represent a large part of the city budget for infrastructure. Last year's mild winter provided some economic relief for the city because fewer repairs were needed. The forecast for the next few years is for continued mild winter weather. For that reason we should defer road repairs this year and use the repair fund for other infrastructure projects instead.

PART IV

VERBAL SECTION

The Verbal section of the GMAT is an important measurement in the graduate school admission application process. The purpose of this section on the GMAT is to evaluate your readiness for business school by testing your ability to critically read, reason, and evaluate written material under time constraints. In order to achieve success on this portion of the test, you must be familiar with interpreting the fundamental concepts of standard written English and respond to questions in a multiple-choice format.

Research suggests that a degree of familiarity with the test format and types of questions increases your odds for greater success on standardized tests, like the GMAT. This is why we have structured this part of the book with three separate chapters that provide you with question types, review material, strategies with sample questions, and practice questions.

As you study the material in each chapter, it is important to observe your mistakes and bracket specific themes that emerge among the questions. Take conscientious notes about material that requires your additional knowledge or understanding. Examining these details will help you to focus on specific areas of improvement and help you to organize your thoughts so that you can develop a study plan to meet your individual needs. As you pace yourself and work through the sample problems and practice questions, you should notice an improvement in your consistent ability to answer questions with greater ease and proficiency.

Research shows that repeated and structured practice is one of the keys to your success on the GMAT so be sure to take advantage of the practice material provided. Sharpen your skills by practicing what you have learned in the full-length practice test at the end of this guide. Three additional practice tests on the accompanying CD-ROM will further your understanding. The official GMAT website at www.mba.com will provide you with an opportunity to practice with computer-simulated questions.

Format

There are three Verbal question types.

Chapter Number	Question Type	Total Number of Questions on GMAT
Chapter 4	**Sentence correction** emphasizes the importance of evaluating and improving sentences that may be grammatically or structurally incorrect.	Approximately 15–16 questions
Chapter 5	**Reading comprehension** questions evaluate your comprehension of long passages that are 200–350 words. Passage topics are drawn from several different sources in business, social science, and science and will test your ability to understand, interpret, and draw conclusions from the written material.	Approximately 12–14 questions
Chapter 6	**Critical reasoning** questions are similar to reading comprehension questions, but emphasize your ability to read critically while analyzing a short argument-type passage. As you read the material, you will be asked to evaluate the passage and find a solution that forms an "action plan" that is logical and reasonable.	Approximately 11–13 questions

Computer-Adaptive Testing

The computer-adaptive Verbal section gives you 75 minutes to answer 41 intermingled questions. This means that you will have about $1\frac{3}{4}$ minutes to answer each question. When factoring the allocated test time, keep in mind that reading passages themselves require additional time. Each question will appear individually on the computer screen starting with a medium-difficulty question. The computer will adapt the level of difficulty in subsequent questions based on your performance on the previous questions.

To select the answer, you must click on the appropriate oval for your selected choice. During the test administration, you will not be allowed to skip questions or navigate back and forth within the section. You are, however, allowed to review a reading passage if it applies to a series of questions. Always remember to fill in an answer before you attempt to move to the next question. In addition, as you work through the computer-adaptive test, take advantage of the noteboard provided to make any notes, graphic organizers, and reminders.

To assist you in understanding explanations and to direct your attention to different questions and answer choices, notice that this study guide numbers the questions and letters the answer choices as (A) through (E). On the actual exam, questions are not numbered and the answer choices are not lettered.

Chapter 4

Introduction to Sentence Correction

Sentence correction questions test your ability to read, evaluate, and identify errors in grammar and sentence structure. This section emphasizes the rules and conventions of standard written English and tests how well you can demonstrate the ability to think critically under time constraints as you apply your knowledge of correct grammar.

Skills and Concepts Tested

Sentence correction questions assess your knowledge of basic grammar and usage (how words are used together to form meaning), and then require you to apply your knowledge to correct errors that break the rules of standard written English. As you answer multiple-choice questions, you will be tested on how well you can demonstrate the ability to think critically under time constraints and apply your knowledge to correct errors that break the rules of stylistic conventions and grammar.

This type of question may contain one of the following common errors in writing:

- Grammar (rules that govern the structure of how words are organized in a sentence)
- Usage (how words are used in a sentence)
- Diction (the right choice of a word in the context of a sentence)
- Idiom (expressions or figures of speech in a sentence)
- Wordiness (redundancy or unnecessary language)

Directions

Part or all of a sentence will be underlined in each question. At the end of each question, you will find five choices, four that offer different possibilities for rephrasing the underlined part of the sentence. The first answer choice repeats the original version of the sentence (see sample sentence correction question below). Sometimes the original sentence is a better choice than the four alternatives. If you find no error, select the first choice. Remember that your answer choice should be a correct and effective expression of standard written English. The correct choice should be clear, unambiguous, and concise. Don't choose any alternative that *changes the meaning* of the sentence, no matter how clear or correct it is. Focus on grammar, word choice, sentence construction, and concision.

Sample Sentence Correction Question

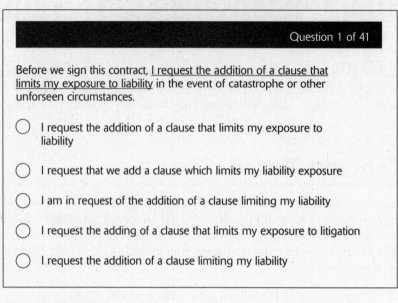

Question 1 of 41

Before we sign this contract, <u>I request the addition of a clause that limits my exposure to liability</u> in the event of catastrophe or other unforseen circumstances.

○ I request the addition of a clause that limits my exposure to liability

○ I request that we add a clause which limits my liability exposure

○ I am in request of the addition of a clause limiting my liability

○ I request the adding of a clause that limits my exposure to litigation

○ I request the addition of a clause limiting my liability

General Strategies

This section describes in detail general and specific strategies, along with practice questions. Before you review specific types of sentence errors, consider the following general strategies that apply to all sentence correction questions.

1. **Observe the rules of standard written English.** This study guide is consistent with the rules of standard written English which are slightly different from spoken English. As you work through the practice exercises, silently read sentences to yourself to *hear* how they sound. Take into account that if a sentence "sounds" accurate, it may still be incorrect if it contains one of the common grammatical or structural errors outlined in this section. Always remember that the guidelines of standard written English prevail over spoken English when you're answering sentence correction questions.

2. **Focus on the underlined words or underlined part of the sentence.** Read the entire sentence actively and focus your attention on the task at hand. After reading the sentence, read all of the possible answer choices. Do not make a hasty assumption that you know the correct answer without reading all of the possible choices.

3. **Manage your time wisely.** Spend about 1¾ minutes per question to have enough time to read and answer all the questions. With sufficient practice, you will know almost automatically when a problem is taking too much time, and when to take an educated guess and move on to the next question.

4. **Use the *elimination strategy*.** Eliminate one or more answer choices whenever possible using the elimination strategy described on page 8. Eliminate answer choices that contain sentence errors as soon as they are identified. If you get stuck on any one question, you may want to reread the question. The answer may become apparent when you take a second look. If not, take an educated guess by eliminating any of the choices that you believe are incorrect and proceed to the next question.

5. **Be on alert for the "attractive distractor" answer choice.** Watch out for answers that look good, but are not the best answer choice. Attractive distractor answer choices are carefully crafted to be *close to the best* answer, but there is never more than one right answer. When you narrow down your choice to two answers, one is probably the attractive distractor. If this happens, read the question again and take an educated guess using the table of common grammar errors in the next section.

Common Grammar Errors

The following table and subsequent sample questions provide you with guidelines and information about grammatical and structural errors that may appear on the GMAT. Take your time to study this list of common mistakes so that you will be able to select the best grammatically correct answer among five choices. Not all of these errors will appear on the exam, but many of them have appeared on previous exams. Some of the errors may appear more than once (such as verb agreement errors and pronoun errors).

Apply what you have learned from this section to the practice questions at the end of this chapter, and continue your practice by completing the full-length practice tests. The extra practice will help you to master the material covered in this section.

Common types of sentence errors appear in nine categories:

Common Types of Grammar Errors		
Type of Error	**Example of Error**	**Corrected Example**
Agreement Errors	<u>New York and Chicago</u> are <u>a city</u> in the United States.	New York and Chicago are cities in the United States.
	The <u>scholars</u> of economics <u>is taking</u> the test.	The scholars of economics are taking the test.
Pronoun Errors	<u>Jerran</u> was late, so we left without <u>them</u>.	Jerran was late, so we left without him.
	<u>He</u> is the coach <u>that</u> trained the dancers.	He is the coach who trained the dancers.
Verb Tense Errors	Last week William <u>buys</u> and a bottle of wine.	Last week William bought a bottle of wine.
Adjective/Adverb Errors	His writing is <u>carelessly</u> because he writes too <u>rapid</u>.	His writing is careless because he writes too rapidly.
Parallel Structure Errors	He is studying <u>biology, physics, and how to swim</u>.	He is studying biology, physics, and swimming.
Idiom Errors	Kelly is eager <u>in seeing</u> the film; she is incapable <u>to answer</u> the question.	Kelly is eager to see the film; she is incapable of answering the question.
	The poetry of Robert Frost is different <u>than</u> any other American poet.	The poetry of Robert Frost is different from any other American poet.
Diction Errors	He will be <u>relapsed</u> from treatment in June.	He will be released from treatment in June.
Faulty Construction: Misplaced Modifier	We saw the boy and <u>his mother in a Batman costume</u> walking.	We saw the boy wearing a Batman costume, walking with his mother.
Faulty Construction: Dangling Modifier	<u>Flowing from the mountain top, he</u> drank from the stream.	He drank from the stream that was flowing from the mountain top.

Agreement Errors

Errors in agreement are one of the most common types of writing errors. Agreement errors will appear on the GMAT in three areas: subject-verb agreement, pronoun-noun agreement, and pronoun-antecedent errors. The following describes errors in subject-verb agreement. The next section will discuss pronoun errors.

Subject-Verb Agreement Errors

Verbs must match their subjects (nouns). An agreement error is the faulty combination of a *singular* and a *plural* in a sentence. A singular subject must agree with a singular verb, and a plural subject must agree with a plural verb. In other words, the *subject must always match the verb*. Nouns ending in *–s* are usually plural and verbs ending in *–s* are usually singular. For example:

The *computer runs* efficiently. (singular noun; singular verb)

The *computers run* efficiently. (plural noun; plural verb)

As long as you know whether the subject is singular or plural, you should have no trouble with this type of problem. Be sure you can identify the subject and the verb of the sentence, and do not let the intervening words distract you.

> 1. Young entrepreneurs, generally lacking the financial backing and seed money necessary to start a new business, <u>is often required, however reluctantly, to ask family and friends for initial assistance</u>.
>
>   Ⓐ is often required, however reluctantly, to ask family and friends for initial assistance
>   Ⓑ is often reluctantly required to ask family and friends for initial assistance
>   Ⓒ often requires, however reluctantly, the asking of family and friends for initial assistance
>   Ⓓ which often requires, however reluctantly, that they ask family and friends for initial assistance
>   Ⓔ are often required, however reluctantly, to ask family and friends for initial assistance

The subject that the underlined verb *is required* refers back to is *young entrepreneurs*, which is a plural noun; the verb should be in its plural form, *are*. The modifying clause beginning with *generally* and ending with *business* creates a large space between the subject and corresponding verb, but does not affect the subject-verb agreement. Choices B and C do not fix this agreement error—*is* and *requires* are both singular verb forms—while choice D is worded awkwardly and passively and does not provide a corresponding verb for the subject *young entrepreneurs*. The correct answer is E.

> 2. The <u>criteria for admission to graduate school includes</u> two years of work experience.
>
>   Ⓐ criteria for admission to graduate school includes
>   Ⓑ criteria for admission to graduate school include
>   Ⓒ criterion for admission to graduate school include
>   Ⓓ criteria for admission to graduate school is
>   Ⓔ criteria for admission to graduate school is at least

Watch for nouns with Greek or Latin endings that form plurals with an *–a*. Words like *data* (plural of *datum*), *phenomena* (plural of *phenomenon*), *media* (plural of *medium*), and *criteria* (plural of *criterion*) are plural forms that can cause subject-verb agreement errors. In this case, *criteria* (plural), must match the verb *include*. Remember that even though the verb *includes* appears to be plural because it ends in an *–s*, it is singular, making choice A incorrect. Choice C, *criterion* is singular, but *include* is plural. Choices D and E show *criteria* (plural), which does not match *is* (singular). The correct answer is B.

Pronoun Errors

Common pronoun errors can be classified into two categories:

- Pronoun-noun agreement errors
- Pronoun-antecedent errors

Pronoun-Noun Agreement Errors

Pronouns can be either singular or plural but must agree with the noun, verb, or other pronoun to which they refer. The *number* of a pronoun (i.e., whether it is singular or plural) must agree in number with its *antecedent* (the word, phrase, or clause to which it refers). Personal pronouns have distinctive singular and plural forms (he/they, his/their, him/them).

Pronouns stand for a word so that writers can avoid using the noun(s) over and over again. For example:

> Robert left *Robert's* workplace, and forgot to take *Robert's* iPad. (*without pronouns*)
> Robert left *his* workplace, and forgot to take *his* iPad. (*substituting pronouns*)

Nouns and pronouns have a *subjective* (nominative) case, a *possessive case,* and an *objective* case (see the table below). Thus, nouns and pronouns can be used as *subjects* (The *cell phone* is small. *I* am tired.), as *objects* (Justin watered the *lawn.* Justin met *him.*), and as *possessors* (*Blake's* guitar is large. *His* arm is broken.).

Because the form of a noun in the subjective case is no different from the form of the same noun in the objective case (The bat hit the ball. The ball hit the bat.), errors are not a problem with nouns. However, several pronouns have different forms as subjects and objects and can sometimes be confusing.

Subjective, Possessive, and Objective Pronouns			
	First Person	**Second Person**	**Third Person**
Subjective Case			
Singular	I	you	he, she, it, who
Plural	we	you	they, who
Possessive Case			
Singular	mine, my	your, yours	his, hers, its, whose
Plural	our, ours	your, yours	their, theirs, whose
Objective Case			
Singular	me	you	him, her, it, whom
Plural	us	you	them, whom

---

3. The director of the animated film, along with the character designer, the 3-D rendering specialist, and the animators, <u>have made their recommendations</u> about the revision of the storyline to the screenwriter.

    (A) have made their recommendations
    (B) has made their recommendations
    (C) made their recommendations
    (D) had made their recommendations
    (E) has made his recommendations

The subject of the sentence is the singular *director.* The phrase beginning with *along with* is parenthetical and is not the subject of the verb or the antecedent of the possessive pronoun that follows. The correct, singular verb form is *has,* and the correct, singular pronoun form is *his.* Choices A, B, C, and D all incorrectly use the plural pronoun *their.* The correct answer is E.

---

4. <u>When one reaches the first plateau, it</u> does not guarantee that you will complete the climb to the summit.

Ⓐ When one reaches the first plateau, it
Ⓑ Because one reaches the first plateau, it
Ⓒ One's reaching the first plateau
Ⓓ Upon reaching the first plateau, it
Ⓔ Reaching the first plateau

This sentence contains an inconsistency in the pronouns; the clause that cannot be changed uses *you,* but the underlined section uses *one.* A correct answer must either use *you* or eliminate the pronoun altogether. Choices A, B, and C are incorrect because they use the pronoun *one.* Choice D eliminates the pronoun, but is incorrect because it contains a dangling modifier (*upon reaching . . .*) that mistakenly refers to the pronoun *it.* Choice E eliminates the pronoun without introducing any additional errors into the sentence. The correct answer is E.

---

5. Anderson's policy allowed an employee to earn a cash bonus <u>if they were able to produce</u> more than the average expected output each week.

Ⓐ if they were able to produce
Ⓑ if they produced
Ⓒ if they overproduced
Ⓓ by producing
Ⓔ producing

The error in the original sentence is an agreement error; *employee* is singular, but the pronoun is the plural *they.* Choice D solves the agreement error problem by omitting the pronoun. Choices B and C do not fix the agreement error, and choice E makes the original meaning unclear by omitting the preposition *by.* The correct answer is D.

---

6. <u>The Rotary Club applauded Fernando and I</u> for our work helping the handicapped in town find secure jobs.

Ⓐ The Rotary Club applauded Fernando and I
Ⓑ The Rotary Club applauded I and Fernando
Ⓒ Fernando and me were applauded by the Rotary Club
Ⓓ The Rotary Club applauded Fernando and me
Ⓔ Me and Fernando were applauded by the Rotary Club

The original sentence uses a subject (*I*) where an object is needed (*me*). Choice D fixes this error without introducing any additional errors. Choice B does not correct the error, and choices C and E use an object (*me*) where a subject is needed. The correct answer is D.

---

7. After extensive trials, the coach chose four swimmers to make up the relay <u>team: Danielle, Alicia, Nicole, and me.</u>

Ⓐ team: Danielle, Alicia, Nicole, and me
Ⓑ team: Danielle, Alicia, Nicole, and I
Ⓒ team: Danielle and I, Alicia, and Nicole
Ⓓ team: I, Danielle, Alicia, and Nicole
Ⓔ team, and they are Danielle, Alicia, Nicole, and me

The original version is correct. The pronoun should be of the objective form (*me*) because the four names are in apposition to *swimmers,* meaning that they are directly following and modified by the noun *swimmers* which, in turn, is the object of the verb *chose.* Therefore, the *I/me* pronoun should be consistent with the verb *chose,* so the subjective *I* in choices B, C, and D is incorrect. Choice E revises the sentence so that the subject of the second clause is *they;* therefore, the pronoun here should be the subjective *I,* not *me.* The correct answer is A.

8. If either Mark or Jack is late again, <u>the bus will leave without them</u>.

 Ⓐ the bus will leave without them
 Ⓑ the bus will leave without him
 Ⓒ the bus will leave without their being on it
 Ⓓ they will miss the bus
 Ⓔ he will miss the bus

The problem here is the choice between the plural *them* and the singular *him*. Because the pronoun refers to either Mark or Jack, but not to both, the singular *him* is the right choice. Choice C incorrectly uses the plural possessive *their*, and choice D incorrectly uses the plural *they*. Choice E changes the meaning of the sentence. The correct answer is B.

Pronoun-Antecedent Errors

The antecedent of a pronoun (the word to which the pronoun refers) should be clear. In spoken conversation and in informal writing, we often use pronouns that have no single word as their antecedent. For example, "This happens all the time." The word *This* is problematic because it refers to a general idea of the preceding sentence, but not to a specific subject. On the GMAT, you should immediately regard a pronoun that does not have a specific noun (or word used as a noun) as its antecedent as an error. *Note:* Sentences in which a pronoun could have two or more possible antecedents should be rewritten.

9. A considerable number of Missouri counties and cities have farmland retention policies, often as part of their general plans, and call for avoiding the best land and developing land more <u>efficiently, which is one of agricultural conservation's most encouraging practices</u>.

 Ⓐ efficiently, which is one of agricultural conservation's most encouraging practices
 Ⓑ efficiently, which is one of the most encouraging practices in agricultural conservation
 Ⓒ efficiently, and this is one of agricultural conservation's most encouraging practices
 Ⓓ efficiently; these policies are one of agricultural conservation's most encouraging practices
 Ⓔ efficiently; this appears to be encouraging to agricultural conservationists

Sentences in which a pronoun has two or more different antecedents should be rewritten. Choices B, C, and E fail to eliminate the ambiguity of the pronouns *which, this,* and *this,* respectively, and are therefore incorrect. The subject *these policies* in choice D clarifies which antecedent is being referenced, and the addition of the semicolon effectively breaks up the long sentence. The correct answer is D.

10. <u>I came in 20 minutes late which</u> made the whole class difficult to understand.

 Ⓐ I came in 20 minutes late which
 Ⓑ I came in 20 minutes late, and this
 Ⓒ I came in 20 minutes late, and this is what
 Ⓓ By coming in 20 minutes late, which
 Ⓔ My coming in 20 minutes late

The pronoun *which* has no specific antecedent here, making choice A incorrect. Choice E eliminates the pronoun altogether and corrects the sentence. Choices B and C are incorrect because the change of *which* to *this* does not correct the pronoun issue, and choice D is a sentence fragment. The correct answer is choice E.

Who and Whom

The pronouns *who* and *whom* are subject and object pronouns. When the pronoun functions as a subject, the doer of an action, use the subjective pronoun *who*. When the pronoun functions as an object, the receiver of an action, use the objective pronoun *whom*. If you have trouble with *who* and *whom*, change the question to a statement and substitute I/me or he/him for who/whom. For example,

Who did that? (*He* did that.)

Whom do you favor to win the MVP? (I favor *him* to win the MVP.)

---

11. Can you tell me <u>whom wrote the new math textbook</u>?

    Ⓐ whom wrote the new math textbook
    Ⓑ which person wrote the new math textbook
    Ⓒ which author wrote the new math textbook
    Ⓓ for whom he wrote the new math textbook
    Ⓔ who wrote the new math textbook

In the original sentence, the person writing the textbook is performing the action rather than being the object of the action, so *whom* is incorrect. Choice E uses the correct subject pronoun by asking *who* performed the action. In choices B and C, the word used to describe the person is *which*; this pronoun should only be used with a very limited set of choices (generally two, and never a person), so these choices are also incorrect. Choice D is incorrect because it changes the meaning of the question. The correct answer is E.

Verb Tense Errors

A verb is a part of speech that expresses a state of being or action. Verb tenses are formed according to person, number, and tense. The tenses (present, past, and future) of the verbs in a sentence must be logical and consistent. Many of the verb tense errors on the GMAT occur in sentences with two verbs, and with past and past participle forms of irregular verbs. Always look carefully at the tenses of the verbs in a sentence, and ask yourself, "Does the *time scheme* make logical sense?" The time scheme will determine the tense. Look carefully at the verbs and the other words in the sentence to establish the time scheme. Adverbs such as *then, subsequently, before, yesterday,* and *tomorrow,* and prepositional phrases such as *in the last decade* and *in the future,* work with verbs to make the time of the actions clearer.

---

12. As of this morning, the trunk containing the <u>cameras, chroma key suits, and body sensors was still not found</u> anywhere in the studio.

    Ⓐ cameras, chroma key suits, and body sensors was still not found
    Ⓑ cameras, chroma key suits, and body sensors are still not found
    Ⓒ cameras, chroma key suits, and body sensors had still not found
    Ⓓ cameras, chroma key suits, and body sensors had still not been found
    Ⓔ cameras, chroma key suits, and body sensors were still not found

---

The verb in the underlined section is in past tense (*was . . . found*), despite describing an action or state that had been occurring in a continuous manner before a specific point in the past. The correct verb form for this situation is past perfect progressive (*had . . . been found*), as in choice D. Choices A and E are therefore incorrect, as they use past tense. Choice B is incorrect because it is worded confusingly and uses the plural verb *are* to refer to the singular subject *trunk*. Choice C is incorrect because it omits *been* from the past perfect progressive verb form. The correct answer is choice D.

13. The convoluted plot, bad acting, and awkward camera work in the 2003 drama *The Room* <u>has been the target of universally bad reviews</u>, although some critics have speculated that the film was intended as a form of subversive comedy.

   Ⓐ has been the target of universally bad reviews
   Ⓑ has been universally targeted by hostile reviewers
   Ⓒ have been the target of universally bad reviews
   Ⓓ is the target of universally bad reviews
   Ⓔ has received universally bad reviews

The subject of this sentence is a compound subject (consisting of *plot, acting,* and *camera work*), and therefore requires the plural form of its operative verb, which is *have.* Only choice C uses this correct plural form of the verb. Choices A, B, D, and E all use singular forms of verbs (*has, has, is,* and *has*), which are inconsistent with the plural subject. The correct answer is C.

14. Facebook users love to update their status and converse with friends, <u>but frequent changes in its privacy policies are often made by the company, which frustrates users.</u>

   Ⓐ but frequent changes in its privacy policies are often made by the company, which frustrates users.
   Ⓑ but the company has often made frequent changes to its privacy policies, which frustrates users.
   Ⓒ and frequent changes in its privacy policies are often made by the company, which frustrates users.
   Ⓓ but the company makes frequent privacy policy changes, which frustrate users.
   Ⓔ but frequent changes in its privacy policies have often been made by the company, which frustrates users.

The first clause is in the preferred, active voice, in that the subjects (*Facebook users*) are acting upon the verbs (*love, update,* and *converse*). However, the second clause is in the passive voice, in that the subject (*changes*) are being acted upon by the verb (*are often made*). When possible, passive voice is to be avoided. Choice D is the best answer because it rephrases the second clause in the active voice without introducing any additional errors. Choice B uses the active voice but changes the verb tense to past tense and is redundant. Choice C does not correct the use of the passive voice, while choice E ambiguously and redundantly rephrases the sentence in the passive voice. The correct answer is D.

15. Although he had appeared as a guest on several popular cable news shows in recent months, yesterday's interview <u>is the first time the governor has admitted</u> his interest in running for senator.

   Ⓐ is the first time the governor has admitted
   Ⓑ was the first time the governor admitted
   Ⓒ will be the first time the governor will admit
   Ⓓ had been the first time the governor had admitted
   Ⓔ shall be the first time the governor admitted

The description of the interview as *yesterday's* places the action in the past. Logically, it follows that the tense of the main verb must then be past tense—therefore, the correct answer is choice B. Choice A uses the present tense of the verb, and choice C uses the future tense of the verb. Choice D uses the past perfect tense of the verb, which should be used to indicate that an event preceded another event in the past. Choice E is not only future tense, but *shall* is a nonstandard form of expression (except with first person). The correct answer is B.

16. Combining flavors from America's melting pot with traditional techniques, <u>New American bistro dining include</u> ethnic twists on old standbys and Old World peasant dishes made from luxury American ingredients.

    Ⓐ New American bistro dining include
    Ⓑ New American bistro dining have included
    Ⓒ New American bistros includes
    Ⓓ New American bistros include
    Ⓔ New American bistro chefs includes

The participle *combining* modifies the plural noun *flavors,* so the participial phrase that begins the sentence can only logically modify *bistros,* not *dining.* The original sentence uses a plural verb (*include*) with a singular noun (*bistro dining*). Choice D corrects this error, making both *bistros* and *include* plural. Choice B changes the verb tense, and choices C and E incorrectly use the singular *includes.* The correct answer is D.

Adjective/Adverb Errors

Adjective or adverb misuse constitutes another type of error. The difference between an adjective and an adverb relates to how they function in a sentence. Adjectives and adverbs are similar because they are both *modifiers* (words or groups of words that *describe* other words). **Adjectives** modify nouns and pronouns. **Adverbs** modify verbs, adjectives, and other adverbs. Several special rules apply to adjectives and adverbs.

- As a rule, many adverbs end in *–ly* (walk *quickly,* walk *slowly*) and point to the place, time, or degree to indicate *how many, how much, what kind,* and *when.* On the GMAT, watch for exceptions to this rule (walk *fast,* walk *often*), and be aware that some adjectives end in *–ly* (*friendly* cat, *deadly* snake).

- Words that answer the question "How?" are adverbs. For example, it is a common error to say, "That's real sad," but *real* modifies *sad,* and the modifier usage is, therefore, incorrect because *real* is an adjective. To understand this rule, ask yourself "*How* sad is it?" The answer is, "It is *very* sad." Therefore, the phrase should use the adverb *really* to modify the adjective. The correct usage is, "That's *really* sad."

- Another rule to follow is to apply *–ly* (the adverbial form) when the senses are verbs (*taste, smell, look, sound,* and *feel*). In this case, ask yourself if the sense verb is used actively. If the answer is yes, then use *–ly.* If not, do not use *–ly* (use the adjectival form). For example, "The man looked angrily" is incorrect because when you ask yourself, "Did the man **look** angry with his eyes?" the answer is no. The correct phrase should read, "The man looked angry." Here's another example: "He feels badly," is incorrect because he cannot **feel** (with his body). Therefore, do not use *–ly.* The correct phrase should read, "He feels bad."

17. <u>The tired mechanic, happily to be finished with a hard day's work,</u> closed the hood over the newly tuned engine.

    Ⓐ The tired mechanic, happily to be finished with a hard day's work
    Ⓑ Happily, the tired mechanic being finished with a hard day's work
    Ⓒ Tired but happy with a hard day's work being done, the mechanic
    Ⓓ The tired mechanic, happy to be finished with a hard day's work
    Ⓔ With the pleasant fatigue of a job well done, the mechanic

Happily is used here to describe a person, the mechanic. The correct part of speech for describing a person or thing is an adjective (*happy*), rather than an adverb (*happily*), so choice A is incorrect. Choice D is correct because it properly uses the adjective form (*happy*) to modify the noun (*mechanic*). Choices B and C are confusing and in passive voice, and choice E changes the meaning of the sentence. The correct answer is D.

18. Though the game was in Charlotte, <u>most every fan in the stands was cheering loud</u> for the Titans.

   Ⓐ   most every fan in the stands was cheering loud
   Ⓑ   almost every fan in the stands was cheering loudly
   Ⓒ   almost every fan in the stands was cheering loud
   Ⓓ   most fans in the stands were cheering loud
   Ⓔ   most every fan in the stands was cheering loudly

Adjectives modify nouns, and adverbs modify verbs. In this example, there are two adjective-adverb problems. *Most* is an adjective, but in this case it is meant to modify the adjective *every,* not the noun *fan.* This means it must take its adverb form *almost. Loud* can be used as an adjective, but here it is meant to modify a verb (*was cheering*). Therefore, it must take the form of an adverb—*loudly.* The correct answer is B, which is the only choice that corrects both of these errors.

Parallel Structure Errors

Errors of parallelism occur when two or more linked words or phrases are expressed in different grammatical structures. The basic rule is that when there are two or more linked words or phrases, they must show the same grammar construction.

Parallel structure errors may include unnecessary shifts in verb tense (past to present, for example) or voice (active to passive, for example). They may also include shifts in pronouns (*you* to *one,* for example). Watch for these errors in lists or series. Be especially careful with sentences that use *correlatives* (*both . . . and; no . . . but; not only . . . but also; not . . . but; either . . . or;* and others). Make sure the construction that follows the second of the correlative conjunctions is the same construction as the one that follows the first.

19. <u>To strive, to seek, to find, and not yielding</u> are the heroic goals of Ulysses in Alfred Lord Tennyson's famous poem by the same name.

   Ⓐ   To strive, to seek, to find, and not yielding
   Ⓑ   To strive, to seek, finding and not yielding
   Ⓒ   To strive, to seek, to find, and not to yield
   Ⓓ   To strive, seeking, to find, and not yielding
   Ⓔ   Striving, seeking, finding, and not to yield

Not yielding is incorrect because it should have the same infinitive form (*to* _____) as the other items. Choices A, B, D, and E all have faulty parallelism, mixing infinitives (verbs with *to*) and gerunds (verbs with *–ing*). Choice C correctly shows all four verbs in the infinitive form. The correct answer is C.

20. <u>After he graduated from college, his parents gave him a new car, ten thousand dollars, and sent him on a</u> trip around the world.

   Ⓐ   After he graduated from college, his parents gave him a new car, ten thousand dollars, and sent him on a
   Ⓑ   After graduating from college, his parents gave him a new car, ten thousand dollars, and a
   Ⓒ   After he graduated from college, his parents gave him a new car, ten thousand dollars, and a
   Ⓓ   After he had graduated from college, his parents gave him a new car, ten thousand dollars, and sent him on a
   Ⓔ   After graduating from college, his parents gave him a new car, ten thousand dollars, and sent him on a

The verb *gave* begins a series with nouns as objects (*car, dollars*) but the third part of the series (*and sent him on*) interrupts the parallelism of the series. Only choices B and C correct this error by making *trip* a third object of *gave.* Choice B cannot be right, though, because it begins with a dangling participle; it appears that the *parents* are graduating from college. The correct answer is C.

21. Hard work and self-discipline often result <u>in not only a rise in one's salary but also your self-esteem</u>.

   Ⓐ in not only a rise in one's salary but also your self-esteem
   Ⓑ not only in a rise in one's salary but also your self-esteem
   Ⓒ not only in a rise in your salary but also your self-esteem
   Ⓓ in a rise not only in one's salary but also in one's self-esteem
   Ⓔ in a rise not only in one's salary but also in your self-esteem

There are two parallelism problems here. First, phrases such as *not only . . . but also* (correlatives) should be followed by phrases that are parallel in structure. Second, the pronouns *one's* and *your* are improperly used in a parallel context. Choice D fixes these issues by following *not only . . . but also* with parallel phrases (*in one's salary* and *in one's self-esteem*) and using the same pronoun (*one's*) in both phrases. None of the other choices fixes both errors. The correct answer is D.

Idiom Errors

On the GMAT, some questions will test your ability to recognize errors of nonstandard expressions. Sentences with these types of errors are called idiom errors and contain an error in a word or a phrase that has not been established as standard usage. Words and phrases with idioms are expressed in a different way from established standard usage and may be incorrect simply because they do not "sound right." There are no general rules for recognizing idiom errors, but most idiom errors arise from the use of prepositions (*to, from, of, by,* and so on). For example, depending upon the sentence, you might say "agree with," "agree to," or "agree upon." The meaning of the sentence will determine the correct usage. Here is a list of common idiom errors.

Correct	Incorrect
except for	excepting for
try to	try and
plan to	plan on
prior to	prior than
type of	type of a
by accident	on accident
on account of	on account that
fewer things	less things
ashamed of	ashamed about
amused by	amused at
at any rate	in any rate
at fault	of fault
is intent on	is intent to
in reference to	in reference of
regarded as	regarded to be
preoccupied with	preoccupied by
used to	use to
should have	should of
supposed to	suppose to
different from	different than

22. The law prohibits passengers <u>to bring liquids in excess of 3 ounces in the plane</u>.

    Ⓐ   to bring liquids in excess of 3 ounces in the plane
    Ⓑ   from bringing liquids in excess of 3 ounces in the plane
    Ⓒ   to bring liquids in excess of 3 ounces on the plane
    Ⓓ   from bringing liquids in excess of 3 ounces onto the plane
    Ⓔ   to bring liquids in excess of 3 ounces to the plane

The original sentence contains two idiomatic errors; first, the parallel idiom for the verb *prohibits* is *from bringing* rather than *to bring*. Second, the idiomatic preposition in this sentence should be *onto* or *on* rather than *in* or *to*. Choice D is the only choice that corrects both of these errors; the correct answer is D.

23. He lacks the ability <u>in running a large company and has no interest to expand</u> its market in Europe and Asia.

    Ⓐ   in running a large company and has no interest to expand
    Ⓑ   in running a large company and has no interest in expanding
    Ⓒ   to run a large company and has no interest in expanding
    Ⓓ   to run a large company and has no interest to expand
    Ⓔ   in the running of a large company and has no interest in the expansion of

This sentence also contains two idiomatic issues. With the phrase *lacks the ability,* the better idiom is the infinitive *to run.* However, with the phrase *has no interest,* the preferred idiom is the preposition *in* and a gerund phrase—here, *expanding.* The correct answer is C.

Diction Errors

Diction errors substitute the wrong word for the meaning intended. Errors in word choice are especially likely to appear on the GMAT with a word that looks or sounds very much like another word: for example, *sit* and *set* or *retain* and *detain.* Diction errors consist of words that you already know but that you confuse easily with one another. Listed below are examples with their definitions for your easy reference. Remember to read *each word* carefully before you answer a question.

Pairs of Commonly Misused Words	
accept (to agree)	except (excluding)
affect (verb—to influence; noun—expression of feeling or emotion)	effect (noun—a result; verb—to bring about)
afflict (cause suffering to)	inflict (impose)
allude (to mention indirectly)	elude (to physically or mental escape from)
allusion (reference)	illusion (false or misleading appearance)
between (when there are only two)	among (three or more)
break (noun—a rest; verb—to fracture)	brake (a device to decelerate)
cite (mention as the source)	site (a place)
complement (to make complete or improve)	compliment (to praise or flatter)
elicit (to bring forth or arrive at by reasoning)	illicit (prohibited by law)
farther (more distant)	further (more time or quantity)
imply (to express indirectly)	infer (to conclude from evidence)

(continued)

its (of it)	it's (it is)
lie (to be in a horizontal position), or lie (to tell something that is not true)	lay (to cause something to be in a certain place, or to produce eggs; past tense form of lie)
precede (to go before)	proceed (to go on, advance, or continue)
principle (a standard rule)	principal (a head of a school, or the initial investment in an account, or first in order of importance)
that (refers to an understood thing or place)	which (refers to a specific thing or place), or who (refers to an understood person)
then (at another time, or next in order)	than (a comparison of unequal parts)
there (in that place)	their (belonging to them)

24. Although she knew the mournful <u>song well, it effected her every time she heard it and brought</u> tears to her eyes.

    Ⓐ song well, it effected her every time she heard it and brought
    Ⓑ song well, it effected her every time she heard it, bringing
    Ⓒ song well, it affected her every time she heard it and brought
    Ⓓ song well, it had an affect on her every time she heard it, bringing
    Ⓔ song well, it effected her time after time, and it brought

The original sentence confuses the noun *effect* with the verb *affect*. When used as a verb, *effect* means *to bring about;* the intended verb here is *affect,* which would imply the song has an emotional impact on the subject. Choice C is the only choice that corrects this error; the correct answer is C.

Lie/Lay

When using *lie* and *lay,* you need to remember that *lie* is an intransitive verb and does not take an object—it does not place an object: "I could lie in bed for hours." *Lay* is transitive; it moves an object: "He lays the book down." He moves an object, the book. Confusion also arises because the past tense of *lie,* the word *lay,* is the same word as the present tense of *lay.*

25. Because George was exhausted yesterday, <u>he had laid in bed for the entire day</u> before his date.

    Ⓐ he had laid in bed for the entire day
    Ⓑ he has lain in bed for the entire day
    Ⓒ he lay in bed for the entire day
    Ⓓ he had laid in bed for the entire day
    Ⓔ he had lain in bed for the entire day

The intransitive verb *lie* needs to be used here, because the verb is not meant to transfer action to an object, and *yesterday . . . before* indicates that the action happened in the past before another event in the past. Therefore, the past perfect form of *lie* must be used (*had lain*), so choice E is correct. Choices A and D are incorrect because *laid* is the past tense and past participle of the transitive verb *lay,* and choice B is incorrect because it uses the present perfect of the verb *lie* (*has lain*). Choice C is incorrect because it uses the simple past tense of the verb *lie* (*lay*). Therefore, the verb tense choice *had lain* in choice E is correct. The correct answer is E.

Faulty Construction Errors

Errors in faulty sentence construction can appear as misplaced or dangling parts, fragmented sentences, awkward or wordy sentences, or comparing two items that are not comparable.

Faulty construction problems appear frequently on the GMAT. Watch for sentences that seem odd or that have an unnatural construction or word order. Also, watch for phrases that have nothing to modify; these phrases are called "dangling modifiers."

---

26. <u>Looking at the tiny image on the screen of her iPhone</u>, Mount Rushmore seemed much smaller and farther away than it had only seconds before.

    A. Looking at the tiny image on the screen of her iPhone
    B. With her iPhone in hand
    C. Via the image displayed by the screen of the iPhone she was looking at
    D. When she looked at the tiny image of it on the screen of her iPhone
    E. Against the screen of her iPhone

Literally interpreted, the original sentence seems to say that Mount Rushmore, rather than the woman, was looking at the iPhone screen, because the modifier (*Looking*) modifies *Mount Rushmore* instead of the woman who was looking at her iPhone. In other words, the modifier "dangles." Choice D eliminates this dangling modifier in a clear and concise way, unlike choice C. By beginning the sentence with *When she looked at the tiny image of it*—a clause that modifies *Mount Rushmore,* rather than the woman—choice D makes the remainder of the sentence flow logically. Choices A and B contain dangling modifiers, and choice E changes the meaning of the sentence. The correct answer is D.

---

27. Fearing criticism of his book, <u>the publisher had to convince Jim that his story would be well received in order to get his signature on the contract</u>.

    A. the publisher had to convince Jim that his story would be well received in order to get his signature on the contract
    B. Jim needed the publisher to convince him that it would be well received before he signed the contract
    C. Jim had to be convinced by the publisher that his story would be well received in order for them to get his signature on the contract
    D. the publisher had to convince Jim that it would be well received before he agreed to sign the contract
    E. the publisher had to convince Jim that his story would be well received before he would sign the contract

---

The original sentence contains a dangling participle, as the clause *Fearing . . . book* is intended to modify *Jim,* rather than *the publisher.* Choice B is the correct choice because it corrects this error so that the participle refers to *Jim,* as intended. Choice C also corrects this error, but is excessively wordy and in passive voice. The correct answer is B.

28. Thanks to his innate aversion to confrontation and inclination to avoid any action that might be construed as antagonistic, <u>the vice-president of the board of directors was elected president by a majority of the voting body primarily as a calming transitional presence</u> in the wake of ongoing turmoil and its consequent depletion in volunteer activity.

    (A) the vice-president of the board of directors was elected president by a majority of the voting body primarily as a calming transitional presence

    (B) the election of the vice-president of the board of directors as president by a majority of the voting body was primarily a calming transitional presence

    (C) a majority of the voting body elected the vice-president of the board of directors as president primarily as a calming transitional presence

    (D) primarily a calming transitional presence, the vice president of the board of directors, was elected president by a majority of the voting body

    (E) the vice-president of the board of directors, which a majority of the voting body elected president primarily as a calming transitional presence

The clause *Thanks . . . antagonistic* is meant to modify *the vice-president,* so the original sentence is constructed correctly. Choices B and C rearrange the sentence in a manner that results in a dangling modifier. Choice D is awkwardly worded, and choice E is incorrect because the word *which* subordinates of the last part of the sentence, creating a sentence fragment. Choice A uses the passive construction *was elected* correctly, because the subject of this sentence is clearly the vice-president. The correct answer is A.

29. Having cashed my refund check and deposited most of the money in my savings account, <u>a small sum was left to spend on new clothes.</u>

    (A) a small sum was left to spend on new clothes
    (B) buying new clothes with the small sum left was possible
    (C) I had a small sum left with which to buy clothes
    (D) new clothes used up the small leftover sum
    (E) the small leftover sum was spent on new clothes

This is another example of dangling participles. The sentence begins with two participles (*having cashed* and *deposited*). These participles will dangle if the first clause is not immediately followed by a reference to the human agent who did the cashing and depositing. Only choice C begins with a human subject (*I*). The correct answer is C.

30. <u>After the shipment of bananas had been unloaded, a tarantula's nest was discovered by the foreman</u> in the hold of the ship.

    (A) After the shipment of bananas had been unloaded, a tarantula's nest was discovered by the foreman
    (B) After unloading the shipment of bananas, a tarantula's nest was discovered by the foreman
    (C) Having unloaded the shipment of bananas, a tarantula's nest was discovered by the foreman
    (D) After the shipment of bananas had been unloaded, the foreman discovered a tarantula's nest
    (E) After the shipment of bananas had been unloaded, the foreman discovers a tarantula's nest

Both choices A and D are grammatically correct, but choice D is the preferable option because it uses the active, rather than passive voice. Choices B and C seem to imply that the *tarantula's nest* unloaded the bananas, and choice E uses improper verb tenses (the past perfect *had been* should be followed by the simple past tense *discovered*). Keep in mind that passively phrased sentences are always wordier than actively phrased ones; you cannot rewrite an active sentence using a passive verb without using at least two additional words. When choosing between two possible correct answers, you should pick the sentence in the active voice.

For example, consider:

I hit the ball. (four words, active)

The ball was hit by me. (six words, passive)

Also note the ambiguity in choice A; it is unclear whether the foreman, the nest, or both are in the hold of the ship. The correct answer is D.

---

31. By the early eleventh century, Muslim scientists <u>knowing the rich medical literature of ancient Greece, as well as</u> arithmetic and algebra.

    Ⓐ knowing the rich medical literature of ancient Greece, as well as
    Ⓑ knew the rich medical literature of ancient Greece, as well as
    Ⓒ know the rich medical literature of ancient Greece, as well as
    Ⓓ having learned the rich medical literature of ancient Greece, as well as
    Ⓔ having been given knowledge of the rich medical literature of ancient Greece, as well as

---

This question is an example of a sentence fragment, with a participle (*knowing*) but no main verb. Choices B and C supply the missing verb, but only choice B is correct because it replaces this participle with a verb in the proper past tense. Choice C eliminates the sentence fragment, but uses the verb in the present tense where past tense is required. Choices D and E are participles in a different tense than in the question. The correct answer is B.

---

32. She wished that her career could be <u>as glamorous as the other women</u>, but was not willing to work as hard as they had.

    Ⓐ as glamorous as the other women
    Ⓑ as glamorous as those of other women
    Ⓒ as glamorous as those of other women's
    Ⓓ more glamorous than the careers of the other women
    Ⓔ glamorous

This question compares two different and therefore incomparable things. In the original sentence, *career* is incorrectly compared to *women*. Choice B clearly corrects this error. Choice C corrects the error, but also unnecessarily adds the possessive *women's*. Choice D is grammatically correct, but more awkward, repetitive, and wordy than choice B, and choice E changes the meaning. The correct answer is B.

---

33. Like the better-known French fashion experts, <u>the clothes of the Italian fashion designers are copied all over the world</u> by fast fashion retailers such as H&M and Zara.

    Ⓐ the clothes of the Italian fashion designers are copied all over the world
    Ⓑ copies of the clothes of Italian fashion designers are made all over the world
    Ⓒ Italian fashion designers make clothes that are copied all over the world
    Ⓓ the clothes copied all over the world are made by Italian fashion designers
    Ⓔ there are copies of the clothes of Italian fashion designers all over the world

---

The correct choice is C, in which the prepositional phrase *Like . . . experts* correctly refers to the subject *Italian fashion designers*. Since the intent of the sentence is to compare the French fashion experts with the Italian designers, answer choices A, B, and D are incorrect; the subjects compared to *French fashion experts* in these choices are *clothes, copies,* and *clothes,* respectively. Choice E also fails to correct the error; the noun being compared with *French fashion experts* should immediately follow the comma, rather than *there are.* The correct answer is C.

Practice Sentence Correction Questions

Easy to Moderate

1. <u>Secretly determined to break up the drug dealer's ring, the undercover agent with the local pushers joined forces,</u> without divulging his identity.

   Ⓐ Secretly determined to break up the drug dealer's ring, the undercover agent with the local pushers joined forces,

   Ⓑ Secretly determined to break up the drug dealer's ring, the undercover agent joined forces with the local pushers

   Ⓒ The undercover agent secretly joined forces with local pushers in order to destroy their ring

   Ⓓ The undercover agent joined forces with the local pushers and secretly determined to destroy their ring

   Ⓔ Secretly determined to destroy the drug dealer's ring, the local pushers were convinced to join forces by the undercover agent, who did so

2. <u>In the study of diabetes, many doctors have concluded</u> that early detection of the disease can permit control through diet.

   Ⓐ In the study of diabetes, many doctors have concluded

   Ⓑ Many doctors, by studying diabetes, have concluded

   Ⓒ Many doctors studying diabetes have concluded

   Ⓓ Diabetes studies have led many doctors to conclude

   Ⓔ The conclusion of those doctors who have studied diabetes is

3. Although he is <u>liable to make</u> political enemies with the decision, the President will propose a moderate tax cut that may stimulate spending in the short term while adding to the country's already burdensome long-term debt.

   Ⓐ liable to make

   Ⓑ reluctant to make

   Ⓒ liable from making

   Ⓓ of a mind to make

   Ⓔ liable for making

4. <u>To the behalf of many citizens who believe that greenhouse gas emissions are excessive and damaging,</u> legislators in California passed the Global Warming Solutions Act by a 46 to 31 vote in 2006.

   Ⓐ To the behalf of many citizens who believe that greenhouse gas emissions are excessive and damaging

   Ⓑ For many citizens believing that greenhouse gas emissions are excessive and damaging

   Ⓒ Believing that greenhouse gas emissions are excessive and damaging

   Ⓓ On the behalf of many citizens who believe that greenhouse gas emissions are excessive and damaging

   Ⓔ To appease the many citizens who are of the belief that greenhouse gas emissions are excessive and damaging

5. <u>On their way to the park last summer, Jason and his father often stopped</u> for ice cream at a local store.

   Ⓐ On their way to the park last summer, Jason and his father often stopped

   Ⓑ On his way to the park, Jason and his father often stopped

   Ⓒ On their ways to the park, Jason and his father often stopped

   Ⓓ On the way to the park, Jason and his father stopped

   Ⓔ On their way to the park, Jason and his father often stop

6. <u>Although most Americans know that they should eat balanced meals and get regular exercise, quite a few</u> of them ignore what they know and continue to indulge themselves.

   Ⓐ Although most Americans know that they should eat balanced meals and get regular exercise, quite a few

   Ⓑ Eating balanced meals and getting regular exercise is something most Americans know, but quite a few

   Ⓒ Although most Americans know to eat balanced meals and getting regular exercise, quite a few

   Ⓓ Although most Americans have known that they should eat balanced meals and exercise regular, quite a few

   Ⓔ To eat balanced meals and to get regular exercise is something that is known by many Americans, however

7. <u>Irregardless of the prevalence of Auto-Tune in popular songs, which produces</u> a flawless, clean vocal, many listeners still prefer a more natural sound.

   Ⓐ Irregardless of the prevalence of Auto-Tune in popular songs, which produces

   Ⓑ Irregardless of the prevalence of Auto-Tune in popular songs, which produce

   Ⓒ Regardless, the prevalence of Auto-Tune in popular songs, which produces

   Ⓓ Regardless of the prevalence of Auto-Tune in popular songs, which produces

   Ⓔ Regardless of the prevalence of Auto-Tune in popular songs, which produce

8. If Jonathan Swift's *Gulliver's Travels* <u>attracts less of a readership in the twenty-first century than he did in the eighteenth century</u>, perhaps the reason is that modern readers do not know enough political history to appreciate the satire.

   Ⓐ attracts less of a readership in the twenty-first century than he did in the eighteenth century

   Ⓑ attracts less readers in the twenty-first century than the eighteenth century did

   Ⓒ attracts fewer readers in the twenty-first century than it did in the eighteenth century

   Ⓓ attracts fewer readers in the twenty-first century than he did in the eighteenth century

   Ⓔ attract less reading in the twenty-first century than it did in the eighteenth century

9. Travelers in a foreign country should be aware of the country's laws and customs <u>so that you won't find yourself in conflict with the authorities or the citizens you encounter</u>.

   Ⓐ so that you won't find yourself in conflict with the authorities or the citizens you encounter

   Ⓑ so that he won't find himself in conflict with the authorities or the citizens he encounters

   Ⓒ in order that one won't find oneself in conflict with the authorities or the citizens one encounters

   Ⓓ in the event that, coming in contact with the authorities or the citizens encountered, you won't find yourself in conflict

   Ⓔ so that they won't find themselves in conflict with the authorities or with the citizens they encounter

Average

10. Although the advisory commission on Pakistan has completed <u>their report that address the political ramifications of Osama bin Laden's death in that area</u>, no easing of tensions has resulted.

    Ⓐ their report that address the political ramifications of Osama bin Laden's death in that area

    Ⓑ their report that addresses the political ramifications of Osama bin Laden's death in that area

    Ⓒ its report that address the political ramifications of Osama bin Laden's death in that area

    Ⓓ its report that addresses the political ramifications of Osama bin Laden's death with that area in mind

    Ⓔ its report that addresses the political ramifications of Osama bin Laden's death in that area

11. <u>To enjoy exploring marine life in general, and so that they could learn in particular about the ways in which certain sea animals possess "human" traits</u>, the university's school of oceanography offered supervised summer field trips for the elementary school children in the area.

   Ⓐ To enjoy exploring marine life in general, and so that they could learn in particular about the ways in which certain sea animals possess "human" traits
   Ⓑ To stress the enjoyment of marine life in general, and particularly the ways in which certain sea animals are "human"
   Ⓒ In order to teach young people about the "human" traits of certain sea animals, and to provide them an opportunity to enjoy marine exploration in general
   Ⓓ Because marine life in general shares certain "human" traits
   Ⓔ Providing education in everything from general marine life to the specifically "human" possessions of sea animals

12. Economists are well aware of the country's dependence on foreign oil, and <u>a steady rise in the price of fuel over the next several years are predicted by them</u>.

   Ⓐ a steady rise in the price of fuel over the next several years are predicted by them
   Ⓑ they predict a steady rise in the price of fuel for the next several years
   Ⓒ a steady rise in the prices of fuel for the next several years is what they predict
   Ⓓ what they predict is that the price of fuel will rise steadily, over the next several years
   Ⓔ the prediction by them is for the rising prices of fuel for the next several years

13. Many of us bemoan our lack of foresight <u>by complaining that if we would have bought stock at bargain levels during the market crash of 2008–2009, we could have taken advantage of the subsequent rebound in prices</u>.

   Ⓐ by complaining that if we would have bought stock at bargain levels during the market crash of 2008–2009, we could have taken advantage of the subsequent rebound in prices
   Ⓑ , looking backward to potential stock purchases in 2008–2009 and wishing we had done so for present purposes
   Ⓒ ; with stock available so cheaply during the 2008–2009 crash, the advantages of the subsequent rebound would be ours for the taking
   Ⓓ , complaining that if we had bought stock at bargain levels during the market crash of 2008–2009, we could have taken advantage of the subsequent rebound in prices
   Ⓔ , the complaint being our lack of purchasing stock during the 2008–2009 crash and the consequent absence of profit in the subsequent rebound in prices

14. Acting selfishly and impulsively, <u>the chairperson adapted the committee's recommendations to meet his own needs, without considering the negative affects of his changes</u>.

   Ⓐ the chairperson adapted the committee's recommendations to meet his own needs, without considering the negative affects of his changes
   Ⓑ without considering the negative affects of his changes, the chairperson adapted the committee's recommendations to meet his own needs
   Ⓒ the chairperson adapted the committee's recommendations to meet his own needs, without considering the negative effects of his changes
   Ⓓ the chairperson had to adopt the committee's recommendations, despite their negative effects
   Ⓔ the chairperson adopted the recommendations of the committee, negative effects notwithstanding.

15. The more the union stubbornly refused to budge from its original demand for a 20 percent across-the-board salary increase, <u>the more the district administration reiterated its original proposal of a mere 1 percent raise</u>.

    (A) the more the district administration reiterated its original proposal of a mere 1 percent raise

    (B) the district administration's original proposal for a mere 1 percent raise was reiterated all the more

    (C) proposing its original and mere 1 percent raise was the district administration's response, more and more

    (D) the district administration reiterated its proposal of a mere 1 percent raise

    (E) the more the district administration's original proposal of a mere 1 percent raise was reiterated

16. Homer's *Odyssey* is often dramatized as a series of hairbreadth escapes from terrible monsters and vengeful god<u>s, and while those episodes are exciting and important literary achievements,</u> they stand apart from the poem's extensive attention to domestic life, to domestic values, and to a hero whose most important achievement is the reestablishment of his home and family.

    (A) , and while those episodes are exciting and important literary achievements,

    (B) , and although in fact these episodes are exciting, important achievements in literature,

    (C) , and while an exciting and important literary achievement,

    (D) ; those episodes are exciting and important literary achievements but

    (E) , and with those episodes as exciting and important literary achievements,

17. <u>Public enthusiasm that had been growing for airline travel, still in its infancy, when Amelia Earhart's plane disappeared in the 1930s, diminished for a while</u>; similarly, many citizens were hesitant to fly in the aftermath of the September 11th attacks.

    (A) Public enthusiasm that had been growing for airline travel, still in its infancy, when Amelia Earhart's plane disappeared in the 1930s, diminished for a while

    (B) Public enthusiasm that had been growing for airline travel, still in its infancy when Amelia Earhart's plane disappeared in the 1930s, diminished for a while

    (C) Growing public enthusiasm for airline travel, still in its infancy, diminished for a while after Amelia Earhart's plane disappeared in the 1930s

    (D) When Amelia Earhart's plane disappeared in the 1930s, growing public enthusiasm for airline travel, still in its infancy, diminished for a while

    (E) Since Amelia Earhart's plane disappeared in the 1930s, the enthusiasm that had been growing for airline travel in its infancy diminished for a while

18. William Golding's most famous novel concerns little boys, <u>once a well-behaved and civilized group, whose</u> resort to murder and savagery during their brief time on a tropical island without adult supervision.

    (A) once a well-behaved and civilized group, whose

    (B) once well-behaved and civilized, who

    (C) once a well-behaved and civilized herd, who

    (D) once civilized and well-behaved, whose

    (E) behaved and civilized, who

19. The company accountant, normally a stringent and reliable watchdog when it came to the expense accounts of sales representatives, <u>were taken off-guard by their unusually high expense totals for the year 2011</u>.

    (A) were taken off-guard by their unusually high expense totals for the year 2011

    (B) were taken off-guard by the unusually high expense totals for the year 2011

    (C) was taken off-guard by the unusually high expense totals for the year 2011

    (D) was taken off-guard by their unusually high expense totals for the year 2011

    (E) was taken off-guard by unusually high expenses in 2011

20. During the French Revolution, especially the Reign of Terror, <u>citizens whom the government suspected of treasonous tendencies were eventually put to death</u> by Monsieur Sanson, the infamous executioner who supervised the killing of hundreds at the guillotine.

    Ⓐ citizens whom the government suspected of treasonous tendencies were eventually put to death
    Ⓑ citizens of which the government had suspicions were eventually put to death
    Ⓒ suspicious citizens were eventually killed
    Ⓓ people which the government suspected of treason were eventually put to death
    Ⓔ citizens who the government had suspicions of were eventually put to death

21. In the popular documentary series *The Deadliest Catch,* vessels depart from the Aleutian Islands port of Dutch Harbor to fish for crab in the Bering Sea, <u>and because each expedition often result in injuries to crew members</u>, the hold is stocked with first-aid supplies before a ship sets sail.

    Ⓐ and because each expedition often result in injuries to crew members
    Ⓑ and because each trip results in injuries to crew members
    Ⓒ and because each expedition often results in injuries to crew members
    Ⓓ and while the trips are dangerous
    Ⓔ and because the trips had been so dangerous

22. <u>As he looked out on an expanse that seemed empty of gods or goddesses</u>, Odysseus must certainly have felt abandoned by the rulers on Olympus.

    Ⓐ As he looked out on an expanse that seemed empty of gods or goddesses
    Ⓑ As he looked out on an empty expanse of gods and goddesses
    Ⓒ With no gods or goddesses as he looked out on the empty expanse
    Ⓓ Facing the empty expanse of gods and goddesses
    Ⓔ As he looked on an expanse that seemed empty of either a god or a goddess

Above Average to Difficult

23. <u>If the majority of your opponents have control, you may become defeated.</u>

    Ⓐ If the majority of your opponents have control, you may become defeated.
    Ⓑ If the majority of your opponents take control, you may lose.
    Ⓒ If the majority of your opponents assumes control, you may see defeat.
    Ⓓ If the majority of your opponents has control, you may lose.
    Ⓔ Most of your opponents will have control, and you may lose.

24. <u>Focusing across several regions of the world</u>, the young filmmaker produced *Wirevolution,* a documentary on the effects of technology on various cultures.

    Ⓐ Focusing across several regions of the world
    Ⓑ Centered around several regions of the world
    Ⓒ Living in several regions of the world
    Ⓓ Focusing on several regions of the world
    Ⓔ Filmed in several regions of the world

25. In the early fourteenth century, almost 200 years before Columbus reached the West Indies, and 250 years before the Reformation, <u>Europe had been Catholic and the Church continued to influence virtually every phase of human life</u>.

    Ⓐ Europe had been Catholic and the Church continued to influence virtually every phase of human life
    Ⓑ the Catholic Church continued to influence every phase of human life
    Ⓒ the Europe that had been Catholic was still influenced in virtually every phase of human life by the Church
    Ⓓ Europe was Catholic and the Church influenced virtually every phase of human life
    Ⓔ every phase of human life bore traces of the European influence of the Catholic Church

26. In an attempt to salvage <u>its ailing relationship, the conference in Madrid provided a forum for executives to try and resolve lingering issues among the two companies</u>.

    Ⓐ its ailing relationship, the conference in Madrid provided a forum for executives to try and resolve lingering issues among the two companies
    Ⓑ the ailing relationship between the two companies, executives tried to resolve lingering issues between their companies at the conference in Madrid
    Ⓒ its ailing relationship, the conference in Madrid provided a forum for executives to try and resolve lingering issues between the two companies
    Ⓓ their ailing relationship, the conference in Madrid provided a forum for executives to try and resolve lingering issues between the two companies
    Ⓔ their ailing relationship, executives from the two companies tried to resolve their lingering issues at the conference in Madrid

27. During the literary renaissance of the 1920s, a large number of new writers—William Faulkner, Ernest Hemingway, John Dos Passos, and F. Scott Fitzgerald—sought to record the inner life of Americans and to scrutinize the American dream, <u>the dream that anyone can earn his own fortune and live happily ever after through hard work, which had become tarnished</u>.

    Ⓐ the dream that anyone can earn his own fortune and live happily ever after through hard work, which had become tarnished
    Ⓑ the tarnished dream that anyone can make his own fortune and live happily ever after through hard work
    Ⓒ which had become tarnished; the dream that anyone can, through hard work, make his own fortune and live happily ever after
    Ⓓ the dream that anyone can earn his own fortune and live happily ever after, though tarnished, through hard work
    Ⓔ that making one's own fortune and living happily ever after, through hard work, had become tarnished

28. Much like Macbeth when he interprets the witches' prophecies all too literally, <u>the mysterious harpooner who Ahab takes aboard the *Pequod* has the captain accepting his strange prophecies without questioning their hidden meaning</u>.

    Ⓐ the mysterious harpooner who Ahab takes aboard the *Pequod* has the captain accepting his strange prophecies without questioning their hidden meaning
    Ⓑ the strange prophecies of the mysterious harpooner he has taken aboard the *Pequod* are accepted by Ahab without questioning their hidden meaning
    Ⓒ the mysterious harpooner whom Ahab takes aboard the *Pequod* has the captain accepting his strange prophecies without questioning their hidden meaning
    Ⓓ Ahab accepts the strange prophecy of the mysterious harpooner whom he has taken aboard the *Pequod,* without questioning their hidden meaning
    Ⓔ Ahab accepts the strange prophecies of the mysterious harpooner he has taken aboard the *Pequod,* without questioning their hidden meaning

29. The weather in San Diego, California, is temperate for most of the year, and although the air is not as clean as it used to be, it has remained virtually smog free through recent years of rapid industrial growth, <u>unlike most urban areas in southern California</u>.

    Ⓐ   unlike most urban areas in southern California

    Ⓑ   unlike the air in most southern California urban areas

    Ⓒ   unlike other southern California air

    Ⓓ   unlike southern California urban areas

    Ⓔ   in contrast to the smog condition elsewhere in urban southern California

30. Brokers who offer foreign cars on the "gray market," thus bypassing the car dealer by shipping directly from the manufacturer to the waiting customer at the dock, claim that their purpose is not to cheat dealerships out of a profit but rather <u>to provide the consumer with the finest value for his or her dollar</u>.

    Ⓐ   to provide the consumer with the finest value for his or her dollar

    Ⓑ   the provision of the finest value for the dollar

    Ⓒ   providing the finest values for consumer dollars

    Ⓓ   that they have an obligation to provide consumers with the finest value for their dollars

    Ⓔ   to provide value for their dollar

31. Two recent statements on the tenure of university professors offer conflicting points of view: <u>those that say that lifetime tenure ensures academic freedom and those that say that lifetime tenure encourages professional laziness and irresponsibility</u>.

    Ⓐ   those that say that lifetime tenure ensures academic freedom and those that say that lifetime tenure encourages professional laziness and irresponsibility

    Ⓑ   Some declare that lifetime tenure ensures academic freedom, and others say that it encourages professional laziness and irresponsibility

    Ⓒ   saying that lifetime tenure either ensures academic freedom or encourages irresponsible laziness

    Ⓓ   One emphasizes the academic freedom that tenure ensures, and one stresses the professional laziness and irresponsibility it encourages

    Ⓔ   advocacies of academic freedom and warnings about professional laziness and irresponsibility

32. <u>With an explosive capacity that can devastate life and property for a radius of hundreds of miles, proponents of peace from several NATO member nations met to discuss the continuing manufacture and deployment of nuclear warheads.</u>

    Ⓐ   With an explosive capacity that can devastate life and property for a radius of hundreds of miles, proponents of peace from several NATO member nations met to discuss the continuing manufacture and deployment of nuclear warheads.

    Ⓑ   Proponents of peace from several NATO member nations met to discuss, due to their explosive capacity that can devastate life and property for a radius of hundreds of miles, the continuing manufacture and deployment of nuclear warheads.

    Ⓒ   Meeting to discuss the continuing manufacture and deployment of nuclear warheads with an explosive capacity that can devastate life and property for a radius of hundreds of miles were several NATO member nations.

    Ⓓ   Proponents of peace from several NATO member nations met to discuss the continuing manufacture and deployment of nuclear warheads that can devastate life and property with its explosive capacity for a radius of hundreds of miles.

    Ⓔ   Proponents of peace from several NATO member nations met to discuss the continuing manufacture and deployment of nuclear warheads that have the explosive capacity to devastate life and property for a radius of hundreds of miles.

33. Economic talks <u>from Prague between France, The Netherlands, Germany, and other European nations may be even more effecting than many world leaders think they would be</u>.

    Ⓐ   from Prague between France, The Netherlands, Germany, and other European nations may be even more effecting than many world leaders think they would be

    Ⓑ   from Prague between France, The Netherlands, Germany, and other European nations may be even more effective than many world leaders suppose

    Ⓒ   in Prague between France, The Netherlands, Germany, and other European nations may be even more affective than many world leaders think they would be

    Ⓓ   in Prague between France, The Netherlands, Germany, and other European nations may be even more effective than many world leaders expect

    Ⓔ   in Prague among France, The Netherlands, Germany, and other European nations may be even more affective than many world leaders expect

34. <u>Acknowledging the volunteers' giving of a great deal of their time to canvass the neighborhood and collect donations from the neighbors, the chairman of the local United Way expressed his sincere gratitude.</u>

    Ⓐ   Acknowledging the volunteers' giving of a great deal of their time to canvass the neighborhood and collect donations from the neighbors, the chairman of the local United Way expressed his sincere gratitude.

    Ⓑ   Acknowledging the time spent by neighborhood volunteers to canvass and to collect neighborhood donations, the chairman of the local United Way expressed his sincere gratitude.

    Ⓒ   With sincere gratitude, the chairman of the local United Way expressed his acknowledgment of the neighborhood donations canvassed and collected on the volunteers' time.

    Ⓓ   The chairman of the local United Way offered sincere thanks to the volunteers who gave so much time to canvass the neighborhood to collect donations.

    Ⓔ   The chairman of the local United Way thanked the neighborhood volunteers, sincerely.

35. A diagonal line connecting two corners of a rectangle is also the hypotenuse of each of two right triangles contained within the rectangle, <u>which is longer than any of the sides</u>.

    Ⓐ   which is longer than any of the sides

    Ⓑ   and the line is longer than any of the sides

    Ⓒ   which is longer than the sides

    Ⓓ   that is longer than any of the sides

    Ⓔ   that is longer than any of the other sides

Answers and Explanations for Practice Sentence Correction Questions

Easy to Moderate

  1. B. Choice B corrects the poor structure of the original wording. Choices C, D, and E change the meaning of the original sentence slightly—because choices C and D suggest that the ring belongs to the *pushers,* not to the *drug dealer,* and choice E implies that the *pushers* were also determined to destroy the ring.

  2. C. All choices are grammatically correct; however, choice C is the clearest and most direct expression of the original wording. Remember that active voice is always preferable, all else being equal. Choice A is worded awkwardly and indirectly, choices D and E change the meaning of the original, and choice B is awkward and introduces a parenthetical phrase.

3. **A.** The correct idiomatic expression is *liable to.* Choice B changes the meaning, as does choice D. Choice C does not make sense as worded, and choice E does not use the correct idiomatic expression for liable.

4. **D.** *To the behalf,* choice A, is not idiomatic; the correct phrase is *On the behalf.* Choice D corrects this error and does not make additional, unnecessary changes. Choice B is awkwardly worded, choice C changes the meaning, and choice E is excessively wordy and awkward in comparison to choice D.

5. **A.** The original sentence is correct; *Jason and his father* is a compound noun (which is treated as a plural noun), so *their* is the correct possessive pronoun. Choice B uses the singular *his* to refer to the plural compound noun, while choice C's phrasing of *their ways* is incorrect. Choice D changes the meaning by omitting *often,* and choice E changes the meaning by changing the sentence to present tense.

6. **A.** The original version contains no errors and is the best choice. Choice B is awkward and wordy; choice C includes a faulty parallel structure; choice D uses an adjective when it is modifying a verb (*exercise regular* instead of *exercise regularly*); and choice E creates a run-on sentence (*however* should be preceded by a semicolon or period here). The correct answer is A.

7. **D.** *Irregardless* is a nonstandard word, so answer choices A and B are incorrect. Apart from this error, the original underlined portion is correct and clear; only choice D corrects the error without introducing additional errors. Choice C would require the proposition *of* in place of the comma after *Regardless* to make sense. Choice E contains an agreement error: *produce* is a plural verb, but it refers to the singular *prevalence.*

8. **C.** *Fewer readers* is more economical than choice A's *less of a readership;* also the correct pronoun here to refer to the book is *it,* not *he.* Choice B is incorrect because less can modify nonquantitative nouns (e.g., *fewer* gallons, *less* gasoline; *fewer* dollars, *less* money), so the word *readers* requires the modifier *fewer.* Choice D is incorrect because it uses the pronoun *he* instead of *it* to refer to the *book.* Choice E incorrectly uses the plural verb *attract* when referring to the singular noun *Gulliver's Travels;* the fact that the title of the book is a plural noun does not make the book itself a plural noun.

9. **E.** This is the only choice that corrects the biggest problem with the sentence, which has the wrong pronouns. The antecedent of the pronoun is *travelers* and therefore the pronouns should be the third person plural: *they* and *themselves.* The correct answer is E.

Average

10. **E.** Both *commission* and *report* are singular, so the singular pronoun *its* and the singular verb *addresses* must be used. Choice E corrects these errors without introducing any additional errors. Choice B does not fix the singular pronoun issue, and choice C does not fix the singular verb issue. The pronoun and verb agreement is correct in choice D, but *with that area in mind* is needlessly wordy.

11. **C.** Along with having inconsistent verb tense and wordiness problems, the original sentence includes the problem of a long dangling modifier. The underlined portion seems to modify *the university's school of oceanography* and suggests that the *school* is enjoying *exploring marine life.* Only choice C offers an introductory phrase that is both correct and unambiguous. Choices B and D, although grammatically correct, significantly change the intended meaning of the original sentence. Choice E is also grammatically correct, but is in passive voice and slightly changes the intended meaning.

12. **B.** This answer makes the clauses parallel (*Economists are . . . they predict*). The other choices are wordy, are not parallel, and use the passive voice unnecessarily. In the original sentence, a singular verb (*is*) should follow the subject of the second clause (*rise*). The correct answer is B.

13. **D.** The correct verb tense in this sentence is past perfect: *had bought stock.* The past conditional form of the verb (*would have bought stock*) is unnecessarily wordy and redundant, because the preceding *if* already implies that the statement is conditional. Choice D supplies the appropriate verb and eliminates the unnecessary *by.* Choices B, C, and E are all worded awkwardly, and each contains additional errors—for example, choice B's correct idiom is *backwards at;* choice C is entirely and incorrectly in present tense; and choice E is entirely in passive voice—which should be avoided if other grammatically correct options exist. Also, the correct idiom should be *profit from,* not *profit in.*

14. **C.** The error in the original sentence is a diction error; *effects,* not *affects,* is the correct word, because the sentence requires a noun rather than a verb. The use of *affects* makes choice B incorrect. Choices D and E correct the diction error but change the meaning of the original sentence significantly while confusing the meaning of the verb *adapt* (*modify*) with *adopt* (*approve*).

15. **A.** The original underlined portion is the clearest and most correct choice. It creates a balanced sentence in which the structure in the second half (i.e., underlined portion) is parallel to the structure of the first half (*the more . . . [subject] . . . [active verb]*). Choices B and C break the parallel structure by moving the word *more* to the end of the sentence. Choice D omits the phrase that makes the structure parallel (*the more*) and doesn't make sense. Choice E has a passive verb.

16. **A.** The original underlined portion is the best choice. Choice B is excessively wordy, and choice C introduces an agreement error (the singular *an* refers to the plural subject *they*). Choice D omits a necessary comma before the word *but* (which connects two independent, complete clauses), and choice E, by omitting *while,* changes the meaning.

17. **C.** The best choice here arranges the parts of the sentence in the clearest, most direct way by keeping the modifiers as close as possible to the words they modify. In addition, choice C replaces *when* with the more appropriate and logical term *after.* Choice B corrects a comma error, but it is still constructed awkwardly, and while choice D is the clearest of the incorrect answers, it does not replace *when* with *after* and it is less direct than choice C. The use of *Since* makes choice E illogical.

18. **B.** Choice B is grammatically correct and concise. In choice C, *herd* introduces a meaning that is not in the original, while choice E omits details. Choices A and D are sentence fragments.

19. **D.** The original sentence contains an agreement error—the plural *were taken* refers back to the singular *company accountant.* Choice B fails to correct the error. Choices C, D, and E all fix this error, but only choice D does so without changing the meaning of the sentence. Choices C and E both omit the word *their,* which removes the clarification that the high expense totals for 2011 were attributable to the sales representatives.

20. **A.** While the original underlined portion is slightly awkward and written in passive voice, it is the best choice available. *Whom* is used when it is the object of a verb; *who* should be used when it is the subject. Choices B and D use *which* instead of *whom* (*who* and *whom* refer to people, *that* and *which* refer to things) and omit the details of the government's suspicions. Choice C omits significant, important information. Choice E incorrectly uses *who* rather than *whom.*

21. **C.** The verb *result* in choice A is a plural verb, but should be in singular form because it refers to the singular noun *expedition.* Choice C corrects this subject-verb agreement discrepancy by matching the singular verb *results* to the plural noun *expedition.* Choice B changes the meaning by omitting *often* and implying that every trip results in injuries, and choice D changes the meaning by eliminating the causative relationship between the two clauses. Choice E changes the meaning by omitting specific information, and it contains a verb tense error; the past perfect form *had been* is inconsistent with the language in the rest of the passage.

22. **A.** The original sentence is clear and contains no grammatical errors. The sentence refers to an expanse that is empty of gods and goddesses; choices B and D change the meaning of this sentence by implying that there is an empty expanse that consists of gods and goddesses. Choice E is needlessly wordy and contains the idiomatically incorrect *looked on,* and choice C is confusingly worded. The original phrasing in answer choice A is correct.

Above Average to Difficult

23. **D.** *Majority* is a collective noun, which may take either a singular or plural verb, depending on whether it emphasizes the group as a whole or the individuals, which means both choice A and choice D are grammatically correct. However, *lose* is a clearer, more active and economical expression than *become defeated,* which makes choice D the better option. Choices B, C, and E change the meaning of the sentence.

24. **D.** *Focusing across* is idiomatically incorrect and also logically unsound, making choice A incorrect. *Focusing on* is the correct idiomatic form, as in choice D. Choices B and E are idiomatically correct but are inconsistent with the clause that follows—they imply that it is the young filmmaker who is *centered around* or *filmed in several regions of the world,* rather than the film itself. Choice C changes the meaning and introduces a fact that was not in the original sentence. Choice D is the correct answer.

25. **D.** The verbs are the problem in the original underlined portion. The context supplied by the rest of the sentence suggests that the verbs should be simple past tense, with both of them indicating what was true in the fourteenth century. As it stands, the underlined portion is internally contradictory. It states that Europe *had been* Catholic, implying that the region is no longer Catholic, but also states that Catholic influence *continued.* Choice D corrects this grammatical/logical problem while retaining the original intended meaning. Choice C is awkwardly worded (*the Europe that had been . . .*) and does not correct the internal contradiction in the original portion. Choices B and E are grammatically correct but omit information contained in the original sentence.

26. **B.** The original sentence contains an unclear, dangling modifier that implies the *conference in Madrid* attempted to salvage the relationship. It also contains two agreement errors: using *its* rather than *their* to refer to the relationship, and using *among* rather than *between* to distinguish between the two companies. Choice B corrects these errors, while rearranging the sentence in a way that upholds the meaning. Choices C and D do not fix the unclear modifier, and choice E changes the meaning by implying that it is the specific executives who have lingering issues rather than the companies themselves.

27. **C.** The original version is confusing because the clause *which had become tarnished* is separated awkwardly from *dream* and the prepositional phrase *through hard work* is separated awkwardly from the verb it modifies, which is *earn.* Choice C eliminates the separation between these phrases without introducing any additional errors. The prepositional phrase is misplaced in choices B, D, and E.

28. **E.** The underlined portion must name Ahab immediately in order to clarify the comparison between Ahab and Macbeth—it is Ahab (not the *harpooner,* as in choices A or C, or the *prophecies,* as in choice B) who is much like Macbeth. Choice D has the right structure but contains an agreement error between *prophecy* and *their.*

29. **B.** The original underlined portion presents an illogical comparison, of *areas* to the topic of the first part of the sentence, *air.* Only choice B clarifies the *air* to *air* comparison without the unnecessary wordiness of choice E. Choice C is awkward and changes the meaning slightly, and choice D does not fix the incorrect comparison.

30. **A.** The original underlined portion is the best choice. By using *to provide,* it maintains parallel structure with the preceding *to cheat.* Choices B and C do not maintain this parallel structure, and choice D is excessively wordy and changes the meaning by introducing the word *obligation.* By omitting *the consumers,* choice E changes the meaning of the clause to suggest that the brokers provide value to the dealerships rather than the consumers.

31. **D.** *Those* is incorrect in the original underlined portion; to respectively express two singular points of view, the noun or pronoun that refers to each viewpoint must be singular, but *those* is plural. *Some* and *others* also indicate plural viewpoints in choice B, as do *advocacies* and *warnings* in choice E. The word *saying* makes choice C awkward and redundant, and it is inconsistent with the setup of the preceding clause. Only choice D provides a clearly singular reference, the word *one,* for each viewpoint.

32. **E.** The introductory clause that precedes the comma (*explosive capacity . . .*) is meant to modify *warheads,* but in the original phrase it modifies *proponents of peace.* Choice B is constructed awkwardly, and the *explosive capacity* clause mistakenly modifies *the continuing manufacture.* Choice C is constructed awkwardly and passively, and changes the meaning of the sentence by omitting *proponents of peace.* Choice D is incorrect because the sentence is awkwardly worded after *warheads.* Only choice E presents the original intent of the sentence in a clear, error-free way.

33. **D.** Answer choice D corrects several errors from the original choice by substituting the preposition *in* for *from* and the adjective *effective* for *effecting.* Choice B is incorrect because it does not correct the *from* preposition error, and choices C and E are incorrect because they mistakenly use the adjective *affective* rather than *effective.* Choice E may initially appear to be correct because it uses *among* instead of *between;* however, *between* may be used when referring to more than two items when each item is a distinct, individual item.

34. **D.** The original underlined sentence as well as choices B and C are unnecessarily wordy. Choice D is an efficient, direct, and clear expression that retains the meaning of the original. Choice E omits essential information.

35. **B.** Though choice B requires more words, it is the only version that avoids the ambiguous pronouns *which* in choices A and C and *that* in choices D and E. *Which* and *that* appear to refer to *rectangle,* but should clearly refer to *hypotenuse,* the *diagonal line.*

Chapter 5

Introduction to Reading Comprehension

Reading is a dynamic, interactive process that is the basis for all problems on the GMAT. Good reading skills develop through consistent practice that helps you to construct meaning from the written passages. As you study the material presented in this chapter, you will be able to apply your knowledge of reading comprehension to answer the assigned questions correctly. You will not be expected to understand every detail presented in the passages, but you must be able to evaluate passages and execute logical thinking processes on the questions presented.

Reading comprehension questions are designed to test your ability to read, understand, and analyze diverse passages that deal with a variety of topics and subject matter. You can anticipate reading about four 200- to 350-word passages. Each passage will be followed by several questions based on its content, structure, or style, for a total of 12 to 14 questions. You are not expected to be familiar with the subject matter of the passage or with its specific content, and you will not be expected to have any prior knowledge of the subject. Everything you need to know will be provided in the passage. Passages are taken from a wide range of categories:

- **Business:** Economics, marketing, management, technology, or human resources
- **Biological or Physical Science:** Medicine, physics, chemistry, astronomy, or botany
- **Social Science:** Philosophy, psychology, sociology, history, law, government, or politics

Skills and Concepts Tested

The questions test your ability to read passages with a critical eye and to answer questions on the basis of what is directly stated or implied. The specific skills you will need to employ include the following tasks:

- Identify and understand the main idea of a passage
- Separate the main idea from the supporting ideas
- Distinguish between what the passage says directly (explicitly) from what it implies indirectly (implicitly)
- Draw reasonable inferences
- Understand and delineate the organizational structure of the passage
- Identify the intended meaning of individual words and phrases
- Apply information from the passage to a hypothetical situation

Directions

Each reading passage is followed by one or more questions based on the passage's content. The reading passage will be split from the question on the computer screen. The passage will appear on one side of the computer screen, and the question with the answer choices will appear on the other side of the screen. Questions appear on the computer screen one at a time, but you will be able to see the corresponding passage related to the question on the split screen. In the heading above the passage, a prompt displays which question you are working on.

After reading a passage, read the question and choose the best answer from among five choices. Mark your answer to the question by selecting the corresponding oval on the screen. You may refer to the passage as necessary when answering the question.

Sample Reading Comprehension Passage and Question

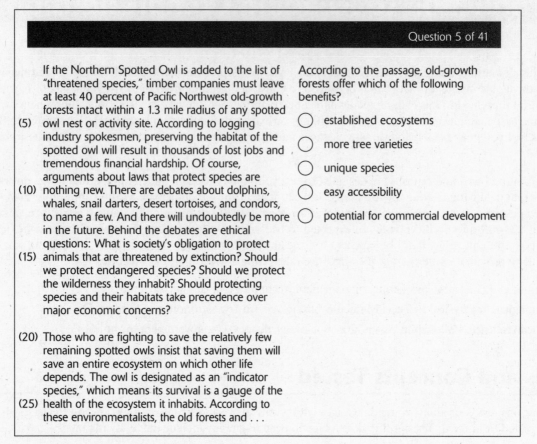

If the Northern Spotted Owl is added to the list of "threatened species," timber companies must leave at least 40 percent of Pacific Northwest old-growth forests intact within a 1.3 mile radius of any spotted (5) owl nest or activity site. According to logging industry spokesmen, preserving the habitat of the spotted owl will result in thousands of lost jobs and tremendous financial hardship. Of course, arguments about laws that protect species are (10) nothing new. There are debates about dolphins, whales, snail darters, desert tortoises, and condors, to name a few. And there will undoubtedly be more in the future. Behind the debates are ethical questions: What is society's obligation to protect (15) animals that are threatened by extinction? Should we protect endangered species? Should we protect the wilderness they inhabit? Should protecting species and their habitats take precedence over major economic concerns?

(20) Those who are fighting to save the relatively few remaining spotted owls insist that saving them will save an entire ecosystem on which other life depends. The owl is designated as an "indicator species," which means its survival is a gauge of the (25) health of the ecosystem it inhabits. According to these environmentalists, the old forests and . . .

According to the passage, old-growth forests offer which of the following benefits?

○ established ecosystems

○ more tree varieties

○ unique species

○ easy accessibility

○ potential for commercial development

Identifying Question Types

The most basic approach to tackling reading comprehension questions is to understand the *author's main idea* of the passage and the *scope* of the questions. The author's main idea is a type of reading comprehension question that will appear on your exam. It is one of six common question types described in this section. As you learn to identify the types of questions on the GMAT, you should be more confident in your ability to answer questions with greater ease and skill.

Let's start by explaining the general *scope* of reading comprehension question types. All reading comprehension questions ask you to respond to information that is directly stated (explicit) or indirectly implied (implicit). Your task is to approach each passage and question with an investigative attitude as you gather clues to help you find direct or indirect evidence to support your answer. If a question asks you for a specific fact or detail, it is a *direct* question. If a question asks you to infer from information presented in the passage, it is an *indirect* question.

Direct questions ask you for explicit information about the passage. Look for information that is stated directly in the passage to answer these types of reading comprehension questions, and remember that you can always find the answer somewhere in the passage. Look for specific words, phrases, or facts that are contained in the passage, and work actively back and forth between the passage and the question.

Indirect questions can be slightly more difficult than direct questions. In indirect questions, you will need to make inferences and find a flow of logic to solve the problem as you draw reasonable conclusions from the passage. Information in this type of question is *not directly stated*. As you search for the answer in the passage, think about gathering words and phrases to understand what is not stated. Look for supporting proof and evidence among the author's words. Do not over-think this type of question. The answer is never vague and is always based on evidence from the passage. Once you understand what the author is communicating in the passage, your inference should make logical sense. Learn to quickly identify direct and indirect questions in one of the following question type categories.

Reading Comprehension Question Type Categories		
Question Type	**Questions May Ask You to**	**What to Look For**
Main Point	❏ Identify main idea ❏ Identify primary purpose ❏ Summarize ❏ Identify author's meaning ❏ Identify author's message ❏ Identify author's objective ❏ Describe passage as	Read the whole passage carefully, and look for the author's central idea and *overall message*. After you read and take notes from the passage, try to synthesize the ideas and ask yourself, "What is the author really saying?" or "What point is the author trying to make?" The best method of isolating the main point of the passage is to *paraphrase* the passage by summarizing and condensing the author's ideas into your own ideas. Practice this type of question first before undertaking other types of questions. After developing a good command of identifying main point questions, you will be ready to tackle the slightly more challenging inference questions.
Supporting Ideas	❏ Identify specific facts ❏ Identify details ❏ Support author's argument ❏ Support author's view ❏ Provide evidence	Look for the author's main ideas, and distinguish them from the supporting ideas. This type of question often requires that you know the difference between ideas stated clearly in the passage and ideas that are implied by the author. These questions require you to break the passage down and examine its smaller components. To develop this skill, practice identifying supporting ideas on a regular basis with newspaper articles, internet news articles, magazine articles, or excerpts from books.
Inference	Identify... ❏ what is implied ❏ what can be inferred ❏ what assumptions can be made ❏ what conclusions can be drawn ❏ the meaning of specific terms or phrases ❏ what is suggested ❏ what is indicated	Look for *supporting proof* and *evidence* among the author's words and *tone* (see below) from the information stated in the passage. "Read between the lines" as you gather evidence to support your conclusion, and write down key words. Ask yourself, "What is not stated directly by the author?" Do not over-think this type of question. The answer is never vague, and is always based on evidence from the passage. Once you understand what the author is communicating in the passage, your inference should make perfect logical sense. Review the five answer choices to determine which answer choice is most plausible *based on the evidence* that you have gathered from the passage.

(continued)

Question Type	Questions May Ask You to	What to Look For
Tone	❏ Describe author's tone ❏ Identify author's attitude ❏ Identify the style of the passage ❏ Describe the mood of the passage	Identify the tone of the passage by looking for and identifying the author's *attitude* and *mood*. The overall tone of the passage is communicated through the author's choice of language and words that help the reader feel a *sense* of connection with the written material. The words that the author uses to describe events, people, or places will help give you a clue about what and how the author wants you to feel or think. Pay careful attention to the *types* of words the author uses. For example, if you read the word *tentative,* you may feel a sense of something *unsure, cautious,* or *hesitant.* Also, look for words that stir up a subtle feeling or emotion. Punctuation marks and/or italicized words or phrases can convey the author's tone, too. Write down key words that signal the author's tone as you read through the passage and then compare these words with the five answer choices. Some key words that set the tone can be as simple as positive or negative words. Avoid selecting extreme ("all-or-nothing") word answer choices unless the written material is clearly compelling. The GMAT typically evaluates your ability to look for subtle differences in word choices, not for obvious extreme answer choices. For example, if you have narrowed your answer choices to *bleak* and *doubtful,* the correct answer would most likely be *doubtful* because the word *doubtful* shows a possibility for hope and the word *bleak* is extremely unhopeful.
Structure and Meaning	❏ Indicate how passage is organized ❏ Evaluate strengths of passage ❏ Compare and contrast ❏ Identify convincing arguments ❏ Determine what supports the author's argument	Look for logic and context clues to understand the author's intent to persuade the readers. Identify the author's reasoning and structure of the given passage, including specific words, phrases, or context that the author develops and presents. For example, a question may ask how one sentence functions within a paragraph or how one paragraph relates to the whole passage. Look for the answer that fits the meaning of the passage. Remember that there may be more than one answer choice that appears to be correct, but there is never more than one right answer. In cases where several choices might fit, select the one that fits the *meaning* of the author's intent most exactly.
Hypothetical Situation	❏ Apply author's main ideas to a situation ❏ Determine if author would agree or disagree ❏ Identify what is alike or unlike ❏ Determine the effect of new information	To distinguish specific and general information in the passage from similar material in comparable situations, use active reading skills to look for and record important points about how the relationship in the passage parallels hypothetical material presented in the question. Focus on finding and understanding the context clues in each passage. Use the logic and context clues to determine if the hypothetical situation is *alike* or *unlike* the author's point of view. Once you select an answer choice, be sure that there is a logical relationship between the answer and the passage.

Three-Step Approach to Improve Reading Comprehension Skills

Improving reading comprehension skills is not about moving your eyes across a page more quickly. It is about forming a mental framework to help you conceptualize words into ideas and thought schemas. Reading is the conscious process of critically "thinking about reading" and actively engaging in the reading passage and questions. For you to attain a higher score, you must *think like an investigator* to search, locate, and extract information in its given context, style, and tone so that you can accurately respond to the questions.

Successful readers use a variety of strategies, including the ability to visualize, pick out details, predict, decode, and summarize reading comprehension passages. If you do not read regularly, be confident in your ability to learn some of these reading skills that will help you develop reading competency. Be patient with yourself as you work through the strategies presented. Remember that repeated and consistent practice is the key to your success. Work through the practice questions and practice tests in this study guide, paying careful attention to the explanations. The explanations provide you with clues about the thinking patterns of the test that help you understand how to determine the correct answer choice.

Now, let's walk through a specific step-by-step approach to improve your reading skills. Apply these steps to the practice questions at the end of this chapter.

STEP ONE
Read the Passage Actively

STEP TWO
Read, then Re-Read the Question

STEP THREE
Respond to the Question

Step One: Read the passage actively.

Active reading is a highly effective technique to use on reading comprehension questions. You must read the passage while thinking purposefully, not casually, to keep your mind actively participating in the reading process. Keep your mind engaged by concentrating on the passage's content and by thinking critically about its ideas as you read. Like an investigator, gather clues from the passage to help you answer the questions. As you become mindful of the passage's content, you will be directing your attention to clues and will be able to respond with a greater sense of awareness. Determine specific types of direct and indirect questions to help you know what to look for in the passages, and use the techniques of paraphrasing, clarifying, and predicting to support your answer.

Paraphrase. Restating written material in your own words will help you concentrate as you read to untangle difficult passages. Always look for the main point of the passage and try to restate or summarize the content of the passage in your own words. When working through the practice questions in this study guide, gather information to paraphrase by writing down key words and phrases. Use these key words and phrases to trigger your memory so that you can summarize and restate the passage in your own words. See if you can use your restatement to answer the question, and keep in mind that selecting the best answer choice is your goal.

You can also practice reading actively by jotting down authors' main ideas in whatever articles you happen to read (magazines, newspapers, scholarly journals, etc.). Read the article, turn it over, and then write down what you remember about the author's main point of view. Compare your written response to the article itself. As you practice this technique and hone your skills, you will find that you will become more efficient and more accurate at paraphrasing.

Clarify. Some passages are difficult to understand, but *the answer to every question is always stated directly within or can be inferred from the information stated in the passage.* Pay attention to the written material, and if there is a word, phrase, or concept that you don't necessarily understand, write a quick note to yourself to seek further clarification. Documenting material that requires clarification will help you complete the task at hand, and often the answers to your questions may appear later in the passage. This strategy helps you to form visual representations of the written material. Your written notes from the passage will often trigger your memory and make mental associations to remember content from the passages. All students have different learning styles, but this technique helps you center on the passage's main ideas and avoid distractions during the exam. You may be surprised at the information you can recall when writing down just a few trigger words to clarify information as you link mental word associations to the context of the reading passage.

Predict. Make predictions so that your mind is continuously guessing at or anticipating what is going to come next. For example, in a passage that introduces "complex carbohydrates" in the first sentence, you might immediately predict that the passage will be a nutrition-based *science* topic.

Step Two: Read, then re-read the question.

Read the question, then reread when necessary to clarify what you should focus on in the passage. Write down important key words to trigger your memory and give you *clues* about what to look for in the passage. This can be especially helpful with unfamiliar reading material. For example, if a question asks you to locate specific facts presented in the passage, write down key words and phrases from the question. If asked to make an inference or to draw a conclusion, write down the words *inference* or *conclusion* to remind you what to look for as you read the passage. Make mental notes of the main points and key words in the question so that you can find the answer in the passage.

Step Three: Respond to the question.

After you have read actively through the passage and read and re-read the question, it's time to answer the question. Be sure that you understand exactly what you are being asked. Reading the questions too quickly can result in your choosing the wrong answer(s)—a common mistake made by test-takers. Always make sure that the answer you choose agrees with the information contained in the passage and that it answers the specific question asked. Use the incorrect answer choices to help guide you toward the correct answer choice. Often, you can arrive at the right answer by eliminating answer choices that are not supported by the passage. If you get stuck on any one question, make an educated guess by eliminating as many of the choices as you can and proceed to the next question.

General Strategies

Read the following general strategies and tips that apply to all reading comprehension questions before you study the suggested strategies, approaches, and exercises that follow.

1. **Use only the information that is directly provided in the passage.** Answer all questions about the passage on the basis of what is *stated* or *implied* in that passage. The passage must support your answer. Do not consider outside information, even if it seems more accurate than the given information.

2. **Develop good reading habits.** Reading is a habit that develops through time and practice. Spend about 15 to 20 minutes per day, at least six to eight weeks before your exam, reading faster than your normal reading speed. As you read, pay special attention to key words, transitional words, and negative words. This process will help strengthen your cognitive reading development. Developing good reading habits is similar to going to the gym to build and strengthen your muscles. You must practice reading skills frequently and consistently to build and strengthen your "brain muscles." You can read newspaper editorials, Internet news, magazine articles, or book excerpts. Don't get hooked into reading only an interesting, thought-provoking article. Try to read material that you might not normally read because you have no interest in the topic. Many GMAT passages you may not normally choose to read.

3. **Manage your time wisely.** At first glance you might calculate that you have about 1¾ minutes to read and answer each reading comprehension question, but this does not include the time it takes you to read the passage. To allow time to read the passages, never spend more than 1 minute on any one question. Reading comprehension questions are time-consuming, so do not let the long passages slow your pace.

4. **Read the passage actively.** As you read each passage, write down main points, key words (names, definitions, places, and numbers) or any other items you feel are important. Do not try to memorize the passage. Instead, think of each paragraph as a "thought unit" and try to move your eyes rapidly down the passage while taking notes. Sometimes it's useful to read peripherally while scanning for information down the page (or screen, on the actual exam) rather than reading left to right. It may seem awkward at first, but it will become more natural as you practice.

5. **Focus on the main point.** Because you are allowed to refer back to the passage, don't try to memorize everything in the passage. Read the passage and focus on the author's main purpose or scope of the entire passage.

6. **Consider all passages.** Test-takers sometimes believe that the shorter passages are easier to read, but this is not necessarily true. All passages require careful consideration and focus.

7. **Line numbers in the passages.** Each passage contains line numbers for easy reference. In questions that mention specific line numbers, you will have the advantage of being able to quickly spot where the information is located. After you spot the location, be sure to read the line(s) just before and after the lines mentioned in the question. The text information that comes before and after the line(s) in the question can be helpful in putting the information in the proper context and answering the question.

8. **Eliminate incorrect answer choices.** If you don't know the answer, try to eliminate some of the obvious wrong choices as soon as you recognize them. Use the elimination strategy discussed on page 8. If you get stuck on any one question, take an educated guess by eliminating as many of the choices as you can and proceed to the next question. Remember to answer every question.

9. **Watch for negative questions.** You may be asked to choose an answer that is *not correct* or is *not true,* which can initially be confusing and challenge your thinking. Keep an eye out for a capitalized *NOT* in the middle of a question or a capitalized *EXCEPT* at the end of a question, as these are the two most common negative question forms. Practice this type of question prior to taking the test to familiarize yourself with it. For example, negative questions can read, "Which of the following is *NOT* true?" or "Which of the following is *least likely* to be true?" or "All of the following are true, *EXCEPT:*." To help answer this type of question, treat the answer choices as *true* or *false* statements, searching for the answer that is *mostly false.* In other words, search among the answer choices and select the one that is false. There may be more than one answer that is false, but follow the flow of logic, context clues, and key words to determine which answer is *not true*, and therefore, the correct choice.

10. **Be on alert for the "attractive distractor" answer choice.** Watch out for answers that look good but are not the *best* answer choice. Just because an answer choice is a true statement, it does not mean that it is the best choice. Attractive distractors are usually the most common wrong answers. The facts and concepts presented on the exam are often in subtle variations of selected answer choices that make it difficult for test-takers to narrow down the correct answer. Attractive distractors are carefully written to be close to the *best* answer, but there is never more than one right answer. When you narrow your choice down to two answers, one is probably the attractive distractor. If this happens, read the question again and select the answer that fits the *meaning* of the question more exactly, and remember that the answer does not have to be perfect, just the *best* among five answer choices.

11. **Use computer tools.** The complete passage may not fit on the screen, so make sure you are comfortable with the method of scrolling up and down on the screen.

Suggested Strategies with Sample Questions

Read the passage below and apply the strategies that you have reviewed so far to answer the five sample questions that follow.

Sample Passage

Woodrow Wilson's rise to the presidency was typical in some ways and unusual in others. He used a state governorship as a stepping-stone to the highest elected office. Many presidents have done so since 1801, when Thomas Jefferson assumed office as President of the United States 22 years after his election as governor of Virginia. In 2009, Barack Obama became the first president without gubernatorial experience to be sworn in (5) since 1989.

Wilson's career trajectory was meteoric, however. After winning his first office in 1910 as governor of New Jersey, he was elected president just two years later in one of the most rapid political rises in American history. Wilson had practiced law for a time but is said to have found it both boring and unprofitable. He then

(10) became a political scientist and ultimately the president of Princeton University. His record at Princeton was outstanding, but when Jim Smith, the Democratic boss of New Jersey, asked him to run for governor, Wilson readily accepted.

Before 1910, Wilson was a conservative Democrat in the Grover Cleveland tradition. He had denounced the Democratic liberal silverite William Jennings Bryan in 1896, and voted instead for John Palmer, the National Democratic third-party candidate who supported gold. Division among the Democrats, however,
(15) gave Republican William McKinley the presidency. Thus, when the Democratic machine first proposed Wilson's nomination in 1912, the young New Jersey progressives were not interested. They decided to work for his election only after Wilson assured them he would champion the progressive cause. Wilson may have acted out of political expediency, but it is also possible that he, along with many other Americans, had changed his views. Between 1910 and 1913, while governor of New Jersey, he carried out his election pledges,
(20) enacting many progressive reforms.

In 1913, Wilson secured the Democratic nomination on the 46th ballot. In the campaign he emerged as a middle-of-the-road candidate between the conservative Republican, William H. Taft, and the more radical Progressive, Theodore Roosevelt. Wilson called his pro-business program the New Freedom, which called for the restoration of free market competition as it had existed before the rise of the trusts. In contrast, Theodore
(25) Roosevelt advocated New Nationalism, which called for major federal interventions in the economic life of the nation. Wilson believed the trusts should be destroyed, but he distinguished between monopoly-seeking trusts and legitimately successful big business. Roosevelt, on the other hand, accepted the trusts as inevitable but believed the government should establish a new regulatory agency to provide oversight and make them accountable.

Strategy: Look for the Main Point

Always look for the main point of the passage. To identify the main idea you might ask yourself questions such as, "What is the main idea?"; "What is the author's main point?"; or "What is the author's purpose?"

> 1. The author's main purpose in writing this passage is to
>
>   Ⓐ   argue that Wilson is one of the great U.S. presidents.
>   Ⓑ   survey the differences among Wilson, Taft, and Roosevelt.
>   Ⓒ   explain Wilson's concept of the New Freedom.
>   Ⓓ   trace major developments in Wilson's political career.
>   Ⓔ   point out the importance of gubernatorial experience for presidential candidates.

Choice A is not implied in the passage, and choices B, C, and E identify supporting details rather than the main purpose, which is expressed in the first sentence of the passage and is implied in choice D. Thus, the importance of gubernatorial experience for prospective presidents (E), Wilson's New Freedom (C), and the differences among the candidates (B) are factors in tracing major developments (D), both typical and unusual, in Wilson's political career. The correct answer is D.

Strategy: Look for Inferences

Some information is not stated directly in the passage but can be gleaned by reading between the lines. This implied information can be valuable in answering some questions, such as the following.

> 2. The author implies which of the following about the New Jersey progressives?
>
>   Ⓐ   They did not support Wilson after he was governor.
>   Ⓑ   They were not conservative Democrats.
>   Ⓒ   They were more interested in political expediency than in political causes or reforms.
>   Ⓓ   Along with Wilson, they were supporters of Bryan in 1896.
>   Ⓔ   They particularly admired Wilson's experience as president of Princeton University.

In the second paragraph, Wilson's decision to champion the progressive cause after 1912 is contrasted with his earlier career, when he seemed to be a conservative Democrat. Thus, you may conclude that the progressives, whom Wilson finally joined, were not conservative Democrats as Wilson was earlier in his career. Choices A and D contradict information in the paragraph, while choices C and E are not suggested by any information given in the passage. The correct answer is B.

Strategy: Draw Conclusions

Watch for important conclusions or information that might support a conclusion.

---

3. The passage supports which of the following conclusions about the progress of Wilson's political career?

   Ⓐ   His rapid progression to higher office was enabled by a willingness to change his core political principles.

   Ⓑ   Failures late in his career caused him to be regarded as a president who regressed instead of progressed.

   Ⓒ   Wilson encountered little opposition once he determined to seek the presidency.

   Ⓓ   The League of Nations marked the end of Wilson's reputation as a strong leader.

   Ⓔ   Wilson's political allies were Bryan and Taft.

The second sentence in paragraph two states that Wilson *was elected president . . . in one of the most rapid political rises in American history,* which supports the first portion of choice A. Paragraph three describes how his 1913 Democratic nomination was made possible by changing from conservative to progressive over the span of several years, which supports the second portion of choice A. Choice B is incorrect because late-career failures are not discussed in the passage. Choice C is never implied and contradicts the opposition from New Jersey progressives described in paragraph three. Choice D is incorrect because the League of Nations is never discussed, and choice E is incorrect because Bryan and Taft are described as Wilson's competition for the presidency. The correct answer is A.

Strategy: Look for Author's Tone

Understand the meaning and possible reason for using certain words or phrases in the passage, and take advantage of the line numbers given.

---

4. The *major federal interventions* mentioned in line 25 of the passage refer to which of the following?

   Ⓐ   Roosevelt's proposal to regulate trusts by establishing a new government agency.

   Ⓑ   Roosevelt's proposal to weaken trusts by subsidizing legitimately successful businesses to encourage competition.

   Ⓒ   Wilson's proposal to destroy the trusts to restore free competition as it had existed before.

   Ⓓ   Wilson's call for the government to take a more active stance in the economic life of the nation.

   Ⓔ   Wilson's New Freedom plan, which opposed monopolies and championed business enterprise.

Major federal interventions were a feature of Roosevelt's New Nationalism, but according to the passage Roosevelt accepted trusts rather than seeking to weaken them and was not pro-business, which eliminates answer choice B. Answer choices C, D, and E are incorrect because they instead refer to features of Wilson's New Freedom plan, which did not call for major federal interventions. The correct answer is A.

Strategy: Look for Supporting Details

Your answer choice must be supported by information either stated or implied in the passage. Eliminate choices that the passage does not support.

> **5.** According to the passage, which of the following was probably true about the presidential campaign of 1912?
>
>   Ⓐ   Woodrow Wilson won the election by an overwhelming majority.
>   Ⓑ   The inexperience of Theodore Roosevelt accounted for his radical position.
>   Ⓒ   Wilson was unable to attract two-thirds of the votes but won anyway.
>   Ⓓ   There were three prominent candidates for the presidency.
>   Ⓔ   Wilson's New Freedom did not represent Democratic interests.

Choices A, B, and C contain information that the passage does not address. You may eliminate them as irrelevant. Choice E contradicts the fact that Wilson was a Democratic candidate. The discussion of Taft and Roosevelt as the candidates who finally ran against Wilson for the presidency supports choice D; the passage states the Wilson *emerged as a middle-of-the-road candidate between [Taft and Roosevelt]*, which implies that they were the three primary candidates in the election. The correct answer is D.

Practice Reading Comprehension Questions

Now let's practice the approaches and strategies you have learned. Read the following eight passages and answer the questions that follow. Question types are intermingled and are not arranged by level of difficulty. Answers and explanations are provided at the end of the section.

Directions: Each reading passage is followed by one or more questions based on the passage's content. After reading a passage, read the question and choose the best answer among five choices to answer the question. Answer all questions about the passage on the basis of what is *stated* or *implied* in that passage.

Questions 1–2 are based on the following passage.

Passage 1

The realization that bacteria are capable of chemical communication first came from investigations of marine bacteria able to glow in the dark. In 1970, Kenneth H. Nealson and John Woodland Hastings of Harvard University observed that luminous bacteria glow at variable intensities and emit no light at all until the population reaches high density.

(5)   Nealson and Hastings knew the glow resulted from chemical reactions catalyzed by the enzyme luciferase inside each bacterial cell. They hypothesized that this enzyme was ultimately controlled not by some mechanism within each cell, but by a molecular messenger that traveled between cells. Once reaching target cells, the messenger, called an autoinducer, induced expression of the genes for luciferase and other proteins involved in light production. That is, the autoinducer stimulated synthesis of the encoded proteins, causing
(10)   the bacteria to glow.

This theory was initially met with skepticism, but has since been confirmed and even hailed as a landmark achievement in bacterial science research. At the turn of the twenty-first century, prominent scientists claimed a lack of progress in research in this field since the work of Nealson and Hastings. Growing sentiment in the scientific community since that time has focused more energy and resources on research based on the
(15)   autoinducer theory, especially as the control of glowing bacteria has valuable potential applications in medicine and bioengineering.

> **1.** According to the passage, Nealson and Hasting's research was instrumental in indicating that
>
>   Ⓐ   bacteria communicate through molecular messengers that travel between cells.
>   Ⓑ   luminous bacteria glow not at a constant density but at various densities.
>   Ⓒ   bacteria are genetically coded by the autoinducer.
>   Ⓓ   the molecular messenger luciferase causes bacteria to glow at high densities.
>   Ⓔ   the autoinducer, not the enzyme luciferase, as was previously believed, produces the luminosity of certain marine bacteria.

2. Which of the following characteristics describes the autoinducer involved in light production in marine bacteria?

(A) It catalyzes chemical reactions inside bacterial cells.
(B) It stimulates synthesis of light-emitting proteins.
(C) It communicates messages between enzymes and bacteria.
(D) It encodes genes.
(E) It signifies lack of progress in bacterial science research.

Questions 3–4 are based on the following passage.

Passage 2

History gives a cruel account of human nature, in showing how exactly the regard for any class of people's life, possessions, and entire earthly happiness was measured by what power the group had to stand up for itself. History shows how all who have made any resistance to authorities with arms in their hands, however dreadful might have been the provocation, have had not only the law of force, but all other laws, and all the (5) notions of social obligation against them; and in the eyes of those whom they resisted, were not only guilty of crime, but of the worst of all crimes, deserving the most cruel chastisement that human beings could inflict. The first small vestige of a feeling of obligation in a superior to acknowledge any right in inferiors began when he had been induced, for convenience, to make some promise to them. Even when sanctioned by the most solemn oaths, these promises were for many ages revoked or violated pursuant to the most trifling (10) provocation or temptation. It is probable, however, that this injustice, except by persons of still worse than average morality, was seldom done without some twinges of conscience.

3. According to the passage, the author implies that laws are based on

(A) the necessity of protecting the weakest members of a society.
(B) the interests of those in a society who possess the most power.
(C) the notions of social obligation that are passed from generation to generation.
(D) promises made to those without power by those with the most power.
(E) the belief that *earthly happiness* is the right of everyone in society, including those who resist authority.

4. The author of this passage would be most likely to agree with which of the following statements about the society presented in this passage?

(A) In order to prevent chaos in a society, authority must be strong and unquestioned.
(B) All men, whether weak or strong, desire justice in their dealings with others.
(C) Social obligation is the most important factor ensuring protection of the weak by the strong.
(D) Rights are granted to those without power when to do so will benefit those with power.
(E) In the past, when rights have been granted to people, only the most extreme circumstances have led to their being rescinded.

Questions 5–8 are based on the following passage.

Passage 3

As the Moorish states in all parts of Spain fell into progressive political, military, and literary decadence, the atmosphere of the established Christian centers became increasingly more favorable to an intensive and varied literary development. The growth of cities had produced a comparatively urban and cultured population with sufficient leisure and security to find time for literary entertainment. The growth of (5) commerce had brought Spaniards into contact with other societies that had developed original and stimulating literary traditions. The growth of a recognized and responsible central government, following the definitive unification of Castile and León under Ferdinand III early in the thirteenth century, had provided a court or central cultural focus toward which men of literary ability could gravitate. The growing

(10) self-awareness of the writer as a unique creative personality, from the anonymity of the *cantares de gesta*[1] to the tentative identification we see in the poetry of Berceo, to intense and affirmative individualism of the later *mester de clerecía*[2] in Juan Ruiz and López de Ayala, demands an ever broader field in which to realize and fulfill itself. In obedience to this sort of aesthetic need and nurtured on the expanding possibilities of a settled and prospering society, the fifteenth century represents a period of great fecundity in the development and widening of literary genres.

(15) The medieval *cantar de gesta,* which had so magnificently served the needs of a society of embattled warriors, undergoes a major change, possibly through the influence of the *mester de clerecía.* In the new society, there was neither time, place, nor public for the recitation of the long and usually complex epic poems, but the great deeds, the great heroes still held their magic for the general public. These survive in a new poetic form, the *romances.* The anonymous *romances* are short poems with regular meter and assonance,

(20) which capture an intense and dramatic moment—of sorrow, of defeat, of parting, of return—in simple and direct language. They are generally fragmentary, combining lyricism and narration taken from the dramatic high points of the epics. Some critics have thought that the oldest *romances* represent a survival of the raw material from which the long *cantares* grew, but the more generally accepted opinion is that they represent the opposite process; as the old *cantares* fell into oblivion, the best moments and the most stirring passages

(25) were conserved and polished and given new life.

Supporting this view is the fact that the earliest *romances* go back only to the middle of the fourteenth century, a time in which the *cantares* were in a period of final decadence and the oldest epic poems already forgotten. They share the realism and directness of the *cantares,* and also the greater polish and lyricism of the *mester de clerecía.* Some thousands of them have been collected and not all relate to the material of the

(30) Spanish epics.

[1]cantares de gesta: "songs of heroic deeds"

[2]mester de clerecía: "ministry of clergy"

5. According to the passage, all of the following probably contributed to increasing the number of literary genres in fifteenth-century Spain EXCEPT:

  Ⓐ growth of Spanish cities.
  Ⓑ Spaniards' increased contact with other societies.
  Ⓒ conflicts between the Moorish and Christian states.
  Ⓓ unification of Castile and León.
  Ⓔ a change in the writer's view of himself.

6. Based on the information in the passage, it can be inferred that the

  Ⓐ *cantares* focus on heroic deeds associated with war, whereas the *romances* are concerned with peace.
  Ⓑ authors of *romances* were well-educated, recognized writers.
  Ⓒ influence of Moorish culture on the *romance* was less strong that it was on the *cantares.*
  Ⓓ *romances* probably influenced the *mester de clerecía.*
  Ⓔ *cantares* were often recited to audiences.

7. According to the passage, the theory that the *romances* come from the same raw material as the *cantares* is questionable because

  Ⓐ *romances* came into being only after the decline of the *cantares.*
  Ⓑ the subject matter of *romances* is the lives of everyday people rather than the lives of heroes.
  Ⓒ *romances* are more lyrical and complex than *cantares.*
  Ⓓ the *cantares* were unavailable to the writers of the *romances.*
  Ⓔ foreign influences are prevalent in the *romances* but not in the *cantares.*

8. The author implies that which of the following statements is true?

    Ⓐ Before the fifteenth century, most Spaniards were illiterate.

    Ⓑ The *cantar* was the only literary genre in Spain before 1600.

    Ⓒ The decline of the Moorish states in Spain resulted in the destruction of much early Spanish literature.

    Ⓓ Fifteenth-century Spanish culture benefited from outside influences.

    Ⓔ The *mester de clerecía* were more popular than the *cantares*.

Questions 9–14 are based on the following passage.

Passage 4

    The Sun is a spinning ball of gas large enough to contain 1.3 million Earths. Its core is a furnace of nuclear fusion, converting 655 million tons of hydrogen into helium every second at a temperature of 28 million degrees Fahrenheit. This fusion creates energy that ultimately reaches us as sunlight. The core and inner layers of the Sun are so dense, however, that it may take a million years for a photon to emerge at what
(5) solar physicists call the convective zone. Above this zone is a thin layer we perceive as the Sun's surface, where photons become visible sunlight. Solar gases continue far into space beyond this visible edge in a blazing hot atmosphere called the corona. Beyond the corona, a thin solar wind blows through the entire solar system.

    The Sun's turbulent convective zone features a dynamic cycle that scientists do not fully understand. Giant gyres of charged gas rise and fall, as in a pot of boiling water, affecting the Sun's magnetic fields. The Sun
(10) rotates about once every 25 days at its equator and about every 34 days at its poles. The difference in rotational velocity shears the boiling charged gas, tangling its electrical currents, which causes the Sun's magnetic fields to flip periodically. The overall magnetic field has a direction, just as Earth's north and south poles attract our compasses. The Sun's magnetic field is full of curves and kinks, however, and every 11 years the poles switch. North becomes south or south becomes north in 11-year cycles. Understanding this dynamic is at the
(15) heart of scientific efforts to understand how the Sun behaves.

    During its flips, the Sun's deep magnetic field becomes gnarled and rises through the visible surface to create sunspots, which appear as dark patches on the Sun's surface. These dark patches of gas are cooler than the rest of the Sun's surface because the knotted magnetic fields act as barriers, preventing some of the Sun's energy from escaping into space. The magnetic fields in sunspots have the potential to erupt, causing them to
(20) loop and swirl through the corona.

9. The primary purpose of the passage is to

    Ⓐ give the reader a sense of the Sun's massive scale.

    Ⓑ describe the Sun's structure and dynamics.

    Ⓒ explain the phenomenon of sunspots.

    Ⓓ warn the reader of dangers presented by the Sun.

    Ⓔ underscore how little scientists understand about the Sun.

10. According to the passage, the convective zone contains or transmits all the following phenomena EXCEPT:

    Ⓐ the dark patches of gas causing sunspots.

    Ⓑ turbulent gyres of charged gas.

    Ⓒ photons of energy.

    Ⓓ the blazing hot corona.

    Ⓔ the Sun's magnetic field.

11. The *difference in rotational velocity* mentioned in lines 10–11 refers to

    Ⓐ season-dependent differences in the Sun's rotational speed.
    Ⓑ how the Sun rotates at a different speed at its equator than at its poles.
    Ⓒ changes in the speed of rotation caused by the Sun's electrical currents.
    Ⓓ changes in the speed of rotation caused by sunspots.
    Ⓔ the difference between the velocities at which the Sun and the Earth spin.

12. According to the information in the passage, each of the following solar events occurs every 11 years EXCEPT:

    Ⓐ the magnetic field flips and changes directions.
    Ⓑ north becomes south and south becomes north.
    Ⓒ the magnetic field pokes through the visible surface to create sunspots.
    Ⓓ magnetic fields within sunspots violently erupt.
    Ⓔ the magnetic field temporarily becomes more twisted, curved, and kinked.

13. With which of the following statements would the author most likely agree?

    Ⓐ The convective zone is never visible to us except potentially during sunspots.
    Ⓑ Sunspots are solar phenomena that occur periodically due to the Sun's magnetic field shifts.
    Ⓒ Scientists generally do not have a good grasp of how the Sun works.
    Ⓓ The journey a photon takes to reach us as visible sunlight takes at least 11 years.
    Ⓔ The Sun's magnetic field is largely uniform and predictable, despite its appearance.

14. According to the passage, which of the following statements most accurately describes the production and transmission of sunlight to Earth?

    Ⓐ Solar gases shoot from the Sun's surface through the corona and out into the solar system.
    Ⓑ The disruptions of the Sun's magnetic field release bursts of photons from the convection zone.
    Ⓒ Chemical reactions in the convective zone create photons of energy that disperse as sunlight.
    Ⓓ Nuclear fusion in the corona creates bursts of energy that escape the magnetic field to be perceived as sunlight.
    Ⓔ The Sun's super-hot core converts hydrogen to helium, creating the energy that eventually reaches Earth as sunlight.

Questions 15–18 are based on the following passage.

Passage 5

    If you make a marked increase in the amount of light falling upon the normal eye, you observe an immediate adjustment of the iris to reduce the size of the pupil. This is called an unconditioned response, and the increased light is called an unconditioned stimulus. Now, if you make numerous trials taking care to sound a buzzer whenever the light is increased, the iris can be "taught," that is to say, conditioned, to reduce
(5) the pupil at the sound of the buzzer alone. This learned response is called a conditioned response, and the sound of the buzzer, a conditioned stimulus.
    Now symbols are our most important conditioned stimuli, and successful communication depends upon complementary conditioning, or complementary experience. Just as we find ourselves shouting at listeners who do not speak our language, so, by a similar irrational impulse, we assume that those with whom we
(10) attempt to communicate are equipped with complementary sets of conditioned responses to our own common stock of symbols. It is easy to see the stupidity of expecting one who does not speak English to converse with you in English. It is not so easy to realize that one who does speak English may not have been conditioned to operate with the same set of senses for the familiar terms common to your vocabulary and to his.

15. The primary purpose of the passage is to

Ⓐ emphasize the importance of symbols in modern, everyday life.

Ⓑ reconcile differing theories on intercultural communication.

Ⓒ provide guidance on how to communicate with those who speak foreign languages.

Ⓓ define and describe the importance of conditioned responses.

Ⓔ explain a possible source of the perceived arrogance of English speakers.

16. According to the author of the passage, which of the following examples best illustrates an unconditioned response?

Ⓐ A businessman reaches for his pocket when he feels a vibration where he usually keeps his cell phone.

Ⓑ Factory workers immediately stop working when a whistle blows at five o'clock every weekday.

Ⓒ A child starts to cry after receiving a poor grade in school.

Ⓓ A cigarette smoker recoils when she accidentally burns her finger on the end of her lit cigarette.

Ⓔ A tired college student immediately presses the snooze button on her alarm when it goes off in the morning.

17. The author of the passage would be most likely to agree with which of the following statements when referring to this similar situation:

A child who begins feeling hungry as the school lunch bell rings each day may be responding to

Ⓐ a developing internal clock.

Ⓑ a conditioned stimulus.

Ⓒ a conditioned response.

Ⓓ an unconditioned stimulus.

Ⓔ an unconditioned response.

18. The passage suggests that those who speak English when attempting to communicate with those who do not speak English are

Ⓐ bound to fail completely.

Ⓑ still dependent upon complementary responses to common symbols.

Ⓒ likely to be more successful if they raise their voices, since listeners are conditioned to respond to louder voices with greater attentiveness.

Ⓓ likely to be able to communicate fully when using words common to both speakers' vocabularies.

Ⓔ inevitably subject to the limitations of third-party translators or translation software.

Questions 19–23 are based on the following passage.

Passage 6

As more people and businesses place greater strain on living systems, limits to prosperity are coming to be determined by natural capital rather than industrial prowess. This is not to say that the world is running out of commodities in the near future. The prices for most raw materials are at a twenty-eight-year low and are still falling. Supplies are cheap and appear to be abundant, due to a number of reasons: the collapse of the

(5) Asian economies, globalization of trade, cheaper transport costs, imbalances in market powers that enable commodities traders and middlemen to squeeze producers, and in large measure the success of powerful new extractive technologies, whose correspondingly extensive damage to ecosystems is seldom given a monetary value. After richer ores are exhausted, skilled mining companies can now level and grind up whole mountains of poorer-quality ores to extract the metals desired. But while technology keeps ahead of depletion, providing

(10) what appear to be ever-cheaper metals, they only appear cheap, because the stripped rainforest and the mountain of toxic tailings spilling into rivers, the impoverished villages, and eroded indigenous cultures—all the consequences they leave in their wake—are not factored into the cost of production.

It is not the supplies of oil or copper that are beginning to limit our development but life itself. Today, our continuing progress is restricted not by the number of fishing boats but by the decreasing numbers of fish;
(15) not by the power of pumps but by the depletion of aquifers; not by the number of chainsaws but by the disappearance of primary forests. While living systems are the source of such desired materials as wood, fish, or food, of utmost importance are the *services* that they offer, services that are far more critical to human prosperity than are nonrenewable resources. A forest provides not only the resources of wood but also the services of water storage and flood management. A healthy environment automatically supplies not only
(20) clean air and water, rainfall, ocean productivity, fertile soil, and watershed resilience, but also such less-appreciated functions as waste processing (both natural and industrial), buffering against the extremes of weather, and regeneration of the atmosphere.

19. The primary purpose of the passage is to

    Ⓐ   propose a solution to economic downturn that does not threaten the natural environment.
    Ⓑ   mourn the loss of natural resources and counsel a return to technologies that are less destructive.
    Ⓒ   clarify that ecological destruction is not an immediate threat to economic growth.
    Ⓓ   identify ecological depletion as a limiting factor to economic productivity and prosperity.
    Ⓔ   compile a short list of unappreciated side effects of ecological depletion.

20. Which of the following statements would the author most likely agree with without reservations?

    Ⓐ   The cost of raw materials is kept artificially low by a failure to account for the unseen cost of ecological damage.
    Ⓑ   Technological advances in the extraction of raw materials are not keeping the supply of these materials abreast of the demand.
    Ⓒ   The explanation for the drop in the cost of raw materials is reasonably well-explained by economic forces such as globalization of trade and cheap transport costs.
    Ⓓ   Ecological depletion, while deeply unfortunate, is the necessary cost of continued economic development and prosperity.
    Ⓔ   The new extraction technologies effectively place the value of human life above that of animal life, vegetation, and the health of the natural environment as a whole.

21. In the view of the author, ecological devastation is most like which of the following?

    Ⓐ   Investing in a company solely on the basis of its overall business model while ignoring the market buzz
    Ⓑ   Gambling the survival of a company on a high-risk venture which, if successful, will yield incalculable benefits
    Ⓒ   Borrowing money at a higher-than-market interest rate, with the understanding that the long-term gain will ultimately justify the short-term costs
    Ⓓ   Spending down the principal of an inheritance without assessing or appreciating the value of its dividends
    Ⓔ   Choosing among the least of several evils, each of which presents unavoidable costs and roughly equivalent prospects for success

22. Which of the following facts, if discovered to be true, would most severely weaken the author's argument in the first paragraph?

    Ⓐ   The depletion of raw commodities is generally overstated by ecologists and not a substantial concern to most economists.
    Ⓑ   Economic factors will continue to keep the cost of raw materials low for the foreseeable future.
    Ⓒ   The negative effects of raw material extraction on the surrounding environment have been overstated.
    Ⓓ   No substantial improvements in extraction technology are expected or likely over the next ten to twenty years.
    Ⓔ   The cost of raw materials continued to decrease since the publication of this passage.

23. The author implies that all of the following statements are true EXCEPT:

    Ⓐ A healthy environment provides resources and services that are currently undervalued by most economists.

    Ⓑ Economic development is not limited so much by a lack of natural resources as by innovations in the technology needed to extract increasingly hard-to-reach resources.

    Ⓒ Not just ecological destruction but its commensurate effect upon humans—for example, eroded indigenous cultures—should be included in the economic cost of certain technological advances.

    Ⓓ While individual natural resources are important, the services that a functional natural environment provides are even more crucial.

    Ⓔ Prosperity is a function not just of human ingenuity in the form of technology and industry, but also of ecological well-being, as evidenced by the continued availability of raw materials.

Questions 24–29 are based on the following passage.

Passage 7

When most labor was agricultural, people generally toiled in the fields until they dropped. The idea of formal retirement did not become feasible until work moved from farms to factories. In 1889, Otto von Bismarck famously introduced the world's first (modest) pension scheme in Germany. In the 20th century, when universal suffrage became widespread, a period of retirement after work was seen as a mark of a
(5)   civilized social democracy.

After the Second World War, pension provision increased markedly, but the number of elderly people was still quite small. In the 1970s and 1980s, caring for them seemed easily affordable. Many countries even reduced their retirement ages.

The demographic picture looks different now that the baby boomers are starting to retire. In 1950, there
(10)   were 7.2 people aged 20 to 64 for every person 65 or older in the 34 member countries of the OECD (Organization for Economic Co-operation and Development). By 1980, the ratio had dropped to 5.1. Now it is around 4.1, and by 2050 it will be just 2.1. In short, every couple will be supporting a pensioner.

Europe and Japan are facing the biggest problems. The average dependency ratio in the European Union is already down to 3.5, and is heading for 1.8 by 2050. In Italy, it is forecasted to be nearly 1.5, and in
(15)   Germany, nearly 1.6 by then. Japan is on track for a startling 1.2. Since the average pensioner currently draws a total of about 60% of median earnings from government and private sources, the system is likely to become unaffordable. In a sense, it does not matter how the benefits are paid for. If they are unfunded, they come from workers' taxes; if funded, they come from investment income. But the income has to be generated by someone.

24. According to the author, a succinct and accurate summary of the passage would be

    Ⓐ a description of how changing concepts of retirement and entitlement programs are becoming unsustainable due to changing demographic trends.

    Ⓑ an attack on underfunded pensions and social security systems.

    Ⓒ a mathematical breakdown of worldwide demographic retirement projections.

    Ⓓ a timeline of retirement norms leading to inevitable economic collapse.

    Ⓔ a call for privatized retirement benefits prefaced by a brief history of retirement customs.

25. It can be inferred from the passage that the *dependency ratio* referred to in line 13 is

    Ⓐ a mathematical way of expressing how economically dependent parents are (or will be) on their children.

    Ⓑ the number of employed citizens divided by the number of citizens receiving pensions or other retirement payments.

    Ⓒ the number of citizens aged 20 to 64 divided by the number of citizens aged 65 or older.

    Ⓓ the ratio of citizens collecting pensions, social security benefits, or welfare benefits to citizens paying taxes and/or funding entitlement programs.

    Ⓔ the ratio of workers to nonworkers in a given country or demographic.

26. Assuming every demographic projection made by the passage comes to fruition, which country or group will have the highest number of citizens aged 65 or older by 2050?

    Ⓐ Japan
    Ⓑ Germany
    Ⓒ the OECD
    Ⓓ the European Union
    Ⓔ insufficient information to determine

27. According to the passage, what does the author imply by claiming that in 2050, *every couple will be supporting a pensioner* (line 12)?

    Ⓐ Once the current system becomes unsustainable, the elderly will inevitably rely on children's families for financial support.
    Ⓑ The only viable, long-term solution to the entitlement crisis will require radical policy changes (e.g., requiring each able couple to support a pensioner).
    Ⓒ If current demographic projections hold, there will be a startling 2-to-1 ratio of working-age citizens to pensioners in Japan.
    Ⓓ The entitlement debt burden will grow to such a high level that citizens will eventually have to subsidize it privately.
    Ⓔ On average, there will be only slightly more than two working-age citizens for every pensioner in OECD countries.

28. The primary purpose of the discussion in the first paragraph is to

    Ⓐ provide evidence that entitlement programs are unnecessary.
    Ⓑ show that the country with the first pension scheme has since become burdened with one of the world's most unsustainable pension obligations.
    Ⓒ give background on the origins and growth of retirement pension plans.
    Ⓓ argue that the concept of *retiring* should not be considered a right or an entitlement.
    Ⓔ point out that universal suffrage contributed to the situation we are facing now.

29. Which of the following statements about the current entitlement situation would the author most likely agree?

    Ⓐ While today's entitlement system is a disaster in the making, it was an inevitable consequence of demographic shifts and could not have been prevented.
    Ⓑ Dramatic changes in both demographics and retirement expectations over the past century have led to a system of promises that will eventually require significant sacrifices to fulfill.
    Ⓒ The projected debt loads generated by retirees over the coming decades are so great that possibly the only solution will be for future retirees to scale back their expectations of benefits.
    Ⓓ The current system is unsustainable, but economic realities will eventually force changes that will result in a long-term, sustainable system.
    Ⓔ While the current situation seems dire, demographic trends should even out the imbalances in payments and obligations over time.

Questions 30–33 are based on the following passage.

Passage 8

Laboratory evidence from a 2009 university study indicates that life originated through chemical reactions in the primordial mixture (water, hydrogen, ammonia, and hydrogen cyanide) that blanketed the earth at its formation. These reactions were brought about by the heat, pressure, and radiation conditions prevailing at the time. One suggestion of the study's report was that nucleosides and amino acids were formed from the
(5)   primordial mixture, and the nucleosides produced nucleotides, which produced the nucleic acids (DNA, the common denominator of all living things, and RNA). The amino acids became polymerized (chemically joined) into proteins, including enzymes, and lipids were formed from fatty acids and glycerol-like molecules. The final step appears to have been the gradual accumulation of DNA, RNA, proteins, lipids, and enzymes into a vital mass, which began to grow, divide, and multiply.
(10)   The evolution of the various forms of life from this biochemical mass must not be considered a linear progression. Rather, the fossil record suggests an analogy between evolution and a bush whose branches go every which way. Like branches, some evolutionary lines simply end, and others branch again. Many biologists believe the pattern of evolution had the following course: Bacteria emerged first and from them branched viruses, red algae, blue-green algae, and green flagellates. From the latter branched green algae,
(15)   from which higher plants evolved, and colorless rhizoflagellates, from which diatoms, molds, sponges, and protozoa evolved. From ciliated protozoa (ciliophora) evolved multinucleate (syncytial) flatworms. These branched into five lines, one of which leads to the echinoderms and chordates. The remaining lines lead to most of the other phyla of the animal kingdom.

30. According to the passage, all the following conclusions can be derived EXCEPT:

Ⓐ   the old metaphor of a bush or tree with branches is still useful for describing the process of evolution.
Ⓑ   evidence indicates that the chemical reactions that produced life required a unique combination of heat, pressure, and radiation.
Ⓒ   some living forms are without DNA.
Ⓓ   some evolutionary chains simply died off without multiplying further.
Ⓔ   the primordial mixture consisted of water, hydrogen, ammonia, and hydrogen cyanide.

31. Which of the following analogies best expresses the relationship between evolution and a bush?

Ⓐ   species : evolution :: bush : branching
Ⓑ   species : branching :: bush : evolution
Ⓒ   evolution : species :: grow : bush
Ⓓ   evolution : species :: bush : branches
Ⓔ   evolution : species :: branches : bush

32. According to the passage, it can be inferred that which of the following life-forms branched off first in the evolutionary process?

Ⓐ   green algae
Ⓑ   blue-green algae
Ⓒ   molds
Ⓓ   flatworms
Ⓔ   ciliated protozoa

33. According to the passage, the evolutionary line of sponges in its proper order is

Ⓐ   bacteria—viruses—green algae—sponges.
Ⓑ   bacteria—viruses—rhizoflagellates—sponges.
Ⓒ   bacteria—red algae—blue-green algae—rhizoflagellates—sponges.
Ⓓ   bacteria—blue-green algae—green flagellates—rhizoflagellates—sponges.
Ⓔ   bacteria—green flagellates—rhizoflagellates—sponges.

Answers and Explanations for Practice Reading Comprehension Questions

Passage 1

1. **A.** Although the research focused on marine bacteria that glow, its broader significance is that it shows the chemical communication between bacteria. Thus, the correct answer is choice A. Choice B is the observation that led to the theory, but it is not the best answer. Choice C is inaccurate; an autoinducer does not code genes but induces their expression. The molecular messenger that causes bacteria to glow is not the enzyme luciferase, so, choice D is incorrect. Choice E might seem correct at first reading, but although the autoinducer allows the expression of the light-producing enzymes such as luciferase, it doesn't produce light itself.

2. **B.** Notice that you must search for specific details in the passage to find the correct answer. Choice A is incorrect because the enzyme luciferase, not the autoinducer, catalyzes the reactions that cause light (line 5). Choice C is incorrect because while the autoinducer acts as a messenger between bacteria cells (line 7), it does not communicate messages between enzymes and bacteria. Choice D is incorrect because the autoinducer stimulates the expression of genes but does not encode them. Choice E is incorrect because the statement is directly contradicted in line 11–12. Choice B is the correct answer and is supported by the following section of the passage (lines 8–10): . . . *the messenger, called an autoinducer, induced expression of the genes for luciferase and other proteins involved in light production. That is, the autoinducer stimulated synthesis of the encoded proteins, causing the bacteria to glow.*

Passage 2

3. **B.** To answer this question correctly, you must pay attention to what the author is *stating directly* versus what the author *is implying.* The author makes it clear that the person with the most power has *not only the law of force, but all other laws* behind him (line 4), implying that the law itself exists to protect the interests of the powerful. Thus, the correct answer is choice B. Choices A and E are incorrect. In fact, the passage suggests the contrary. Choice C is also inaccurate: *all the notions of social obligation* support the powerful, according to the passage (line 4–5). Choice D might be tempting, but according to the author, promises are made only for the convenience of the powerful; laws are made to protect their interests.

4. **D.** This type of question requires that you recognize the tone and author's purpose of the passage. According to the passage, the rights of the weak were acknowledged only when the strong were induced to do so for their own convenience (lines 8–9). Thus, the correct answer is choice D. Choice A is irrelevant: The author doesn't advocate strong, unquestioned authority, but only defines what he or she sees as the realistic situation. Choice B is incorrect: The author states that the powerful are concerned with their own interests, not with justice. Choice C is also incorrect: Notions of social obligation are, like laws, based on the needs of the powerful. Choice E is refuted in the passage: The author states that rights have been *revoked or violated pursuant to the most trifling provocation* (lines 9–10).

Passage 3

5. **C.** This negative type of question reverses your line of thinking. Be sure to note the word *EXCEPT* when considering your answer. The passage indicates that more literary genres developed in Spain because the Christian states provided a *settled and prospering society* (line 13), not because of conflicts between Moors and Christians. Thus, choice C is the correct answer. Choices A, B, D, and E are all mentioned as contributing to the developing literary climate in fifteenth-century Spain and are, therefore, correct. Remember, you are looking for a *false* statement.

6. **E.** The implication in lines 16–18 is that the *cantares* were more often recited in public than read in private. Thus, choice E is the correct answer. Choice A is incorrect because the *romances* combine lyricism with narration taken from the dramatic high points of the epics, and nothing suggests that they are concerned with peace rather than war. Notice that defeat is mentioned as one of the moments captured by *romances,* which further eliminates choice A. Choice B is contradicted in line 19, where the *romances* are characterized as anonymous, and therefore incorrect. The passage does not refer to Moorish influence on any of the genres, so choice C can be eliminated. Choice D is a reversal of what the passage suggests (lines 22–25), so it can be eliminated. Although only choice E remains, you need to read it anyway to make sure that it is correct and that you have not misread one of the other choices.

7. **A.** Use logic and reasoning to answer this question. According to the author, the *cantares* were in a period of *final decadence* at the time the *romances* were born, so it is unlikely that they came from the same raw material. Thus, choice A is the correct answer. Choice B is incorrect because the subject matter of *romances* was not the lives of everyday people. In line 17, the *cantares* are described as *usually complex,* whereas in lines 20–21, the *romances* are characterized as written in *simple and direct language,* making choice C also incorrect. Since the subject matter of *romances* often derives from the epics, choice D is incorrect, too. Foreign influences on the genres, choice E, are not addressed in the passage.

8. **D.** The author cites Spaniards' contact with other societies as a positive influence on Spain's literary development (lines 4–7). Thus, the correct answer is choice D. The statements in both choices A and B are far too sweeping, based on information in the passage. Choice C is not mentioned or implied, and nothing suggests that the *mester de clerecía* were more popular than the epics, making choice E incorrect.

Passage 4

9. **B.** The passage provides a comprehensive description of the Sun, including its size, scale, temperature, atmosphere, composition, and inner processes. Therefore, this is the underlying theme and the focus of all three paragraphs; choice B is the correct answer. Choices A and C are incorrect because they represent secondary purposes: They are supporting details discussed in paragraphs one and three, respectively. Choice D is not implied in this passage. While paragraph two states that scientists do not fully understand the Sun's magnetic fields, the overall passage focuses on what scientists do know about the Sun, making choice E incorrect.

10. **D.** According to the passage, the corona is beyond the visible layer of the Sun, which is beyond the convective zone. Thus, choice D is the correct answer. Choices A and B are incorrect because paragraphs two and three make it clear that the gases burst through the convective layer to create the sunspots. Choice C is incorrect because paragraph one states that while it may take millions of years, photons of energy reach the convective layer. Choice E is incorrect because the magnetic field is part of the convective zone. The only phenomenon that does not involve the zone is the corona, choice D.

11. **B.** Paragraph two states that the Sun rotates at different speeds *about once every 25 days at its equator* and **more slowly**, *about every 34 days,* at its poles. This explicitly supports answer choice B. Thus, choice B is correct. Choice A is never mentioned in the passage, and choice C is incorrect because the causal sequence is reversed; according to the passage, rotational velocity produces electrical currents, not vice versa. Choice D is incorrect because the passage never makes a connection between rotational velocity and sunspots. Choice E is also incorrect, because the discussion of rotational velocity does not reference this difference.

12. **D.** The passage states only that sunspots *have the potential to erupt* (line 19) during the events that occur every 11 years. Thus, choice D is the correct answer. Choices A and B are incorrect because they explicitly define the 11-year cycle of magnetic shifting. Choices C and E are incorrect because the passage expressly identifies them as events associated with the 11-year cycle of magnetic shifts.

13. **B.** Paragraph three describes sunspots as phenomena that occur every 11 years when the Sun's magnetic field reverses; in other words, "that occur periodically due to the Sun's magnetic field shifts." Thus, choice B is correct. Choice A is incorrect because the convective zone is defined as the thin layer above the magnetic field that we perceive as the Sun's surface, thus making it visible. Choice C is incorrect because aside from the Sun's magnetic reversal, the passage implies that scientists have an advanced understanding of how the Sun works. Choice D is incorrect because the passage states that the time between the production of photons and their delivery as visible sunlight *may take a million years.* Choice E is incorrect because the passage implies the opposite about the magnetic field.

14. **E.** The first paragraph describes the Sun's core as *a furnace of nuclear fusion*, in which the high-heat conversion of hydrogen to helium creates the photons of energy that eventually reach us as sunlight. Thus, choice E is correct. Sunlight does not have to do with solar gasses (choice A), or the magnetic field (choice B), or with the convection zone (choice C), or the corona (choice D).

Passage 5

15. **D.** The first half of the passage is devoted to defining the concept of the conditioned response, while the second half emphasizes the importance of these responses in communication and everyday life. Therefore, choice D is correct. The discussion of communication with non-English speakers is merely an example to underscore this main point, which makes answer choices B, C, and E incorrect. The discussion of symbols in everyday life is prominent in the second paragraph but completely absent from the first paragraph, which makes choice A incorrect. The primary purpose of the passage should be discussed in most, if not all paragraphs of the passage.

16. **D.** An unconditioned response is unlearned and unaffected by previous knowledge, experiences, or expectations. Recoiling from unexpected pain is an example. Thus, the correct answer is choice D. The other behaviors are conditioned responses. The businessman (choice A), has been conditioned to reach for his cell phone upon feeling a vibration; the workers (choice B), have been conditioned to stop work when the whistle blows; the child (choice C), has been conditioned through negative reinforcement to react negatively to poor grades; and the college student (choice E), has been conditioned to press a button to stop an unwanted noise.

17. **B.** The bell elicits the child's response, just as the buzzer elicits the eye's response in the example in the passage. That is, after many days of associating the bell with lunch, the child has been "conditioned" to feel hungry when the bell rings. Therefore, the child is responding to a conditioned stimulus. Thus, choice B is correct. Choices C and E are incorrect because one cannot respond to a response. Choice D is incorrect because the stimulus is conditioned, not unconditioned. Choice A is not mentioned in the passage and contradicts the passage's logic.

18. **B.** The passage suggests that complementary responses to common symbols are crucial in communication, even when there is no common language. Thus, choice B is correct. It does not imply that communication is hopeless, as answer choice A suggests, and if anything, implies the opposite of answer choice C (calling a raised voice an *irrational impulse*). Choice D is incorrect because the passage implies that differences in complementary responses to symbols may prevent complete communication, even with shared vocabulary. Choice E is not mentioned in the passage.

Passage 6

19. **D.** Throughout the passage, the author continues to return to one specific problem with ecological depletion—that it has become a key limiting factor to economic growth—and the rest of the passage is in service to this point. The correct answer is choice D. Choice A is incorrect because neither economic downturn nor a solution to it is mentioned in the passage. Rule out choice B because, while the passage focuses on natural resources, it does not discuss returning to technologies that are less destructive. Choice C is wrong because the passage argues that ecological destruction does affect economic growth. Eliminate choice E because, while the passage does mention unappreciated side effects of economic depletion, it does so in service to a larger point.

20. **A.** The first paragraph argues precisely that the unseen cost of ecological damage is not figured into the cost of raw material extraction, which is thereby kept artificially low. The correct answer is choice A. Choice B is incorrect because line 4 states that supply is keeping up with demand. Choice C is wrong because the first paragraph argues that economic forces alone are inadequate to explain the low cost of raw materials. Eliminate choice D because the author's whole thrust is that economic depletion limits prosperity rather than supports it. Rule out choice E because lines 9–12 express a lack of concern for the human cost of extraction technologies in terms of impoverished villages and eroded indigenous cultures.

21. **D.** The first paragraph details the unnoticed costs of ecological devastation, and the second paragraph details the unappreciated economic value of a healthy environment. Thus, ecological balance can be likened to an inheritance that provides benefits that are not managed properly and, thus, are in danger of depletion. The correct answer is D. Choice A is wrong because ignoring the market buzz does not correlate well with an ignorance of the unseen costs of economic depletion. Choice B is wrong because the passage enumerates risks but not benefits. Choice C is incorrect because the passage presents short-term gains with long-term costs rather than the reverse. Choice E can be ruled out because the passage does not present a pair of alternatives with roughly equivalent prospects for success, but rather two alternatives with decidedly different outcomes.

22. **C.** In the first paragraph, the author argues that advances in extraction techniques make harder-to-reach resources available and, in the process, keep prices artificially low by passing unseen costs on to the environment. Thus, if the negative effects of these extraction techniques were not really a problem, the argument would be weakened. The correct answer is choice C. Eliminate choice A because the argument does not hinge on the depletion of raw commodities. Rule out choice B for similar reasons. Choice D is wrong because possible improvements in extraction technology are not at issue. Choice E is incorrect because the cost of raw materials is also not central to the argument.

23. **B.** The main idea of the passage, as expressed in lines 1–2, is that the environment itself rather than industrial prowess, such as modern extraction technologies, is the limiting factor to economic development. Choice B is in direct contradiction with this thesis, so the correct answer is choice B. Choice A is incorrect because lines 13–23 list resources and services that are generally not considered in economics. Rule out choice C because lines 9–12 address the effect of technology on humans and suggest that these costs should be factored in. Choice D is wrong because lines 16–18 stress the importance of natural services over natural resources. Eliminate choice E because the author's main point throughout the passage is that economic prosperity is a function of ecological well-being.

Passage 7

24. **A.** The question asks for the most succinct summary that is accurate. The word *attack* in choice B implies a much stronger tone than the article has, and the author never explicitly criticizes the concepts as inherently negative. The point, rather, is that demographic trends are driving them toward unsustainability. Thus, choice A is correct. However, the passage focuses on the consequences of these demographic changes rather than simply on the mathematical trends, so choice C is also incorrect. Choice D is incorrect because the passage does not suggest "inevitable economic collapse," and E is incorrect because the author is indifferent toward the sources of funding for benefits.

25. **C.** While the term is never explicitly defined, one can infer that the term refers to the ratio described in choice C. The initial ratio introduced in paragraph three is the number of *people aged 20 to 64 for every person of 65 or older,* and the ratios produced by this definition are compared to the ratios associated with the term *dependency ratio* in paragraph four. Choice A is not mentioned in the passage, and while choices B, D, and E *sound* like they could define the term, they are inferences not directly supported by the passage.

26. **E.** The passage only gives projections on what countries or groups will have the highest *ratios* of elderly citizens, not the nominal amounts, so choices A, B, and D are all incorrect. Choice C is incorrect because the OECD is not a country.

27. **E.** The context for the quote is discussing the projected ratio of 20- to 64-year-olds to pensioners in the OECD. The projection for 2050 is 2:1, or basically, one pensioner for every "couple" in what the author implies to be the working-age demographic. Thus, choice E is correct. Choices A, B, and D are never implied, and while choice C gets the ratio right, it mistakenly assigns the ratio to Japan (which will have an even lower ratio of 1.2 working-age adults to elderly citizens, according to the passage's projections).

28. **C.** The purpose of this paragraph is to give a brief history of retirement concepts and the beginnings of entitlement programs, on which the rest of the passage elaborates. Thus, the correct answer is choice C. It does not argue against the concept of entitlement programs (choice A). The fact that Germany and universal suffrage are mentioned (choices C and E) is merely in the interest of historical accuracy; neither is a focus of the passage. The passage also does not argue that people should not be allowed to or expect to retire, as implied in strongly worded choice D.

29. **B.** Choice B is the correct answer. The author points to both an aging populace and changes in the concepts of retirement and pensions over the last 100 or so years as the cause of an untenable situation that will either require massive subsidization from workers' taxes or from investment income in the future. As the author says, *the income has to be generated by someone.* Choice C is therefore incorrect. Choice A is incorrect because the author points to preventable measures, such as countries not reducing retirement ages in the 1970s and 1980s. Finally, the passage never fields the concept of long-term sustainability working itself out (as mentioned in choices D and E).

Passage 8

30. **C.** The passage states that DNA is *the common denominator of all living things.* Thus, choice C is correct. All of the other answer choices are true, making them incorrect in this context. Choices A and D can be concluded from statements about the branching nature of evolution. Choices B and E can be concluded because they are presented as accepted fact.

31. **D.** *Evolution* is to *species* as *bush* is to *branches.* Just as the branches of a bush reach out every which way in varying lengths, the results of evolution (forms of life, species) have expanded in irregular "branches." This is the main point of the second paragraph. Thus, choice D is correct. Choices A and E get the order of the comparison wrong, and choice B pairs the compared items incorrectly. Choice C is an illogical analogy that compares a noun-noun relationship to a verb-noun relationship.

32. **B.** Of the answer choices, blue-green algae are the earliest step on the evolutionary ladder, as we can see from the following section of the passage: *Bacteria emerged first and from them branched viruses, red algae, blue-green algae* (choice B), *and green flagellates. From the latter branched green algae* (choice A), *from which higher plants evolved, and colorless rhizoflagellates, from which diatoms, molds* (choice C), *sponges, and protozoa evolved. From ciliated protozoa (ciliophora)*—choice E—*evolved multinucleate (syncytial) flatworms* (choice D).

33. **E.** The passage presents sponges as evolving from rhizoflagellates, which came from green flagellates, which came from bacteria. Thus, choice E is correct. Choices A, B, C, and D all show a different evolutionary pattern, and therefore are incorrect.

Chapter 6

Introduction to Critical Reasoning

Critical reasoning tests your ability to analyze argument-style passages and apply your knowledge of reasoning and logic to answer questions. Questions present you with specific conditions, and your task is to analyze written material to determine the logical relationship among the passage, the question, and the answer choices. Many of the thinking skills required in this section are necessary to a successful business executive. This is why critical reasoning is especially relevant for many future MBA students. The systematic thinking skills required to strategize solutions focus on your ability to analyze a written argument, decide upon the logical relationships in the argument, determine unstated assumptions in the argument, find evidence to support or oppose the argument, or form a plan of action to answer each question.

You are encouraged to pace yourself as you become familiar with each of the thinking skills required to be successful in critical reasoning. After you review the specific concepts and strategies for each type of critical reasoning question, you will be ready to practice what you have learned in the practice questions in this chapter's final section. Repeated practice is the key to your success on the GMAT. The final chapter of this study guide is a full-length practice test with complete answer explanations, and the accompanying CD-ROM contains three additional full-length practice tests. Apply the rules, concepts, and strategies you learn in this chapter to the practice tests, and review the strategies and questions regularly before your test to maximize your chances for greater success on the actual test.

Skills and Concepts Tested

Critical reasoning tests your ability to use common sense standards of logic to form and evaluate arguments and strategize solutions. It does not require knowledge of formal logic or special expertise. Candidates who read critically and understand simple logic and reasoning do well in this section.

Directions

As you read each passage, follow its line of reasoning and choose the best answer. Keep in mind that several answer choices may be technically correct, but only one answer choice is *best*. Always remember to choose the *best* answer choice.

Use only the information that the passage presents or implies. Do not make leaps in logic to arrive at your answer choice; in other words, do not read anything into the passage that isn't stated or directly implied. Spend no more than $1\frac{3}{4}$ minutes on each problem set (passage, question, and answer choices). Critical reasoning questions can be time-consuming, so remember not to over-think the meaning of a passage because doing so can slow you down.

General Strategies

Each question in this section is a stand-alone question, but all questions share a common strategic approach. The following four-step approach will be referenced throughout this chapter and apply to most types of questions. As you study the material, keep these steps in mind as a reminder to focus on objectives that will guide you to the correct answer.

1. Identify the question type (main idea, assumptions/inferences, draw a conclusion, strengthen or weaken an argument, or faulty reasoning).
2. Read the passage (argument).
3. Look for underlying assumptions and inferences that will support the argument's conclusion.
4. Formulate a conclusion (hypothesis).

Basic Key Terms and Concepts

This chapter provides basic logic and reasoning concepts that you can refer to again and again during your preparation. They are integral to your understanding of the arguments and the critical reasoning questions that follow each one. In addition to learning about the problem structure and question types, it is important to become familiar with these terms and concepts.

Term	Definition
Argument	Critical reasoning passages are also called argument passages. Argument passages attempt to convince the reader to agree with an author's basic position regarding a statement or claim. Argument passages include an *assumption*, a *conclusion*, and *evidence* to support the argument. Evidence may support the conclusion explicitly (directly) or implicitly (indirectly).
Deductive Reasoning	Deductive reasoning refers to a logical flow of reasoning from *general to specific* that leads to a solution or hypothesis. Many critical reasoning questions follow a line of deductive reasoning. A deductive reasoning argument is called a *syllogism*. Deductive reasoning arguments must have two *premises* and a *conclusion* in order to be valid. Furthermore, for a deductive conclusion to be true, both of its premises must be true. For example: Premise: When the school semester ends, final grades will be posted. (true) Premise: School has ended. (true) Conclusion: Therefore, final grades are now posted.
Premise	A premise is the basis of a statement or argument from which you draw a conclusion. Words that signal a premise include: *for example, given that, because, since, due to, for the reason that, as indicated by; in addition,* and *furthermore.*
Conclusion	A conclusion is a statement that logically follows one or more premises. *Conclusions can be logical without necessarily being true.* For example, if Steve is a basketball player who practices three hours each day, and Mark is a basketball player who practices one hour each day, the logical conclusion might appear to be that Steve is a better basketball player than Mark if you assume that the amount of practice is proportional to improved basketball skills. Although this conclusion seems logical, it is not necessarily true. Mark may be a better basketball player than Steve, even though he practices only one hour each day. The conclusion that Steve is the better basketball player is based on an *assumption.* Conclusions that are based on assumptions may or may not be true. Conclusions are typically found in the last sentence of the passage. Words that signal a conclusion include: *consequently, therefore, thus, conclude that,* and *as a result.*
Assumption	Assumptions are underlying principles or presuppositions that the author supposes or assumes to be true, but they are typically unstated, and they are not necessarily true. Assumptions are essential to reaching a conclusion. Although the terms premise and assumption are often used interchangeably, there is a distinction. A premise is explicit—it is stated. An assumption is implied. Therefore, premises are always found written within the passage, but an assumption is not.
Inference	Inferences are unstated implications that the reader draws from an argument. Inferences are not stated by the author, but are directly derived from the passage, argument, or discussion.

Problem Set vs. Question Types

To answer critical reasoning questions correctly, become familiar with the *problem set* structure and the different question *types.* The diagram below illustrates how critical reasoning problems are structured. Each problem consists of a passage, a question stem, and five answer choices.

Five common *types* of critical reasoning questions shown in the following diagram (outer circles) represent the most common types of questions. A critical reasoning question will ask you to:

1. identify the main idea;
2. look for assumptions;
3. draw a conclusion;
4. decide what strengthens or weakens the argument; or
5. find faulty reasoning.

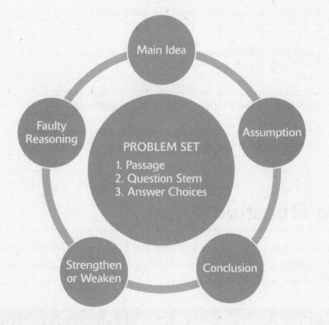

Analyzing the Problem Set

The critical reasoning *problem set* comprises three basic components: the passage, the question stem, and the answer choices. Examine the sample question below as you consider each part of the question, and then use your knowledge of problem sets to help you strategize how to solve the different types of questions.

Critical Reasoning Sample Question

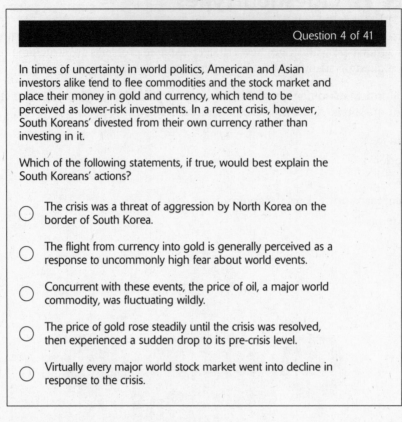

In times of uncertainty in world politics, American and Asian investors alike tend to flee commodities and the stock market and place their money in gold and currency, which tend to be perceived as lower-risk investments. In a recent crisis, however, South Koreans' divested from their own currency rather than investing in it.

Which of the following statements, if true, would best explain the South Koreans' actions?

○ The crisis was a threat of aggression by North Korea on the border of South Korea.

○ The flight from currency into gold is generally perceived as a response to uncommonly high fear about world events.

○ Concurrent with these events, the price of oil, a major world commodity, was fluctuating wildly.

○ The price of gold rose steadily until the crisis was resolved, then experienced a sudden drop to its pre-crisis level.

○ Virtually every major world stock market went into decline in response to the crisis.

Identifying the Question Types

There are predictable patterns in every type of question on the GMAT. The table below categorizes the five most common types of critical reasoning questions. As you become familiar with these question types, you will be able to quickly identify and respond to most problem sets.

Identifying Critical Reasoning Question Types		
Question Type	**Sample Questions**	**Strategies to Use**
Main Point or Idea	Which of the following, if true, most helps to explain . . . in the argument? Which of the following most logically completes the argument? Each of the following statements provides support for the passage EXCEPT: In the argument given, the two boldfaced portions play which of the following roles? In evaluating the passage, it would be useful to know which of the following?	Although this is not a typical type of question in the critical reasoning section, it is listed first as an important first step reminder to view the passage through the lens of the author. Looking for the author's main point will always provide you with a holistic view of the argument and give you insights into its content. Read the whole passage (also called *argument* or *discussion*) carefully, and determine the central conclusion and *overall message*. After you've read and taken notes from the passage, try to synthesize the ideas while separating facts from inferences. The best method to help you focus on the main point is to *paraphrase* the passage by summarizing and distilling the author's argument into your own words.

Question Type	Sample Questions	Strategies to Use
Assumptions	The argument above logically depends on which of the following assumptions? Which of the following is an assumption that supports the conclusion in the argument above? In the argument above, the author assumes that . . . Which of the following can be inferred from the passage above? Which of the following inferences can most reliably be drawn from the passage above? Based on the passage, the author implies that . . .	Look for an unstated assumption that is the foundation upon which the argument rests. **Assumptions** An assumption is an unstated premise necessary for a logical conclusion. You may need to make assumptions in order to determine what is behind the author's argument. To make accurate assumptions, consider the author's overall attitude about the argument and notice the author's language and choice of words. When you identify an assumption question, ask yourself, "What is the foundation from which the author based the argument?" or "What is assumed by the author to be true (but is not stated by the author) that will provide evidence to support the conclusion?" In other words, look for clues about the author's underlying presuppositions. Do not over-think the answer. Always keep in mind that most assumptions are *unstated* and may not necessarily be true. For example, in the statement, "legislative action is necessary in order to improve the quality of air in our community," there are two unstated assumptions. First, it assumes that present air conditions are unsatisfactory and need to be improved. Second, the statement assumes that such proposed legislative action can be effective in resolving the air problem.
Inferences		**Inferences** The process of "inferring" logically proceeds from one statement or judgment to the next. The dictionary defines *inferring* as the act or process of deriving logical conclusions from a "line of reasoning." For example, you can infer from the statement, "Only a minority of children under the age of six have visited a dentist," that "A majority of children under the age of six have not visited a dentist." The distinction between the meanings of *infer* and *imply* is not very important in the critical reasoning section. Thus you can use some of the same assumption strategies for both assumption and inference questions. Look for *supporting proof* by reading between the lines to support the conclusion. Remember to ask yourself, "What does the author not state directly, but rather infers to be true, in order for the conclusion to be valid?"

(continued)

Question Type	Sample Questions	Strategies to Use
Draw a Conclusion	Which of the following conclusions about . . . is best supported by the passage? Which of the following most logically completes the argument above? Which of the following conclusions can be drawn from the information above? The above statements, if true, support which of the following as a conclusion? The claims above, if true, most strongly support which of the following conclusions? Based on the passage above, the author would conclude . . .	A conclusion must logically follow the conditions presented in the argument. A conclusion can be logical, but may not be true unless a valid statement precedes it. Several answer choices will be logically feasible, but you are to choose the one option that not only is possible, but that follows from the reasoning in the argument. If you are asked to draw a conclusion, your answer must be supported by evidence from the premise(s) and the written material within the argument. There must be a relationship between the premise(s) and the answer choices. As you read the passage, immediately start considering the premises and assumptions that might help you draw a conclusion. When in doubt, one of the best strategies for answering this type of question is to plug in each answer choice to see which one best fits the premises provided.
Strengthen or Weaken an Argument	Which of the following, if true, most strongly supports the argument [or conclusion]? Which of the following, if true, helps to provide support for the argument's hypothesis? Which of the following, if true, provides the strongest evidence for . . .? Which of the following, if true, most strengthens [or weakens] the conclusion? Which of the following, if true, most seriously weakens the argument above? The argument is most vulnerable to which of the following criticisms?	Strengthening an argument is the most common type of question you will see in the critical reasoning section of the GMAT. For this reason, be sure that you practice this type of question frequently. Here's how to analyze each statement in the answer choices and how to look for information that "supports" or "disproves" the argument's conclusion. (1) Read the passage and quickly write down key words or phrases that will help you understand the main point of the argument. (2) Analyze the statements in the answer choices and look for information that strengthens or weakens the argument's conclusion. That is, look for information in the answer choices that is not stated in the argument. (3) If an answer choice provides a *different* assumption, immediately eliminate that choice as a possible answer. (4) Once you have narrowed down your answer choices, read the remaining choices to check for relevance. Eliminate any answer choice that is irrelevant to the argument's topic.

Question Type	Sample Questions	Strategies to Use
Look for Faulty Reasoning	Which of the following indicates a flaw in the reasoning above? Which of the following, if true, undermines the argument? The argument is flawed primarily because the author . . . The argument is flawed because it fails to consider . . .	Look for an inconsistency or a break in the flow of logic in the argument to solve a faulty reasoning question. Identify the author's reasoning behind the given argument, including specific words and phrases that help to point to the flaw. When you approach questions that ask you to determine the flaw in reasoning, it is helpful to summarize the main point of the argument by paraphrasing the argument in your own words. You should look for the answer choice that is only *partially true* and *partially wrong*. Therefore, any answer that is completely true can be eliminated immediately because you are only looking for the incorrect choice. Remember, the correct answer is implausible. Look for irrelevant reasoning—reasons that do not support the argument—and look for the answer choice that most undermines the accurate meaning of the passage. Other common flaws in reasoning include arguments that make unsupported comparisons or that provide unlikely cause-and-effect relationships (relationships that do not match). Also, watch for parts of an argument that focus on a small piece of evidence but apply this evidence broadly to all parts of the argument. When this is the case, you should select the answer choice that uses all-or-nothing words and phrases (*always, forever, never,* or *none*).

Analysis of Problem Sets

The following section is a detailed review of problem sets: the question stem, the passage, and the answer choices. As you read through the material presented, remember that your objective is to increase your ability to think critically and to strategize solutions for critical reasoning questions. Take time to read through this section to make sure you understand the concepts and strategies presented, and apply your learning to the practice questions that follow.

The Question Stem

Critical reasoning question stems provide you with essential details about what to look for in the passage. In most instances, only one question follows each passage. Question stems are usually short and to the point, but may be the most important part of the problem set because they help you to stay focused on the task at hand.

A good strategy to follow is to read the question stem *before* the passage to identify the question type. Knowing ahead of time what you're expected to answer will keep you focused on the most pertinent concepts in the passage and help lead you to the best answer. Many GMAT candidates have found that prereading the question stem eliminates having to read the passage a second time, thus saving valuable minutes.

However, if prereading the question stem does not help you narrow your response to one best answer choice, rereading the question and writing down key words can help remind you about what is being asked. For example, take a look at the following question stem.

> Which of the following, if true, most strongly supports the author's explanation for this position?

The words *strongly supports* identify the problem as a *strengthening the argument* question type. The answer choice, therefore, should strengthen the author's argument found in the passage. Practice can help you determine if and when prereading the question stem will be a good strategy for you.

Tip: Do not preread critical reasoning answer choices. It is a waste of time and energy. Four of the five answer choices are either incorrect or not the best answer choice. Thus scanning all of the answer choices exposes you to irrelevant and inconsistent information.

You may be asked to choose an answer that is *not true* or that is an *exception.* For example, take a look at the following negative question stem.

> All of the following statements, if true, provide an explanation EXCEPT:

To help answer this type of question, treat the answer choices as *true* or *false* statements. Search among the answer choices and select the one that is *false.* If there is more than one false answer, follow the flow of logic and evaluate key words to help you determine which answer is *not* true, and therefore, the correct choice. Be sure to practice a variety of negative questions prior to taking the GMAT to familiarize yourself with the different types of thought processes.

The Passage

Critical reading passages, also called *arguments* or *discussions,* are usually brief. You will notice that they are similar to reading comprehension passages, but the questions require you to apply logic and reasoning in addition to comprehending the author's meaning. As in reading comprehension passages, topics address a wide variety of business, science, or social science topics. As you read each passage, continue to practice the same skills that helped you with reading comprehension questions.

After you read the question stem, read the passage carefully while focusing on the specific question type. Your ability to analyze the passage's argument depends upon the logical relationship you can form between the passage and the question. Three reading skills that are especially useful in helping you with passages are:

1. **Understand the main point.** Use the strategies from the reading comprehension section of this study guide (pages 152–153) to help you concentrate on the main point or overall thrust of the entire passage. To help you focus on the main point, separate the author's facts from inferences. An especially useful strategy is to restate the passage's content in your own words. Doing so will help you clarify what the passage is intended to communicate. After you determine the main point of the argument, look at the question again to find the logical relationship between the passage's main point and the question.

2. **Identify the conclusion.** In addition to approaching each passage with a critical eye, try to identify its conclusion. The conclusion is a statement that sums up the main point of the passage and leads you to the evidence that supports your answer. It is often the last sentence in the passage. Use the *deductive reasoning* and *conclusion* skills identified earlier in "Basic Key Terms and Concepts" (page 172) to help you identify conclusions.

3. **Read actively and take notes.** Read actively and take notes to activate *critical thinking* skills that will help you reach logical conclusions that support your answer choice. Critical thinking is the process of thinking about and actively engaging in the written passage to formulate a hypothesis. Consider each passage a "thought unit," and if the argument appears somewhat unclear, but you have a vague idea about the author's reasoning, make a brief note to yourself. You will be amazed at your ability to organize the passage's content, facts, or details that you can then use to make logical assumptions that clarify your understanding of the passage and support your selected answer choice. Sometimes just one word can trigger associations that will point you to the correct answer. The key is to read actively and keep moving. Do not get tied up on any one question.

The Answer Choices

Critical reasoning questions are followed by five answer choices. After reading the question and passage, read all five answer choices before making your selection. If you don't know the answer, try to eliminate some of the obviously wrong choices as soon as you recognize them. If you get stuck on any one question, it may help to reread it because the answer may become more apparent when you take a second look. If rereading doesn't work, take an educated guess and eliminate all but the best of the choices that you haven't already eliminated.

Watch out for answer choices that look good, but are not the *best* answer choice. Just because an answer choice is a true statement, it does not mean that it is the best choice. Some questions present distracting answer choices to make it difficult for test-takers to narrow down the correct answer. These answer choices are often subtle variations of the correct answer choice and are commonly called "attractive distractors." Attractive distractors are designed to be similar to the *best* answer, and are statistically the most common wrong answers. When you narrow your choice to two answers, one is probably the attractive distractor. If you are having a difficult time deciding between two answer choices, read the question again and take an educated guess by selecting the choice that fits the *meaning* of the question more exactly. Remember that the correct answer choice is not necessarily perfect; it just has to be the *best* answer among the five choices.

Suggested Strategies with Sample Questions

This section illustrates common critical reasoning questions types. Use the general and specific strategies to learn how to use logic and reasoning to analyze the sample questions. As you study this material and practice the problems, recall the four-step approach suggested in the introduction of this chapter to direct your line of reasoning to the correct answer choice.

1. Identify the question type (main idea, assumptions/inferences, draw a conclusion, strengthen or weaken an argument, or faulty reasoning).
2. Read the passage (argument).
3. Look for underlying assumptions and inferences that will support the argument's conclusion.
4. Formulate a conclusion (hypothesis).

Strategy: Look for the Main Idea

Although critical reasoning problems do not strictly follow the "main idea" format found in some reading comprehension questions, we list this strategy first because it is the *first step* in solving critical reasoning problems. More commonly, the argument may leave the main point unstated and the question may ask you to formulate a logical connection from the content of the passage.

It is important to keep in mind that most critical reasoning problems require you to 1) identify the main point, argument, or conclusion that the author is attempting to make, and then 2) analyze this point in some manner. Therefore, it is usually necessary to identify the main idea of the passage before proceeding to the analysis portion of the problem.

1. *Jason:* Ticketing companies are scamming concertgoers out of their money by nickel-and-diming them on every ticket sale. For example, a customer might end up paying close to $60 for a $40 ticket once all of the excessive venue fees and processing fees are added to the ticket price. Additionally, since several companies hold a virtual monopoly on the market, consumers are generally forced to pay whatever the companies charge if they want to see their favorite performers.

    Jason's argument is most vulnerable to which of the following criticisms?

    Ⓐ It ignores the possibility that there may be alternate avenues through which consumers can purchase tickets.
    Ⓑ It ignores the possibility that the fees referenced may only apply to certain tickets.
    Ⓒ It ignores the possibility that the fees referenced may be legitimately necessary or out of the ticketing companies' control.
    Ⓓ It confuses the correlation between high overall ticket prices and ticketing fees with causation.
    Ⓔ It conflates *nickel-and-diming* with scamming.

Start by prereading the question to quickly determine what to look for in the argument. The main point will be the overall thrust of the entire passage.

The main point that Jason is trying to make is that ticketing companies are scamming consumers by charging *excessive* fees on top of ticket prices. However, the only evidence Jason provides to back this accusation is the fact that the companies charge substantial fees when selling tickets. Therefore, Jason is assuming that the fees are unwarranted without providing any support for this assumption; choice C correctly points out this flaw in reasoning. Choice A is addressed by Jason's *virtual monopoly on the market* comment, and choice B is addressed by Jason's *every ticket sale* comment. Choice D is incorrect because Jason provides a specific example of how fees can substantially increase a ticket's price. Choice E is incorrect because *nickel-and-diming* is a term with negative, exploitative connotations and supports Jason's argument. The correct answer is C.

2. Democracy is a political system of government that allows Americans to voice their opinion in free-choice elections to choose leaders. Critics of the election process, however, cite that the Electoral College does not accurately represent the popular vote. Whatever else might be said about American elections, they are quite unlike those in totalitarian countries in that Americans are totally free to make choices. And one choice Americans can make in this free country is to stay home and not vote at all.

    Which of the following, if true, most strongly supports the author's main argument?

    Ⓐ Americans who do decide to vote make more choices than those who do not.
    Ⓑ American elections embody many negative aspects, most of which are not embodied by elections in totalitarian countries.
    Ⓒ Choosing not to vote is the prerogative of a free citizen.
    Ⓓ All citizens vote in every election in totalitarian countries.
    Ⓔ Most American voters are not well informed enough to vote wisely.

When considering the answer choices, immediately eliminate those items that are (1) irrelevant to the question and/or the major issue of the argument and (2) not at all addressed by the argument. Consider the passage above. The author's point is necessarily connected with the major issues of the argument—in this case, free choice. The author stresses the free choice *not to vote* by making the point that Americans can choose to *stay home.* You may eliminate all choices that do not address the free choice not to vote. Choice A is irrelevant because it addresses the number of choices rather than the freedom of choice. Choice B raises issues scarcely addressed in the passage—that is, the negative aspects of elections. Choice D does not address the issue of choosing not to vote; although it notes that all citizens in totalitarian countries must vote, it neglects the main point—that Americans' free choice may be not to vote! Choice E is irrelevant to the issue of free choice, stressing voter information instead. *Choosing not to vote is the prerogative of a free citizen* addresses the major issue, free choice, and also the author's specific point, the free choice not to vote. Therefore, the correct answer is C.

Strategy: Look for Assumptions

An assumption is an *unstated* notion on which an argument rests and is necessary for the reader to reach a conclusion. In an assumption question, you are asked to determine what the author assumes but has not stated overtly in the argument. As you answer the sample questions below, remember to ask yourself, "What is assumed to be true and is not stated by the author, but is necessary in order to have evidence to support the conclusion?"

3. An actor must remain free to interpret a character in any way that strikes him or her as most deeply true to what the character would actually do in a given scene of a play. But every play has a director whose job it is to manage the action of the play as a whole. Therefore, no play provides a true opportunity for an actor to do what he or she does best.

   Which of the following is an assumption in the argument above?

   (A) Some directors will not under any circumstances compromise, regardless of what an individual actor believes to be the best way to interpret his or her role in the play.
   (B) An audience grants a certain amount of leeway in its expectation that a character in a play be entirely consistent from one scene to another.
   (C) An actor's true interpretation of a character is always inconsistent with the director's duty to manage the play as a whole.
   (D) Not every actor is entirely committed to an uncompromised interpretation of his or her role on stage.
   (E) No director would expect an actor to do something on stage that is entirely out of keeping with his or her character.

The author argues that *no play provides a true opportunity for an actor* to truly and freely interpret a character, because the director's responsibility *to manage the action of the play as a whole* will conflict with this type of interpretation in every play. Therefore, the assumption in choice C is correct. Choice A is incorrect because it refers only to the actions of *some* directors, and choice B is wrong because the audience expectation is irrelevant to the argument. Choice D is incorrect because it would actually contradict the author's argument, and choice E is incorrect because it rules out only some cases in which a director's decisions limit an actor's choices. The correct answer is C.

4. Surpluses in hydroelectric power are not always advantageous. For example, during years with heavy precipitation in the winter and spring season, the Pacific Northwest often experiences a power surplus from its hydroelectric dams. This surplus has allowed the region to lessen its dependency on more dangerous, environmentally damaging power sources such as coal and nuclear plants. However, the surplus also comes with potentially negative consequences: the leading power provider in the region could be forced to shut down many of its wind farms—a major blow to the burgeoning wind power industry—and inconsistent river surges could result in unstable employment conditions at coal and nuclear power plants in the region.

   Which of the following is an assumption made in drawing the conclusion above?

   (A) Excess power cannot be stored or sold to other energy providers in regions of need.
   (B) Employees of coal and nuclear power plants in the region cannot find alternative employment.
   (C) Hydroelectric power is the only viable alternative to more dangerous, environmentally damaging power sources such as coal and nuclear plants.
   (D) During years without heavy precipitation, hydroelectric dams do not produce significant energy.
   (E) Wind power is less environmentally damaging than hydroelectric power.

In emphasizing negative consequences, the author assumes that surplus power provides no benefit, and that power supply must be reduced if a surplus occurs. Therefore, choice A is correct. Choice B is incorrect because the passage does not mention alternative employment opportunities for coal and nuclear power plant workers. Choice C is incorrect because the passage identifies wind power as another viable alternative power source. Choice D is incorrect because the author implies only that hydroelectric dams do not produce *excess* power during years without heavy precipitation. Choice E is not implied in the passage. The correct answer is A.

Strategy: Draw a Conclusion

To draw a conclusion you must refer to the given premises and assumptions in the passage. You must always support your answer choice with material provided in the argument. Be careful to derive only what is directly indicated in the passage. A jump in logic may take you beyond the scope of the passage. Remember, if you are struggling with this type of question, plug in each answer choice to see which answer best fits the argument.

---

5. *Elisa:* Every time a new technology takes the place of human labor, workers suffer because jobs are lost. For example, if a machine were invented to cut hair automatically, hair salons would go out of business, a disaster which would throw thousands of hair stylists out of work.

   Niki: But that's not entirely true. Although hair stylists would have to find other work, other jobs would be created building, selling, and repairing those machines, and this might offset the job loss or even result in a net increase in jobs.

   Niki responds to Elisa's argument by

   Ⓐ agreeing with her conclusion, but pointing out an unexpected outcome.
   Ⓑ calling into question a key unstated assumption on which her whole argument rests.
   Ⓒ providing evidence that one of her premises is false.
   Ⓓ demonstrating how, upon further examination, her example does not support her conclusion.
   Ⓔ pointing out the absurdity of her conclusion by taking it to its logical extreme.

Elisa's conclusion is, in essence, "When technology advances, jobs are lost." She exemplifies this argument by discussing hair stylists. Niki responds by showing how this example fails to support Elisa's conclusion because new jobs would be created; therefore choice D is correct. Choice A is incorrect because Niki disagrees with Elisa's conclusion, saying, *But that's not entirely true.* Choices B and C are incorrect because Niki does not address an underlying assumption upon which Elisa's entire premise rests, but instead questions her example. Choice E is incorrect because Niki's first sentence implies that Elisa's premise may be partially true, and therefore not absurd. The correct answer is D.

---

6. In compliance with legislation enacted by the Obama administration, the county legislature has finally passed an antipollution ordinance. If its language is any indication, this legislation promises to be one of the most effective bills in the history of the state.

   Which of the following conclusions can be deduced from the passage?

   Ⓐ Pollution problems will be eliminated or reduced in the county.
   Ⓑ Previous ordinances have not had effective language.
   Ⓒ County, state, and federal antipollution measures overlap.
   Ⓓ Pollution has never been a serious problem in the county.
   Ⓔ The county will now be in compliance with recent federal legislation.

When selecting a conclusion based on a passage, select the one choice that must necessarily be true based on the information given, not just a choice that may possibly be true. Choice A is possible, for example, but not necessary to answer the question. Choices B, C, and D may be true, but they are unwarranted assumptions because they are not based on evidence that the author actually wrote in the passage. Choice E is the only conclusion that can be drawn safely, because the passage states that the ordinance was necessary to bring the county into compliance. The correct answer is E.

7. Which of the following most logically completes the passage below?

In the 1980s, the introduction of the compact disk (or CD) completely changed the way we listen to music. The low-fidelity, unreliable audiocassette soon disappeared from the marketplace. Today, digital audio, which is unmatched in sound clarity and convenience, is replacing the compact disk, and will _____

   Ⓐ   expand the music-buying public.
   Ⓑ   erode the profits of the music industry.
   Ⓒ   drive audiocassettes from the second-hand market.
   Ⓓ   make CD players obsolete.
   Ⓔ   encourage new musical talent.

The passage compares the obsolescence of the audiocassette when the CD was introduced with the present-day situation in which, according to the author, digital audio will soon replace the compact disk. This implies that CDs will soon become obsolete, which means that the manufacture of the machines that play them will become unnecessary. Therefore, answer choice D is correct. Choices A and B are incorrect because the passage offers no information about the profitability of the industry or size of the market, and choice C is incorrect because the passage tells us nothing of the effect of digital audio on audiocassettes. Choice E is incorrect because, even if true, there is nothing in the passage that supports this conclusion. The correct answer is D.

Strategy: Look for Evidence That Supports or Weakens the Conclusion

This type of question asks you to identify the answer choice that best supports (strengthens) or weakens (undermines) the conclusion or the argument. This question type may be the most common in the critical reasoning section. Be sure to practice this type of question as often as you can.

Looking for evidence that supports or weakens the conclusion does not suggest that you must identify how the author structures the line of reasoning. It asks you to identify *parallel* evidence that supports or undermines the conclusion. That is to say, you need to select the answer choice that is *different* from the same method of reasoning in the argument. Remember that this type of question supports or weakens the assumption but is not essential for a conclusion to be made.

Sometimes these types of questions ask you to determine what is relevant to the reasoning. The answer choice that would either strengthen or weaken the logic would be the relevant choice. Also, notice that this question type may contain the words *if true*. That means you should automatically accept all of the choices as being true: do not challenge their reasonableness or the possibility of their occurring. Rather, accept all of the choices as being true and from there decide which one would most strengthen or weaken the argument, whichever the question requires.

8. Ethologists, people who study animal behavior, have traditionally divided an organism's actions into two categories: learned behavior (based on experience) and instinctive behavior (based on genotype). Contemporary scholars reject this distinction, claiming that all behavior is a predictable interaction of genetic and environmental factors.

Which of the following statements, if true, would most strengthen the claim of the contemporary scholars?

   Ⓐ   All organisms with identical genotypes and identical experience sometimes respond differently in different situations.
   Ⓑ   All organisms with different genotypes and identical experience always respond identically in identical situations.
   Ⓒ   All organisms with similar genotypes and similar experience always respond differently in identical situations.
   Ⓓ   All organisms with identical genotypes and identical experience always respond identically in identical situations.
   Ⓔ   All organisms with identical genotypes and different experience always respond identically in identical situations.

The question expects you to find a statement that supports the claim of the contemporary scholars—that behavior is derived from an interaction of both experience and genotype. Choice A is wrong because it weakens this claim, implying the existence of a third factor other than genotype or experience. Choices B and E are both wrong because each relies on the distinction between genotypes and experience that contemporary scholars have rejected. Choice C is wrong because the word *similar* is undefined and too vague to be of any use in this context. Choice D is the only option that does not weaken the contemporary scholars' claim. It says that if identical organisms have identical experiences, then the organisms will always respond identically. This statement allows for both environmental and genetic factors to be tested at once. Note that this statement does not prove their claim; it merely provides more evidence that their thinking could be right. The correct answer is D.

Read the following passage and answer questions 9–10.

Research that compares children of cigarette-smoking parents in Virginia with children of nonsmoking parents in West Virginia found that children of smoking parents in Virginia have lower test scores than children of nonsmokers in West Virginia. Therefore, secondhand cigarette smoke is a cause of the lower test scores.

9. Which of the following, if true, most seriously weakens the conclusion above?

Ⓐ Children in Virginia have lower test scores than children in West Virginia, whether or not their parents smoke.
Ⓑ More people smoke in Virginia than in West Virginia.
Ⓒ Some children of nonsmoking parents in Virginia have low test scores.
Ⓓ Nonsmoking parents in Virginia have more children, on average, than those in most other states.
Ⓔ Research has shown that smoking is not only unhealthy for the smoker, but for others in the nearby vicinity.

If children in Virginia have lower test scores than children in West Virginia, whether or not their parents smoke, then the cigarette-smoking parents cannot logically be claimed to be the cause of the lower test scores. The correct answer, therefore, is choice is A because this choice weakens the conclusion. Choices B and D are incorrect; they would not affect the specific evidence presented in the passage. The evidence in choice C is too vague and anecdotal to be relevant to the author's conclusion. Choice E is incorrect because it strengthens the author's conclusion. The correct answer is A.

10. Which of the following, if true, would most strengthen the logic of the argument?

Ⓐ Recent data show that average test scores in Virginia are similar to those in West Virginia.
Ⓑ Parents in any particular state will always have different test scores than parents in other states.
Ⓒ The specific tests referenced in the research are limited in their ability to measure content areas.
Ⓓ Some children of nonsmoking parents are healthier than children of smoking parents.
Ⓔ Some children of smoking parents in Virginia have good test scores.

If average test scores in the two states are similar, then the discrepancy in the specific scores found by the research is more likely to be caused by the variable being tested in the study, which is parents who smoke. Choice B is incorrect because parents' test scores are irrelevant. Choice C is incorrect because the effectiveness of the tests does not affect the discrepancy found in the test scores themselves. Choices D and E are incorrect because they are vague and anecdotal. The correct answer is A.

11. *Political Activist:* The First Amendment of the U.S. Constitution guarantees that no law shall be made that infringes on free speech. Yet everywhere you look, laws do exactly that. Laws against libel and slander prohibit speech that is false and harmful, safety laws prohibit yelling "Fire!" in a crowded public place, and obscenity laws limit how and when certain words and phrases can be used. Some people may argue that the First Amendment acts as a safeguard that provides a check upon the creation of laws that egregiously prohibit free speech. In my opinion, it would be better to admit that the First Amendment, as stated, is unrealistic and dismantle it, even if it were to result in some cumbersome restrictions on free speech.

The argument exemplifies the political activist's wider belief that

Ⓐ passing laws that cannot be properly enforced is a necessary evil.
Ⓑ in law as in life, the end justifies the means.
Ⓒ integrity of the law should outweigh practical considerations.
Ⓓ no system of laws, however well conceived, can consistently administer justice.
Ⓔ individual liberty is more important than social harmony.

The argument concludes that it would be *better* to dismantle the First Amendment. Implied here is the political activist's belief that the benefit in doing so—that is, protecting and restoring the integrity of the law—outweighs the cost (that is, the practical consideration that free speech may be restricted). Choice A is wrong because the activist rejects the argument that the First Amendment is a necessary evil and, therefore, must remain in place. Similarly, choice B is incorrect because the activist directly rejects the belief that the end justifies the means, instead placing the means above the end. Choice D can be ruled out because the activist's larger point is not about how laws bring about justice, but rather about how a greater concept of justice overrules the importance of individual laws. Choice E is incorrect because the argument doesn't address the question of the individual versus society. The correct answer is C.

Strategy: Look for Faulty Reasoning

As you read the passage, look for an inconsistency or flaw in logic. For example, the argument may use a generalization to prove a specific point, or vice versa. Or it may use a false analogy (an invalid or unrelated comparison) to further an argument. It may present a conclusion without adequately supporting it, or it may contradict its original premise within the passage.

As you can see, a line of reasoning may be structured—and faulty—in many ways. Be aware that it usually does not matter whether you agree or disagree with the logic presented in the given passage, because faulty reasoning questions do not ask you to determine the passage's validity. Rather, you need to identify in structural (sequential) terms how the author has set up the argument and then identify any errors in logic.

If you know what you're looking for from prereading the question, you will quickly recognize the error as soon as you reach it. Typically, logical errors are so striking that, even if you are not looking for them, they will cause you to stop in realization that the logic of the passage has somehow been broken. You will find yourself wondering why you are having trouble with the reasoning. That's when you discover that you have uncovered the flaw in reasoning.

12. It is no wonder that most metropolitan cities have a significant increase in homeless populations. As a result of gentrification, middle- and high-income populations are renovating and settling in the low-rent areas of cities. Property values and rents have escalated, resulting in the inability of the lower income tenants to pay increased rents. If the governing bodies of cities could impose rent control, then the problem of homelessness would be virtually eliminated.

Which of the following, if true, would most seriously weaken the argument's reasoning that rent-control housing solves the problem of homelessness?

Ⓐ Homelessness was a problem before low-rent areas became gentrified.
Ⓑ Homeless populations are eager to find affordable housing.
Ⓒ The renovation of the low-rent areas has created more jobs and therefore more income for low-income city inhabitants.
Ⓓ Some homeless people cannot afford to pay for low-income housing.
Ⓔ Jobs and training are already available to the homeless through county job service programs.

In this question, you need to find a statement that argues *against* the idea that rent-control housing will end homelessness. The best choice here is A. Choices B, C, and E strengthen the argument's reasoning by implying that homeless populations are "eager to find affordable housing" (choice B) or are willing to secure "jobs" (choices C and E). If homelessness was a problem even when rents were low, then making rents low again by controlling rent logically *would not solve the homeless problem*. The next best choice is D, but without more information on what "some homeless people" means, choice A is better because choice D implies that some homeless people *can* afford low-income housing. The correct answer is A.

13. *Speaker:* One need not look very far to find abundant examples of incivility and brutality in the most genteel corners of American society.

Questioner: Then why don't we step up law enforcement in the slums of our cities?

The questioner reveals which of the following misunderstandings?

Ⓐ Incivility and brutality have become more common.
Ⓑ Law enforcement is related to problems of incivility and brutality.
Ⓒ The speaker is from genteel society.
Ⓓ The phrase *genteel corners* has something to do with *slums*.
Ⓔ Incivility is synonymous with brutality.

The speaker says incivility and brutality are issues in genteel American society—or in other words, affluent communities. By proposing increased law enforcement in city slums, rather than in affluent communities, the questioner reveals a misunderstanding of the meaning of the phrase, *genteel corners*. Choices A and B are incorrect because neither the speaker or the questioner implies disagreement with either of these sentiments. Choice C is incorrect because the origins of the speaker are irrelevant, and choice E is incorrect because it is an irrelevant distinction. The correct answer is D.

Practice Critical Reasoning Questions

Easy to Moderate

1. Worldwide, in all demographics over the age of 25, women tend to play social games such as *Farmville* more than men. Within all demographics, a slow and steady rise in social gaming is expected over the next five years. In the country of Fredonia, however, a sharp increase in the ratio of female social gamers to men is predicted, even though no increase in the population of women is expected.

   Which of the following, if true, best explains the apparent discrepancy in this prediction?

   Ⓐ Husbands of married women who play social games are more likely to be gamers themselves than single men.
   Ⓑ A slight rise in the birth rate is expected in each of the next five years.
   Ⓒ Women are far less likely than men to play video games that lack a social element.
   Ⓓ Fredonia's ongoing civil war is projected to have a devastating effect on the male population.
   Ⓔ Virtually no people in any demographic stop playing social games once they begin.

2. Deliberations of our governing bodies are held in public in order to allow public scrutiny of each body's actions to question those actions that citizens feel are not, for whatever reason, in their best interests.

   Which of the following statements is an assumption on which the passage depends?

   Ⓐ Government action should reflect the will of the people.
   Ⓑ Public scrutiny usually results in criticisms of our governing bodies.
   Ⓒ The best interests of the public usually do not coincide with the interests of our governing bodies.
   Ⓓ No government deliberations should be kept from the public.
   Ⓔ Citizens in countries without public scrutiny are not well served by their governments.

Read the following passage and answer questions 3–4.

A significant number of criminologists cite a definite correlation between an increase in temperature and an increase in crime activity. Additional research shows a close connection between atmospheric conditions, especially in July and August, and most forms of crime. Recent studies indicate that more violent crimes are committed during hot weather than during cold weather. Thus, if we could control the weather, the violent crime rate would drop.

3. The argument makes which of the following assumptions about the relationship between weather conditions and crime rates?

   Ⓐ If atmospheric conditions change, most forms of crime will decrease.
   Ⓑ The relationship between weather conditions and crime rates is causal.
   Ⓒ If weather conditions could be controlled, crime activity will cease.
   Ⓓ The relationship between weather conditions and crime rates is negligible.
   Ⓔ The relationship between weather conditions and crime rates is proportional.

4. Which of the following statements, if true, would most strengthen the argument?

Ⓐ The annual violent crime statistics for New York are higher than for Los Angeles.
Ⓑ Empirical evidence shows that increased heat caused an increase in aggressive behavior.
Ⓒ In addition to the increase in crime rates during hot summer months, violent crime also increases when students are on vacation.
Ⓓ New technology is making weather control a possibility in the future.
Ⓔ Many cities in warmer climates have more wide-scale poverty than cities in cooler climates.

5. The state's vacant multimillion-dollar governor's mansion on the banks of the Capitol River may be a sort of "suburban Taj Mahal," as the governor once stated. But given the state's current financial situation, the prudent solution is to sell the mansion.

Which of the following statements is an assumption on which the argument depends?

Ⓐ The governor's mansion is out of place in the suburbs.
Ⓑ Selling the mansion would ease the state's budgetary defect.
Ⓒ No one has yet lived in the governor's mansion.
Ⓓ The state is already trying to sell the governor's mansion.
Ⓔ The current market value of the mansion has decreased.

6. Following a season of devastating tornadoes in a rural town in Missouri, several members of the town council have proposed the construction of an underground community tornado shelter. Residents could take shelter during severe tornado warnings and live in the structure for short periods during the aftermath if tornadoes damaged or destroyed their homes. The council members claim that such a shelter could be built without raising municipal tax rates and would benefit the entire community by providing a safety net for any citizens unlucky enough to fall in the paths of destruction.

Which of the following statements, if true, would most weaken the council members' argument?

Ⓐ Town residents are already unhappy with high municipal tax rates.
Ⓑ Several similar proposals in nearby towns have failed to pass.
Ⓒ Most residents have tornado shelters in their homes or in municipal buildings nearby.
Ⓓ An aboveground tornado shelter in a nearby town was recently destroyed by a tornado.
Ⓔ Meteorologists are unable to predict the severity of future tornado seasons.

7. *Store owner:* Recently, a department store opened nearby, threatening to lure away some of my customers. This competing department store sells heavily insulated UGG boots, which my store does not carry. Therefore, only those customers of mine who buy UGG boots will patronize my competitor.

The store owner's conclusion is flawed because he illogically assumes that

Ⓐ his other customers do not find the boots attractive.
Ⓑ customers are not buying other products from the competition.
Ⓒ customers will wear the boots in all seasons and weather conditions.
Ⓓ some customers wearing UGG boots bought them from stores other than that of his competitor.
Ⓔ the competition is outselling the store owner.

8. Marketing literature for a brand of netbook computer cites a study in which high school students who used the product to take and organize their class notes scored 15 percent higher on tests than students who did not use the product. The company that produces the netbooks asserts that using the netbook will therefore increase a student's school grades by 15 percent.

   Which of the following statements, if true, would most seriously weaken the company's claim?

   Ⓐ The netbook comes with note-taking and test-preparation software.
   Ⓑ Students who did not use the netbook benefited from private tutoring.
   Ⓒ Netbook users in the study who performed poorly were less likely to report their grades.
   Ⓓ Students who used note-taking software with other products did equally well.
   Ⓔ The use of netbooks in classrooms is already fairly widespread.

Average

9. *Councilperson:* Without sign ordinances, anyone with a can of spray paint could decide to publicly create his or her own Picassos, and soon the entire town would start to look like something out of *Alice in Wonderland.* Therefore, we need sign ordinances to prevent this scenario from happening.

   The councilperson asserts each of the following basic assumptions EXCEPT:

   Ⓐ Spray paint is often used to make signs.
   Ⓑ The entire town looking like *Alice in Wonderland* is undesirable.
   Ⓒ Sign ordinances will prevent the town from looking like *Alice in Wonderland.*
   Ⓓ Given the opportunity, many citizens would create their own signs.
   Ⓔ Limiting access to spray paint would prevent the scenario from happening.

10. The SmartWay Supermarket chain recently began advertising its new policy to prevent long checkout lines: Whenever more than three customers are waiting in any line, the store manager opens a new checkout station. Yet within two months, upper-level management has noticed a rise in complaints from gold-level customers (shoppers who typically buy more than $750 in groceries from SmartWay every month) that their wait time in checkout lines has increased rather than decreased.

    Which of the following, if true, would best explain this rise in complaints by gold-level shoppers?

    Ⓐ During peak shopping hours, many store managers open more lines than necessary to keep lines to three customers or less.
    Ⓑ People who tend to buy more groceries usually budget a larger block of time for their shopping than those who buy only a few items at a time.
    Ⓒ This new policy also included an initiative to increase the proportion of lines reserved for customers with 20 items or less.
    Ⓓ An increase in the number of checkout lines tends to result in a commensurate decrease in floor staff to answer questions and direct customers to items that they cannot find by themselves.
    Ⓔ Since the new policy has begun, upper management has become aware of an increase in staff tardiness and absenteeism.

11. In most economies, the government plays a role in the market system. Governments enforce laws that regulate the financial markets and often control prices through price ceilings, price supports, currency controls, and other fiscal policies. Government actions can create short-term shortages or surpluses in the markets, but even fiscal conservatives accept the necessity of government taking an active role in the economy.

Which of the following viewpoints does the information in the passage most strongly support?

Ⓐ Economic surpluses and low prices are good for the economy.
Ⓑ Occasional market shortages are a price of government intervention in the economy.
Ⓒ Consistently higher prices strengthen the economy.
Ⓓ Most fiscal conservatives believe that government should not interfere in financial markets.
Ⓔ Surpluses and shortages are usually unintended consequences of fiscal policy.

Read the following passage and answer questions 12–13.

> A more stringent smog test is needed as part of the required vehicle inspection program to protect the quality of the state's air for us its citizens. Auto exhausts are a leading contributor to respiratory ailments and air pollution. The state's long-term interests in the health of its citizens and its viability as a place to live, work, and conduct business depend on clean air.

12. Which of the following, if true, would most seriously weaken the argument?

Ⓐ Since automotive anti-smog devices were made mandatory thirty-eight years ago, the contribution of auto emissions to air pollution is now negligible.
Ⓑ Air pollution problems are increasing in other states at a faster rate than in this state.
Ⓒ Respiratory ailments may be caused by phenomena other than air pollution.
Ⓓ Vehicle inspection programs need to be more comprehensive.
Ⓔ Home buyers and businesses prefer to locate in areas with clean air.

13. Which of the following statements represents an underlying assumption of the argument?

Ⓐ People's health is more important than attracting businesses to the area.
Ⓑ The state's short-term interests are at stake the most.
Ⓒ Exhaust emissions contribute to air pollution.
Ⓓ A more stringent smog test would be effective to reduce auto emissions.
Ⓔ Air pollution is unavoidable.

14. An under-recognized and unfortunate consequence of the piracy of digitized music—and the resulting decline in album sales—is the decline of the professional songwriter. In genres such as country, pop, and R&B, many songs traditionally have been written by professional songwriters to be performed by the artists, whose vocal talents often outshone their writing gifts. Songwriters received a few cents in royalties each time one of their songs was played on the radio (performance royalties), in addition to a few cents per song each time an album or CD was sold containing one of their songs (mechanical royalties). Artists received no performance royalties for songs they did not write, but received mechanical royalties for every song on every album or CD they sold. However, the virtual disappearance of album sales because of the digitization of music has resulted in more artists writing all of their own material instead of relying on professional songwriters.

In the passage above, the author implies each of the following EXCEPT:

Ⓐ The trend of increasing numbers of artists writing their own songs is a positive development for the music industry.

Ⓑ An artist whose recording of a songwriter's song receives millions of plays on radio stations receives no compensation for the airplay.

Ⓒ If a songwriter's song is recorded on an artist's best-selling album but is never played on the radio, the songwriter would receive mechanical but not performance royalties.

Ⓓ The recent trend of artists writing more of their own material is primarily financially, rather than artistically, driven.

Ⓔ Many artists in the country, pop, and R&B genres are better singers than they are songwriters.

15. In 1951, cells from a cancerous tumor in a poor tobacco farmer named Henrietta Lacks were taken for research without her knowledge. These specific cells reproduced so rapidly and prolifically in laboratory tests that her reproduced cells have since been bought and sold in the scientific community. The combined weight of these cells measured well into the tons, despite the miniscule weight of each individual cell. Henrietta's descendents, however, are still too poor to afford the very health care that her cells helped make possible.

If the above statements are true, which of the following must also be true?

Ⓐ Neither Henrietta Lacks nor her descendents ever received any compensation for her cells, despite their scientific and commercial value.

Ⓑ It is theoretically possible to combine cells to collectively weigh them.

Ⓒ Henrietta Lacks never found out that her cells were taken from her.

Ⓓ The fact that Henrietta's cells reproduced quickly and abundantly in laboratory tests made them valuable to the scientific community.

Ⓔ Reproductions of Henrietta Lacks' cells are still bought and sold today.

16. The older we get, the less sleep we desire. Because of the advanced knowledge and capabilities naturally acquired through aging, awake hours are more enjoyable. Therefore, "mindless" sleep becomes a waste of time.

    Which of the following, if true, would most logically strengthen the argument?

    Ⓐ Advanced knowledge is often manifested in creative dreams.
    Ⓑ While certain areas of the brain are active during certain types of sleep, other types of sleep produce very little activity in the brain.
    Ⓒ Several empirical studies have shown that sleeping more than a minimum threshold can actually impede intellectual stimulation.
    Ⓓ Advanced capabilities are not necessarily mind-associated.
    Ⓔ Dreams have the potential to teach us how to use waking experiences more intelligently.

17. Cooking dinner at home tends to cost less than going to restaurants. At the same time, a home-cooked meal can be assured to be lower in calories, because the ingredients that go into the meal can be monitored. However, eating at a restaurant is a common social activity among friends. So when choosing where to eat dinner, a tradeoff needs to be made between economy and health on the one hand and friendship on the other.

    Which of the following, if true, most strongly undermines the conclusion in the argument above?

    Ⓐ The cost of cooking a single dinner at home may be higher than eating a meal at a restaurant because a variety of staple items, such as flour, may need to be purchased in bulk.
    Ⓑ A man may be reluctant to invite a woman over to his house for a home-cooked meal, fearing that she will perceive him to be financially incapable of paying for dinner at a restaurant.
    Ⓒ In most eateries, competition for dinner-hour customers is so intense that most restaurants cannot afford to lower their prices.
    Ⓓ Friends can turn cooking healthy, inexpensive meals together into an enjoyable shared activity.
    Ⓔ Most cookbooks focus much more on the gustatory pleasure that a recipe provides than either its cost to prepare or its calorie count.

18. *President of a developing nation:* We are considering whether to seek a substantial loan to finance the construction of a nationwide electrical grid powered by a hydroelectric dam. The dam would, however, cut off downriver water supplies that many people rely on for subsistence.

    Advisor: The electrical grid plan will have two positive effects on every citizen in the country. First, it will significantly increase the country's GDP, an economic projection that should encourage economic investment. Second, it will provide electrical power to those who currently do not have it at all, or who have it only sporadically. On this basis, I encourage you to move forward on this proposal.

    Each of the following, if true, is an assumption in the advisor's argument EXCEPT:

    Ⓐ The advisor's economic projections are accurate.
    Ⓑ Increasing the GDP is more important to the country than maintaining the welfare of citizens who depend on the river for subsistence.
    Ⓒ Increasing the GDP is a desirable prospect for the country.
    Ⓓ The hydroelectric dam would generate sufficient power for the entire electrical grid.
    Ⓔ The country would be able to secure the loan needed to finance the investment.

19. Before evidence of the state's upcoming budget crisis began to surface, state legislators enacted a variety of bills that had saddled the state with $5 billion in long-term debt. Now the legislature has voted to put five more general obligation bond issues on the November ballot, which would add approximately $1.5 billion to the state's long-term debt. Budget items on the November agenda include $500 million for building and remodeling public schools, $450 million to extend the veterans home loan program, $200 million to subsidize subprime mortgages on the verge of default, $85 million to acquire land for environmental protection, and $280 million to help counties expand or remodel their jails.

Which of the following, if true, most weakens the argument for approving five new bond issues?

 Ⓐ Environmental protection is not an overriding concern of the constituency.
 Ⓑ The state's long-term debt cannot lawfully exceed $6 billion.
 Ⓒ Voters favor improvements in education, the environment, corrections, and the real-estate market.
 Ⓓ Similar bond proposals in other states have not been successful.
 Ⓔ Voters are not happy about the prospect of sinking more money into the housing of criminals.

Above Average to Difficult

20. Low sales figures are typically an indicator of how a sales department is doing its job. This makes no sense, because these numbers are almost always a function of a variety of other factors, none of which is the responsibility of the sales department: for example, _____.

All of the following would logically complete the example above by strengthening the argument EXCEPT:

 Ⓐ when the buyers for an electronics store select items that the public doesn't wish to purchase
 Ⓑ when management sets prices so high that customers simply refuse to pay
 Ⓒ when the marketing department designs products that misinterpret the needs of the end user
 Ⓓ when technology becomes so complicated that consumers cannot accurately assess the benefits of a product
 Ⓔ when a company environment is disorganized or hostile and the delivery of quality, on-time services to clients becomes impossible

21. In 2010, when implementing an employee evaluation program, the gross income of Staritec Corporation reached an all-time high. After dropping the program during 2011, however, Staritec's income dropped by 50 percent. It is clear, therefore, that Staritec's employees perform better when being evaluated.

Which of the following statements, if true, most weakens the conclusion?

 Ⓐ Company executives also received performance evaluations in 2010.
 Ⓑ Economic conditions in the industry during 2011 significantly deteriorated.
 Ⓒ Staritec department managers noted that employees seemed to work harder when they knew they were being evaluated.
 Ⓓ An optional survey suggested that the employee evaluation program increased company morale during 2010.
 Ⓔ Staritec's drop in income could not be attributed to other factors.

22. One form of paper recycling draws from post-consumer waste products. This means that the paper is produced from paper products that were once used in homes or industry. However, another kind of paper can also be called "recycled." This paper is produced from byproducts of the paper-making process itself, which means the paper has never been used by a consumer. Although the former method is more environmentally sound, the latter produces a paper with a higher aesthetic quality.

If the passage above is true, then it is also true that people who buy the best-looking recycled paper are

    Ⓐ   buying paper that was once used in homes and industry.

    Ⓑ   inspecting the byproducts of the paper-making process.

    Ⓒ   insisting on a high-quality paper made from post-consumer waste.

    Ⓓ   purchasing paper that does not come from the most environmentally sound process.

    Ⓔ   reducing the amount of paper they use.

23. The *Financial Times* magazine takes pride in being one of the longest-standing financial periodicals still in production, dating back to the mid-1920s. However, while the fledgling periodical devoted two pages to the stock market crash of 1929 in its weekly issue following the initial drop, the magazine covered the market crash of 2008 with 25 pages in the weekly issue following *its* initial drop. This occurred despite the fact that the initial drop in the first week of the 1929 crash was of a larger percentage than that of the 2008 crash.

Based on the information in the passage, the most likely explanation for the discrepancy in coverage is that

    Ⓐ   at the time, the crash of 1929 was a largely unprecedented event, and as such, the scale of its effects were more widely debated.

    Ⓑ   while the initial percentage drop of the 1929 crash was greater than that of the 2008 crash, the drop was much smaller than that of the 2008 crash in nominal terms.

    Ⓒ   there was much less transparency in the financial markets in 1929 than there was in 2008.

    Ⓓ   the size of the magazine increased significantly since the 1929 crash, so editors could devote more space to the 2008 story.

    Ⓔ   given the sensitive climate of the time, the press in 1929 devoted more time to covering positive stories, rather than negative and potentially damaging news.

Answers and Explanations for Practice Critical Reasoning Questions

1. **D.** With no increase in the population of women, the only way to explain a sharp increase in the ratio of women who play social games is an increase in the ratio of women over 25. Given a constant population of women, the ratio of women to men over 25 is growing if and only if the ratio of women under 25 is shrinking. The correct answer is choice D. Choice A is wrong because whether men play social games is irrelevant to the argument. Eliminate choice B because a slight rise in the birth rate coupled with a stable population of women would tend to decrease the population of women over 25, which would not help explain the discrepancy. Choice C can be ruled out because video games that lack a social element do not enter into the discussion. Rule out choice E because the fact that people who start playing social games tend not to stop is extraneous, given that the argument assumes a slight rise in the total number of women who play social games.

2. **A.** The passage states that deliberations of governing bodies are held in public to allow citizens to challenge any decisions that are not in their best interests; therefore, choice A states an assumption that the passage depends on—namely, the value judgment that good governance reflects the will of those governed. Choices B and C are incorrect because the argument does not address the frequency of specific consequences of public scrutiny. Choices D and E are overgeneralizations that are not explicitly supported in the argument to the extent of choice A.

3. **B.** The argument assumes hot weather causes crime, when all that can be concluded from the evidence presented is a correlation. The correct answer is choice B. Choice A is incorrect, because the author makes the opposite assumption. Choices C, D, and E are incorrect because they are not implied in the passage.

4. **B.** The scientific evidence presented in choice B directly supports the argument, making it the correct response. Choice A does not support the argument because no information is given about crime rates in the New York and Los Angeles. Choices C and E are incorrect because they refer to variables other than weather that may affect crime rates. Choice D is irrelevant to the argument.

5. **B.** The author's reason for selling the mansion is *the state's current financial situation;* thus it can be assumed that the state needs the money that selling the mansion would bring. The correct answer is choice B. None of the other choices is implied in the passage.

6. **C.** If true, choice C would suggest that the proposed community tornado shelter is not needed. The correct answer is choice C. Choice A contradicts the stated claim that the proposal would not increase tax rates. Choices B and E are not relevant to the proposal, as the desirability of a community tornado shelter does not depend on specific events in other towns or the ability to predict tornadoes. Choice D is incorrect because the failure of an aboveground shelter does not imply that an underground shelter would similarly fail.

7. **B.** The store owner ignores the possibility that *other* customers may be buying *other* products from his competitor besides UGG boots. The correct answer is choice B. Choices A, C, and E are irrelevant to the store owner's assertion. Choice D may be true, but it is not an assumption the store owner is making; to the contrary, he ignores the possibility altogether.

8. **C** The correct answer is C. If students who did poorly after using the netbooks reported their grades inaccurately, it would indicate that the study results were invalid and that the 15% increase in performance was an inflation of the actual performance increase. Choice A supports the company's claim, while choices B and E are irrelevant to the company's claim. Choice D is incorrect because the fact that other products may produce an equal benefit is irrelevant.

9. **E.** The councilperson does not mean to imply that spray paint is the only medium people would use to create signs. The correct answer is choice E. All of the other answers choices are assumptions the councilperson does make, and that the passage implies; therefore, choices A, B, C, and D are incorrect in this context.

10. **C.** The passage states that gold-level shoppers purchase more per month than shoppers who have not reached gold-level status, a condition that implies that they typically purchase more items at a time than nongold-level shoppers; therefore, it follows that they would be more likely to purchase more than 20 items at a time, which would prevent them from using an increased portion of the lines. The correct answer is choice C. Choice A is irrelevant because the passage mentions nothing about peak hours, and choices B and D are irrelevant to time spent waiting in line. Choice E is illogical because it would not explain why the policy causes only the gold-level shoppers to wait longer in line.

11. **B.** The passage most explicitly supports the viewpoint expressed in choice B. The passage actually implies the opposite of choice A, while choice C is never addressed. Choice D is directly contradicted by the final sentence. A weak argument could be made for choice E, but it is not nearly as clearly implied as choice B is; the question asks for the viewpoint that the passage "most strongly supports," which is choice B.

12. **A.** The argument for more stringent inspections would be most weakened by evidence that existing measures have effectively removed auto emissions as a source of air pollution. The correct answer is choice A. Choice C does not weaken the argument because auto exhaust is cited as only a contributing cause of respiratory ailments. Choice B is irrelevant to the argument, and choices D and E support rather than weaken the argument.

13. **D.** The author of the argument assumes that testing to new standards would reduce emissions, which according to the argument would lower air pollution. The correct answer is choice D. Answer choices A, B, and E are not supported in the passage. Choice C is incorrect because it expresses stated information rather than an unstated assumption.

14. **A.** The author does not imply that the decline of the professional songwriter is a positive development; in fact, the opposite. The correct answer is choice A. Choices B, C, D, and E are incorrect because they are all implied in the passage.

15. **D.** The explicit and sole reasoning given for the widespread use of Henrietta's cells (implying value) was that they reproduced *rapidly and prolifically,* (synonyms for the adjectives used in choice D), which means that these characteristics must have given them value in the scientific community. The correct answer is choice D. Choice A is *suggested* by the passage, but cannot be *deduced.* It is possible that Henrietta's descendants are poor despite receiving some form of compensation along the way. Choice B is incorrect because you can add the individual weights to come up with a combined weight; the cells don't have to be physically combined. Choice E is incorrect because while the passage describes a general amount of cells that were bought and sold in the time since 1951, it cannot be deduced that the cells are still being traded today. Choice C is incorrect because while Henrietta was unaware of her cells being taken *at the time,* it is never stated that she never found out about them being taken and their use.

16. **C.** Choice C supports the idea that sleep operates against the use of advanced knowledge and capabilities. Choices A and E present information that supports the value of sleep, which contradicts the argument. Choice B does not strengthen the argument because it implies sleep is *not* entirely "mindless" as the author asserts. Choice D is incorrect because it implies that "mindless" sleep may not impede our advanced capabilities after all.

17. **D.** The conclusion of the argument is that people must choose between economy and health (by cooking at home) and friendship (by eating at a restaurant). This is most undermined by the insight that friends can decide to cook at home as a social event. The correct answer is choice D. Choice A can be ruled out because an additional impediment to cooking at home doesn't particularly affect the conclusion of the argument. Choice B is incorrect for the same reason; it is a distractor because its logic is correct, but it does not conflict with the author's conclusion. Choice C is wrong because the cost of eating at a restaurant doesn't come into the argument. Eliminate choice E because the content of cookbooks also doesn't enter into the discussion.

18. **B.** The advisor's argument does not address the president's concern for the welfare of certain citizens; it only addresses two benefits to the populace as a whole. The correct answer is choice B. The rest of the choices all contain basic assumptions upon which his argument relies. The advisor's economic projections (choice A), provide the foundation for his argument, as does the assumption that increasing GDP is desirable, choice C. Choice D is inherently assumed if the plan is to positively affect all of the citizens. Choice E is also essential for the plan to move forward.

19. **B.** The strongest deterrent to approving the bond issues is that passage would raise the debt over the legal limit. The correct answer is B. Choices A and E may weaken the argument somewhat, but not nearly to the extent of choice B. Choice C supports the argument, and choice D is irrelevant.

20. **D.** A good answer should be an example of how sales were negatively affected by a factor that the sales department has no power over. Thus, a bad example would point out a factor that is within the control of sales department. A sales department is responsible for keeping abreast of technology well enough to educate the consumer on product benefits, so the correct answer is choice D. Eliminate choice A because poor choices by electronics store buyers are out of the control of the sales department. Choice B is wrong because management decisions to raise prices are also out of the control of the sales department. Similarly, choice C is incorrect because bad marketing decisions are out of the control of the sales department. Choice E can be ruled out because a company-wide dysfunctional work environment that affects the service that clients receive is also out of the sales department's control.

21. **B.** The conclusion attributes the drop in income solely to the evaluation program. If economic conditions were different in the two years, however, other factors may have contributed to the loss of income. The correct answer is B. Choice A is irrelevant to the conclusion, and choices C and E support the conclusion. Choice D is incorrect because it does not weaken the conclusion, although it may call into question the validity of the survey.

22. **D.** This question requires you to read through the information on recycled paper and then draw a conclusion based on that information. The question here is if people insist on the best-looking recycled paper, which paper have they purchased? The passage states that post-consumer waste paper is not the best looking. So these people won't buy this kind of paper; instead, they will buy paper made from byproducts. To find the right choice, you also have to remember that using post-consumer waste is the most environmentally sound process. Once you put these facts together (the best-looking paper does not come from the most environmentally sound process), you have your answer, choice D. Choices A and C are incorrect because the passage explicitly states that the more aesthetic paper has *not* been used in homes and industry. Choice B is incorrect because it is never implied that the consumers are "inspecting" the raw materials used to create their paper. Choice E is incorrect because a reduction in usage is never implied.

23. **D.** The passage tells us that the magazine was founded in the mid-1920s, so it logically follows that it would likely have been a much smaller publication in 1929 compared to the 80-some year-old institution it would have become by the 2008 crash; the passage even calls the magazine "fledgling" at the time of the crash. The correct answer is D. Choice A is incorrect, because more debate would imply more coverage. Choices C and E are incorrect, because, while logical, they are never implied by information in the passage. Choice B is incorrect, because not only is it never implied by the passage, the nominal drop would be less important than the percentage drop in terms of its effect on society and, thus, its level of media coverage.

PART V

QUANTITATIVE SECTION

The Quantitative section of the GMAT measures your ability to reason quantitatively and think critically as you solve math problems. This section covers fundamental math topics in arithmetic, algebra, geometry, data analysis, word problems, and data interpretation presented within specific *question types* that appear on the GMAT. The problem solving and data sufficiency chapters provide suggested strategies, sample questions, and practice questions to help you become familiar with the test format. The math skills review chapter is a comprehensive review of arithmetic, algebra, geometry, data analysis, word problems, and data interpretation. This chapter includes diagnostic tests, math terminology, formulas, and concepts with step-by-step examples and practice questions.

You are encouraged to pace yourself and become familiar with the question types by completing the practice exercises outlined in each chapter. To enhance individual learning styles, we have organized practice exercises by level of difficulty starting with easy to moderate questions, average questions, and finally above average to difficult questions. As you repeat the practice questions, you will be steadily increasing your comfort level with the question types and increasing your ability to solve more difficult questions. Sharpen your skills by actively working through the four full-length practice tests, one in this study guide and the three additional tests on the accompanying CD-ROM.

Format

Chapter Number	Question Type	Total Number of Questions on GMAT
Chapter 7	**Problem solving** questions are straightforward math problems.	Approximately 22–24 questions
Chapter 8	**Data sufficiency** problem sets require that you to draw upon math and reasoning skills to determine if the information provided in the problem is *sufficient* to answer the question.	Approximately 12–15 questions

The diagram on the following page identifies the format of Quantitative topics with possible corresponding question types. Notice that there are six different math *content topics* AND each question topic may be matched with any one of the two different *question types*. For example, you may be asked to solve an algebra problem that is presented as a problem solving question, or you may be asked to solve an algebra problem that is presented as a data sufficiency question.

Question Types vs. Content Topics

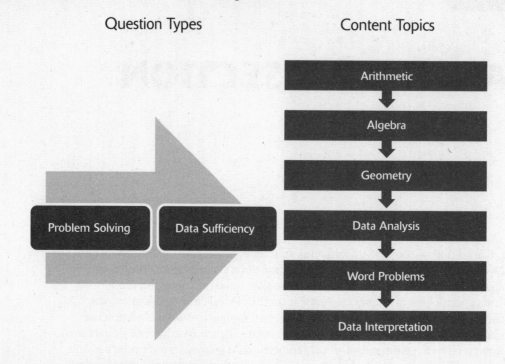

Question Types

Content Topics

Problem Solving | Data Sufficiency

Arithmetic

Algebra

Geometry

Data Analysis

Word Problems

Data Interpretation

Computer-Adaptive Testing

The Quantitative section of the exam is comprised of 37 questions with a 75-minute time limit. Each question will appear individually on the computer screen or will appear as part of a data interpretation set of questions that are based on facts related to tables, graphs, or other forms of graphic information. Since this is a computer-adaptive test wherein the computer analyzes each response in order to determine the difficulty level of future questions, you will not have the ability to skip questions and return to them later. Keep in mind that because the GMAT is a computer-adaptive test, your overall Quantitative score is a combination of your performance (how many questions were answered correctly) and the difficulty level of each question.

To assist you in understanding explanations and to direct your attention to different questions and answer choices, notice that this study guide numbers the questions and letters the answer choices as (A) through (E). On the actual exam, questions are not numbered and the answer choices are not lettered.

Quantitative General Directions

Consider reviewing the on-screen instructions *before* the day of your test to save you valuable testing time. As you become more familiar with the instructions, you only need to scan the written directions to confirm that no changes have been made to the instructions. The on-screen instructions for the Quantitative section depend on the type of question asked.

As a reminder, in this study guide, answer choices appear with capital letters (A, B, C, D, and E), but on the actual computer test, answer choices will appear with circles. Your task is to click on the oval that best represents your selected answer.

Specific directions for each question type are described in chapters 7 and 8. In general, all Quantitative questions have assumptions about symbols, diagrams, and numerical values. These assumptions include, but are not limited, to the following:

- All numbers used are real numbers.
- Geometric figures or diagrams, such as lines, circles, triangles, and quadrilaterals, are drawn to scale unless otherwise indicated and can be used to estimate sizes by measurement.
- Lines that appear straight can be assumed to be straight.
- A symbol that appears repeatedly within a question represents the same value or object each time it appears.
- Points on a line are in the order shown and all angle measures are positive values. On a number line, positive numbers are to the right of zero and increase to the right, and negative numbers are to the left of zero and decrease to the left.
- Distances are always either zero or a positive value.

General Strategies

Read the following general strategies and tips that apply to all Quantitative problems before you study the chapters' suggested strategies, approaches, and practice questions that follow.

1. **Practice.** Memorize and practice the two types of questions before your exam date to save time the day of the test. Make sure you are comfortable solving math problems using a computer by practicing prior to your exam date at www.mba.com.

2. **Manage your time wisely.** Quantitative questions can be time consuming so do not let questions slow your pace. You have about 2 minutes to read and answer each question, but this does not include the time it takes you to perform calculations. To allow time to read and perform computations, shorten your practice time in this study guide to no more than $1\frac{1}{2}$ minutes per question.

3. **Use the noteboard to organize your computations.** Write down key words, numbers and computations to help take a closer look at the question. This visual organization process is especially helpful with complex problems that require you to break the problem into sequential parts.

4. **Questions are intermingled and computer adaptive.** Problem solving and data sufficiency questions are mixed together. The first question will be medium difficulty. If you get the question right, the computer will offer you a slightly more difficult question next. If you answer the first question incorrectly, the computer will adapt and offer you a slightly less difficult question next. The computer will continue to adapt the level of questions you receive based on your responses to all the previous questions.

Chapter 7

Introduction to Problem Solving

The problem solving question type requires you to solve math problems and then choose the single given response that best answers the question.

Skills and Concepts Tested

Multiple-choice problem solving questions test your ability to use mathematical insight, approximations, simple calculations, or common sense to choose the one correct or best answer. This question type tests concepts presented in secondary mathematics classes through first-year algebra and first-year geometry. It also includes statistical concepts usually presented as part of a second-year algebra course in high school. There are no concepts tested from trigonometry, calculus, or other higher level mathematics courses.

Directions

Solve each problem in this section by using the information given and your own mathematical calculations. Select the one correct (best) answer choice from the five given answers.

Format

The format of problem solving questions is straightforward. Each problem consists of one question and five answer choices. Some questions will refer to a geometric figure, graph, chart, or table. The sample problem below illustrates a typical problem solving question.

Sample Problem Solving Question

Question 21 of 37

If the value of x is both the median and the mean of the data set consisting of 12, 5, 18, 7, and x, then in what range of values will you find x?

    ◯ $7 < x \leq 8$

    ◯ $8 < x \leq 9$

    ◯ $9 < x \leq 10$

    ◯ $10 < x \leq 11$

    ◯ $11 < x \leq 12$

Suggested Strategies with Sample Questions

- The correct answer is always on the list provided. If your final calculations show an answer that is not on the list, your calculations contain an error.

- In some questions, you are asked which answer choice meets certain requirements. This usually involves examining each answer choice individually. You may notice some relationship among the answer choices that allows you to settle on the correct answer more quickly.

- Working backward from the answers is an accepted method for solution, although it usually takes longer than using logical reasoning to find the correct answer.

- Some questions require approximation. It may be useful to look at the answer choices and see how close together or far apart they are. This will guide you in determining how close your approximation needs to be to choose the correct answer. Some questions require accurate computations; for others, estimation may be all you need to arrive at the correct choice.

- Use the answer choices to help guide you. For example, whole number answer choices may suggest less accuracy needed in computations than fractions.

- Use the elimination strategy whenever possible to eliminate one or more answer choices. Read all of the answer choices carefully and try to eliminate obvious wrong answers as soon as you recognize them. The elimination approach is described on page 8 of the Introduction.

Sample Questions

Sample problem solving questions are provided in this section and are organized by content topics: arithmetic, algebra, geometry, data analysis, word problems, and data interpretation. Use what you have learned about the suggested strategies to help you answer the sample questions in this section.

On the actual exam, the five possible answer choices will appear with the question on the left side of your computer screen. The letters (A, B, C, D, E) will not be assigned to the answer choices on the actual GMAT. To select your answer, you must click on the oval that matches your selected answer choice.

Arithmetic

1. If the ratio of males to females at a party is 4 to 5 and the ratio of adults to children at that party is 3 to 2, which of the following could be the number of people at that party?

   Ⓐ 18
   Ⓑ 28
   Ⓒ 35
   Ⓓ 45
   Ⓔ 60

Given that the ratio of males to females is 4 to 5, the number of males must be a multiple of 4 and the number of females must be a multiple of 5. If $4x$ and $5x$ represent these numbers, then $9x$ would represent the total number of males and females combined, indicating that the number of people at the party must be a multiple of 9. This eliminates choices B, C, and E. In a similar manner, because the ratio of adults to children is 3 to 2, this indicates that the number of people at the party must be a multiple of 5. This eliminates choice A. Only choice D is both a multiple of 9 and 5. The correct answer is D.

Sometimes, combining terms, performing simple operations, or simplifying the problem in some other way will give you insight and make the problem easier to solve.

2. Which of the following fractions expresses the product of 1.5 and 0.4 in simplest form?

   Ⓐ $\frac{2}{5}$

   Ⓑ $\frac{1}{2}$

   Ⓒ $\frac{3}{5}$

   Ⓓ $\frac{2}{3}$

   Ⓔ $\frac{4}{5}$

To simplify this problem, first change 1.5 to $\frac{3}{2}$. Next, change 0.4 to $\frac{4}{10}$. The product is the answer attained from multiplication, therefore, $\frac{3}{\underset{1}{\cancel{2}}} \times \frac{\overset{2}{\cancel{4}}}{10} = \frac{6}{10} = \frac{3}{5}$. Notice that simplifying can make a problem much easier to solve. The correct answer is C.

If you immediately recognize the method or proper formula to solve the problem, go ahead and do the work directly.

3. Which of the following is an approximation of the value for $0.26 \times 0.67 \times 0.5 \times 0.9$?

   Ⓐ 0.04
   Ⓑ 0.08
   Ⓒ 0.13
   Ⓓ 0.32
   Ⓔ 0.8

Focus on the key phrase, *is an approximation*. One fast method for approximating is to find simple fractions to represent the decimal values, multiply them together, and then convert that answer to a decimal. Use $\frac{1}{4}$ for an approximation of 0.26 since 0.26 is approximately 0.25 and $0.25 = \frac{1}{4}$. Use $\frac{2}{3}$ as an approximation for 0.67. Use $\frac{1}{2}$ for 0.5, and use $\frac{9}{10}$ for 0.9. Thus $0.26 \times 0.67 \times 0.5 \times 0.9 \approx \frac{1}{\underset{2}{\cancel{4}}} \times \frac{\overset{1}{\cancel{2}}}{\underset{1}{\cancel{3}}} \times \frac{1}{2} \times \frac{\overset{3}{\cancel{9}}}{10} = \frac{3}{40} = 0.075 \approx 0.08$. Another fast method would be to round each decimal to one decimal place and do the multiplication. First, 0.26 is approximately 0.3 and 0.67 is approximately 0.7. Then $0.3 \times 0.7 \times 0.5 \times 0.9 = (0.21) \times 0.5 \times 0.9 = (0.105) \times 0.9 = 0.0945$. The best answer choice would be 0.08. The correct answer is B.

If you don't immediately recognize a method or formula, or if using the method or formula might require a great deal of time, try working backward from the answer choices. Because the answer choices are usually given in ascending or descending order, almost always start by plugging in choice C first. Then you'll know whether to go up or down on your next try. Another option is to plug in one of the simple answer choices first.

4. The number 24 is 20 percent of what number?

   Ⓐ 12
   Ⓑ 28
   Ⓒ 100
   Ⓓ 120
   Ⓔ 480

This question illustrates the strategy of working backward from the answer choices to find the solution. Although you can easily solve this question directly, try practicing to work backward starting with answer choice C. Since 20% of 100 is 20, and you want 24 as a result, you will quickly notice that the answer must be larger than 100. Therefore either choices D or E are possible answers. Now find 20% of 120. Since that is 24, the answer is 120. The correct answer is D.

If you don't immediately recognize a method or formula to use to solve the problem, you may want to try a reasonable approach and then work from the answer choices.

5. If the price of apples is decreased from two dozen for $5 to three dozen for $6, how many more apples can be purchased for $30 now than could be purchased before?

 Ⓐ 36
 Ⓑ 48
 Ⓒ 72
 Ⓓ 144
 Ⓔ 180

At two dozen for $5, $30 will allow you to purchase six groups of two dozen apples, or $6 \times 2 \times 12 = 144$ apples. At three dozen for $6, $30 can purchase five groups of three dozen apples, or $5 \times 3 \times 12 = 180$ apples. The question asked, "How many more apples can be purchased for $30 now than could be purchased before?" Therefore, $180 - 144 = 36$ more apples can be purchased now. Be sure to answer the question asked. The correct answer is A.

If it appears that extensive calculations are going to be necessary to solve a problem, check to see how far apart the choices are and then approximate. The reason for checking the answer choices first is to give you a guide for how freely you can approximate.

6. If 28 zippos are equivalent to 2.8 hippos, how many zippos are there in 50 hippos?

 Ⓐ 0.5
 Ⓑ 5
 Ⓒ 50
 Ⓓ 500
 Ⓔ 5,000

Before starting any computations, take a glance at the answers to see how far apart they are. Notice that the only close answers are choices A or B. If you were to round 2.8 hippos to 3 hippos, you could quickly see that 50 hippos is about 16 to 17 times as many as 3 hippos. Thus you would have approximately 16 to 17 times 28 zippos. The closest answer is choice D. Notice that choices A, B, and E are not reasonable. The correct answer is D.

Algebra

7. If $x = -3$ and $y = (x + 5)(x - 5)$, then what is the value of $y + 2$?

 Ⓐ −16
 Ⓑ −14
 Ⓒ 9
 Ⓓ 16
 Ⓔ 64

First focus on $y + 2$ because this is what you are solving for. Replacing x with -3 in $y = (x + 5)(x - 5)$, you get $y = (-3 + 5)(-3 - 5) = (2)(-8) = -16$.

Remember, you are solving for $y + 2$, not just y. Therefore, $y + 2 = -16 + 2 = -14$. Make sure that you stay focused on answering the question that was asked. The correct answer is B.

---

8. If $\dfrac{x}{10} + \dfrac{4}{5} = 1\dfrac{2}{5}$, what is the value of x?

Ⓐ -22

Ⓑ -6

Ⓒ 0

Ⓓ 6

Ⓔ 22

First, if you know how to solve this type of equation, then solve it directly.

$$\frac{x}{10} + \frac{4}{5} = 1\frac{2}{5} \qquad \text{Rewrite } 1\frac{2}{5} \text{ as an improper fraction.}$$

$$\frac{x}{10} + \frac{4}{5} = \frac{7}{5} \qquad \text{Subtract } \frac{4}{5} \text{ from both sides.}$$

$$\frac{x}{10} = \frac{3}{5}$$

$$x = \frac{30}{5} \qquad \text{Multiply each side by 10 to isolate } x.$$

$$x = 6$$

Remember, you should first focus on "the value of x." If you've forgotten how to solve this kind of equation, work backward by plugging in answer choices. Start with choice C. Plug in 0:

$$\frac{0}{10} + \frac{4}{5} \neq 1\frac{2}{5}$$

Because this answer is too small, try choice D, a larger number. Plugging in 6 gives you:

$$\frac{6}{10} + \frac{4}{5} = 1\frac{2}{5}$$

$$\frac{3}{5} + \frac{4}{5} = 1\frac{2}{5}$$

$$\frac{7}{5} = 1\frac{2}{5}$$

Since replacing x with 6 makes the sentence true, 6 is the correct answer.

Working from the answers is a valuable technique that you should practice frequently. The correct answer is D.

Some problems may not ask you to solve for a numerical answer or even an answer including variables. Rather, you may be asked to set up the equation or expression without performing calculations to solve the problem. A quick glance at the answer choices will help you know what is expected.

---

9. Mark is five times as old as Janice, and Gloria is six years younger than Janice. If Gloria is z years old, what is the sum of the ages of Mark, Janice, and Gloria in terms of z?

Ⓐ $5z + 30$

Ⓑ $z + 6$

Ⓒ $7z + 36$

Ⓓ $6z + 36$

Ⓔ $7z + 30$

The question provides Gloria's age as z. Each additional piece of information allows us to work toward the desired result:

z = Gloria's age

z = Janice's age − 6 (Gloria is six years younger than Janice)

Therefore, $z + 6$ = Janice's age.

$5(z + 6)$ = Mark's age (Mark is five times as old as Janice)

Therefore, Mark's age + Gloria's age + Janice's age $= 5(z+6) + z + z + 6$
$$= 5z + 30 + z + z + 6$$
$$= 7z + 36$$

The correct answer is C.

> In some problems, you may be given special symbols that may be unfamiliar. Don't let these special symbols cause you to be apprehensive. Special symbols typically represent an operation or combination of operations that you are familiar with. Look for the definition of the special symbol and how it might be substituted to help you solve the problem.

---

10. If $\boxed{\Delta}$ is a binary operation such that $x\boxed{\Delta}y$ is defined as $\dfrac{(x+y)^2 - (x-y)^2}{-4xy}$, then what is the value of $-5\boxed{\Delta}3$?

Ⓐ −2

Ⓑ −1

Ⓒ $-\dfrac{1}{2}$

Ⓓ 0

Ⓔ 1

Start with the definition: $x\boxed{\Delta}y = \dfrac{(x+y)^2 - (x-y)^2}{-4xy}$

Replace x with −5 and y with 3.

$$x\boxed{\Delta}y = \frac{(x+y)^2 - (x-y)^2}{-4xy}$$

$$-5\boxed{\Delta}3 = \frac{(-5+3)^2 - (-5-3)^2}{-4(-5)(3)}$$

$$-5\boxed{\Delta}3 = \frac{(-2)^2 - (-8)^2}{-4(-5)(3)}$$

$$-5\boxed{\Delta}3 = \frac{4-64}{60}$$

$$-5\boxed{\Delta}3 = \frac{-60}{60}$$

$$-5\boxed{\Delta}3 = -1$$

The correct answer is B.

Geometry

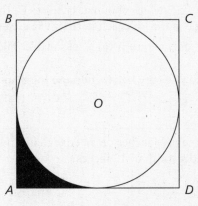

---

11. In the figure above, circle O is inscribed in square $ABCD$. The area of the square is 100 square units.

What is the approximate area, in square units, of the shaded region?

- Ⓐ 6
- Ⓑ 12
- Ⓒ 15
- Ⓓ 20
- Ⓔ 25

Many quantitative problems can be solved using multiple methods. This problem can be solved *directly* or by using an *estimation approach*.

$$\textbf{Direct approach:} \quad \text{shaded region} = \frac{\text{area of the square} - \text{area of the circle}}{4}$$

The information provided shows that the area of the square is 100.

Given that the area of a square is found by squaring one side, each side of the square must be 10, which is then the diameter of the circle. Half the diameter is the radius; thus, the radius of the circle is 5.

Now calculate the area of the circle with a radius of 5: $A = \pi r^2 \approx (3.14)(5^2) \approx 78$.

Subtract to find the difference and then divide by 4: $\frac{100 - 78}{4} = \frac{22}{4} = 5.5$. Clearly, answer choice A (6) is the closest and therefore the correct answer.

Estimation approach: Sketch a diagram. Divide the diagram into fourths.

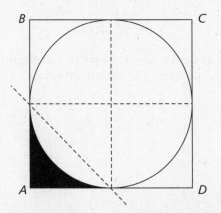

Since the area of each fourth of the square is $\frac{100}{4} = 25$, and the shaded area is clearly less than half of that, the correct answer choice must be less than 12.5, which eliminates choices C, D, and E. Notice also that the shaded area is about half the area of the triangle in the lower left corner. The area of that triangle is 12.5, so the shaded area is about $\frac{1}{2}(12.5) = 6.25$. Therefore, only choice A (6) is reasonable. The correct answer is A.

> **Sketching diagrams or simple pictures can be very helpful because the diagram may tip off either a simple solution or a method for solving the problem.**

---

12. What is the maximum number of cubes 3 inches on an edge that can be packed into a box with a length of 30 inches, a height of 7 inches, and a width of 12 inches?

   A. 70
   B. 84
   C. 80
   D. 88
   E. 93

Sketching the box and showing the cube within it helps to simplify the problem.

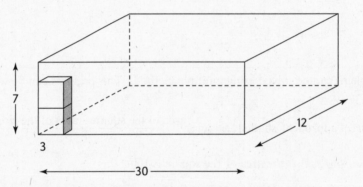

With a diagram, you can see that 10 cubes can fit along the length, 4 cubes along the width, and only 2 cubes along the height. Therefore, the maximum number of cubes is $10 \times 4 \times 2 = 80$ cubes.

If you had approached the problem by finding the volume of the box and dividing it by the volume of the cube, you would have calculated a larger number than 80.

Volume of the box = $30 \times 12 \times 7 = 2,520$.

Volume of the cube = $3 \times 3 \times 3 = 27$.

$$\frac{2,520}{27} \approx 93$$

Notice that cubes will fit exactly only along the length and width, but not the height. Therefore, using the volume method is an incorrect approach to this problem. The correct answer is C.

13. If point P lies on $\overline{ON}$ such that $\overline{OP} = 3\overline{PN}$ and point Q lies on $\overline{OP}$ such that $\overline{OQ} = \overline{QP}$, what is the ratio of $\overline{OQ}$ to $\overline{QN}$?

Ⓐ $\frac{1}{3}$

Ⓑ $\frac{1}{2}$

Ⓒ $\frac{3}{5}$

Ⓓ $\frac{2}{3}$

Ⓔ $\frac{4}{5}$

A sketch that represents the relationship might look like this:

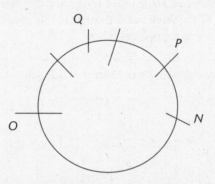

One method is to assign values on $\overline{OPN}$ such that $\overline{OP} = 3\overline{PN}$. Let $\overline{PN} = 1$, then $\overline{OP} = 3$. Since Q lies on $\overline{OP}$ such that $\overline{OQ} = \overline{QP}$ and $\overline{OP} = 3$, then $\overline{OQ} = 1.5$ and $\overline{QP} = 1.5$. Since $\overline{QN} = \overline{QP} + \overline{PN}$, this makes $\overline{QN} = 1.5 + 1 = 2.5$. Therefore, the ratio of $\overline{OQ}$ to $\overline{QN}$ is $\frac{1.5}{2.5} = \frac{15}{25} = \frac{3}{5}$.

The correct answer is C.

> Redrawing and marking in diagrams on your noteboard as you read them can save you valuable time. Marking can also give you insight into how to solve a problem because you will have the complete picture clearly in front of you.

14. In the figure below, $\overline{CD}$ is an angle bisector, $\angle ACD = 24°$, and $\angle ABC$ is a right angle. What is the value of x?

Ⓐ 11

Ⓑ 22

Ⓒ 24

Ⓓ 33

Ⓔ 66

After redrawing the diagram on your noteboard, read the problem and mark it as follows: In the previous triangle, $\overline{CD}$ is an angle bisector (*stop and mark it in the drawing*), $\angle ACD = 24°$ (*stop and mark it in the drawing*), and $\angle ABC$ is a right angle (*stop and mark it in the drawing*). What is value of x in degrees? (*Stop and mark or circle what you're looking for in the drawing.*)

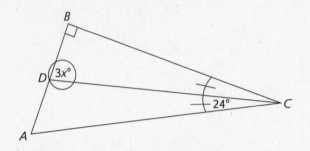

With the drawing marked, it is evident that since $\angle ACD = 24°$, $\angle BCD = 24°$. This is because these angles were formed by an *angle bisector,* which divides an angle into two equal parts. Because $\angle ABC$ is 90° (right angle) and $\angle BCD = 24°$, $3x$ is 66° since the sum of the angles of a triangle is 180°. However, the question asked for the value of x. Since $3x = 66$, then $x = 22$. The correct answer is B.

---

15. If each small square in the figure below has a perimeter of 12, what is the perimeter of the entire figure?

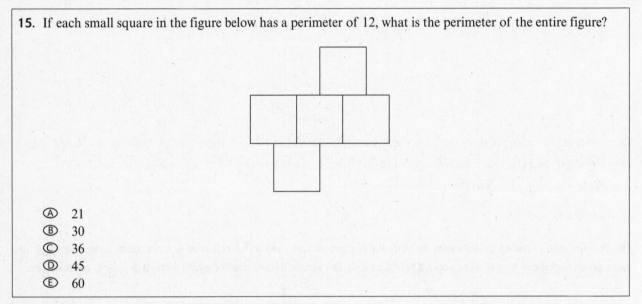

    Ⓐ   21
    Ⓑ   30
    Ⓒ   36
    Ⓓ   45
    Ⓔ   60

Since each small square has a perimeter of 12, each side of the small squares is 3. Redraw and mark in the information given.

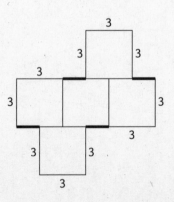

The perimeter is 30 *plus* the darkened parts. Now look carefully at the top two darkened parts. The total width of the three central squares is 9. A total of 6 is already accounted for. Thus, the two darkened parts have a sum of 3. The darkened parts are not necessarily equal in length. The same is true for the bottom two darkened parts. They will also have a sum of 3.

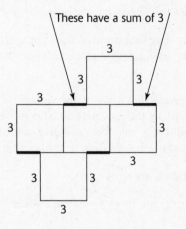

Thus, the total perimeter is 30 + 6 = 36.

A different approach would be to "slide" the squares at the top and bottom so that they are directly above and below the middle square.

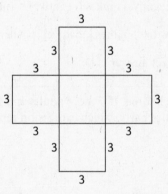

After completing this step, you can see that the perimeter will be 12 groups of 3, or 36. Be careful to note the difference between perimeter and area. Each square in the figure has an area of 9. Thus the area of the entire figure is 9 times 5, or 45. Therefore, answer choice D represents the area, not the perimeter of the figure. The correct answer is C.

Data Analysis

16. Given that $x^3y^2z^4 < 0$, $x^2yz < 0$, and $xyz^2 > 0$, which one of the following expressions <u>must</u> be negative?

   Ⓐ xyz
   Ⓑ $xy + z$
   Ⓒ $xy - z$
   Ⓓ $xz + y$
   Ⓔ $(xy)^3z$

Look for key words when approaching problems. The key word in this problem is "must." If an answer choice could create a negative value, it may not necessarily be correct.

Now consider each fact and the implications.

$x^3y^2z^4 < 0$ says that the product is negative. Therefore, none of the variables can be zero. Regardless of whether y or z is positive or negative, when its value is raised to an even power, the result is positive. When a negative value is raised to an odd power, the result is still a negative number. The only way a product of numbers can be negative is to have an odd number of negative factors. Therefore, the only way $x^3y^2z^4 < 0$ is for x to be a negative number.

$x^2yz < 0$ says the product is negative, implying that none of the variables is zero. Since x^2 is positive regardless of whether x is positive or negative, the only way the product can be negative is for either the y or z to be negative, but not both.

$xyz^2 > 0$ says the product is positive, implying that none of the variables is zero. Since z^2 is positive regardless of whether it is positive or negative, the only way the product can be positive is for x and y to be both positive, or to be both negative. Since it was established that x must be a negative number, then that now implies that y is a negative number. Since both y and z could not be negative, it implies that z is positive.

Now with $x < 0$, $y < 0$, and $z > 0$, check each answer choice.

Choice A: xyz (negative)(negative)(positive) produces a positive answer.

Choice B: $xy + z$ (negative)(negative) + (positive) makes (positive) + (positive), which is positive.

Choice C: $xy - z$ (negative)(negative) – (positive) makes (positive) – (positive), which could be negative, positive, or zero. Remember, you are looking for what <u>must</u> be negative.

Choice D: $xz + y$ (negative)(positive) + (negative) makes (negative) + (negative), which <u>must</u> be negative.

Choice E: $(xy)^3z$ [(negative)(negative)]^3(positive) makes [positive]^3(positive), which is positive.

Only choice D <u>must</u> be negative. The correct answer is D.

---

17. At a party, there are a adults and c children. If 3 more adults and 2 more children arrive and one person is then randomly selected from the entire party, which expression represents the probability that person is an adult?

    Ⓐ $\dfrac{a}{c}$

    Ⓑ $\dfrac{a+3}{c+2}$

    Ⓒ $\dfrac{a}{a+c+5}$

    Ⓓ $\dfrac{a+3}{a+c+3}$

    Ⓔ $\dfrac{a+3}{a+c+5}$

Probability is the comparison of the number of favorable outcomes to the number of total outcomes. After 3 more adults and 2 more children arrive, the total number of people will be $a + c + 5$. Therefore, the probability expression must have this value in its denominator. With this information, only choices C and E are possible solutions. After 3 more adults arrive, there will be $a + 3$ adults. Therefore, the probability of randomly selecting an adult is $\dfrac{a+3}{a+c+5}$. The correct answer is E.

18. A fair coin has a picture of a bird on one side and a picture of a head on its other side. If the coin is flipped four times, what is the probability that exactly two times the picture of a bird will turn up?

    Ⓐ 0.0625
    Ⓑ 0.125
    Ⓒ 0.25
    Ⓓ 0.375
    Ⓔ 0.5

When an event has two possibilities, and is repeated four times, there are 16 possible outcomes ($2^4 = 16$). If you let b represent the bird side turning up and h represent the head side turning up, then the 16 possibilities become the following:

$(hhhh)$, $(hhhb, hhbh, hbhh, bhhh)$, $(hhbb, hbhb, bbhh, hbbh, bhbh, bhhb)$, $(bbbh, bbhb, bhbb, hbbb)$, $(bhhb)$

(all 4 heads)   (exactly 3 heads and 1 bird)   (exactly 2 heads and 2 birds)   (exactly 1 head and 3 birds)   (all 4 birds)

There are 16 total possibilities, of which 6 involve exactly two birds turning up. The probability of exactly two birds is then $\frac{6}{16} = \frac{3}{8} = 0.375$.

Another way to approach this type of question is to use the combinations formula, $_nC_r = \frac{n!}{r!(n-r)!}$. With four flips, how many ways can you get two birds?

$$_4C_2 = \frac{4!}{2!(4-2)!} = \frac{4 \times 3 \times 2 \times 1}{(2 \times 1)(2 \times 1)} = 6$$

So now you have 6 of 16 possibilities for a probability of 0.375. The correct answer is D.

19. Ten horses are in a race. Assuming all 10 horses complete the race, how many different first-, second-, and third-place finishes are possible?

    Ⓐ 27
    Ⓑ 30
    Ⓒ 120
    Ⓓ 720
    Ⓔ 1,000

A direct approach to answering this question would look like this:

Any one of the 10 horses could finish first. After that, any one of the remaining 9 horses could finish second, followed by any one of the remaining 8 horses finishing third: $10 \times 9 \times 8 = 720$.

Since the order of selection matters, you could use the permutations formula, $_nP_r = \frac{n!}{(n-r)!}$.

$$_{10}P_3 = \frac{10!}{(10-3)!} = \frac{10 \times 9 \times 8 \times 7!}{7!} = 720$$

The correct answer is D.

20. If x is a positive integer, then in the data set $\{x, x + 1, x + 2, x + 4\}$, find the absolute difference between the mean and the median and state which is greater.

   Ⓐ $\frac{1}{4}$, median

   Ⓑ $\frac{1}{4}$, mean

   Ⓒ $3x + 4$, median

   Ⓓ $3x + 4$, mean

   Ⓔ $2x + 3\frac{1}{4}$, mean

The mean for the data set is found by taking the sum of the data and dividing by the number of data values.

$$\text{Mean} = \frac{x + (x+1) + (x+2) + (x+4)}{4} = \frac{4x+7}{4} = \frac{4x}{4} + \frac{7}{4} = x + 1\frac{3}{4}$$

Since there are four data values, the median is found by taking the sum of the two middle values and dividing it by 2.

$$\text{Median} = \frac{(x+1) + (x+2)}{2} = \frac{2x+3}{2} = \frac{2x}{2} + \frac{3}{2} = x + 1\frac{1}{2}$$

Since x is the same value in each case, you can see that the mean is greater by the difference between $1\frac{3}{4}$ and $1\frac{1}{2}$, which is $\frac{1}{4}$.

The correct answer is B.

21. A sequence is defined by the formula $a_n = 3a_{n-1} + \frac{1}{4}(a_{n-2})$ for all $n \geq 2$. If $a_0 = 16$ and $a_1 = 8$, what is the value of a_3?

   Ⓐ 28
   Ⓑ 36.5
   Ⓒ 50
   Ⓓ 72
   Ⓔ 86

You are given that $a_0 = 16$ and $a_1 = 8$. According to the formula $a_n = 3a_{n-1} + \frac{1}{4}(a_{n-2})$, $a_2 = 3a_{2-1} + \frac{1}{4}a_{2-2} = 3a_1 + \frac{1}{4}a_0 = 3(8) + \frac{1}{4}(16) = 24 + 4 = 28$ and $a_3 = 3a_{3-1} + \frac{1}{4}a_{3-2} = 3a_2 + \frac{1}{4}a_1 = 3(28) + \frac{1}{4}(8) = 84 + 2 = 86$.

The correct answer is E.

Word Problems

22. Machine A can do a job in 12 hours. Machine B can do the same job in 18 hours. Machine C can do the job in 8 hours. Which will be faster and by approximately how much: Machine A and Machine B together or Machine C alone?

   Ⓐ Machine A and Machine B together by approximately 1 hour

   Ⓑ Machine A and Machine B together by approximately $\frac{1}{2}$ hour

   Ⓒ Machine C alone by approximately 7 hours

   Ⓓ Machine C alone by approximately 1 hour

   Ⓔ They will take the same amount of time, 8 hours

Suppose that you are unfamiliar with the type of equation. Try an *estimating approach* to help you solve the problem.

If machines A and B each worked at the same rate, together they would need half the time. Thus, if each machine needed 12 hours individually, together they would do the job in 6 hours. Similarly, if individually they needed 18 hours, then together they would do the job in 9 hours. Since Machine A does the job in 12 hours and Machine B does it in 18 hours, together they do the job in 6 hours to 9 hours. A rough approximation would be that they do the job in about $7\frac{1}{2}$ hours. This would lead you to choose choice B, which unfortunately is incorrect. Had answer choices A and B not been so close, this method would save some time. At this point you would select either choice A or B.

Using an equations approach, the problem would translate into the following.

$$\frac{1}{12} + \frac{1}{18} = \frac{1}{x}$$

Where $\frac{1}{12}$ represents the part of the job Machine A could do in 1 hour, $\frac{1}{18}$ represents the part of the job Machine B could do in 1 hour, and $\frac{1}{x}$ represents the amount of job done in 1 hour working together.

$$\frac{1}{12} + \frac{1}{18} = \frac{1}{x} \qquad \text{Multiply each side by } 36x$$
$$36x\left(\frac{1}{12} + \frac{1}{18}\right) = 36x\left(\frac{1}{x}\right)$$
$$3x + 2x = 36$$
$$5x = 36$$
$$x = \frac{36}{5} = 7\frac{1}{5}$$

Together, machines A and B need $7\frac{1}{5}$ hours and Machine C needs 8 hours. Machines A and B together need $\frac{4}{5}$ of an hour less time, and $\frac{4}{5}$ of an hour is closer to 1 hour than it is to $\frac{1}{2}$ hour. The correct answer is A.

---

23. After an increase of $30 per hour, an employee's hourly pay is now $100. In what range was the approximate percent increase in the employee's salary?

  Ⓐ   less than 27%
  Ⓑ   27%–32%
  Ⓒ   33%–38%
  Ⓓ   39%–44%
  Ⓔ   more than 44%

In this type of question, you must look for words in the question to help you focus on what to look for. In this case, *percent increase*.

In general percent change $= \dfrac{\text{amount of change}}{\text{original amount}} \times 100\%$. If the employee's salary was increased $30 per hour to a new salary of $100 per hour, then the starting salary was $100 – $30 = $70 per hour. Therefore,

percent increase $= \dfrac{\text{amount of increase}}{\text{original salary}} \times 100\% = \dfrac{30}{70} \times 100\% = \dfrac{3}{7} \times 100\% \approx 43\%.$

The correct answer is D.

"Pulling" information out of a word problem structure can often give you a better look at what you are working with, and therefore can help you gain additional insight into the problem. Organize this information on your notebook.

---

24. Six years from now, Ed will be six years less than twice Sharon's age. Four years ago, Ed was four years less than three times Sharon's age. How old is Ed now?

    Ⓐ 8 years old
    Ⓑ 12 years old
    Ⓒ 16 years old
    Ⓓ 20 years old
    Ⓔ 24 years old

Construct a grid that organizes the information you are given. Let E represent Ed's age now and S represent Sharon's age now.

	Now	In 6 Years	4 Years Ago
Ed	E	$E + 6$	$E - 4$
Sharon	S	$S + 6$	$S - 4$

This solution method involves setting up two equations. One equation represents the time frame "in six years." The other equation represents the time frame "four years ago." After you have set this up, solve to get the variable for the correct age today (now).

"Six years from now, Ed will be six years less than twice Sharon's age." translates into

$$E + 6 = 2(S + 6) - 6$$
$$E + 6 = 2S + 12 - 6$$
$$E = 2S$$

"Four years ago, Ed was four years less than three times Sharon's age." translates into

$$E - 4 = 3(S - 4) - 4$$
$$E - 4 = 3S - 12 - 4$$
$$E = 3S - 12$$

Since E is expressed as two different expressions, but represents the same value, set the expressions equal to one another and solve for S:

$$3S - 12 = 2S$$
$$S = 12$$

Therefore, Sharon is 12 years old now. *Be careful to choose the correct answer at this stage.* You must continue to work the problem. The question asked for Ed's current age, not Sharon's. Don't be misled and choose answer choice B, 12 years old, since this is Sharon's age now.

Find Ed's age now by substituting back in either of the previous equations:

$$E = 2S \quad \text{or} \quad E = 3S - 12$$
$$E = 2(12) \qquad E = 3(12) - 12$$
$$E = 24 \qquad\quad E = 24$$

If you try to solve for Ed's age directly, you will probably create a more complex algebraic equation. It is usually best to solve for the easiest value in the table and then adjust your answer. The correct answer is E.

Data Interpretation

Question 25 is based on the following graphs.

Product	Total Unit Sales
V	600
W	1,000
X	800
Y	700
Z	900

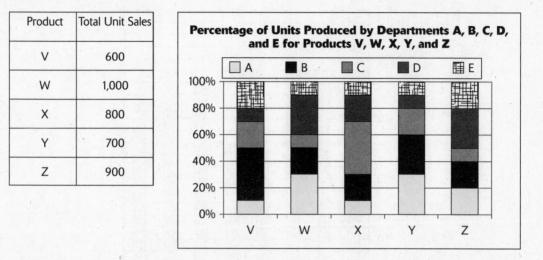

Percentage of Units Produced by Departments A, B, C, D, and E for Products V, W, X, Y, and Z

25. If x is the total Unit Sales for Department B, then what is the correct range of values for x?

   Ⓐ $950 < x \leq 1,000$
   Ⓑ $900 < x \leq 950$
   Ⓒ $850 < x \leq 900$
   Ⓓ $800 < x \leq 850$
   Ⓔ $x \leq 800$

Calculate the number of units produced by Department B for each of the five products and add them together.

For Product V, the bar for Company B started at 10% and ended at 50%. This means that Company B had 40% of the sales for Product V (50% – 10% = 40%). Using the table, you see that there were 600 units of Product V sold. Therefore, Company B sold 40% of 600 units of Product V.

Continue to do this line of reasoning for each of the five products.

V	W	X	Y	Z	
(40% of 600) +	(20% of 1,000) +	(20% of 800) +	(30% of 700) +	(20% of 900) =	
240 +	200 +	160 +	210 +	180 =	990

The correct answer is A.

Question 26 is based on the following graph.

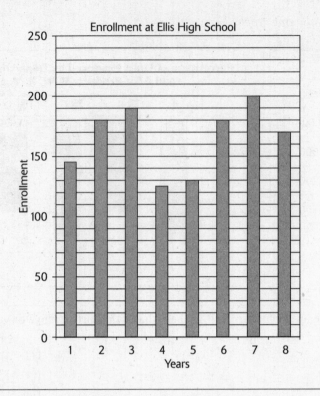

26. Based on the above bar graph of the enrollment at Ellis High for its first 8 years, what would be the closest value to the median number of students for years 1 through 8 inclusive?

Ⓐ 127
Ⓑ 130
Ⓒ 145
Ⓓ 170
Ⓔ 175

The *median* is the middle value when the values are listed from least to greatest. Listing the approximate values from least to greatest you list 125, 130, 145, 170, 180, 180, 190, and 200. Since there are eight values, the median will be the average of the 4th and 5th values from least to greatest, which are 170 and 180. Therefore, the median is 175.

To calculate the *mean* (the sum of the values divided by the number of values), the answer would have been 165. To calculate the *mode* (the value repeated most often), the answer would have been 180. If you had simply found the average of the 4th and 5th values, reading from left to right on the chart, your answer would have been about 127.5. The correct answer is E.

Practice Problem Solving Questions

Easy to Moderate

1. What is the value of $x^2 - 2x + 4$, if $3x^3 + 25 = 1$?

   (A) −4
   (B) −2
   (C) 4
   (D) 8
   (E) 12

2. What is the next number in the sequence 2, 9, 28, 65, . . . ?

   (A) 84
   (B) 111
   (C) 126
   (D) 152
   (E) 210

3. The ratio of Fords to Hondas to Buicks is 12:15:18. If there is a total of 1,800 of these automobiles on a car lot, how many of them are Buicks?

   (A) 40
   (B) 120
   (C) 480
   (D) 600
   (E) 720

4. What is the value of $8a + 4b$, if $4a + 2b = 12$?

   (A) 5
   (B) 16
   (C) 20
   (D) 24
   (E) It cannot be determined from the given information.

5. Which of the following is an approximation of $\left(\frac{3}{7}\right)(0.5)\left(66\frac{2}{3}\%\right)$ to the nearest hundredth?

   (A) 0.1
   (B) 0.14
   (C) 0.142
   (D) 0.143
   (E) 0.15

6. In a survey of middle school students, each was asked to indicate which of three classes they liked best. Students were allowed to select one or more of the classes. The survey indicated that the classes that students liked best were math, English, and physical education. All students are required to take each of these classes. Only 5% of the students liked both English and math but not physical education; 10% liked both English and physical education but not math; 7% liked both math and physical education but not English; and 3% liked all three subjects. Overall, 30% of the students said they liked their math classes and 20% of the students said they liked their English classes.

What percent of the students only liked physical education classes but neither their math or English classes?

Ⓐ 46%
Ⓑ 50%
Ⓒ 54%
Ⓓ 58%
Ⓔ 62%

7. Mr. Brown has 80 students in his class. One-fifth of them are averaging 65% on tests, 30% of them are averaging 75% on tests, and the remaining students are averaging 85% on tests. What is the class percent average?

Ⓐ 75%
Ⓑ 76%
Ⓒ 77%
Ⓓ 78%
Ⓔ 79%

8. A restaurant survey has found that 18% of the patrons order a beef entrée, 26% order a chicken entrée, 34% order a fish entrée, 12% order a lamb entrée, and the remaining patrons order a vegetarian entrée. If a random patron did not order a lamb or vegetarian entrée, what is the probability that they ordered a chicken entrée?

Ⓐ 0.220
Ⓑ 0.260
Ⓒ 0.333
Ⓓ 0.380
Ⓔ 0.780

9. The following table represents the student population at a local college.

	Daytime Students	Nighttime Students
Male	290	277
Female	395	38

What percentage of students are daytime students?

Ⓐ 32%
Ⓑ 40%
Ⓒ 46%
Ⓓ 54%
Ⓔ 69%

Average

10. The cube pictured below has a surface area of 300 square inches. Which of the following is the best approximation of its volume?

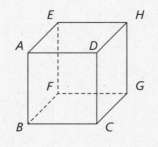

    Ⓐ 5^3 cubic inches
    Ⓑ 7^3 cubic inches
    Ⓒ 9^3 cubic inches
    Ⓓ 11^3 cubic inches
    Ⓔ 13^3 cubic inches

11. Which of the following correctly places the values in order from least to greatest?

    Ⓐ $\left(\sqrt[3]{64}\right)^2$, $33\frac{1}{3}\%$ of 50, $4\frac{1}{7} \div \frac{1}{4}$

    Ⓑ $\left(\sqrt[3]{64}\right)^2$, $4\frac{1}{7} \div \frac{1}{4}$, $33\frac{1}{3}\%$ of 50

    Ⓒ $33\frac{1}{3}\%$ of 50, $\left(\sqrt[3]{64}\right)^2$, $4\frac{1}{7} \div \frac{1}{4}$

    Ⓓ $33\frac{1}{3}\%$ of 50, $4\frac{1}{7} \div \frac{1}{4}$, $\left(\sqrt[3]{64}\right)^2$

    Ⓔ $4\frac{1}{7} \div \frac{1}{4}$, $33\frac{1}{3}\%$ of 50, $\left(\sqrt[3]{64}\right)^2$

12. If $n! = 1 \times 2 \times 3 \times \ldots \times n$, which expression has the greatest value?

    Ⓐ $\dfrac{6!}{2!4!}$

    Ⓑ $\dfrac{7!}{3!4!}$

    Ⓒ $\dfrac{6!4!}{5!3!}$

    Ⓓ $\dfrac{6!}{4!}$

    Ⓔ $4! + 3! + 2!$

13. In parallelogram *AEFG* below, if $AB = BC = CD = DE$, and the area of the parallelogram is 48 square inches, what is the area of triangle *BEF*?

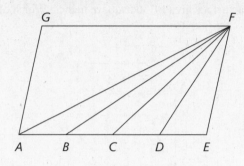

   Ⓐ   24 square inches

   Ⓑ   22 square inches

   Ⓒ   20 square inches

   Ⓓ   18 square inches

   Ⓔ   The area cannot be determined from the information given.

14. The table below represents how the members of different political parties view a particular issue.

	Democratic	Republican	Green	Independent
In Favor	180	110	130	115
Against	45	320	25	75

Which political party had an approval percentage closest to the overall approval percentage for all the parties combined?

   Ⓐ   Democratic

   Ⓑ   Republican

   Ⓒ   Green

   Ⓓ   Independent

   Ⓔ   Not enough information is given in the table to determine the answer.

15. The average of nine numbers is x, and the average of x numbers is 9. What is the average of all the numbers?

   Ⓐ $\dfrac{x+9}{2}$

   Ⓑ $\dfrac{9x}{2}$

   Ⓒ $9x$

   Ⓓ $\dfrac{9x}{x+9}$

   Ⓔ $\dfrac{18x}{x+9}$

16. Which of the following equations or systems of equations produce the same value for the variable x?

    I. $x^2 - 5x - 24 = 0$

    II. $2x + 3y = 12$
          $2x + 2y = 4$

    III. $4(3x + 2) = 2(x - 11)$

    Ⓐ I and II
    Ⓑ I and III
    Ⓒ II and III
    Ⓓ I, II, and III
    Ⓔ Each equation produces a different value(s) for x.

17. The sum of the ages of Anna, Barbara, and Chris is 45 years. Anna is 12 years older than Barbara, while Barbara is 3 years younger than Chris. How old will Chris be three years from now?

    Ⓐ 10
    Ⓑ 13
    Ⓒ 16
    Ⓓ 22
    Ⓔ 25

18. If $2x + 3y = 8$ and $3x + 2y = 17$, what is the value of $x + y$?

    Ⓐ −14
    Ⓑ −2
    Ⓒ 5
    Ⓓ 7
    Ⓔ 9

19. In the right triangle below, $c° = 2a°$ and $d° = 2b°$. What is the degree measure of angle b?

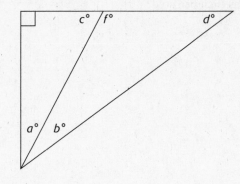

    Ⓐ 10°
    Ⓑ 20°
    Ⓒ 30°
    Ⓓ 45°
    Ⓔ 60°

20. What is the slope of $\overline{EF}$ if point E has coordinates $(-3, 5)$ and point F has coordinates $(6, -7)$?

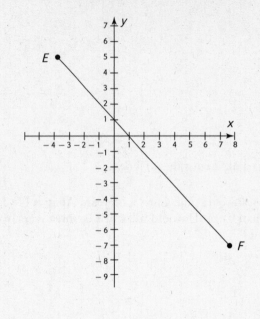

Ⓐ $-\dfrac{4}{3}$

Ⓑ $-\dfrac{3}{4}$

Ⓒ $\dfrac{3}{4}$

Ⓓ $\dfrac{4}{3}$

Ⓔ 15

21. Fifty identical pens were bought for a total cost of p dollars. Each pen was sold at 25% above its original cost. In cents, for how much was each pen sold?

Ⓐ $\dfrac{p}{200}$

Ⓑ $\dfrac{p}{40}$

Ⓒ $\dfrac{p}{50} + 0.25$

Ⓓ $\dfrac{p}{2}$

Ⓔ $\dfrac{5p}{2}$

22. An area rug is 3 square yards in area. What is the equivalent measurement in square inches?

Ⓐ $2^2 3^2$

Ⓑ $2^2 3^3$

Ⓒ $2^3 3^3$

Ⓓ $2^3 3^5$

Ⓔ $2^4 3^5$

23. If a store has a sale such that electronics are now $33\frac{1}{3}\%$ off and clothing is 25% off, what percent is saved when purchasing a TV that originally cost \$240 and a suit that originally cost \$400?

   Ⓐ Less than 27%

   Ⓑ More than 27% but less than 30%

   Ⓒ More than 30% but less than $33\frac{1}{3}\%$

   Ⓓ More than $33\frac{1}{3}\%$ but less than 50%

   Ⓔ More than 50%

24. If $x > 1$ and $\dfrac{x^2-1}{x^2+2x+1} > 0$, then which of the following has the greatest value?

   Ⓐ $\dfrac{x-1}{x+1}$

   Ⓑ $\left(\dfrac{x-1}{x+1}\right)^2$

   Ⓒ $\dfrac{x+1}{x-1}$

   Ⓓ $\left(\dfrac{x+1}{x-1}\right)^2$

   Ⓔ $\left(\dfrac{x-1}{x+1}\right)^3$

25. Everyone who enters Thien's store always buys one of three products: A, B, or C. For those who buy Product A, there is a 5% chance they will return it. For those who buy Product B, there is a 10% chance they will return it. For those who buy Product C, there is a 15% chance they will return it. Product A is purchased by 10% of the people, Product B is purchased by 30% of the people, and Product C is purchased by the remaining number of people. Which of the following is the best approximation for the probability that an item was purchased and then returned?

   Ⓐ 10%

   Ⓑ 20%

   Ⓒ 30%

   Ⓓ 40%

   Ⓔ 50%

26. If m and n are positive integers and $\sqrt{mn} = 6$, which of the following CANNOT be a value of $m + n$?

   Ⓐ 12

   Ⓑ 13

   Ⓒ 15

   Ⓓ 25

   Ⓔ 37

Above Average to Difficult

27. If $(17)(24) = x$ and $(12)(18) = y$, then in terms of x and y what would represent $\dfrac{(18)(23)}{(13)(19)}$?

    (A) $\dfrac{x}{y}$

    (B) $\dfrac{x+1}{y-1}$

    (C) $\dfrac{x-1}{y+1}$

    (D) $\dfrac{x+6}{y+31}$

    (E) $\dfrac{x+6}{y+27}$

28. If x, y, and z are consecutive positive integers greater than 1, such that $x < y < z$, and x is odd, which of the following might not always be an integer?

    (A) $\dfrac{x+y+z}{2}$

    (B) $\dfrac{x+y+z}{3}$

    (C) $\dfrac{x+2y+z}{4}$

    (D) $\dfrac{x+2y-z}{6}$

    (E) $\dfrac{2x+3y+2z}{7}$

29. A 75% saltwater solution is mixed with a 50% saltwater solution to make 10 gallons of a 60% saltwater solution. If G represents the number of gallons of the 75% solution used, then in what range of values is G?

    (A) $G < 3$
    (B) $3 \leq G < 4$
    (C) $4 \leq G < 5$
    (D) $5 \leq G < 6$
    (E) $G \geq 6$

30. Given the following two sets of data:

    Set P: {3, 4, 5, 5, 5, 6}

    Set Q: {1, 2, 3, 4, 5}

    If one number is randomly selected from each set, what is the approximate probability that the sum of the two numbers will be a multiple of 3?

    (A) 0.2
    (B) 0.3
    (C) 0.4
    (D) 0.5
    (E) 0.6

31. If $-5 < x < -1$ and $y > 0$, which of the following expressions would have the least value?

    Ⓐ $x^2 + y^2$

    Ⓑ $x^2 + y$

    Ⓒ $(x + y)^2$

    Ⓓ $2x - y^2$

    Ⓔ Cannot be determined from the given information.

32. If for all integers a, $a^{\#} = a^2 + 3a - 4$, then what is the value of $\left((-2)^{\#} \right)^{\#}$?

    Ⓐ -6

    Ⓑ -4

    Ⓒ -2

    Ⓓ 6

    Ⓔ 14

33. The product of x and y is 12. If the value of x is decreased by 25%, by what percent must the value of y be increased, so the product of the new numbers is still 12?

    Ⓐ 75%

    Ⓑ 50%

    Ⓒ $66\frac{2}{3}\%$

    Ⓓ $33\frac{1}{3}\%$

    Ⓔ 25%

34. The table below represents the relative frequency of test scores on a recent exam taken by students in Mr. Ed's math class.

Test Score	Frequency
30	2
45	5
55	3
60	5
75	6

Approximately what percentage of students scored above the class median?

    Ⓐ 20%

    Ⓑ 30%

    Ⓒ 42%

    Ⓓ 55%

    Ⓔ 67%

35. With a plug in place, an empty water tank can be filled two-thirds full in 24 minutes. If the plug is removed from a full tank, then five-eighths of the tank can be emptied in 40 minutes. If the tank starts out empty without the plug in place, and is now being filled with water, after 48 minutes the tank will be approximately

    Ⓐ one-sixth full
    Ⓑ one-fourth full
    Ⓒ one-half full
    Ⓓ three-fourths full
    Ⓔ overflowing

36. If $x + y = 37$ and $x - y + z = 41$, what is the value of $6x + 3z$?

    Ⓐ Between 50 and 100
    Ⓑ Between 100 and 150
    Ⓒ Between 150 and 200
    Ⓓ Between 200 and 250
    Ⓔ Cannot be determined from the given information.

Answers and Explanations for Practice Problem Solving Questions

Easy to Moderate

1. **E.** If $3x^3 + 25 = 1$, then $3x^3 = -24$, $x^3 = -8$, $x = -2$.

   Replace x with -2 in the expression $x^2 - 2x + 4$.

   $$x^2 - 2x + 4 = (-2)^2 - 2(-2) + 4$$
   $$= 4 + 4 + 4$$
   $$= 12$$

2. **C.** At first there does not seem to be a specific pattern to follow. However, if you subtract 1 from each number in the sequence, a pattern does emerge. The original sequence is 2, 9, 28, 65, . . . With 1 subtracted from each number, the new sequence is 1, 8, 27, 64, . . . These are consecutive perfect cubes. The original sequence is one more than the next perfect cube. Thus the next number should be one more than 5^3, or one more than 125, which is 126.

3. **E.** Since the ratio of Fords to Hondas to Buicks is 12:15:18, let the number of Fords be represented by $12x$, the number of Hondas by $15x$, and the number of Buicks by $18x$. Then

   $$12x + 15x + 18x = 1,800$$
   $$45x = 1,800$$
   $$x = 40$$

   The number of Buicks $= 18x = 18(40) = 720$.

4. D. At first it appears that the answer cannot be determined since you are only given one equation and it has two variables. However, notice that the quantity $8a + 4b$ is twice the value of $4a + 2b$: $2(4a + 2b) = 8a + 4b$. This allows you to find the value of $8a + 4b$ without first finding values for a and b.

$$4a + 2b = 12$$
$$2(4a + 2b) = 2(12)$$
$$8a + 4b = 24$$

5. B. This problem is easily solved by rewriting each value in its simplest fraction form and then simplifying before multiplying.

Next, find the decimal name for the resulting fraction, but first notice that the question asks for the answer to the nearest *hundredth*. Only choices B and E give answers rounded to the hundredths place.

$$0.5 = \frac{1}{2} \text{ and } 66\frac{2}{3}\% = \frac{2}{3}$$

$$\left(\frac{3}{7}\right)(0.5)\left(66\frac{2}{3}\%\right) = \frac{\overset{1}{\cancel{3}}}{7} \times \frac{1}{\underset{1}{\cancel{2}}} \times \frac{\overset{1}{\cancel{2}}}{\underset{1}{\cancel{3}}} = \frac{1}{7} \approx 0.142857\ldots \text{ rounded to the nearest hundredth is } 0.14.$$

6. D. This problem is made easier to visually follow with the use of a Venn diagram. Let M represent the oval for the percentage of students that like math, E for the English, and PE for the physical education classes. Since there is an overlap for all three subjects, begin by drawing three ovals that overlap each other.

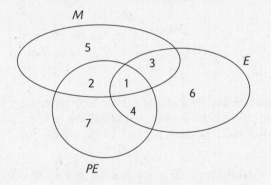

Region 1 represents the percentage of students that liked all three subjects.

Region 2 represents the percentage of students that liked both math and physical education but not English.

Region 3 represents the percentage of students that liked math and English but not physical education.

Region 4 represents the percentage of students that liked English and physical education, but not math.

Region 5 represents the percentage of students that liked math only.

Region 6 represents the percentage of students that like English only.

Region 7 represents the percentage of students that like PE only.

The sum of the percentages of all seven regions is 100%.

Next, fill in the known percentages into the overlapping regions. Begin with the most overlapped region, Region 1. Since 3% liked all three subjects, place 3% in Region 1. Since 7% liked both math and physical education but not English, place 7% in Region 2. Since 5% of the students liked both English and math but not physical education, place 5% in Region 3. Since 10% liked both English and physical education but not math, place 10% in Region 4.

The total percent of students who liked math was 30%. The total percent of students who liked math is comprised of Regions 1, 2, 3, and 5. The sum of Regions 1, 2, and 3 is 15%. Therefore Region 5 is 15%: (30% – 15% = 15%).

The total percent of students who liked English was 20%. The total percent of students who liked English is comprised of Regions 1, 3, 4, and 6. The sum of Regions 1, 3, and 4 is 18%. Therefore Region 6 is 2%: (20% – 18% = 2%).

All that remains is Region 7, the percentage of students that only like physical education. Since the sum of all seven regions is 100%, the remaining region has 58%: (100% – 42% = 58%).

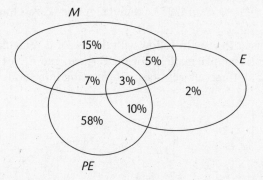

7. **D.** The class percent average is found by finding the class total percentage and dividing that by the number of students in the class. The class has 80 students with one-fifth of them averaging 65%. One-fifth of 80 is 16, so the total percentage for the 16 students is $16 \times 65\%$. Similarly, 30% of 80 is 24, so $24 \times 75\%$ is their percentage total.

Since 16 + 24 = 40, 40 of the 80 students are accounted for, leaving 40 students who averaged 85% for a total percentage of $40 \times 85\%$. The class percent average is:

$$\frac{16 \times 65\% + 24 \times 75\% + 40 \times 85\%}{80} = \frac{1040\% + 1800\% + 3400\%}{80} = \frac{6240\%}{80} = 78\%$$

One method to speed up this arithmetic is to do the following. Notice that the 16, 24, and 40 in the numerator and the 80 in the denominator are each divisible by 8. Divide each by 8 before doing any multiplying.

$$\frac{\overset{2}{\cancel{16}} \times 65\% + \overset{3}{\cancel{24}} \times 75\% + \overset{5}{\cancel{40}} \times 85\%}{\underset{10}{\cancel{80}}} = \frac{130\% + 225\% + 425\%}{10} = \frac{780\%}{10} = 78\%$$

8. **C.** Since the patron did not order a lamb or vegetarian entrée, the patron was in the remaining 78% of patrons (18% + 26% + 34% = 78%). Now, to find the probability of having ordered a chicken entrée, divide the percentage for the chicken entrée (26%) by the total possible remaining percentage, 78%.

$$\text{Probability of } B = \frac{26\%}{78\%} = \frac{1}{3} \approx 0.333$$

9. **E.** To find the percent of students that are daytime students, find the total number of daytime students and divide by the total number of students.

$$\frac{\text{daytime students}}{\text{total students}} = \frac{290\,(\text{male}) + 395\,(\text{female})}{567\,(\text{male}) + 433\,(\text{female})} = \frac{685}{1,000} = 0.685 \approx 69\%$$

Average

10. **B.** The cube is made up of six identical squares. Since the surface area of the cube is 300 square inches, each square will have an area of 50 square inches: $(300 \div 6 = 50)$. The area of a square is found by squaring the length of one side, so to find the length, knowing the area, take the square root of the area. The square root of 50 is approximately 7. The volume of a cube is found by cubing the length of one side. So the volume of this cube is approximately 7^3 cubic inches.

11. **B.**

$$\left(\sqrt[3]{64}\right)^2 = (4)^2 = 16, \quad 33\tfrac{1}{3}\% \text{ of } 50 = \tfrac{1}{3} \times 50 = 16\tfrac{2}{3}, \quad 4\tfrac{1}{7} \div \tfrac{1}{4} = \tfrac{29}{7} \times \tfrac{4}{1} = \tfrac{116}{7} = 16\tfrac{4}{7}$$

Since 16 is the least value, the answer can only be either choice A or B. What is left is to compare $\tfrac{2}{3}$ with $\tfrac{4}{7}$. You can compare by converting each fraction to its decimal form or rewriting each fraction with a common denominator.

$$\tfrac{2}{3} = 0.666..., \quad \tfrac{4}{7} = 0.571428...$$

$$\tfrac{2}{3} = \tfrac{14}{21}, \quad \tfrac{4}{7} = \tfrac{12}{21}$$

In either case, you can see that $\tfrac{2}{3}$ is greater than $\tfrac{4}{7}$, thus $33\tfrac{1}{3}\%$ of 50 is the greatest value and should be listed last.

12. **B.**

Choice A: $\dfrac{6!}{2!4!} = \dfrac{\overset{3}{\cancel{6}} \times 5 \times \cancel{4 \times 3 \times 2 \times 1}}{(\cancel{2} \times 1)(\cancel{4 \times 3 \times 2 \times 1})} = 15$

Choice B: $\dfrac{7!}{3!4!} = \dfrac{7 \times \cancel{6} \times 5 \times \cancel{4 \times 3 \times 2 \times 1}}{(\cancel{3 \times 2} \times 1)(\cancel{4 \times 3 \times 2 \times 1})} = 35$

Choice C: $\dfrac{6!4!}{5!3!} = \dfrac{(6 \times \cancel{5 \times 4 \times 3 \times 2 \times 1})(4 \times \cancel{3 \times 2 \times 1})}{(\cancel{5 \times 4 \times 3 \times 2 \times 1})(\cancel{3 \times 2 \times 1})} = 24$

Choice D: $\dfrac{6!}{4!} = \dfrac{6 \times 5 \times \cancel{4 \times 3 \times 2 \times 1}}{\cancel{4 \times 3 \times 2 \times 1}} = 30$

Choice E: $4! + 3! + 2! = (4 \times 3 \times 2 \times 1) + (3 \times 2 \times 1) + (2 \times 1) = 24 + 6 + 2 = 32$

Choice B produces the greatest value.

13. **D.**

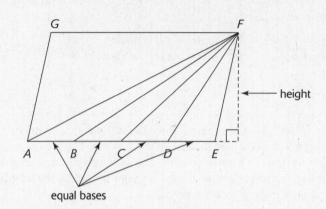

In the parallelogram, draw the segment from F perpendicular to the extension of side $\overline{AE}$. This segment becomes the height for each of the four small triangles. In parallelogram $AEFG$, since $AB = BC = CD = DE$, all the small triangles have the same size base and they all meet at F, giving them all the same height. Therefore, each of the small triangles has the same area since the area of a triangle is found by multiplying the base and height and dividing that by two. The diagonal from A to F cuts the parallelogram in half. Since the area of the parallelogram was given as 48 square inches, the area of triangle AEF is 24 square inches. Triangle AEF is broken into four triangles of equal area, so each small triangle has an area of 6 square inches. Triangle BEF comprises three of these smaller triangles, hence its area is 18 square inches.

14. **D.** The table below includes all the totals necessary for solving the problem.

	Democratic	Republican	Green	Independent	Totals
In Favor	180	110	130	115	535
Against	45	320	25	75	465
Totals	225	430	155	190	1,000

There are a total of 1,000 people who voiced an opinion on the issue. There were 535 people who were in favor of the issue. The overall approval percentage is $\frac{535}{1,000} = 0.535 \approx 54\%$.

The approval ratings for the different political parties are:

$$\text{Democratic: } \frac{180}{225} = 80\%$$

$$\text{Republican: } \frac{110}{430} \approx 26\%$$

$$\text{Green: } \frac{130}{155} \approx 84\%$$

$$\text{Independent: } \frac{115}{190} \approx 61\%$$

The closest political party approval percentage to the overall percentage is Independent.

15. **E.** If the average of nine numbers is x, then the sum of these nine numbers must be $(9)(x)$. If the average of x numbers is 9, then the sum of these x numbers must be $(x)(9)$ or also $9x$. There are $x + 9$ numbers whose sum is $9x + 9x$ or $18x$. Therefore, the average of all $x + 9$ numbers must be $\frac{18x}{x+9}$.

16. B.

I. $x^2 - 5x - 24 = 0$ Solve using factoring

$(x-8)(x+3) = 0$

$x - 8 = 0$ or $x + 3 = 0$

$x = 8$ or $x = -3$

II. $2x + 3y = 12$ Subtract to eliminate x

$\underline{2x + 2y = 4}$

$y = 8$

Replace 8 for y in either equation and solve for x:

$$2x + 2(8) = 4$$
$$2x + 16 = 4$$
$$2x = -12$$
$$x = -6$$

III. $4(3x + 2) = 2(x - 11)$

$12x + 8 = 2x - 22$

$10x = -30$

$x = -3$

Only I and III produced the same value for x.

17. C.

Anna's current age = A

Barbara's current age = B

Chris's current age = C

Since the sum of their current ages is 45, $A + B + C = 45$.

Anna is 12 years older than Barbara: $A = B + 12$.

Barbara is 3 years younger than Chris: $B = C - 3$, or $B + 3 = C$.

In the equation $A + B + C = 45$, replace A with $B + 12$ and replace C with $B + 3$ to calculate Barbara's current age and Chris's current age. Then you can determine Chris's age three years from now.

$$A + B + C = 45$$
$$(B + 12) + B + (B + 3) = 45$$
$$3B + 15 = 45$$
$$3B = 30$$
$$B = 10$$

Barbara is currently 10 years old, thus Chris is currently 13 years old. Three years from now, Chris will be 16 years old.

18. **C.** Solve the two equations simultaneously, or recognize a shortcut.

Shortcut approach: Add the two equations and see that there is a common factor of 5. Divide each side of the resulting equation by 5 to get the desired result without first finding out what either x or y equals.

$$
\begin{array}{l}
2x + 3y = 8 \\
\underline{3x + 2y = 17} \quad \text{Add the two equations} \\
5x + 5y = 25 \quad \text{Now divide the sum by 5} \\
\,x + y = 5
\end{array}
$$

Solving the two equations simultaneously:

$$
2x + 3y = 8
$$
$$
3x + 2y = 17
$$

Multiply the top equation by 3 and the bottom equation by –2 and add the two new equations together. This will eliminate the x-variable and then you can solve for y.

$$
\begin{array}{rcl}
3(2x + 3y) = 3(8) & \rightarrow & 6x + 9y = \;\;24 \\
-2(3x + 2y) = -2(17) & \rightarrow & \underline{-6x - 4y = -34} \\
& & 5y = -10 \\
& & y = -2
\end{array}
$$

Now replace y with –2 in one of the original equations.

$$
\begin{array}{l}
2x + 3y = 8 \;\rightarrow\; 2x + 3(-2) = 8 \\
2x - 6 = 8 \\
2x = 14 \\
x = 7
\end{array}
$$

Therefore, $x + y = 7 + (-2) = 5$.

19. **B.** In the right triangle, $a° + c° = 90°$, since the sum of the angles in a triangle is 180°. Since $c° = 2a°$, then $a° + 2a° = 90°$, or $3a° = 90°$. So $a = 30°$ and $c = 60°$. Since angle c and angle f form a straight line, $c + f = 180°$. With $c = 60°$, then $f = 120°$. Now refer to the figure below with the above information included.

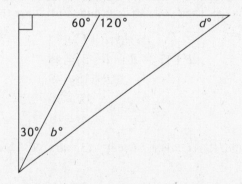

Since the sum of the angles of a triangle equals 180°, $120° + (b + d) = 180°$. Therefore, $b + d = 60°$. With $d° = 2b°$, then $3b° = 60°$, so $b° = 20°$.

20. A. If two points have coordinates (x_1, y_1) and (x_2, y_2), the slope of the line that joins them is defined to be $m = \dfrac{y_2 - y_1}{x_2 - x_1}$. Since point E has coordinates of $(-3, 5)$ and point F has coordinates of $(6, -7)$, the slope of $\overline{EF}$ is: $m = \dfrac{-7-5}{6-(-3)} = \dfrac{-12}{9} = -\dfrac{4}{3}$.

21. E. The question asks for your final answer to be represented in cents. You must then convert dollars into cents. The 50 pens cost a total of p dollars, therefore they cost a total of $p(100 \text{ cents})$ or $100p$ cents. Each pen then costs $\dfrac{100p}{50} = 2p$ cents. If each pen was sold at 25% above its cost, it was sold at 125% of its original cost. Since the answers are given in fraction form, convert 125% to its fraction form and multiply it with $2p$.

$$125\% = \frac{125}{100} = \frac{5}{4}, \quad \left(\frac{\cancel{5}}{\cancel{4}_2}\right)\left(\frac{\cancel{2}p}{1}\right) = \frac{5p}{2}$$

22. E. Notice that all the answers are given in factored form. Try to express the arithmetic to be done but do not multiply it out; instead, rewrite in factored form. One yard equals 3 feet. One square yard is 9 square feet, as can be seen in the picture below.

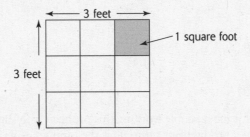

Each square foot is 144 square inches. Thus 1 square yard is 9(144) square inches. Therefore, 3 square yards is (3)(9)(144) square inches. Now rewrite this product in factored form.

$$144 = (12)(12) = (2^2 3)(2^2 3) = 2^4 3^2$$

Therefore, $(3)(9)(144) = (3)(3^2)(2^4 3^2) = 2^4 3^5$.

23. B. To determine what percent you saved, you cannot merely add the percentages together. That is, you cannot simply add $33\frac{1}{3}\%$ and 25% and say that $58\frac{1}{3}\%$ was saved. You need to find the dollar amount saved and compare it to what would have been the total original price to determine the percent saved. Electronics are $33\frac{1}{3}\%$ off. You saved $33\frac{1}{3}\%$ of $240 on the TV. Hence, $33\frac{1}{3}\%$ is equivalent to $\frac{1}{3}$, so you saved $\frac{1}{3}$ of $240, or $80. Since clothing is 25% off and the original price of the suit was $400, you saved 25% of $400, or $100. Therefore, you saved $180 out of what would have been a total cost of $640.

$$\frac{180}{640} = \frac{9}{32} \approx 28\%$$

24. D. The expression $\dfrac{x^2-1}{x^2+2x+1}$ can be simplified to $\dfrac{\left(\cancel{x+1}\right)(x-1)}{\left(\cancel{x+1}\right)(x+1)}=\dfrac{x-1}{x+1}$.

Since $x > 1$, this fraction will always be positive and its numerator will always be less than the denominator, making the value of the fraction always less than 1. When any positive value less than 1 is multiplied by itself, the value gets smaller. Thus the value of choice B is less than that of choice A and similarly, the value of choice E is less than that of choice A. Choice C is the reciprocal of $\dfrac{x-1}{x+1}$. The reciprocal of any positive number less than 1 is a positive number greater than 1, hence choice C is greater than choice A. Choice D is the square of a positive number greater than 1, which makes it greater than what it was. Therefore, choice D has the greatest value.

If you were to replace x with a value greater than 1, and solve by trial and error, you would also find that choice D has the greatest value. For example, if $x = 2$, then

A. $\dfrac{x-1}{x+1}=\dfrac{2-1}{2+1}=\dfrac{1}{3}$

B. $\left(\dfrac{x-1}{x+1}\right)^2=\left(\dfrac{1}{3}\right)^2=\dfrac{1}{9}$

C. $\dfrac{x+1}{x-1}=\dfrac{3}{1}$

D. $\left(\dfrac{x+1}{x-1}\right)^2=\left(\dfrac{3}{1}\right)^2=9$

E. $\left(\dfrac{x-1}{x+1}\right)^3=\left(\dfrac{1}{3}\right)^3=\dfrac{1}{27}$

25. A. The first source of error for most people working this problem is to simply add the return percentages together. The probability that a product gets returned is the product of its probability of being purchased with the probability of its being returned. This problem may be solved with the help of drawing a simple table.

Product	Probability of Being Purchased	Probability of Being Returned
A	10%	(5%)(10%) = (0.05)(0.1) = 0.005 = 0.5%
B	30%	(10%)(30%) = (0.1)(0.3) = 0.03 = 3%
C	60%	(15%)(60%) = (0.15)(0.6) = 0.09 = 9%

Therefore, the probability of a product being purchased and returned is 0.5% + 3% + 9% = 12.5%. The best answer is 10%.

26. D. Squaring both sides of $\sqrt{mn}=6$ gives $mn = 36$. The following are the possible positive integer pairs that multiply to make 36: 1 and 36, 2 and 18, 3 and 12, 4 and 9, and 6 and 6. The question asked which answer CANNOT be the value of $m + n$. The only sum *not* possible is 25.

Above Average to Difficult

27. **D.** Do not multiply out the expressions and intend to do a lot of substituting into the various answers. Instead, try to look for some relationships in the question to what was given. Notice that in the expression $\frac{(18)(23)}{(13)(19)}$, 18 is 1 more than 17 and 23 is 1 less than 24. Therefore, the numerator can be expressed as $(17 + 1)(24 - 1)$. Multiplying this out using the method done in algebra, you get $(17)(24) - 17 + 24 - 1 = (17)(24) + 6$.

But you were told that $(17)(24) = x$, thus the numerator can be expressed as $x + 6$. Therefore, the answer now is either choice D or E. In a similar manner, notice that $13 = 12 + 1$ and $19 = 18 + 1$. Therefore, the denominator can be expressed as $(12 + 1)(18 + 1)$. Again, multiplying this out using the algebraic multiplying method, you get $(12)(18) + 12 + 18 + 1 = (12)(18) + 31$.

But you were told that $(12)(18) = y$, thus the denominator can now be expressed as $y + 31$ and then $\frac{(18)(23)}{(13)(19)} = \frac{x+6}{y+31}$.

28. **D.** Since x, y, and z are consecutive positive integers greater than 1, with $x < y < z$ and x is odd, you could try plugging in values to test each choice. The smallest set of consecutive positive integers would be 3, 4, and 5.

Choice A: $\frac{3+4+5}{2} = \frac{12}{2} = 6$, an integer

Choice B: $\frac{3+4+5}{3} = \frac{12}{3} = 4$, an integer

Choice C: $\frac{3+2(4)+5}{4} = \frac{16}{4} = 4$, an integer

Choice D: $\frac{3+2(4)-5}{6} = \frac{6}{6} = 1$, an integer

Choice E: $\frac{2(3)+3(4)+2(5)}{7} = \frac{28}{7} = 4$, an integer

It appears each answer will produce an integer. The question asks for which one might not always produce an integer. So start with another possible set of integers. With x being odd, the next set would be 5, 6, and 7.

Choice A: $\frac{5+6+7}{2} = \frac{18}{2} = 9$, an integer

Choice B: $\frac{5+6+7}{3} = \frac{18}{3} = 6$, an integer

Choice C: $\frac{5+2(6)+7}{4} = \frac{24}{4} = 6$, an integer

Choice D: $\frac{5+2(6)-7}{6} = \frac{10}{6} = 1\frac{2}{3}$, NOT an integer

Choice E: $\frac{2(5)+3(6)+2(7)}{7} = \frac{42}{7} = 6$, an integer

Therefore, the answer is choice D.

A different method that does not involve trial and error is to represent the consecutive integers x, y, and z, as x, $x + 1$, and $x + 2$ and test each choice with these replacements.

Choice A: $\dfrac{x+(x+1)+(x+2)}{2} = \dfrac{3x+3}{2}$ Since x is odd, $3x$ is odd, and $3x + 3$ is even. Any even integer divided by 2 is an integer.

Choice B: $\dfrac{x+(x+1)+(x+2)}{3} = \dfrac{3x+3}{3} = x + 1$ Since x is an integer, so is $x + 1$.

Choice C: $\dfrac{x+2(x+1)+(x+2)}{4} = \dfrac{x+2x+2+x+2}{4} = \dfrac{4x+4}{4} = x + 1$ Since x is an integer, so is $x + 1$.

Choice D: $\dfrac{x+2(x+1)-(x+2)}{6} = \dfrac{x+2x+2-x-2}{6} = \dfrac{2x}{6} = \dfrac{x}{3}$ This will only be an integer when x is a multiple of 3. Therefore, this expression will not always be an integer.

Choice E: $\dfrac{2(x)+3(x+1)+2(x+2)}{7} = \dfrac{2x+3x+3+2x+4}{7} = \dfrac{7x+7}{7} = x + 1$ Since x is an integer, so is $x + 1$.

Only choice D is not always going to have an integer result.

29. **C.** Since the final solution is 60% saltwater, and 60% is closer to 50% than it is to 75%, this means more of the 50% than the 75% solution will be used. Since the end mixture has 10 gallons, more than 5 gallons of it will come from the 50% solution and less than 5 gallons will come from the 75% solution. Since you are looking for how much of the 75% solution is used, this eliminates choices D and E.

Below is an *algebraic approach* to solving this problem; this method uses a chart to organize the given information.

G = # gallons of 75% saltwater solution

$10 - G$ = # gallons of 50% saltwater solution

	# Gallons in the Solution	% of Salt in the Solution	Amount of Salt in the Solution
75% Solution	G	75%	$0.75G$
50% Solution	$10 - G$	50%	$0.50(10 - G)$
Mixture	10	60%	$0.60(10)$

$$\underbrace{\text{salt in the 75\% solution}}_{0.75G} \underbrace{\text{plus}}_{+} \underbrace{\text{salt in the 50\% solution}}_{0.50(10-G)} \underbrace{\text{equals}}_{=} \underbrace{\text{salt in the mixture}}_{0.60(10)}$$

$$0.75G + 5 - 0.50G = 6$$
$$0.25G + 5 = 6$$
$$0.25G = 1$$
$$G = 4$$

Be careful now; $G = 4$, which is not in the range of values in choice B. It is in the range of values of choice C.

30. B. The only multiples of 3 that are possible as a sum of two numbers, one from Set P and one from Set Q, are 6 and 9. The probability can be calculated by using a chart approach. Write the numbers from Set P written across the chart horizontally and the numbers from Set Q written down vertically. Then within the chart, make checks at the pairs of numbers that satisfy that their sum is a multiple of 3.

	3	4	5	5	5	6
1			✓	✓	✓	
2		✓				
3	✓					✓
4			✓	✓	✓	
5		✓				

You can see that there are 30 locations, of which 10 are checked. Therefore, the probability of getting a multiple of 3 from selecting two numbers is $\frac{10}{30} = \frac{1}{3} \approx 0.33$.

31. D. Since x must be a negative value, x^2 must be positive. Since $y > 0$, it is positive. See whether the expressions given must be positive or negative before using any trial and error approaches. If only one expression represents a negative value and the others represent positive or zero values, the negative expression must have the least value.

Choice A: $x^2 + y^2$ is positive + positive = positive.

Choice B: $x^2 + y$ is positive + positive = positive.

Choice C: $(x + y)^2$. Since x is less than -1 and y is positive, then $x + y$ can be negative, zero, or positive. In any of these possibilities, $(x + y)^2$ is either zero or positive.

Choice D: $2x - y^2$. Since x is negative, then $2x$ is negative.

Therefore, $2x - y^2$ is negative – positive = negative. Only choice D is negative, while the other expressions are either positive or could be zero. Therefore, choice D is the expression with the least value.

32. E. The expression $\left((-2)^{\#}\right)^{\#}$ requires you to use the definition of $a^{\#} = a^2 + 3a - 4$ twice. First, a is replaced with -2 and evaluated. Then that result is replaced for a and evaluated once again.

$$a^{\#} = a^2 + 3a - 4$$
$$\left((-2)^{\#}\right)^{\#} = \left((-2)^2 + 3(-2) - 4\right)^{\#}$$
$$= (4 - 6 - 4)^{\#}$$
$$= (-6)^{\#}$$
$$= \left((-6)^2 + 3(-6) - 4\right)$$
$$= 36 - 18 - 4$$
$$= 14$$

33. D. If x is decreased by 25%, it becomes $(100\%)x - (25\%)x = (75\%)x = \frac{3}{4}x$. In order for $\frac{3}{4}x$ to multiply with some amount of y to produce the same value as the original xy, you must multiply it by $\frac{4}{3}y$ so that $\left(\frac{3}{4}x\right)\left(\frac{4}{3}y\right) = \left(\frac{3}{4} \times \frac{4}{3}\right)(xy) = xy$. To find the percent change from the original y to $\frac{4}{3}y$, use percent change $= \dfrac{\text{amount of change}}{\text{original amount}} \times 100\%$.

$$\frac{\frac{4}{3}y - y}{y} \times 100\% = \frac{\frac{1}{3}y}{y} \times 100\%$$

$$= \frac{1}{3} \times 100\%$$

$$= 33\frac{1}{3}\%$$

You could have used a form of trial and error to find the solution. If $xy = 12$, let x be 4 and y be 3. If x is decreased by 25%, it will now become 3. Therefore, $4 - 25\%(4) = 4 - 1 = 3$. Therefore, the new number it must multiply with so the product is still 12 will be 4. Now find the percent increase from the original y value of 3 to the new value of 4.

$$\text{percent change} = \frac{\text{amount of change}}{\text{original amount}} \times 100\%$$

$$\frac{1}{3} \times 100\% = 33\frac{1}{3}\%$$

34. B. Use the chart to first find the total number of scores by adding the frequencies for the different score values: $2 + 5 + 3 + 5 + 6 = 21$. The median (middle score) is the eleventh score on the tests, or 60%. Six students scored above the class median with a score of 75%. Therefore, 6 out of 21 scores were above the class median. $\frac{6}{21} \times 100\% \approx 29\%$

Choice B is the closest at 30%.

35. C. This word problem involves adding and taking away water from the tub. Since it takes 24 minutes to fill the tub two-thirds full with water, it takes 12 minutes to fill it one-third full, thus it would take 36 minutes to completely fill the tub. This could also be seen using proportions.

$$\frac{24 \text{ minutes}}{x \text{ minutes}} = \frac{2}{3}$$

$$2x = (24)(3)$$

$$x = \frac{\left(\overset{12}{\cancel{24}}\right)(3)}{\underset{1}{\cancel{2}}}$$

$$x = 36$$

Therefore, water enters the tank at the rate of $\frac{1}{36}$ of the tank per minute.

Similarly, since it takes 40 minutes to empty five-eighths of a full tank, then in 8 minutes, one-eighth of the tank is emptied. Therefore, it would take 64 minutes to empty a full tank. Again, you could use proportions to see this.

$$\frac{40 \text{ minutes}}{y \text{ minutes}} = \frac{5}{8}$$

$$5y = (40)(8)$$

$$y = \frac{\left(\overset{8}{\cancel{40}}\right)(8)}{\left(\dfrac{\cancel{5}}{1}\right)}$$

$$y = 64$$

Therefore, water is emptied from the tank at the rate of $\frac{1}{64}$ of a tank per minute.

In 48 minutes the portion of the tank that is filled is

$$48\left(\frac{1}{36} - \frac{1}{64}\right) = \frac{48}{36} - \frac{48}{64}$$
$$= \frac{4}{3} - \frac{3}{4}$$
$$= \frac{16-9}{12}$$
$$= \frac{7}{12}$$

$\frac{7}{12}$ is between one-half and three-fourths. The question now is which is it closer to?

$$\frac{1}{2} = \frac{6}{12} \text{ and } \frac{3}{4} = \frac{9}{12}$$

$\frac{7}{12}$ is closer to one-half than it is to three-fourths.

36. **D.** At first glance it appears that there is insufficient information to determine a solution. However, look again at what is being asked to see if there is a relationship to the given information. The expression $6x + 3z$ can be rewritten as $3(2x + z)$. Now review the problem again to see if the expression $2x + z$ can be related to the original information. Adding the two original equations together gives the following.

$$\begin{array}{r} x + y = 37 \\ \underline{x - y + z = 41} \\ 2x + z = 78 \end{array}$$

Therefore, $6x + 3z = 3(2x + z) = 3(78) = 234$. This is between 200 and 250.

Chapter 8

Introduction to Data Sufficiency

Data sufficiency tests your ability to *reason* and *think* quantitatively about arithmetic, algebra, geometry, data analysis, word problems, and data interpretation. This question type emphasizes your knowledge of mathematical insight, approximations, simple calculations, and common sense to sufficiently determine if a question can be answered.

Math calculations are not necessarily required to answer specific questions. Each question is presented in a format that is unique to other forms of standardized math test problems. Your task is to examine problem sets, draw upon your math skills, and reason deductively to decide if the information provided will solve the problem. To reach the correct answer, you must determine whether each statement provided is *sufficient* to arrive at the requested solution.

Skills and Concepts Tested

Data sufficiency questions test the concepts presented in secondary mathematics classes through second-year algebra and first-year geometry. You will also need to be familiar with statistical concepts that are usually presented as part of a second-year algebra course in high school. There are no advanced concepts tested from trigonometry, calculus, or other higher level mathematics courses.

Format

The format of data sufficiency questions is uniquely different from straightforward math problems, and each of the individual problems have the same *problem set* layout. Look at the sample problem set below and notice that each contains:

1. One question
2. Two math data statements
3. Five answer choice statements

Sample Data Sufficiency Question

Question 7 of 37

Is x greater than y?

  (1) $xy < 0$

  (2) $y^3 > 0$

○ Statement (1) ALONE is sufficient, but statement (2) alone is not sufficient to answer the question asked.

○ Statement (2) ALONE is sufficient, but statement (1) alone is not sufficient to answer the question asked.

○ BOTH statements (1) and (2) TOGETHER are sufficient to answer the question asked, but NEITHER statement ALONE is sufficient.

○ EACH statement ALONE is sufficient to answer the question asked.

○ Statements (1) and (2) TOGETHER are NOT sufficient to answer the question.

Directions

Each of the problems consists of a question and two statements, labeled (1) and (2), which contain certain data. You must determine whether the data provided in the statements are *sufficient* to provide an answer to the question. Use your knowledge of mathematics to determine which of the five possible answer choices (shown in the previous sample) is correct.

All questions share the following assumptions:

- All numerical values used are real numbers.
- Geometric figures, such as lines, circles, triangles, and quadrilaterals, are drawn to scale. That is, they are intended to provide information useful in solving the problems. Lines that appear jagged on the computer screen are actually straight, points on a line are in the order shown, and more generally, all geometric objects are in the relative position shown. Angles have positive measures.
- Lines that appear straight can be assumed to be straight.
- A symbol that appears in repeated quantities represents the same value or object for each quantity.
- On a number line, positive numbers are to the right of zero and increase to the right, and negative numbers are to the left of zero and decrease to the left.

Suggested Strategies with Sample Questions

1. **Learn the sequence of the answer choices.** Memorize and practice the five possible answer choices *before* your exam date to save you time the day of the test. These choices will always be presented in the exact order shown in this guide.

2. **Paraphrase the directions using the acronym "12-TEN."** The wording to data sufficiency statements can often be confusing and difficult to understand. Use the following memory aid to help you avoid rereading the answer choices again and again when trying to determine the correct answer. Remember that this section tests your reasoning and thinking skills along with your math skills. Your goal is to stay focused on determining the correct answer choice. Paraphrasing the answer choice statements should help you quickly reason why your selected answer is the correct solution.

12-TEN Approach		
12-TEN Code	**Answer Choice Letter**	**Say to Yourself**
1 One	A	Statement **(1)** alone is sufficient.
2 Two	B	Statement **(2)** alone is sufficient.
T Together	C	Both statements (1) and (2) must be used **together** to be sufficient.
E Either	D	**Either** statement (1) or (2) alone is sufficient.
N Neither	E	**Neither** statement (1), nor statement (2) is sufficient—either alone or taken together. Additional data specific to the problem are needed to answer the question.

3. **Avoid calculations that are not necessary.** When comparing data statements, remember that you are being asked to match information to a unique statement. The question does not usually require you to actually solve the problem. For instructional purposes, calculations are included with detailed explanations in this guide to help you understand *how* to arrive at correct solutions. In a data sufficiency problem, however, you will probably never need to perform calculations to solve the problem. You will just need to identify if the problem *can* be solved. For example, if you can identify that a problem containing two different equations with the same two unknowns is solvable, STOP! Answer the question and move on to the next question.

4. **Use the process of elimination.** If you are able to say whether a statement is sufficient or not, you can eliminate two or three choices immediately to narrow down your answer.

   - If statement (1) alone is sufficient, the answer is A or D.

   - If statement (1) alone is not sufficient, the answer is B, C, or E.

   - If statement (2) alone is sufficient, the answer is B or D.

   - If statement (2) alone is not sufficient, the answer is A, C, or E.

5. **Watch for *yes* and *no* answers, such as, "Is *x* positive?"** Questions that are set up as *yes* or *no* answers can be tricky. Remember that you are *not necessarily trying to calculate a specific mathematical solution* to find the right answer choice; you are determining whether the question can be answered using the information provided. For example, if the question asks, "Is *x* positive?" and you know that *x* is −3, then *you do have sufficient information* to answer the question.

6. **Read math data statements correctly.**

   - **Answers must reference the math data.** If you think you could answer the question without making reference to either of the *two math data statements,* then you have either misread the question or assumed something that was not stated. Each data sufficiency question requires additional information from the math data statements in order to answer the question. Be sure you read the question correctly.

   - **Math data must be considered independently.** Do not bring the information from math data statement (1) when you read math data statement (2) for the first time. When you read statement (2) for the first time, you must see it as a stand-alone statement. For example, one of the answer choice statements is, "Statement (2) ALONE is sufficient, but statement (1) alone is not sufficient to answer the question asked."

   Example:

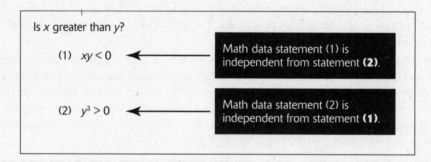

7. **Manage your time wisely.** Spend about 1½ minutes per question to have enough time to read and answer all of the questions. With sufficient practice, you will know almost automatically when a problem is taking too much time, and when to take an educated guess and move on to the next question.

8. **Practice, practice, practice.** Data sufficiency questions require a shift in your ability to conceptualize math problems. Approximately one-third of the quantitative problems relate to data sufficiency, so it is important that you are comfortable with this type of question before you take the GMAT. Consistent practice is critical if you are to succeed on this section of the test.

Sample Questions

This section provides sample data sufficiency questions organized by content topics: arithmetic, algebra, geometry, data analysis, word problems, and data interpretation. Use what you have learned about problem sets and strategies, and the sample questions to help you answer the practice questions that follow this section.

On the actual exam, the five possible answer choice statements will appear with the question on the computer screen. They are included below for your reference in answering the sample questions. Remember that although we letter the answer choices in this guide for easy reference, no letters or numbers will be assigned to the answer choices on the actual GMAT. To select your answer, you must click on the oval that matches your selected answer choice.

- Ⓐ Statement (1) ALONE is sufficient, but statement (2) alone is not sufficient to answer the question asked.
- Ⓑ Statement (2) ALONE is sufficient, but statement (1) alone is not sufficient to answer the question asked.
- Ⓒ BOTH statements (1) and (2) TOGETHER are sufficient to answer the question asked, but NEITHER statement ALONE is sufficient.
- Ⓓ EACH statement ALONE is sufficient to answer the question asked.
- Ⓔ Statements (1) and (2) TOGETHER are NOT sufficient to answer the question asked, and additional data specific to the problem are needed.

Arithmetic

---

1. Is the positive integer j greater than 59?

   (1)   The numbers 2, 3, and 4 are each factors of j.

   (2)   The numbers 3, 4, and 5 are each factors of j.

The correct answer is B. Statement (2) ALONE is sufficient.

From statement (1), you can determine that j is a multiple of 12, since the smallest positive integer with factors of 2, 3, and 4 is 12. Therefore, j can be found in the following list: (12, 24, 36, 48, 60, 72, . . .). Using statement (1), you cannot definitely say whether j is or is not greater than 59.

From statement (2), you can determine that j is a multiple of 60, since the smallest positive integer with factors of 3, 4, and 5 is 60. Hence, j must be greater than 59 and you can definitely answer the question with a *yes*.

Remember, you are not being asked for the value of j, but whether it is greater than 59.

---

2. What percent of the class passed the test?

   (1)   25% of the boys passed the test.

   (2)   30% of the girls passed the test.

The correct answer is E. Statements (1) and (2) TOGETHER are NOT sufficient.

In order to find the percent of the class that passed the test, you would need to know how many students are in the class. Neither statement, alone nor together, provides that information.

---

3. What is the average weight of Bill, Tom, and Mark?

   (1)   The sum of the weights of Bill, Tom, and Mark is 165 pounds.

   (2)   Tom weighs 10 pounds more than Mark, and Mark weighs 10 pounds more than Bill.

The correct answer is A. Statement (1) ALONE is sufficient.

In order to find the average weight of Bill, Tom, and Mark you would need to know their combined weight, and then divide that sum by 3. Statement (1) gives their combined weight, thus it has sufficient information.

Statement (2) merely tells you that the weights of the three people differ by 10 pounds each. It does not give their combined weights.

One might argue that if you put the facts together you can find the weights of each individual person. That is correct, but the question did not ask for the weight of any individual person, but only what the average weight was for all three people.

---

4. Is the positive integer w a prime number?

(1) w is odd.

(2) w^2 lies between 1 and 10.

The correct answer is B. Statement (2) ALONE is sufficient.

Since some odd integers are prime and others are not, statement (1) is not sufficient. Since the only positive integers whose square is between 1 and 10 are the integers 2 and 3, $1 < 2^2 < 10$ and $1 < 3^2 < 10$, and each is a prime number, statement (2) is sufficient. With the knowledge of statement (2), you can definitely say that w is a prime number.

---

5. If the percent increase from A to B is 20%, what is the value of A?

(1) $B = 60$

(2) The percent decrease from B to A is $16\frac{2}{3}\%$.

The correct answer is D. EACH statement ALONE is sufficient.

Knowing the final value and the percent increase, you can calculate the original amount. Therefore, statement (1) is sufficient. Remember, you are not being asked to answer the question, but whether a unique answer is possible from the given statement or statements. Below is a method of finding the answer.

$$\text{Let } x = \text{ original amount}$$
$$x + 0.20x = 60 \text{ (after a 20\% increase, the value is 60)}$$
$$1.2x = 60 \text{ (divide each side by 1.2)}$$
$$x = 50$$

The original amount of A is 50.

Knowing the final value and the percent decrease from it to the original value, you can calculate the original amount. Therefore, statement (2) is sufficient. Below is a method of finding the answer.

$$\text{Let } x = \text{ original amount}$$
$$100\%(60) - 16\frac{2}{3}\%(60) = x \text{ (after a } 16\frac{2}{3}\% \text{ decrease from 60, the value is } x)$$
$$83\frac{1}{3}\%(60) = x \text{ (change } 83\frac{1}{3}\% \text{ to a fraction)}$$
$$\frac{5}{6}(60) = x$$
$$50 = x$$

The original amount of A is 50.

---

6. An arithmetic sequence has 100 terms. What is the 75th term?

(1) The 80th term is 395 and the 90th term is 325.

(2) The sum of the 1st and 100th terms is the same as the sum of the 49th and 50th terms.

The correct answer is A. Statement (1) ALONE is sufficient.

In an arithmetic sequence, the same value is added to a term to get to the next term. That value is referred to as the common difference. If you know the values of any two terms along with their positions in the sequence, you have sufficient information to find the common difference. Therefore, statement (1) is sufficient. Below is a method for finding the answer.

Let $a_n = n$th term in the sequence, a_x any other term in the sequence.

Let d = the common difference.

$$a_n = a_x + (n - x)d$$
$$a_{90} = 395,\ a_{80} = 325$$
$$a_{90} = a_{80} + (90 - 80)d$$
$$395 = 325 + 10d$$
$$70 = 10d$$
$$7 = d$$
$$a_{75} = a_{80} + (75 - 80)d$$
$$a_{75} = 325 - 5(7)$$
$$a_{75} = 290$$

Therefore, knowing the 80th and 90th terms of an arithmetic sequence is sufficient information to be able to find the 75th term of the sequence.

Statement (2) merely states something that is true for all arithmetic sequences. That is, the sum of the first and last terms is the same as the sum of the second and second to last terms, the same as the sum of the third and third from last terms, etc. This fact will not allow you to find the value of any term in the sequence.

---

7. A sales person makes 8% commission on each sale. What was the sales price?

  (1)   The sales price was $3\frac{1}{2}$ times the original price of $24.

  (2)   The difference between the sales price and the commission was $77.28.

The correct answer is D. EACH statement ALONE is sufficient.

Statement (1) states that if you multiply $3\frac{1}{2}$ times $24 you get the sales price. Hence, statement (1) is sufficient: $\left(3\frac{1}{2}\right) \times \$24 = \$84$.

Using statement (2), you can create an equation that allows you to find the sales price. Therefore, statement (2) is sufficient. Below is a method for finding the answer.

If you let s be the sales price, then 8% of s, or $0.08s$ will be the commission. "The difference between the sales price and the commission was $77.28" can now be translated into the following equation, which is then solved.

$$1s - 0.08s = \$77.28$$
$$0.92s = \$77.28$$
$$s = \$84$$

---

8. The symbol @ represents either addition or multiplication.

  What is the value of 3 @ 5?

  (1)   2 @ 2 = 4

  (2)   3 @ 3 ≠ 6

The correct answer is B. Statement (2) ALONE is sufficient.

Using statement (1), suppose @ was addition: 2 @ 2 becomes 2 + 2 = 4, thus @ could be addition. Suppose @ was multiplication: 2 @ 2 becomes 2 × 2 = 4, thus @ could be multiplication. Statement (1) is not sufficient to conclude which arithmetic operation @ is.

Using statement (2), suppose @ was addition: 3 @ 3 becomes 3 + 3 = 6, but statement (2) says 3 @ 3 ≠ 6. Hence, @ is not addition. Since there were only two options for @, either addition or multiplication, and @ is not addition, @ must be multiplication. Therefore, the question can be answered with statement (2) because knowing that @ is multiplication, then 3 @ 5 must be 15.

Algebra

> **9.** What is the ratio of r to p?
>
> (1) $2r + p = 4$
> (2) $2r - 3p = 0$

The correct answer is B. Statement (2) ALONE is sufficient.

In order to use a single equation to express the ratio of r to p, that equation must only consist of expressions involving both r and p with no other expressions, including constants. The equation in statement (1) does not meet the above requirements, hence it is not sufficient. The equation in statement (2) does meet the above requirements, hence it is sufficient. Below is a method using statement (2) to answer the question.

$$2r - 3p = 0 \qquad \text{Add } 3p \text{ to each side.}$$
$$2r = 3p \qquad \text{Divide each side by } p.$$
$$\frac{2r}{p} = 3 \qquad \text{Divide each side by 2.}$$
$$\frac{r}{p} = \frac{3}{2}$$

The ratio of r to p is 3 to 2.

> **10.** Bill makes a profit of $12 for each box of candy and a profit of $16 for each floral arrangement he sells. How many boxes of candy did he sell last week?
>
> (1)   Last week, Bill sold 5 more boxes of candy than floral arrangements.
> (2)   Last week, his total profit from the candy boxes was equal to his total profit from the floral arrangements.

The correct answer is C. BOTH statements TOGETHER are sufficient.

Using statement (1), if you let C = the number of candy boxes sold and F = the number of floral arrangements sold, then you could make the equation $C = F + 5$. You cannot get a unique answer to the question from this equation.

Using statement (2), if you let C = the number of candy boxes sold and F = the number of floral arrangements sold, then you could make the equation $12C = 16F$. You cannot get a unique answer to the question from this equation.

If you now use both statements together, you have two different equations involving the same two variables, which you can solve and find the answer to the question. *Remember, you are not finding the answer to the question, but whether the question can be answered with the statement or statements provided.* Below is a method that uses the information from both statements to answer the question.

$$C = F + 5$$
$$12C = 16F \qquad \text{Replace } C \text{ with } F + 5.$$
$$12(F + 5) = 16F$$
$$12F + 60 = 16F \qquad \text{Subtract } 12F \text{ from each side.}$$
$$60 = 4F \qquad \text{Divide each side by 4.}$$
$$15 = F$$
$$C = 15 + 5$$
$$C = 20$$

Bill sold 20 boxes of candy last week.

---

11. Of the three values, x, y, and z, which has the greatest value?

   (1)   The average of x and y is equal to z.

   (2)   The sum of x and y is equal to z.

The correct answer is E. Statements (1) and (2) TOGETHER are NOT sufficient.

Statement (1) translates into $\frac{x + y}{2} = z$ or $x + y = 2z$. With experiments, you can find that sometimes one variable will be the greatest and other times it will not be the greatest. For example, if $x = 0$ and $y = 1$, then $z = \frac{1}{2}$, making y the greatest of the three variables. If $x = 1$ and $y = 0$, then $z = \frac{1}{2}$, making x the greatest of the three variables. Hence, statement (1) is not sufficient.

Statement (2) translates into $x + y = z$. As before, with experiments, you can find that sometimes one variable will be the greatest and other times it will not be the greatest. For example, if $x = 1$ and $y = -1$, then $z = 0$, making x the greatest of the three variables. If $x = -1$ and $y = 1$, then $z = 0$, making y the greatest of the three variables. Hence, statement (2) is not sufficient.

Using the two statements together, you have the following.

$$x + y = 2z$$
$$x + y = z$$

Subtracting the lower equation from the upper one, you get $0 = z$. This means that $x + y = 0$. Even with this information, it cannot be determined which of the three variables is the greatest.

---

12. $3x - 5y = ?$

   (1) $x = 7$

   (2) $12x - 20y = 36$

The correct answer is B. Statement (2) ALONE is sufficient.

Statement (1) alone cannot help you find the value of $3x - 5y$ since it lacks information about y. At first glance, it seems that statement (2) would not be helpful since it does not provide information as to what are the values of x and y. But on closer inspection, notice that each side of the equation can be divided by 4. After dividing each side of the equation by 4, you get $3x - 5y = 9$. Therefore, statement (2) provided sufficient information to answer the question. Remember, you were not asked to find the values of x and y, but what the value of the expression $3x - 5y$ will be.

13. $x = ?$

    (1) $x^2 = 49$

    (2) $x^2 - 8x + 7 = 0$

The correct answer is C. BOTH statements TOGETHER are sufficient.

For a statement to be sufficient, you must be able to get a unique answer to the question. That is, there can only be one answer. From statement (1), $x^2 = 49$, there are two possible answers, namely $x = 7$ or $x = -7$. Since you cannot give the **_unique_** value that x is, statement (1) is not sufficient.

Statement (2), $x^2 - 8x + 7 = 0$, can be solved using factoring.

$$x^2 - 8x + 7 = 0$$
$$(x - 7)(x - 1) = 0$$

$$x - 7 = 0 \quad \text{or} \quad x - 1 = 0$$
$$x = 7 \quad \text{or} \quad x = 1$$

Since you cannot give the **_unique_** value that x is, statement (2) is not sufficient. However, when both statements are used, then $x = 7$ is the only answer. From statement (1), substitute 49 for x^2 and 7 for x in statement (2) to double-check:

$$49 - 8(7) + 7 = 0$$
$$49 - 56 + 7 = 0$$
$$0 = 0$$

14. Is the slope of line CD greater than the slope of line AB?

    (1) Line AB passes through $(2, 5)$ and $(-3, 4)$ and line CD has a negative slope.

    (2) The equation of line CD is $x + 4y = 8$.

The correct answer is A. Statement (1) ALONE is sufficient.

If a line passes through (x_1, y_1) and (x_2, y_2), then its slope $= \dfrac{y_2 - y_1}{x_2 - x_1}$.

Using statement (1), the slope of $\overrightarrow{AB} = \dfrac{4 - 5}{-3 - 2} = \dfrac{-1}{-5} = \dfrac{1}{5}$. You were told that the slope of line CD is negative.

Now you have sufficient information to answer the question. In this case, the answer is *no*. Don't let the fact that the answer to the question is no make you think the information was not sufficient.

Using statement (2), you can only find the slope of line CD. You will not be able to compare its slope to that of line AB. Below is a method you could use to find the slope of line CD.

To find the slope of a line when given its equation, rewrite the equation in the $y = mx + b$ form. The value of m is the slope of the line.

$$x + 4y = 8$$
$$4y = -1x + 8$$
$$y = -\frac{1}{4}x + 2$$

The slope of $\overrightarrow{CD} = -\dfrac{1}{4}$.

15. What are the coordinates of point *F*?

    (1) *F* lies on the line $15x - 10y = 20$.

    (2) *F* lies on the line $6x - 4y = 8$.

The correct answer is E. Statements (1) and (2) TOGETHER are NOT sufficient.

The fact that *F* lies on a line of a given equation means that its coordinates satisfy the equation. There are an endless number of points that lie on a line, thus an endless number of *x* and *y* combinations that satisfy its equation.

If you are told that a point lies on the equations of two *different lines,* then you can find that unique point since two *different lines* only intersect at one point. At first glance, it would appear that the equations given in the two statements represent different lines, and as such, statements (1) and (2) together should be sufficient information to find the point of intersection. But upon closer inspection, notice that each side of equation (1) can be divided by 5 and each side of equation (2) can be divided by 2. After doing each of the divisions, both equations become the one equation $3x - 2y = 4$. Therefore, you do not have two different equations of lines, but one equation written in two different ways. Both statements together are still not sufficient.

16. What is the value of $3r + 4s$?

    (1) $2q + 6r + 8s = 60$

    (2) $6q + 9r + 12s = 120$

The correct answer is C. BOTH statements TOGETHER are sufficient.

You might think that since there are only two equations and three unknowns, the question cannot be answered. You are not being asked to solve the system of equations for all three unknowns. You are being asked for the value of the expression $3r + 4s$. Use that as a clue.

Statement (1) can be rewritten in a different way. Factor out a 2 from the expression $6r + 8s$ and statement (1) becomes $2q + 2(3r + 4s) = 60$. It still is not sufficient to answer the question.

Statement (2) can also be rewritten in a different way. Factor out a 3 from the expression $9r + 12s$ and it becomes $6q + 3(3r + 4s) = 120$. It still is not sufficient to answer the question.

Put the statements together, rename the expression $3r + 4s$ as *x*, and you have the following system of equations.

$$2q + 2x = 60$$
$$6q + 3x = 120$$

Since these are two different equations in *q* and *x*, they can be used to find the value of *x*, or $3r + 4s$. Hence, the statements together are sufficient. Remember, you are not asked to solve the problem, but only to recognize when it is solvable. Below is a method for finding the value of *x*.

$$6q + 3x = 120 \xrightarrow{\text{Divide each side by 3}} 2q + x = 40$$
$$2q + 2x = 60 \xrightarrow{\text{Divide each side by 2}} q + x = 30$$

Subtract the lower equation from the upper equation to get $q = 10$. With $q = 10$, you can find that $x = 20$, which means that $3r + 4s = 20$.

Geometry

---

17. What is the perimeter of $\triangle ABC$?

    (1) $\triangle ABC$ is an isosceles triangle with a base length of 10 inches.

    (2)   The largest angle in $\triangle ABC$ has a measure of 60°.

The correct answer is C. BOTH statements TOGETHER are sufficient.

An isosceles triangle has two, possibly all three, sides of equal length. If only two sides are equal in length, the remaining side is referred to as the base. The perimeter of a triangle refers to the distance around it, and can be calculated by adding the lengths of its three sides. Statement (1) only gives you the length of one side, the one that is not one of the equal sides of the isosceles triangle. Therefore, statement (1) is not sufficient.

Statement (2) says the largest angle in a triangle has the measure of 60°. This, together with the fact that the sum of the angles of a triangle are 180°, allows you to conclude that the other two angles, which have equal measures, must also be 60° each. This would make the triangle an equilateral triangle, a triangle with all sides of equal length. Statement (2) does not provide the length of any side, and thus is not sufficient to find the perimeter of the triangle.

Using the statements together, you have an equilateral triangle with one side of 10 inches. Therefore, you can find the perimeter. Using the statements together, you can conclude that the perimeter is 30 inches (10 + 10 + 10 = 30).

---

18. Is the volume of right circular cylinder A greater than the volume of right circular cylinder B?

    (1)   The circumference of the bases of cylinders A and B are 6π inches and 8π inches, respectively.

    (2)   The areas of the bases of cylinders A and B are 9π square inches and 16π square inches, respectively.

The correct answer is E. Statements (1) and (2) TOGETHER are NOT sufficient.

The volume of a right circular cylinder requires knowing its height. Since the height is not provided in either statement, no comparisons are possible.

---

19. In the figure below, what is the measure of $\angle CAD$?

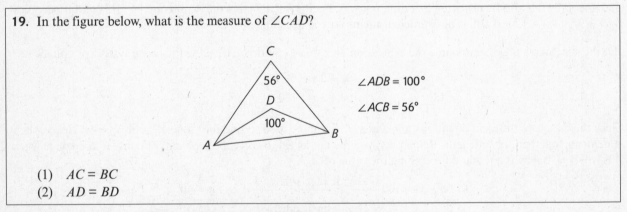

$\angle ADB = 100°$

$\angle ACB = 56°$

    (1) $AC = BC$

    (2) $AD = BD$

The correct answer is C. BOTH statements TOGETHER are sufficient.

If two sides in a triangle have equal lengths, then the angles opposite those sides have equal measure. From statement (1), you can conclude that $\angle CAB = \angle CBA$, and since the sum of the angles of a triangle is 180°, then $\angle CAB = \angle CBA = 62°$. This is not sufficient to answer the question of how big is $\angle CAD$.

From statement (2), you can conclude that ∠*DAB* = ∠*DBA,* and since the sum of the angles of a triangle is 180°, then ∠*DAB* = ∠*DBA* = 40°. This is not sufficient to answer the question of how big is ∠*CAD.*

Using the statements together, and the fact that ∠*CAD* = ∠*CAB* – ∠*DAB,* you now have sufficient information to answer the question. If you wanted to answer the question, then ∠*CAD* = ∠*CAB* – ∠*DAB* = 62° – 40° = 22°.

---

20. In the diagram below, what is the perimeter of figure *GROW*?

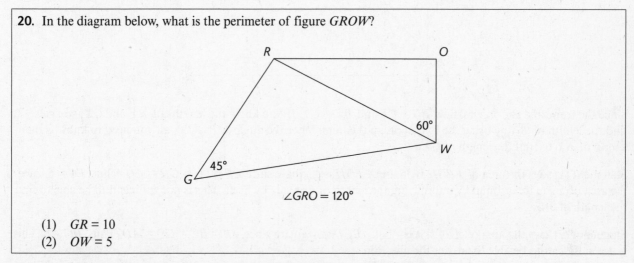

∠*GRO* = 120°

    (1) *GR* = 10
    (2) *OW* = 5

The correct answer is E. Statements (1) and (2) TOGETHER are NOT sufficient.

Despite the fact that ∠*O* and ∠*GRW* appear to be right angles, you cannot assume they are. Even though you have the special angles of 45° and 60°, you cannot assume that the triangles that have them are right triangles. Neither statement gives you information that would allow you to make that conclusion. Had you been able to conclude that the two triangles are the special 45-45-90 and the 30-60-90 right triangles, then knowing one side of either triangle would allow you to find all the other sides. In that case, each statement alone would have been sufficient to find the perimeter of figure *GROW*.

---

21. In the figure below, how long is $\overline{BG}$?

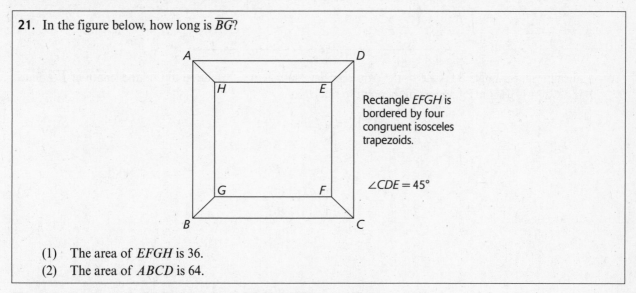

Rectangle *EFGH* is bordered by four congruent isosceles trapezoids.

∠*CDE* = 45°

    (1) The area of *EFGH* is 36.
    (2) The area of *ABCD* is 64.

The correct answer is C. BOTH statements TOGETHER are sufficient.

Since the four isosceles trapezoids are congruent, that would make $AB = BC = CD = AD$, $EF = FG = GH = EH$, and $\angle CDE = \angle DCF = \angle BCF = \angle CBG = \angle BAH = \angle ABG = \angle DAH = \angle ADE = 45°$.

Now consider trapezoid $BGFC$ with heights drawn from G and F to X and Y, respectively, on side $\overline{BC}$.

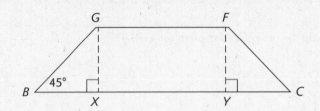

Since the trapezoid is isosceles, then $BG = CF$ and $BX = CY$. If you know the lengths of $\overline{BX}$ and $\overline{GX}$, you can find the length of $\overline{BG}$ by using the Pythagorean theorem. Since the angle at B is 45°, all you need to know is the length of $\overline{BX}$ to find the length of $\overline{GX}$.

Statement (1) says the area of $EFGH$ is 36, but $EFGH$ is a square since $EF = FG = GH = EH$. Thus, $FG = 6$ since the area of a square is found by multiplying the length of one side by itself. This is not sufficient to be able to find the length of $\overline{BG}$.

Statement (2) says the area of $ABCD$ is 64, but $ABCD$ is a square since $AB = BC = CD = AD$. Thus, $BC = 8$. This is not sufficient to be able to answer the question.

Using the two statements together, you can make the following conclusions. Since $XY = GF = 6$ and $BC = 8$, then $BX + CY = 2$. But $BX = CY$, so $BX = CY = 1$. Now draw trapezoid $BGFC$ with the above information included.

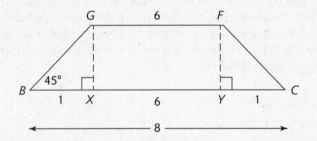

$GX = 1$ since in right triangle BXG $\angle B = 45°$. You now have sufficient information to find the length of $\overline{BG}$. Since $BX = 1$ and $GX = 1$, use the Pythagorean theorem to find BG.

$$(BX)^2 + (GX)^2 = (BG)^2$$
$$1^2 + 1^2 = (BG)^2$$
$$1 + 1 = (BG)^2$$
$$\sqrt{2} = BG$$
$$1.414 \approx BG$$

22. In the figure below, what is the shaded area?

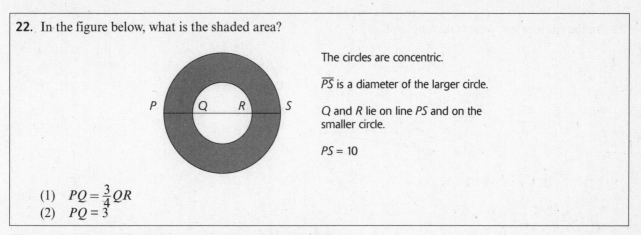

The circles are concentric.

$\overline{PS}$ is a diameter of the larger circle.

Q and R lie on line PS and on the smaller circle.

$PS = 10$

(1) $PQ = \frac{3}{4}QR$
(2) $PQ = 3$

The correct answer is D. EACH statement ALONE is sufficient.

Since the circles are concentric (have the same center), you can conclude that $PQ = RS$. To calculate the shaded area, you would find the larger area and subtract the smaller area. Since the diameter of the larger circle is known to be 10, you only need to find the diameter of the smaller circle, QR, to calculate the shaded area. From statement (1), together with the fact that $PQ = RS$ and $PS = 10$, you can find QR. Hence, statement (1) is sufficient. Below you will find a method for getting the value of QR.

You are given $PQ = \frac{3}{4}QR$, and $PS = 10$. You know that $PQ = RS$, so $RS = \frac{3}{4}QR$.

$$PQ + QR + RS = PS$$

Making all the replacements in the above equation, you get the following equation.

$$\frac{3}{4}QR + QR + \frac{3}{4}QR = 10$$
$$\frac{6}{4}QR + QR = 10$$
$$\frac{10}{4}QR = 10$$
$$QR = 4$$

From statement (2), together with $PS = 10$ and $PQ = RS$, you can find QR. Hence, statement (2) is sufficient.

Below you will find a method to find QR.

$$PQ + QR + RS = PS$$
$$3 + QR + \ 3\ = 10$$
$$QR = 4$$

To actually find the shaded area, you would use the formula for the area of a circle, $A = \pi r^2$, which uses the length of a radius (half the diameter). The diameter of the large circle is PS, which is given as 10. The radius of the large circle is then 5, and the area of the large circle becomes 25π. Each statement allowed you find that $QR = 4$, so the radius of the smaller circle would be 2, and the area of the small circle would be 4π. Thus, the shaded area would be $25\pi - 4\pi = 21\pi$.

23. In the circle below, what is the length of $\overset{\frown}{AC}$?

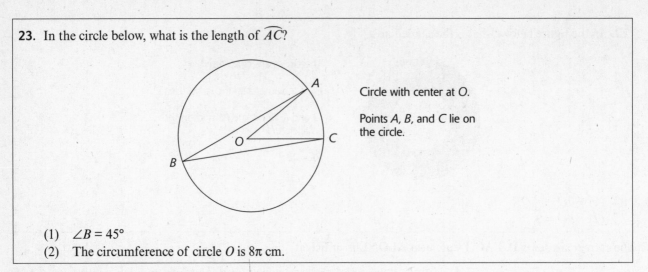

Circle with center at O.

Points A, B, and C lie on the circle.

    (1) $\angle B = 45°$

    (2)   The circumference of circle O is 8π cm.

The correct answer is C. BOTH statements TOGETHER are sufficient.

To find the arc length, you need to know what portion of the circle's circumference the arc occupies. This portion is found by comparing the measure of the central angle to 360°, the degree measure of a full rotation. $\angle AOC$ is a central angle. A central angle has the same degree measure as its intercepted arc. $\angle ABC$ is an inscribed angle. An inscribed angle's measure is equal to half the number of degrees of its intercepted arc. Therefore, $\angle ABC = \frac{1}{2}\angle AOC = \frac{1}{2}\overset{\frown}{AC}$. Statement (1) gives you $\angle B = 45°$. So $\angle AOC = 90°$. Now compare the part circle to the whole circle: $\dfrac{\text{part circle in degrees}}{\text{whole circle in degrees}} = \dfrac{90}{360} = \dfrac{1}{4}$. Hence, $\overset{\frown}{AC}$ is one-fourth of the entire circumference.

This does not provide sufficient information to find the actual length of the arc, so statement (1) alone is not sufficient.

Statement (2) provides you with the circumference, but not what portion $\overset{\frown}{AC}$ is of the circle.

Using the statements together you know the entire circumference and what portion of that is the length of $\overset{\frown}{AC}$. Hence, together the statements are sufficient. The length of $\overset{\frown}{AC}$ is $\frac{1}{4}(8\pi) = 2\pi$ cm.

Data Analysis

24. $S = \{a, b, c, d, e, f, g, h, i, j, k, l\}$

$a, b, c, d, e, f, g, h, i, j, k$, and l are real numbers.

What is the average (arithmetic mean) of a, b, and c?

    (1)   The average (arithmetic mean) of set S is 6.

    (2)   The average (arithmetic mean) of d, e, f, g, h, i, j, k, and l is 3.

The correct answer is C. BOTH statements TOGETHER are sufficient.

To find the average of a, b, and c you do not need to know their individual values, but only their sum. That sum divided by 3 will be the average. From statement (1), you can determine the sum of all 12 variables in set S by multiplying 12 with the average of 6. Therefore, $a + b + c + d + e + f + g + h + i + j + k + l = (12)(6) = 72$. But this is not sufficient to be able to answer the question.

From statement (2), you can determine the sum of $d, e, f, g, h, i, j, k,$ and l by multiplying the number of variables, 9, by the average, 3. Therefore, $d + e + f + g + h + i + j + k + l = (9)(3) = 27$. But this is not sufficient to be able to answer the question. Take the statements together and then subtract the lower equation from the upper one.

$$a + b + c + d + e + f + g + h + i + j + k + l = 72$$
$$\underline{d + e + f + g + h + i + j + k + l = 27}$$
$$a + b + c \qquad\qquad\qquad\qquad = 45$$

This is now sufficient to be able to answer the question. The average of a, b, and $c = \dfrac{45}{3} = 15$.

---

25. What is the probability of selecting a dime from a set of coins?

    (1)   The set only consists of dimes and nickels.

    (2)   There are 4 more dimes than nickels.

The correct answer is E. Statements (1) and (2) TOGETHER are NOT sufficient.

In order to calculate the probability of selecting a dime from the set, you need to know the number of dimes and the total number of coins in the set. Probability is the comparison of favorable outcomes to the total number of outcomes. Neither statement alone or together provides sufficient information to find the total number of coins.

---

26. In the diagram below, is the probability of selecting the path from A to D greater than the probability of selecting the path from A to G?

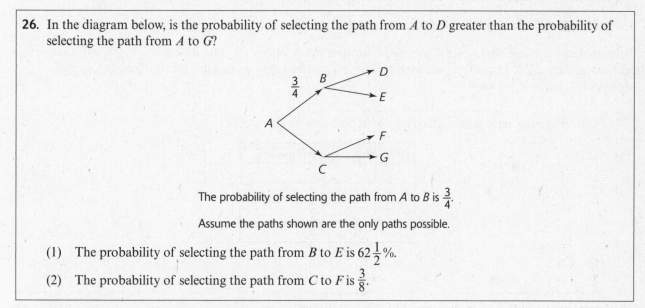

The probability of selecting the path from A to B is $\dfrac{3}{4}$.

Assume the paths shown are the only paths possible.

    (1)   The probability of selecting the path from B to E is $62\dfrac{1}{2}\%$.

    (2)   The probability of selecting the path from C to F is $\dfrac{3}{8}$.

The correct answer is A. Statement (1) ALONE is sufficient.

In order to calculate the probability of selecting the path from A to D, you multiply the probability of selecting the path from A to B with the probability of selecting the path from B to D. Similarly, in order to calculate the probability of selecting the path from A to G, you multiply the probability of selecting the path from A to C with the probability of selecting the path from C to G. Since the probability of selecting the path from A to B is $\dfrac{3}{4}$, the probability of selecting the path from A to C is $\dfrac{1}{4}$. Statement (1) gives the probability of selecting the path from B to E as $62\dfrac{1}{2}\%$, therefore the probability of selecting the path from B to D is $37\dfrac{1}{2}\%$. This provides sufficient information to calculate the probability of selecting the path from A to D to be $\dfrac{3}{4} \times \dfrac{3}{8} = \dfrac{9}{32}$, which is approximately 28%. To calculate the probability for the path from A to G, you multiply $\dfrac{1}{4}$ with the probability of selecting the path from C to G. The probability of selecting the path from C to G is a value that is less than or equal to 1, hence the probability of selecting the path from A to G will be less than or equal to $\dfrac{1}{4}$, or 25%. The probability of selecting the path from A to D will be greater than that of selecting the path from A to G. Therefore, statement (1) is sufficient to answer the question.

Statement (2) gives the probability of selecting the path from C to F as $\frac{3}{8}$; therefore, the probability of selecting the path from C to G is $\frac{5}{8}$. Thus, the probability of selecting the path from A to G is $\frac{1}{4} \times \frac{5}{8} = \frac{5}{32}$, or approximately 16%.

The probability of going from A to B is $\frac{3}{4}$, so you can conclude that the probability of selecting the path from A to D will be less than, or equal to $\frac{3}{4}$, or 75%. Simply being less than 75% is not sufficient to determine if it is greater than 16%, or not. Therefore, statement (2) is not sufficient.

To illustrate, below is a completed diagram with all the probabilities.

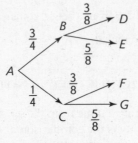

The probability of selecting the path from A to D is $\frac{3}{4} \times \frac{3}{8} = \frac{9}{32}$.

The probability of selecting the path from A to G is $\frac{1}{4} \times \frac{5}{8} = \frac{5}{32}$.

This problem may have been easier if you used both statements together, but because this is a data sufficiency problem you are asked to see if either statement alone would be sufficient to solve the problem. In this case, statement (1) alone is sufficient.

---

27. In the frequency table below, which is greater, the mean or the median?

Data Value	Frequency
3	x
4	6
y	3
11	2

    (1) $x = 2$

    (2)   The median is 4.

The correct answer is D. EACH statement ALONE is sufficient.

In a frequency table, the data values are listed in numerical order. Thus, y is more than 4 but less than 11. The median of a set of data is the middle value when the values are listed from least to greatest. The mean of a set of data is found by finding the sum of all the data values and dividing by how many data values there are. Statement (1) says $x = 2$, so the value 3 is repeated 2 times. Therefore, there are 13 data values. With 13 data values, the 7th (from least to greatest) is the median, which means that the median has the value 4. The missing data value is given as y. The mean of the data set can then be found by doing the following arithmetic.

$$\frac{3(2) + 4(6) + y(3) + 11(2)}{13} = \frac{6 + 24 + 3y + 22}{13}$$

$$= \frac{52 + 3y}{13}$$

$$= \frac{52}{13} + \frac{3y}{13}$$

$$= 4 + \frac{3y}{13}$$

Since y is greater than 4, the mean must have a value greater than $4 + \dfrac{3(4)}{13} = 4\dfrac{12}{13}$. Thus, the mean is greater than the median. Statement (1) is sufficient.

Statement (2) says the median is 4. With some trial and error, you can find that x can be any integer from 1 to 10, and the median remains at 4. When x is 11, there will be 22 data values, and then the median will be the average of the 11th and 12th scores, making the median become $\dfrac{3+4}{2} = 3\dfrac{1}{2}$. With the missing score as y and the value 3 repeated x times, the mean is expressed by

$$\frac{3(x)+4(6)+y(3)+11(2)}{11+x} = \frac{3x+24+3y+22}{11+x}$$
$$= \frac{3x+46+3y}{11+x}$$

Now look at the value of this expression for all x's from 1 to 10. Remember that y is a value greater than 4. Use y as 4, and replace x with the integers from 1 through 10. Then calculate the resulting mean. The actual value for the mean will be more than what is calculated since the actual value of y is greater than 4.

$$x \qquad \frac{3x+46+3(y)}{11+x}$$

$$1 \qquad \frac{3(1)+46+3(4)}{11+1} = \frac{61}{12} > 4$$

$$2 \qquad \frac{3(2)+46+3(4)}{11+2} = \frac{64}{13} > 4$$

$$3 \qquad \frac{3(3)+46+3(4)}{11+3} = \frac{67}{14} > 4$$

Skip all the way to $x = 10$

$$10 \qquad \frac{3(10)+46+3(4)}{11+10} = \frac{88}{21} > 4$$

For every value of x from 1 to 10, the mean is greater than the median. Statement (2) is sufficient.

---

28. How many combinations of n things taken r at a time are there?

 (1) The permutations of n things taken r at a time is 60 when r is 3.
 (2) The permutations of n things taken r at a time is 60 when n is 5.

The correct answer is D. EACH statement ALONE is sufficient.

The combinations formula for n things taken r at a time is $_nC_r = \dfrac{n!}{r!(n-r)!}$.

The permutations formula for n things taken r at a time is $_nP_r = \dfrac{n!}{(n-r)!}$.

Notice that the combinations formula can be expressed as $_nC_r = \dfrac{_nP_r}{r!}$.

Statement (1) gives the value of $_nP_r$ as 60 and the value of r as 3. Use the alternative form of the combinations formula, $_nC_r = \dfrac{_nP_r}{r!}$, to find $_nC_r$: $_nC_r = \dfrac{60}{3!} = \dfrac{60}{(3)(2)(1)} = 10$.

Statement (2) gives the value of $_nP_r$ as 60 and the value of n as 5. Use the permutations formula, $_nP_r = \dfrac{n!}{(n-r)!}$, to find the value of r.

$$60 = \frac{5!}{(5-r)!}$$

$$60 = \frac{5 \cdot 4 \cdot 3 \cdot 2 \cdot 1}{(5-r)!}$$

$$60 = \frac{120}{(5-r)!}$$

$$60(5-r)! = 120$$

$$(5-r)! = 2$$

The only value of r that makes this last equation true, is $r = 3$. So now, as before, you can find that $_nC_r = \dfrac{60}{3!} = \dfrac{60}{(3)(2)(1)} = 10$.

Word Problems

29. How many minutes will it take to go directly from point A to point B at an average rate of 35 miles per hour?

   (1) The time it takes to go from point A to point B at 40 miles per hour is 2 hours less than it takes at 30 miles per hour.
   (2) A car that averages 20 miles per gallon uses 12 gallons to go from A to B.

The correct answer is D. EACH statement ALONE is sufficient.

Statement (1) provides enough information to find the distance between A and B. Knowing the distance traveled and the average rate for the distance traveled, you can find the time it will take to go from A to B. Statement (1) is sufficient. Below you will find a method to solve the problem.

Let x = the distance from A to B in miles. Since total distance divided by average rate equals total time, the sentence, "The time it takes to go from point A to point B at 40 miles per hour is 2 hours less than it takes at 30 miles per hour," can be translated into:

$$\frac{x\text{ mi}}{40\text{ mi/hr}} = \frac{x\text{ mi}}{30\text{ mi/hr}} - 2\text{ hr}$$

$$\frac{x}{40} = \frac{x}{30} - 2 \qquad \text{Multiply each side by 120.}$$

$$3x = 4x - 240$$

$$240 = x$$

The distance from A to B is 240 miles. At an average rate of 35 miles per hour, it will take $\dfrac{240\text{ mi}}{35\text{ mi/hr}} = 6\frac{6}{7}$ hr. This can be converted to minutes by multiplying by 60, since there are 60 minutes in one hour. Therefore, statement (1) is sufficient.

Statement (2) provides enough information to find the distance between A and B and is therefore sufficient. At an average of 20 miles per gallon, 12 gallons will allow you to go 20 mi/gal × 12 gal = 240 miles. Now you could proceed as above to find the number of minutes it would take to go that distance at 35 mi/hr.

30. How long will it take John to do the job alone if working together with Bill and Mary it takes all three people 12 hours to do the job together?

(1)   John's alone time is 12 hours more than the combined alone times of Bill and Mary.

(2)   John needs three times as long as Mary and twice as long as Bill to do the job alone.

The correct answer is B. Statement (2) ALONE is sufficient.

If you let j = amount of time John needs to do the job alone, b = the amount of time Bill needs to do the job alone, and m = the amount of time Mary needs to do the job alone, then the initial information can be translated into the following algebraic equation.

$$\frac{1}{j} + \frac{1}{b} + \frac{1}{m} = \frac{1}{12}$$

If you get sufficient information to replace the b and m with exact values or expressions in terms of j, then you can solve for how much time John needs to do the job alone.

Statement (1) can be translated into $j = b + m + 12$. This allows you to replace the j with $b + m + 12$, but will not allow you to eventually solve for j. Statement (1) is not sufficient.

Statement (2) can be translated into the following. Since John needs three times as much time as Mary, then Mary's time is $\frac{1}{3}$ of John's time, or $m = \frac{1}{3} j = \frac{j}{3}$. Since John needs twice as much time as Bill, Bill's time is $\frac{1}{2}$ of John's time, or $b = \frac{1}{2} j = \frac{j}{2}$. Replacing the b and m in the equation above, you get an equation that only involves j and then can be solved by getting John's time alone. Statement (2) is sufficient. The following is a method for solving the equation for j.

$$\frac{1}{j} + \frac{1}{b} + \frac{1}{m} = \frac{1}{12}$$

$$\frac{1}{j} + \frac{1}{\frac{j}{2}} + \frac{1}{\frac{j}{3}} = \frac{1}{12}$$

$$\frac{1}{j} + \frac{2}{j} + \frac{3}{j} = \frac{1}{12}$$

$$\frac{6}{j} = \frac{1}{12}$$

$$j = 72$$

Therefore, John needs 72 hours to do the job alone. Statement (2) is sufficient.

31. In State A, the sales tax is a% and in State B, the sales tax is b%. In State A, the retail cost of a certain car is x dollars; in State B, the same car retails for y dollars. In which state will the cost of the car with tax be greater?

(1) $a > b$

(2) $y > x$

The correct answer is E. Statements (1) and (2) TOGETHER are NOT sufficient.

Since there are four variables involved, neither statement alone could be sufficient. With some simple numbers, it can be shown that even with both statements together, it is possible to create opposite results.

Suppose $a = 5$, $x = \$10,000$, $b = 4$, and $y = \$11,000$.

Then the total cost of the car in State A is (1.05)($10,000) = $10,500 and the total cost of the car in State B is (1.04)($11,000) = $11,440. In this scenario, the total cost of the car in State B is greater.

Now suppose $a = 5$, $x = \$10,000$, $b = 3$, and $y = \$10,100$.

The cost of the car in State A is still $10,500, and the cost of the car in State B becomes (1.03)($10,100) = $10,403. Now the total cost of the car in State A is greater. Even together, the statements are not sufficient.

---

32. Will Laura need more than 5 pounds of peanuts to make her nut mixture?

    (1)   The 10-pound mixture only contains peanuts and cashews.

    (2)   The mixture is to sell for 75 cents per ounce. Peanuts cost 50 cents per ounce and cashews cost twice as much per ounce as peanuts.

The correct answer is C. BOTH statements TOGETHER are sufficient.

Taking the statements together, you know the mixture had 10 pounds of peanuts and cashews and that peanuts cost 50 cents per ounce, while cashews cost $1.00 per ounce. If an equal amount of peanuts and cashews are mixed together, their average cost would be $\frac{50+100}{2} = 75$ cents per ounce. Since the mixture is selling for 75 cents per ounce, then you know an equal amount of each type of nut is used. If there are 10 pounds of nuts, then there will be 5 pounds of each type of nut used. Thus, taking the statements together is sufficient information. Don't be mislead by the fact that the answer to the question of "Will Laura need more than 5 pounds of peanuts to make her nut mixture?" is *no*. Since you can answer the question, you have sufficient information.

---

33. How old are José and Gloria?

    (1)   In 5 years, José will be twice as old as Beatriz.

    (2)   15 years ago, Gloria was 20 years older than twice Beatriz's age.

The correct answer is E. Statements (1) and (2) TOGETHER are NOT sufficient.

Neither statement alone involves both José and Gloria. Use a table to help organize the ages of the three people.

	Current Age	Age in 5 Years	Age 15 Years Ago
Beatriz	B	$B + 5$	$B - 15$
José	J	$J + 5$	$J - 15$
Gloria	G	$G + 5$	$G - 15$

Now translate each statement into an algebraic sentence.

In 5 years, José will be twice as old as Beatriz:

$$J + 5 = 2(B + 5)$$
$$J + 5 = 2B + 10 \quad (\text{Isolate } J)$$
$$J = 2B + 5$$

15 years ago, Gloria was 20 years older than twice Beatriz's age:

$$G - 15 = 2(B - 15) + 20$$
$$G - 15 = 2B - 30 + 20 \quad (\text{Isolate } G)$$
$$G = 2B + 5$$

All you can get from taking the statements together is that José and Gloria are the same age, $(2B + 5)$. You cannot say how old either one of them is.

Data Interpretation

34. Use the pie chart with diameter $\overline{PR}$ below to answer the question that follows.

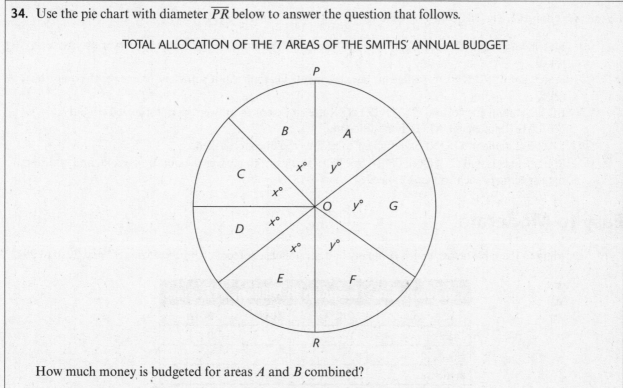

TOTAL ALLOCATION OF THE 7 AREAS OF THE SMITHS' ANNUAL BUDGET

How much money is budgeted for areas *A* and *B* combined?

(1) The total budget for all 7 areas of the Smiths' annual budget is $120,000.
(2) The annual budget for area *F* of the Smiths' annual budget exceeds the annual budget of area *E* by $5,000.

The correct answer is D. EACH statement ALONE is sufficient.

From the pie chart, you can conclude that areas *A*, *G*, and *F* have equal amounts since the central angle for each region is given as *y* degrees. Furthermore, since the three *y*'s make up half the circle, then each of these regions represents $\frac{1}{6}$ of the annual budget $\left(\frac{1}{2} \times \frac{1}{3} = \frac{1}{6}\right)$. In a similar manner, you can conclude that regions *B*, *C*, *D*, and *E* each represent $\frac{1}{8}$ of the annual budget $\left(\frac{1}{2} \times \frac{1}{4} = \frac{1}{8}\right)$. Statement (1) says the annual budget is $120,000. Therefore, Region A has $\frac{1}{6}$ of $120,000 and Region B has $\frac{1}{8}$ of $120,000. From this you can calculate their combined values. Statement (1) is sufficient.

Statement (2) can be translated into an algebraic equation that allows you to find the annual budget. Then you have the same information as what is derived from statement (1). Statement (2) is sufficient. Below is a method for making and solving the equation.

Let *X* = the annual budget.

$$\text{Region F} = \frac{1}{6}X \text{ and Region E} = \frac{1}{8}X$$
$$\frac{1}{6}X - \frac{1}{8}X = 5,000 \quad \text{Multiply each side by 24.}$$
$$4X - 3X = 120,000$$
$$X = 120,000$$

Practice Data Sufficiency Questions

The answer choices are listed below for reference:

Ⓐ Statement (1) ALONE is sufficient, but statement (2) alone is not sufficient to answer the question asked.

Ⓑ Statement (2) ALONE is sufficient, but statement (1) alone is not sufficient to answer the question asked.

Ⓒ BOTH statements (1) and (2) TOGETHER are sufficient to answer the question asked, but NEITHER statement ALONE is sufficient.

Ⓓ EACH statement ALONE is sufficient to answer the question asked.

Ⓔ Statements (1) and (2) TOGETHER are NOT sufficient to answer the question asked, and additional data specific to the problem are needed.

Easy to Moderate

1. According to the table below, which company had the greatest percent change in earnings from 2010 to 2012?

Company Gross Earnings in Millions of Dollars			
	2010	**2011**	**2012**
Titan	10	x	8
Huge	y	15	16
Immense	12	15	z

(1) $y + z = 30$
(2) y and z are consecutive even integers.

2. Bill is fined for his delinquent return of materials. Each day the fine is 20 cents more than the previous day's fine. What was the total amount of the fine?

(1) If Bill had returned the materials three days earlier, his fine would have been $2.00.
(2) Bill's total fine equaled four times the fine for the last day.

3. Who earned the greater dollar increase in salary?

(1) José's salary increased by 20%.
(2) Maria's salary increased by 25%.

4. Is triangle ABC a right triangle?

(1) $AB = 5$, $BC = 12$, $AC = 13$
(2) The sum of the two smallest angles equals the largest angle.

5. If points A, B, and C are collinear with B between A and C, how long is $\overline{AC}$?

(1) $AB = \frac{2}{3} BC$

(2) The midpoints of $\overline{AB}$ and $\overline{BC}$ are 10 units apart.

6. Is the prime number p greater than 15?

(1) The difference between the next larger prime number and p is 4.
(2) The difference between p and the previous prime number is 2.

7. How much salt is in the saltwater mixture?

    (1) The mixture is 25% water.
    (2) After 75% of the mixture is removed, 20 ounces remain.

8. Did Mike or Ed travel farther?

    (1) Mike's speed was twice Ed's speed.
    (2) Ed traveled 15 miles.

9. Is the percent change from a to b greater than the percent change from b to a?

    (1) $a > b > 0$
    (2) $a = b + 1$ and $2a = b + 8$

Average

10. Is x greater than zero?

    (1) $x^2 = 49$
    (2) $|x + 8| = 15$

11. What is the ratio of a to b?

    (1) $a^2 = 16b^2$
    (2) $6a + 3b = 5a - b$

12. What is the smallest of the three numbers a, b, and c?

    (1) The median of the three numbers is a.
    (2) $5b = 3c$

13. All students at Emory High are enrolled in Algebra 2, Chemistry, or both Algebra 2 and Chemistry. How many students are enrolled in only Algebra 2?

    (1) Of the 200 students at Emory High, 80 are enrolled in both Algebra 2 and Chemistry.
    (2) There are 75% as many students enrolled in Chemistry as in Algebra 2.

14. What is the area of $\triangle ABC$?

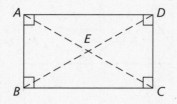

    (1) $AD = 12$ and $BD = 13$
    (2) $AE = 6.5$ and $CD = 5$

15. How long would it take Mary to do the job alone?

(1) Working together, Mary and Jorge need 15 minutes to complete half the job.

(2) Jorge can do $\frac{1}{3}$ of the job in 20 minutes.

16. On individual index cards are written the integers from 20 to x with x being greater than 20 and a multiple of 4. What is the probability of randomly selecting an index card with a prime number on it?

(1) There is only one prime between 20 and x.

(2) x is a multiple of 7.

17. The * symbol represents either multiplication or addition. How much is 5 * 3?

(1) 2 * 2 = 4

(2) 0 * 0 = 0

18. Which figure below has the greater perimeter?

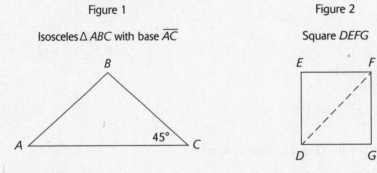

Figure 1

Isosceles $\triangle ABC$ with base $\overline{AC}$

Figure 2

Square $DEFG$

(1) $AB = 6$ and $DF = 4\sqrt{2}$

(2) Area $\triangle ABC = 18$ and area $DEFG = 16$

19. A sequence of numbers uses the following rule: $a_{n+2} = a_n + 2a_{n+1}$. How big is a_6?

(1) $a_3 = 12$

(2) $a_1 = 2$

20. What is the measure of $\angle A$?

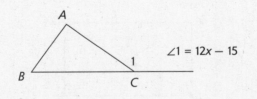

$\angle 1 = 12x - 15$

(1) $\angle B = 3x + 2$

(2) $\angle A = 4x + 48$

21. Were more hot dogs or hamburgers eaten by people living in Tarzana in 2011?

    (1) In 2011, one-fifth of Tarzana's population ate hot dogs.
    (2) In 2011, one-half of Tarzana's population ate hamburgers.

22. A regular hexagon is inscribed in a circle. What is its area?

    (1) The circumference of the circle is 12π inches.
    (2) The area of the circle is 36π square inches.

23. A basket has 120 colored balls that are only red, white, or blue. What is the probability of randomly selecting a ball from the basket that is not blue?

    (1) The ratio of red to not red is 1:4.
    (2) The ratio of red to white balls is 2:3.

24. Gary and Paul live in Encino and Woodland Hills, respectively. The two cities are connected by a straight road between them. They left their respective cities at the same time, with neither one stopping, and met at a location somewhere between the two cities. To which city is the location closer?

    (1) Gary traveled for 10 minutes and Paul traveled for 15 minutes.
    (2) Gary traveled at a rate that was 1.5 times faster than Paul.

25. How old is the youngest of six children?

    (1) The children's ages are consecutive even numbers.
    (2) The oldest child is twice the age of the youngest child.

26. What is the volume of the cube?

    (1) The ratio of the numerical values of surface area to volume is 3 to 2.
    (2) The surface area is 96 square inches.

Above Average to Difficult

27. What is the value of $f[g(x)]$, if $g(x) = 3x - 2$?

    (1) $g(x) = 16$
    (2) $f(x) = 2x + 1$

28. If a and b are integers with $a > 2$, is $b^3 > 10$?

    (1) $2 < ab < 20$
    (2) $|ab| < 6$

29. Is $6x + 3$ divisible by 9?

    (1) $x = 3a + 1$ for some integer a
    (2) $2x + 1$ is divisible by 3

30. Hexagon $QRSTUV$ is inscribed in a circle with center O. What is the measure of $\angle QOR$?

    (1) Hexagon $QRSTUV$ is a regular polygon.
    (2) $QR = RS = ST = TU = UV = QV$

31. What is the three-digit number?

    (1) The ten's digit is three times the hundred's digit.
    (2) The sum of the digits is 18.

32. What is the value of x?

    (1) A line that passes through the points $(x, 5)$ and $(3, y)$ has a slope of 4.
    (2) A line that passes through the points $(x, 3)$ and $(5, y)$ has a slope of -2.

33. A, B, and C are points on the circle below with center at O. What is the area of the circle?

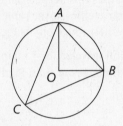

    (1) $\angle C = 45°$ and the length of $\overset{\frown}{AB}$ is 3π inches.
    (2) $\overset{\frown}{AC}$ and $\overset{\frown}{BC}$ each are 1.5 times the measure of $\overset{\frown}{AB}$.

34. What is the value of $4^{2x} + 4^{-2x}$?

    (1) $2^{2x} + 2^{-2x} = 8$
    (2) $4^{x} + 4^{-x} = 8$

35. In one year, the value of A increased by 20% at the same time the value of B decreased by 5%. The new value of A is what percent of the new value of B?

    (1) At the beginning of the year, A's value was 50 more than B's value.
    (2) At the beginning of the year, A's value was twice B's value.

36. What is the standard deviation for data set X?

    (1) The data set has seven values.
    (2) The data set consists of consecutive integers.

Answers and Explanations for Practice Data Sufficiency Questions

Easy to Moderate

1. **C. BOTH statements TOGETHER are sufficient.**

   The percent change in earnings from 2010 to 2012 does not require knowing any values in 2011, therefore the value of x is not necessary. To find the percent changes for Huge and Immense you need to find the values of y and z. With neither statements (1) nor (2) alone can you find the unique values for y and z. With the statements together you can find that y must be 14 and z must be 16, since these are the only consecutive even integers with a sum of 30. The actual calculations of the percent changes are not necessary, since you are not being asked for the answer to the question, but rather if the question can be answered.

   To calculate the percent changes you could use the following formula:

   $$\text{percent change} = \frac{\text{amount of change}}{\text{starting amount}} \times 100\%$$

   Below is a method for calculating the values with which you can make the comparisons and eventually answer the question.

   Titan's percent decrease from 10 to 8 $= \frac{2}{10} \times 100\% = 20\%$.

   Huge's percent increase from 14 to 16 $= \frac{2}{14} \times 100\% = 14\frac{2}{7}\%$.

   Immense's percent increase from 12 to 16 $= \frac{4}{12} \times 100\% = 33\frac{1}{3}\%$.

   Thus, Immense had the greatest percent change from 2010 to 2012.

2. **D. EACH statement ALONE is sufficient.**

   Statement (1) tells you that Bill would have paid a fine of $2.00 had he returned the materials three days earlier. Bill pays a fine of 20 cents the first day, 40 cents the second day, 60 cents the third day, and 80 cents the fourth day for a total of $2.00. Therefore, three days later he would have paid an additional $1.00 + $1.20 + $1.40 or an additional $3.60 above the $2.00, or a total fine of $5.60. Statement (1) is sufficient.

   Statement (2) tells you that Bill's total fine equals four times the fine on the last day. By making a table of accumulated fines, you can determine when this occurs, and then you can find the total for his fines. Therefore, statement (2) is sufficient. Below is such a table that allows you to find the answer, but remember, you are not being asked for the answer, only if a unique answer can be found with the given information.

Day	Fine	Accumulated Fine	4 times Last Day's Fine
1	0.20	0.20	4(0.20) = 0.80
2	0.40	0.20 + 0.40 = 0.60	4(0.40) = 1.60
3	0.60	0.60 + 0.60 = 1.20	4(0.60) = 2.40
4	0.80	1.20 + 0.80 = 2.00	4(0.80) = 3.20
5	1.00	2.00 + 1.00 = 3.00	4(1.00) = 4.00
6	1.20	3.00 + 1.20 = 4.20	4(1.20) = 4.80
7	**1.40**	**4.20 + 1.40 = 5.60**	**4(1.40) = 5.60**

3. **E. Statements (1) and (2) TOGETHER are NOT sufficient.**

Each statement only refers to one person, therefore neither statement alone is sufficient. The question asked, "who earned the greater _dollar_ increase in salary." Even with the two statements together, no dollar amounts were given. You cannot determine who receives the greater dollar amount when only given information on percentage increases. For example, had José started with a salary of $100, his 20% increase would have been $20. Had Maria started with a salary of $80, her 25% increase would also be $20. In this scenario, they had an equal dollar increase despite the fact they had an unequal percent increase. Had they each started with a salary of $100, then Maria would have had the greater dollar increase.

4. **D. EACH statement ALONE is sufficient.**

Statement (1) gives you the three sides of a triangle. Knowing these lengths you can determine the type of triangle it is. Statement (1) is sufficient. To determine the type of triangle, do the following:

Let c be the longest of the three sides and let a and b represent each of the smaller lengths. If $c^2 = a^2 + b^2$, it is a right triangle; if $c^2 > a^2 + b^2$, it is an obtuse triangle; if $c^2 < a^2 + b^2$, it is an acute triangle. Since $13^2 = 5^2 + 12^2$ ($169 = 25 + 144$), you can answer the question. The answer is _yes;_ triangle ABC is a right triangle.

Statement (2) gives you information regarding the angle measures of the triangle, which you can use to determine the measure of the largest angle and then use to determine the type of triangle it is. Statement (2) is sufficient. If the largest angle in a triangle equals 90°, it is a right triangle. If the largest angle is less than 90°, it is an acute triangle. If the largest angle is more than 90°, it is an obtuse triangle. If C represents the measure of the largest angle, and A and B represents the measures of the two smaller angles, then statement (2) can be translated into $C = A + B$. Since the sum of the angles of a triangle is 180°, then $A + B + C = 180°$. By replacing $A + B$ with C, you get $2C = 180°$, or $C = 90°$. With the information derived from statement (2), you can answer the question. The answer is _yes;_ triangle ABC is a right triangle.

5. **C. BOTH statements TOGETHER are sufficient.**

Neither statement alone is sufficient. The figure below will help you understand how the statements together can be used to solve the problem. Let $3x$ represent the length of $\overline{BC}$, then $\overline{AB}$ can be represented by using fractions. Since $AB = \frac{2}{3} BC$, then $AB = 2x$, and $AC = 5x$. If the value of x can be determined, then the length of $\overline{AC}$ can be determined. The midpoints of $\overline{AB}$ and $\overline{BC}$ have been marked and the lengths of each of the smaller segments have been indicated.

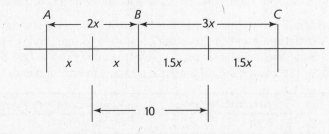

You now can see that $x + 1.5x = 10$, $2.5x = 10$, $x = 4$. Therefore, $AC = 20$.

6. **E. Statements (1) and (2) TOGETHER are NOT sufficient.**

Begin by making a list of prime numbers: 2, 3, 5, 7, 11, 13, 17, 19, 23, 29, etc.

Statement (1) says that the difference between the next larger prime number and p is 4.

Notice that the difference between 13 and 17 is 4, and that the difference between 19 and 23 is also 4. Statement (1) does not provide sufficient information to conclusively say whether the prime number p is greater than 15 or less than 15, so it is not sufficient.

Statement (2) says that the difference between p and the previous prime number is 2. Notice that the difference between 11 and 13 is 2, and the difference between 17 and 19 is also 2. Statement (2) does not provide sufficient information to conclusively say whether the prime number p is greater than 15 or less than 15.

Even using the statements together is not sufficient. For example, look at 5, 7, and 11. In this case, p is 7 since it is 2 more than its previous prime number and 4 less than the next larger one. Now look at 17, 19, and 23. Here p is 19 since it is 2 more than its previous prime number and 4 less than the next larger one. Even together, the statements do not provide sufficient information to conclusively say whether or not the prime number p is greater than 15.

7. C. BOTH statements TOGETHER are sufficient.

Statement (1) indicates what percentage of the mixture is water, from which you can determine the percentage of the mixture that is salt. This does not allow you to find the actual amount of the mixture that is salt. Statement (1) is not sufficient.

Statement (2) tells you the amount of mixture after 75% has been removed, which allows you to find the original amount of the mixture, but not how much of it is salt. Statement (2) is not sufficient.

Using the statements together, you can find how much salt was in the original mixture. Remember, you are not being asked to answer the question, but whether the question can be answered. Below is the work necessary if you actually wanted to answer the question.

Let x = the original amount of the mixture. Then $0.25x = 20$. (75% has been removed, 25% remains).

Therefore, $x = 80$. If the mixture is 25% water, then it is 75% salt, and 75% of 80 is 60. Therefore, the original mixture had 60 ounces of salt.

8. E. Statements (1) and (2) TOGETHER are NOT sufficient.

Statement (1) says that Mike's speed was twice Ed's speed. If you cannot determine how much time either one traveled, you cannot conclude which one traveled farther. For example, suppose Mike's speed was 20 miles per hour and Ed's speed was 10 miles per hour. If Mike travels for 1 hour and Ed travels for 2 hours, they will have traveled the same distance, since distance = rate × time. If Mike travels for 1 hour and Ed travels for 3 hours, Ed will have traveled farther. Therefore, statement (1) is not sufficient. Statement (2) provides no information regarding Mike, thus it is not sufficient. Taking the statements together still is not sufficient information to determine how far Mike traveled and no comparison can be made.

9. D. EACH statement ALONE is sufficient.

Statement (1) says both a and b are positive with $a > b$. The percent change from a smaller number to a larger one is greater than the percent change from the larger to a smaller. Statement (1) is sufficient.

From statement (2), you can determine the values of a and b, from which you can determine the percent change from one to the other and can determine which percent change is greater. Statement (2) is sufficient.

To actually find the values of a and b, you could do the following. Replace a in the following equation with $b + 1$ and solve for b, from which you can determine a.

If $a = b + 1$ and $2a = b + 8$, then

$$2(b+1) = b+8$$
$$2b+2 = b+8$$
$$b = 6$$

Therefore, since $a = b + 1$, $a = 6 + 1$, and $a = 7$.

To calculate the percent changes you could use the following formula:

$$\text{percent change} = \frac{\text{amount of change}}{\text{starting amount}} \times 100\%$$

Therefore, the percent change from a to b (from 7 to 6) $= \frac{1}{7} \times 100\% = 14\frac{2}{7}\%$ and the percent change from b to a (6 to 7) $= \frac{1}{6} \times 100\% = 16\frac{2}{3}\%$. The percent change from b to a is greater, making the answer to the question *no*.

Average

10. **C. BOTH statements TOGETHER are sufficient.**

    From statement (1) you can conclude that $x = 7$, or $x = -7$. Statement (1) is not sufficient.

    From statement (2) you can conclude that either $x + 8 = 15$, or $x + 8 = -15$, which means that $x = 7$, or $x = -23$. Statement (2) is not sufficient.

    The only value of x that makes both statements true at the same time is 7. Hence, statements (1) and (2) together are sufficient.

11. **B. Statement (2) ALONE is sufficient.**

    From statement (1), you can determine that $a = 4b$ or $a = -4b$. Therefore, $\frac{a}{b} = 4$ or $\frac{a}{b} = -4$. Statement (1) is not sufficient to determine a unique answer.

    From statement (2), you can get a unique ratio value. Statement (2) is sufficient. See the work below.

    $$6a + 3b = 5a - b \qquad \text{Subtract } 5a \text{ and } 3b \text{ from each side.}$$
    $$a = -4b \qquad \text{Divide each side by } b.$$
    $$\frac{a}{b} = -4$$

12. **E. Statements (1) and (2) TOGETHER are NOT sufficient.**

    Statement (1) allows you to determine that a is not the smallest value, but does not allow you to determine which is the smallest. Statement (1) is not sufficient.

    Statement (2) does not make any comparison with the value of a. Statement (2) is not sufficient.

    Using the statements together, you determine that either b or c is the smallest and that $5b = 3c$. The error made here is assuming that both a and b are positive. If that were the case, then c would be greater than b. (For example, if $b = 3$ and $c = 5$, then $5b = 3c$.) But if both b and c were negative values, then b would be greater than c. (For example, if $b = -3$ and $c = -5$, then $5b = 3c$.) Even together, the statements are not sufficient.

13. **C. BOTH statements TOGETHER are sufficient.**

    Neither statement alone is sufficient. The use of a Venn diagram will help you see why the statements together are sufficient. Let the oval on the left represent all students enrolled in Algebra 2, with x being the number of students in Algebra 2, but not in Chemistry. Let the oval on the right represent all of the students enrolled in Chemistry, with y being the number of students enrolled in Chemistry, but not Algebra 2. The overlap represents the students enrolled in both Algebra 2 and Chemistry.

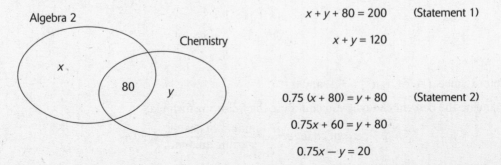

$x + y + 80 = 200 \qquad$ (Statement 1)

$x + y = 120$

$0.75\,(x + 80) = y + 80 \qquad$ (Statement 2)

$0.75x + 60 = y + 80$

$0.75x - y = 20$

You can now solve this system of equations and find the values of each variable.

$$x + y = 120$$
$$\underline{0.75x - y = 20} \qquad \text{Add the equations.}$$
$$1.75x = 140 \qquad \text{Divide by 1.75.}$$
$$x = 80$$
$$\text{Hence, } y = 40$$

Since $x + y = 120$, and $y = 40$, then $x + 40 = 120$ or $x = 80$. Therefore, there are 80 students enrolled only in Algebra 2.

14. **D. EACH statement ALONE is sufficient.**

Since all angles in the quadrilateral are right angles, the figure is a rectangle. Opposite sides and diagonals of a rectangle have equal lengths. The diagonals of a rectangle bisect each other.

Therefore, $AD = BC$, $AB = CD$, $AC = BD$, $AE = EC$, and $BE = ED$. The area of $\triangle ABC$ can be found using $\frac{1}{2}(AB)(BC)$. $\triangle ABC$ is a right triangle, so $(AB)^2 + (BC)^2 = (AC)^2$.

Statement (1) gives you $AD = 12$, so $BC = 12$. It gives you $BD = 13$, so $AC = 13$ and with these values you can find AB. Statement (1) is sufficient. Below is the work for finding the area of $\triangle ABC$.

$$(AB)^2 + (BC)^2 = (AC)^2 \qquad \text{area } \triangle ABC = \frac{1}{2}(AB)(BC)$$
$$(AB)^2 + (12)^2 = (13)^2$$
$$(AB)^2 + 144 = 169 \qquad \qquad = \frac{1}{2}(5)(12)$$
$$(AB)^2 = 25 \qquad \qquad = 30$$
$$AB = 5$$

Statement (2) gives you $AE = 6.5$, so $AC = 13$. It gives you $CD = 5$, so $AB = 5$. With $AC = 13$ and $AB = 5$, you can find BC, and then the area of $\triangle ABC$. Statement (2) is sufficient.

Below is the work for finding the area of $\triangle ABC$ with this information.

$$(AB)^2 + (BC)^2 = (AC)^2 \qquad \text{area } ABC = \frac{1}{2}(AB)(BC)$$
$$(5)^2 + (BC)^2 = (13)^2$$
$$25 + (BC)^2 = 169 \qquad \qquad = \frac{1}{2}(5)(12)$$
$$(BC)^2 = 144 \qquad \qquad = 30$$
$$BC = 12$$

15. **C. BOTH statements TOGETHER are sufficient.**

Neither statement alone is sufficient. Taking the statements together, you are given how long it takes the two people together and how long it takes one person alone. This is sufficient information to find the time it takes the other person alone. Remember, you are not asked for the answer to the question, but whether a unique answer to the question can be found with the given information.

Below is the work necessary to find the answer.

Since Jorge can do $\frac{1}{3}$ of the job in 20 minutes, he does the whole job in 60 minutes.

Since working together, Mary and Jorge need 15 minutes to complete half the job, they would need 30 minutes together to complete the whole job.

Let m = the amount of time, in minutes, that Mary needs to do the job alone. Then

$$\frac{1}{m} + \frac{1}{60} = \frac{1}{30}$$

Multiply each side by $60m$.

$$60m\left(\frac{1}{m} + \frac{1}{60}\right) = 60m\left(\frac{1}{30}\right)$$

$$60 + m = 2m$$

$$60 = m$$

It would take Mary 60 minutes to do the job alone.

16. C. BOTH statements TOGETHER are sufficient.

With statement (1), the fact that there is only one prime number between 20 and x with x a multiple of 4, x could be either 24 or 28, since the only prime number between 20 and 24 is 23 and the only prime number between 20 and 28 is also 23. Not knowing how many integers are involved from 20 to x, you cannot determine the probability of selecting a prime number. Statement (1) is not sufficient.

With statement (2), the fact that x is a multiple of 7, it is now both a multiple of 4 and 7. That means x is a multiple of 28. It could be 28, 56, 84, etc. Not knowing what specific value x is, you cannot determine the probability of selecting a prime number from 20 to x. Statement (2) is not sufficient.

Using the statements together, x can only be the value 28, and the probability can now be determined.

If you actually wanted to calculate the answer, you would use the definition of probability.

$$\text{probability} = \frac{\#\text{ favorable outcomes}}{\#\text{ total outcomes}}$$

From 20 to 28, there are 9 integers (20, 21, 22, 23, 24, 25, 26, 27, 28). Only one of them is a prime number. Therefore, the probability is $\frac{1}{9}$.

17. E. Statements (1) and (2) TOGETHER are NOT sufficient.

From statement (1), 2 * 2 = 4, the * could be either addition or multiplication. Statement (1) is not sufficient.

From statement (2), 0 * 0 = 0, the * could be either addition or multiplication. Statement (2) is not sufficient.

Even using the statements together, which operation * represents cannot be determined.

18. D. EACH statement ALONE is sufficient.

Using the first part of statement (1), $AB = 6$, together with the fact that $\triangle ABC$ is isosceles with base $\overline{AC}$ and $\angle C = 45°$ provides enough information to find the perimeter of the triangle. Using the second part of statement (1), $DF = 4\sqrt{2}$, together with the fact that $DEFG$ is a square, provides enough information to find the perimeter of the square. Therefore, the comparison can be made. Statement (1) is sufficient.

Using the first part of statement (2), area $\triangle ABC = 18$, together with the fact that $\triangle ABC$ is isosceles with base $\overline{AC}$ and $\angle C = 45°$ provides enough information to find the perimeter of the triangle. Using the second part of statement (2), area $DEFG = 16$, together with the fact that $DEFG$ is a square, provides enough information to find the perimeter of the square. Therefore, the comparison can be made. Statement (2) is sufficient.

Remember, you are not answering the question, but whether the question can be answered with the given information. Below is how the perimeter of each figure can be derived from the given information.

Using statement (1): First draw a segment from B to D on $\overline{AC}$ so that $\overline{BD}$ is perpendicular to $\overline{AC}$.

In the isosceles triangle, $AB = BC = 6$.

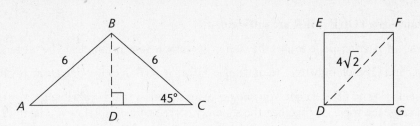

In the 45-45-90 right triangle BDC, $BD = CD$ and $BC = CD\sqrt{2}$. Since $BC = 6$, then $CD = \dfrac{6}{\sqrt{2}} = 3\sqrt{2}$. Therefore, $AC = 2\left(3\sqrt{2}\right) = 6\sqrt{2}$. The perimeter of $\triangle ABC = 6\sqrt{2} + 12$.

The diagonal of a square divides it into two 45-45-90 right triangles. In $\triangle DFG$, $DG = FG$ and $DF = DG\sqrt{2}$. Since $DF = 4\sqrt{2}$, then $DG = 4$ and the perimeter of the square is 16.

The perimeter of the triangle is greater than the perimeter of the square.

Using statement (2):

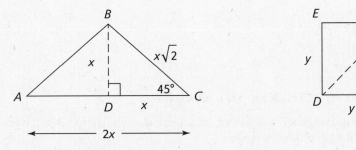

Area $\triangle ABC = 18$ and area $DEFG = 16$. Therefore,

$$\frac{1}{2}(2x)(x) = 18 \qquad\qquad y^2 = 16$$
$$x^2 = 18 \qquad\qquad y = 4$$
$$x = \sqrt{18} = 3\sqrt{2}$$

The perimeter of $\triangle ABC = 2x + 2x\sqrt{2} = 6\sqrt{2} + 12$. The perimeter of $DEFG = 16$.

The perimeter of the triangle is greater than the perimeter of the square.

19. **C. BOTH statements TOGETHER are sufficient.**

Since the formula for a term in the sequence uses its two previous terms, you must know at least two terms to find another term. Neither statement alone is sufficient. Using the statements together, you can find the second term. Then knowing the second and third terms, you can find the fourth term. Eventually, you can find the sixth term. Below is the work necessary to find the sixth term.

$$a_{n+2} = a_n + 2a_{n+1} \qquad \text{Let } n = 1$$
$$a_{1+2} = a_1 + 2a_{1+1}$$
$$a_3 = a_1 + 2a_2$$
$$12 = 2 + 2a_2$$
$$10 = 2a_2$$
$$5 = a_2$$

$$a_4 = a_2 + 2a_3 = \ 5 + 2(12) = 29$$
$$a_5 = a_3 + 2a_4 = 12 + 2(29) = 70$$
$$a_6 = a_4 + 2a_5 = 29 + 2(70) = 169$$

20. C. BOTH statements TOGETHER are sufficient.

In any triangle, an exterior angle equals the sum of its remote interior angles. Therefore, $\angle 1 = \angle A + \angle B$.

Statements (1) and (2) each only refer to one angle, either A or B. Neither one alone is sufficient.

Using statements (1) and (2) together, you can make an equation that is solvable for x, which in turn allows you to find a value for angle A. Together, the statements are sufficient. Below is a method for finding x and then angle A.

$$\angle 1 = \angle A + \angle B$$

$$12x - 15 = (3x + 2) + (4x + 48)$$
$$12x - 15 = 7x + 50 \qquad \text{Subtract } 7x \text{ and add } 15 \text{ to each side.}$$
$$5x = 65$$
$$x = 13$$

$$\angle A = 4x + 48$$
$$\angle A = 4(13) + 48$$
$$\angle A = 100°$$

21. E. Statements (1) and (2) TOGETHER are NOT sufficient.

Neither statement alone nor together is sufficient since there is no indication that the people in Tarzana only ate one of either hot dogs or hamburgers.

22. D. EACH statement ALONE is sufficient.

A regular hexagon is one where all sides are the same length and all angles have the same measure. The area of a regular hexagon inscribed in a circle can be calculated if the length of one side is known, its perimeter is known, or the radius of the circumscribed circle is known.

Statement (1) gives the circumference of the circle, from which the radius can be found. Statement (1) is sufficient.

Statement (2) gives the area of the circle, from which the radius can be found. Statement (2) is sufficient. Below is the work necessary to find the area of the regular hexagon.

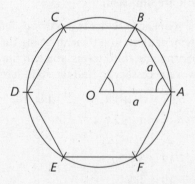

When the radius of the regular hexagon is drawn, it is also the radius of the circle. Points A, B, C, D, E, and F around the circle form equal arcs. Since there are 360° in one rotation of a circle, each arc has a measure of 60°. It can eventually be shown that $\triangle AOB$ is an equilateral triangle. The regular hexagon consists of six of these equilateral triangles. If the area of one triangle can be found, then six times that area is the area of the regular hexagon. If you know one side of an equilateral triangle, you can find its area the following way.

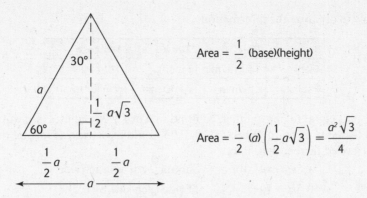

Statement (1) gives the circumference as 12π inches $= (2)(\text{radius})\pi$. Therefore, the radius of the circle is 6 inches. The area of the equilateral triangle is $\frac{6^2\sqrt{3}}{4} = \frac{36\sqrt{3}}{4} = 9\sqrt{3}$ square inches. Therefore the area of the regular hexagon is $6\left(9\sqrt{3}\right) = 54\sqrt{3}$ square inches.

Statement (2) gives the area of the circle as 36π square inches $= (\text{radius})^2(\pi)$. Therefore, the radius is again 6 inches and the work described above calculates the area of the regular hexagon.

23. **C. BOTH statements TOGETHER are sufficient.**

Using statement (1), you can find how many balls are red and how many are not red. If you let x represent how many balls are red and $4x$ represents how many are not red, then $x + 4x = 120$, $5x = 120$ or $x = 24$. Therefore, there are 24 red balls and 96 balls that are either white or blue. This does not tell you how many are not blue. Statement (1) is not sufficient.

Statement (2) gives the ratio of red to white balls, but that is not enough information to relate it to the 120 total balls. Statement (2) is not sufficient.

Using the statements together, there are 24 red balls and the ratio of red to white is 2:3, which means there are 36 white balls $\left(\frac{24}{36} = \frac{2}{3}\right)$. Therefore, there are 60 balls that are not blue, $(24 + 36 = 60)$, and the probability of selecting a ball that is not blue can be calculated. The probability is $\frac{60}{120} = \frac{1}{2}$.

24. **E. Statements (1) and (2) TOGETHER are NOT sufficient.**

Statement (1) says Paul traveled for a longer time, but not knowing the speed either traveled, you cannot determine who traveled farther. Statement (1) is not sufficient.

Statement (2) says Gary traveled faster than Paul, but not knowing how much time either spent traveling, you cannot determine who traveled farther. Statement (2) is not sufficient.

Using the statements together, you still cannot determine who traveled farther.

For example, suppose Paul's speed was 2 miles per minute. This would make Gary's speed 3 miles per minute. Suppose Paul traveled for 15 minutes at 2 miles per minute. He would have traveled 30 miles. Then Gary traveled for 5 minutes at 3 miles per minute for a distance of 15 miles. They would have met closer to Gary's home in Encino. Now suppose that Paul's speed was still 2 miles per minute but he traveled for 40 minutes. He would have traveled 80 miles. Gary would still have traveled at 3 miles per minute but for 30 minutes. He would then have traveled 90 miles. Now the meeting location was closer to Paul's home in Woodland Hills.

It can be determined at what amount of time they would have met at a location exactly halfway between them. Then at any time other than that, the location would have been closer to one of them than the other.

Let r = Paul's rate in miles per minutes, then $1.5\, r$ = Gary's rate in miles per minute.

Let t = # minutes Gary travels, then $t + 10$ = # minutes Paul travels.

Use the chart below to organize the information.

	Rate	Time	Distance
Gary	1.5 r mi/min	t min	1.5 rt mi
Paul	r mi/min	$t + 10$ min	$rt + 10r$ mi

If you set the distances equal to one another, you find that at $t = 20$ minutes (see work below), they would each have traveled the same distance. When $t < 20$, Paul would have traveled farther than Gary. When $t > 20$, Gary would have traveled farther than Paul.

$$1.5rt = rt + 10r \qquad \text{Subtract } rt \text{ from each side.}$$
$$0.5rt = 10r \qquad \text{Divide each side by } 0.5r.$$
$$t = 20$$

25. C. BOTH statements TOGETHER are sufficient.

Statement (1) simply states that the children's ages are consecutive even numbers from which you cannot determine what specifically is the age of the youngest child. Statement (2) says the oldest child is twice the age of the youngest, but this is not sufficient to determine the specific age of the youngest. Neither statement alone is sufficient. Using the statements together, the age of each of the six children can be determined. Below is a method using the information from both statements.

Let x = age of the youngest child (call this the first child), then $x + 2$ = age of second child, $x + 4$ = age of third child, $x + 6$ = age of fourth child, $x + 8$ = age of fifth child, $x + 10$ = age of sixth child (the oldest).

Then $x + 10 = 2x$, which means that $x = 10$. The youngest child is 10 years old.

26. D. EACH statement ALONE is sufficient.

If each edge of the cube was length x inches, then its volume would be x^3 cubic inches and its surface area would be $6x^2$ square inches. Statement (1) says that $\dfrac{6x^2}{x^3} = \dfrac{3}{2}$. From this, you can determine the value of x and then you can find the volume of the cube. Statement (1) is sufficient. Below is the work to find the value of x.

$$\frac{6x^2}{x^3} = \frac{3}{2} \qquad \text{Simplify the fraction on the left.}$$
$$\frac{6}{x} = \frac{3}{2}$$
$$3x = 12$$
$$x = 4$$

Statement (2) says that $6x^2 = 96$. Then $x^2 = 16$, or $x = 4$. Now you can find the volume of the cube. Since the volume of a cube is found by raising the length of an edge to the third power, the volume of this cube is $4^3 = 64$ cubic inches. Statement (2) is sufficient.

Above Average to Difficult

27. C. BOTH statements TOGETHER are sufficient.

Using statement (1), you can determine the value of x, but not the value of $f[g(x)]$. Statement (1) is not sufficient.

Statement (2) gives you what $f(x)$ is, but not what to replace x with. Statement (2) is not sufficient.

Using the two statements together,

$$f[g(x)] = f(16) \qquad \text{Replace } g(x) \text{ with 16.}$$
$$= 2(16) + 1 \qquad f(x) = 2x + 1$$
$$= 33$$

28. **B. Statement (2) ALONE is sufficient.**

    Dividing each side of the inequality statement in statement (1) by a, you get $\frac{2}{a} < b < \frac{20}{a}$. Since a is an integer and $a > 2$, the smallest value a can be is 3. Replacing a with 3, you get $\frac{2}{3} < b < \frac{20}{3}$. Since b is also an integer, then when $a = 3$, b could only be 1, 2, 3, 4, 5, or 6. For certain of these values, $b^3 > 10$. For other values of b, $b^3 < 10$. Statement (1) is not sufficient.

    Translating what absolute value means, statement (2) becomes $-6 < ab < 6$. Since a is an integer and $a > 2$, the smallest value a can be is 3. Replacing a with 3, you get $-6 < 3b < 6$. Divide each side of the inequality by 3 to get $-2 < b < 2$. Since b is also an integer, then when $a = 3$, b could only be -1, 0, or 1. In each case, $b^3 < 10$. Statement (2) is sufficient. Be careful—just because the answer to the question is *no* does not mean the information is not sufficient.

29. **D. EACH statement ALONE is sufficient.**

    Replace x with $3a + 1$ in statement (1).

    $$\begin{aligned}
    6x + 3 &= 6(3a + 1) + 3 \\
    &= 18a + 6 + 3 \\
    &= 18a + 9 \\
    &= 9(2a + 1)
    \end{aligned}$$

    Since $6x + 3$ is now represented as 9 times some integer expression, it is divisible by 9. Statement (1) is sufficient.

    Statement (2) says that $2x + 1$ is divisible by 3. That would mean that $3(2x + 1)$ would be divisible by 9. Since $3(2x + 1) = 6x + 3$, $6x + 3$ is divisible by 9. Statement (2) is sufficient.

30. **D. EACH statement ALONE is sufficient.**

    A regular hexagon is a six-sided figure with all sides of equal lengths and all interior angles equal in measure. Angle QOR is a central angle of the circle. The measure of a central angle in a circle is the same as the measure, in degrees, of its intercepted arc. If two chords in a circle have the same length, then the arcs they cut off have the same measure. Therefore, if a regular polygon (statement 1) is inscribed in a circle, the central angle can be calculated. If a polygon inscribed in a circle has sides of equal lengths (statement 2), each central angle can be calculated. Hence, each statement alone is sufficient. In this case, each central angle is $\frac{1}{6}(360°) = 60°$.

31. **C. BOTH statements TOGETHER are sufficient.**

    In order to know the three-digit number, you need its unit's, ten's, and hundred's digits. Statement (1) makes no reference to the unit's digit. Statement (2) does not provide sufficient information to get the unique values for the unit's, ten's, and hundred's digits. Neither statement alone is sufficient.

    Initially, taking the statements together, it appears that there is not sufficient information since you only have two sentences relating three unknowns. But if the ten's digit is three times the hundred's digit, the only possibilities are that the hundred's digit is 1 and the ten's digit is 3, the hundred's digit is 2 and the ten's digit is 6, or the hundred's digit is 3 and the ten's digit is 9. If the sum of the digits is 18, the only possibility becomes the hundred's digit is 3, the ten's digit is 9, and the unit's digit is 6. The number is 396.

32. **C. BOTH statements TOGETHER are sufficient.**

    If a line passes through (x_1, y_1) and (x_2, y_2), then its slope $= \frac{y_2 - y_1}{x_2 - x_1}$. From statement (1), you can get the equation $\frac{y - 5}{3 - x} = 4$, or $y - 5 = 4(3 - x)$. Statement (1) is not sufficient. From statement (2), you can get the equation $\frac{y - 3}{5 - x} = -2$, or $y - 3 = -2(5 - x)$. Statement (2) is not sufficient.

Together, you have two different equations involving x and y which can be solved for each variable. Thus, the statements together are sufficient. Remember, you are not finding the answer, but whether an answer can be found. Below is a method for finding the answer.

$$y - 5 = 4(3 - x) \qquad y - 3 = -2(5 - x)$$
$$y - 5 = 12 - 4x \qquad y - 3 = -10 + 2x$$
$$y = 17 - 4x \qquad y = -7 + 2x$$

Now set the two expressions for y equal to one another.

$$-7 + 2x = 17 - 4x \qquad \text{Add } 4x \text{ and 7 to each side.}$$
$$6x = 24$$
$$x = 4$$

33. **A. Statement (1) ALONE is sufficient.**

The area of the circle can be found if you know its radius or its circumference.

Statement (1) says that $\angle C = 45°$ and since point C lies on the circle, it makes $\angle C$ become an inscribed angle. An inscribed angle has as its measure, half the number of degrees in its intercepted arc. Thus, $\overset{\frown}{AB}$ has a measure of $90°$, making it $\frac{90}{360} = \frac{1}{4}$ of the circumference of the circle. Statement (1) also says that $\overset{\frown}{AB}$ has a length of 3π inches. Thus, the circumference is 12π inches, from which the radius can be calculated and then the area. Statement (1) is sufficient. Below is a method to find the desired area using the information from statement (1):

The formula for the circumference of a circle is $C = 2\pi r$. Since the circumference was calculated to be 12π, you have $12\pi = 2\pi r$, which means that $r = 6$ inches. The formula for the area of a circle is $A = \pi r^2$. With $r = 6$, the area becomes $\pi(6)^2 = 36\pi$ square inches.

Statement (2) says that $\overset{\frown}{AC}$ and $\overset{\frown}{BC}$ each are 1.5 times the measure of $\overset{\frown}{AB}$. Since the sum of the arcs in a circle is $360°$, you can eventually determine the measure of $\overset{\frown}{AB}$ is $90°$. But not knowing what the lengths of any of the arcs are, neither the circumference nor the radius can be calculated. Statement (2) is not sufficient.

34. **D. EACH statement ALONE is sufficient.**

The trick in this question is to recognize the following two concepts.

First, $2^{2x} = (2^2)^x = 4^x$ and $2^{-2x} = (2^2)^{-x} = 4^{-x}$.

Second, $\left(4^x + 4^{-x}\right)^2 = \left(4^x\right)^2 + 2\left[\left(4^x\right)\left(4^{-x}\right)\right] + \left(4^{-x}\right)^2$

$$= 4^{2x} + 2\left(4^0\right) + 4^{-2x}$$
$$= 4^{2x} + 2(1) + 4^{-2x}$$
$$= 4^{2x} + 4^{-2x} + 2$$

Now notice that statement (1) and statement (2) say exactly the same thing.

Using the information as presented in statement (2), you can square each side and get $4^{2x} + 4^{-2x} + 2 = 64$, or $4^{2x} + 4^{-2x} = 62$.

35. B. Statement (2) ALONE is sufficient.

Using statement (1), if you let B = original B value, then $B + 50$ = original A value. The value of A increased by 20%, which means the new A is 1.2 times the original A. So, the new $A = 1.2(B + 50) = 1.2B + 60$. The new B was decreased by 5%, which means the new B is 0.95 times the original B. So, the new $B = 0.95B$. You can attempt to find what percent the new A is of the new B, but you find that the equation you make has two variables which cannot be simplified into one with only one variable.

$$1.2B + 60 = \frac{x}{100}(0.95B)$$
$$\frac{1.2B + 60}{0.95B} = \frac{x}{100}$$

Statement (1) is not sufficient.

Using statement (2), let B = the original B value, then $2B$ = the original A value. The value of A increased by 20%, which means the new $A = 1.2(2B) = 2.4B$. The new B decreased by 5%, which means the new $B = 0.95B$. Now when you make the equation to find the percentage, you find that one of the two variables simplifies out. Thus, you can find what percent of the new B is the value of the new A. Statement (2) is sufficient. Below is a method to find the percentage.

$$2.4B = \frac{x}{100}(0.95)B$$
$$\frac{2.4 \overset{1}{\cancel{B}}}{0.95 \underset{1}{\cancel{B}}} = \frac{x}{100}$$
$$2.53 \approx \frac{x}{100}$$
$$253 \approx x$$

The new A is about 253% of the new B.

36. C. BOTH statements TOGETHER are sufficient.

Statement (1) says you have seven data values but not what those data values are, hence you cannot express their sum, and therefore cannot determine the mean value, which is a necessary value in order to calculate the standard deviation. Statement (1) is not sufficient.

Statement (2) says you have consecutive integers, but not how many of them you have. Again, you cannot determine the mean value, which is necessary to find the standard deviation. Statement (2) is not sufficient.

To calculate standard deviation, you do a five-step process.

1) Calculate the mean.

2) For each data value, do the following: (data value – mean)^2.

3) Add together the results from step 2.

4) Divide the result of step 3 by the number of data values.

5) Take the square root of the result in step 4.

Using both statements, the seven consecutive integers can be represented as n, $n + 1$, $n + 2$, $n + 3$, $n + 4$, $n + 5$, and $n + 6$. Then the mean can be calculated as follows:

$$\text{mean} = \frac{n + (n+1) + (n+2) + (n+3) + (n+4) + (n+5) + (n+6)}{7}$$
$$= \frac{7n + 21}{7}$$
$$= n + 3$$

Now, when you do (data value – mean)^2, the variable n gets removed and you have only integer values from which you can eventually find the standard deviation. Below is the work to actually find that value.

$$\left[n-(n+3)\right]^2 = (-3)^2 = 9$$
$$\left[(n+1)-(n+3)\right]^2 = (-2)^2 = 4$$
$$\left[(n+2)-(n+3)\right]^2 = (-1)^2 = 1$$
$$\left[(n+3)-(n+3)\right]^2 = (0)^2 = 0$$
$$\left[(n+4)-(n+3)\right]^2 = (1)^2 = 1$$
$$\left[(n+5)-(n+3)\right]^2 = (2)^2 = 4$$
$$+\left[(n+6)-(n+3)\right]^2 = (3)^2 = 9$$
$$\overline{28}$$

$$\sqrt{\frac{28}{7}} = \sqrt{4} = 2$$

As you continue to study, keep in mind the following plan of attack for data sufficiency questions:

A PATTERNED PLAN OF ATTACK
Data Sufficiency

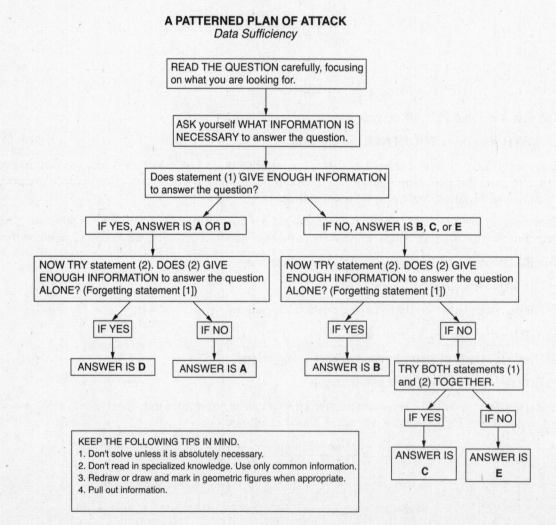

KEEP THE FOLLOWING TIPS IN MIND.
1. Don't solve unless it is absolutely necessary.
2. Don't read in specialized knowledge. Use only common information.
3. Redraw or draw and mark in geometric figures when appropriate.
4. Pull out information.

Chapter 9

Math Skills Review

GMAT math questions cover the basic properties of mathematics that support your success as a graduate business student. You will need to have a solid understanding of arithmetic, algebra, geometry, data analysis, word problems, and data interpretation to do well on this section of the exam. This comprehensive chapter is designed to review basic math concepts and increase your ability to *think critically* as you use math insights, simple calculations, and common sense to solve GMAT questions.

As you review this chapter, assess your strengths and evaluate areas in which you feel you may need improvement. Even if your cumulative knowledge of math is strong, you should at least skim through the topic headings to help trigger your memory of forgotten math concepts.

The first part of this chapter begins with an *overview* section that contains commonly encountered math symbols and terminology. The next part of the chapter consists of a thorough review of six math topic areas. Each topic begins with a *diagnostic test* to help you assess your knowledge of that topic and is followed by a *review section* that provides you with illustrated examples, explanations, and clarifications about solving basic math problems. After you have taken the diagnostic test and systematically reviewed the explanations with examples in a topic area, you will be ready to practice what you have learned with the *practice exercises* provided at the end of each topic area subject.

Pace yourself as you work through each topic area, and remember that the Quantitative Reasoning section of the GMAT measures your ability to use your *cumulative knowledge* of mathematics and your ability to *reason quantitatively*. Try to focus your attention on one math concept at a time (i.e., finish the arithmetic diagnostic and arithmetic review before you begin the algebra diagnostic and algebra review, etc.).

GMAT Math Review Topic Areas					
Arithmetic (pages 291–328)	**Algebra (pages 328–368)**	**Geometry (pages 368–406)**	**Data Analysis (pages 406–416)**	**Word Problems (pages 417–426)**	**Data Interpretation (pages 427–439)**
❏ Arithmetic diagnostic test	❏ Algebra diagnostic test	❏ Geometry diagnostic test	❏ Data analysis diagnostic test	❏ Word problems diagnostic test	❏ Data interpretation diagnostic test
❏ Sets of numbers	❏ Set notations	❏ Lines, segments, rays, and angles	❏ Methods for counting	❏ Motion problems	❏ Circle or pie graphs
❏ Divisibility rules	❏ Variables	❏ Polygons and their angles	❏ Permutations	❏ Work problems	❏ Bar graphs
❏ Grouping symbols	❏ Solving linear equations in one or two variables	❏ Triangles	❏ Combinations	❏ Mixture problems	❏ Line graphs
❏ Order of operations	❏ Solving linear inequalities in one variable	❏ Quadrilaterals	❏ Probability	❏ Age problems	❏ Venn diagrams
❏ Integers	❏ Polynomials	❏ Circles	❏ Basic statistics	❏ Integers problems	❏ Charts and tables
❏ Fractions	❏ Algebraic fractions	❏ Perimeter, circumference, and area of plane figures	❏ Frequency table and measure of central tendency		
❏ Decimals	❏ Solving quadratic equations in one variable	❏ Surface area, volume, and diagonal lengths of 3-dimensional figures	❏ Five steps to calculate the standard deviation		
❏ Ratios and proportions	❏ Coordinate geometry	❏ Congruence and similarity			
❏ Percents	❏ Functions and function notation				
❏ Exponents					
❏ Square roots					

Overview

This overview section contains basic references that you will refer to again and again during your GMAT math preparation. These fundamental facts and formulas were compiled so that you can easily have important basic math concepts at your fingertips. As you review different math topics, keep in mind that these basic references will help you solve math problems so that you don't spend valuable time trying to search math information and formulas. The math overview includes the following: common math symbols, vocabulary related to sets of numbers, common math conventions and terminology, geometric formulas (perimeter, area, and volume), important fraction-decimal-percent equivalents, and measurement equivalents (English and metric systems).

Common Math Symbols

$x = 5$	x is equal to 5
$x \neq 5$	x is not equal to 5
$x \approx 5$	x is approximately equal to 5
$x \leq 5$	x is less than or equal to 5
$x < 5$	x is less than 5
$x \geq 5$	x is greater than or equal to 5
$x > 5$	x is greater than 5
$|x|$	the absolute value of x
$\sqrt{x}$	the nonnegative square root of x when $x \geq 0$
$-\sqrt{x}$	the nonpositive square root of x when $x \geq 0$
$n!$	the product of the positive integers 1, 2, 3, ..., n
$0!$	is defined to have the value of 1
$k \parallel p$	line k is parallel to line p
$k \perp p$	line k is perpendicular to line p

Numbers Vocabulary

Natural numbers	{1, 2, 3, 4, ...} The counting numbers.
Whole numbers	{0, 1, 2, 3, 4, ...} The counting numbers and zero.
Integers	{0, ±1, ±2, ±3, ±4, ...} The whole numbers and their opposites.
Positive integers	{1, 2, 3, 4, ...} The natural numbers.
Non-negative integers	{0, 1, 2, 3, 4, ...} The whole numbers.
Negative integers	{−1, −2, −3, −4, ...} The opposites of the natural numbers.
Nonpositive integers	{0, −1, −2, −3, −4, ...} The opposites of the whole numbers.
Rational numbers	Any value that can be expressed as $\frac{p}{q}$, where p is any integer and q is any nonzero integer. In decimal form, it either terminates or has a block of repeating digits. For example, $\frac{3}{4} = 0.75$, $\frac{1}{12} = 0.08333... = 0.08\overline{3}$
Irrational numbers	Any value that exists that cannot be expressed as $\frac{p}{q}$, where p is any integer and q is any nonzero integer. In decimal form, it neither terminates nor has any block of repeating digits. For example, $\sqrt{2}$, π.
Real numbers	All the rational numbers and irrational numbers.
Prime numbers	Any integer, greater than 1, that only has 1 and itself as divisors. The first 10 prime numbers are 2, 3, 5, 7, 11, 13, 17, 19, 23, 29.

Composite numbers	Any integer greater than 1 that is not prime. The first 10 composite numbers are 4, 6, 8, 9, 10, 12, 14, 15, 16, 18.
Even integers	{0, ±2, ±4, ±6, ...} Integers that are perfectly divisible by 2.
Odd integers	{±1, ±3, ±5, ±7, ...} Integers that are not perfectly divisible by 2.
Squares	{(±1)^2, (±2)^2, (±3)^2, (±4)^2, ...} = {1, 4, 9, 16, ...} The squares of the nonzero integers.
Cubes	{(±1)^3, (±2)^3, (±3)^3, (±4)^3, ...} = {±1, ±8, ±27, ±64, ...} The cubes of the nonzero integers.

Common Mathematical Conventions and Terminology

All numbers used on the GMAT are **real numbers.** Imaginary values such as $\sqrt{-1}$ are not considered. Expressions that have no value, real or imaginary, such as $\frac{8}{0}$, $\frac{0}{0}$, 0^0, are not considered.

Exponents can be positive, negative, or zero. For example, $5^2 = 5 \times 5 = 25$, $5^{-2} = \frac{1}{5^2} = \frac{1}{25}$, and $5^0 = 1$.

When **function notation** is used on the test, it will be standard function notation. For example, $f(x) = 2x$ and $g(x) = x + 3\sqrt{x}$. Replacements for the variable are assumed to be all real numbers except for those that produce values not allowed. For the function called f, $f(x) = 2x$, all real numbers can be used for replacements. For the function called g, $g(x) = x + 3\sqrt{x}$, only nonnegative replacements are allowed for the variable. The composition of the two functions, g with f, is shown by $g(f(x))$, which requires you to evaluate $f(x)$ first, and then bring its value to the g function. For example, using the f and g functions described above, $g(f(50))$ has you first find $f(50)$. Since $f(x) = 2x$, then $f(50) = 2 \times 50 = 100$. Now use this value to replace the variables in the g function. Since $g(x) = x + 3\sqrt{x}$, then $g(100) = 100 + 3\sqrt{100} = 100 + 3(10) = 130$. Hence, $g(f(50)) = 130$.

Geometric Figures on the GMAT

- Lines are assumed to be straight and extend indefinitely in opposite directions.
- Triangles will have interior angle sums of 180 degrees.
- Angle measures will be assumed to be positive and less than or equal to 360 degrees.
- All closed geometrical figures are assumed to be convex.
- The area of a figure refers to the region enclosed by the figure.
- The perimeter of a figure, or circumference in the case of circles, refers to the distance around the figure.
- If A and B refer to two points on a line, AB can refer to the line containing A and B, the segment joining A and B, or the distance between A and B. Which one is being represented is determined by its context. However, the following convention is also used. The symbol $\overleftrightarrow{AB}$ is used to denote line AB, $\overline{AB}$ is used to denote the line segment AB, and AB with no symbol above it is used to denote the distance between A and B.
- Figures are drawn as accurately as possible except when it is specifically stated that the "figure is not drawn to scale."

The diagram below will illustrate some things that can and cannot be assumed from a figure.

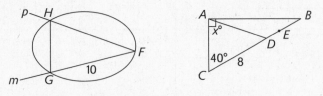

Note: Figures are not drawn to scale.

For the figures above, you _can assume_:

- *ABD, ACD, ABC,* and *FGH* are triangles
- *D* lies between *C* and *E* on segment *BC, E* lies between *D* and *B* on segment *BD*
- *CD* = 8

- $BC > 8$
- Angle C has a measure of 40 degrees
- Angle CAB has a measure of 90 degrees (indicated by the small square symbol at A)
- x has a measure less than 90 degrees
- The area of triangle ABC is greater than the area of triangle ABD
- F, G, and H lie on the closed curve
- H and F lie on line p, F and G lie on line m
- Lines p and m intersect at F
- $FG = 10$
- The area of the closed curve region is greater than the area of triangle FGH

For the figures above, since they were not drawn to scale, you _cannot assume_:

- $BD < 8$
- Angle $BAD < x$ degrees
- Area of triangle ABD < area triangle ACD
- Angles FGH, FHG, and HFG are each less than 90 degrees
- Line HG is parallel to line AC
- Area of the region between $\overline{FH}$ and the closed curve > area of the region between $\overline{GH}$ and the closed curve

Important Geometric Formulas

The table below is a reference with formulas of basic shapes: perimeter, area, and volume. The Pythagorean theorem follows the table to illustrate how the lengths of the sides of a right triangle relate to one another.

Shape	Illustration	Perimeter	Area
Square		$P = 4a$	$A = a^2$
Rectangle		$P = 2b + 2h$ or $P = 2(b + h)$	$A = bh$
Parallelogram		$P = 2a + 2b$ or $P = 2(a + b)$	$A = bh$
Triangle		$P = x + y + b$	$A = \dfrac{bh}{2}$ or $A = \dfrac{1}{2}bh$
Rhombus		$P = 4a$	$A = ah$
Trapezoid		$P = b_1 + b_2 + x + y$	$A = \dfrac{h(b_1 + b_2)}{2}$ or $A = \dfrac{1}{2}h(b_1 + b_2)$

Shape	Illustration	Perimeter	Area
Circle		$C = \pi d$ or $C = 2\pi r$	$A = \pi r^2$

Shape	Illustration	Surface Area	Volume
Cube		$SA = 6a^2$	$V = a^3$
Rectangular prism		$SA = 2(lw + lh + wh)$ or $SA = (\text{Perimeter of base})h + 2(\text{Area of base})$	$V = lwh$ or $V = (\text{Area of base})h$
Prisms in general		$SA = (\text{Perimeter of base})h + 2(\text{Area of base})$	$V = (\text{Area of base})h$
Cylinder		$SA = (\text{Perimeter of base, or Circumference})h + 2(\text{Area of base})$ or $SA = 2\pi rh + 2\pi r^2$ or $SA = 2\pi r(h + r)$	$V = (\text{Area of base})h$ or $V = \pi r^2 h$
Sphere		$SA = 4\pi r^2$	$V = \frac{4}{3}\pi r^3$

Pythagorean Theorem

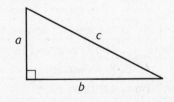

Pythagorean theorem: The sum of the squares of the legs of a right triangle equals the square of the hypotenuse ($a^2 + b^2 = c^2$).

Fraction-Decimal-Percent Equivalents

A time-saving tip is to try to memorize some of the following equivalents before you take the GMAT to eliminate unnecessary computations on the day of the exam.

$\frac{1}{100} = 0.01 = 1\%$

$\frac{1}{10} = 0.1 = 10\%$

$\frac{1}{5} = \frac{2}{10} = 0.2 = 0.20 = 20\%$

$\frac{3}{10} = 0.3 = 0.30 = 30\%$

$\frac{2}{5} = \frac{4}{10} = 0.4 = 0.40 = 40\%$

$\frac{1}{2} = \frac{5}{10} = 0.5 = 0.50 = 50\%$

$\frac{3}{5} = \frac{6}{10} = 0.6 = 0.60 = 60\%$

$\frac{7}{10} = 0.7 = 0.70 = 70\%$

$\frac{4}{5} = \frac{8}{10} = 0.8 = 0.80 = 80\%$

$\frac{9}{10} = 0.9 = 0.90 = 90\%$

$\frac{1}{4} = \frac{25}{100} = 0.25 = 25\%$

$\frac{3}{4} = \frac{75}{100} = 0.75 = 75\%$

$\frac{1}{3} = 0.33\frac{1}{3} = 33\frac{1}{3}\%$

$\frac{2}{3} = 0.66\frac{2}{3} = 66\frac{2}{3}\%$

$\frac{1}{8} = 0.125 = 0.12\frac{1}{2} = 12\frac{1}{2}\%$

$\frac{3}{8} = 0.375 = 0.37\frac{1}{2} = 37\frac{1}{2}\%$

$\frac{5}{8} = 0.625 = 0.62\frac{1}{2} = 62\frac{1}{2}\%$

$\frac{7}{8} = 0.875 = 0.87\frac{1}{2} = 87\frac{1}{2}\%$

$\frac{1}{6} = 0.16\frac{2}{3} = 16\frac{2}{3}\%$

$\frac{5}{6} = 0.83\frac{1}{3} = 83\frac{1}{3}\%$

$1 = 1.00 = 100\%$

$2 = 2.00 = 200\%$

$3\frac{1}{2} = 3.50 = 350\%$

Customary English and Metric System Measurements

Length	
English	**Metric**
12 inches (in) = 1 foot (ft)	10 millimeter (mm) = 1 centimeter (cm)
3 feet = 1 yard (yd)	10 centimeters = 1 decimeter (dm)
36 inches = 1 yard	10 decimeters = 1 meter (m)
5,280 feet = 1 mile (mi)	10 meters = 1 decameter (dam)
1,760 yards = 1 mile	10 decameters = 1 hectometer (hm)
	10 hectometers = 1 kilometer (km)
One meter is about 3 inches more than a yard	
One kilometer is about 0.6 mile	

Weight	
English	**Metric**
16 ounces (oz) = 1 pound (lb)	10 milligram (mg) = 1 centigram (cg)
2,000 pounds = 1 ton (T)	10 centigrams = 1 decigram (dg)
	10 decigrams = 1 gram (g)
	10 grams = 1 decagram (dag)
	10 decagrams = 1 hectogram (hg)
	10 hectograms = 1 kilogram (kg)
One kilogram is about 2.2 pounds	
1,000 kilograms is a metric ton	

Volume (capacity)	
English	**Metric**
1 cup (cp) = 8 fluid ounces (fl oz)	10 milliliter (ml or mL) = 1 centiliter (cl or cL)
2 cups = 1 pint (pt)	10 centiliters = 1 deciliter (dl or dL)
2 pints = 1 quart (qt)	10 deciliters = 1 liter (l or L)
4 quarts = 1 gallon (gal)	10 liters = 1 decaliter (dal or daL)
	10 decaliters = 1 hectoliter (hl or hL)
	10 hectoliters = 1 kiloliter (kl or kL)
One liter is a little more than 1 quart	

Arithmetic

Arithmetic Diagnostic Test

1. Which of the following are integers? $\frac{1}{2}$, -2, 0, 4, $\sqrt{25}$, $-\frac{15}{3}$, 7.5

2. Which of the following are rational numbers? 5.8, -4, $\sqrt{7}$, π, $2\frac{5}{8}$

3. List the prime numbers between 0 and 50.

4. List the perfect cubes between 1 and 100.

5. Which integers between 1 and 10 divide 2,730?

6. $3\left[3^2 + 2(4+1)\right] =$

7. $-4 + 8 =$

8. $-12 - 6 =$

9. $(-6)(-8) =$

10. $\dfrac{-48}{3} =$

11. Change $5\frac{3}{4}$ to an improper fraction.

12. Change $\frac{59}{6}$ to a mixed number in lowest terms.

13. $\frac{2}{7} + \frac{3}{5} =$

14. $1\frac{3}{8} + 2\frac{5}{6} =$

15. $11 - \frac{2}{3} =$

16. $6\frac{1}{8} - 3\frac{3}{4} =$

17. $-\frac{7}{8} - \frac{5}{9} =$

18. $-\frac{1}{6} \times \frac{1}{3} =$

19. $2\frac{3}{8} \times 1\frac{5}{6} =$

20. $-\frac{1}{4} \div \frac{9}{14} =$

21. $2\frac{3}{7} \div 1\frac{1}{4} =$

22. $\dfrac{1}{3 + \dfrac{2}{1 + \frac{1}{3}}} =$

23. Round 4.4584 to the nearest thousandth.

24. Round –3.6 to the nearest integer.

25. $0.08 + 1.3 + 0.562 =$

26. $0.45 - 0.003 =$

27. $8.001 \times 2.4 =$

28. $0.147 \div 0.7 =$

29. Change $\frac{3}{20}$ to a decimal.

30. Change 7% to a decimal.

31. Solve the proportion for x: $\frac{4}{x} = \frac{7}{5}$

32. Change $\frac{1}{8}$ to a percent.

33. 79% of 64 =

34. 40% of what is 20?

35. What percent of 45 is 30?

36. What is the percent increase of a rise in temperature from 80° to 100°?

37. $8^3 \times 8^7 =$

38. $9^5 \div 9^{-2} =$

39. $(5^3)^2 =$

40. $\sqrt{135}$ is between what two consecutive integers and to which is it closer?

41. Simplify $\sqrt{80}$.

42. $-\sqrt{9} =$

Arithmetic Diagnostic Test Answers

The diagnostic test explanations listed below include topic headings that correspond with step-by-step learning tools and examples to help you solve specific problem types. Corresponding topic headings can be found in the Arithmetic Review section on pages 295–328.

Sets of Numbers

1. $-2, 0, 4, \sqrt{25}, -\dfrac{15}{3}$

2. $5.8, -4, 2\dfrac{5}{8}$

3. 2, 3, 5, 7, 11, 13, 17, 19, 23, 29, 31, 37, 41, 43, 47

4. 8, 27, 64

Divisibility Rules

5. 2, 3, 5, 6, 7

Grouping Symbols and Order of Operations

6. 57

Integers

7. 4

8. –18

9. 48

10. –16

Fractions

11. $\dfrac{23}{4}$

12. $9\dfrac{5}{6}$

13. $\dfrac{31}{35}$

14. $4\dfrac{5}{24}$

15. $10\frac{1}{3}$

16. $2\frac{3}{8}$

17. $-\frac{103}{72} = -1\frac{31}{72}$

18. $-\frac{1}{18}$

19. $\frac{209}{48} = 4\frac{17}{48}$

20. $-\frac{7}{18}$

21. $\frac{68}{35} = 1\frac{33}{35}$

22. $\frac{2}{9}$

Decimals

23. 4.458

24. –4

25. 1.942

26. 0.447

27. 19.2024

28. 0.21

29. 0.15

30. 0.07

Ratios and Proportions

31. $x = \frac{20}{7}$ or $2\frac{6}{7}$

Percents

32. $12\frac{1}{2}\%$ or 12.5%

33. 50.56

34. 50

35. $66\frac{2}{3}\%$

36. 25%

Exponents

37. 8^{10}

38. 9^7

39. 5^6

Square Roots

40. 11 and 12, closer to 12

41. $4\sqrt{5}$

42. -3

Arithmetic Review Section

Preliminaries (Sets of Numbers)

You should already be familiar with the fundamentals of addition, subtraction, multiplication, and division of sets of numbers found under "Numbers Vocabulary" in the "Overview" section on page 286. Here are corresponding examples for your review.

Examples:

> **1.** Which of the following are integers? $\frac{1}{2}$, -2, 0, 4, $\sqrt{25}$, $-\frac{15}{3}$, 7.5

Integers are only whole numbers or their opposites. Only the numbers -2, 0, 4, $\sqrt{25} = 5$, and $-\frac{15}{3} = -5$ are integers.

> **2.** Which of the following are rational numbers? 5.8, -4, $\sqrt{7}$, π, $2\frac{5}{8}$

Any value that can be expressed as $\frac{\text{integer}}{\text{nonzero integer}}$, or as a decimal that either ends or has a repeating pattern is a rational number. Only the numbers 5.8, –4, and $2\frac{5}{8}$ are rational numbers.

> **3.** List the prime numbers between 0 and 50.

A prime number is an integer greater than 1 that can only be divided by itself or 1. Only the numbers 2, 3, 5, 7, 11, 13, 17, 19, 23, 29, 31, 37, 41, 43, and 47 satisfy this definition for integers between 1 and 50.

> **4.** List the perfect cubes between 1 and 100.

Cubes are integers raised to the third power. The perfect cubes between 1 and 100 come from $2^3 = 8$, $3^3 = 27$, and $4^3 = 64$. The value 1 is not between 1 and 100; thus, $1^3 = 1$ is not included in this list. The perfect cubes between 1 and 100 are 8, 27, and 64.

Practice: Sets of Numbers

1. Name a number less than 100, but greater than 1, that is both a perfect square and a perfect cube.

2. What is the largest sum that a composite number and a prime number can make if each is less than 97?

Answers: Sets of Numbers

1. 64

Only 64 is both a perfect square and a perfect cube and less than 100.

2. 185

The largest prime number less than 97 is 89 (90, 92, 94, 96 are divisible by 2, 91 is divisible by 7, 93 is divisible by 3, and 95 is divisible by 5) and the largest composite number less than 97 is 96. The largest sum of a prime number and a composite number each less than 97 is 89 + 96 = 185.

Divisibility Rules

The following divisibility chart will help you to quickly evaluate and rule out wrong answer choices.

If a number is divisible by	Divisibility Rule
2	it ends in 0, 2, 4, 6, or 8
3	the sum of its digits is divisible by 3
4	the number formed by the last two digits is divisible by 4
5	it ends in 0 or 5
6	it is divisible by 2 and 3 (use the rules for both)
7	N/A (no simple rule)
8	the number formed by the last three digits is divisible by 8
9	the sum of its digits is divisible by 9

Examples:

> **1.** Which integers between 1 and 10 divide 2,730?

2 – 2,730 ends in a 0

3 – the sum of the digits is 12, which is divisible by 3

5 – 2,730 ends in a 0

6 – the rules for 2 and 3 both work

7 – $2,730 \div 7 = 390$

Even though 2,730 is divisible by 10, 10 is not between 1 and 10.

> **2.** Which integers between 1 and 10 divide 2,648?

2 – 2,648 ends in 8

4 – 48, the number formed by the last two digits, is divisible by 4

8 – 648, the number formed by the last three digits is divisible by 8

Practice: Divisibility Rules

1. Which integers between 1 and 10 divide 4,620?

2. Which integers between 1 and 10 divide 13,131?

Answers: Divisibility Rules

1. 2, 3, 4, 5, 6, and 7

2 – 4,620 ends in a 0.

3 – the sum of the digits is 12, which is divisible by 3.

4 – the number formed by the last two digits, 20, is divisible by 4.

5 – 4,620 ends in 0.

6 – the number is divisible by 2 and 3.

7 – 4,620 ÷ 7 = 660.

2. 3 and 9

3 – the sum of the digits is 9 which is divisible by 3

9 – the sum of the digits is 9, which is divisible by 9

Grouping Symbols

Parentheses are used to group numbers or variables. Calculations inside parentheses take precedence and should be performed before any other operations.

$$50(2 + 6) = 50(8) = 400$$

If a parenthesis is preceded by a minus sign, the parentheses must be removed before calculations can be performed. To remove the parentheses, change the plus or minus sign of each term within the parentheses.

$$6 - (-3 + a - 2b + c) = 6 + 3 - a + 2b - c = 9 - a + 2b - c$$

Brackets and *braces* are also used to group numbers or variables. Sometimes, instead of brackets or braces, you'll see the use of larger parentheses:

$$((3+4)\cdot 5)+2$$

An expression using all three grouping symbols might look like this:

$$2\{1+[4(2+1)+3]\}$$

This expression can be simplified as follows (notice that you work from the inside out):

$$2\{1+[4(2+1)+3]\} = 2\{1+[4(3)+3]\}$$
$$= 2\{1+[12+3]\}$$
$$= 2\{1+[15]\}$$
$$= 2\{16\}$$
$$= 32$$

Order of Operations

If multiplication, division, exponents, addition, subtraction, or parentheses are all contained in one problem, the *order of operations* is as follows:

1. Parentheses
2. Exponents
3. Multiplication or Division in the order it occurs from left to right
4. Addition or Subtraction in the order it occurs from left to right

An easy way to remember the order of operations is Please Excuse My Dear Aunt Sally (Parentheses, Exponents, Multiplication, Division, Addition, Subtraction).

Examples:

1. $3[3^2 + 2\underline{(4+1)}] = 3[3^2 + 2(5)]$ (most inside parentheses first)

   $3[\underline{3^2} + 2(5)] = 3[9 + 2(5)]$ (exponents next)

   $3[9 + \underline{2(5)}] = 3[9 + 10]$ (mult./div. in order from left to right next)

   $3[\underline{9 + 10}] = 3[19]$ (add/subtract in order from left to right)

   $3[19] = 57$

2. $10 - 3 \times 6 + 10^2 + \underline{(6+1)} \times 4 = 10 - 3 \times 6 + 10^2 + 7 \times 4$ (parentheses first)

   $10 - 3 \times 6 + \underline{10^2} + 7 \times 4 = 10 - 3 \times 6 + 100 + 7 \times 4$ (exponents next)

   $10 - \underline{3 \times 6} + 100 + \underline{7 \times 4} = 10 - 18 + 100 + 28$ (mult./div. in order from left to right)

   $\underline{10 - 18} + 100 + 28 = -8 + 100 + 28$ (add/subtract in order from left to right)

   $\underline{-8 + 100} + 28 = 92 + 28$ (add/subtract in order from left to right)

   $92 + 28 = 120$

3. $-3^2 + (-2)^3 = -1(3)^2 + (-2)^3$ $\left(\begin{array}{l}\text{the exponent 2 only applies to the 3, while} \\ \text{the exponent 3 applies to the entire } (-2)\end{array}\right)$

   $\quad\quad\quad\quad\quad = -1(9) + (-8)$

   $\quad\quad\quad\quad\quad = -9 + (-8)$

   $\quad\quad\quad\quad\quad = -17$

Remember: An easy way to remember the order of operations is **P**lease **E**xcuse **M**y **D**ear **A**unt **S**ally (**P**arentheses, **E**xponents, **M**ultiplication, **D**ivision, **A**ddition, **S**ubtraction).

Practice: Order of Operations

Simplify:

1. $6 + 4 \times 3^2$

2. $3^2 + 6(4+1)$

3. $12 - 2(8+2) + 5$

4. $8[3(3^2 - 8) + 1]$

5. $6\{4[2(3+2) - 8] - 8\}$

Answers: Order of Operations

1. 42

   $6 + 4 \times \underline{3^2} = 6 + 4 \times 9$

   $6 + \underline{4 \times 9} = 6 + 36$

   $6 + 36 = 42$

2. 39

$$3^2 + 6\underline{(4+1)} = 3^2 + 6(5)$$
$$\underline{3^2} + 6(5) = 9 + 6(5)$$
$$9 + \underline{6(5)} = 9 + 30$$
$$9 + 30 = 39$$

3. -3

$$12 - 2\underline{(8+2)} + 5 = 12 - 2(10) + 5$$
$$12 - \underline{2(10)} + 5 = 12 - 20 + 5$$
$$\underline{12 - 20} + 5 = -8 + 5$$
$$-8 + 5 = -3$$

4. 32

$$8\left[3\left(\underline{3^2 - 8}\right) + 1\right] = 8\left[3\left(\underline{3^2} - 8\right) + 1\right]$$
$$8\left[3\left(\underline{3^2} - 8\right) + 1\right] = 8\left[3(9 - 8) + 1\right]$$
$$8\left[3\underline{(9 - 8)} + 1\right] = 8\left[3(1) + 1\right]$$
$$8\left[\underline{3(1)} + 1\right] = 8\left[3 + 1\right]$$
$$8\underline{[3 + 1]} = 8[4]$$
$$8[4] = 32$$

5. 0

$$6\left\{4\left[2\underline{(3+2)} - 8\right] - 8\right\} = 6\left\{4\left[2(5) - 8\right] - 8\right\}$$
$$6\left\{4\left[\underline{2(5)} - 8\right] - 8\right\} = 6\left\{4\left[\underline{2(5)} - 8\right] - 8\right\}$$
$$6\left\{4\left[\underline{2(5)} - 8\right] - 8\right\} = 6\left\{4[10 - 8] - 8\right\}$$
$$6\left\{4\underline{[10 - 8]} - 8\right\} = 6\left\{4[2] - 8\right\}$$
$$6\left\{\underline{4[2]} - 8\right\} = 6\{8 - 8\}$$
$$6\{\underline{8 - 8}\} = 6(0)$$
$$6(0) = 0$$

Integers

Number Line

On a ***number line,*** the numbers to the right of 0 are *positive*. Numbers to the left of 0 are *negative* as follows:

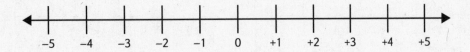

Given any two integers on a number line, the integer located furthest to the right is always larger, regardless of its sign (positive or negative). Note that fractions may also be placed on a number line and can be similarly compared.

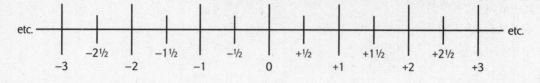

Examples:

For each pair of values, select the one with the greater value.

> **1.** $-8, -3$

$-3 > -8$ since -3 is farther to right on the number line.

> **2.** $0, -3\frac{1}{4}$

$0 > -3\frac{1}{4}$ since 0 is farther to the right on the number line.

Absolute Value

The *absolute value* of a number is its distance from 0 on a number line. It can also be interpreted as the value of the number disregarding its sign. The symbol denoting the absolute value of 5, for example, is |5|. Two vertical lines are placed around the number.

The absolute value of -5 is denoted as $|-5|$ and its value is 5.

Examples:

> **1.** $|-12| = 12$

> **2.** $\left|-3\frac{1}{2}\right| = 3\frac{1}{2}$

> **3.** $-|-5| = -5$

First find $|-5|$, which is 5; then find the negative of this result, which is -5.

Adding Two Integers with the Same Sign

To *add two integers with the same sign* (either both positive or both negative), add the absolute values of the integers and keep their same sign.

Examples:

> $\begin{array}{r} +5 \\ \textbf{1.} \underline{++7} \\ +12 \end{array}$ $\quad |+5| = 5, |+7| = 7, 5 + 7 = 12$

> $\begin{array}{r} -8 \\ \textbf{2.} \underline{+-3} \\ -11 \end{array}$ $\quad |-8| = 8, |-3| = 3, 3 + 8 = 11$

Adding Two Integers with Different Signs

To **add two integers with different signs** (one positive and one negative), subtract their absolute values and keep the sign of the integer with the greater absolute value.

Examples:

1. $-4 + 8 = 4$ $|-4| = 4, |8| = 8$ $8 - 4 = 4$ $|8| > |-4|$

2. $\begin{array}{r} +5 \\ +-7 \\ \hline -2 \end{array}$ $|+5| = 5, |-7| = 7$ $7 - 5 = 2$ $|-7| > |+5|$

Subtracting Positive and/or Negative Integers

To **subtract positive and/or negative integers,** just change the sign of the number being subtracted and then add.

Examples:

1. $-12 - 6 = -12 + -6 = -18$

2. $\begin{array}{r} +12 \\ -+4 \\ \hline \end{array}$ becomes $\begin{array}{r} +12 \\ +-4 \\ \hline +8 \text{ or } 8 \end{array}$

3. $\begin{array}{r} -14 \\ --4 \\ \hline \end{array}$ becomes $\begin{array}{r} -14 \\ ++4 \\ \hline -10 \end{array}$

When number values are positive, the "+" is dropped, $+5 = 5$.

Minus Sign Precedes a Parenthesis

If a **minus sign precedes a parenthesis,** it means everything within the parentheses is to be subtracted. Therefore, using the same rule as in subtraction of integers, simply change every sign within the parentheses to its opposite, and then add.

Examples:

1. $\begin{aligned} 9 - (3 - 5 + 7 - 6) &= 9 + [(-3) + 5 + (-7) + 6] \\ &= 9 + 1 \\ &= 10 \end{aligned}$

2. $\begin{aligned} 20 - (35 - 50 + 100) &= 20 + [(-35) + 50 + (-100)] \\ &= 20 + (-85) \\ &= -65 \end{aligned}$

Multiply or Divide Integers with Negative Signs

To multiply or divide integers with a negative sign use these rules:

- Multiplying or dividing with an odd number of negative signs will produce a negative answer.
- Multiplying or dividing with an even number of negative signs will produce a positive answer.

Examples:

1. $(-3)(8)(-5)(-1)(-2) = 240$

2. $(-3)(8)(-1)(-2) = -48$

3. $\dfrac{-64}{-2} = 32$

4. $\dfrac{-64}{2} = -32$

Zero Times Any Number

Zero times any number equals zero.

Examples:

1. $(0)(5) = 0$

2. $(-3)(0) = 0$

3. $(8)(9)(0)(3)(-4) = 0$

Zero Divided by a Nonzero Number

Similarly, zero divided by any *nonzero* number is zero.

Examples:

1. $0 \div 5$ also written as $\dfrac{0}{5} = 0$

2. $\dfrac{0}{-3} = 0$

Important note: Dividing by zero is "undefined" and is not permitted. $\dfrac{6}{0}$ and $\dfrac{0}{0}$ are not permitted because there are no values for these expressions. The answer is *not* zero.

Practice: Integers

1. Which is larger, $-11\frac{2}{3}$ or -12?

2. $|-4.6| =$

3. $-\left|-2\frac{1}{2}\right| =$

4. $-3 - \left[4 - 7 - (-9)\right] =$

5. $[5 - 8][4 - 9][-5 + 7] =$

6. $\dfrac{-32}{(10 - 18)} =$

7. $\dfrac{(11 - 13) + (14 - 12)}{(-3)(-2)} =$

8. $\dfrac{6(-1)(-2)}{100 - 10^2} =$

Answers: Integers

1. $-11\frac{2}{3}$

$-11\frac{2}{3}$ is the larger value since it is farther to the right on the number line.

2. 4.6

$|-4.6| = 4.6$ because absolute value is the value disregarding the sign.

3. $-2\frac{1}{2}$

Find $\left|-2\frac{1}{2}\right|$, then find the negative of that: $-\left|-2\frac{1}{2}\right| = -2\frac{1}{2}$.

4. -9

$$-3 - [4 - 7 - (-9)] = -3 - [4 + (-7) + 9]$$
$$= -3 - [6]$$
$$= -9$$

5. 30

$[5 - 8][4 - 9][-5 + 7] = [-3][-5][2] = 30$

6. 4

$$\dfrac{-32}{(10 - 18)} = \dfrac{-32}{-8} = 4$$

7. 0

$$\dfrac{(11 - 13) + (14 - 12)}{(-3)(-2)} = \dfrac{-2 + 2}{6} = \dfrac{0}{6} = 0$$

8. no such value

$$\dfrac{6(-1)(-2)}{100 - 10^2} = \dfrac{12}{100 - 100} = \dfrac{12}{0}$$

You cannot divide by zero, so no such value exists.

Fractions

Fractions compare two values. The ***numerator*** is written above the fraction bar and the ***denominator*** is written below the fraction bar. The fraction bar indicates division.

$$\dfrac{1}{2} \quad \dfrac{1 \text{ is the numerator}}{2 \text{ is the denominator}}$$

All rules for the arithmetic operations involving integers also apply to fractions.

Fractions may be *negative* as well as *positive*. However, negative fractions are typically written $-\frac{3}{4}$, not $\frac{-3}{4}$ or $\frac{3}{-4}$ (although they are all equal): $-\frac{3}{4} = \frac{-3}{4} = \frac{3}{-4}$.

A fraction with a value less than 1, like $\frac{3}{5}$, where the numerator is smaller than the denominator, is called a **proper fraction**. A fraction with a value greater than or equal to 1, like $\frac{12}{7}$ or $\frac{6}{6}$, where the numerator is larger than or equal to the denominator, is called an **improper fraction**.

Mixed Numbers

When a term contains both a whole number and a fraction, it is called *a **mixed number**.* For instance, $5\frac{1}{4}$ and $290\frac{3}{4}$ are both mixed numbers. To change an improper fraction to a mixed number, you divide the denominator into the numerator to get the whole number portion and then place the remainder over the divisor to get the fraction portion.

$$\frac{18}{7} = 2\frac{4}{7} \quad \begin{array}{l} \leftarrow \text{remainder} \\ \leftarrow \text{divisor} \end{array} \qquad \begin{array}{r} 2 \\ 7\overline{)18} \\ \underline{14} \\ 4 \end{array}$$

To change a mixed number to an improper fraction, you multiply the denominator of the fraction portion with the whole number, then add the numerator portion to that product, and then put that total over the original denominator.

$$4\frac{1}{2} = \frac{9}{2} \qquad \frac{2\times 4+1}{2} = \frac{9}{2}$$

Examples:

1. Change $5\frac{3}{4}$ to an improper fraction.

$$5\frac{3}{4} = \frac{23}{4} \qquad 4\times 5+3 = 23$$

2. Change $\frac{59}{6}$ to a mixed number.

$$\frac{59}{6} = 9\frac{5}{6} \qquad \begin{array}{r} 9 \\ 6\overline{)59} \\ \underline{54} \\ 5 \end{array}$$

Simplified Fractions

On the GMAT, fractions should be *simplified*. This is done by dividing both the numerator and denominator by the largest number that will divide both without a remainder.

Examples:

1. $\frac{30}{50} = \frac{30 \div 10}{50 \div 10} = \frac{3}{5}$

2. $\frac{8}{40} = \frac{8 \div 8}{40 \div 8} = \frac{1}{5}$

3. $\frac{9}{15} = \frac{9 \div 3}{15 \div 3} = \frac{3}{5}$

Changing the Denominator

The *denominator* of a fraction may be changed by multiplying both the numerator and the denominator by the same number.

Examples:

1. Change $\frac{1}{2}$ into tenths.

$$\frac{1}{2} = \frac{1 \times 5}{2 \times 5} = \frac{5}{10}$$

2. Change $\frac{3}{4}$ into fortieths.

$$\frac{3}{4} = \frac{3 \times 10}{4 \times 10} = \frac{30}{40}$$

Factors

Factors of a number are those whole numbers that divide the number with no remainder.

Examples:

1. What are the factors of 8?

$$8 = 1 \times 8 \text{ and } 8 = 2 \times 4$$

Therefore, the factors of 8 are 1, 2, 4, and 8.

2. What are the factors of 24?

$$24 = 1 \times 24, \ 24 = 2 \times 12, \ 24 = 3 \times 8, \ 24 = 4 \times 6$$

Therefore, the factors of 24 are 1, 2, 3, 4, 6, 8, 12, and 24.

Common Factors

Common factors are those factors that are the same for two or more numbers.

Examples:

1. What are the common factors of 6 and 8?

Number	List of factors
6	1 2 3 6
8	1 2 4 8

1 and 2 are common factors of 6 and 8.

Note: Some numbers may have many common factors.

2. What are the common factors of 24 and 36?

Number	List of factors
24	1 2 3 4 6 8 12 24
36	1 2 3 4 6 9 12 18 36

The common factors of 24 and 36 are 1, 2, 3, 4, 6, and 12.

Greatest Common Factor

The *greatest common factor* (GCF), also known as the greatest common divisor, is the largest factor common to two or more numbers.

Example:

1. What is the greatest common factor of 24 and 36?

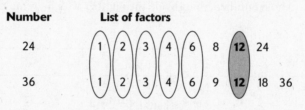

Number	List of factors
24	1 2 3 4 6 8 **12** 24
36	1 2 3 4 6 9 **12** 18 36

Notice that while, 1, 2, 3, 4, 6, and 12 are all common factors of 24 and 36, 12 is the greatest common factor.

Multiples

Multiples of a number are found by multiplying that number by 1, by 2, by 3, by 4, by 5, and so on.

Examples:

1. Multiples of 3 are: 3, 6, 9, 12, 15, 18, 21, and so on.

2. Multiples of 4 are: 4, 8, 12, 16, 20, 24, 28, 32, and so on.

3. Multiples of 7 are: 7, 14, 21, 28, 35, 42, 49, 56, and so on.

Common Multiples

Common multiples are those multiples that are the same for two or more numbers.

Example:

1. What are the common multiples of 2 and 3?

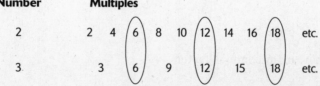

Number	Multiples
2	2 4 6 8 10 12 14 16 18 etc.
3	3 6 9 12 15 18 etc.

The common multiples of 2 and 3 are 6, 12, 18,... Notice that common multiples may go on indefinitely.

Least Common Multiple

The *least common multiple* (LCM) is the smallest multiple that is common to two or more numbers.

Example:

1. What is the least common multiple of 2 and 3?

Number	Multiples
2	2 4 **6** 8 10 12 14 16 18 etc.
3	3 **6** 9 12 15 18 etc.

The least common multiple of 2 and 3 is 6.

Least Common Denominator

To add fractions, you must first change all denominators to their *least common denominator* (LCD). The LCD is also known as the least common multiple of the denominators. After all the denominators are the same, add fractions by simply adding the numerators (notice the denominator remains the same).

Examples:

1. $\dfrac{2}{7}+\dfrac{3}{5}=\left(\dfrac{5}{5}\right)\left(\dfrac{2}{7}\right)+\left(\dfrac{7}{7}\right)\left(\dfrac{3}{5}\right)=\dfrac{10}{35}+\dfrac{21}{35}=\dfrac{31}{35}$

35 is the LCD and $\dfrac{2}{7}=\dfrac{10}{35}$, $\dfrac{3}{5}=\dfrac{21}{35}$

2. $\begin{aligned}\dfrac{3}{8}&=\dfrac{3}{8} \quad \left\{8 \text{ is the LCD and } \dfrac{3}{8}=\dfrac{3}{8}\right.\\ +\dfrac{1}{2}&=\dfrac{4}{8} \quad \left\{8 \text{ is the LCD and } \dfrac{1}{2}=\dfrac{4}{8}\right.\\ &\;\;\dfrac{7}{8}\end{aligned}$

3. $\dfrac{4}{11}+\dfrac{9}{11}=\dfrac{13}{11}$ or $1\dfrac{2}{11}$

Since the denominators are the same, it is not necessary to find an LCD.

Adding and Subtracting Positive and Negative Fractions

The rules for integers apply to adding or subtracting positive and negative fractions.

Examples:

1. $-\dfrac{1}{2}+\dfrac{1}{3}=-\dfrac{3}{6}+\dfrac{2}{6}=\dfrac{-3+2}{6}=-\dfrac{1}{6}$

2. $\begin{aligned}\dfrac{3}{4}&=\quad\dfrac{9}{12}\\ +\left(-\dfrac{1}{3}\right)&=+\left(-\dfrac{4}{12}\right)\\ &\quad\;\;\dfrac{5}{12}\end{aligned}$

3. $-\dfrac{7}{8} - \dfrac{2}{3} = -\dfrac{7}{8} + \left(-\dfrac{2}{3}\right)$

$\quad\quad = \left(\dfrac{3}{3}\right)\left(-\dfrac{7}{8}\right) + \left(\dfrac{8}{8}\right)\left(-\dfrac{2}{3}\right)$

$\quad\quad = \dfrac{-21}{24} + \dfrac{-16}{24}$

$\quad\quad = \dfrac{-37}{24}$ or $-1\dfrac{13}{24}$

4. $\quad\quad \dfrac{9}{10} = \dfrac{9}{10} = \dfrac{9}{10}$

$\quad -\left(-\dfrac{1}{5}\right) = +\dfrac{1}{5} = +\dfrac{2}{10}$

$\quad\quad\quad\quad\quad\quad \dfrac{11}{10}$ or $1\dfrac{1}{10}$

Adding Mixed Numbers

The rules for adding and subtracting integers also apply to mixed numbers. To **add mixed numbers,** add the fraction portions together, add the whole numbers, then combine the two results.

Example:

1. $1\dfrac{3}{8} + 2\dfrac{5}{6} = (1+2) + \left(\dfrac{3}{8} + \dfrac{5}{6}\right) \quad\quad \dfrac{3}{8} = \dfrac{9}{24}$ and $\dfrac{5}{6} = \dfrac{20}{24}$

$\quad\quad\quad\quad = 3 + \left(\dfrac{9}{24} + \dfrac{20}{24}\right)$

$\quad\quad\quad\quad = 3 + \dfrac{29}{24}$

$\quad\quad\quad\quad = 3 + 1\dfrac{5}{24}$

$\quad\quad\quad\quad = 4\dfrac{5}{24}$

Subtracting Mixed Numbers

When you subtract mixed numbers, sometimes you may have to "borrow" from the whole number, just as you sometimes borrow from the next column when subtracting ordinary numbers.

Examples:

1. $\begin{array}{r} \overset{\displaystyle 3\ \overset{7}{6}}{\cancel{4}\ \cancel{\dfrac{1}{6}}} \\ -2\dfrac{5}{6} \\ \hline 1\dfrac{2}{6} = 1\dfrac{1}{3} \end{array}$ $\leftarrow \begin{cases} \text{borrowed 1 in the form } \dfrac{6}{6} \text{ from the 4} \\ \text{and added it to the } \dfrac{1}{6} \text{ to get } \dfrac{7}{6} \end{cases}$

To subtract a mixed number from a whole number, you have to "borrow" from the whole number.

2.
$$6 = 5\frac{5}{5} \leftarrow \left\{ \text{borrow 1 in the form of } \frac{5}{5} \text{ from the 6} \right.$$
$$\frac{-3\frac{1}{5} = -3\frac{1}{5}}{2\frac{4}{5}}$$

3.
$$11 = 10\frac{3}{3} \leftarrow \left\{ \text{borrow 1 in the form of } \frac{3}{3} \text{ from the 11} \right.$$
$$\frac{-\frac{2}{3} = -\frac{2}{3}}{10\frac{1}{3}}$$

4. $6\frac{1}{8} - 3\frac{3}{4} = 6\frac{1}{8} - 3\frac{6}{8} = \overset{\overset{9}{\cancel{8}}}{\cancel{6}}\overset{5}{\cancel{}}\frac{\cancel{1}}{\cancel{8}} - 3\frac{6}{8} = 2\frac{3}{8}$

5. $-\frac{7}{8} - \frac{5}{9} = -\frac{63}{72} + \left(-\frac{40}{72}\right) \qquad \frac{7}{8} = \frac{63}{72}, \frac{5}{9} = \frac{40}{72}$
$$= -\frac{103}{72} \text{ or } -1\frac{31}{72}$$

Multiplying Fractions

The rules for multiplying and dividing of integers also apply to multiplying and dividing of fractions. To **multiply fractions,** simply multiply the numerators, and then multiply the denominators. Simplify if possible.

Examples:

1. $-\frac{1}{6} \times \frac{1}{3} = -\frac{1 \times 1}{6 \times 3} = -\frac{1}{18}$

2. $\left(-\frac{3}{4}\right)\left(-\frac{5}{7}\right) = +\frac{3 \times 5}{4 \times 7} = \frac{15}{28}$

3. $\frac{2}{3} \times \frac{5}{12} = \frac{10}{36}$ Simplify $\frac{10}{36}$ to $\frac{5}{18}$.

Notice the answer was simplified because $\frac{10}{36}$ was not in lowest terms.

Whole numbers can be written as fractions: $\left(3 = \frac{3}{1}, 4 = \frac{4}{1}, \text{ and so on}\right)$.

4. $3 \times \frac{3}{8} = \frac{3}{1} \times \frac{3}{8} = \frac{9}{8} = 1\frac{1}{8}$

When multiplying fractions, it is often possible to simplify the problem by **canceling.** To cancel, find a number that divides one numerator and one denominator. In the next example, 2 in the numerator and 12 in the denominator are both divisible by 2.

5. $\dfrac{\overset{1}{\cancel{2}}}{3} \times \dfrac{5}{\underset{6}{\cancel{12}}} = \dfrac{5}{18}$

Remember: You can cancel only when *multiplying* fractions.

6. $\dfrac{1}{4} \times \dfrac{2}{7} = \dfrac{1}{\underset{2}{\cancel{4}}} \times \dfrac{\overset{1}{\cancel{2}}}{7} = \dfrac{1}{14}$

7. $\left(-\dfrac{\overset{1}{\cancel{3}}}{\underset{2}{\cancel{8}}} \right) \times \left(-\dfrac{\overset{1}{\cancel{4}}}{\underset{3}{\cancel{9}}} \right) = \dfrac{1}{6}$

Multiplying Mixed Numbers

To *multiply mixed numbers,* change any mixed numbers or whole numbers to improper fractions, then multiply as previously shown.

Examples:

1. $2\dfrac{3}{8} \times 1\dfrac{5}{6} = \dfrac{19}{8} \times \dfrac{11}{6} = \dfrac{209}{48}$ or $4\dfrac{17}{48}$

2. $\left(-3\dfrac{1}{3} \right)\left(2\dfrac{1}{4} \right) = \left(-\dfrac{\overset{5}{\cancel{10}}}{\underset{1}{\cancel{3}}} \right)\left(\dfrac{\overset{3}{\cancel{9}}}{\underset{2}{\cancel{4}}} \right) = -\dfrac{15}{2}$ or $-7\dfrac{1}{2}$

Dividing Fractions or Mixed Numbers

To *divide fractions or mixed numbers* invert (turn upside down) the second fraction (the one "divided by") and multiply. Simplify where possible.

Examples:

1. $-\dfrac{1}{4} \div \dfrac{9}{14} = \left(-\dfrac{1}{\underset{2}{\cancel{4}}} \right)\left(\dfrac{\overset{7}{\cancel{14}}}{9} \right) = -\dfrac{7}{18}$

2. $6 \div 2\dfrac{1}{3} = \dfrac{6}{1} \div \dfrac{7}{3} = \dfrac{6}{1} \times \dfrac{3}{7} = \dfrac{18}{7}$ or $2\dfrac{4}{7}$

Complex Fractions

Sometimes a division-of-fractions problem may appear in the form below. Division problems in this form are called *complex fractions.*

$$\dfrac{\dfrac{3}{4}}{\dfrac{7}{8}}$$

The line separating the two fractions means "divided by." This problem may be rewritten as $\frac{3}{4} \div \frac{7}{8}$. Now follow the same procedure as previously shown.

$$\frac{3}{4} \div \frac{7}{8} = \frac{3}{\overset{}{\underset{1}{4}}} \times \frac{\overset{2}{8}}{7} = \frac{6}{7}$$

Some complex fractions require applying the order of operations.

Example:

> 1. $\dfrac{1}{3 + \dfrac{2}{1 + \frac{1}{3}}}$

This problem can be rewritten using grouping symbols.

$$\frac{1}{3 + \dfrac{2}{1 + \frac{1}{3}}} = 1 \div \left\{ 3 + \left[2 \div \left(1 + \frac{1}{3} \right) \right] \right\} \text{ Start with the most inside grouping.}$$

$$= 1 \div \left\{ 3 + \left[2 \div \left(\frac{4}{3} \right) \right] \right\} \text{ Do the next most inside grouping.}$$

$$= 1 \div \left\{ 3 + \left[\frac{\overset{1}{2}}{1} \times \frac{3}{\underset{2}{4}} \right] \right\}$$

$$= 1 \div \left\{ 3 + \left[\frac{3}{2} \right] \right\} \text{ Do the next most inside grouping.}$$

$$= 1 \div \left\{ \frac{9}{2} \right\}$$

$$= 1 \times \frac{2}{9}$$

$$= \frac{2}{9}$$

Practice: Fractions

1. When $4\frac{5}{8}$ is made into a fraction, what will be the numerator?

2. Change $-\frac{42}{16}$ into a mixed number in simplest form.

3. What is the GCF of 36 and 60?

4. What is the LCM of 12 and 16?

5. $\frac{3}{4} + \left(-\frac{1}{2} \right) =$

6. $\left(-\frac{3}{4} \right) + \frac{1}{3} + \left(-\frac{1}{6} \right) =$

7. $\frac{1}{6} - \left(-\frac{1}{3} \right) =$

8. $-\frac{7}{12} - \frac{5}{6} =$

9. $2\frac{1}{2} \times 3\frac{1}{4} =$

10. $-5\frac{1}{4} \times 3\frac{3}{7} =$

11. $\left(-2\frac{3}{4}\right) \div (-7) =$

12. $\dfrac{2 - \frac{7}{8}}{1 + \frac{3}{4}} =$

13. $\dfrac{1 + \dfrac{1}{2 + \frac{1}{2}}}{3} =$

Answers: Fractions

1. 37

   $4\frac{5}{8} = \frac{37}{8}$. The numerator is 37.

2. $-2\frac{5}{8}$

   $-\frac{42}{16} = -\frac{21}{8} = -2\frac{5}{8}$

3. 12

   Factors of 36 are 1, 2, 3, 4, 6, 9, **12**, 18, 36. Factors of 60 are 1, 2 ,3, 4, 5, 6, 10, **12**, 15, 20, 30, 60.

   The GCF of 36 and 60 is 12.

4. 48

   Multiples of 12 are 12, 24, 36, **48**, 60,... Multiples of 16 are 16, 32, **48**, 64,...

   The LCM of 12 and 16 is 48.

5. $\frac{1}{4}$

   $\frac{3}{4} + \left(-\frac{1}{2}\right) = \frac{3}{4} + \left(-\frac{2}{4}\right) = \frac{1}{4}$

6. $-\frac{7}{12}$

   $\left(-\frac{3}{4}\right) + \frac{1}{3} + \left(-\frac{1}{6}\right) = \left(-\frac{9}{12}\right) + \frac{4}{12} + \left(-\frac{2}{12}\right) = -\frac{7}{12}$

7. $\frac{1}{2}$

   $\frac{1}{6} - \left(-\frac{1}{3}\right) = \frac{1}{6} + \frac{1}{3} = \frac{1}{6} + \frac{2}{6} = \frac{3}{6} = \frac{1}{2}$

8. $-\frac{17}{12}$ or $-1\frac{5}{12}$

   $-\frac{7}{12} - \frac{5}{6} = -\frac{7}{12} + \left(-\frac{5}{6}\right) = -\frac{7}{12} + \left(-\frac{10}{12}\right) = -\frac{17}{12}$ or $-1\frac{5}{12}$

9. $\dfrac{65}{8}$ or $8\dfrac{1}{8}$

$$2\dfrac{1}{2}\times 3\dfrac{1}{4}=\left(\dfrac{5}{2}\right)\left(\dfrac{13}{4}\right)=\dfrac{65}{8}\ \text{or}\ 8\dfrac{1}{8}$$

10. -18

$$-5\dfrac{1}{4}\times 3\dfrac{3}{7}=\left(-\dfrac{\overset{3}{\cancel{21}}}{\underset{1}{\cancel{4}}}\right)\left(\dfrac{\overset{6}{\cancel{24}}}{\underset{1}{\cancel{7}}}\right)=-18$$

11. $\dfrac{11}{28}$

$$\left(-2\dfrac{3}{4}\right)\div(-7)=\left(-\dfrac{11}{4}\right)\div\left(-\dfrac{7}{1}\right)=\left(-\dfrac{11}{4}\right)\left(-\dfrac{1}{7}\right)=\dfrac{11}{28}$$

12. $\dfrac{9}{14}$

$$\dfrac{2-\dfrac{7}{8}}{1+\dfrac{3}{4}}=\dfrac{1\dfrac{1}{8}}{1\dfrac{3}{4}}=\dfrac{9}{8}\div\dfrac{7}{4}=\left(\dfrac{9}{\underset{2}{\cancel{8}}}\right)\left(\dfrac{\overset{1}{\cancel{4}}}{7}\right)=\dfrac{9}{14}$$

13. $\dfrac{7}{15}$

$$\dfrac{1+\dfrac{1}{2+\dfrac{1}{2}}}{3}=\dfrac{1+\dfrac{1}{\frac{5}{2}}}{3}=\dfrac{1+\left(1\div\dfrac{5}{2}\right)}{3}=\dfrac{1+\left(1\times\dfrac{2}{5}\right)}{3}=\dfrac{1+\dfrac{2}{5}}{3}=\dfrac{1\dfrac{2}{5}}{3}=\dfrac{\frac{7}{5}}{3}=\dfrac{7}{5}\div\dfrac{3}{1}=\dfrac{7}{5}\times\dfrac{1}{3}=\dfrac{7}{15}$$

Decimals

Each position in any decimal number has **_place value._** For instance, in the number 485.03, the 4 is in the hundreds place, the 8 is in the tens place, the 5 is in the ones place, the 0 is in the tenths place, and the 3 is in the hundredths place. The following chart will help you identify place value.

millions	hundred thousands	ten thousands	thousands	hundreds	tens	ones	tenths	hundredths	thousandths	ten thousandths	hundred thousandths
							1/10	1/100	1/1,000	1/10,000	1/100,000
1,000,000	100,000	10,000	1,000	100	10	1	0.1	0.01	0.001	0.0001	0.00001
10^6	10^5	10^4	10^3	10^2	10^1	10^0	10^{-1}	10^{-2}	10^{-3}	10^{-4}	10^{-5}
				4	8	5	0	3			

Rounding Off

To *round off* any **positive number:**

1. Underline the place value to which you're rounding off.
2. Look to the immediate right (one place) of the underlined place value.
3. Identify the number (the one to the right). If it is 5 or higher, round off the underlined place value up 1. If the number (the one to the right) is 4 or less, leave your underlined place value as it is and change all the other numbers to the right of it to zeros, or drop them if it is to the right of the decimal point.

To *round off* any **negative number:**

1. Take the absolute value of the number.
2. Do the 3 steps as above.
3. Replace the negative sign on the number.

Examples:

> **1.** Round 4.4584 to the nearest thousandth.

The 8 is in the thousandth place. To its right is a 4. Thus, the 8 is left unchanged and to its right the digits are dropped. The rounded off answer becomes 4.458.

> **2.** Round 3456.12 to the nearest ten.

The 5 is in the tens place. To its right is a 6. Thus, the 5 is increased by 1 and the digits until the decimal become zeros, then the remaining digits are dropped. The rounded-off answer is 3460.

> **3.** Round –3.6 to the nearest integer.

|–3.6| = 3.6. Rounding to the nearest integer is the same as rounding to the nearest one. The 3 is in the one's place and to its right is a 6. Thus, 3.6 rounded to the nearest one is 4. Therefore, –3.6 rounded to the nearest integer is –4.

Fractions Written in Decimal Form

Fractions and mixed numbers can be written in decimal form (**decimal fractions**) by using a *decimal point.* All numbers to the left of the decimal point are whole numbers. All numbers to the right of the decimal point are fractions with denominators of powers of 10 (10^1, 10^2, 10^3, …).

Examples:

> **1.** $0.6 = \dfrac{6}{10} = \dfrac{3}{5}$

> **2.** $3.25 = 3\dfrac{25}{100} = 3\dfrac{1}{4}$

Adding and Subtracting Decimals

To ***add or subtract decimals,*** line up the decimal points and then add or subtract in the same manner you would add or subtract regular numbers. Placing zeros at the right of the number can make the problem look better.

Examples:

> **1.** $0.08 + 1.3 + 0.562 = $
> $$\begin{array}{r} 0.080 \\ 1.300 \\ +\,0.562 \\ \hline 1.942 \end{array}$$

$$2. \quad 0.45 - 0.003 = 0.4 \overset{4}{\cancel{5}} \overset{10}{\cancel{0}}$$
$$\underline{-0.0\,0\,3}$$
$$0.4\,4\,7$$

A whole number has an understood decimal point to its right.

$$3. \quad 17 - 8.43 = 1\overset{6}{\cancel{7}}.\overset{9}{\cancel{0}}\overset{10}{\cancel{0}}$$
$$\underline{-8\,.\,4\,3}$$
$$8\,.\,5\,7$$

Multiplying Decimals

To *multiply decimals,* multiply as usual. Place the decimal point in the answer so that the number of digits to the right of the decimal point is equal to the sum of the number of digits to the right of the decimal point in both numbers multiplied (the multiplier and multiplicand). It is sometimes necessary to insert zeros immediately to the right of the decimal point in the answer to have the correct number of digits.

Examples:

1. $\quad 8.001 \quad \leftarrow \{ 3$ digits to the right of the decimal point

    $\quad \underline{\times 2.4} \quad \leftarrow \{ 1$ digit to the right of the decimal point

    $\quad 32004$

    $\quad \underline{16002}$

    $\quad 19.2024 \quad \begin{cases} \text{decimal point placed so there is the same number of} \\ \text{digits to the right of the decimal point } (1+3=4) \end{cases}$

2. $\quad 3.02 \quad \leftarrow \{ 2$ digits to the right of the decimal point

    $\quad \underline{\times 0.004} \quad \leftarrow \{ 3$ digits to the right of the decimal point

    $\quad 0.01208 \quad \begin{cases} \text{zero inserted on the left so that there is the same number of} \\ \text{digits to the right of the decimal point } (2+3=5) \end{cases}$

Dividing Decimals

To *divide decimals,* divide as usual, except that if the *divisor* (the number you're dividing by) has a decimal, move it to the right as many places as necessary until it's a whole number. Then move the decimal point in the *dividend* (the number being divided into) to the right the same number of places. Sometimes you may have to insert zeros in the *dividend* (the number inside the division bracket).

Examples:

1. $0.147 \div 0.7$ becomes $0.7\overline{)0.147} = 7\overline{)1.47}^{\,0.21}$

The decimal point was moved to the right 1 place in each number.

2. $0.002\overline{)26.} = 2\overline{)26000.}^{\,13000.}$

The decimal point was moved 3 places to the right in each number. This required inserting 3 zeros in the dividend.

Changing a Fraction to a Decimal

To *change a fraction to a decimal,* divide the numerator by the denominator. Every fraction, when changed to a decimal, either terminates (comes to an end) or has a repeating pattern in its decimal portion.

Examples:

Change each fraction into its decimal name.

1. $\dfrac{3}{20}$ becomes $20\overline{)3.00}^{\displaystyle 0.15} = 0.15$

2. $\dfrac{5}{8}$ becomes $8\overline{)5.000}^{\displaystyle 0.625} = 0.625$

3. $\dfrac{7}{12}$ becomes $12\overline{)7.00000}^{\displaystyle 0.58333} = 0.58333\ldots$ or $0.58\overline{3}$

Practice: Decimals

1. Round −123.456 to the nearest hundredth.

2. $12.005 + 6.3 =$

3. $-4.45 - (-3.617) =$

4. $(-3.5)(0.001) =$

5. $\dfrac{-16.2}{0.81} =$

6. Change $\dfrac{4}{15}$ into a decimal.

Answers: Decimals

1. −123.46

   $|-123.456| = 123.456$. The 5 is in the hundredth place and to its right is a 6; 5 becomes 6 and to its right the digits are dropped. Replace the negative sign on the number.

2. 18.305

   $$12.005 + 6.3 = \begin{array}{r} 12.005 \\ +\,6.300 \\ \hline 18.305 \end{array}$$

3. −0.833

   $-4.45 - (-3.617) = -4.45 + 3.617$

   $|-4.45| > |3.617|$; therefore, the result will be negative and the arithmetic is to subtract the absolute values.

   $$\begin{array}{r} 4.450 \\ -\,3.617 \\ \hline 0.833 \end{array}$$

4. −0.0035

$$-3.5 \leftarrow \{\text{total of 4 digits that are to the right of the decimal points}$$
$$\underline{\times 0.001} \swarrow$$
$$-0.0035 \quad \begin{cases} \text{decimal point placed so there is the same number of digits to the right} \\ \text{of the decimal point, which required inserting two zeros to the left of the 3} \end{cases}$$

5. −20

$$0.81\overline{)16.2} = 81\overline{)1620}^{\,20}$$

Each number had its decimal point moved 2 places to the right, which required inserting one zero in the dividend.

6. $0.2\bar{6}$

$$
\begin{array}{r}
0.26.... \\
15\overline{)4.0000} \\
\underline{30} \\
100 \\
\underline{90} \\
100
\end{array}
$$

The "6" keeps repeating, so a bar is placed over the 6.

Ratios and Proportions

A *ratio* is a comparison of two values usually written in fraction form. The ratio of 3 to 5 can be expressed as 3:5 or $\frac{3}{5}$. A *proportion* is a statement that states that two ratios are equal. Because $\frac{5}{10}$ and $\frac{4}{8}$ both have values of $\frac{1}{2}$, it can be stated that $\frac{5}{10} = \frac{4}{8}$.

Cross-Products Fact

In a proportion, the cross products (multiplying across the equal sign) always produce equal answers. In the example of $\frac{5}{10} = \frac{4}{8}$, $5 \times 8 = 10 \times 4$.

You can use this cross-products fact to solve proportions.

Examples:

1. Solve for x: $\frac{4}{x} = \frac{7}{5}$.

Applying the cross-products fact, you get

$$7x = (4)(5)$$
$$7x = 20$$
$$x = \frac{20}{7} = 2\frac{6}{7}$$

2. Solve for x: $\frac{x}{100} = \frac{4}{25}$.

Applying the cross-products fact, you get

$$25x = (4)(100)$$
$$25x = 400$$
$$x = \frac{400}{25} = 16$$

Practice: Ratios and Proportions

1. Express the ratio of 15 to 29 in two different ways.

2. Solve for x: $\frac{x}{12} = \frac{3}{4}$.

Answers: Ratios and Proportions

1. 15:29 or $\frac{15}{29}$

2. 9

$$\frac{x}{12} = \frac{3}{4}$$
$$4x = (12)(3)$$
$$4x = 36$$
$$x = \frac{36}{4}$$
$$x = 9$$

Percents

The symbol for *percent* is %. The word percent means hundredths (per hundred). The expression 37% is read as 37 hundredths and can be expressed either as the fraction $\frac{37}{100}$ or decimal 0.37.

Changing Decimals to Percents

Decimals to Percents	Steps to change decimals to percents	Examples: Changing decimals to percents
	1. Move the decimal point two places to the right. 2. Insert a percent sign.	1. 0.75 = 75% 2. 0.005 = 0.5% 3. 1.85 = 185% 4. 20.3 = 2,030%
Percents to Decimals	**Steps to change percents to decimals:**	**Examples: Changing percents to decimals**
	1. Eliminate the percent sign. 2. Move the decimal point two places to the left. 3. Notice that sometimes inserting zeros will be necessary as in Examples 1 and 3.	1. 7% = 0.07 2. 23% = 0.23 3. 0.2% = 0.002

Changing Fractions to a Percent

There are two methods for changing a fraction to a percent.

Method 1: Changing Fractions to a Percent

1. Change the fraction to a decimal.

2. Change the decimal to a percent.

Examples:

Change each fraction into a percent.

1. $\frac{1}{8}$ $\frac{1}{8} = 0.125 = 12.5\%$ or $12\frac{1}{2}\%$

2. $\frac{2}{5}$ $\frac{2}{5} = 0.4 = 40\%$

3. $\frac{5}{2}$ $\frac{5}{2} = 2.5 = 250\%$

Method 2: Changing Fractions to a Percent

1. Create a proportion that sets the fraction equal to $\frac{x}{100}$.
2. Solve the proportion for x. Place a percent sign next to the x.

Examples:

Change each fraction into a percent.

1. $\frac{3}{8}$

$$\frac{3}{8} = \frac{x}{100}$$
$$8x = 300$$
$$x = \frac{300}{8} = 37\frac{1}{2} \text{ or } 37.5$$
$$\frac{3}{8} = 37\frac{1}{2}\% \text{ or } 37.5\%$$

2. $\frac{2}{3}$

$$\frac{2}{3} = \frac{x}{100}$$
$$3x = 200$$
$$x = \frac{200}{3} = 66\frac{2}{3}$$
$$\frac{2}{3} = 66\frac{2}{3}\%$$

Tip: To eliminate many unnecessary computations and save you time, try to make time to memorize important equivalents presented in "Fraction-Decimal-Percent Equivalents" at the beginning of this chapter (page 290).

Percentage-Type Problems

Percentage-type problems are of the form A is $B\%$ of C. If the B and C are known, the process is simply to multiply the B-percent value with the C-value.

Examples:

---
1. What is 79% of 64?

Using fractions: 79% of $64 = \dfrac{79}{100} \times \dfrac{64}{1} = \dfrac{5056}{100}$ or 50.56

Using decimals: 79% of $64 = (0.79)(64) = 50.56$

---
2. What is 15% of 50?

Using fractions: 15% of $50 = \dfrac{\overset{3}{\cancel{15}}}{\underset{\underset{2}{20}}{\cancel{100}}} \times \dfrac{\overset{5}{\cancel{50}}}{1} = \dfrac{15}{2} = 7\dfrac{1}{2}$ or 7.5

Using decimals: 15% of $50 = 0.15 \times 50 = 7.5$

---
3. What is $33\dfrac{1}{3}\%$ of 36?

The fraction method works best in this case.

$33\dfrac{1}{3}\%$ of $36 = \dfrac{1}{\underset{1}{\cancel{3}}} \times \dfrac{\overset{12}{\cancel{36}}}{1} = \dfrac{12}{1} = 12$

If the A value is known and one of the B or C values is unknown, then there are two methods that make solving the problem easier.

Equation and Proportion Methods

Method 1 - Percentage-Type Problems: Equation Method

1. Turn the question word-for-word into an equation. (Change percents to decimals or fractions, whichever you find easier.)
2. Solve the equation. (To review solving simple equations, see pages 336–337 in the Algebra section).

Method 2 - Percentage-Type Problems: Proportion Method

1. Use x to replace the unknown value.
2. Replace *is* with an *equal sign* (=) and replace *of* with *multiplication*. The proportion will look like this:

$$\frac{\%\text{-number}}{100} = \frac{\text{"is"-number}}{\text{"of"-number}}$$

Examples:

---
1. 40% of what is 20?
---

equation method	proportion method
$0.4(x) = 20$	$\dfrac{40}{100} = \dfrac{20}{x}$
$x = \dfrac{20}{0.4}$	$40x = 2000$
$x = 50$	$x = 50$

Therefore, 40% of 50 is 20.

2. What percent of 45 is 30?

equation method	proportion method
$\left(\dfrac{x}{100}\right)(45)=30$	$\dfrac{x}{100}=\dfrac{30}{45}$
$\dfrac{45}{100}x=30$	$45x=3000$
$x=\left(\dfrac{\overset{2}{\cancel{30}}}{1}\right)\left(\dfrac{100}{\underset{3}{\cancel{45}}}\right)$	$x=\dfrac{3000}{45}$
$x=\dfrac{200}{3}$ or $66\dfrac{2}{3}$	$x=\dfrac{200}{3}$ or $66\dfrac{2}{3}$

Therefore, $66\dfrac{2}{3}\%$ of 45 is 30.

Percent Change

To find *percent change* (increase or decrease), use this formula:

$$\frac{\text{amount of change}}{\text{starting amount}}\times100\%=\text{percent change}$$

Examples:

1. What is the percent increase of a rise in temperature from 80° to 100°?

The amount of change is the difference between 100 and 80 or 20.

$$\frac{\text{amount of change}}{\text{starting amount}}\times100\%=\frac{\overset{1}{\cancel{20}}}{\underset{4}{\cancel{80}}}\times100\%=25\%\text{ increase}$$

2. What is the percent decrease of Jon's salary if it went from $150 per hour to $100 per hour?

$$\frac{\text{amount of change}}{\text{starting amount}}\times100\%=\frac{\overset{1}{\cancel{50}}}{\underset{3}{\cancel{150}}}\times100\%=\left(\frac{100}{3}\right)\%=33\frac{1}{3}\%\text{ decrease}$$

3. What is the percent change from 2,100 to 1,890?

$$\frac{\text{amount of change}}{\text{starting amount}}\times100\%=\frac{\overset{1}{\cancel{210}}}{\underset{10}{\cancel{2,100}}}\times100\%=10\%\text{ change}$$

Note: The terms percentage rise, percentage difference, and percentage change are the same as percent change.

Practice: Percents

1. Change $\dfrac{11}{12}$ into a percent.

2. Change 0.25% into a decimal.

3. 25% of 72 is what?

4. $16\frac{2}{3}\%$ of what is 15?

5. What percent of 60 is 45?

6. Which is greater, the percent change from 5 to 8 or the percent change from 8 to 5?

Answers: Percent

1. $91\frac{2}{3}\%$

$$\frac{11}{12} = \frac{x}{100}$$
$$12x = 1100$$
$$x = \frac{\overset{275}{\cancel{1100}}}{\underset{3}{\cancel{12}}} = 91\frac{2}{3}$$
$$\frac{11}{12} = 91\frac{2}{3}\%$$

2. 0.0025

   0.25% = 0.0025 Drop the %-sign and move the decimal 2 places to the left.

3. 18

   fraction method: $25\% = \frac{1}{4}$ decimal method: $25\% = 0.25$

   $$\left(\frac{1}{\underset{1}{\cancel{4}}}\right)\left(\frac{\overset{18}{\cancel{72}}}{1}\right) = 18 \qquad\qquad (0.25)(72) = 18$$

4. 90

   Making $16\frac{2}{3}\%$ into a fraction is the best way to begin.

   $$16\frac{2}{3}\% = \left(\frac{\overset{1}{\cancel{50}}}{3}\right)\left(\frac{1}{\underset{2}{\cancel{100}}}\right) = \frac{1}{6}$$

   equation method   proportion method

   $$\left(\frac{1}{6}\right)x = 15 \qquad\qquad \frac{16\frac{2}{3}}{100} = \frac{15}{x}$$
   $$x = \left(\frac{15}{1}\right)\left(\frac{6}{1}\right) \qquad\qquad \frac{1}{6} = \frac{15}{x}$$
   $$x = 90 \qquad\qquad x = (15)(6)$$
   $$x = 90$$

   $16\frac{2}{3}\%$ of 90 is 15.

5. 75%

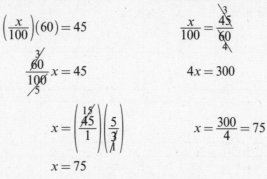

equation method   proportion method

75% of 60 is 45. In this example, in the proportion method, once $\frac{45}{60}$ was simplified to $\frac{3}{4}$, you may have recognized that the percent is 75%.

6. percent change from 5 to 8

Percent change from 5 to 8: $\dfrac{\text{amount of change}}{\text{starting amount}} \times 100\% = \dfrac{3}{5} \times 100\% = 60\%$ change

Percent change from 8 to 5: $\dfrac{\text{amount of change}}{\text{starting amount}} \times 100\% = \dfrac{3}{8} \times 100\% = 37\frac{1}{2}\%$ change

The percent change from 5 to 8 is greater than the percent change from 8 to 5.

Exponents

An *exponent* is a positive, negative, or zero number placed above and to the right of a quantity. The quantity is known as the base, and the exponent expresses the power to which the base is to be raised. In 4^3, 4 is the base and 3 is the exponent. It shows that 4 is to be used as a factor three times: $4^3 = (4)(4)(4)$ and is read as *four to the third power* or *four cubed*.

Examples:

1. $2^5 = (2)(2)(2)(2)(2) = 32$

2. $(-3)^3 = (-3)(-3)(-3) = -27$

3. $\left(-\dfrac{1}{4}\right)^2 = \left(-\dfrac{1}{4}\right)\left(-\dfrac{1}{4}\right) = \dfrac{1}{16}$

More Exponents

Remember that $x^1 = x$ for all replacements of x and $x^0 = 1$ as long as $x \neq 0$.

Examples:

1. $(-5)^0 = 1$

2. $-6^0 = -1$ (in this case, the 0 exponent is only applied to the 6 since the negative sign was not in a parentheses as in example 1 above.)

3. $(2.4)^0 = 1$

4. $6^1 = 6$

Negative Exponents

If the **exponent is negative**, such as 3^{-2}, then the base and its exponent may be dropped under the number 1 in a fraction to remove the negative sign.

Examples:

> **1.** $6^{-1} = \dfrac{1}{6^{1}} = \dfrac{1}{6}$

> **2.** $3^{-2} = \dfrac{1}{3^{2}} = \dfrac{1}{9}$

> **3.** $(-2)^{-3} = \dfrac{1}{(-2)^{3}} = \dfrac{1}{-8} = -\dfrac{1}{8}$

Multiplying Two Numbers with the Same Base

To multiply two numbers with the same base, you add their exponents and keep the same base.

Examples:

> **1.** $8^{3} \times 8^{7} = 8^{3+7} = 8^{10}$

> **2.** $(-2)^{6}(-2)^{-3} = (-2)^{6+(-3)} = (-2)^{3}$

Dividing Two Numbers with the Same Base

To divide two numbers with the same base, you subtract the exponent on the dividing number from the exponent on the number being divided.

Examples:

> **1.** $9^{5} \div 9^{-2} = 9^{5-(-2)} = 9^{5+2} = 9^{7}$

> **2.** $\dfrac{3^{7}}{3^{4}} = 3^{7-4} = 3^{3}$

Exponents Base and Exponent to a Power

To raise an expression involving a base and exponent to a power, keep the base and use the product of the exponent and the power as the new exponent.

Examples:

> **1.** $\left(5^{3}\right)^{2} = 5^{(2)(3)} = 5^{6}$

> **2.** $\left[(-4)^{-4}\right]^{-2} = (-4)^{(-4)(-2)} = (-4)^{8}$

Practice: Exponents

Simplify each of the following into expressions without exponents.

1. $\left(-\frac{1}{4}\right)^3$

2. 5.6^0

3. -3^0

4. $(-7)^1$

5. 4^{-3}

6. $(-5)^{-2}$

Express each of the following with a base and one exponent.

7. $(7^6)(7^2)$

8. $\dfrac{(-3)^{12}}{(-3)^{-4}}$

9. $(6^3)^5$

Answers: Exponents

1. $-\dfrac{1}{64}$

$$\left(-\frac{1}{4}\right)^3 = \left(-\frac{1}{4}\right)\left(-\frac{1}{4}\right)\left(-\frac{1}{4}\right) = -\frac{1}{64}$$

2. 1

Any nonzero number to the zero power is 1.

3. -1

The zero exponent only is applied to the 3 and $3^0 = 1$.

4. -7

Any value to the 1st power is that value.

5. $\dfrac{1}{64}$

$$4^{-3} = \frac{1}{4^3} = \frac{1}{(4)(4)(4)} = \frac{1}{64}$$

6. $\dfrac{1}{25}$

$$(-5)^{-2} = \frac{1}{(-5)^2} = \frac{1}{(-5)(-5)} = \frac{1}{25}$$

7. 7^8

$$(7^6)(7^2) = 7^{6+2} = 7^8$$

8. $(-3)^{16}$

$$\frac{(-3)^{12}}{(-3)^{-4}}=(-3)^{12-(-4)}=(-3)^{12+4}=(-3)^{16}$$

9. 6^{15}

$$(6^3)^5=6^{(5)(3)}=6^{15}$$

Square Roots

Square Roots of Perfect Squares

The square roots of *perfect squares* have exact answers. $\sqrt{5^2}=\sqrt{25}=5$ and $\sqrt{(-4)^2}=\sqrt{16}=4$. If a negative sign precedes a square root, the answer is the negative of the square root.

Example:

1. $-\sqrt{9}=-3$

2. $-\sqrt{(-4)^2}=-\sqrt{16}=-4$

Square Roots of Nonperfect Squares

To find the square root of a number that is *not a perfect square,* it is necessary to find an approximate answer by using the procedure given in the examples below.

Example:

1. Between what two consecutive integers is $\sqrt{135}$ and to which is it closer?

$$\sqrt{135} \text{ is between } \sqrt{121} \text{ and } \sqrt{144}$$

$$\sqrt{121}<\sqrt{135}<\sqrt{144}, \text{ and } \sqrt{121}=11, \sqrt{144}=12$$
$$11<\sqrt{135}<12$$

Since 135 is closer to 144 than 121, $\sqrt{135}$ is closer to 12 than to 11.

Tip: After calculating the square root, use your knowledge of rounding off to determine the desired place value.

Simplifying a Square Root

Sometimes you will have to *simplify square roots,* or write them in simplest form. In fractions, $\frac{2}{4}$ can be simplified to $\frac{1}{2}$. In square roots, $\sqrt{32}$ can be simplified to $4\sqrt{2}$.

Methods to Simplify a Square Root	
Method 1	**Method 2**
Factor the number under the $\sqrt{}$ into two factors, one of which is the largest possible perfect square that divides the number. (Perfect squares are 1, 4, 9, 16, 25, 36, 49, ...)	Completely factor the number under the $\sqrt{}$ into prime factors and then simplify by bringing out any factors that came in pairs.

Examples:

1. Simplify $\sqrt{32}$.

Method 1.

$\sqrt{32} = \sqrt{16 \times 2}$

$\qquad = \sqrt{16} \times \sqrt{2}$

Take the square root of the perfect square number

$\qquad = 4 \times \sqrt{2}$

Finally, write it as a single expression.

$\qquad = 4\sqrt{2}$

Method 2.

$\sqrt{32} = \sqrt{2 \times 16}$

$\qquad = \sqrt{2 \times 2 \times 8}$

$\qquad = \sqrt{2 \times 2 \times 2 \times 4}$

$\qquad = \sqrt{2 \times 2 \times 2 \times 2 \times 2}$

Rewrite with pairs under the radical

$\qquad = \sqrt{2 \times 2} \times \sqrt{2 \times 2} \times \sqrt{2}$

$\qquad = 2 \times 2 \times \sqrt{2}$

$\qquad = 4\sqrt{2}$

In example 1, the largest perfect square is easy to see so Method 1 is probably the faster method to use.

2. Simplify $\sqrt{80}$.

Method 1.

$\sqrt{80} = \sqrt{16 \times 5}$

$\qquad = \sqrt{16} \times \sqrt{5}$

$\qquad = 4\sqrt{5}$

Method 2.

$\sqrt{80} = \sqrt{2 \times 40}$

$\qquad = \sqrt{2 \times 2 \times 20}$

$\qquad = \sqrt{2 \times 2 \times 2 \times 10}$

$\qquad = \sqrt{2 \times 2 \times 2 \times 2 \times 5}$

$\qquad = \sqrt{2 \times 2} \times \sqrt{2 \times 2} \times \sqrt{5}$

$\qquad = 2 \times 2 \times \sqrt{5}$

$\qquad = 4\sqrt{5}$

In Method 1, it might not be so obvious that the largest perfect square is 16, so Method 2 might be the faster method to use.

3. Simplify $\sqrt{\dfrac{384}{8}}$.

First, do the division under the square root, then proceed with the simplifying.

$$\sqrt{\frac{384}{8}} = \sqrt{48}$$

Method 1.

$\sqrt{48} = \sqrt{16 \times 3}$

$\qquad = \left(\sqrt{16}\right)\left(\sqrt{3}\right)$

$\qquad = 4\sqrt{3}$

Method 2.

$\sqrt{48} = \sqrt{2 \times 24}$

$\qquad = \sqrt{2 \times 2 \times 12}$

$\qquad = \sqrt{2 \times 2 \times 2 \times 6}$

$\qquad = \sqrt{2 \times 2 \times 2 \times 2 \times 3}$

$\qquad = \left(\sqrt{2 \times 2}\right)\left(\sqrt{2 \times 2}\right)\sqrt{3}$

$\qquad = (2)(2)\sqrt{3}$

$\qquad = 4\sqrt{3}$

Practice: Square Roots

1. $-\sqrt{(-5)^2} =$

The square roots in practice questions 2 and 3 fall between two consecutive integers. (a) Find the two integers that each square root is between, and (b) determine which of the two integers is closer to the square root.

2. $\sqrt{110}$

3. $\sqrt{26}$

4. Simplify $\sqrt{75}$

5. Simplify $\sqrt{\dfrac{156}{13}}$

Answers: Square Roots

1. -5

$$-\sqrt{(-5)^2} = -\sqrt{25} = -5$$

2. 10 and 11, closer to 10

$$\sqrt{100} < \sqrt{110} < \sqrt{121}$$
$$10 < \sqrt{110} < 11$$

$\sqrt{110}$ is closer to 10.

3. 5 and 6, closer to 5

$$\sqrt{25} < \sqrt{26} < \sqrt{36}$$
$$5 < \sqrt{26} < 6$$

$\sqrt{26}$ is closer to 5.

4. $5\sqrt{3}$

$$\sqrt{75} = \sqrt{25}\sqrt{3} = 5\sqrt{3}$$

5. $2\sqrt{3}$

$$\sqrt{\dfrac{156}{13}} = \sqrt{12} = \sqrt{4}\sqrt{3} = 2\sqrt{3}$$

Algebra

Algebra Diagnostic Test

1. $\{1, 3, 5\} \cap \{1, 2, 3\} =$

2. $\{2, 5\} \cup \{3, 4, 5\} =$

3. $\{1, 2, 3\} \cap \{4, 5\} =$

4. $|\{3, 5, 7, 9\}| =$

5. $|\varnothing| =$

6. Evaluate the diagram below and determine which statement is correct.

$A \cap B = C, A \cup B = C, A \cap C = B, A \cup C = B, B \cap C = A, B \cup C = A$

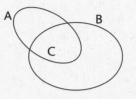

7. Express algebraically: five increased by three times x.

8. Evaluate: $-3x^2 - 4x - 6$ if $x = -5$.

9. Evaluate: $\dfrac{x}{3} - \dfrac{x + 2y}{y}$ if $x = 2$ and $y = 6$.

10. Solve for x: $2x - 9 = 21$.

11. Solve for y: $\dfrac{4}{7}y + 6 = 18$.

12. Solve for x: $3x - 5 = -2x - 25$.

13. Solve for x: $ax + by = c$.

14. Solve for y: $\dfrac{8}{y-3} = \dfrac{2}{y+3}$.

15. Solve this system for x and y: $8x + y = 4$.
$$2x - y = 6$$

16. Solve for x: $|x| = 12$.

17. Solve for x: $|x - 3| = 10$.

18. Solve for x: $-3x + 5 > 14$.

19. Solve for x: $8x + 4 \geq 6x - 10$.

20. $12x + 4x - 23x - (-3x) =$

21. $(4x - 7z) - (3x - 4z) =$

22. $6x^2y(4xy^2) =$

23. $(-2x^4y^2)^3 =$

24. $\dfrac{a^{10}b^3}{a^2b^6} =$

25. $\dfrac{-5(a^3b^2)(2a^2b^5)}{a^4b^3} =$

26. $(5^3)(2^3) =$

329

27. $-8(2x - y) =$

28. $(4x + 2y)(3x - y) =$

29. $\dfrac{16x^2y + 18xy^3}{2xy} =$

30. Factor: $8x^3 - 12x^2$

31. Factor: $16a^2 - 81$

32. Factor: $x^2 - 2x - 63$

33. Factor: $3a^2 - 4a + 1$

34. Simplify: $\dfrac{x^2 - 3x + 2}{3x - 6}$

35. $\left(\dfrac{x^3}{2y}\right)\left(\dfrac{5y^2}{6x}\right) =$

36. $\left(\dfrac{x - 5}{x}\right)\left(\dfrac{x + 2}{x^2 - 2x - 15}\right) =$

37. $\dfrac{6x - 3}{2} \div \dfrac{2x - 1}{x} =$

38. $\dfrac{3x - 2}{x + 1} - \dfrac{2x - 1}{x + 1} =$

39. $\dfrac{5}{x} + \dfrac{7}{y} =$

40. $\dfrac{3}{a^3b^5} + \dfrac{2}{a^4b^2} =$

41. $\dfrac{2x}{x - 1} - \dfrac{x}{x + 2} =$

42. Solve for x: $3x^2 - 4x - 5 = 2x^2 + 4x - 17$

43. Solve for x: $9x^2 - 49 = 0$

44. Name the quadrant(s) in which points have positive x-coordinates.

45. Name the quadrant(s) in which points have negative x-coordinates and positive y-coordinates.

Use the graph below to answer questions 46–51.

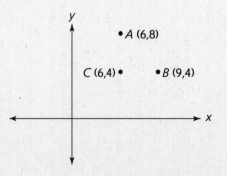

46. What is the distance between A and B?

47. What are the coordinates of the midpoint between A and B?

48. What is the slope of the line joining A and B?

49. What is the equation of the line, in slope-intercept form, joining A and B?

50. If the line joining A and B was extended, what would be its exact y-intercept?

51. Given that points A, B, and C are connected to form a triangle, what would be the area of $\triangle ABC$? What would be the perimeter of $\triangle ABC$?

52. If $f(x) = x^2 - 3x$, then $f(3) - f(1) = ?$

53. If $h(x) = |x|$, then $\dfrac{4}{h(4)} - \dfrac{-2}{h(-2)} = ?$

54. If $m(x) = 3x + 2$ and $t(x) = x^2$, then $t[m(-2)] = ?$

Algebra Diagnostic Test Answers

The diagnostic test explanations listed below include topic headings that correspond with step-by-step learning tools and examples to help you solve specific problem types. Topic headings can be found in the Algebra Review section on pages 333–368.

Set Notations

1. $\{1, 3\}$
2. $\{2, 3, 4, 5\}$
3. $\varnothing$
4. 4
5. 0
6. $A \cap B = C$

Variables and Algebraic Expressions

7. $5 + 3x$
8. -61
9. $-\dfrac{5}{3}$

Solving Linear Equations in One or Two Variables

10. $x = 15$
11. $y = 21$
12. $x = -4$
13. $x = \dfrac{c - by}{a}$
14. $y = -5$
15. $x = 1, y = -4$
16. $x = 12$ or $x = -12$
17. $x = 13$ or $x = -7$

Solving Linear Inequalities in One Variable

18. $x < -3$

19. $x \geq -7$

Polynomials

20. $-4x$

21. $x - 3z$

22. $24x^3y^3$

23. $-8x^{12}y^6$

24. $\dfrac{a^8}{b^3}$

25. $-10ab^4$

26. $\left[(5)(2)\right]^3 = 10^3 = 1{,}000$

27. $-16x + 8y$

28. $12x^2 + 2xy - 2y^2$

29. $8x + 9y^2$

30. $4x^2(2x - 3)$

31. $(4a + 9)(4a - 9)$

32. $(x - 9)(x + 7)$

33. $(3a - 1)(a - 1)$

Algebraic Fractions

34. $\dfrac{x-1}{3}$

35. $\dfrac{5x^2y}{12}$

36. $\dfrac{x+2}{x(x+3)}$

37. $\dfrac{3x}{2}$

38. $\dfrac{x-1}{x+1}$

39. $\dfrac{5y+7x}{xy}$ or $\dfrac{7x+5y}{xy}$

40. $\dfrac{3a+2b^3}{a^4b^5}$

41. $\dfrac{x^2+5x}{(x-1)(x+2)}$

Solving Quadratic Equations in One Variable

42. $x = 6$ or $x = 2$

43. $x = \dfrac{7}{3}$ or $x = -\dfrac{7}{3}$

Coordinate Geometry

44. I and IV

45. II

46. 5

47. $\left(\frac{15}{2}, 6\right)$ or $(7.5, 6)$

48. $-\frac{4}{3}$

49. $y = -\frac{4}{3}x + 16$

50. 16 or $(0, 16)$

51. area = 6, perimeter = 12

Functions and Function Notation

52. 2

53. 2

54. 16

Algebra Review

Set Notations

The *intersection* of two sets is a set containing only the members that are in each set at the same time. The symbol for finding the intersection of two sets is $\cap$. If two sets are *disjointed,* then they have no common members. The intersection of disjointed sets is called the *empty set* (or *null set*) and is indicated by the symbol $\varnothing$.

The *union* of two sets is a set containing all the numbers in those sets. Any duplicates are only written once. The symbol for finding the union of two sets is $\cup$.

The size or *magnitude of a set* refers to how many elements are in the set. This usually expressed by placing absolute value symbols around the set. The magnitude of the empty set is zero.

Venn diagrams (or *Euler circles*) is a method of pictorially describing sets as shown in the figure below.

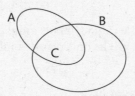

In the Venn diagram above, A represents all the elements in the smaller oval, B represents all the elements in the larger oval, and C represents all the elements that are in both ovals at the same time.

Examples:

> **1.** $\{1, 3, 5\} \cap \{1, 2, 3\} = \{1, 3\}$

The intersection of the set with members 1, 3, 5 together with the set with members 1, 2, 3 is the set that only has the 1 and 3.

2. $\{2, 5\} \cup \{3, 4, 5\} = \{2, 3, 4, 5\}$

The union of the set with members 2, 5 together with the set with members 3, 4, 5 is the set with members 2, 3, 4, 5.

3. $\{1, 2, 3\} \cap \{4, 5\} = \varnothing$

The intersection of disjointed sets is the empty set.

4. $|\{3, 5, 7, 9\}| = 4$

The set consisting of the elements 3, 5, 7, and 9 has 4 elements in it.

5. $|\varnothing| = 0$

The empty set has no elements in it. The value zero indicates this.

6. $A \cap B = C$

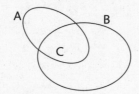

The intersection, or overlapping area, of sets A and B is C.

Practice: Set Notations

1. $\{\text{prime numbers}\} \cup \{\text{composite numbers}\} =$

2. $|\{\text{even integers}\} \cap \{\text{prime numbers}\}| =$

Answers: Set Notations

1. $\{2, 3, 4, 5, 6, ...\}$

Prime numbers and composite numbers are each integers greater than 1. The union will be all integers greater than 1.

2. 1

The correct answer is 1 since the absolute value symbols around the set notations is asking for how many values are in the set, *not* what the value is. The only prime number that is also even is the value 2. This set has only one member in it.

Variables and Algebraic Expressions

A *variable* is a symbol used to denote any element of a given set—often a letter used to stand for a number. Variables are used to change verbal expressions into *algebraic expressions.*

Important Key Words	
Addition	sum, more than, enlarge, plus
Subtraction	difference, less than, diminish, minus
Multiplication	product, times, of, twice
Division	quotient, ratio, divided by, half

Examples:

Express each of the following algebraically.

> **1.** Five increased by three times x: $5 + 3x$

> **2.** The sum of twice x and y: $2x + y$

> **3.** Twice the sum of x and y: $2(x + y)$

> **4.** The product of six and the difference between x and y: $6(x - y)$

> **5.** The ratio of x and y decreased by the quotient of s and r: $\dfrac{x}{y} - \dfrac{s}{r}$

Evaluate an Expression

To *evaluate an expression,* replace the unknowns with grouping symbols, insert the *value* for the unknowns, and then do the arithmetic, making sure to follow the rules for the order of operations.

Examples:

> **1.** Evaluate $-3x^2 - 4x - 6$ if $x = -5$.

$$
\begin{aligned}
-3x^2 - 4x - 6 &= -3(-5)^2 - 4(-5) - 6 \\
&= -3(25) + 20 - 6 \\
&= -75 + 20 - 6 \\
&= -61
\end{aligned}
$$

> **2.** Evaluate $\dfrac{x}{3} - \dfrac{x + 2y}{y}$ if $x = 2$ and $y = 6$.

$$
\begin{aligned}
\frac{x}{3} - \frac{x + 2y}{y} &= \frac{(2)}{3} - \frac{(2) + 2(6)}{6} \\
&= \frac{2}{3} - \frac{2 + 12}{6} \\
&= \frac{2}{3} - \frac{14}{6} \\
&= \frac{2}{3} - \frac{7}{3} \\
&= -\frac{5}{3}
\end{aligned}
$$

Practice: Variables and Algebraic Expressions

1. Express algebraically: 15 less than the ratio of x and y.

2. Evaluate $-3x^2 - \dfrac{4x - 3}{3}$ if $x = -6$.

Answers: Variables and Algebraic Expressions

1. $\dfrac{x}{y} - 15$

"15 less than" says to subtract 15 from something.

2. -99

$$-3x^2 - \frac{4x-3}{3} = -3(-6)^2 - \frac{4(-6)-3}{3}$$
$$= -3(36) - \frac{-24-3}{3}$$
$$= -108 - \frac{-27}{3}$$
$$= -108 - (-9)$$
$$= -108 + 9$$
$$= -99$$

Solving Linear Equations in One or Two Variables

An equation is like a balance scale. In order to maintain the balance, the arithmetic operations you perform to one side of the equation must be performed to the other side of the equation. To solve a linear equation with one variable, cancel the numbers that are added or subtracted by using the opposite operation on both sides of the equation. Then divide by the number in front of the variable to get the variable by itself.

Examples:

1. Solve for x: $2x - 9 = 21$

$$2x - 9 = 21 \quad \text{(add 9 to each side)}$$
$$\underline{\;+9 \quad +9\;}$$
$$2x \;\;\;\; = 30 \quad \text{(divide each side by 2)}$$
$$\frac{2x}{2} = \frac{30}{2}$$
$$x = 15$$

2. Solve for y: $\dfrac{4}{7}y + 6 = 18$

$$\frac{4}{7}y + 6 = 18 \qquad \text{(subtract 6 from each side)}$$
$$\underline{\;-6 \quad -6\;}$$
$$\frac{4}{7}y \;\;\;\; = 12 \qquad \left(\text{divide each side by } \frac{4}{7}, \text{ which is the same as multiplying each side } \frac{7}{4}\right)$$
$$\frac{7}{4}\left(\frac{4}{7}y\right) = \frac{7}{4}\left(\frac{12}{1}\right)$$
$$y = 21$$

3. Solve for x: $3x - 5 = -2x - 25$

$$\begin{aligned}
3x - 5 &= -2x - 25 \qquad &\text{(add } 2x \text{ to each side to get all the } x\text{'s on one side)}\\
\underline{+2x} \quad &\quad \underline{+2x}\\
5x - 5 &= \quad\ -25 \qquad &\text{(add 5 to each side)}\\
\underline{+5} \quad &\quad \underline{+5}\\
5x &= \quad\ -20 \qquad &\text{(divide each side by 5)}\\
\frac{5x}{5} &= \frac{-20}{5}\\
x &= -4
\end{aligned}$$

4. Solve for x: $ax + by = c$

$$\begin{aligned}
ax + by &= c \qquad &\text{(subtract } by \text{ from each side)}\\
\underline{-by} \quad &\quad \underline{-by}\\
ax \quad &= c - by \qquad &\text{(divide each side by } a\text{)}\\
\frac{ax}{a} &= \frac{c - by}{a}\\
x &= \frac{c - by}{a}
\end{aligned}$$

5. Solve for y: $\dfrac{8}{y-3} = \dfrac{2}{y+3}$

Solve using the proportions method (refer to the proportions method discussed in the arithmetic section on page 317).

$$\begin{aligned}
\frac{8}{y-3} &= \frac{2}{y+3} \qquad &\text{(cross multiply to clear the denominators)}\\
8(y+3) &= 2(y-3) \qquad &\text{(multiply out each side)}\\
8y + 24 &= 2y - 6 \qquad &\text{(subtract } 2y \text{ from each side to get the } y\text{'s on one side)}\\
\underline{-2y} \quad &\quad \underline{-2y}\\
6y + 24 &= \quad\ -6 \qquad &\text{(subtract 24 from each side)}\\
\underline{-24} \quad &\quad \underline{-24}\\
6y \quad &= \quad -30 \qquad &\text{(divide each side by 6)}\\
\frac{6y}{6} &= \frac{-30}{6}\\
y &= -5
\end{aligned}$$

Solving Two Equations Involving the Same Two Variables

To solve *two equations involving the same two variables,* you can use either of two algebraic methods: *elimination method* and *substitution method.*

Method 1 - The Elimination Method

1. Arrange each equation so that it has all the variables on one side.
2. Multiply each side of one equation so that the numbers to the left of the same variable in each equation are exact opposites. *(Note: Sometimes you will have to multiply each equation by different numbers to accomplish this.)*

3. Add the two equations to eliminate one variable.

4. Solve for the remaining variable.

5. Replace this value into one of the original equations to find the second variable.

Examples:

> **1.** Solve for x and y: $3x + 3y = 24$
> $$2x + y = 13$$

Both equations are already in the required form. Multiply each side of the bottom equation by –3. Now the y is preceded by exact opposites in the two equations.

$$3x + 3y = 24 \quad \rightarrow \quad 3x + 3y = 24$$
$$-3(2x + y) = -3(13) \quad \rightarrow \quad \underline{-6x - 3y = -39}$$

Add the equations, eliminating the y terms.

$$3x + 3y = 24$$
$$\underline{-6x + -3y = -39}$$
$$-3x \quad\quad = -15$$

Solve for the remaining variable.

$$\frac{-3x}{-3} = \frac{-15}{-3}$$
$$x = 5$$

Replace x with 5 in one of the original equations to solve for y:

$$2x + y = 13$$
$$2(5) + y = 13$$
$$10 + y = 13$$
$$\underline{-10 \quad\quad -10}$$
$$y = 3$$

Answer: $x = 5$ and $y = 3$

Of course, if the numbers to the left of a variable are already opposites in each equation, you don't have to change either equation. Simply add the equations. See example 2 below.

> **2.** Solve for x and y: $x + y = 7$
> $$x - y = 3$$

$$x + y = 7$$
$$\underline{x - y = 3}$$
$$2x \quad = 10$$
$$\frac{2x}{2} = \frac{10}{2}$$
$$x = 5$$

Replacing x with 5 in the first equation gives:

$$5 + y = 7$$
$$\underline{-5 \qquad -5}$$
$$y = 2$$

Answer: $x = 5$ and $y = 2$

Note that this method will not work when the two equations *are the same equation* but written in two different forms. See example 3 below.

---

3. Solve for a and b: $3a + 4b = 2$

$\qquad\qquad\qquad\quad 6a + 8b = 4$

The second equation is actually the first equation multiplied by 2. In this instance, the system does not have a unique solution. Any replacements for a and b that make one of the sentences true will also make the other sentence true. In this situation, the system has an infinite number of solutions for a and b.

Sometimes each equation will have to be multiplied by different numbers to get the numbers to the left of one variable to be opposites of one another. See example 4 below.

---

4. Solve for x: $3x + 2y = 8$

$\qquad\qquad\qquad\quad 2x - 5y = 18$

The equations are already in the required form. Since it is the x value desired, find a way to eliminate the y variable. The numbers to the left of the y-terms are already of the opposite sign. Multiply the upper equation with the coefficient of y from the lower equation and multiply the lower equation by the coefficient of y from the upper equation.

$$5(3x + 2y) = 5(8) \quad \rightarrow \quad 15x + 10y = 40$$
$$2(2x - 5y) = 2(18) \quad \rightarrow \quad \underline{4x - 10y = 36}$$

Add the equations.

$$15x + 10y = 40$$
$$\underline{4x - 10y = 36}$$
$$19x \qquad\; = 76$$
$$\frac{19x}{19} = \frac{76}{19}$$
$$x = 4$$

Answer: $x = 4$

Method 2 - The Substitution Method

1. Solve one equation for one of its variables in terms of the other variable.
2. Replace this expression for that variable in the other equation.
3. Solve the equation for that variable.
4. Replace this value into one of the original equations to find the second variable.

Examples:

---

1. Solve for x and y: $x = y + 8$

$\qquad\qquad\qquad\qquad x + 3y = 48$

The first equation already has been solved for x in terms of y. Replace x with $(y + 8)$ in the second equation.

$$x + 3y = 48$$
$$(y + 8) + 3y = 48$$

Solve for y.

$$y + 3y + 8 = 48$$
$$4y + 8 = 48$$
$$\underline{-8 \quad -8}$$
$$4y \quad\; = 40$$
$$\frac{4y}{4} = \frac{40}{4}$$
$$y = 10$$

Replace y with 10 in one of the original equations and solve for x.

$$x = y + 8$$
$$x = 10 + 8$$
$$x = 18$$

Answer: $x = 18$ and $y = 10$

---

2. Solve for x and y: $8x + y = 4$
$2x - y = 6$

This problem can now be solved by using *Method 1 - The Elimination Method*.

$$8x + y = 4$$
$$\underline{2x - y = 6}$$
$$10x \quad\;\; = 10$$
$$\frac{10x}{10} = \frac{10}{10}$$
$$x = 1$$

Using the top equation:

$$8x + y = 4$$
$$8(1) + y = 4$$
$$8 + y = 4$$
$$\underline{-8 \qquad -8}$$
$$y = -4$$

Answer: $x = 1$ and $y = -4$

Equations Involving Absolute Value

Recall that the numerical value when direction or sign is not considered is called the ***absolute value.*** The absolute value of x is written $|x|$. If $|x| = 2$, then $x = 2$ or $x = -2$ since $|2| = 2$ and $|-2| = 2$.

Examples:

1. Solve for x: $|x| = 12$

$$x = 12 \text{ or } x = -12$$

2. Solve for x: $|x - 3| = 10$

$$
\begin{array}{llll}
x - 3 = 10 & \text{or} & x - 3 = -10 \\
\underline{+3 \quad +3} & & \underline{+3 \quad \ +3} \\
x \quad = 13 & \text{or} & x \quad \ = -7
\end{array}
$$

3. Solve for x: $|2x - 1| = 7$

$$
\begin{array}{llll}
2x - 1 = 7 & \text{or} & 2x - 1 = -7 \\
\underline{+1 \ +1} & & \underline{\quad +1 \ +1} \\
2x \quad = 8 & \text{or} & 2x \quad = -6 \\
\dfrac{2x}{2} = \dfrac{8}{2} & \text{or} & \dfrac{2x}{2} = \dfrac{-6}{2} \\
x = 4 & \text{or} & x = -3
\end{array}
$$

4. Solve for x: $|x| = -3$

There is no solution because the absolute value of any number is never negative.

5. Solve for x: $|2x - 1| \geq 0$.

The answer is all real numbers, because the absolute value of any number is always positive or zero.

Practice: Solving Linear Equations in One or Two Variables

Solve each equation for x:

1. $3x + 5 = -16$

2. $\frac{3}{4}x - 5 = 19$

3. $8x - 12 = 5x - 27$

4. $wx - y = z$

5. $\frac{x+2}{3} = \frac{3x-4}{8}$

Solve each system of equations for x and y.

6. $3x + y = 8$
$x - y = 4$

7. $y = 5x - 2$
$2x + y = 19$

Solve each equation for x.

8. $|x| = 6$

9. $|3x - 5| = 10$

Answers: Solving Linear Equations in One or Two Variables

1. $x = -7$

$$3x + 5 = -16$$
$$3x = -21$$
$$x = -7$$

2. $x = 32$

$$\frac{3}{4}x - 5 = 19$$
$$\frac{3}{4}x = 24$$
$$x = 32$$

3. $x = -5$

$$8x - 12 = 5x - 27$$
$$3x - 12 = -27$$
$$3x = -15$$
$$x = -5$$

4. $x = \dfrac{y+z}{w}$ or $x = \dfrac{z+y}{w}$

$$
\begin{array}{ccc}
wx - y = z & & wx - y = z \\
wx = y + z \quad \text{or} & & wx = z + y \\
x = \dfrac{y+z}{w} & & x = \dfrac{z+y}{w}
\end{array}
$$

5. $x = 28$

$$\frac{x+2}{3} = \frac{3x-4}{8}$$
$$8(x+2) = 3(3x-4)$$
$$8x + 16 = 9x - 12$$
$$-x + 16 = -12$$
$$-x = -28$$
$$x = 28$$

6. $x = 3, y = -1$

$$
\begin{array}{r}
3x + y = 8 \\
\underline{x - y = 4} \\
4x \quad\;\; = 12 \\
x = 3
\end{array}
$$
$$3x + y = 8 \rightarrow 3(3) + y = 8$$
$$9 + y = 8$$
$$y = -1$$

7. $x = 3$, $y = 13$

$$y = 5x - 2$$
$$2x + y = 19$$
$$2x + (5x - 2) = 19$$
$$7x - 2 = 19$$
$$7x = 21$$
$$x = 3$$
$$y = 5x - 2 \rightarrow y = 5(3) - 2$$
$$y = 15 - 2$$
$$y = 13$$

8. $x = 6$, $x = -6$

9. $x = 5$, $x = -\dfrac{5}{3}$

$$|3x - 5| = 10$$
$$3x - 5 = 10 \quad \text{or} \quad 3x - 5 = -10$$
$$3x = 15 \quad \text{or} \qquad 3x = -5$$
$$x = 5 \quad \text{or} \qquad x = -\dfrac{5}{3}$$

Solving Linear Inequalities in One Variable

An inequality sentence is one involving $\leq$, $<$, $\geq$, or $>$ separating the two sides of the sentence. Solving an inequality sentence involves the same procedures as solving an equation with one exception: When you multiply or divide each side of an inequality sentence by a negative number, the direction of the inequality switches.

Examples:

1. Solve for x: $-3x + 5 > 14$

$$-3x + 5 > 14 \qquad (\text{subtract 5 from each side})$$
$$\underline{ -5 \quad -5}$$
$$-3x \quad > \quad 9 \qquad (\text{divide each side by } -3, \text{ switch the direction of the inequality})$$
$$\frac{-3x}{-3} < \frac{9}{-3}$$
$$x < -3$$

2. Solve for x: $8x + 4 \geq 6x - 10$

$$8x + 4 \geq 6x - 10 \qquad (\text{subtract } 6x \text{ from each side to get all the } x\text{'s on one side})$$
$$\underline{-6x \qquad -6x}$$
$$2x + 4 \geq \quad -10 \qquad (\text{subtract 4 from each side})$$
$$\underline{ -4 > \qquad -4}$$
$$2x \quad \geq \quad -14 \qquad (\text{divide each side by 2})$$
$$\frac{2x}{2} \geq \frac{-14}{2}$$
$$x \geq -7$$

3. Solve for x: $-\dfrac{3}{8}x - 2 < 13$

$$-\frac{3}{8}x - 2 < 13 \qquad \text{(add 2 to each side)}$$
$$\underline{+2 \quad +2}$$
$$-\frac{3}{8}x \quad < 15 \qquad \left(\begin{array}{l}\text{divide each side by } -\frac{3}{8}, \text{ which is the same as multiplying each}\\ \text{side by } -\frac{8}{3}, \text{ and then switch the direction of the inequality}\end{array}\right)$$

$$\left(\frac{\cancel{8}}{\cancel{3}}\right)\left(\frac{\cancel{3}^{\,1}}{\cancel{8}}x\right) > \left(-\frac{8}{\cancel{3}_{1}}\right)\left(\frac{\cancel{15}^{\,5}}{1}\right)$$

$$x > -40$$

Practice: Solving Inequalities in One Variable

Solve for x.

1. $3x - 12 < 36$

2. $-\dfrac{5}{6}x - 4 < 26$

3. $6x - 11 \ge 3x - 53$

Answers: Solving Inequalities in One Variable

1. $x < 16$

$$3x - 12 < 36 \qquad \text{(add 12 to each side)}$$
$$3x < 48 \qquad \text{(divide each side by 3)}$$
$$x < 16$$

2. $x > -36$

$$-\frac{5}{6}x - 4 < 26 \qquad \text{(add 4 to each side)}$$
$$-\frac{5}{6}x < 30 \qquad \left(\text{multiply each side by } -\frac{6}{5}, \text{ switch the direction of the inequality}\right)$$
$$x > -36$$

3. $x \ge -14$

$$6x - 11 \ge 3x - 53 \qquad \text{(subtract } 3x \text{ from each side to get all the } x\text{'s on one side)}$$
$$3x - 11 \ge -53 \qquad \text{(add 11 to each side)}$$
$$3x \ge -42 \qquad \text{(divide each side by 3)}$$
$$x \ge -14$$

Polynomials

A *monomial* is an algebraic expression that consists of only one term. (A *term* is a numerical or literal expression with its own sign.) For instance, $9x$, $4a^2$, and $3mpxz^2$ are all monomials. When there are variables with exponents, the exponents must be whole numbers.

A *polynomial* consists of two or more terms. For instance, $x + y$, $y^2 - x^2$, and $x^2 + 3x + 5y^2$ are all polynomials. A *binomial* is a polynomial that consists of exactly two terms. For instance, $x + y$ is a binomial. A *trinomial* is a polynomial that consists of exactly three terms. For instance, $y^2 + 9y + 8$ is a trinomial. The number to the left of the variable is called the *numerical coefficient*. In $9y$, the 9 is the numerical coefficient.

Polynomials are usually arranged in one of two ways.

- *Ascending order* is when the power of a term increases for each succeeding term. For example, $x + x^2 + x^3$ or $5x + 2x^2 - 3x^3 + x^5$ are arranged in ascending order.

- *Descending order* is when the power of a term decreases for each succeeding term. For example, $x^3 + x^2 + x$ or $2x^4 + 3x^2 + 7x$ are arranged in descending order. Descending order is more commonly used.

Adding and Subtracting Polynomials

To **add** or **subtract polynomials,** follow the same rules as with integers introduced in the Arithmetic section (see pages 300–301), provided that the terms are alike. Notice that you add or subtract the coefficients only and leave the variables the same.

Examples:

1. $12x + 4x - 23x - (-3x) = [12 + 4 - 23 - (-3)]x = [12 + 4 - 23 + 3]x = -4x$

2. $(4x - 7z) - (3x - 4z) = 4x - 7z - 3x + 4z = (4 - 3)x + (-7 + 4)z = x - 3z$

3. $15x^2yz$
   $\underline{-18x^2yz}$
   $-3x^2yz$

Multiplying and Dividing Monomials

To **multiply** or **divide monomials,** follow the rules and definitions for powers and exponents introduced in the preceding Arithmetic section (see page 324).

Examples:

1. $6x^2y(4xy^2) = (6)(4)(x^2x)(yy^2) = 24x^{2+1}y^{1+2} = 24x^3y^3$

2. $(-2x^4y^2)^3 = (-2)^3 x^{(4)(3)} y^{(2)(3)} = -8x^{12}y^6$

3. $\dfrac{a^{10}b^3}{a^2b^6} = \left(\dfrac{a^{10}}{a^2}\right)\left(\dfrac{b^3}{b^6}\right) = a^{10-2}b^{3-6} = a^8b^{-3} = a^8\left(\dfrac{1}{b^3}\right) = \dfrac{a^8}{b^3}$

Note: You might have solved example 3 quickly by recognizing that the remaining exponent ends up where the larger exponent was originally.

4. $\dfrac{-5(a^3b^2)(2a^2b^5)}{a^4b^3} = \dfrac{-5(2)(a^3a^2)(b^2b^5)}{a^4b^3}$
   $= \dfrac{-10}{1}\left(\dfrac{a^{3+2}}{a^4}\right)\left(\dfrac{b^{2+5}}{b^3}\right)$
   $= \dfrac{-10}{1}\left(\dfrac{a^5}{a^4}\right)\left(\dfrac{b^7}{b^3}\right)$
   $= -10a^{5-4}b^{7-3}$
   $= -10ab^4$

5. $(5^3)(2^3) = [(5)(2)]^3 = 10^3$ or $1,000$

Multiply Polynomials

To **multiply polynomials,** multiply each term in one polynomial by each term in the other polynomial. Simplify if possible.

Examples:

1. $-8(2x - y) = -8(2x) - (-8)(y)$
$$= -16x + 8y$$

2. $(4x + 2y)(3x - y) = \left[(4x)(3x)\right] + \left[(4x)(-y)\right] + \left[(2y)(3x)\right] + \left[(2y)(-y)\right]$
$$= 12x^2 - 4xy + 6xy - 2y^2$$
$$= 12x^2 + 2xy - 2y^2$$

You may wish to use the **FOIL method** when multiplying a pair of binomials together. FOIL stands for *first terms, outside terms, inside terms, last terms.* After multiplying, simplify if possible. See the example below.

$$(3x + a)(2x - 2a)$$

Multiply *first terms* from each quantity. The first terms are the "$3x$" from the left parentheses and the "$2x$" from the right parentheses.

$$(3x + a)(2x - 2a) = \underline{6x^2}$$

Then multiply *outside terms.* The outside terms are the "$3x$" from the left parentheses and the "$-2a$" from the right parentheses.

$$(3x + a)(2x - 2a) = 6x^2 \underline{-6ax}$$

Then multiply *inside terms.* The inside terms are the "a" from the left parentheses and the "$2x$" from the right parentheses.

$$(3x + a)(2x - 2a) = 6x^2 - 6ax \underline{+2ax}$$

Finally, multiply *last terms.* The last terms are the "a" from the left parentheses and the "$-2a$" from the right parentheses.

$$(3x + a)(2x - 2a) = 6x^2 - 6ax + 2ax \underline{-2a^2}$$

Now simplify.

$$(3x + a)(2x - 2a) = 6x^2 - 6ax + 2ax - 2a^2 = 6x^2 - 4ax - 2a^2$$

Divide a Polynomial by a Monomial

To *divide a polynomial by a monomial,* divide each term in the polynomial by the monomial.

Examples:

1. $\dfrac{16x^2y + 18xy^3}{2xy} = \dfrac{16x^2y}{2xy} + \dfrac{18xy^3}{2xy}$

   $= \left(\dfrac{16}{2}\right)\left(\dfrac{x^2}{x}\right)\dfrac{y}{y} + \left(\dfrac{18}{2}\right)\left(\dfrac{x}{x}\right)\left(\dfrac{y^3}{y}\right)$

   $= \quad 8x \quad + \quad 9y^2$

2. $\left(6x^2 + 2x\right) \div \left(2x\right) = \dfrac{6x^2 + 2x}{2x} = \dfrac{6x^2}{2x} + \dfrac{2x}{2x} = 3x + 1$

Factor Each Polynomial Using a Common Factor

To *factor* means to find two or more quantities whose product equals the original quantity. To *factor out a common factor:*

1. Find the largest common monomial factor of each term.
2. Divide the original polynomial by this factor to obtain the second factor. The second factor will also be a polynomial.

Examples:

1. $8x^3 - 12x^2$

The largest common factor of $8x^3$ and $12x^2$ is $4x^2$. $\dfrac{8x^3}{4x^2} = 2x$, $\dfrac{12x^2}{4x^2} = 3$. Therefore, $8x^3 - 12x^2 = 4x^2(2x - 3)$.

2. $x^5 - 4x^3 + x^2$

The largest common factor of x^5, $4x^3$, and x^2 is x^2. $\dfrac{x^5}{x^2} = x^3$, $\dfrac{4x^3}{x^2} = 4x$, $\dfrac{x^2}{x^2} = 1$.

Therefore, $x^5 - 4x^3 + x^2 = x^2(x^3 - 4x + 1)$.

Factor Each Polynomial Using Difference of Squares

The difference of two squares refers to the subtraction of two expressions that are each the results of the squares of other expressions. To *factor the difference of two squares:*

1. Find the square root of the first term and the square root of the second term.
2. Express your answer as the product of the sum of the quantities from step 1 times the difference of those quantities.

Examples:

1. $16a^2 - 81$

$$\sqrt{16a^2} = 4a, \ \sqrt{81} = 9$$

Therefore, $16a^2 - 81 = (4a + 9)(4a - 9)$.

2. $9y^2 - 1$

$$\sqrt{9y^2} = 3y, \sqrt{1} = 1$$

Therefore, $9y^2 - 1 = (3y + 1)(3y - 1)$.

Note: $x^2 + 144$ is *not* factorable using difference of squares. Even though both x^2 and 144 are both square numbers, the expression $x^2 + 144$ is not a *difference* of squares.

Factor Polynomials Having Three Terms of the Form $ax^2 + bx + c$ when $a = 1$

To *factor polynomials having three terms of the form $ax^2 + bx + c$ when $a = 1$* (that is, the first term is simply x^2):

1. Use double parentheses and place an x at the left sides of the parentheses: $(x\ \ )(x\ \ )$.
2. Find two numbers that multiply to make the c value and at the same time add to make the b value.
3. Place these numbers, with their appropriate signs, in the parentheses with the x's.

Examples:

1. Factor $x^2 - 2x - 63$.

This is a polynomial in the form of $ax^2 + bx + c$ with $a = 1$, $b = -2$, $c = -63$. Find two numbers that multiply to make -63 and add to make -2. Only the numbers -9 and $+7$ do that. Therefore, $x^2 - 2x - 63 = (x - 9)(x + 7)$. The two parentheses expressions could be written in reverse order as well: $(x + 7)(x - 9)$.

2. Factor $x^2 - 8x + 15$.

This is a polynomial in the form of $ax^2 + bx + c$ with $a = 1$, $b = -8$, $c = 15$. Find two numbers that multiply to make $+15$ and add to make -8. Only the numbers -3 and -5 do that. Therefore, $x^2 - 8x + 15 = (x - 3)(x - 5)$. The two parentheses expressions could be written in reverse order as well: $(x - 5)(x - 3)$.

Factor Polynomials Having Three Terms of the Form $ax^2 + bx + c$ when $a \neq 1$

To *factor polynomials having three terms of the form $ax^2 + bx + c$ when $a \neq 1$* requires a trial-and-error approach. The following problems will demonstrate what type of thinking is required.

Examples:

1. Factor $3a^2 - 4a + 1$.

This is a polynomial in the form of $ax^2 + bx + c$ with $a = 3$, $b = -4$, $c = 1$. Set up two parentheses expressions: $(\ \ )(\ \ )$. The values that will be in the *first* positions must multiply to make $3a^2$. These could be $3a$ and a. The values in the *last* position need to make $+1$. These could either be $+1$ and $+1$ or -1 and -1. The values in the inner and outer positions need to multiply and combine to make $-4a$. Consider the possibilities:

$$(3a + 1)(a + 1) \quad \text{Here, the } outer \text{ and } inner \text{ products combine to make } +4a$$
$$(3a - 1)(a - 1) \quad \text{Here, the } outer \text{ and } inner \text{ products combine to make } -4a.$$

Therefore, $3a^2 - 4a + 1 = (3a - 1)(a - 1)$.

2. Factor $4x^2 + 5x + 1$.

To get $4x^2$, the *first terms* could be $2x$ and $2x$ or $4x$ and x. To get $+1$, the *last terms* could be $+1$ and $+1$ or -1 and -1. Experiment with $2x$ and $2x$ together with $+1$ and $+1$ and multiply.

$$(2x + 1)(2x + 1) = 4x^2 + 2x + 2x + 1 = 4x^2 + 4x + 1$$

This expression has $4x$ as the result of the *outer* and *inner* multiplications, but the original expression has $5x$ as the result of the *outer* and *inner* multiplications. Thus, $(2x + 1)(2x + 1)$ is not the correct factored form.

If the 1's were replaced with –1's, the only change would be that the result of the *inner* and *outer* multiplications would have the result of $-4x$. Thus, $(2x - 1)(2x - 1)$ is not the correct factored form.

Experiment with $4x$ and x together with $+1$ and $+1$ and multiply.

$$(4x + 1)(x + 1) = 4x^2 + 4x + x + 1 = 4x^2 + 5x + 1$$

Therefore, $4x^2 + 5x + 1 = (4x + 1)(x + 1)$.

Some factoring problems combine one or more of the methods described:

> **3.** Factor $4a^2 + 6a + 2$.

Notice that the expression $4a^2 + 6a + 2$ has a common factor of 2. Factoring out a 2 gives $2(2a^2 + 3a + 1)$. The expression $2a^2 + 3a + 1$ can be further factored into $(2a + 1)(a + 1)$. Therefore, $4a^2 + 6a + 2 = 2(2a + 1)(a + 1)$.

> **4.** Factor $x^4 - 81$.

$\sqrt{x^4} = x^2$ and $\sqrt{81} = 9$, therefore, $x^4 - 81 = (x^2 + 9)(x^2 - 9)$. Notice that $x^2 - 9$ is a difference of squares.

$\sqrt{x^2} = x$ and $\sqrt{9} = 3$, therefore $x^2 - 9 = (x + 3)(x - 3)$. Therefore, $x^4 - 81 = (x^2 + 9)(x + 3)(x - 3)$.

Practice: Polynomials

1. $-15x - 32x + 34x - (-4x) =$

2. $(3x^2 - 7x - 6) - (6x^2 - 4x - 5) =$

3. $-3x^4y(-2x^2y^7) =$

4. $(-3x^2y^5)^3 =$

5. $\dfrac{x^{12}y^8}{x^{16}y^6} =$

6. $\dfrac{4(-3x^2y^5)(x^4y^3)}{x^3y^4} =$

7. $(25^4)(4^4) =$

8. $-12(3x - 5y) =$

9. $(4x - 5y)(3x + 2y) =$

10. $\dfrac{24x^3y^5 - 36x^2y^3}{12xy} =$

11. Factor: $45x^3 - 60x^2$

12. Factor: $144x^2 - 49$

13. Factor: $x^2 - 5x - 36$

14. Factor: $2x^2 + x - 28$

Answers: Polynomials

1. $-9x$

   $-15x - 32x + 34x - (-4x) = -15x - 32x + 34x + 4x = -9x$

2. $-3x^2 - 3x - 1$

   $(3x^2 - 7x - 6) - (6x^2 - 4x - 5) = 3x^2 - 7x - 6 - 6x^2 + 4x + 5 = -3x^2 - 3x - 1$

3. $6x^6y^8$

   $-3x^4y(-2x^2y^7) = (-3)(-2)(x^4x^2)(yy^7) = 6x^6y^8$

4. $-27x^6y^{15}$

   $(-3x^2y^5)^3 = (-3)^3(x^2)^3(y^5)^3 = -27x^6y^{15}$

5. $\dfrac{y^2}{x^4}$

   $\dfrac{x^{12}y^8}{x^{16}y^6} = \left(\dfrac{x^{12}}{x^{16}}\right)\left(\dfrac{y^8}{y^6}\right) = \left(\dfrac{1}{x^4}\right)\left(\dfrac{y^2}{1}\right) = \dfrac{y^2}{x^4}$

6. $-12x^3y^4$

   $\dfrac{4(-3x^2y^5)(x^4y^3)}{x^3y^4} = ((4)(-3))\left(\dfrac{x^2x^4}{x^3}\right)\left(\dfrac{y^5y^3}{y^4}\right) = -12\left(\dfrac{x^6}{x^3}\right)\left(\dfrac{y^8}{y^4}\right) = -12x^3y^4$

7. 100^4 or $100{,}000{,}000$

   $(25^4)(4^4) = [(25)(4)]^4 = 100^4$ or $100{,}000{,}000$

8. $-36x + 60y$

   $-12(3x - 5y) = -12(3x) - 12(-5y) = -36x + 60y$

9. $12x^2 - 7xy - 10y^2$

   $(4x - 5y)(3x + 2y) = 12x^2 + 8xy - 15xy - 10y^2 = 12x^2 - 7xy - 10y^2$

10. $2x^2y^4 - 3xy^2$

    $\dfrac{24x^3y^5 - 36x^2y^3}{12xy} = \left(\dfrac{24x^3y^5}{12xy}\right) - \left(\dfrac{36x^2y^3}{12xy}\right) = 2x^2y^4 - 3xy^2$

11. $15x^2(3x - 4)$

    The GCF of $45x^3 - 60x^2$ is $15x^2$; $\dfrac{45x^3}{15x^2} = 3x$; $\dfrac{60x^2}{15x^2} = 4$. Therefore, $45x^3 - 60x^2 = 15x^2(3x - 4)$.

12. $(12x + 7)(12x - 7)$

    $144x^2 - 49$ is a difference of squares.

    $144x^2 - 49 = (12x + 7)(12x - 7)$

13. $(x + 4)(x - 9)$

    To factor $x^2 - 5x - 36$, find two numbers whose product is -36 and sum is -5. Only -9 and 4 satisfy the conditions.

    $x^2 - 5x - 36 = (x + 4)(x - 9)$

14. $(2x - 7)(x + 4)$

    To factor $2x^2 + x - 28$, use the trial-and-error method.

    $2x^2 + x - 28 = (2x - 7)(x + 4)$

Algebraic Fractions

Algebraic fractions are fractions using a variable in the numerator, denominator, or both numerator and denominator such as $\frac{3}{x}$, $\frac{x+1}{2}$, or $\frac{x^2-x-2}{x+1}$. Since division by 0 is impossible, variables in the denominator have certain restrictions. The denominator can *never* equal 0. Therefore in $\frac{5}{x}$, $x \neq 0$; in $\frac{2}{x-3}$, $x \neq 3$; in $\frac{3}{a-b}$, $a-b \neq 0$, which implies $a \neq b$; and in $\frac{4}{a^2 b}$, $a \neq 0$ and $b \neq 0$. Be aware of these types of restrictions.

Simplify an Algebraic Fraction

To *simplify an algebraic fraction,* first factor the numerator and the denominator; then cancel (or divide out) common factors.

Examples:

1. Simplify: $\dfrac{x^2-3x+2}{3x-6}$

$$\frac{x^2-3x+2}{3x-6} = \frac{(x-1)(x-2)}{3(x-2)} = \frac{(x-1)\cancel{(x-2)}}{3\cancel{(x-2)}} = \frac{(x-1)}{3}$$

2. Simplify: $\dfrac{(3x-3)}{(4x-4)}$

$$\frac{(3x-3)}{(4x-4)} = \frac{3(x-1)}{4(x-1)} = \frac{3\cancel{(x-1)}}{4\cancel{(x-1)}} = \frac{3}{4}$$

Warning: Do *not* cancel through an addition or subtraction sign. The following is NOT allowed:

$$\frac{x+1}{x+2} \neq \frac{\cancel{x}+1}{\cancel{x}+2} \text{ or } \frac{x+6}{6} \neq \frac{x+\cancel{6}}{\cancel{6}}$$

Multiply Algebraic Fractions

To *multiply algebraic fractions,* first factor the numerators and denominators that are polynomials then cancel where possible. Multiply the remaining numerators and denominators together. *If you've canceled properly, your answer will be in simplified form.*

Examples:

1. $\left(\dfrac{x^3}{2y}\right)\left(\dfrac{5y^2}{6x}\right) = \dfrac{\cancel{x^3}\,5\cancel{y^2}}{2\cancel{y}\,6\cancel{x}} = \dfrac{5x^2y}{12}$

2. $\left(\dfrac{x-5}{x}\right)\left(\dfrac{x+2}{x^2-2x-15}\right) = \dfrac{\cancel{(x-5)}}{x}\,\dfrac{x+2}{\cancel{(x-5)}(x+3)} = \dfrac{x+2}{x(x+3)}$

Divide Algebraic Fractions

To *divide algebraic fractions,* invert the second fraction (the divisor) and then multiply the fractions. **Remember:** You can cancel only after you invert.

Examples:

1. $\dfrac{3x^2}{5} \div \dfrac{2x}{y} = \dfrac{3x^2}{5} \times \dfrac{y}{2x} = \dfrac{3x^{\overset{1}{2}}}{5} \times \dfrac{y}{2\underset{1}{x}} = \dfrac{3xy}{10}$

2. $\dfrac{6x-3}{2} \div \dfrac{2x-1}{x} = \dfrac{6x-3}{2} \times \dfrac{x}{2x-1} = \dfrac{3\overset{1}{(2x-1)}}{2} \dfrac{x}{\underset{1}{(2x-1)}} = \dfrac{3x}{2}$

Add or Subtract Algebraic Fractions with a Common Denominator

To *add or subtract algebraic fractions having a common denominator,* simply keep the denominator and combine (add or subtract) the numerators. Simplify if possible.

Examples:

1. $\dfrac{4}{x} + \dfrac{5}{x} = \dfrac{4+5}{x} = \dfrac{9}{x}$

2. $\dfrac{3x-2}{x+1} - \dfrac{2x-1}{x+1} = \dfrac{3x-2-(2x-1)}{x+1} = \dfrac{3x-2-2x+1}{x+1} = \dfrac{x-1}{x+1}$

Add or Subtract Algebraic Fractions with Different Denominators

To *add or subtract algebraic fractions having different denominators,* first find the lowest common denominator (LCD) and change each fraction to an equivalent fraction with the common denominator. Finally, combine the numerators and simplify if possible.

Examples:

1. $\dfrac{5}{x} + \dfrac{7}{y} =$

LCD = xy.

$$\left(\dfrac{5}{x} \times \dfrac{y}{y}\right) + \left(\dfrac{7}{y} \times \dfrac{x}{x}\right) = \dfrac{5y}{xy} + \dfrac{7x}{xy} = \dfrac{5y+7x}{xy} \text{ or } \dfrac{7x+5y}{xy}$$

2. $\dfrac{3}{a^3b^5} + \dfrac{2}{a^4b^2} =$

LCD = a^4b^5.

$$\left(\dfrac{3}{a^3b^5} \times \dfrac{a}{a}\right) + \left(\dfrac{2}{a^4b^2} \times \dfrac{b^3}{b^3}\right) = \dfrac{3a}{a^4b^5} + \dfrac{2b^3}{a^4b^5} = \dfrac{3a+2b^3}{a^4b^5}$$

3. $\dfrac{2x}{x-1}-\dfrac{x}{x+2}=$

LCD $=(x-1)(x+2)$

$$\left(\frac{2x}{x-1}\times\frac{(x+2)}{(x+2)}\right)-\left(\frac{x}{x+2}\times\frac{(x-1)}{(x-1)}\right)=\frac{2x^2+4x}{(x-1)(x+2)}-\frac{x^2-x}{(x-1)(x+2)}$$

$$=\frac{2x^2+4x-\left(x^2-x\right)}{(x-1)(x+2)}$$

$$=\frac{2x^2+4x-x^2+x}{(x-1)(x+2)}$$

$$=\frac{x^2+5x}{(x-1)(x+2)}$$

Practice: Algebraic Fractions

1. Simplify: $\dfrac{x^2+6x-27}{x^2-9}$

2. $\left(\dfrac{x^5y}{5z^3}\right)\left(\dfrac{15z^5}{4x^3y^4}\right)=$

3. $\dfrac{3x^2-2x-1}{x^2+x}\left(\dfrac{x+1}{x-1}\right)=$

4. $\dfrac{4x-8}{6}\div\dfrac{x-2}{3}=$

5. $\dfrac{2x+7}{x+4}-\dfrac{x-5}{x+4}=$

6. $\dfrac{1}{x}+\dfrac{3}{y}=$

7. $\dfrac{2}{x^2y}+\dfrac{3}{xy^3}=$

8. $\dfrac{4x}{x-3}-\dfrac{x}{x+1}=$

Answers: Algebraic Fractions

1. $\dfrac{x+9}{x+3}$

$$\frac{x^2+6x-27}{x^2-9}=\frac{\cancel{(x-3)}(x+9)}{\cancel{(x-3)}(x+3)}=\frac{x+9}{x+3}$$

2. $\dfrac{3x^2z^2}{4y^3}$

$$\left(\frac{x^5y}{5z^3}\right)\left(\frac{15z^5}{4x^3y^4}\right)=\left(\frac{x^2\ \ 1}{\cancel{5}\ z^3}\cdot\frac{\cancel{x^5}\ \cancel{y}}{\cancel{5}\ z^3}\right)\left(\frac{3\ \ z^2}{\cancel{15}\ \cancel{z^5}}\cdot\frac{}{4x^3\ y^4}\right)=\frac{3x^2z^2}{4y^3}$$

353

3. $\dfrac{3x+1}{x}$

$$\left(\dfrac{3x^2-2x-1}{x^2+x}\right)\left(\dfrac{x+1}{x-1}\right)=\dfrac{(3x+1)\cancel{(x-1)}^{1}}{x\cancel{(x+1)}}\dfrac{\cancel{(x+1)}^{1}}{\cancel{(x-1)}_{1}}=\dfrac{3x+1}{x}$$

4. 2

$$\dfrac{4x-8}{6}\div\dfrac{x-2}{3}=\dfrac{4x-8}{6}\times\dfrac{3}{x-2}=\dfrac{4\cancel{(x-2)}^{1}}{\cancel{6}_{2}}\times\dfrac{\cancel{3}^{1}}{\cancel{(x-2)}_{1}}=\dfrac{4}{2}=2$$

5. $\dfrac{x+12}{x+4}$

$$\dfrac{2x+7}{x+4}-\dfrac{x-5}{x+4}=\dfrac{2x+7-(x-5)}{x+4}=\dfrac{2x+7-x+5}{x+4}=\dfrac{x+12}{x+4}$$

6. $\dfrac{y+3x}{xy}$ or $\dfrac{3x+y}{xy}$

$$\dfrac{1}{x}+\dfrac{3}{y}=\left(\dfrac{1}{x}\times\dfrac{y}{y}\right)+\left(\dfrac{3}{y}\times\dfrac{x}{x}\right)=\dfrac{y}{xy}+\dfrac{3x}{xy}=\dfrac{y+3x}{xy}\ \text{or}\ \dfrac{3x+y}{xy}$$

7. $\dfrac{2y^2+3x}{x^2y^3}$ or $\dfrac{3x+2y^2}{x^2y^3}$

$$\dfrac{2}{x^2y}+\dfrac{3}{xy^3}=\left(\dfrac{2}{x^2y}\times\dfrac{y^2}{y^2}\right)+\left(\dfrac{3}{xy^3}\times\dfrac{x}{x}\right)=\dfrac{2y^2}{x^2y^3}+\dfrac{3x}{x^2y^3}=\dfrac{2y^2+3x}{x^2y^3}\ \text{or}\ \dfrac{3x+2y^2}{x^2y^3}$$

8. $\dfrac{3x^2+7x}{(x-3)(x+1)}$

$$\dfrac{4x}{x-3}-\dfrac{x}{x+1}=\left(\dfrac{4x}{x-3}\times\dfrac{(x+1)}{(x+1)}\right)-\left(\dfrac{x}{x+1}\times\dfrac{(x-3)}{(x-3)}\right)$$

$$=\dfrac{4x^2+4x}{(x-3)(x+1)}-\dfrac{x^2-3x}{(x-3)(x+1)}$$

$$=\dfrac{4x^2+4x-x^2+3x}{(x-3)(x+1)}$$

$$=\dfrac{3x^2+7x}{(x-3)(x+1)}$$

Solving Quadratic Equations in One Variable

A *quadratic equation* is an equation that can be written as ax^2+bx+c with $a\neq0$. Some quadratic equations can be solved quickly by *factoring*, but factoring is not always possible. Quadratic equations can also be solved by using the *quadratic formula*.

Steps to Solve a Quadratic Equation Using Factoring

1. Place all terms on one side of the equal sign, leaving zero on the other side.
2. Factor the quadratic expression.
3. Set each factor equal to zero.
4. Solve each of these equations.

Examples:

> **1.** Solve for x by factoring: $x^2 - 6x = 16$

Following the steps above:

$x^2 - 6x = 16$ becomes $x^2 - 6x - 16 = 0$

$x^2 - 6x - 16 = 0$ becomes $(x - 8)(x + 2) = 0$

$$x - 8 = 0 \quad \text{or} \quad x + 2 = 0$$
$$x = 8 \quad \text{or} \quad x = -2$$

> **2.** Solve for x by factoring: $3x^2 - 4x - 5 = 2x^2 + 4x - 17$

$3x^2 - 4x - 5 = 2x^2 + 4x - 17$ becomes $x^2 - 8x + 12 = 0$

$x^2 - 8x + 12 = 0$ becomes $(x - 6)(x - 2) = 0$

$$x - 6 = 0 \quad \text{or} \quad x - 2 = 0$$
$$x = 6 \quad \text{or} \quad x = 2$$

> **3.** Solve for x by factoring: $9x^2 - 49 = 0$

The quadratic is already in the "= 0" form.

$9x^2 - 49 = 0$ becomes $(3x + 7)(3x - 7) = 0$

$$3x + 7 = 0 \quad \text{or} \quad 3x - 7 = 0$$
$$3x = -7 \quad \text{or} \quad 3x = 7$$
$$x = -\frac{7}{3} \quad \text{or} \quad x = \frac{7}{3}$$

> **4.** Solve for x by factoring: $x^2 = 6x$

$x^2 = 6x$ becomes $x^2 - 6x = 0$

$x^2 - 6x = 0$ becomes $x(x - 6) = 0$

$$x = 0 \quad \text{or} \quad x - 6 = 0$$
$$x = 0 \quad \text{or} \quad x = 6$$

The Quadratic Formula

Frequently, even when a quadratic equation can be factored, finding the appropriate factors is difficult. When finding the appropriate factors becomes difficult, use the quadratic formula.

The *quadratic formula* is a rule that allows you to solve all quadratic problems, even the quadratic equations that are not factorable. The general quadratic equation is $ax^2 + bx + c = 0$.

The quadratic formula says $x = \dfrac{-b \pm \sqrt{b^2 - 4ac}}{2a}$. In order to use the formula, all terms must be on one side of the equation set equal to zero.

The following examples are taken from the previous original four examples. Each problem begins with the original problem rewritten in the **"= 0"** form. Notice that the answers are the same as when the problems were solved by factoring.

Examples:

> **1.** Solve for x using the quadratic formula: $x^2 - 6x - 16 = 0$

$a = 1$, $b = -6$, $c = -16$

$$x = \frac{-(-6) \pm \sqrt{(-6)^2 - 4(1)(-16)}}{2(1)}$$

$$= \frac{6 \pm \sqrt{36 + 64}}{2}$$

$$= \frac{6 \pm \sqrt{100}}{2}$$

$$= \frac{6 \pm 10}{2}$$

$$= \frac{6 + 10}{2} = \frac{16}{2} = 8 \text{ or } \frac{6 - 10}{2} = \frac{-4}{2} = -2$$

> **2.** Solve for x using the quadratic formula: $x^2 - 8x + 12 = 0$

$a = 1$, $b = -8$, $c = 12$

$$x = \frac{-(-8) \pm \sqrt{(-8)^2 - 4(1)(12)}}{2(1)}$$

$$= \frac{8 \pm \sqrt{64 - 48}}{2}$$

$$= \frac{8 \pm \sqrt{16}}{2}$$

$$= \frac{8 \pm 4}{2}$$

$$= \frac{8 + 4}{2} = \frac{12}{2} = 6 \text{ or } \frac{8 - 4}{2} = \frac{4}{2} = 2$$

> **3.** Solve for x using the quadratic formula: $9x^2 - 49 = 0$

$a = 9$, $b = 0$, $c = -49$

$$x = \frac{-(0) \pm \sqrt{(0)^2 - 4(9)(-49)}}{2(9)}$$

$$= \frac{\pm \sqrt{4(9)(49)}}{18}$$

$$= \frac{\pm (2)(3)(7)}{18}$$

$$= \frac{\pm 42}{18}$$

$$= \frac{42}{18} = \frac{7}{3} \text{ or } \frac{-42}{18} = -\frac{7}{3}$$

4. Solve for x using the quadratic formula: $x^2 - 6x = 0$

$a = 1$, $b = -6$, $c = 0$

$$x = \frac{-(-6) \pm \sqrt{(-6)^2 - 4(1)(0)}}{2(1)}$$

$$= \frac{6 \pm \sqrt{36 - 0}}{2}$$

$$= \frac{6 \pm \sqrt{36}}{2}$$

$$= \frac{6 \pm 6}{2}$$

$$= \frac{6 + 6}{2} = \frac{12}{2} = 6 \text{ or } \frac{6 - 6}{2} = \frac{0}{2} = 0$$

Practice: Solving Quadratic Equations in One Variable

Solve for x in the following quadratic equations using either factoring or the quadratic formula.

1. $x^2 = -7x + 8$

2. $4x^2 - 81 = 0$

3. $3x^2 + 9x = 0$

Answers: Solving Quadratic Equations in One Variable

1. -8 or 1

Using factoring

$x^2 + 7x - 8 = 0$

$(x + 8)(x - 1) = 0$

$x + 8 = 0 \quad \text{or} \quad x - 1 = 0$

$x = -8 \quad \text{or} \quad x = 1$

Using the quadratic formula

$x^2 + 7x - 8 = 0$, $a = 1$, $b = 7$, $c = -8$

$$x = \frac{-(7) \pm \sqrt{(7)^2 - 4(1)(-8)}}{2(1)}$$

$$= \frac{-7 \pm \sqrt{49 + 32}}{2}$$

$$= \frac{-7 \pm \sqrt{81}}{2}$$

$$= \frac{-7 \pm 9}{2}$$

$$= \frac{-7 + 9}{2} = \frac{2}{2} = 1 \text{ or } \frac{-7 - 9}{2} = \frac{-16}{2} = -8$$

2. $-\dfrac{9}{2}$ or $\dfrac{9}{2}$

Using factoring

$4x^2 - 81 = 0$

$(2x + 9)(2x - 9) = 0$

$2x + 9 = 0 \quad \text{or} \quad 2x - 9 = 0$

$2x = -9 \quad \text{or} \quad 2x = 9$

$x = -\dfrac{9}{2} \quad \text{or} \quad x = \dfrac{9}{2}$

Using the quadratic formula

$4x^2 - 81 = 0$, $a = 4$, $b = 0$, $c = -81$

$$x = \frac{-(0) \pm \sqrt{(0)^2 - 4(4)(-81)}}{2(4)}$$

$$= \frac{0 \pm \sqrt{1296}}{8}$$

$$= \frac{\pm 36}{8}$$

$$= \frac{\pm 9}{2}$$

3. 0 or −3

Using factoring	Using the quadratic formula

Using factoring

$3x^2 + 9x = 0$

$3x(x+3) = 0$

$3x = 0$ or $x+3 = 0$

$x = 0$ or $x = -3$

Using the quadratic formula

$3x^2 + 9x = 0,\ a = 3,\ b = 9,\ c = 0$

$$x = \frac{-(9) \pm \sqrt{(9)^2 - 4(3)(0)}}{2(3)}$$

$$= \frac{-9 \pm \sqrt{81}}{6}$$

$$= \frac{-9 \pm 9}{6}$$

$$= \frac{-9 + 9}{6} = \frac{0}{6} = 0$$

$$= \frac{-9 - 9}{6} = \frac{-18}{6} = -3$$

Coordinate Geometry

Each point on a number line is assigned a number. In the same way, each point in a plane is assigned a pair of numbers. These numbers represent the placement of the point relative to two intersecting lines. In **coordinate graphs,** two perpendicular number lines are used and are called the *coordinate axes.* One axis is horizontal and is called the *x-axis.* The other is vertical and is called the *y-axis.* The point of intersection of the two number lines is called the *origin* and is represented by the coordinates (0,0).

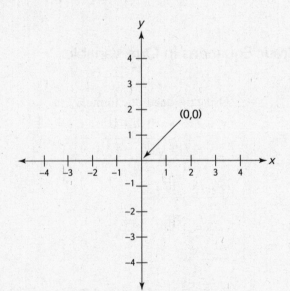

Each point on a plane is located by a unique pair of ordered numbers called the *coordinates.* Some coordinates are noted below.

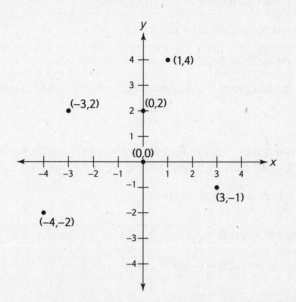

Notice that on the *x*-axis, numbers to the right of 0 are positive and to the left of 0 are negative. On the *y*-axis, numbers above 0 are positive and below 0 are negative. The first number in the ordered pair is called the *x-coordinate,* or *abscissa,* while the second number is the *y-coordinate,* or *ordinate.* The *x*-coordinate shows the right or left direction, and the *y*-coordinate shows the up or down direction. The coordinate graph is divided into four regions (quarters) called *quadrants.* These quadrants are labeled below.

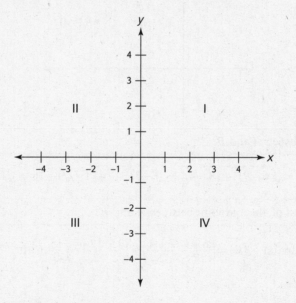

In quadrant I, *x* is always positive and *y* is always positive.

In quadrant II, *x* is always negative and *y* is always positive.

In quadrant III, *x* and *y* are both always negative.

In quadrant IV, *x* is always positive and *y* is always negative.

Examples:

> **1.** In which quadrant(s) do points have positive x-coordinates?

Points have positive x-coordinates in quadrants I and IV.

> **2.** In which quadrant(s) do points have negative x-coordinates and positive y-coordinates?

Only in quadrant II do points have negative x-coordinates and positive y-coordinates.

Distance and Midpoint

Given the coordinates of any two points, you can find the *distance* between them, the *length* of the segment, and the *midpoint* (the point that is located halfway between them) by using appropriate formulas.

Given that A (x_1, y_1) and B (x_2, y_2) are any two points then:

$$\text{Distance between A and B} = \sqrt{(x_2 - x_1)^2 + (y_2 - y_1)^2} \text{ or } \sqrt{(x_1 - x_2)^2 + (y_1 - y_2)^2}$$

$$\text{Midpoint between A and B} = \left(\frac{x_1 + x_2}{2}, \frac{y_1 + y_2}{2}\right) \text{ or } \left(\frac{x_2 + x_1}{2}, \frac{y_2 + y_1}{2}\right)$$

Examples:

Use the following graph for example questions 1 and 2.

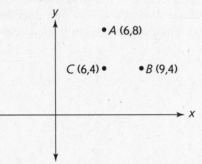

> **1.** What is the distance between A and B?

$$AB = \sqrt{(6-9)^2 + (8-4)^2} = \sqrt{(-3)^2 + (4)^2} = \sqrt{9+16} = \sqrt{25} = 5$$

> **2.** What are the coordinates of the midpoint between A and B?

$$\text{Midpoint}\,(AB) = \left(\frac{6+9}{2}, \frac{8+4}{2}\right) = \left(\frac{15}{2}, \frac{12}{2}\right) = \left(\frac{15}{2}, 6\right) \text{ or } (7.5, 6)$$

Constructing a Graph

Given the equation of a line, you can ***construct the graph*** of this line by finding ordered pairs that make the equation true. One method for finding the solutions begins with giving a value to one variable and solving the resulting equation for the other value. Repeat this process to find other solutions. (Note: When giving a value for one variable, start with 0, then try 1, and so on.) Then graph the solutions.

Example:

1. Graph the equation $x + y = 6$.

If x is 0, then y is 6: $(0) + y = 6$; $y = 6$.

If x is 1, then y is 5: $(1) + y = 6$; $y = 5$.

If x is 2, then y is 4: $(2) + y = 6$; $y = 4$.

Using a simple chart is helpful.

x	y
0	6
1	5
2	4

Now plot these coordinates and connect them.

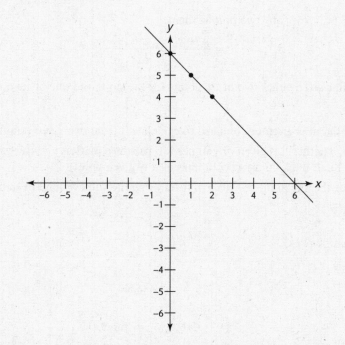

Notice that these solutions form a straight line when plotted. Equations whose solution sets form a straight line are called *linear equations*. Equations that have a variable raised to a power, show division by a variable, involve variables with square roots, or have variables multiplied together will not form straight lines when their solutions are graphed. These are called *nonlinear equations*.

Slope and *y*-intercept

There are two relationships between the graph of a linear equation and the equation itself. One involves the *slope of the line*, and the other involves the point of intersection of the line with the *y*-axis, known as the *y-intercept*. When a linear equation is written in the $y = mx + b$ form, the m value becomes the slope of the line, and the b value is the location on the *y*-axis where the line intercepts the *y*-axis. Thus, the $y = mx + b$ form is called the *slope-intercept form* for the equation of a line.

Example:

1. Find the slope and y-intercept of the line with equation $3x - 4y = 12$.

$$3x - 4y = 12 \qquad \text{(Solve for } y \text{ by first subtracting } 3x \text{ from each side.)}$$
$$\underline{-3x \qquad -3x}$$
$$-4y = -3x + 12 \qquad \text{(Divide each term on each side by } -4.)$$
$$\frac{-4y}{-4} = \frac{-3x}{-4} + \frac{12}{-4}$$
$$y = \frac{3}{4}x - 3$$

Therefore, the slope of the line is $\frac{3}{4}$, and its y-intercept is at -3.

Slope-Intercept

Given any two points on a line, you can locate the equation of the line that passes through these points. This will require finding the slope of the line and the y-intercept.

Given that A (x_1, y_1) and B (x_2, y_2) are any two points, then:

$$m = \frac{y_2 - y_1}{x_2 - x_1} \text{ or } \frac{y_1 - y_2}{x_1 - x_2}$$

To find an equation of a line given either two of its points (or the slope and one of its points), use the following step-by-step approach.

1. Find the slope, m (either it is given or you need to calculate it from two given points).
2. Find the y-intercept, b (either it is given or you need to use the equation $y = mx + b$ and substitute the slope value found in Step 1 and the x- and y-coordinates of any given point).
3. Write the equation of the line in the $y = mx + b$ form using the values found in steps 1 and 2.

Examples:

Use the graph below for questions 1–3.

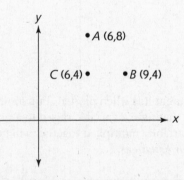

1. What is the slope of the line joining A and B?

$$m = \frac{4 - 8}{9 - 6} = -\frac{4}{3} \left(\text{or } \frac{8 - 4}{6 - 9} = -\frac{4}{3} \right)$$

2. What is the equation of the line, in slope-intercept form, joining A and B?

$$y = mx + b \qquad \left(\text{Replace } m \text{ with } -\frac{4}{3}.\right)$$

$$y = -\frac{4}{3}x + b \qquad \left(\begin{array}{l}\text{Use the point } (6,8) \text{ and replace } x \text{ with } 6 \text{ and } y \text{ with } 8 \\ \text{then solve the resulting equation for } b.\end{array}\right)$$

$$8 = -\frac{4}{\cancel{3}_{1}}\left(\frac{\cancel{6}^{2}}{1}\right) + b$$

$$8 = -8 + b$$

$$16 = b$$

Therefore, the equation is $y = -\frac{4}{3}x + 16$.

3. If the line joining A and B were extended, what would be its exact y-intercept?

The b-value represents the y-intercept, thus the exact y-intercept is 16.

Finding Perimeter and Area

Once the coordinates of a figure are known, certain measurements regarding the figure can be calculated. That is, you can find its *perimeter* (distance around), and its **area.**

Examples:

Use the graph below for questions 1 and 2.

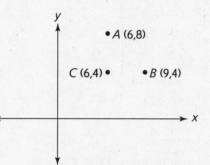

Points A, B, and C, when connected, form a triangle.

1. What is the perimeter of $\triangle ABC$?

To find the perimeter of a triangle, simply add the lengths of its sides.

$$AB = \sqrt{(6-9)^{2} + (8-4)^{2}} = \sqrt{(-3)^{2} + (4)^{2}} = \sqrt{9+16} = \sqrt{25} = 5$$

$$AC = \sqrt{(6-6)^{2} + (8-4)^{2}} = \sqrt{(0)^{2} + (4)^{2}} = \sqrt{16} = 4$$

$$BC = \sqrt{(9-6)^{2} + (4-4)^{2}} = \sqrt{(3)^{2} + (0)^{2}} = \sqrt{9} = 3$$

Therefore, the perimeter of $\triangle ABC = 5 + 4 + 3 = 12$.

> **2. What is the area of $\triangle ABC$?**

Since point A is directly above point C and point B is directly to the right of point C, then $\triangle ABC$ is a right triangle. Now use BC as a base and AC as a height, and find the area of $\triangle ABC$ using the formula $A = \frac{1}{2}bh$, where b is the length of the base and h is the length of the height.

Area of $\triangle ABC = \frac{1}{2}(3)(4) = \frac{1}{2}(12) = 6$.

Practice: Coordinate Geometry

1. In which quadrant is $(-4,-2)$ located?

Use the graph below for questions 2–8.

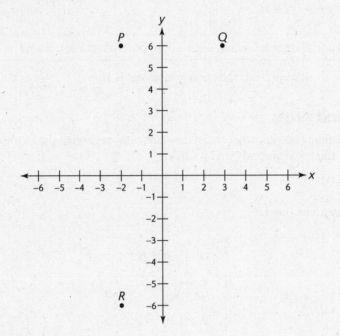

2. What is the distance from Q to R?

3. What are the coordinates of the midpoint between Q and R?

4. What is the slope of the line joining Q and R?

5. What is the equation of the line, in slope-intercept form, joining Q and R?

6. What is the exact y-intercept of the line joining Q and R?

7. What is the perimeter of $\triangle PQR$?

8. What is the area of $\triangle PQR$?

Answers: Coordinate Geometry

1. III

(–4,–2) is located in quadrant III.

2. 13

Point Q is at (3,6) and point R is at (–2,–6).

$$QR = \sqrt{(-2-3)^2 + (-6-6)^2}$$
$$= \sqrt{(-5)^2 + (-12)^2}$$
$$= \sqrt{25+144}$$
$$= \sqrt{169}$$
$$= 13$$

3. $\left(\frac{1}{2},0\right)$

$$\text{Midpoint } QR = \left(\frac{-2+3}{2}, \frac{-6+6}{2}\right)$$
$$= \left(\frac{1}{2}, \frac{0}{2}\right)$$
$$= \left(\frac{1}{2}, 0\right)$$

4. $\frac{12}{5}$

$$m = \frac{-6-6}{-2-3} = \frac{-12}{-5} = \frac{12}{5} \text{ or } m = \frac{6-(-6)}{3-(-2)} = \frac{12}{5}$$

5. $y = \frac{12}{5}x - \frac{6}{5}$

From question 4, slope of line $QR = \frac{12}{5}$. Use point Q (3,6) and the slope value to substitute into $y = mx + b$.

$$y = mx + b$$
$$6 = \frac{12}{5}\left(\frac{3}{1}\right) + b$$
$$6 = \frac{36}{5} + b \qquad \left(\frac{6}{1} - \frac{36}{5} = \frac{30}{5} - \frac{36}{5} = -\frac{6}{5}\right)$$
$$-\frac{6}{5} = b$$

The equation of the line passing through Q and R is $y = \frac{12}{5}x - \frac{6}{5}$.

6. $-\frac{6}{5}$ or $-1\frac{1}{5}$

The y-intercept is the b-value from the slope-intercept form of the equation of the line joining Q and R, which is $-\frac{6}{5}$ or $-1\frac{1}{5}$.

7. 30

Perimeter $\Delta PQR =$ PR $+$ PQ $+QR$

$$= \sqrt{\left(-2-(-2)\right)^2 + (-6-6)^2} + \sqrt{(-2-3)^2 + (6-6)^2} + 13$$

$$= \sqrt{(0)^2 + (-12)^2} \qquad + \sqrt{(-5)^2 + (0)^2} \qquad + 13$$

$$= \sqrt{144} \qquad\qquad + \sqrt{25} \qquad\qquad + 13$$

$$= 12 \qquad\qquad + 5 \qquad\qquad + 13$$

Perimeter $\Delta PQR = 30$

8. 30

Since P and Q are directly across from one another and P and R are directly one above the other, ΔPQR is a right triangle. Use PQ as a base and PR as a height.

$$\text{Area } \Delta PQR = \frac{1}{2}(PQ)(PR)$$
$$= \frac{1}{2}(5)(12)$$
$$= 30$$

Functions and Function Notation

A *function* is an equation that expresses an output for any acceptable input. Often the letters f, g, or h are used to denote functions. Consider the function $f(x) = x^2 - 2x$. The English phrase "find the value of the function when x is 6" is expressed as $f(6) = ?$

The function is then evaluated by replacing each x with the value 6.

$$f(x) = x^2 - 2x$$
$$f(6) = (6)^2 - 2(6)$$
$$f(6) = 36 - 12$$
$$f(6) = 24$$

Examples:

---
1. If $f(x) = x^2 - 3x$, then $f(3) - f(1) = ?$

First find $f(3)$ and $f(1)$. Then solve the subtractions of these results.

$$f(x) = x^2 - 3x \qquad\qquad f(x) = x^2 - 3x$$
$$f(3) = (3)^2 - 3(3) \qquad\qquad f(1) = (1)^2 - 3(1)$$
$$f(3) = 9 - 9 \qquad\qquad f(1) = 1 - 3$$
$$f(3) = 0 \qquad\qquad f(1) = -2$$

$$f(3) - f(1) = 0 - (-2) = 2$$

2. If $h(x)=|x|$ then $\dfrac{4}{h(4)}-\dfrac{-2}{h(-2)}=?$

First find $h(4)$ and $h(-2)$. Then make the appropriate replacements and evaluate the results.

$$h(x)=|x| \qquad h(4)=|4| \qquad h(-2)=|-2|$$
$$h(4)=4 \qquad h(-2)=2$$
$$\frac{4}{h(4)}=\frac{4}{4}=1 \qquad \frac{-2}{h(-2)}=\frac{-2}{2}=-1$$
$$\frac{4}{h(4)}-\frac{-2}{h(-2)}=1-(-1)=2$$

3. If $m(x)=3x+2$ and $t(x)=x^2$, then $t[m(-2)]=?$

First find $m(-2)$, then use its value to replace the x and $t(x)$ function.

$$m(x)=3x+2 \qquad t(x)=x^2$$
$$m(-2)=3(-2)+2 \qquad t[m(-2)]=[m(-2)]^2$$
$$m(-2)=-6+2 \qquad t[m(-2)]=[-4]^2$$
$$m(-2)=-4 \qquad t[m(-2)]=16$$

Practice: Functions and Function Notation

1. If $f(x)=5x+3$, then $f(4)-f(-2)=?$

2. If $f(x)=x^2-3x+7$ and $g(x)=|-2x-5|$, then $f(-2)-g(-2)=?$

3. If $g(x)=x-2$ and $h(x)=x^2+1$, then $g[h(0)]=?$ and $h[g(0)]=?$

Answers: Functions and Function Notation

1. 30

$$f(x)=5x+3,$$
$$f(4)=5(4)+3 \qquad f(-2)=5(-2)+3$$
$$f(4)=20+3 \qquad f(-2)=-10+3$$
$$f(4)=23 \qquad f(-2)=-7$$
$$f(4)-f(-2)=23-(-7)=30$$

2. 16

$$f(x)=x^2-3x+7 \text{ and } g(x)=|-2x-5|$$
$$f(-2)=(-2)^2-3(-2)+7 \qquad g(-2)=|-2(-2)-5|$$
$$f(-2)=4+6+7 \qquad g(-2)=|4-5|$$
$$f(-2)=17 \qquad g(-2)=|-1|=1$$
$$f(-2)-g(-2)=17-1=16$$

3. $g[h(0)] = -1$, $h[g(0)] = 5$

$$g(x) = x - 2 \qquad\qquad h(x) = x^2 + 1$$
$$g(0) = 0 - 2 = -2 \qquad\qquad h(0) = (0)^2 + 1 = 1$$
$$g[h(0)] = \qquad\qquad h[g(0)] =$$
$$g(1) = 1 - 2 = -1 \qquad\qquad h(-2) = (-2)^2 + 1 = 5$$

Geometry

Geometry Diagnostic Test

1. Lines that stay the same distance apart and never meet are called _____ lines.

2. Lines that meet to form right angles are called _____ lines.

3. A(n) _____ angle measures less than 90 degrees.

4. A(n) _____ angle measures 90 degrees.

5. A(n) _____ angle measures more than 90 degrees but less than 180 degrees.

6. A(n) _____ angle measures 180 degrees.

7. Find the smaller angle of a pair of complementary angles such that the larger one is 30 degrees greater than twice the smaller one.

8. Find the larger of two supplementary angles such that the smaller one is half the larger one.

9. In the diagram below, find the measure of $\angle 1$, $\angle 2$, and $\angle 3$.

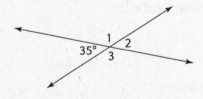

10. In the diagram below, find the value of x, then find the measure of all the numbered angles.

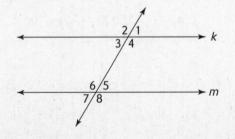

$k \parallel m$; $\angle 1 = 2x + 6$ and $\angle 6 = 10x + 30$

Questions 11 and 12 refer to the figure below.

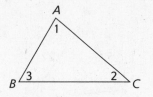

11. Name ∠*A* of this triangle in three different ways.

12. ∠1 + ∠2 + ∠3 = _____°.

13. What are the generic names of polygons with 4, 5, 6, 7, 8, 9, and 10 sides?

14. What are the interior angle sums of convex polygons having 4, 5, 6, 7, 8, 9, or 10 sides?

15. What is the sum of all the exterior angles, one at each vertex, for any convex polygon?

16. What is the measure of one interior angle and one exterior angle of a regular dodecagon (12-sided polygon)?

17. In △*ABC* below,

segment *BD* is a(n) _____

segment *BE* is a(n) _____

segment *BF* is a(n) _____

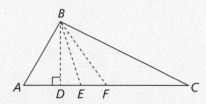

$\overline{BD} \perp \overline{AC}$, *AF* = *FC*, ∠*ABE* = ∠*CBE*

18. A(n) _____ triangle has three equal sides. Therefore, each interior angle measures _____°.

19. In the diagram below, *ABC* is an isosceles triangle with base *BC* and ∠*B* = 38°. Find ∠*A* and ∠*C*.

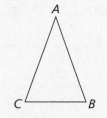

Questions 20 and 21 refer to the diagram below.

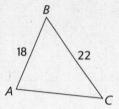

20. In $\triangle ABC$, what is the range of possible values for AC?

21. In $\triangle ABC$, which angle is smaller, $\angle A$ or $\angle C$?

22. In the diagram below, what is the measure of $\angle RST$ if it is an exterior angle of $\triangle QRS$ and $\angle Q = 4x - 3$, $\angle R = 6x - 7$, and $\angle RST = 9x + 5$?

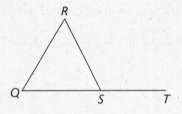

Questions 23–26 refer to the diagram below.

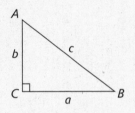

23. If $b = 8$ and $a = 15$, find c.

24. If $b = 10$ and $c = 26$, find a.

25. If $\angle A = 45°$ and $a = 9$, find $\angle B$, b, and c.

26. If $\angle B = 60°$ and $a = 12$, find $\angle A$, b, and c.

27. If in trapezoid $ABCD$ below, $\angle A = 45°$, $\angle B = 30°$, $CD = 10$, and $BC = 12$, find the exact length of AB.

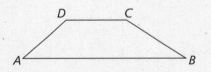

28. Examine the table of quadrilaterals below and place a check mark (✓) next to the statements that *must* be true?

Property Statements	Square	Rectangle	Rhombus	Parallelogram	Trapezoid
Diagonals are equal					
Diagonals bisect each other					
Diagonals are perpendicular					
Diagonals bisect the angles					
All sides are equal in length					
All angles are equal in measure					
Opposite angles are equal in measure					
Opposite sides are equal in length					
At least one pair of opposite sides are parallel					
At least two pairs of consecutive angles are supplementary					

Questions 29–36 relate to the circle with diameter at AC, center at O; points A, B, C, and D lie on the circle, and segment EF is tangent to the circle at point C.

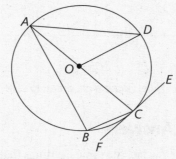

Note: Figure is not drawn to scale.

29. Name all the radii.

30. Name all the chords. What is the longest chord in a circle called?

31. Name all the central angles.

32. Name all the inscribed angles.

33. Name all the angles that *must* have a measure of 90°.

34. If $\overset{\frown}{CD} = 80°$ and $\overset{\frown}{BC} = 50°$, find $\angle DOC$ and $\angle DAB$.

35. If $AC = 12$ inches, find the exact area and circumference of the circle.

36. If $\angle DOC = 40°$ and $DO = 10$ inches, find the exact length of $\overset{\frown}{CD}$ and the exact area of sector DOC.

37. Find the perimeter and area of the trapezoid below.

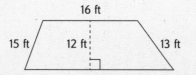

38. Find the area and perimeter of a rhombus if its diagonals have lengths of 24 inches and 10 inches.

39. The area of a triangle with a base of 20 inches is 32 square inches. What is the height associated with this base?

40. Find the exact volume and surface area of a right circular cylinder with a base radius of 12 inches and a height of 10 inches.

41. Find the volume of a cube whose surface area is 24 square inches.

42. A rectangular prism has a diagonal length of $\sqrt{61}$ feet. It has a length of 4 feet and a height of 3 feet. What is its width?

43. If $\triangle ABC \cong \triangle EFG$ and $\angle A = 35°$, $\angle B = 75°$, then $\angle G = ?$

44. Use the diagram below to find x and y.

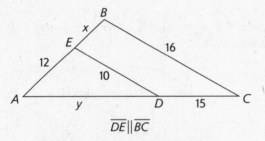

$\overline{DE} \| \overline{BC}$

Note: Figure is not drawn to scale.

Geometry Diagnostic Test Answers

The diagnostic test explanations listed below include topic headings that correspond with step-by-step learning tools and examples to help you solve specific problem types. Topic headings can be found in the Geometry Review section on pages 374–406.

Lines, Segments, Rays, and Angles

1. parallel

2. perpendicular

3. acute

4. right

5. obtuse

6. straight

7. 20 degrees

8. 120 degrees

9. $\angle 1 = \angle 3 = 145°$, $\angle 2 = 35°$

10. $x = 12$, $\angle 1 = \angle 3 = \angle 5 = \angle 7 = 30°$, $\angle 2 = \angle 4 = \angle 6 = \angle 8 = 150°$

Polygons and their Angles

11. $\angle BAC$, $\angle CAB$, $\angle 1$

12. 180

13. 4 sides – quadrilateral, 5 sides – pentagon, 6 sides – hexagon, 7 sides – septagon or heptagon, 8 sides – octagon, 9 sides – nonagon, 10 sides – decagon

14. 4 sides – 360°, 5 sides – 540°, 6 sides – 720°, 7 sides – 900°, 8 sides – 1080°, 9 sides – 1260°, 10 sides – 1440°

15. 360°

16. each interior angle is 150°, each exterior angle is 30°

Triangles

17. BD is an altitude, BE is an angle bisector, BF is a median

18. equilateral, 60

19. $\angle A = 104°$, $\angle C = 38°$

20. AC can be any value between 4 and 40

21. $\angle C$

22. $\angle RST = 140°$

23. 17

24. 24

25. $\angle B = 45°$, $b = 9$, $c = 9\sqrt{2}$

26. $\angle A = 30°$, $b = 12\sqrt{3}$, $c = 24$

27. $16 + 6\sqrt{3}$

Quadrilaterals

28.

Property Statements	Square	Rectangle	Rhombus	Parallelogram	Trapezoid
Diagonals are equal	✓	✓			
Diagonals bisect each other	✓	✓	✓	✓	
Diagonals are perpendicular	✓		✓		
Diagonals bisect the angles	✓		✓		
All sides are equal in length	✓		✓		
All angles are equal in measure	✓	✓			
Opposite angles are equal in measure	✓	✓	✓	✓	
Opposite sides are equal in length	✓	✓	✓	✓	
At least one pair of opposite sides are parallel	✓	✓	✓	✓	✓
At least two pairs of consecutive angles are supplementary	✓	✓	✓	✓	✓

Circles

29. $\overline{OA}$, $\overline{OC}$, $\overline{OD}$

30. $\overline{AB}$, $\overline{AC}$, $\overline{AD}$, $\overline{BC}$; diameter

31. $\angle AOD$, $\angle DOC$

32. $\angle DAC$, $\angle DAB$, $\angle CAB$, $\angle ABC$, $\angle ACB$

33. $\angle ABC$, $\angle ACE$, $\angle ACF$

34. $\angle DOC = 80°$, $\angle DAB = 65°$

Perimeter, Circumference, and Area of Plane Figures

35. area = 36π sq. in., circumference = 12π in.

36. $\overset{\frown}{CD} = \dfrac{20}{9}\pi$ in., area of sector $DOC = \dfrac{100}{9}\pi$ sq. in.

37. perimeter = 74 ft., area = 276 sq. ft.

38. perimeter = 52 in., area = 120 sq. in.

39. height = 3.2 in. or $3\dfrac{1}{5}$ in.

Surface Area, Volume, and Diagonal Lengths

40. volume = 1440π cu. in., surface area = 528π sq. in.

41. volume = 8 cu. in.

42. width = 6 ft.

Congruence and Similarity

43. $\angle G = 70°$

44. $x = 7.2$ or $7\dfrac{1}{5}$, $y = 25$

Geometry Review

Lines, Segments, Rays, and Angles

A *line* will always be considered to be straight. It continues forever in opposite directions. A line consists of an infinite number of points and is named by any two points on it. A line may also be named by one lowercase letter.

The above line can be referred to as line *AB*, line *BA*, or line *k*.

A *line segment* is a portion of a line that contains two endpoints and all the points that are in between them. A line segment is named by its two endpoints. A segment has a length and is expressed by stating the two endpoints next to one another. On the GMAT, a line segment and its length will occasionally be expressed using the same expression. It is important to recognize the context of the expression that is being referenced.

The segment that has endpoints at *A* and *B* can be referred to as $\overline{AB}$, *AB*, or segment *AB*. The distance between *A* and *B*, or the length of segment *AB* is also referred to as *AB*.

A **midpoint** of a line segment is the halfway point, or the point equidistant from the endpoints.

If *AM* = *MB*, then *M* is the midpoint of *AB*. In the previous sentence, the *AM* and *MB* are considered to be lengths, and the *AB* is considered to be the segment itself.

A **ray** is a portion of a line with one endpoint and continues forever in only one direction. Referring to figure above, ray *AB* would be the portion of the line starting at *A*, its endpoint, passing through *B* and continuing on in that direction. Ray *BA* would start at *B*, its endpoint, pass through *A* and continue forever in that direction. Notice that ray *AB* and ray *BA* are not the same ray, yet ray *AB* and ray *AM* represent the same ray.

An **angle** is formed by two rays that have the same endpoint (or two lines that intersect at a point). The endpoint of intersection of an angle is called the **vertex of the angle** and the rays are called the **sides** of the angle. An angle is measured in degrees from 0 to 360. The number of degrees indicates the size of the angle. The angle symbol $\angle$ is often used instead of the word "angle."

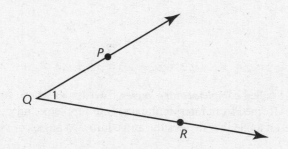

In the figure above, there are several common ways to name the angle:

- by the letter of the vertex, $\angle Q$
- by the number in its interior, $\angle 1$.
- by three letters with the middle letter the vertex of the angle, $\angle PQR$ or $\angle RQP$.

A **right angle** has a measure of 90°. In the figure below, the small square symbol in the interior of the angle means a right angle. Angle *T* is a right angle.

Any angle whose measure is less than 90° is called an **acute angle.** Any angle whose measure is larger than 90° but smaller than 180° is called an **obtuse angle.** A **straight angle** has a measure of 180°.

In the figure below, ∠*PQR* is an acute angle, ∠*PQS* is an obtuse angle, and ∠*RQS* is a straight angle.

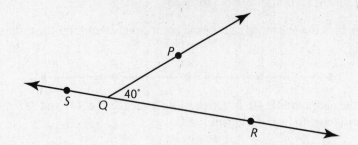

When lines intersect, four angles are formed. The angles opposite each other are called ***vertical angles.*** The angles sharing a common side and a common vertex are ***adjacent angles.*** Vertical angles are always equal in measure and adjacent angles formed by intersecting lines will always have a sum of 180°.

In the figure below, line *n* and line *m* intersect.

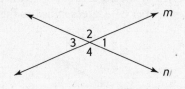

$$\angle 1 = \angle 3, \angle 2 = \angle 4, \angle 1 + \angle 2 = \angle 2 + \angle 3 = \angle 3 + \angle 4 = \angle 4 + \angle 1 = 180°$$

Two angles whose sum is 90° are called ***complementary angles.*** Two angles whose sum is 180° are called ***supplementary angles.*** Adjacent angles formed from intersecting lines are supplementary. An ***angle bisector*** is a ray, segment, or line from the vertex of an angle that divides the angle into two angles of equal measure.

Two lines that meet to form right angles are called ***perpendicular lines.*** The symbol ⊥ is used to denote perpendicular lines. Two or more lines that remain the same distance apart at all times are called ***parallel lines.*** Parallel lines never meet. The symbol ∥ is used to denote parallel lines.

In the figure below, ray *m* is an angle bisector. *k* ⊥ *n* and *l* ⊥ *n*. *k* ∥ *l*.

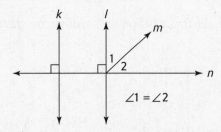

When two parallel lines are both intersected by a third line, eight angles, none of which are straight angles, are formed. Angles in the same relative positions will have equal measures. With this, knowing any one angle, or how any two angles are related, the measures of all 8 angles can be determined.

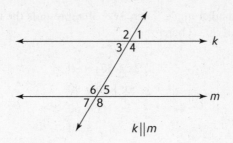

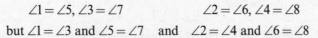

$$\angle 1 = \angle 5, \angle 3 = \angle 7 \qquad \angle 2 = \angle 6, \angle 4 = \angle 8$$

but $\angle 1 = \angle 3$ and $\angle 5 = \angle 7$ and $\angle 2 = \angle 4$ and $\angle 6 = \angle 8$

because vertical angles are equal

therefore,

$$\angle 1 = \angle 3 = \angle 5 = \angle 7 \quad \text{and} \quad \angle 2 = \angle 4 = 6 = \angle 8$$

When two parallel lines are intersected by a third line, any two angles will either have equal measures or be supplementary.

Examples:

1. Lines that stay the same distance apart and never meet are called _____ lines.

This is a definition of parallel lines.

2. Lines that meet to form right angles are called _____ lines.

This is the definition of perpendicular lines.

3. A(n) _____ angle measures less than 90 degrees.

This is the definition of an acute angle.

4. A(n) _____ angle measures 90 degrees.

This is the definition of a right angle.

5. A(n) _____ angle measures more than 90 degrees but less than 180 degrees.

This is the definition of an obtuse angle.

6. A(n) _____ angle measures 180 degrees.

This is the definition of a straight angle.

7. Find the smaller angle of a pair of complementary angles such that the larger one is 30 degrees greater than twice the smaller one.

Let x represent the measure of the smaller angle. Then $2x + 30$ represents the measure of the larger angle. Complementary angles have a sum of 90°. Therefore,

$$x + (2x + 30) = 90$$
$$3x + 30 = 90$$
$$3x = 60$$
$$x = 20$$

The smaller angle has a measure of 20 degrees.

---

8. Find the larger of two supplementary angles such that the smaller one is half the larger one.

Let x represent the measure of the larger angle. Then $\frac{1}{2}x$ represents the measure of the smaller angle. Supplementary angles have a sum of 180°. Therefore,

$$x + \frac{1}{2}x = 180$$
$$\frac{3}{2}x = 180$$
$$x = 120$$

The larger angle has a measure of 120 degrees.

---

9. In the diagram below, find the measure of $\angle 1$, $\angle 2$, and $\angle 3$.

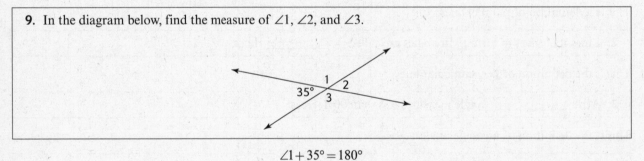

$$\angle 1 + 35° = 180°$$
$$\angle 1 = 145°$$

And since vertical angles have equal measure, $\angle 2 = 35°$, $\angle 3 = 145°$.

---

10. In the diagram below, find the value of x, then find the measure of all the numbered angles.

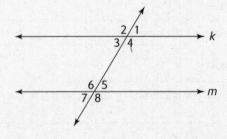

$k \| m$; $\angle 1 = 2x + 6$ and $\angle 6 = 10x + 30$

Lines k and m are parallel. Since $\angle 1$ and $\angle 6$ are not equal, then they must be supplementary. Therefore,

$$\angle 1 + \angle 6 = 180$$
$$(2x+6)+(10x+30)=180$$
$$12x+36=180$$
$$12x=144$$
$$x=12$$

$\angle 1 = 2x+6 = 2(12)+6 = 24+6 = 30, \quad \angle 6 = 10x+30 = 10(12)+30 = 120+30 = 150$

$\angle 1 = \angle 3 = \angle 5 = \angle 7 = 30° \qquad \angle 2 = \angle 4 = \angle 6 = \angle 8 = 150°$

Practice: Lines, Segments, Rays, and Angles

1. Find the value of $x + y$. All measures are in degrees.

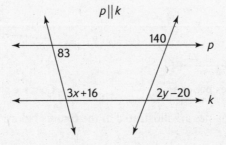

2. If in the figure below, the measure of angle 2 is twice that of angle 1, how big is angle ABC and what type of angle is it?

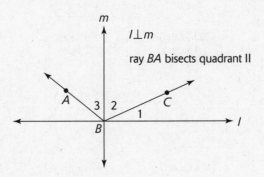

Answers: Lines, Segments, Rays, and Angles

1. 57

Since $p \parallel k$, then

$$2y-20+140=180 \qquad \text{and} \qquad (3x+16)+83=180$$
$$(2y-20 \neq 140) \qquad\qquad (3x+16 \neq 83)$$
$$\text{Then, } 2y-20+140=180 \qquad 3x+16+83=180$$
$$2y+120=180 \qquad\qquad 3x+99=180$$
$$2y=60 \qquad\qquad 3x=81$$
$$y=30 \qquad\qquad x=27$$

Therefore, $x + y = 27 + 30 = 57$.

2. 105°, obtuse

Since $l \perp m$, then $\angle 1 + \angle 2 = 90°$.

Since $\angle 2$ is twice as large as $\angle 1$, then $\angle 2$ is 60° and $\angle 1$ is 30°. Since ray *BA* bisects quadrant II, then $\angle 3 = 45°$. $\angle ABC = \angle 3 + \angle 2 = 45 + 60 = 105$.

Since $\angle ABC$ is between 90 and 180, $\angle ABC$ is obtuse.

Polygons and their Angles

Closed shapes, or figures in a plane, with three or more sides are called *polygons. Poly* means "many," and *gon* means "sides." Thus, polygon means "many sides."

Convex polygons are polygons such that regardless of what side is extended, the polygon always remains on one side of the extension. *Concave polygons* have at least one side, and when extended there is a polygon on each side of the extension. The GMAT examination only deals with convex polygons. Examples of convex and concave polygons are provided below.

Convex polygon   Concave polygon

Convex polygons, and their generic names are illustrated in the figures below.

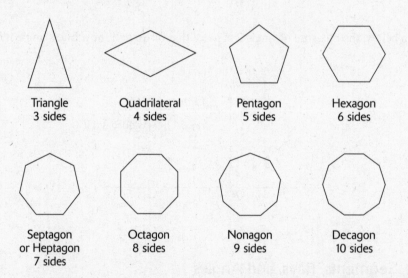

| Triangle | Quadrilateral | Pentagon | Hexagon |
| 3 sides | 4 sides | 5 sides | 6 sides |

| Septagon or Heptagon | Octagon | Nonagon | Decagon |
| 7 sides | 8 sides | 9 sides | 10 sides |

Regular polygons are polygons that have all sides the same length and all angles the same measure. A regular three-sided polygon is the *equilateral triangle.* A regular four-sided polygon is the *square.* A regular five-sided polygon is called a *regular pentagon.* A regular six-sided polygon is called a *regular hexagon.*

A *diagonal of a polygon* is a line segment that connects one vertex with another vertex and is not itself a side.

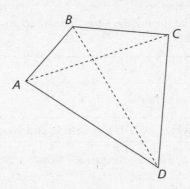

In quadrilateral *ABCD*, $\overline{AC}$, and $\overline{BD}$ are both diagonals. If all the diagonals from one vertex of a polygon were drawn, it would divide the polygon into nonoverlapping triangles. The figure below illustrates nonoverlapping triangles in a quadrilateral, pentagon, and hexagon.

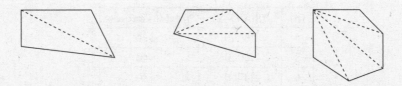

In each case, the number of triangles created is 2 less than the number of sides of the polygon. Since the sum of the angles of any triangle is 180°, you can now find the sum of the angles of any convex polygon by taking 2 less than the number of sides times 180°. That is, if *n* is how many sides a polygon has, then $180(n - 2)$ is the sum of all its interior angles.

Another interesting fact about the angles of any convex polygon is that if each side was extended in one direction, and the exterior angles at the vertices were measured, then the sum of all the exterior angles, one at each vertex would equal 360°.

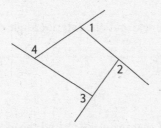

In the case of the quadrilateral above, $\angle 1 + \angle 2 + \angle 3 + \angle 4 = 360°$.

A 15-sided polygon would have 15 exterior angles, one at each vertex, and the sum of those 15 angles would also be 360°.

Examples:

Questions 1 and 2 refer to the figure below.

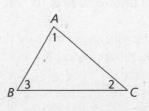

---

1. Name $\angle A$ of this triangle in three different ways.

If three letters are used, the vertex must be the middle letter. The three possible answers are $\angle BAC$, $\angle CAB$, and $\angle 1$.

---

2. $\angle 1 + \angle 2 + \angle 3 = \underline{\qquad}°$.

The sum of the angles of a triangle is always 180°.

---

3. What are the generic names of polygons with 4, 5, 6, 7, 8, 9, and 10 sides?

4 sides – quadrilateral, 5 sides – pentagon, 6 sides – hexagon, 7 sides – septagon or heptagon, 8 sides – octagon, 9 sides – nonagon, 10 sides – decagon

---

4. What are the interior angle sums of convex polygons having 4, 5, 6, 7, 8, 9, or 10 sides?

The formula for the sum of the interior angle sums is $180(n-2)$, where n is the number of sides of the polygon.

n	$180(n-2)$	Total (in degrees)
4	180(2)	360
5	180(3)	540
6	180(4)	720
7	180(5)	900
8	180(6)	1080
9	180(7)	1260
10	180(8)	1440

---

5. What is the sum of all the exterior angles, one at each vertex, for any convex polygon?

The sum is always 360°.

---

6. What is the measure of one interior angle and one exterior angle of a regular dodecagon (12-sided polygon)?

There are two methods to do this problem.

Method 1:

Find the interior angle, then subtract that from 180 to find the exterior angle. The sum of the interior angles is $180(12-2) = 180(10) = 1800°$.

Since there are 12 angles in a 12-sided figure, and a regular polygon has each of its interior angles equal to one another, each angle will have a measure of $\frac{1800°}{12} = 150°$.

Then each exterior angle has a measure of $180° - 150° = 30°$.

Method 2:

Find each exterior angle, then subtract that from 180 to find the interior angle. The sum of all the exterior angles is 360°.

Since the figure is regular, each of its exterior angles will have the same measure. There are 12 exterior angles; therefore, each exterior angle has the measure $\frac{360°}{12} = 30°$, which means each interior angle has the measure $180° - 30° = 150°$.

Practice: Polygons and their Angles

1. How many sides does a polygon have if the interior angle sum of a polygon is 1980°?

2. How many sides does a regular polygon have if each exterior angle measures 18°?

Answers: Polygons and their Angles

1. 13

   The sum of the angles of any convex polygon with n sides is $180(n-2)$.

   $$180(n-2)=1980 \quad \text{(divide each side by 180)}$$
   $$n-2=11$$
   $$n=13$$

   The polygon has 13 sides.

2. 20

   The sum of the exterior angles of any polygon is 360°. A regular polygon has each of its exterior angles equal in measure. Let n be the number of sides, then

   $$\frac{360°}{n}=18°$$
   $$18n=360$$
   $$n=20$$

   The polygon has 20 sides.

Triangles

Triangles can be classified by the lengths of their sides.

- A triangle having all three sides equal in measure is called an ***equilateral triangle.***
- A triangle having at least two equal sides is called an ***isosceles triangle.***
- A triangle having no equal sides is called a ***scalene triangle.***

Triangles can also be classified by their angles.

- A triangle having all three angles equal in measure is called an ***equiangular triangle.***
- A triangle having a right angle in its interior is called a ***right triangle.***
- A triangle having an obtuse angle in its interior is called an ***obtuse triangle.***
- A triangle having all acute angles in its interior is called an ***acute triangle.***

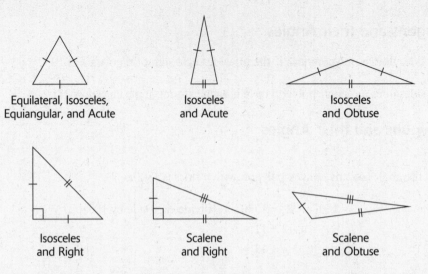

Equilateral, Isosceles, Equiangular, and Acute

Isosceles and Acute

Isosceles and Obtuse

Isosceles and Right

Scalene and Right

Scalene and Obtuse

In any triangle, if two of its sides have equal length, the angles opposite those sides have equal measure, and if any two angles in a triangle have equal measure, then the sides opposite those angles have equal length. If all three sides in a triangle are equal, then all three angles in the triangle are equal and vice versa. In any triangle, if one side is longer than another side, then the angle opposite the longer side will be greater than the angle opposite the shorter side and vice versa.

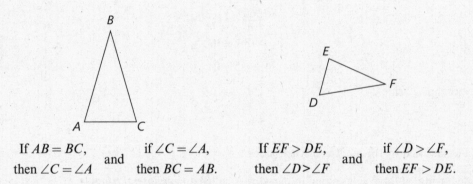

If $AB = BC$, then $\angle C = \angle A$ and if $\angle C = \angle A$, then $BC = AB$.

If $EF > DE$, then $\angle D > \angle F$ and if $\angle D > \angle F$, then $EF > DE$.

Any side of a triangle can be called a ***base.*** With each base, there is an associated ***height*** (or *altitude*). Each height segment is the perpendicular segment from a vertex to its opposite side or the extension of the opposite side. The height, ***h,*** can go inside the triangle to its associated base, ***b,*** it can be one of the sides of the triangle, or it can go outside the triangle as shown in the diagram below.

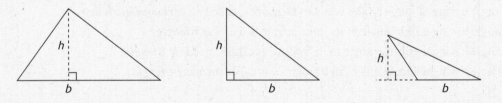

Every triangle has three medians. A *median* is a line segment drawn from a vertex to the midpoint of the opposite side. In the figure below, $\overline{BD}$ is a median to side AC.

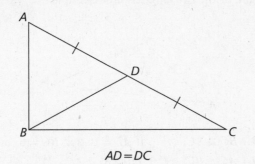

$$AD = DC$$

Every triangle has three *angle bisectors.* The angle bisector divides an angle into two smaller angles that are equal in measure. In the figure below, $\overline{GI}$ is the angle bisector from vertex G.

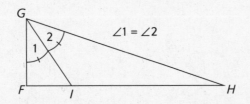

$$\angle 1 = \angle 2$$

An interesting fact: In any triangle, if one segment is any two of the three special segments in a triangle (altitude, median, angle bisector), then it is automatically the third one, and the triangle is isosceles. The vertex from which the segments are drawn becomes the vertex of the isosceles triangle, and it is at the vertex of the isosceles triangle where the equal sides meet. See figure below.

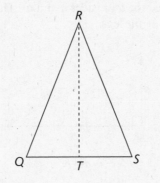

- If $\overline{RT}$ is an altitude <u>and</u> an angle bisector or
- If $\overline{RT}$ is an altitude <u>and</u> a median or
- If $\overline{RT}$ is an angle bisector <u>and</u> a median

The sum of the lengths of any two sides of a triangle must be larger than the length of the third side. This statement can be interpreted as, "given any two sides of a triangle, the remaining side must be greater than the difference of the two lengths, but less than the sum of the two lengths." For example:

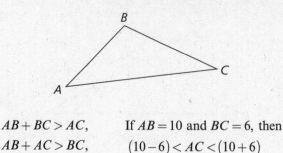

$$AB + BC > AC,$$
$$AB + AC > BC,$$
$$AC + BC > AB$$

If $AB = 10$ and $BC = 6$, then
$$(10 - 6) < AC < (10 + 6)$$
$$4 < AC < 16$$

If one side of a triangle is extended, the exterior angle formed by that extension is equal to the sum of the remote interior angles. For example:

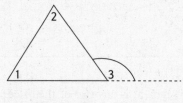

$$\angle 3 = \angle 1 + \angle 2$$

In any right triangle, the relationship between the lengths of the sides is stated by the ***Pythagorean theorem.*** The side opposite the right angle is called the ***hypotenuse*** (side c). The hypotenuse will always be the longest side in a right triangle. The other two sides are called the ***legs*** (sides a and b). The theorem states that the square of the hypotenuse equals the sum of the squares of the legs.

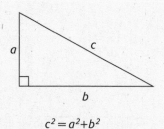

$$c^2 = a^2 + b^2$$

An extension of this theorem can be used to determine the type of triangle based on knowing its angle measures or the lengths of its three sides. If a, b, and c are the lengths of the sides of any triangle with c being the longest side, then the following is true:

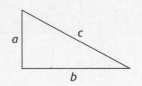 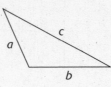 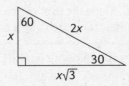

If $c^2 = a^2 + b^2$, then the triangle is a right triangle and the angle opposite c is 90°.

If $c^2 > a^2 + b^2$, then the triangle is an obtuse triangle and the angle opposite c is greater than 90°.

If $c^2 < a^2 + b^2$, then the triangle is an acute triangle and the angle opposite c is less than 90°.

If the angle opposite c is 90°, the triangle is a right triangle and $c^2 = a^2 + b^2$.

If the angle opposite c is greater than 90°, the triangle is an obtuse triangle and $c^2 > a^2 + b^2$.

If the angle opposite c is less than 90°, the triangle is an acute triangle and $c^2 < a^2 + b^2$.

There are two very special right triangles whose side relationships you should know. One is called the *30-60-90 right triangle* and the other is the *45-45-90 right triangle.*

In the 30-60-90 right triangle, the side opposite the 30 degrees is the shortest side, the hypotenuse is twice as long as the shortest side, and the side opposite the 60 degrees is the shortest side times $\sqrt{3}$. This is shown in the figure below.

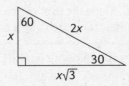

In the 45-45-90 right triangle, the legs have equal lengths and the length of the hypotenuse is a leg times $\sqrt{2}$. This is shown in the figure below.

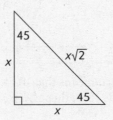

Besides these two special right triangles, right triangles with sides 3-4-5, 5-12-13, 7-24-25, and 8-15-17 are often used on tests.

Examples:

1. In △*ABC* below,

   segment *BD* is a(n) _____.

   segment *BE* is a(n) _____.

   segment *BF* is a(n) _____.

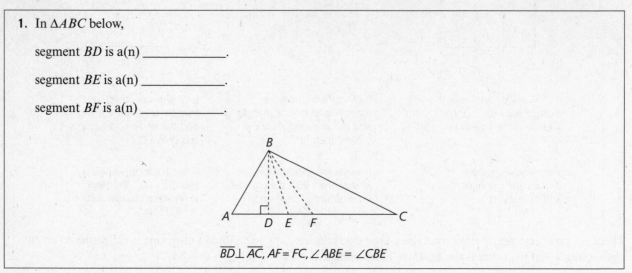

$$\overline{BD} \perp \overline{AC}, AF = FC, \angle ABE = \angle CBE$$

Since $\overline{BD} \perp \overline{AC}$, $\overline{BD}$ is an altitude. Since $\angle ABE = \angle CBE$, $\overline{BE}$ is an angle bisector. Since $AF = FC$, $\overline{BF}$ is a median.

2. A(n) _____ triangle has three equal sides. Therefore, each interior angle measures ____°.

An equilateral triangle has all three sides equal. Since the sum of the angles of any triangle is 180°, and equal sides means opposite angles are equal in a triangle, then each angle measures 60°.

3. In the diagram below, *ABC* is an isosceles triangle with base $\overline{BC}$ and $\angle B = 38°$. Find $\angle A$ and $\angle C$.

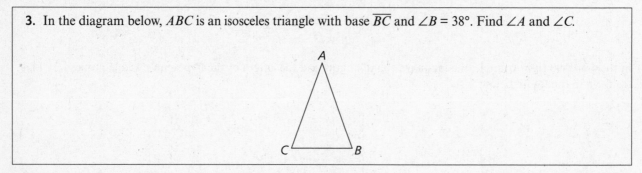

Since $\overline{BC}$ is the base of the isosceles triangle, that means that $AC = AB$, which in turn means $\angle B = \angle C$. Hence, $\angle C = 38°$. The sum of the angles of a triangle is 180°, thus $\angle A + 38° + 38° = 180°$, then $\angle A = 104°$.

Questions 4 and 5 refer to the figure below.

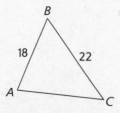

4. In △*ABC* above, what is the range of possible values for *AC*?

AC is greater than the difference of the two given lengths and less than their sum, thus $4 < AC < 40$.

5. In $\triangle ABC$ above, which angle is smaller, $\angle A$ or $\angle C$?

Since $BC > AB$, then $\angle A > \angle C$, which means $\angle C$ is the smaller angle.

6. In the diagram below, what is the measure of $\angle RST$ if it is an exterior angle of $\triangle QRS$ and $\angle Q = 4x - 3$, $\angle R = 6x - 7$, and $\angle RST = 9x + 5$?

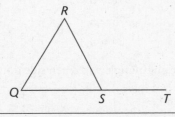

The exterior angle of a triangle equals the sum of its remote interior angles, thus

$$\angle RST = \angle Q + \angle R$$
$$9x + 5 = (4x - 3) + (6x - 7)$$
$$9x + 5 = 10x - 10$$
$$5 = x - 10$$
$$15 = x$$
$$\angle RST = 9x + 5$$
$$= 9(15) + 5$$
$$= 135 + 5$$
$$= 140°$$

Questions 7–10 refer to the figure below.

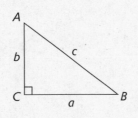

7. If $b = 8$ and $a = 15$, find c.

$$c^2 = a^2 + b^2$$
$$c^2 = (15)^2 + (8)^2$$
$$c^2 = 225 + 64$$
$$c^2 = 289$$
$$c = \sqrt{289}$$
$$c = 17$$

This is an example of the special 8-15-17 right triangle.

8. If $b = 10$ and $c = 26$, find a.

$$c^2 = a^2 + b^2$$
$$26^2 = a^2 + (10)^2$$
$$676 = a^2 + 100$$
$$576 = a^2$$
$$\sqrt{576} = a$$
$$24 = a$$

This is an example of the special 5-12-13 right triangle with each side doubled.

9. If $\angle A = 45°$ and $a = 9$, find $\angle B$, b, and c.

Since the angle at C is 90° and the sum of the angles of a triangle is always 180°, then $\angle B = 45°$. In the 45-45-90 right triangle, the legs are equal and the hypotenuse is a leg times $\sqrt{2}$. Therefore, $b = 9$ and $c = 9\sqrt{2}$.

10. If $\angle B = 60°$ and $a = 12$, find $\angle A$, b, and c.

Since the angle at C is 90° and the sum of the angles of a triangle is always 180°, then $\angle A = 30°$. In the 30-60-90 right triangle, the side opposite the 30° angle is the short leg, the hypotenuse is twice that value, and the long leg is the short leg times $\sqrt{3}$. Therefore, $b = 12\sqrt{3}$ and $c = 2(12) = 24$.

Practice: Triangles

Use the figure below for questions 1–3.

The angles of a triangle are given by $\angle Q = 3x + 12$, $\angle R = 4x - 3$, $\angle S = 2x + 18$.

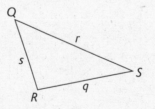

1. Find the value of x.

2. Classify the triangle.

3. Find the relationship between q^2, r^2, and s^2.

4. Which of the following could be the third side of a triangle with sides of 2 and 3?

Ⓐ 1
Ⓑ 3
Ⓒ 5

Answer: Triangles

1. 17

$$\angle Q \quad + \quad \angle R \quad + \quad \angle S \; = 180°$$
$$(3x+12) \; + \; (4x-3) \; + \; (2x+18) = 180$$
$$9x+27 = 180$$
$$9x = 153$$
$$x = 17$$

2. acute and scalene

$$\begin{array}{lll}
\angle Q = 3x+12 & \angle R = 4x-3 & \angle S = 2x+18 \\
\quad = 3(17)+12 & \quad = 4(17)-3 & \quad = 2(17)+18 \\
\quad = 51+12 & \quad = 68-3 & \quad = 34+18 \\
\quad = 63 & \quad = 65 & \quad = 52
\end{array}$$

Since the angles are each different, then the opposite sides are all of different lengths. Therefore the triangle is a scalene triangle. Since each of the angles is less than 90°, the triangle is also an acute triangle.

3. $r^2 < q^2 + s^2$

Since the triangle is an acute triangle, then the square of the longest side is less than the sum of the squares of the other two sides. $\angle R$ is the largest angle, thus its opposite side, r, is the longest side. Therefore, $r^2 < q^2 + s^2$.

4. B

The third side of the triangle must be greater than the difference of 3 and 2 but less than the sum of 3 and 2. The only value that satisfies both conditions is 3.

Quadrilaterals

A polygon having four sides is called a *quadrilateral.* There are four angles in its interior. The sum of the measures of these interior angles will always be 360°. A quadrilateral is named by using the four letters of its vertices named in order either clockwise or counterclockwise.

A *square* is a quadrilateral with four equal sides and four right angles. Both pairs of opposite sides are parallel. Diagonals of a square are equal, bisect each other, are perpendicular to each other, and bisect the angles through which they pass. Figure *ABCD* below is a square.

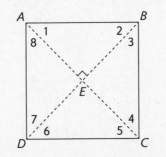

$$\overline{AB} \parallel \overline{CD}, \; \overline{AD} \parallel \overline{BC}, \; AB = BC = CD = AD$$
$$\angle ABC = \angle BCD = \angle CDA = \angle DAB = 90°$$
$$AC = BD, \; \overline{AC} \perp \overline{BD}, \; AE = EC = BE = DE$$
$$\angle 1 = \angle 2 = \angle 3 = \angle 4 = \angle 5 = \angle 6 = \angle 7 = \angle 8 = 45°$$

A *rectangle* has opposite sides equal and parallel and four right angles. Diagonals of a rectangle are equal and bisect each other. Figure *ABCD* below is a rectangle.

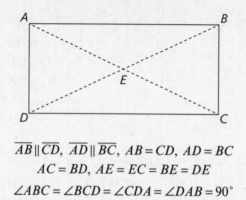

$$\overline{AB} \parallel \overline{CD}, \ \overline{AD} \parallel \overline{BC}, \ AB = CD, \ AD = BC$$

$$AC = BD, \ AE = EC = BE = DE$$

$$\angle ABC = \angle BCD = \angle CDA = \angle DAB = 90°$$

A *parallelogram* has opposite sides equal and parallel, opposite angles equal, and consecutive angles supplementary. Diagonals of a parallelogram are not necessarily equal, but they do bisect each other. Figure *ABCD* below is a parallelogram.

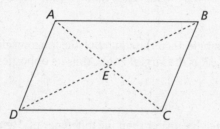

$$\overline{AB} \parallel \overline{CD}, \ \overline{AD} \parallel \overline{BC}, \ AB = CD, \ AD = BC$$

$$AE = EC, \ BE = DE$$

$$\angle ABC = \angle BCD = 180°, \ \angle BCD = \angle CDA = 180°$$

$$\angle CDA + \angle DAB = 180°, \ \angle DAB + \angle ABC = 180°$$

$$\angle ABC = \angle CDA, \ \angle DAB = \angle BCD$$

A *rhombus* *is* a parallelogram with four equal sides but not necessarily four equal angles. Diagonals of a rhombus are not necessarily equal, but they do bisect each other, are perpendicular to each other, and bisect the angles through which they pass. Figure *ABCD* below is a rhombus.

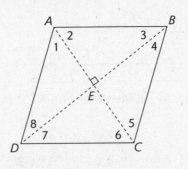

$$\overline{AB} \parallel \overline{CD}, \ \overline{AD} \parallel \overline{BC}, \ AB = CD = AD = BC$$

$$AE = EC, \ BE = DE, \ \overline{AC} \perp \overline{BD}$$

$$\angle ABC = \angle BCD = 180°, \ \angle BCD = \angle CDA = 180°$$

$$\angle CDA + \angle DAB = 180°, \ \angle DAB + \angle ABC = 180°$$

$$\angle ABC = \angle CDA, \ \angle DAB = \angle BCD$$

$$\angle 1 = \angle 2 = \angle 5 = \angle 6, \ \angle 3 = \angle 4 = \angle 7 = \angle 8$$

A *trapezoid* has only one pair of parallel sides. The parallel sides are called the *bases*. The nonparallel sides are called the *legs*. The *median* of a trapezoid is a line segment that is parallel to the bases and bisects the legs (connects the midpoints of the legs). An *isosceles trapezoid* is a trapezoid whose legs are equal in length. Only in the isosceles trapezoid are the diagonals equal in length but do not bisect each other. In an isosceles trapezoid, each pair of angles on the same base are equal in measure. Figure *ABCD* below is a trapezoid with median *EF*.

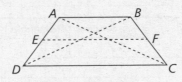

$$\overline{AB} \parallel \overline{CD} \ (\text{the bases})$$

$$AE = ED, \ BF = FC, \ \overline{FE} \parallel \overline{AB} \ \text{and} \ \overline{FE} \parallel \overline{CD}, \ \left(\overline{FE} \text{ is a median}\right)$$

$$\angle ABC + \angle BCD = 180°, \ \angle BAD + \angle CDA = 180°$$

If $AD = BC$ (an isosceles trapezoid), then $AC = BD$, $\angle DAB = \angle CBA$, $\angle ADC = \angle BCD$.

Examples:

1. If in trapezoid *ABCD* below, $\angle A = 45°$, $\angle B = 30°$, $CD = 10$, and $BC = 12$, find the exact length of *AB*.

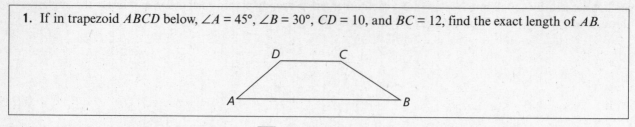

Begin by drawing a perpendicular segment to $\overline{AB}$ from *D* and from *C* creating two special right triangles.

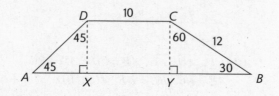

In the 30-60-90 right triangle *BCY*, $\overline{CY}$ will be half as long as $\overline{BC}$; therefore, $CY = 6$. *BY* will then be $6\sqrt{3}$. The figure *DCYX* is a rectangle; therefore, $DC = XY$ and $DX = CY$. So $XY = 10$ and $DX = 6$. In the 45-45-90 right triangle *DXA*, the legs are equal in length; therefore, $AX = 6$. The length of $\overline{AB}$ is the sum of the lengths of $\overline{AX}$, $\overline{XY}$, and $\overline{BY}$.

$$AB = AX + XY + BY$$
$$= 6 + 10 + 6\sqrt{3}$$
$$= 16 + 6\sqrt{3}$$

2. In chart form, summarize the properties of quadrilaterals.

Property Statements	Square	Rectangle	Rhombus	Parallelogram	Trapezoid
Diagonals are equal	✓	✓			
Diagonals bisect each other	✓	✓	✓	✓	
Diagonals are perpendicular	✓		✓		
Diagonals bisect the angles	✓		✓		
All sides are equal in length	✓		✓		
All angles are equal in measure	✓	✓			
Opposite angles are equal in measure	✓	✓	✓	✓	
Opposite sides are equal in length	✓	✓	✓	✓	
At least one pair of opposite sides are parallel	✓	✓	✓	✓	✓
At least two pairs of consecutive angles are supplementary	✓	✓	✓	✓	✓

Practice: Quadrilaterals

1. A rhombus has a side of length 5 and the longer of its two diagonals has a length of 8. Find the length of the shorter diagonal.

2. The opposite angles of a parallelogram have measures of $12x + 18$ and $4x + 58$. Find the measure of the largest angle in this parallelogram.

Answers: Quadrilaterals

1. 6

The sides of a rhombus are all equal. The diagonals of a rhombus bisect each other and are perpendicular to one another. If the longer diagonal is 8, half of it will be 4. Since there is a right triangle, use the Pythagorean theorem. Refer to the diagram below.

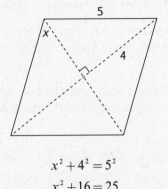

$$x^2 + 4^2 = 5^2$$
$$x^2 + 16 = 25$$
$$x^2 = 9$$
$$x = 3$$

Since half the shorter diagonal is 3, the entire diagonal will be 6.

2. 102°

Opposite angles in a parallelogram have equal measure. Therefore,

$$12x + 18 = 4x + 58$$
$$8x + 18 = 58$$
$$8x = 40$$
$$x = 5$$
$$12x + 18 = 12(5) + 18$$
$$= 60 + 18$$
$$= 78$$

Therefore, one set of opposite angles are each 78° and the other pair of opposite angles are each 102° since consecutive angles in a parallelogram have a sum of 180°. The largest angle in this parallelogram has a measure of 102°.

Circles

A *radius* of a circle can either be the segment that joins the center to any point on the circle or the length of that segment. All radii of the same circle have the same length.

A *diameter* of a circle can either be the segment that joins any two points on a circle and passes through the center of the circle or the length of that segment. In any circle, all diameters have the same length and a diameter equals two radii in length. A *chord* of a circle is a line segment whose endpoints lie on the circle. The *diameter* is the longest chord in any circle.

An *arc* is the portion of a circle between any two points on the circle. Arcs are measured in degree units or in length units. In degrees, it is a portion of the 360° that is a full rotation. In length, it is a portion of the circumference, which is the distance around the circle.

A *central angle* in a circle has the center as its vertex and two radii as its sides. The measure of a central angle in degrees is the same as the number of degrees in the arc it intercepts.

An *inscribed angle* in a circle has its vertex on the circle and two chords as its sides. The measure of an inscribed angle in degrees is half the number of degrees of the arc it intercepts.

A *tangent* to a circle is a line that intersects a circle at only one point. That point is referred to as *the point of tangency*. When a diameter or a radius meet a tangent at the point of tangency, they form a 90° angle.

The symbol $\overparen{AB}$ is used to denote the arc between points A and B. It is written on top of the two endpoints that form the arc. It is in the context of use that you would know whether the measure is intended to be a degree measure or a length measure.

When an arc involves half or more than half of a circle, three letters must be used with the first and third indicating the ends of the arc and the middle letter indicating an additional point through which the arc passes.

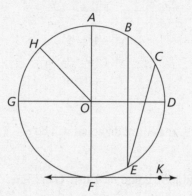

The diagram above is of circle O. (A circle is named by its center.) Points A, B, C, D, E, F, G, and H lie on the circle. The radii shown are $\overline{OA}$, $\overline{OD}$, $\overline{OF}$, $\overline{OG}$, and $\overline{OH}$. The diameters shown are $\overline{AF}$ and $\overline{DG}$. $DG = 2(OH)$. Chords shown that are not diameters are BE and CE.

The shortest path along the circle from point A to point E is $\overparen{AE}$. The longest path along the circle from point A to point E can be shown by $\overparen{AFE}$. The central angles shown are $\angle AOD$, $\angle DOF$, $\angle FOG$, $\angle FOH$, $\angle GOH$, $\angle GOA$, and $\angle HOA$. In degrees, $\overparen{AH} = \angle AOH$, $\overparen{ADH} = 360° - \angle AOH$.

The inscribed angle shown is $\angle BEC$. In degrees, $\frac{1}{2}\overparen{BC} = \angle BEC$. Line FK is tangent to circle O. The point of tangency is F. $\angle AFK = 90°$.

Examples:

Questions 1–7 relate to the circle with diameter $\overline{AC}$, center at O; points A, B, C, and D lie on the circle, and segment EF is tangent to the circle at point C.

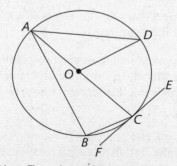

Note: Figure is not drawn to scale.

1. Name all the radii.

$\overline{OA}$, $\overline{OC}$, $\overline{OD}$

2. Name all the chords.

$\overline{AB}$, $\overline{AC}$, $\overline{AD}$, $\overline{BC}$

3. What is the longest chord in a circle called?

diameter

4. Name all the central angles.

$\angle AOD$, $\angle DOC$

5. Name all the inscribed angles.

$\angle ABC$, $\angle ACB$, $\angle BAD$, $\angle CAD$, $\angle CAB$

6. Name all the angles that *must* have a measure of 90°.

$\angle ACE$, $\angle ACF$ (where a tangent and diameter meet, they form a 90° angle).

$\angle ABC$ (it is an inscribed angle that intercepts a half circle, so it is $\frac{1}{2}$ of 180°).

7. If $\overset{\frown}{CD} = 80°$ and $\overset{\frown}{BC} = 50°$, find $\angle DOC$ and $\angle DAB$.

$\overset{\frown}{CD} = \angle DOC$ therefore, $\angle DOC = 80°$.

$\angle DAB = \frac{1}{2}\overset{\frown}{DB}$ and $\overset{\frown}{DB} = \overset{\frown}{DC} + \overset{\frown}{CB}$, therefore, $\angle DAB = \frac{1}{2}(80° + 50°) = 65°$.

Practice: Circles

Questions 1–2 relate to the circle with diameter at AC, center at O; points A, B, C, and D lie on the circle, and segment EF is tangent to the circle at point C.

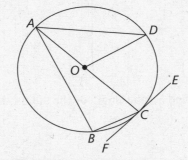

Note: Figure is not drawn to scale.

1. If $\angle BCA = 37°$, then $\angle CAB = $?

2. If $\angle CAB = 30°$, how does BC compare to OD?

Answers: Circles

1. 53°

   Since $\overline{AC}$ is a diameter, then inscribed angle ABC intercepts a semicircle, which makes its measure $\frac{1}{2}(180°) = 90°$. The sum of angles of a triangle is always 180°.

$$\angle CAB + \angle BCA + \angle ABC = 180$$
$$\angle CAB + \quad 37 \quad + \quad 90 \quad = 180$$
$$\angle CAB + \qquad 127 \qquad = 180$$
$$\angle CAB = 53$$

2. $BC = OD$

   As discussed above, $\angle ABC = 90°$. With $\angle CAB = 30°$, triangle ABC is a 30-60-90 right triangle, which makes $BC = \frac{1}{2}(AC)$. Since OD is a radius and AC is a diameter, $OD = \frac{1}{2}(AC)$. Therefore, $BC = OD$.

Perimeter, Circumference, and Area of Plane Figures

Perimeter is the distance around the outside of a polygon. **Circumference** is the distance around a circle. **Area** is the number of square units that fill the interior of a plane figure.

For the circle, the **circumference** and **area** formulas use the symbol π. This is a value that is approximately 3.14 in decimal form or about $\frac{22}{7}$ in fraction form. See "Important Geometric Formulas" on pages 288–289 for **perimeter**, **circumference**, and **area** formulas of the most common geometric figures.

In addition to these fundamental formulas, there are the formulas for the length of an arc of a circle and the area of a sector of a circle. The length of an arc is a portion of the circumference. The sector of a circle is a portion of the area of a circle between two radii. In order to calculate either of these quantities, you need to know a central angle and the length of a radius.

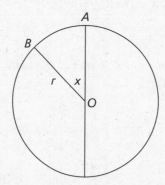

If x is the measure of the central angle and r is the length of the radius, then the length of $\overparen{AB}$ is $\overparen{AB} = \frac{x}{360}(2\pi r)$ and area of sector $AOB = \frac{x}{360}(\pi r^2)$.

Examples:

1. Find the perimeter and area of the trapezoid below.

16 ft

15 ft / 12 ft ⌐ 13 ft

In order to make this easier to solve, draw the perpendicular segments from the ends of the upper base to the lower base, creating two right triangles. Then use the Pythagorean theorem to find missing lengths.

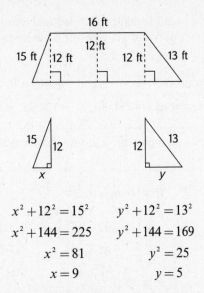

$$x^2 + 12^2 = 15^2 \qquad y^2 + 12^2 = 13^2$$
$$x^2 + 144 = 225 \qquad y^2 + 144 = 169$$
$$x^2 = 81 \qquad\qquad y^2 = 25$$
$$x = 9 \qquad\qquad y = 5$$

Now the figure can be redrawn with all the measurements indicated.

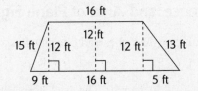

The trapezoid now can be seen as having base lengths of 16 ft. and 30 ft., (9 + 16 + 5 = 30), and a height of 12 ft.

$$\text{perimeter} = \text{ sum of all the sides} = (15 + 16 + 13 + 30)\,\text{ft} = 74 \text{ ft}$$
$$\text{area} = \frac{h(b_1 + b_2)}{2} = \frac{(12)(16 + 30)}{2}\,\text{sq. ft.} = 276 \text{ sq. ft.}$$

---

2. Find the area and perimeter of a rhombus if its diagonals have lengths of 24 inches and 10 inches.

A rhombus is a quadrilateral with all sides equal in length. The diagonals of a rhombus are perpendicular to one another and bisect each other. If one diagonal has length of 24 inches, then each half would be 12 inches. If the other diagonal has length of 10 inches, then each half would be 5 inches. Now you have a right triangle with legs of 5 and 12. Use the Pythagorean theorem to find the hypotenuse, which is the length of one side of the rhombus.

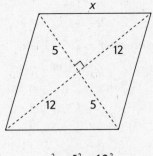

$$x^2 = 5^2 + 12^2$$
$$x^2 = 25 + 144$$
$$x^2 = 169$$
$$x = 13$$

Each side of the rhombus is 13 inches; therefore, its perimeter is 4(13) or 52 inches.

To find the area of the rhombus, find the area of each of the identical four triangles created with the intersecting diagonals. Each is a right triangle with legs of 5 and 12. Use one of these as the height and the other as the base.

$$\text{Area triangle} = \frac{bh}{2} = \frac{(5)(12)}{2} \text{ sq. in.} = 30 \text{ sq. in.}$$
$$\text{Area rhombus} = 4(30) \text{ sq. in.} = 120 \text{ sq. in.}$$

---

3. The area of a triangle with a base of 20 inches is 32 square inches. What is the height associated with this base?

$$\text{Area triangle} = \frac{bh}{2}$$
$$32 = \frac{(20)(h)}{2}$$
$$64 = 20h$$
$$3.2 = h$$

The height is 3.2 inches or $3\frac{1}{5}$ inches.

Practice: Perimeter, Circumference, and Area of Plane Figures

1. The length of a diagonal in a rectangle is 13 inches and one side has a length of 5 inches. Find the perimeter and area of this rectangle.

2. An arc of a circle has a central angle of 30 degrees. The arc length is 12π inches. Find the area of this circle.

Answers: Perimeter, Circumference, and Area of Plane Figures

1. perimeter = 34 in., area = 60 sq. in.

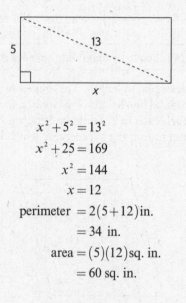

$$x^2 + 5^2 = 13^2$$
$$x^2 + 25 = 169$$
$$x^2 = 144$$
$$x = 12$$
$$\text{perimeter} = 2(5+12)\text{in.}$$
$$= 34 \text{ in.}$$
$$\text{area} = (5)(12)\text{sq. in.}$$
$$= 60 \text{ sq. in.}$$

2. 5184π sq. in.

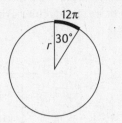

Arc length $= \frac{x}{360}(2\pi r)$, where x is the measure of the central angle.

$$12\pi = \frac{\overset{1}{\cancel{30}}}{\underset{12}{\cancel{360}}}(2\pi r)$$

$$12\pi = \frac{2\pi r}{12}$$

$$144\pi = 2\pi r$$

$$72 = r$$

$$\text{Area} = \pi r^2$$

$$= \pi(72)^2$$

$$= 5184\pi \text{ sq. in.}$$

Surface Area, Volume, and Diagonal Lengths of 3-Dimensional Figures

Surface area is the sum of all the areas of the surfaces of a 3-dimensional figure. **Volume** is the number of cubic units that fill the interior of a 3-dimensional figure. See "Important Geometric Formulas" on pages 288–289 for the surface area and volume formulas of the most common 3-dimensional geometric figures.

In a rectangular prism, besides the length, width, and height, there is a diagonal that goes from one corner to the extreme opposite corner. Refer to the figure below.

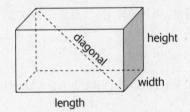

The relationship between the length (l), width (w), height (h), and the diagonal (d) of a rectangular prism is illustrated with the following formula:

$$d = \sqrt{l^2 + w^2 + h^2}$$

Examples:

1. Find the exact volume and surface area of a right circular cylinder with a base radius of 12 inches and a height of 10 inches.

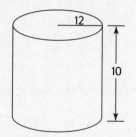

$$\text{Surface area} = 2\pi r^2 + 2\pi rh \qquad\qquad \text{Volume} = \pi r^2 h$$
$$= 2\pi(12)^2 + 2\pi(12)(10) \qquad\qquad = \pi(12)^2(10)$$
$$= 2\pi(144) + 2\pi(120) \qquad\qquad = \pi(144)(10)$$
$$= 288\pi + 240\pi \qquad\qquad = 1440\pi \text{ cu. in.}$$
$$= 528\pi \text{ sq. in.}$$

2. Find the volume of a cube whose surface area is 24 square inches.

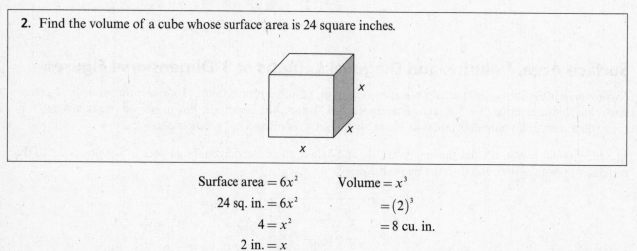

$$\text{Surface area} = 6x^2 \qquad\qquad \text{Volume} = x^3$$
$$24 \text{ sq. in.} = 6x^2 \qquad\qquad = (2)^3$$
$$4 = x^2 \qquad\qquad = 8 \text{ cu. in.}$$
$$2 \text{ in.} = x$$

3. A rectangular prism has a diagonal length of $\sqrt{61}$ feet. It has a length of 4 feet and a height of 3 feet. What is its width?

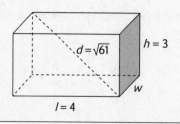

$$d = \sqrt{l^2 + w^2 + h^2}$$
$$\sqrt{61} = \sqrt{4^2 + w^2 + 3^2}$$
$$\sqrt{61} = \sqrt{16 + w^2 + 9} \quad \text{(square both sides)}$$
$$61 = w^2 + 25$$
$$36 = w^2$$
$$6 = w$$

The width is 6 feet.

Practice: Surface Area, Volume, and Diagonal Lengths of 3-Dimensional Figures

1. Find the surface area and diagonal length of a cube whose volume is 343 cubic feet.

2. A cylinder has a height of 3 feet and a volume of 147π cubic feet. Find the surface area of this cylinder.

Answers: Surface Area, Volume, and Diagonal Lengths of 3-Dimensional Figures

1. surface area = 294 cu. ft., diagonal = $7\sqrt{3}$ ft.

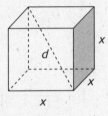

$$\text{Volume} = x^3 \qquad \text{Surface area} = 6x^2 \qquad \text{diagonal} = \sqrt{x^2 + x^2 + x^2}$$
$$343 \text{ cu. ft.} = x^3 \qquad\qquad = 6(7)^2 \qquad\qquad\qquad = \sqrt{3x^2}$$
$$7 \text{ ft.} = x \qquad\qquad\quad = 6(49) \qquad\qquad\qquad = x\sqrt{3}$$
$$\qquad\qquad\qquad = 294 \text{ cu. ft.} \qquad\qquad = 7\sqrt{3} \text{ ft.}$$

2. 140π sq. ft.

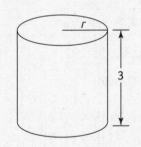

$$\text{Volume} = \pi r^2 h \qquad \text{Surface area} = 2\pi r^2 + 2\pi rh$$
$$147\pi \text{ cu. ft.} = \pi r^2 (3) \qquad\qquad = 2\pi(7)^2 + 2\pi(7)(3)$$
$$49 = r^2 \qquad\qquad\qquad = 2\pi(49) + 2\pi(21)$$
$$7 \text{ ft.} = r \qquad\qquad\qquad = 98\pi + 42\pi$$
$$\qquad\qquad\qquad = 140\pi$$

Congruence and Similarity

Two figures are said to be *congruent* if they have the same shape and have exactly the same size. The symbol for "is congruent to" is ≅. When congruent figures are named, the order in which their vertices are named indicates which angles and sides have the same measure. If $\triangle ABC \cong \triangle DEF$, then $\angle A = \angle D$, $\angle B = \angle E$, $\angle C = \angle F$ and $AB = DE$, $AC = DF$, $BC = EF$.

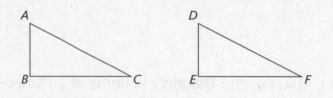

$$\triangle ABC \cong \triangle DEF$$

If two figures are *similar,* they have exactly the same shape but are not necessarily the same size. When similar figures are named, the order in which their vertices are named also indicates which angles are equal in measure and which sides are proportional in measure. The symbol for "is similar to" is ~. If $\triangle ABC \sim \triangle DEF$, then $\angle A = \angle D$, $\angle B = \angle E$, $\angle C = \angle F$ and $\dfrac{AB}{DE} = \dfrac{AC}{DF} = \dfrac{BC}{EF}$.

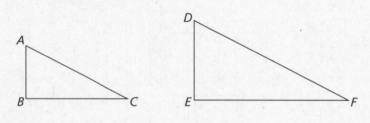

$$\triangle ABC \sim \triangle DEF$$

Triangles that Are Similar

The easiest way to show that two triangles are similar is to show that two angles in one of them have the same measure as two angles in the other.

Examples:

1. If $\triangle ABC \cong \triangle EFG$ and $\angle A = 35°$, $\angle B = 75°$, then $\angle G = ?$

If $\triangle ABC \cong \triangle EFG$, then $\angle A = \angle E$, $\angle B = \angle F$, and $\angle C = \angle G$.

In any triangle, the sum of its angles is 180°. Therefore,

$$\angle A + \angle B + \angle C = 180°$$
$$35° + 75° + \angle C = 180°$$
$$110° + \angle C = 180°$$
$$\angle C = 70°$$
$$\text{but } \angle C = \angle G, \text{ therefore}$$
$$\angle G = 70°$$

2. Use the diagram below to find x and y.

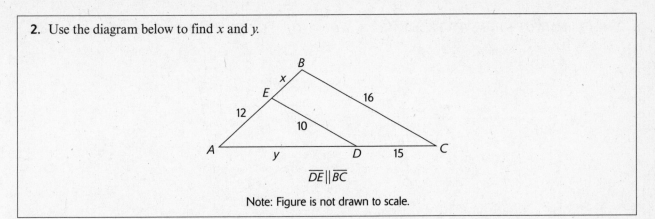

$$\overline{DE} \parallel \overline{BC}$$

Note: Figure is not drawn to scale.

There are two triangles in the figure above: $\triangle ADE$ and $\triangle ACB$. Angle A is the same measure in each triangle. Since $\overline{DE} \parallel \overline{BC}$, then $\angle ADE$ and $\angle C$ have the same measure. This makes $\triangle ADE \sim \triangle ACB$. Redraw the triangles separately with their corresponding measures.

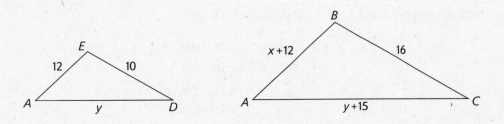

Therefore,

$$\frac{AD}{AC} = \frac{DE}{BC} \qquad \text{and} \qquad \frac{AE}{AB} = \frac{DE}{BC}$$

$$\frac{y}{y+15} = \frac{\overset{5}{\cancel{10}}}{\underset{8}{\cancel{16}}} \qquad\qquad \frac{12}{x+12} = \frac{\overset{5}{\cancel{10}}}{\underset{8}{\cancel{16}}}$$

$$8y = 5(y+15) \qquad\qquad 5(x+12) = 8(12)$$

$$8y = 5y + 75 \qquad\qquad 5x + 60 = 96$$

$$3y = 75 \qquad\qquad 5x = 36$$

$$y = 25 \qquad\qquad x = \frac{36}{5} \text{ or } 7\frac{1}{5} \text{ or } 7.2$$

Practice: Congruence and Similarity

1. If figure $ABCD \cong$ figure $GHIJ$ and $\angle A = \angle B = \angle C = 80°$, find $\angle I + \angle J$.

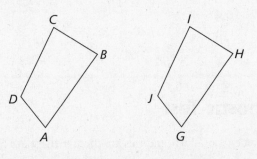

2. If figure $MNOP \sim$ figure $WXYZ$ and $MN = 6$, $NO = 8$, $OP = 10$, $PM = 4$, $WX = 9$, find the perimeter of figure $WXYZ$.

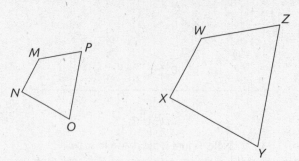

Answers: Congruence and Similarity

1. 200°

The sum of the measures of the angles of a quadrilateral is 360°.

$$\angle A + \angle B + \angle C + \angle D = 360°$$
$$80° + 80° + 80° + \angle D = 360°$$
$$240° + \angle D = 360°$$
$$\angle D = 120°$$

Since figure $ABCD \cong$ figure $GHIJ$, $\angle C = \angle I$ and $\angle D = \angle J$ so $\angle I = 80°$ and $\angle J = 120°$.

$\angle I + \angle J = 80° + 120° = 200°$

2. 42

Since figure $MNOP \sim$ figure $WXYZ$, then

$$\frac{MN}{WX} = \frac{NO}{XY} = \frac{OP}{YZ} = \frac{PM}{ZW}$$

$$\frac{MN}{WX} = \frac{NO}{XY} \qquad \frac{MN}{WX} = \frac{OP}{YZ} \qquad \frac{MN}{WX} = \frac{PM}{ZW}$$

$$\frac{\overset{2}{\cancel{6}}}{\underset{3}{\cancel{9}}} = \frac{8}{XY}, \qquad \frac{\overset{2}{\cancel{6}}}{\underset{3}{\cancel{9}}} = \frac{10}{YZ}, \qquad \frac{\overset{2}{\cancel{6}}}{\underset{3}{\cancel{9}}} = \frac{4}{ZW}$$

$$2XY = 24 \qquad 2YZ = 30 \qquad 2ZW = 12$$
$$XY = 12 \qquad\; YZ = 15 \qquad\;\; ZW = 6$$

The perimeter of figure $WXYZ = WX + XY + YZ + ZW$
$$= 9 + 12 + 15 + 6$$
$$= 42$$

Data Analysis

Data Analysis Diagnostic Test

1. How many different arrangements of shirts and ties are there if there are 5 shirts and 3 ties?

2. In how many different ways can 5 people sit in a row of 5 chairs if all 5 have to be seated?

3. In how many different ways can 3 of out 7 horses finish 1st, 2nd, 3rd if all 7 horses finish the race?

4. How many committees of 4 can be made from a group of 7 people?

5. Pizza Joe's offers customers a choice of five different toppings from column A and four different toppings from column B. You are to select two toppings from each column to make a four-item pizza. How many different possibilities are there?

6. The positive integers 4 through 20 are individually written on index cards and placed in a bowl. What is the probability of randomly selecting a prime number?

Use the spinner with 12 equally divided sections pictured below for questions 7–9.

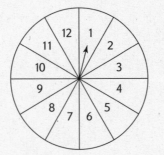

7. What is the probability of spinning a number that is both a multiple of 2 and a multiple of 3 in one spin?

8. What is the probability of *not* spinning a factor of 8 in one spin?

9. If the spinner is spun twice, what is the probability that the spinner will stop on the number 6 the first time and the number 2 the second time?

Use the frequency table below for question 10.

x	f
1	2
2	2
3	1
5	2
7	3

10. Use the frequency table above to find each of the following:

a) mean

b) median

c) mode

d) range

e) 1st quartile

f) 75th percentile

g) interquartile range

h) standard deviation

Data Analysis Diagnostic Test Answers

The diagnostic test explanations listed below include topic headings that correspond with step-by-step learning tools and examples to help you solve specific problem types. Topic headings can be found in the Data Analysis Review section on pages 408–416.

Methods for Counting

1. 15

2. 5! or 120 different ways

3. 210

4. 35

5. 60

Probability

6. $\frac{6}{17}$

7. $\frac{1}{6}$

8. $\frac{2}{3}$

9. $\frac{1}{144}$

Basic Statistics

10. a) mean = 4

   b) median = 4

   c) mode = 7

   d) range = 6

   e) 1st quartile = 2

   f) 75th percentile = 7

   g) interquartile range = 5

   h) standard deviation = $\sqrt{5.6}$

Data Analysis Review

Methods for Counting

The *counting principle*, or *multiplying principle* states that if there are a number of successive choices to be made, and the choices are independent of each other (order makes no difference), the total number of possible choices is the product of each of the choices at each stage.

Example:

1. How many different arrangements of shirts and ties are there if there are 5 shirts and 3 ties?

There are 5 choices for shirts and 3 choices for ties; therefore, there are $5 \times 3 = 15$ possible choices. The 15 choices can be illustrated. Let the 5 choices for shirts be called S1, S2, S3, S4, and S5. Let the 3 choices for ties be called T1, T2, and T3.

The 15 possible pairings are as follows:

S1-T1, S1-T2, S1-T3
S2-T1, S2-T2, S2-T3
S3-T1, S3-T2, S3-T3
S4-T1, S4-T2, S4-T3
S5-T1, S5-T2, S5-T3

Permutations

If there are a number of successive choices to make and the choices are affected by the previous choice or choices (dependent upon order), then *permutations* are involved.

Example:

> **2.** In how many different ways can 5 people sit in a row of 5 chairs if all 5 have to be seated?

$$\underbrace{\begin{array}{c}\text{\# of choices}\\\text{for 1st chair}\end{array}}_{5} \times \underbrace{\begin{array}{c}\text{\# of choices}\\\text{for 2nd chair}\end{array}}_{4} \times \underbrace{\begin{array}{c}\text{\# of choices}\\\text{for 3rd chair}\end{array}}_{3} \times \underbrace{\begin{array}{c}\text{\# of choices}\\\text{for 4th chair}\end{array}}_{2} \times \underbrace{\begin{array}{c}\text{\# of choices}\\\text{for 5th chair}\end{array}}_{1}$$

The product $5 \times 4 \times 3 \times 2 \times 1$ can be written as 5! (read *5 factorial* or *factorial 5*). Thus, there are 5! or 120 different ways to arrange 5 people in 5 chairs in a row.

Sometimes permutation problems do not use all the choices available. In these situations, the use of a *permutations formula* can simplify matters. The symbol to denote this is $P(n, r)$ or $_nP_r$, which is read as "the permutations of n things taken r at a time."

The formula used is $P(n,r) = {_nP_r} = \dfrac{n!}{(n-r)!}$.

Permutations Formula

Example:

> **3.** In how many different ways can 3 out of 7 horses finish 1st, 2nd, and 3rd if all 7 horses finish the race?

The order in which the horses finish the race makes a difference. That is why this situation is referred to as a permutation. In this case, we are taking 7 things 3 at a time.

Since $n = 7$ and $r = 3$, (7 taken 3 at a time) the equation becomes

$$P(7, 3) = {_7P_3} = \frac{7!}{(7-3)!} = \frac{7!}{4!} = \frac{7 \times 6 \times 5 \times \overset{1}{\cancel{(4 \times 3 \times 2 \times 1)}}}{\underset{1}{\cancel{(4 \times 3 \times 2 \times 1)}}} = 7 \times 6 \times 5 = 210$$

This problem could also have been solved using the counting principle.

$$\underbrace{\begin{array}{c}\text{\# of choices}\\\text{for 1st place}\end{array}}_{7} \times \underbrace{\begin{array}{c}\text{\# of choices}\\\text{for 2nd place}\end{array}}_{6} \times \underbrace{\begin{array}{c}\text{\# of choices}\\\text{for 3rd place}\end{array}}_{5} \qquad 7 \times 6 \times 5 = 210$$

Combinations

There are situations in which the order that items are selected does not matter. Those situations are referred to as *combinations*. The symbol used to denote this situation is $C(n, r)$ or $_nC_r$, which is read as "the number of combinations of n things taken r at a time." The formula used is $C(n,r) = {}_nC_r = \dfrac{n!}{r!(n-r)!}$.

Example:

> 4. How many committees of 4 can be made from a group of 7 people?

Notice that the order of selection makes no difference. Since $n = 7$ and $r = 4$ (7 people taken 4 at a time), the equation is as follows:

$$C(7, 4) = {}_7C_4 = \frac{7!}{4!(7-4)!} = \frac{7 \times 6 \times 5 \times 4 \times 3 \times 2 \times 1}{4 \times 3 \times 2 \times 1 \times (3)!} = \frac{7 \times \cancel{6} \times 5 \times \cancel{(4 \times 3 \times 2 \times 1)}}{\cancel{(4 \times 3 \times 2 \times 1)} \; \cancel{3 \times 2 \times 1}} = 35$$

Therefore, 35 committees of 4 can be made from a group of 7 people.

Counting Principle and Combinations Formula

Sometimes you might see a problem on the GMAT that involves both the counting principle and the combinations formula.

Example:

> 5. Pizza Joe's offers customers a choice of five different toppings from column A and four different toppings from column B. You are to select two toppings from each column to make a four-item pizza. How many different possibilities are there?

Here we have two key choices: which two toppings from column A and which two toppings from column B. The number of possibilities for each will be multiplied together by the counting principle. To find how many topping choices there are from each column, you will need to use the combinations formula.

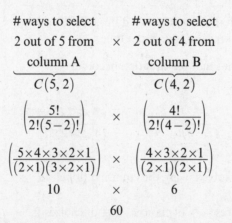

Therefore, there are 60 different possibilities.

Probability

Probability is the numerical measure of the chance of an outcome or event occurring. When all outcomes are equally likely to occur, the probability of the occurrence of a given outcome can be found by using the following formula:

$$\text{probability} = \frac{\text{number of favorable outcomes}}{\text{number of possible outcomes}}$$

The probability of an event not occurring is 1 – (probability that it does occur).

Examples:

1. The positive integers 4 through 20 are individually written on index cards and placed in a bowl. What is the probability of randomly selecting a prime number?

The integers 4 through 20 are 4, 5, 6, 7, 8, 9, 10, 11, 12, 13, 14, 15, 16, 17, 18, 19, and 20.

There are 17 integers from 4 to 20. The integers that are prime numbers are 5, 7, 11, 13, 17, and 19. There are 6 prime integers from 4 to 20.

$$\text{probability} = \frac{\#\ \text{favorable}}{\#\ \text{total}} = \frac{6}{17}$$

Use the spinner with 12 equally divided sections pictured below for questions 2–4.

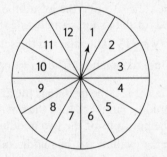

2. What is the probability of spinning a number that is both a multiple of 2 and a multiple of 3 in one spin?

To be a multiple of 2 and 3 means to be a multiple of 6. Of the 12 numbers, only 6 and 12 are multiples of 6.

$$\text{probability} = \frac{\#\ \text{favorable}}{\#\ \text{total}} = \frac{2}{12} = \frac{1}{6}$$

3. What is the probability of *not* spinning a factor of 8 in one spin?

The factors of 8 are 1, 2, 4, and 8. The probability of spinning a factor of 8 becomes
$\text{probability} = \frac{\#\ \text{favorable}}{\#\ \text{total}} = \frac{4}{12} = \frac{1}{3}$. Therefore, the probability of not spinning a factor of 8 is $1 - \frac{1}{3} = \frac{2}{3}$.
You could also have found the numbers that were not factors of 8, namely 3, 5, 6, 7, 9, 10, 11, and 12 (there are 8 of them), and then said the probability of not spinning a factor of 12 is $\frac{8}{12} = \frac{2}{3}$.

> **4.** If the spinner is spun twice, what is the probability that the spinner will stop on the number 6 the first time and the number 2 the second time?

This problem can be solved in two ways. One way is to first find the individual probabilities and multiply them together. The probability of spinning a 6 the first time is $\frac{1}{12}$. There is only one 6 and there are 12 numbers. Similarly, the probability of spinning a 2 on the second spin is also $\frac{1}{12}$. Therefore, the probability of spinning a 6 on the first spin followed by spinning a 2 on the second spin is $\frac{1}{12} \times \frac{1}{12} = \frac{1}{144}$.

The second method is to use the counting principle to find the total number of ways of spinning a first number followed by a second number. There are 12 numbers possible for each spin; therefore, there are $12 \times 12 = 144$ possibilities. Of these, only one is a 6 followed by a 2. Therefore, the probability is $\frac{1}{144}$.

Basic Statistics

Any measure indicating a center of a distribution is called a **_measure of central tendency._** The three basic measures of central tendency are mean (or arithmetic mean), median, and mode.

The **_mean_** (arithmetic mean) is what is usually called the average. To determine the arithmetic mean, find the sum of the data values and then divide by the number of data values.

The **_median_** of a set of numbers arranged in ascending or descending order is the middle number. If there is an odd number of data values in the set, then one of the data values is the median and there will be an equal number of data values on either side of this middle value. To find the location of the median value when there is an odd number of data values, add 1 to the number of data values and divide that number by 2. This then is the position of the median value. For example, if there were 15 data values in the set, then $\frac{15+1}{2} = \frac{16}{2} = 8$, the 8th data value would be the median value with 7 data values to its left and 7 data values to its right.

If there is an even number of data values in the set, the median is the arithmetic mean of the middle two numbers. To find the position of the two middle numbers, take the number of data values in the set and divide by 2. That number and the next integer are the positions of the two middle values. For example, if the data set has 20 values, then $\frac{20}{2} = 10$, the 10th and 11th data values are the middle values and the median would be the average of these two values. The median is easy to calculate and is not influenced by extreme measurements.

The **_mode_** is the data value that appears most, or whose frequency is the greatest. In order to have a mode, there must be a repetition of a data value.

The **_range_** for a set of data values is the difference between the largest and the smallest values.

When a set of data values is listed from least to greatest, the median value is sometimes referred to as the _2nd quartile_ or the _50th percentile_ value. To the left of the median are a set of data values called the lower values, and to the right of the median are a set of data values called the upper values. The median of the lower values is called the _1st quartile_ or _25th percentile_ value, and the median of the upper values is called the _3rd quartile_ or the _75th percentile_ value.

The difference between the 3rd quartile and the 1st quartile (or the 75th percentile and the 25th percentile) is called the **_interquartile range._**

The *standard deviation* of a set of data is a measure of how far data values of a population are from the mean value of the population. A small standard deviation indicates that the data values tend to be very close to the mean value. A large standard deviation indicates that the data values are "spread out" from the mean value.

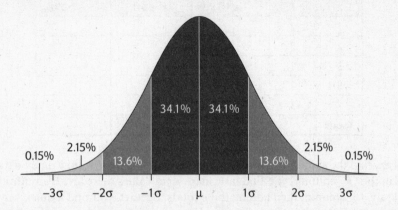

The figure above represents a set of data that has a normal distribution. In it, μ represents the mean value of the set of data. Each shaded band has a width of one standard deviation. For normally distributed data, you will find approximately 68% of all the data values within one standard deviation from the mean. You will find approximately 95.5% of all the data values within two standard deviations from the mean. At three standard deviations from the mean, approximately 99.8% of all the data values are found.

The basic method for calculating the standard deviation for a population is lengthy and time consuming. It involves five steps:

1. Find the mean value for the set of data.
2. For each data value, find the difference between it and the mean value; then square that difference.
3. Find the sum of the squares found in Step 2.
4. Divide the sum found in Step 3 by how many data values there are.
5. Find the square root of the value found in Step 4.

The result found in Step 4 is referred to as the *variance.* The square root of the variance is the standard deviation. This form of the standard deviation assumes all the data values are used, not merely a sample of all the data.

Frequency Table and Measure of Central Tendency

A *frequency table* or a *frequency chart* is often used to summarize the data information. Generally there is a column on the left, the data values, and a column on the right, the frequency, which indicates how many of each data value are in the data set.

By adding the values in the frequency column, you find the total number of data values. By multiplying each data value with its frequency, then adding these totals together, you can quickly find the sum of all the data values.

Example:

1. Use the frequency table at the right to find each of the following:
   a) mean
   b) median
   c) mode
   d) range
   e) 1st quartile
   f) 75th percentile
   g) interquartile range
   h) standard deviation

x	f
1	2
2	2
3	1
5	2
7	3

In order to make all the calculations, add three more columns and one more row to the table. The "m" will be the mean value.

x	f	$(x)(f)$	$(x - m)^2$	$(x - m)^2(f)$
1	2			
2	2			
3	1			
5	2			
7	3			
Totals				

a) To *calculate the mean,* find the sum of all the data values and divide that by how many data values there are. By adding the values in the "f" column, you find how many data values there are. By multiplying each data value by its frequency, the "$(x)(f)$" column, then adding these totals together, you find a quick way to get the sum of all the data values.

x	f	$(x)(f)$	$(x - m)^2$	$(x - m)^2(f)$
1	2	2		
2	2	4		
3	1	3		
5	2	10		
7	3	21		
Totals	10	40		

Therefore, $m = \dfrac{40}{10} = 4$, the mean has a value of 4.

b) To find the *median value,* notice that there are 10 data values. The median will be the average of the data values in the 5th and 6th positions. Based on the frequency table, the 1st and 2nd values are each 1, and the 3rd and 4th values are each 2. The 5th value is 3 and the 6th value is 5. The average of 3 and 5 is 4. The median value is 4. If the data values were all listed in order, it would look like this:

$$\underset{\text{1st}}{1}, \underset{\text{2nd}}{1}, \underset{\text{3rd}}{2}, \underset{\text{4th}}{2}, \underset{\text{5th}}{3}, \underset{\text{6th}}{5}, \underset{\text{7th}}{5}, \underset{\text{8th}}{7}, \underset{\text{9th}}{7}, \underset{\text{10th}}{7}$$

$$\uparrow$$
$$\text{median}$$

c) The *mode* is the value repeated most often. Based on the frequency table, the value 7 occurs 3 times, which is more than any other value occurred. The mode is the value 7.

d) The *range* is the difference between the greatest value, 7, and the least value, 1. Since $7 - 1 = 6$, the range is 6.

e) The *1st quartile,* or the *25th percentile,* is the median of the lower values. The median of the original data set was the average between the 5th and 6th values. Therefore, there are 5 values in the lower portion. The 1st quartile then is the median of these 5 values. Since $\dfrac{5+1}{2} = \dfrac{6}{2} = 3$, the 1st quartile will be the 3rd value. The 3rd value is 2; therefore, the 1st quartile is 2.

414

f) The **75th percentile,** or the **3rd quartile,** is the median of the upper values. There are 5 data values in the upper portion, so the 75th percentile will also be the 3rd value of the upper values. This would make it the 8th data value. The 75th percentile is 7.

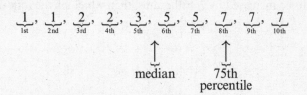

g) The **interquartile range** is the difference between the 3rd quartile and the 1st quartile values. The 3rd quartile value was 7; the 1st quartile value was 2, 7 – 2 = 5. The interquartile range is 5.

Five Steps to Calculate the Standard Deviation

The additional columns in the frequency table are now used.

1. Calculate the mean. For this data set the mean, *m,* was 4.
2. For each data value, find (data value – mean)^2:

x	f	(x)(f)	(x – m)^2	(x – m)^2(f)
1	2	2	$(1 - 4)^2 = 9$	
2	2	4	$(2 - 4)^2 = 4$	
3	1	3	$(3 - 4)^2 = 1$	
5	2	10	$(5 - 4)^2 = 1$	
7	3	21	$(7 - 4)^2 = 9$	
Totals	10	40		

3. Find the sum of the squares found in Step 2. This is done by taking each (data value – mean)^2 result and multiplying it by the frequency of the data value, then adding these results together.

x	f	(x)(f)	(x – m)^2	(x – m)^2(f)
1	2	2	$(1 - 4)^2 = 9$	$(9)(2) = 18$
2	2	4	$(2 - 4)^2 = 4$	$(4)(2) = 8$
3	1	3	$(3 - 4)^2 = 1$	$(1)(1) = 1$
5	2	10	$(5 - 4)^2 = 1$	$(1)(2) = 2$
7	3	21	$(7 - 4)^2 = 9$	$(9)(3) = 27$
Totals	10	40		56

4. Divide the results of Step 4 by the number of data values:

$$\frac{56}{10} = 5.6$$

5. Find the square root of the answer to Step 4. This is then the standard deviation. Standard deviation is $\sqrt{5.6}$.

Practice: Data Analysis

1. A scientist discovered that the instrument used for an experiment was off by 2 milligrams. If each weight in his experiment needed to be increased by 2 milligrams, then which of the following statistical measures would not be affected?

   Ⓐ mean
   Ⓑ median
   Ⓒ mode
   Ⓓ range
   Ⓔ standard deviation

2. Three green marbles, two blue marbles, and five yellow marbles are placed in a jar. What is the probability of selecting at random a yellow marble followed by a green marble if the first marble is not replaced before drawing the second marble?

3. There are 9 players on a basketball team. Only 5 of them can play at any one time. How many different teams of 5 are possible?

Answers: Data Analysis

1. range and standard deviation

   The values of the mean, median, and mode will each increase by 2. The range and standard deviation values will remain unaffected.

2. $\frac{1}{6}$

   There are 3 + 2 + 5 = 10 total marbles. The probability that the first draw will be yellow is $\frac{5}{10} = \frac{1}{2}$. Without replacing a marble, there will only be 9 marbles remaining, 3 of which are green. The probability of now selecting a green marble is $\frac{3}{9} = \frac{1}{3}$. The probability of both events is $\frac{1}{2} \times \frac{1}{3} = \frac{1}{6}$.

   Another approach is to first find the number of ways to select a yellow marble followed by a green marble. Using the counting principle: $5 \times 3 = 15$. Then use the counting principle to find the number of ways to select one marble followed by another one: $10 \times 9 = 90$. Then the probability becomes $\frac{15}{90} = \frac{1}{6}$.

3. 126

   The order in which the players are selected does not matter; therefore, use the combinations formula. Since $n = 9$ and $r = 5$ (9 players taken 5 at a time), the equation is as follows:

   $$C(9,5) = \frac{9!}{(5!)(9-5)!} = \frac{\overset{3}{\cancel{9}} \times \overset{2}{\cancel{8}} \times 7 \times \overset{3}{\cancel{6}} \times \overset{1}{\cancel{(5!)}}}{\underset{1}{\cancel{(5!)}} \times \underset{1}{\cancel{4}} \times \underset{1}{\cancel{3}} \times \underset{1}{\cancel{2}} \times 1} = 126$$

Word Problems

Word Problems Diagnostic Test

1. Traveling from point A to point B, John averages 30 miles per hour. The return trip is along the same route and he averages 40 miles per hour. Find John's average speed for the entire trip, to the nearest tenth of a mile per hour.

2. Jim can do a job in 8 hours by himself that would take Tom 12 hours to do by himself. Working together, how long should it take Jim and Tom to do the job?

3. A chemist wants to dilute 50 ml of a 40% acid solution into a 30% acid solution. How much pure water must be added?

4. Carlos is 5 years older than three times his daughter's age. Two years ago, he was 4 years older than four times her age. How many years from today will he be twice her age?

5. Find the product of three consecutive odd integers such that twice the smallest increased by the largest is thirteen less than four times the middle integer.

Word Problems Diagnostic Test Answers

The diagnostic test explanations listed below include topic headings that correspond with step-by-step learning tools and examples to help you solve specific problem types. Topic headings can be found in the Word Problems Review section on pages 418–426.

Motion Problem

1. 34.3 miles/hour

Work Problem

2. $4\frac{4}{5}$ hours or 4.8 hours

Mixture Problem

3. $16\frac{2}{3}$ ml

Age Problem

4. 12 years

Integer Problems

5. 1,287

Word Problems Review

Motion Problems

Motion problems all use the basic formula of (average rate)(total time) = (total distance) or more simply $r \times t = d$.

Usually a chart that organizes the given information is helpful in creating an equation to be solved that can answer the question. Such a chart could look like this:

	Average Rate	Total Time	Total Distance
A			
B			

Examples:

> 1. Traveling from point A to point B, John averages 30 miles per hour. On the return trip along the same route, he averages 40 miles per hour. Find John's average speed for the entire trip to the nearest tenth of a mile per hour.

The most common error made on this type of problem is to add the rates together and divide by 2. Average speed is found by taking the total distance traveled and dividing by the total time it took to travel that distance. To make the problem more simple, assume the distance traveled was 120 miles, a number that is easily divided by both 30 and 40.

	Average Rate	Total Time	Total Distance
A to B	30 mi/hr	x	120 mi
B to A	40 mi/hr	y	120 mi

Then $30x = 120$ and $40y = 120$, which means that the entire trip of 240 miles took 7 hours. Thus, the average
$\quad\quad x = 4 \quad\quad\quad\quad y = 3$

speed becomes $\dfrac{240 \text{ miles}}{7 \text{ hours}} \approx 34.29$ mi/hr, which rounded off to the nearest tenth of a mile per hour is 34.3 mi/hr.

The problem can also be solved algebraically:

Let d be the one-way distance, then $\dfrac{d \text{ mi}}{30 \text{ mi/hr}} = \dfrac{d}{30}$ hr is the time used going from A to B and $\dfrac{d \text{ mi}}{40 \text{ mi/hr}} = \dfrac{d}{40}$ hr is the time used going from B to A.

$$\text{average speed} = \frac{\text{total distance}}{\text{total time}}$$

$$= \frac{2d}{\dfrac{d}{30} + \dfrac{d}{40}}$$

$$= \frac{2d}{\dfrac{70d}{1200}}$$

$$= \frac{\overset{1}{\cancel{2d}}}{1} \times \frac{1200}{\underset{35}{\cancel{70d}}}$$

$$\approx 34.29$$

You should also be able to get an estimate before starting the problem. To travel a certain distance going 30 miles per hour will take longer than going that distance at 40 miles per hour, which means that the average speed will be closer to 30 mi/hr than to 40 mi/hr. Had this been a multiple-choice question and only one answer was between 30 and 35, it is the one, and calculations would have been unnecessary.

2. If a girl can run m miles in h hours, how fast will she run k miles at the same rate?

Let x be the rate for each direction and t the time for the second run.

	Average Rate	Total Time	Total Distance
A	x mi/hr	h hr	m mi
B	x mi/hr	t hr	k mi

$$xh = m \quad \text{and} \quad xt = k$$
$$x = \frac{m}{h} \qquad x = \frac{k}{t}$$
$$\text{Therefore, } \frac{m}{h} = \frac{k}{t}$$
$$tm = hk$$
$$t = \frac{hk}{m}$$

It will take $\frac{hk}{m}$ hours to run k miles.

3. A boat travels 30 miles against a current in 3 hours. It travels the same 30 miles with the current in 1 hour. How fast is the current and what is the boat's speed in still water?

Let b be the boat's speed in still water, and let c be the current's speed. Going with the current, the boat's speed will be $b + c$ mi/hr. Going against the current, the boat's speed will be $b - c$ mi/hr. Use a chart to organize the information.

	Average Rate	Total Time	Total Distance
With the current	$b + c$ mi/hr	1 hr	30 mi
Against the current	$b - c$ mi/hr	3 hr	30 mi

This now translates into the following system of equations:

$$(b+c)(1) = 30 \qquad \rightarrow \qquad b + c = 30$$
$$\rightarrow$$
$$(b-c)(3) = 30 \quad \text{(divide each side by 3)} \qquad \underline{b - c = 10} \quad \text{(add the equations)}$$
$$2b = 40$$
$$b = 20$$

Since $b + c = 30$ and $b = 20$, then $c = 10$. The current's speed is 10 mi/hr, and the boat's speed in still water is 20 mi/hr.

Work Problems

Work problems, which usually involve how much time it takes each of two ways to complete a job or one way to complete a job and the other to undo a job, can be quickly calculated. If two methods of completing a job are given, to find the time it would take working together, take the product of the two times and divide by the sum of the two times. If one method undoes the job, then take the product of the two times and divide by the difference of the two times.

If the work problem involves more than two methods of either completing or undoing the job, then an algebraic approach to get the answer would look like this:

$$\frac{1}{\text{first's person's time}} + \frac{1}{\text{second's person's time}} + \frac{1}{\text{third's person's time}} + \cdots = \frac{1}{\text{time together}}$$

Examples:

> **1.** Jim can do a job in 8 hours by himself that would take Tom 12 hours to do himself. Working together, how long should it take to do the job?

Using the fast method: $\dfrac{(8)(12)}{8+12} = \dfrac{96}{20} = 4\dfrac{4}{5}$ or 4.8.

Using the algebraic method, let x be the amount of time it takes together:

$$\frac{1}{8} + \frac{1}{12} = \frac{1}{x} \qquad \text{(multiply each side by the LCD of } 24x\text{)}$$
$$24x\left(\frac{1}{8} + \frac{1}{12}\right) = 24x\left(\frac{1}{x}\right)$$
$$3x + 2x = 24$$
$$5x = 24$$
$$x = \frac{24}{5} = 4\frac{4}{5} \text{ or } 4.8$$

It will take them $4\dfrac{4}{5}$ or 4.8 hours together.

> **2.** If it takes 6 hours to fill a tank with water and 15 hours to drain it, how long would it take to fill the tank if the drain was accidently left open?

Using the fast method: $\dfrac{(15)(6)}{15-6} = \dfrac{90}{9} = 10$.

Using the algebraic method, let x be the amount of time it takes together:

$$\frac{1}{6} - \frac{1}{15} = \frac{1}{x} \qquad \text{(multiply each side by the LCD of } 30x\text{)}$$
$$30x\left(\frac{1}{6} - \frac{1}{15}\right) = 30x\left(\frac{1}{x}\right)$$
$$5x - 2x = 30$$
$$3x = 30$$
$$x = 10$$

With the drain open, it will take 10 hours to fill the tank.

> **3.** Working alone, Bill can do a job in 4 hours. With Fred's help, it takes only $2\dfrac{2}{9}$ hours. How long should it take Fred working alone to do the job?

Using the fast method: First change $2\dfrac{2}{9}$ to $\dfrac{20}{9}$. Let x be how long it would take Fred alone: $\dfrac{4x}{4+x} = \dfrac{20}{9}$. You can quickly see that x is 5.

Using the algebraic method:

$$\frac{1}{4} + \frac{1}{x} = \frac{1}{2\frac{2}{9}} \qquad \left(\frac{1}{2\frac{2}{9}} = \frac{1}{\frac{20}{9}} = \frac{9}{20} \right)$$

$$\frac{1}{4} + \frac{1}{x} = \frac{9}{20} \qquad \text{(multiply each side by the LCD of } 20x\text{)}$$

$$20x\left(\frac{1}{4} + \frac{1}{x}\right) = 20x\left(\frac{9}{20}\right)$$

$$5x + 20 = 9x$$

$$20 = 4x$$

$$5 = x$$

It would take Fred 5 hours to do the job alone.

Mixture Problems

Mixture problems, like motion problems, are more easily solved using a chart to organize the given information. Depending on the type of mixture problem, different organizing charts can be used.

Examples:

1. A chemist wants to dilute 50 ml of a 40% acid solution into a 30% acid solution. How much pure water must be added?

This problem involves acid and water. We begin with 50 ml of a solution of which 40% is acid and 60% is not acid. Pure water is being added and then the new mixture will only be 30% acid and 70% not acid.

Let x be how many ml of water is being added.

	Start	Add	Totals
Mixture	50 ml	x ml	x + 50 ml
Acid	(0.40)(50) ml	0 ml	(0.30)(x + 50) ml
Not acid	(0.60)(50) ml	x ml	(0.70)(x + 50) ml

There are now two different equations that can be used to find x.

$$(0.40)(50) + 0 = (0.30)(x + 50) \text{ or } (0.60)(50) + x = (0.70)(x + 50)$$

The easier one is the one on the left since the x only appears on one side of the equation.

$$(0.40)(50) + 0 = (0.30)(x + 50)$$

$$20 = 0.3x + 15$$

$$5 = 0.3x$$

$$\frac{50}{3} = x \text{ or } x = 16\frac{2}{3}$$

The chemist must add $16\frac{2}{3}$ ml of pure water.

2. One solution is 75% saltwater and another solution is 50% saltwater. How many gallons of each should be used to make 10 gallons of a solution that is 60% saltwater?

Let x be the number of gallons of the 75% saltwater solution. Then $10 - x$ will be the number of gallons of the 50% solution since there will be a total of 10 gallons in the final mixture.

	Start	Add	Totals
Mixture	x gal	$10 - x$ gal	10 gal
Salt	$(0.75)(x)$ gal	$(0.50)(10 - x)$ gal	$(0.60)(10)$
Water	$(0.25)(x)$ gal	$(0.50)(10 - x)$ gal	$(0.40)(10)$

There are now two different equations that can be used to find x.

$$(0.75)(x) + (0.50)(10 - x) = (0.60)(10) \text{ or } (0.25)(x) + (0.50)(10 - x) = (0.40)(10)$$

Selecting the first equation:

$$(0.75)(x) + (0.50)(10 - x) = (0.60)(10)$$
$$0.75x + 5 - 0.50x = 6$$
$$0.25x + 5 = 6$$
$$0.25x = 1$$
$$x = \frac{1}{0.25}$$
$$x = 4 \text{ and } 10 - x = 6$$

Therefore, 4 gallons of 75% and 6 gallons of 50% solutions are used.

3. Nuts worth $1.50 per pound are mixed with nuts worth $1.75 per pound to make 20 pounds of nuts worth $1.65 per pound. How many pounds of each type is used?

Let x be the number of pounds of $1.75/lb nuts. Then $20 - x$ would be the number of pounds of $1.50/lb nuts since there will be 20 pounds in the final mixture.

A slightly different chart will be used to organize the information.

	Cost/lb	# Pounds	Total Cost
Mixture	$1.65	20	($1.65)(20)
$1.75/lb	$1.75	x	($1.75)(x)
$1.50/lb	$1.50	$20 - x$	($1.50)(20 - x)

The total cost of the individual type of nuts should equal the total cost of the mixture:

$$1.75x + 1.50(20 - x) = 1.65(20)$$
$$1.75x + 30 - 1.50x = 33$$
$$0.25x + 30 = 33$$
$$0.25x = 3$$
$$x = \frac{3}{0.25}$$
$$x = 12 \text{ and } 20 - x = 8$$

Therefore, 12 pounds of the $1.75/lb and 8 pounds of the $1.50/lb nuts are used.

Age Problems

Age problems usually require a representation of ages now, ages in the past, and/or ages in the future. Use a chart to keep the information organized.

Examples:

1. Currently, Carlos is 5 years older than three times his daughter, Juanita's, age. Two years ago, he was 4 years older than four times her age. How many years from now will he be twice her age?

Let J represent Juanita's current age. Then $3J + 5$ is Carlos' current age.

Person	Current Age	Age 2 Years Ago
Juanita	J	$J - 2$
Carlos	$3J + 5$	$(3J + 5) - 2$

Translating the sentence "Two years ago, he was 4 years older than four times her age" algebraically, you get

$$\overbrace{(3J+5)-2}^{\substack{\text{Carlos'} \\ \text{age} \\ \text{2 years} \\ \text{ago}}} = 4\overbrace{(J-2)}^{\substack{\text{Juanita's} \\ \text{age} \\ \text{2 years} \\ \text{ago}}}+4$$

$$3J+5-2 = 4J-8+4$$
$$3J+3 = 4J-4$$
$$3 = J-4$$
$$7 = J$$

Therefore, currently, Juanita is 7 years old and Carlos is $3(7) + 5$ or 26 years old. The question asks when in the future he will be twice as old as his daughter.

Let t be how many years into the future this takes place and set up a new chart.

Person	Current Age	Age t Years from Now
Juanita	7	$7 + t$
Carlos	26	$26 + t$

"Carlos will be twice his daughter's age" translates into

$$26+t = 2(7+t)$$
$$26+t = 14+2t$$
$$26 = 14+t$$
$$12 = t$$

Therefore, in 12 years, Carlos will be twice his daughter's age. In 12 years he will be 38 and his daughter will be 19, hence his age will be twice hers.

2. Ed is 12 years older than Jim. Five years ago, the sum of their ages was 42. What will be the product of their ages in 5 years?

Let x be Jim's age now and $12 + x$ Ed's age now.

Person	Current Age	Age 5 Years Ago
Jim	x	$x - 5$
Ed	$12 + x$	$12 + x - 5$ or $x + 7$

Translate "Five years ago, the sum of their ages was 42" into an algebraic equation.

$$(x-5)+(12+x-5)=42$$
$$2x+2=42$$
$$2x=40$$
$$x=20 \quad \text{and} \quad 12+x=32$$

Therefore, Jim is currently 20 years old and Ed is 32 years old. In 5 years, Jim will be 25 and Ed will be 37 years old, and the product of their ages will be $(25)(37) = 925$.

Integer Problems

Integer problems usually involve consecutive integers, consecutive even integers, or consecutive odd integers. If you let x represent any integer, then $x + 1$ would represent the next larger integer, $x + 2$ would be the next larger after that, then $x + 3$, and so on.

If you let x represent either an odd or an even integer, then the next odd or even integer would be 2 more than that, or $x + 2$, and the one after that would be $x + 4$ and so on.

Examples:

1. Find the product of three consecutive odd integers such that twice the smallest increased by the largest is thirteen less than four times the middle integer.

Let x be the smallest of the 3 consecutive odd integers. Then $x + 2$ and $x + 4$ would be the next two consecutive odd integers.

Translate "twice the smallest increased by the largest is thirteen less than four times the middle integer" into

$$2x+(x+4)=4(x+2)-13$$
$$3x+4=4x+8-13$$
$$3x+4=4x-5$$
$$4=x-5$$
$$9=x \quad \text{and} \quad x+2=11, x+4=13$$

The integers are 9, 11, and 13 and their product is $(9)(11)(13) = 1,287$.

> 2. The sum of four consecutive even integers is 60. What is the largest integer?

Let x, $x + 2$, $x + 4$, and $x + 6$ represent the 4 consecutive even integers.

$$x + (x + 2) + (x + 4) + (x + 6) = 60$$
$$4x + 12 = 60$$
$$4x = 48$$
$$x = 12 \quad \text{and} \quad x + 2 = 14, x + 4 = 16, x + 4 = 18$$

Therefore, the largest integer is 18.

Practice: Word Problems

1. Part one of a trip was a distance of 1,120 miles at 280 miles per hour. Part two of that trip was the same distance at 70 miles per hour. What was the average speed for the two parts combined?

2. Roberto and Julio do a whole job in $2\frac{1}{10}$ days. Had Roberto worked alone, he would have needed 7 days. How long would it have taken Julio to do the job alone?

3. Two quarts of a 25% acid solution are mixed with one quart of 40% acid solution. What percent acid is the mixture?

4. Kobe is 12 years younger than his brother Caleb. Last year, the sum of their ages was 30. What will be the product of their ages in 5 years?

5. The product of two consecutive positive even integers is 168. What is their sum?

Answers: Word Problems

1. 112 miles per hour.

   Average speed is found by taking total distance and dividing it by total time. The total distance is 1,120 + 1,120 or 2,240 miles.

   To find the total time, find the individual times by taking distance and dividing it by rate. The time for part one of the trip is $\frac{1,120 \text{ mi}}{280 \text{ mi/hr}} = 4 \text{ hr}$. The time for part two of the trip is $\frac{1,120 \text{ mi}}{70 \text{ mi/hr}} = 16 \text{ hr}$.

   The total time for the trip is 20 hours. The average speed is $\frac{2,240 \text{ mi}}{20 \text{ hr}} = 112 \text{ mi/hr}$.

2. 3 days

   Fast method: Let x represent the amount of time Julio needs:

   $$\frac{\text{product of their times}}{\text{sum of their times}} = \text{total time together}$$

   $$\frac{7x}{x + 7} = \frac{21}{10} \quad \left(2\frac{1}{10} = \frac{21}{10}\right)$$

   Visually, it can be seen that if x is 3, the above equation is true. Therefore, Julio would need 3 days.

Algebraic method: Let x represent the amount of time Julio needs.

$$\frac{1}{x}+\frac{1}{7}=\frac{1}{2\frac{1}{10}}$$

$$\frac{1}{x}+\frac{1}{7}=\frac{1}{\frac{21}{10}}$$

$$\frac{1}{x}+\frac{1}{7}=\frac{10}{21} \qquad \text{(multiply each side by the LCD of } 21x\text{)}$$

$$21x\left(\frac{1}{x}+\frac{1}{7}\right)=21x\left(\frac{10}{21}\right)$$

$$21+3x=10x$$

$$21=7x$$

$$3=x$$

3. 30%

Since the question only involves acid, find the amount of total acid there is and divide that by the three quarts that the final mixture contains.

Two quarts that are 25% acid have 2(0.25) or 0.5 quarts of acid. One quart that is 40% acid has 1(0.4) quarts of acid. Therefore, the final solution has $\frac{0.5+0.4}{3}=\frac{0.9}{3}=0.3=30\%$ acid.

4. 405

Let x represent Caleb's age now. Then $x-12$ represents Kobe's age now.

Person	Current Age	Age 1 Year Ago
Caleb	x	$x-1$
Kobe	$x-12$	$(x-12)-1$

"Last year the sum of their ages was 30" translates into $x-1+(x-12)-1=30$.

$$x-1+(x-12)-1=30$$

$$2x-14=30$$

$$2x=44$$

$$x=22 \quad \text{then } x-12=10$$

Caleb is currently 22 years old, and Kobe is currently 10 years old. In 5 years, Caleb will be 27 and Kobe will be 15. The product of their ages will be (27)(15) = 405.

5. 26

Let x be the smaller of the two positive even integers. Then $x+2$ will be the larger integer. "The product of two consecutive positive even integers is 168" translates into

$$x(x+2)=168$$

$$x^2+2x=168$$

$$x^2+2x-168=0 \qquad \text{(solve by factoring)}$$

$$(x-12)(x+14)=0$$

$$x-12=0 \quad \text{or} \quad x+14=0$$

$$x=12 \quad \text{or} \qquad x=-14$$

The smaller integer is 12 or –14, but the problem said the integers were positive. Therefore, the smaller integer is 12, the larger one is 14, and their sum is 26.

Data Interpretation

Data Interpretation Diagnostic Test

Questions 1–4 refer to the following circle graphs.

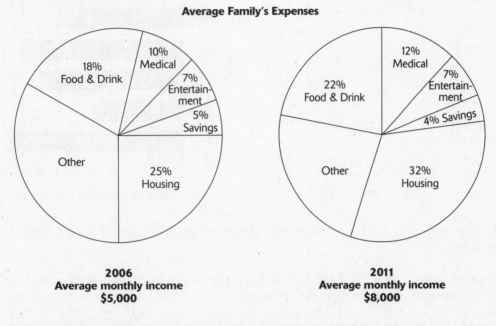

Average Family's Expenses

2006
Average monthly income
$5,000

2011
Average monthly income
$8,000

1. For the year in which the average family's monthly medical expenses were $500, what was the family's average monthly expense on savings?

2. What is the ratio of average monthly medical expenses in 2006 to the average monthly medical expenses in 2011?

3. To the nearest tenth of a percent, what was the percent increase from 2006 to 2011 in the percentage spent on food and drink?

4. How much more did the average family spend monthly on "other" in 2011 than they did in 2006?

Questions 5 and 6 refer to the following bar graph.

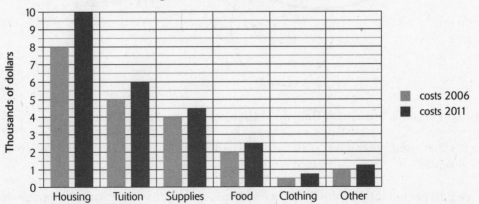

Glendale College: Costs in thousands of dollars

5. Which category of expenses had the greatest percent increase in costs from 2006 to 2011?

6. To the nearest whole percent, by what percent did the total expenses increase from 2006 to 2011?

Questions 7–9 refer to the following graphs.

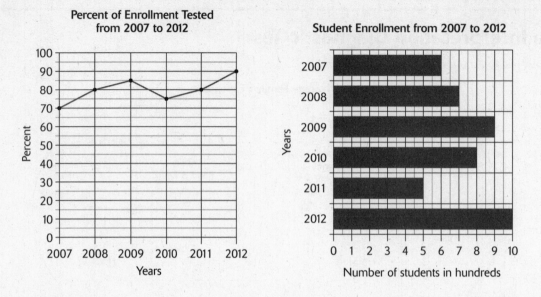

**Percent of Enrollment Tested
from 2007 to 2012**

Student Enrollment from 2007 to 2012

7. For the years 2007 to 2012, when the percentage of students tested exceeded 80%, how many total students were actually tested?

8. For which consecutive years was the percent change in the number of students enrolled the least? To the nearest whole percent, what was that percent change?

9. For the odd-numbered years, what was the approximate lowest score that any student tested achieved on the test?

Questions 10–12 refer to the following Venn diagram.

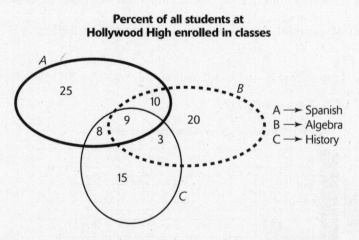

**Percent of all students at
Hollywood High enrolled in classes**

A ⟶ Spanish
B ⟶ Algebra
C ⟶ History

10. What percent of all the students at Hollywood High are not enrolled in history?

11. If there are 2,000 students enrolled at Hollywood High, how many are taking exactly two of the three courses indicated?

12. If 300 students are not enrolled in any of the indicated courses, how many students are enrolled at Hollywood High?

Questions 13–15 refer to the following table.

Profile of the Neighborhood		
# People Living at Even-numbered Addresses	Favorite Baseball League	# People Living at Odd-numbered Addresses
30	American	42
25	National	27
16	Neither	20
	Sex	
42	Male	54
29	Female	35

13. To the nearest percent, what percent of the neighborhood prefers the National league?

14. In this neighborhood, how many people living in odd-numbered addresses are younger than 36 years?

15. What would be the ratio of females to males in the even-numbered addresses if 5 of the males were replaced with females?

Data Interpretation Diagnostic Test Answers

The diagnostic test explanations listed below include topic headings that correspond with step-by-step learning tools and examples to help you solve specific problem types. Topic headings can be found in the Data Interpretation Review section on pages 430–439.

Circle or Pie Graphs

1. $250

2. $\frac{25}{48}$

3. 22.2%

4. $90

Bar Graphs

5. Clothing, 50%

6. 22%

Line Graphs

7. 1,665

8. 2009–2010, 11%

9. cannot be determined from the given information

Venn Diagrams

10. 65%

11. 420

12. 3,000

Charts and Tables

13. 33%

14. cannot be determined from the given information

15. $\frac{34}{37}$

Data Interpretation Review

Circle or Pie Graphs

A *circle* or *pie graph* shows the relationship between the whole circle (100%) and the various slices that represent portions of that 100%. The larger the slice, the greater the percentage it represents.

Examples:

Questions 1–4 refer to the following circle graphs.

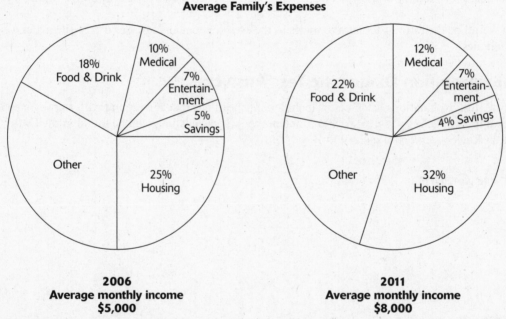

Average Family's Expenses

2006
Average monthly income
$5,000

2011
Average monthly income
$8,000

---

1. For the year in which the average family's monthly medical expenses were $500, what was the family's average monthly expense on savings?

In 2011, the medical expenses were 12% of $8,000, which is $960. In 2006, the medical expenses were 10% of $5,000, which is $500. Therefore, the question is referring to the 2006 graph. In that year, savings were 5% of the total monthly income, and 5% of $5,000 is $250. You could also have said that since 5% is half of 10%, the savings amount would be half the medical amount and arrived at the same answer.

---

2. What is the ratio of average monthly medical expenses in 2006 to the average monthly medical expenses in 2011?

The average monthly medical expenses in 2006 was 10% of $5,000, or $500. The average monthly medical expenses in 2011 was 12% of $8,000, or $960. The ratio becomes $\frac{500}{960} = \frac{25}{48}$.

3. To the nearest tenth of a percent, what was the percent increase from 2006 to 2011 in the percentage spent on food and drink?

Note that the question is not referring to money, but to the change in the percentage values. The 2006 average monthly percentage spent on food and drink was 18% and in 2011 it was 22%.

Percent change $= \dfrac{\text{amount of change}}{\text{starting amount}} \times 100\% = \dfrac{4\%}{18\%} \times 100\% = 22.2\bar{2}\%$, which is 22.2% when rounded to the nearest tenth of a percent.

4. How much more did the average family spend monthly on "other" in 2011 than they did in 2006?

In the 2006 graph, the sum of the given percentages is 65% (18% + 10% + 7% + 5% + 25% = 65%), leaving 35% (100% – 65% = 35%) for the "other" category. The average monthly amount of money spent on "other" in 2006 was 35% of $5,000, or $1,750. In the 2011 graph, the sum of the given percentages is 77%, (22% + 12% + 7% + 4% + 32% = 77%), leaving 23% (100% – 77% = 23%) for the "other" category. The average monthly amount spent on "other" in 2011 was 23% of $8,000, or $1,840. The family spent, on average, $90 more per month in 2011 on "other" than in 2006 ($1,840 – $1,750 = $90).

Bar Graphs

Bar graphs convert information into separate bars or columns. The bars can either be vertical or horizontal. You must be able to determine the relationship between the bars in the graph.

Examples:

Questions 1 and 2 refer to the following bar graph.

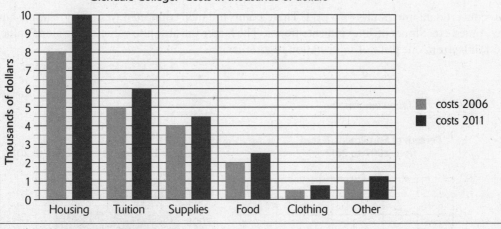

Glendale College: Costs in thousands of dollars

1. Which category of expenses had the greatest percent increase in costs from 2006 to 2011?

In this bar graph, different categories of expenditures are listed horizontally, and costs, in thousands of dollars, are shown vertically. The light gray bar above the "housing" category indicates that housing in 2006 cost $8,000.

Recall that percent change $= \dfrac{\text{amount of change}}{\text{starting amount}} \times 100\%$.

Category	2006	2011	Percent Change
Housing	8,000	10,000	$\frac{2,000}{8,000} \times 100\% = 25\%$
Tuition	5,000	6,000	$\frac{1,000}{5,000} \times 100\% = 20\%$
Supplies	4,000	4,500	$\frac{500}{4,000} \times 100\% = 12.5\%$
Food	2,000	2,500	$\frac{500}{2,000} \times 100\% = 25\%$
Clothing	500	750	$\frac{250}{500} \times 100\% = 50\%$
Other	1,000	1,250	$\frac{250}{1,000} \times 100\% = 25\%$

Clothing had the greatest percentage increase in costs from 2006 to 2011. Its costs increased by 50%.

2. To the nearest whole percent, by what percent did the total expenses increase from 2006 to 2011?

Total expenses in 2006 were $8,000 + $5,000 + $4,000 + $2,000 + $500 + $1,000 = $20,500.

Total expenses in 2011 were $10,000 + $6,000 + $4,500 + $2,500 + $750 + $1,250 = $25,000.

percent change $= \dfrac{\text{amount of change}}{\text{starting amount}} \times 100\% = \dfrac{4,500}{20,500} \times 100\% \approx 21.95\%$, which is 22% when rounded to the nearest whole percent.

Line Graphs

Line graphs convert data into points on a grid. These points are then connected to show a relationship between items, dates, times, etc. Slopes of lines indicate trends. The larger the absolute value of the slope value, the greater the change will be from one piece of information to another.

Examples:

Questions 1–3 refer to the following graphs.

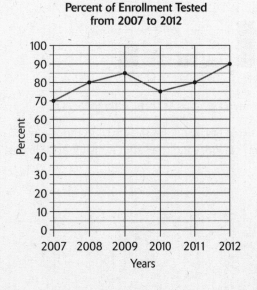

Percent of Enrollment Tested from 2007 to 2012

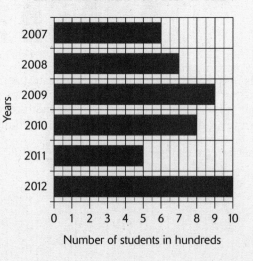

Student Enrollment from 2007 to 2012

> **1.** For the years 2007 to 2012, when the percentage of students tested exceeded 80%, how many total students were actually tested?

This question requires the use of both the line graph on the left and the bar graph on the right. Note that the bar graph measures the number of students in hundreds.

In 2009, 85% of the students were tested. In 2009, there were 900 students enrolled. Therefore, 765 students were tested in 2009 (85% of 900 = 765). Similarly, in 2012, 900 students were tested (90% of 1,000 = 900). The years 2009 and 2012 were the only years in which more than 80% of the students were tested. Therefore, for the years 2007 through 2012, when more than 80% of the students were tested, a total of 765 + 900 = 1,665 students were tested.

> **2.** For which consecutive years was the percent change in the number of students enrolled the least? To the nearest whole percent, what was that percent change?

Recall that percent change $= \dfrac{\text{amount of change}}{\text{starting amount}} \times 100\%$.

Consecutive Years	Number of Students Enrolled	Percent Change
2007 2008	600 700	$\dfrac{100}{600} \times 100\% = 16\dfrac{2}{3}\%$ or $16.\overline{6}\%$
2008 2009	700 900	$\dfrac{200}{700} \times 100\% = 28\dfrac{4}{7}\%$ or $28.\overline{571428}\%$
2009 2010	900 800	$\dfrac{100}{900} \times 100\% = 11\dfrac{1}{9}\%$ or $11.\overline{1}\%$
2010 2011	800 500	$\dfrac{300}{800} \times 100\% = 37\dfrac{1}{2}\%$ or 37.5%
2011 2012	500 1,000	$\dfrac{500}{500} \times 100\% = 100\%$

For the years 2009 to 2010 the percent change was the least. Rounded to the nearest whole percent, it is 11%.

> **3.** For the odd-numbered years, what was the approximate lowest score that any student tested achieved on the test?

The information given cannot provide an answer. The line graph indicates the percent of enrollment tested, not what any single student received as a test score.

Venn Diagrams

Venn diagrams show sets of objects with certain characteristics using geometric figures, usually ovals or circular regions. Numbers placed within a region indicate the number of objects, or percent of the total number of objects, that have that particular characteristic. When a number is placed in an area of overlapping regions, then that is how many objects, or the percent of objects, that share the characteristics of the overlapping regions.

Examples:

Questions 1–3 refer to the following Venn diagram.

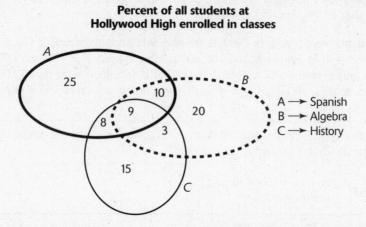

**Percent of all students at
Hollywood High enrolled in classes**

In this Venn diagram, region A represents the percent of the students at Hollywood High that are taking Spanish, region B represents the percent of students at Hollywood High taking algebra, and region C represents the percent of students at Hollywood High taking history.

Only looking at region A and the regions it overlaps, we can make the following conclusions from the diagram:

a) 25% of the students at Hollywood High take Spanish but do not take either algebra nor history

b) 10% of the students at Hollywood High take Spanish and algebra, but not history

c) 9% of the students at Hollywood High take Spanish, algebra, and history

d) 8% of the students at Hollywood High take Spanish and history, but not algebra

If all the percentage numbers are added together, you get 90%. Thus, 10% of the students at Hollywood High do not take any of the three listed classes.

> **1.** What percent of all the students at Hollywood High are not enrolled in history?

One approach is to take the percentage of students that are enrolled in history, then subtract that from 100%. Another approach is to add the percentages indicated outside of history, and be sure to add in the 10% that are not taking any of the three classes.

According to the diagram, there are 8% + 9% + 3% + 15% = 35% of the students taking history; thus, there are 100% – 35% = 65% of the students not taking history.

> **2.** If there are 2,000 students enrolled at Hollywood High, how many are taking exactly two of the three courses indicated?

The overlap of regions A and B, but not including region C, only has 10% in it. The overlap of regions A and C, but not including region B, only has 8% in it. The overlap of regions B and C, but not including region A, only has 3% in it. Thus, there are 10% + 8% + 3% = 21% of the 2,000 students, or 420 students taking exactly 2 of the 3 courses indicated.

3. If 300 students are not enrolled in any of the indicated courses, how many students are enrolled at Hollywood High?

Since 10% of the students are not enrolled in any of the indicated courses, then 10% of the enrollment is 300. This can be solved as an equation or as a proportion.

$$0.10x = 300 \qquad \frac{\text{part}}{\text{whole}} : \quad \begin{array}{cc} \% & \text{\# of students} \\ \dfrac{10}{100} = \dfrac{300}{x} \end{array}$$

$$x = \frac{300}{0.10} = 3{,}000 \qquad\qquad 10x = 30{,}000$$

$$x = 3{,}000$$

There are 3,000 students enrolled at Hollywood High.

Charts and Tables

Charts and tables are often used to give an organized picture of data. You must pay close attention to column or row headings for important information.

Examples:

Questions 1–3 refer to the following table.

# People Living at Even-numbered Addresses	Favorite Baseball League	# People Living at Odd-numbered Addresses
30	American	42
25	National	27
16	Neither	20
	Sex	
42	Male	54
29	Female	35

1. To the nearest percent, what percent of the neighborhood prefers the National league?

First, find the total number of people in the neighborhood, then find how many prefer the National league.

$$\text{Total: } (30 + 25 + 16) + (42 + 27 + 20) = 160$$

Prefer National league: $25 + 27 = 52$

$$\frac{52}{160} = \frac{x}{100}$$

$$160x = 5200$$

$$x = 32.5$$

Therefore, to the nearest percent, 33% prefer the National league.

2. In this neighborhood, how many people living in odd-numbered addresses are younger than 36 years?

The answer cannot be determined from the given information. There are 89 people living in odd-numbered addresses. Therefore, the median age is the number in the 45th position when the ages are listed from least to greatest. This means that there are 44 people whose ages would be to the left of the 36, but this does not guarantee that all of them are less than 36. The age in the 44th position could be 36 as well as the age in the 45th position.

3. What would be the ratio of females to males in the even-numbered addresses if 5 of the males were replaced with females?

Prior to making the replacement, there are 42 males and 29 females in the even-numbered addresses. After the replacement, there will be 37 males and 34 females. The ratio of *females* to *males* will then become $\frac{34}{37}$.

Practice: Data Interpretation

Use the following graph for questions 1 and 2.

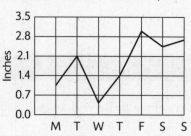

Rainfall—Portland—Dec. 5–11, 2011

1. What was the median rainfall for the week shown?

2. Between which two consecutive days was the change the greatest?

Use the following graph for questions 3 and 4.

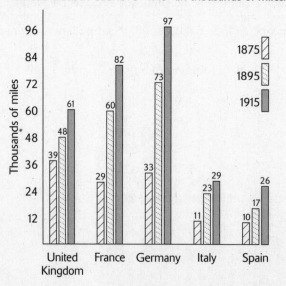

Railroad Track in Use 1875–1915 (in thousands of miles)

3. How many countries showed a larger increase in miles from 1875 to 1895 than from 1895 to 1915?

4. In hundreds of miles of track, how much more was in use in France in 1895 than in Spain in 1915?

Use the following graphs for questions 5 and 6.

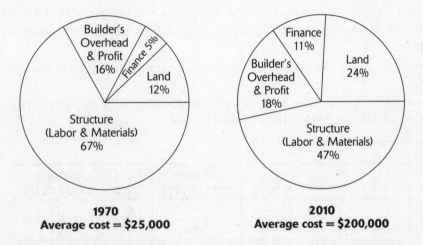

1970
Average cost = $25,000

2010
Average cost = $200,000

5. Based on the average cost at the time, by what percent did the cost of financing the building of a house increase from 1970 to 2010?

6. Based on the average cost at the time, how much more went into structure in 2010 than in 1970?

Use the following graph for questions 7 and 8.

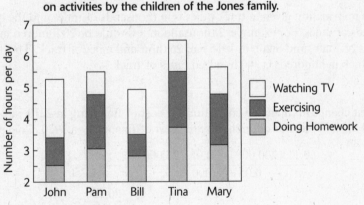

7. For which activity was the average daily hours the least?

8. What is the average amount of television, in hours and minutes, that all 5 children watch per day?

Answers: Data Interpretation

1. 2.1

The median of the 7 values will be the 4th when listed from least to greatest. Even though most of the values can only be approximated, the 4th value is exactly 2.1. The values when written from least to greatest are as follows:

approximately 0.4, approximately 1.0, exactly 1.4, **exactly 2.1**,
approximately 2.4, approximately 2.7, approximately 2.9

2. **Tuesday to Wednesday**

   From Monday to Tuesday, the change was from approximately 1.0 to 2.1 or about +1.1

   From Tuesday to Wednesday, the change was from 2.1 to approximately 0.4 or about –1.7

   From Wednesday to Thursday, the change was from approximately 0.4 to 1.4 or about +1

   From Thursday to Friday, the change was from 1.4 to approximately 2.9 or about +1.5

   From Friday to Saturday, the change was from approximately 2.9 to approximately 2.4 or about –0.5

   From Saturday to Sunday, the change was from approximately 2.4 to approximately 2.7 or about +0.3.

The greatest change took place from Tuesday to Wednesday. This could also have been done visually by finding the segment with the greatest slope in absolute value.

3. **three (France, Germany, and Italy)**

Country	1875	1895	Change 1875 to 1895	1915	Change 1895 to 1915
U.K	39	48	+9	61	+13
France	29	60	**+31**	82	+22
Germany	33	73	**+40**	97	+24
Italy	11	23	**+12**	29	+6
Spain	10	17	+7	26	+9

Three countries, France, Germany, and Italy, showed a larger increase in miles from 1875 to 1895 than from 1895 to 1915.

4. **340 hundreds**

Be aware that the information given in track miles is in thousands of miles and the question asked for an answer in hundreds of miles. For example, 2 thousand miles would be 20 hundred miles. France in 1895 had 60 thousand miles of track, and Spain in 1915 had 26 thousand miles of track. The difference is 34 thousand miles of track, which in hundreds is 340 hundred miles of track.

5. **1,660%**

To find the percent change in financing costs, find the cost of financing in 2010, subtract the cost of financing in 1970, then divide this difference by the cost of financing in 1970. Convert this to a percentage.

$$\frac{(0.11)(200,000)-(0.05)(25,000)}{(0.05)(25,000)} = \frac{22,000-1,250}{1,250}$$

$$= \frac{20,750}{1,250}$$

$$= 16.6$$

$$= 1,660\%$$

6. **$77,250**

Structure costs for 2010 minus structure costs in 1970: $(0.47)(\$200,000) - (0.67)(\$25,000) = \$77,250$

7. Television watching

   This graph is an example of an accumulation bar graph. Be careful when looking at it. Consider the information for John. The first bar ends at 2.5 hours, meaning that John spends, on average, 2.5 hours per day doing homework. The bar above this goes from 2.5 hours to 3.5 hours, meaning John spends about 1 hour per day (3.5 − 2.5 = 1) exercising. The last bar goes from about 3.5 hours to about 5.25 hours, meaning John spends about 1.75 hours per day (5.25 − 3.5 = 1.75) watching television.

   The chart below is a summary for the children and their average hours spent doing the activities.

Child	Homework	Exercise	TV
John	2.5	3.5 − 2.5 = 1	5.25 − 3.5 = 1.75
Pam	3	4.75 − 3 = 1.75	5.5 − 4.75 = 0.75
Bill	2.75	3.5 − 2.75 = 0.75	5 − 3.5 = 1.5
Tina	3.75	5.5 − 3.75 = 1.75	6.5 − 5.5 = 1
Mary	3.25	4.75 − 3.25 = 1.5	5.75 − 4.75 = 1
TOTALS	15.25	6.75	6

8. 1 hour and 12 minutes

   Using the chart above, all 5 children combined watch 6 hours of television per day.

   Therefore, on average they watch $\frac{6}{5} = 1.2$ hours of TV per day. The question wanted the answer in hours and minutes. 0.2 hours means $0.2\,\text{hr} \times \frac{60\,\text{min}}{\text{hr}} = 12$ minutes.

PART VI

FULL-LENGTH PRACTICE TEST

Answers and explanations for Practice Test 1 can be found on pages 481–511.

This section contains one full-length GMAT practice test designed to give you extra practice and insight into problem solving. While this practice test does not adapt based upon your right or wrong answers (as the computer-adaptive test does), you will gain valuable test-taking skills and insight into your strengths and weaknesses. The practice test is followed by an answer key, complete answer explanations, and analysis techniques.

When taking this practice test, try to simulate the test conditions. Budget your time effectively when you take this written practice test. If you need a break, stop the clock and take a 10-minute break after the second section. Try to spend no more than $1\frac{1}{2}$ minutes on each multiple-choice question and 30 minutes on the writing task and 30 minutes on the Integrated Reasoning section.

The total testing time for this practice test is 3 hours and 30 minutes.

Section 1: Analytical Writing Assessment – Analysis of an Argument

Section 2: Quantitative

Section 3: Verbal

Section 4: Integrated Reasoning

REMEMBER: The answer choices for multiple-choice questions on the actual computer version of the GMAT are not labeled with letters. Answer choices in this study guide have lettered choices A, B, C, D, and E for clarity. On the actual exam, you will be required to click on the appropriate oval to select your answer.

Chapter 10

Practice Test 1

Section 1: Analytical Writing Assessment— Analysis of an Argument

Time: 30 minutes
1 Essay

Directions: This section will require you to critique the argument given. Note that you are NOT being asked to present your own viewpoint. Questioning the underlying assumptions, finding alternative explanations or counterexamples, and delineating evidence to strengthen or weaken an argument are some possible approaches.

Your response will be evaluated for its overall quality, based on how well you:

- respond to the specific instructions.
- organize, develop, and communicate your ideas.
- support your evaluation with relevant reasons and/or examples.
- use standard written English.

It is important to simulate the actual computer-adaptive exam; therefore, it is recommended that you type your response into your home computer. Before you begin writing, you may want to think for a few minutes about the passage and instructions, and then plan your response by prewriting on scratch paper. Be sure to develop your evaluation fully and organize it coherently, but leave time to read what you have written and make any revisions you think are necessary.

Argument Topic

The following is a memo from the National Binding Company:

> A recent study of workplace behaviors found that employees who regularly eat lunch with their colleagues have higher productivity levels. At our Bridgeton site there are a large number of employees who eat lunch in their offices and at their desks. Over the past two months, total office sales for the Bridgeton office have declined. Therefore, to increase productivity and improve sales, as well as morale, we should make it company policy that employees not eat in their offices or at their desks.

Write a critique of the argument. Your essay should consider its line of reasoning and how well it uses evidence. You should consider what doubtful assumptions undermine the reasoning, and consider what other evidence might support or weaken the argument. Your essay may also consider how the argument could be made more persuasive and its conclusion more convincing.

IF YOU FINISH BEFORE TIME IS CALLED, CHECK YOUR WORK ON THIS SECTION ONLY. DO NOT WORK ON ANY OTHER SECTION IN THE TEST.

Section 2: Quantitative

The answer choices for multiple-choice questions on the actual computer version of the GMAT are not labeled with letters. Answer choices in this study guide have lettered choices A, B, C, D, and E for clarity. On the actual exam, you will be required to click on the appropriate oval to select your answer.

Time: 75 Minutes
37 Questions

General Directions: Your score on the Quantitative section will be based on how well you do on the questions presented and on the number of questions you answer. You should try to pace yourself so that you have sufficient time to consider every question. If possible, answer all 37 questions in this section and guess if necessary. Select the best answer choice for each question. Use a blank sheet of paper to record your answers. Use scratch paper for any necessary calculations.

Note: Some problems may be accompanied by figures or diagrams. These figures are drawn as accurately as possible except when it is stated in a specific problem that the *figure is not drawn to scale.* The figure is meant to provide information useful in solving the problem. Unless otherwise stated or indicated, all figures lie in a plane and angle measures are greater than zero. All numbers used are real numbers.

Data Sufficiency Directions: Each of the data sufficiency questions below consists of a question and two statements, labeled (1) and (2), in which certain data are given. You must decide whether the data given in the statements are *sufficient* to answer the question. Using the data given in the statements plus your knowledge of mathematics and everyday facts (such as the number of days in July or the meaning of *counterclockwise*), choose the best answer choice.

    (A) Statement (1) ALONE is sufficient, but statement (2) alone is not sufficient to answer the question asked.

    (B) Statement (2) ALONE is sufficient, but statement (1) alone is not sufficient to answer the question asked.

    (C) BOTH statements (1) and (2) TOGETHER are sufficient to answer the question asked, but NEITHER statement ALONE is sufficient.

    (D) EACH statement ALONE is sufficient to answer the question asked.

    (E) Statements (1) and (2) TOGETHER are NOT sufficient to answer the question asked, and additional data specific to the problem are needed.

Problem Solving Directions: Answer each problem-solving question in this section by using the information given and your own mathematical calculations. Then select the correct answer of the five choices given.

---

1. If $1,500 = 2^x 3^y 5^z$, then $x + z - y =$

    (A) 0

    (B) 2

    (C) 4

    (D) 5

    (E) 6

2. If $x > 0$, then $x =$

   (1) $|2x - 5| = 11$
   (2) $x^2 - 10x + 16 = 0$

   Ⓐ Statement (1) ALONE is sufficient, but statement (2) alone is not sufficient to answer the question asked.
   Ⓑ Statement (2) ALONE is sufficient, but statement (1) alone is not sufficient to answer the question asked.
   Ⓒ BOTH statements (1) and (2) TOGETHER are sufficient to answer the question asked, but NEITHER statement ALONE is sufficient.
   Ⓓ EACH statement ALONE is sufficient to answer the question asked.
   Ⓔ Statements (1) and (2) TOGETHER are NOT sufficient to answer the question asked, and additional data specific to the problem are needed.

3. In the rhombus below, $BC = 8$, $AE = 4$, and $\angle DAE = 60°$. $\overline{AD}$ is the diameter of the circle.

   If a man starts at C and follows around the outer edge of this figure to D, F, A, G, E, B, and back to C, exactly how far will he travel?

   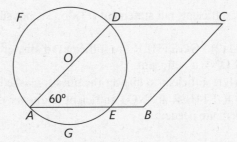

   Note: Figure not drawn to scale.

   Ⓐ $20 + 8\pi$

   Ⓑ $20 + \dfrac{16\pi}{3}$

   Ⓒ $20 + \dfrac{8\pi}{3}$

   Ⓓ $16 + 8\pi$

   Ⓔ $16 + \dfrac{16\pi}{3}$

4. At a party, there were children under the age of 12, teenagers, and adults over the age of 18. A person is randomly selected from this party. What is the probability that the person is a teenager?

   (1) The total number of people at the party was 20, with twice as many teenagers as children.
   (2) The number of teenagers and adults were the same.

   Ⓐ Statement (1) ALONE is sufficient, but statement (2) alone is not sufficient to answer the question asked.
   Ⓑ Statement (2) ALONE is sufficient, but statement (1) alone is not sufficient to answer the question asked.
   Ⓒ BOTH statements (1) and (2) TOGETHER are sufficient to answer the question asked, but NEITHER statement ALONE is sufficient.
   Ⓓ EACH statement ALONE is sufficient to answer the question asked.
   Ⓔ Statements (1) and (2) TOGETHER are NOT sufficient to answer the question asked, and additional data specific to the problem are needed.

5. Juan is at least 4 years older than Brandy, and he is at least 3 years younger than Julian. If Juan's age is b, Brandy's age is c, and Julian's age is d, then which of the following could be true?

   I. $c + 3 < b + 1 < d + 2$

   II. $b - 2 < c - 1 < d + 1$

   III. $c - 1 < d - 2 < b + 2$

   Ⓐ   I only

   Ⓑ   II only

   Ⓒ   III only

   Ⓓ   I and III only

   Ⓔ   II and III only

6. If x and y are positive integers, is $x + y > 20$?

   (1) x is a prime number between 5 and 12

   (2) y is a prime number between 8 and 14

   Ⓐ   Statement (1) ALONE is sufficient, but statement (2) alone is not sufficient to answer the question asked.

   Ⓑ   Statement (2) ALONE is sufficient, but statement (1) alone is not sufficient to answer the question asked.

   Ⓒ   BOTH statements (1) and (2) TOGETHER are sufficient to answer the question asked, but NEITHER statement ALONE is sufficient.

   Ⓓ   EACH statement ALONE is sufficient to answer the question asked.

   Ⓔ   Statements (1) and (2) TOGETHER are NOT sufficient to answer the question asked, and additional data specific to the problem are needed.

7. A large corporation offers its employees one of two different pension plans, Plan A or Plan B. Records show that 70% of the employees choose Plan A and the rest of the employees choose Plan B. In addition, 60% of those employees who choose Plan A are married and 70% of those who choose Plan B are married. If a married employee is selected at random, what is the probability the employee is in Plan A?

   Ⓐ $\dfrac{1}{3}$

   Ⓑ $\dfrac{4}{7}$

   Ⓒ $\dfrac{3}{5}$

   Ⓓ $\dfrac{2}{3}$

   Ⓔ $\dfrac{3}{4}$

8. Point *O* is the center of the circle shown below.

   What is the area of the shaded region?

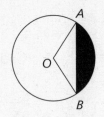

   (1) $AB = 6\sqrt{3}$
   (2) $\angle AOB = 120°$

   (A) Statement (1) ALONE is sufficient, but statement (2) alone is not sufficient to answer the question asked.
   (B) Statement (2) ALONE is sufficient, but statement (1) alone is not sufficient to answer the question asked.
   (C) BOTH statements (1) and (2) TOGETHER are sufficient to answer the question asked, but NEITHER statement ALONE is sufficient.
   (D) EACH statement ALONE is sufficient to answer the question asked.
   (E) Statements (1) and (2) TOGETHER are NOT sufficient to answer the question asked, and additional data specific to the problem are needed.

9. Alex leaves point *X* at 8:15 a.m. and drives north on the highway at an average speed of 52 miles per hour. Andrew leaves point *X* at 9:00 a.m. and drives north on the same highway at an average speed of 65 miles per hour. Andrew will

   (A) overtake Alex at 11:15 a.m.
   (B) overtake Alex at 12 noon.
   (C) overtake Alex at 12:15 p.m.
   (D) overtake Alex at 1:00 p.m.
   (E) never overtake Alex.

10. The sum of four positive integers is 36. What is the smallest integer?

    (1) The largest integer is 12 more than the smallest and is also 6 more than the *second* largest integer.
    (2) The largest integer is four times the smallest integer and is also the sum of the *remaining* two integers.

    (A) Statement (1) ALONE is sufficient, but statement (2) alone is not sufficient to answer the question asked.
    (B) Statement (2) ALONE is sufficient, but statement (1) alone is not sufficient to answer the question asked.
    (C) BOTH statements (1) and (2) TOGETHER are sufficient to answer the question asked, but NEITHER statement ALONE is sufficient.
    (D) EACH statement ALONE is sufficient to answer the question asked.
    (E) Statements (1) and (2) TOGETHER are NOT sufficient to answer the question asked, and additional data specific to the problem are needed.

11. In the figure below, each circle has a radius of length x and is tangent to the other two circles. If triangle PQR is formed by joining the centers of the three circles, what is the area of the portion that is inside the triangle but outside each of the circles?

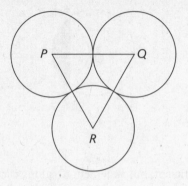

Ⓐ $x^2\sqrt{3} - \dfrac{\pi x^2}{2}$

Ⓑ $\dfrac{x^2\sqrt{3}}{4} - \dfrac{\pi x^2}{2}$

Ⓒ $x^2\sqrt{3} - \dfrac{\pi x^2}{6}$

Ⓓ $\dfrac{x^2\sqrt{3}}{4} - \dfrac{\pi x^2}{6}$

Ⓔ $\dfrac{x^2\sqrt{3}}{2} - \dfrac{\pi x^2}{3}$

12. Is x greater than y?

(1) $xy < 0$
(2) $y^3 > 0$

Ⓐ Statement (1) ALONE is sufficient, but statement (2) alone is not sufficient to answer the question asked.

Ⓑ Statement (2) ALONE is sufficient, but statement (1) alone is not sufficient to answer the question asked.

Ⓒ BOTH statements (1) and (2) TOGETHER are sufficient to answer the question asked, but NEITHER statement ALONE is sufficient.

Ⓓ EACH statement ALONE is sufficient to answer the question asked.

Ⓔ Statements (1) and (2) TOGETHER are NOT sufficient to answer the question asked, and additional data specific to the problem are needed.

13. The numerator of a fraction is decreased by 30% at the same time its denominator is increased by 40%. The new fraction is what percent of the original fraction?

Ⓐ 25%

Ⓑ $33\dfrac{1}{3}\%$

Ⓒ 50%

Ⓓ $66\dfrac{2}{3}\%$

Ⓔ 75%

14. What is the sum of the least and greatest of seven consecutive odd integers?

(1) The mean of the seven integers is 15.
(2) The median of the four smallest integers is 12.

Ⓐ Statement (1) ALONE is sufficient, but statement (2) alone is not sufficient to answer the question asked.

Ⓑ Statement (2) ALONE is sufficient, but statement (1) alone is not sufficient to answer the question asked.

Ⓒ BOTH statements (1) and (2) TOGETHER are sufficient to answer the question asked, but NEITHER statement ALONE is sufficient.

Ⓓ EACH statement ALONE is sufficient to answer the question asked.

Ⓔ Statements (1) and (2) TOGETHER are NOT sufficient to answer the question asked, and additional data specific to the problem are needed.

15. Machine A can do a certain job alone in 10 hours. Machine B can do the same job alone in 12 hours. Both machines start working on the job at 9:00 a.m. Machine A stops working at 1:00 p.m. and Machine B continues working on the job until it is complete. To the nearest minute, at what time will Machine B finish the job?

Ⓐ 4:04 p.m.
Ⓑ 4:10 p.m.
Ⓒ 4:12 p.m.
Ⓓ 4:20 p.m.
Ⓔ 4:40 p.m.

16. In the figure below, how long is $\overline{MN}$?

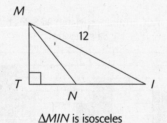

$\triangle MIN$ is isosceles

(1) $\angle MNI = 120°$
(2) $MT = 6$

Ⓐ Statement (1) ALONE is sufficient, but statement (2) alone is not sufficient to answer the question asked.

Ⓑ Statement (2) ALONE is sufficient, but statement (1) alone is not sufficient to answer the question asked.

Ⓒ BOTH statements (1) and (2) TOGETHER are sufficient to answer the question asked, but NEITHER statement ALONE is sufficient.

Ⓓ EACH statement ALONE is sufficient to answer the question asked.

Ⓔ Statements (1) and (2) TOGETHER are NOT sufficient to answer the question asked, and additional data specific to the problem are needed.

17. If the average (arithmetic mean) of two numbers is *y*, and one of numbers is equal to *z*, then the other number is equal to which of the following?

    Ⓐ $2z - y$

    Ⓑ $\dfrac{y+z}{2}$

    Ⓒ $z - y$

    Ⓓ $2y - z$

    Ⓔ $y + 2z$

18. *x*, *y*, and *z* are integers. Is $xy + z$ odd?

    (1) *x* is odd
    (2) The sum of *y* and *z* is even.

    Ⓐ Statement (1) ALONE is sufficient, but statement (2) alone is not sufficient to answer the question asked.
    Ⓑ Statement (2) ALONE is sufficient, but statement (1) alone is not sufficient to answer the question asked.
    Ⓒ BOTH statements (1) and (2) TOGETHER are sufficient to answer the question asked, but NEITHER statement ALONE is sufficient.
    Ⓓ EACH statement ALONE is sufficient to answer the question asked.
    Ⓔ Statements (1) and (2) TOGETHER are NOT sufficient to answer the question asked, and additional data specific to the problem are needed.

19. Review the graph below. If Salesperson D's total sales for Auto, Home, and Life were $28,000, then what were the total Auto sales for the four salespersons?

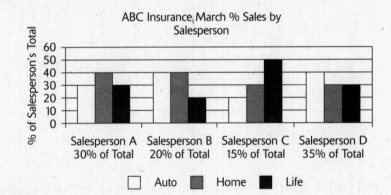

    Ⓐ $20,000–$24,000
    Ⓑ $24,000–$28,000
    Ⓒ $28,000–$32,000
    Ⓓ $32,000–$36,000
    Ⓔ $36,000–$40,000

20. What is the value of x in the data set $\{x, y, 45, 3, 10\}$?

    (1) $x < y$
    (2) The median of the data set is 3.

    Ⓐ Statement (1) ALONE is sufficient, but statement (2) alone is not sufficient to answer the question asked.
    Ⓑ Statement (2) ALONE is sufficient, but statement (1) alone is not sufficient to answer the question asked.
    Ⓒ BOTH statements (1) and (2) TOGETHER are sufficient to answer the question asked, but NEITHER statement ALONE is sufficient.
    Ⓓ EACH statement ALONE is sufficient to answer the question asked.
    Ⓔ Statements (1) and (2) TOGETHER are NOT sufficient to answer the question asked, and additional data specific to the problem are needed.

21. For which replacement of x is the expression $\dfrac{12+x}{x}$ NOT an integer?

    Ⓐ 1
    Ⓑ 2
    Ⓒ 3
    Ⓓ 4
    Ⓔ 5

22. What is the ratio of a to b?

    (1) $5a - 3b = 2a + 7b$
    (2) $a = b + 6$

    Ⓐ Statement (1) ALONE is sufficient, but statement (2) alone is not sufficient to answer the question asked.
    Ⓑ Statement (2) ALONE is sufficient, but statement (1) alone is not sufficient to answer the question asked.
    Ⓒ BOTH statements (1) and (2) TOGETHER are sufficient to answer the question asked, but NEITHER statement ALONE is sufficient.
    Ⓓ EACH statement ALONE is sufficient to answer the question asked.
    Ⓔ Statements (1) and (2) TOGETHER are NOT sufficient to answer the question asked, and additional data specific to the problem are needed.

23. If $\dfrac{1}{x+2} + \dfrac{1}{x+5} = \dfrac{1}{x+1}$, then what could the value of x be?

    Ⓐ −1
    Ⓑ −2
    Ⓒ −3
    Ⓓ −4
    Ⓔ −5

24. What is the perimeter of triangle *PRI* below?

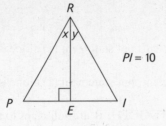

(1) $x = 30°$

(2) $\angle I = 60°$

Ⓐ   Statement (1) ALONE is sufficient, but statement (2) alone is not sufficient to answer the question asked.

Ⓑ   Statement (2) ALONE is sufficient, but statement (1) alone is not sufficient to answer the question asked.

Ⓒ   BOTH statements (1) and (2) TOGETHER are sufficient to answer the question asked, but NEITHER statement ALONE is sufficient.

Ⓓ   EACH statement ALONE is sufficient to answer the question asked.

Ⓔ   Statements (1) and (2) TOGETHER are NOT sufficient to answer the question asked, and additional data specific to the problem are needed.

25. The mean of three numbers is 57. The second number is one more than twice the first number. The third number is four less than three times the second number. What is the difference between the mean and the median of these three numbers?

Ⓐ   16

Ⓑ   17

Ⓒ   18

Ⓓ   19

Ⓔ   20

26. How long would it take Jorge to do a job alone if, when working with Taylor and Gary, it takes 6 hours to do the job?

(1)   Gary would need 45 hours to do the job alone.

(2)   Taylor and Gary would need 18 hours to do the job working together.

Ⓐ   Statement (1) ALONE is sufficient, but statement (2) alone is not sufficient to answer the question asked.

Ⓑ   Statement (2) ALONE is sufficient, but statement (1) alone is not sufficient to answer the question asked.

Ⓒ   BOTH statements (1) and (2) TOGETHER are sufficient to answer the question asked, but NEITHER statement ALONE is sufficient.

Ⓓ   EACH statement ALONE is sufficient to answer the question asked.

Ⓔ   Statements (1) and (2) TOGETHER are NOT sufficient to answer the question asked, and additional data specific to the problem are needed.

27. The ratio of w to x is 4 to 5. The ratio of x to y is 7 to 8. The ratio of y to z is 3 to 2. If q is the ratio of w to z, then in what range of values is q?

   Ⓐ $0.25 < q < 0.5$
   Ⓑ $0.5 < q < 0.75$
   Ⓒ $0.75 < q < 1.0$
   Ⓓ $1.0 < q < 1.25$
   Ⓔ $1.25 < q < 1.5$

28. Is the positive integer n divisible by 24?

   (1) n is divisible by 16 and 3.
   (2) n is divisible by 12 and 4.

   Ⓐ   Statement (1) ALONE is sufficient, but statement (2) alone is not sufficient to answer the question asked.
   Ⓑ   Statement (2) ALONE is sufficient, but statement (1) alone is not sufficient to answer the question asked.
   Ⓒ   BOTH statements (1) and (2) TOGETHER are sufficient to answer the question asked, but NEITHER statement ALONE is sufficient.
   Ⓓ   EACH statement ALONE is sufficient to answer the question asked.
   Ⓔ   Statements (1) and (2) TOGETHER are NOT sufficient to answer the question asked, and additional data specific to the problem are needed.

29. The length and width of a rectangle are each an integer, and the width is from one-third to two-thirds of its length. If the perimeter of the rectangle is 40, which of the following could NOT be the area of the rectangle?

   Ⓐ   96
   Ⓑ   91
   Ⓒ   84
   Ⓓ   75
   Ⓔ   64

30. Is $x > y$?

   (1) $|x - 3| = 2$
   (2) $y^2 - 6y + 5 = 0$

   Ⓐ   Statement (1) ALONE is sufficient, but statement (2) alone is not sufficient to answer the question asked.
   Ⓑ   Statement (2) ALONE is sufficient, but statement (1) alone is not sufficient to answer the question asked.
   Ⓒ   BOTH statements (1) and (2) TOGETHER are sufficient to answer the question asked, but NEITHER statement ALONE is sufficient.
   Ⓓ   EACH statement ALONE is sufficient to answer the question asked.
   Ⓔ   Statements (1) and (2) TOGETHER are NOT sufficient to answer the question asked, and additional data specific to the problem are needed.

31. Review the graph below. Which of the following is NOT true about the number of degrees awarded from 2010 to 2011?

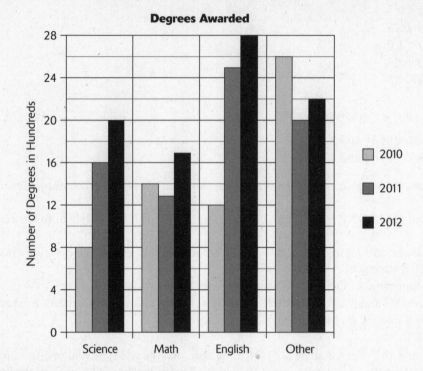

Degrees Awarded

Ⓐ Both science and math increased in number.

Ⓑ English increased in number while math decreased in number.

Ⓒ Both science and English increased in number.

Ⓓ The combined number of degrees awarded for science, math, and English increased by more than 1,900 degrees.

Ⓔ The combined *Other* category for these two years had less than twice as many degrees awarded than the combined number of degrees awarded for math in these two years.

32. How old is Anthony?

(1) Five years ago Anthony was 4 years older than Bai, yet 5 years from now he will be 12 years older than half her age.

(2) Bai is 11 years old.

Ⓐ Statement (1) ALONE is sufficient, but statement (2) alone is not sufficient to answer the question asked.

Ⓑ Statement (2) ALONE is sufficient, but statement (1) alone is not sufficient to answer the question asked.

Ⓒ BOTH statements (1) and (2) TOGETHER are sufficient to answer the question asked, but NEITHER statement ALONE is sufficient.

Ⓓ EACH statement ALONE is sufficient to answer the question asked.

Ⓔ Statements (1) and (2) TOGETHER are NOT sufficient to answer the question asked, and additional data specific to the problem are needed.

33. All possible arrangements using five letters A, B, C, D, and E are written in a row and are placed on separate index cards using each letter exactly once. All the index cards are then placed in a box, and an index card is then randomly selected. What is the probability that the index card selected will have the letter A as the first letter on the left and the letter E as the last letter on the right?

   Ⓐ 0.05
   Ⓑ 0.1
   Ⓒ 0.2
   Ⓓ 0.4
   Ⓔ 0.5

34. What is the value of positive integer J if it is less than 30?

   (1) When J is divided by 5, the remainder is 1.
   (2) When J is divided by 3, the remainder is 2.

   Ⓐ Statement (1) ALONE is sufficient, but statement (2) alone is not sufficient to answer the question asked.
   Ⓑ Statement (2) ALONE is sufficient, but statement (1) alone is not sufficient to answer the question asked.
   Ⓒ BOTH statements (1) and (2) TOGETHER are sufficient to answer the question asked, but NEITHER statement ALONE is sufficient.
   Ⓓ EACH statement ALONE is sufficient to answer the question asked.
   Ⓔ Statements (1) and (2) TOGETHER are NOT sufficient to answer the question asked, and additional data specific to the problem are needed.

35. If w is a positive multiple of 3 and k is a positive multiple of 5, which of the following CANNOT be the value of $w + k$?

   Ⓐ 14
   Ⓑ 15
   Ⓒ 16
   Ⓓ 17
   Ⓔ 18

36. If $2a + 5c = 3b$, what is the value of c?

   (1) $3a = 39$
   (2) $3b + 25 = 2a$

   Ⓐ Statement (1) ALONE is sufficient, but statement (2) alone is not sufficient to answer the question asked.
   Ⓑ Statement (2) ALONE is sufficient, but statement (1) alone is not sufficient to answer the question asked.
   Ⓒ BOTH statements (1) and (2) TOGETHER are sufficient to answer the question asked, but NEITHER statement ALONE is sufficient.
   Ⓓ EACH statement ALONE is sufficient to answer the question asked.
   Ⓔ Statements (1) and (2) TOGETHER are NOT sufficient to answer the question asked, and additional data specific to the problem are needed.

37. If $\begin{vmatrix} a & b \\ c & d \end{vmatrix} = ad - bc$, and $r = \begin{vmatrix} 2 & 4 \\ 6 & 8 \end{vmatrix}$, then what is the value of $\begin{vmatrix} 10 & 5 \\ 2r & 4 \end{vmatrix}$?

Ⓐ −120

Ⓑ −40

Ⓒ −8

Ⓓ 40

Ⓔ 120

IF YOU FINISH BEFORE TIME IS CALLED, CHECK YOUR WORK ON THIS SECTION ONLY. DO NOT WORK ON ANY OTHER SECTION IN THE TEST.

Section 3: Verbal

Time: 75 Minutes

41 Questions

General Directions: Your score on the Verbal section will be based on how well you do on the questions presented and also on the number of questions you answer. Try to pace yourself so that you have sufficient time to consider every question. If possible, answer all 41 questions in this section. Guess if you need to. Select the best answer choice for each question. Use a blank sheet of paper to record your answers. You will encounter three kinds of questions in this section: sentence correction, reading comprehension, and critical reasoning.

Sentence Correction Directions: Some part of each sentence is underlined; sometimes the whole sentence is underlined. Five choices for rephrasing the underlined part follow each sentence; the first choice repeats the original, and the other four are different. If the first choice seems better than the alternatives, choose that answer; if not, choose one of the others.

For each sentence, consider the requirements of standard written English. Your choice should be a correct and effective expression, not awkward or ambiguous. Focus on grammar, word choice, sentence construction, and punctuation. If a choice changes the meaning of the original sentence, do not select it.

Reading Comprehension Directions: A reading passage will be followed by questions based on its content. After reading the passage, choose the best answer to each question. Answer all questions about the passage on the basis of what is *stated* or *implied* in the passage. You may refer back to the passage.

Critical Reasoning Directions: You will read a brief passage and determine the author's line of reasoning using only commonsense standards of logic. No knowledge of formal logic is required. Then choose the best answer, realizing that several choices may be possible, but only one is best.

---

1. Perhaps too eager to learn from "The Lost Decade," debt is piling up at an unsustainable rate in Japan.

    (A) Perhaps too eager to learn from "The Lost Decade," debt is piling up at an unsustainable rate in Japan.
    (B) Perhaps too eager to learn from "The Lost Decade," Japan is piling up debt at an unsustainable rate.
    (C) Perhaps to eager to learn from "The Lost Decade," Japan is continually piling up debt at an unsustainable rate.
    (D) Due to the "The Lost Decade," Japan is currently piling up debt at an unsustainable rate.
    (E) Perhaps too eager to learn from "The Lost Decade," Japan piled up debt at an unsustainable rate.

2. Since its founding in 1927, the Northern Tallahassee Ice Factory (NTIF) has greatly evolved as a business. In its first several decades, the company earned revenue exclusively from weekly deliveries for iceboxes. Following the spread of electric refrigeration, NTIF's business focus quickly shifted to the production of bagged, cubed ice. In the early 1980s, the company's core business began to shift toward commercial contracts, a change accelerated by the proliferation of electric ice machines in refrigerators. The company now deals almost exclusively with catering and event-related services, providing everything from portable refrigeration devices to exquisite ice sculptures.

Which of the following conclusions may be drawn from the passage above?

   Ⓐ The advent of electric ice machines negatively affected NTIF's business.

   Ⓑ NTIF deals exclusively with ice and refrigeration-related goods and services.

   Ⓒ The spread of electric refrigeration did not occur until several decades after NTIF's founding.

   Ⓓ NTIF's revenues during the 1920s came entirely from the sale of cubed ice.

   Ⓔ NTIF has remained relatively financially stable over the years.

Questions 3–5 refer to the following passage.

Cloud computing represents a significant shift in how we use information technology. Storage space for digital files, processing power, and services and software are abstracted away from the user's own computing device to servers accessed through the Internet. Google's online office software, the new Amazon Cloud Player, and photo gallery tools such as Flickr are examples of cloud services. Users can work with and use

(5)   their data on multiple devices and networks from almost any location either for free or by paying a service provider for access.

Researchers Kashif Kifayat, Madjid Merabti, and Qi Shi of the Liverpool John Moores University, UK, point out that cloud computing has many advantages, including a high degree of redundancy at both the hardware and software levels and also geographic independence. Cloud services can also cope with individual

(10)   increases in user demand without users having to upgrade their systems. However, there are concerns regarding security and other risks. After all, users must trust the service provider with potentially sensitive data as well as cope with the possibility of system outages that might disrupt their workflow significantly.

The research team cites International Data Corporation, who analyzed the worldwide forecast for cloud service in 2009 as around $17.4 billion and estimated revenues for 2013 as potentially amounting to $44.2

(15)   billion. The European market alone ranged from $971 million in 2008 to a projected $6,005 million in 2013. In terms of blue skies thinking, then, the future is almost certainly cloudy. With the rise of cloud computing in mind, the issues of availability, manageability and monitoring, data protection, scalability and adaptability, privacy, and security must all be addressed urgently.

3. The primary purpose of the passage is to

   Ⓐ illustrate the global nature of the cloud computing market.

   Ⓑ warn against the drawbacks and dangers of cloud computing.

   Ⓒ summarize the risks and benefits of cloud computing.

   Ⓓ provide a comprehensive technical definition of cloud computing.

   Ⓔ interpret results of an industry analysis and forecast.

4. According to the passage, all of the following are benefits of cloud computing EXCEPT:

   Ⓐ high degrees of redundancy at the software level

   Ⓑ lack of geographic dependence

   Ⓒ allowances for increases in individual usage demand without requiring a system upgrade

   Ⓓ reduced risk of potentially disrupting local system outages

   Ⓔ high degrees of redundancy at the hardware level

5. Based on the passage, it can most safely be inferred that

   Ⓐ   the market for cloud service is currently larger in Asia than in Europe.

   Ⓑ   the author of the passage would advise against the use of cloud computing until certain urgent issues are addressed.

   Ⓒ   users of digital files have traditionally stored them on their own computers.

   Ⓓ   most cloud services charge a fee for the use of their servers.

   Ⓔ   the cloud computing industry is ultimately destined to fail.

6. <u>I had been playing Angry Birds on my phone in the lobby for almost 30 minutes when the assistant called</u> me back for my interview.

   Ⓐ   I had been playing Angry Birds on my phone in the lobby for almost 30 minutes when the assistant called

   Ⓑ   I had been playing Angry Birds on my phone in the lobby for almost 30 minutes when the assistant had called

   Ⓒ   I played Angry Birds on my phone in the lobby for almost 30 minutes until the assistant called

   Ⓓ   I was playing Angry Birds on my phone in the lobby for almost 30 minutes when the assistant called

   Ⓔ   I was playing Angry Birds on my phone in the lobby for almost 30 minutes, then the assistant called

7. A major multinational company recently announced that it was investing a substantial sum in research on the enrichment of uranium through a process using lasers. The announcement was met with controversy. On the one hand, such a breakthrough could significantly reduce electricity costs and environmental damage from power plants. Critics worried, however, that if information was leaked on the laser process used to enrich uranium, terrorist groups would be able to produce nuclear weapons.

Concerns about research into the process of using lasers to enrich uranium are based on each of the following assumptions EXCEPT:

   Ⓐ   Terrorist groups likely possess enough scientific knowledge and aptitude to enrich uranium if they had access to the same equipment and instructions as the multinational company's scientists.

   Ⓑ   The uranium-enriching process would inevitably be leaked and become accessible to terrorists.

   Ⓒ   Terrorist groups would be able to obtain the type of lasers necessary for the enrichment process.

   Ⓓ   The enrichment process would not involve any other hard-to-obtain equipment besides the lasers.

   Ⓔ   Nothing prevents terrorist groups from producing nuclear weapons besides the enrichment of uranium.

8. Some hedge fund managers are not particularly concerned with public perception; from their actions, <u>you would think that losses, recessions, and having extravagant parties goes</u> hand in hand.

   Ⓐ   you would think that losses, recessions, and having extravagant parties goes

   Ⓑ   you would think that losses, recessions, and having extravagant parties go

   Ⓒ   losses, recessions, and extravagant parties would seem to go

   Ⓓ   you would think that losses, recessions, and extravagant parties go

   Ⓔ   you would think that losses, recessions and extravagant parties goes

9. As ridiculous as it may seem, the marketing firm is not interviewing any applicants with less than 200 followers on Twitter.

  Ⓐ As ridiculous as it may seem, the marketing firm is not interviewing any applicants with less than 200 followers on Twitter.

  Ⓑ As ridiculous as it may seem; the marketing firm is not interviewing any applicants with less than 200 followers on Twitter.

  Ⓒ As ridiculous as it may seem, the marketing firm is not interviewing any applicants with fewer than 200 followers on Twitter.

  Ⓓ The marketing firm is not interviewing any applicants with fewer than 200 followers on Twitter, despite it seeming ridiculous.

  Ⓔ The marketing firm is not interviewing any applicants with fewer than 200 followers on Twitter.

10. Marketing studies have consistently shown that people rated by test subjects as attractive are more successful in their careers than their less attractive peers, even when performance is equal. This "beauty gap" is greatest in industries such as modeling and retail clothing customer service, where physical appearance is predictably a valuable quality. However, the gap extends to professions where good looks do not seem to merit additional value; despite equal performance, a positive relationship between attractiveness and salary has been observed in positions ranging from investment bankers and corporate lawyers to NFL quarterbacks. This represents an irrational bias toward attractive people in business.

Which of the following, if true, most contradicts the author's conclusion?

  Ⓐ Physical appearance has been considered a point of emphasis and pride in investment banking firms.

  Ⓑ The value of NFL quarterbacks to their franchises is based not only on on-field performance but on marketability.

  Ⓒ Attractive people may be better at their jobs than unattractive people.

  Ⓓ In the field of corporate law, charm and appearance are considered important qualities.

  Ⓔ Attractiveness is a subjective quality and therefore cannot be studied scientifically.

Questions 11–14 refer to the following passage.

Cultures differ in all sorts of ways—their greetings, clothing, expectations about how children should behave, coming-of-age rituals, expressions of sexuality, numbers of husbands or wives, beliefs in god, gods, or lack thereof. People celebrate but also wage wars over these differences. Usually such variety is attributed to the vagaries of history and chance. Some things, such as religious expression and differences or, say, the
(5) fleeting popularity of tube socks, seem simply beyond the realm of explanation. And yet haven't you ever wondered whether there is some reason we are all so different, some underlying cause of our great cultural diversity?

Recently a group of biologists has offered a theory that they say explains, if not tube socks, then nearly everything else. In a series of high-profile papers, Corey Fincher and Randy Thornhill, both at the University
(10) of New Mexico, and Mark Schaller and Damian Murray of the University of British Columbia argue that one factor, disease, ultimately determines much of who we are and how we behave.

Their theory is simple. Where diseases are common, individuals are mean to strangers. Strangers may carry new diseases and so one would do best to avoid them. When people avoid strangers—those outside the tribe—communication among tribes breaks down. That breakdown allows peoples, through time, to become
(15) more different.

Differences accumulate until in places with more diseases, for example Nigeria or Brazil, there are more cultures and languages. Sweden, for example, has few diseases and only 15 languages; Ghana, which is a similar size, has many diseases and 89 languages. Cultural diversity is, in this view, a consequence of disease.

Then Fincher and colleagues go even further. Where people are more xenophobic and cultures more
(20) differentiated from one another, wars are more likely. Democratic governments are less likely because the tribe or group comes first; the nation and individuals in other tribes within the nation come second. And finally, poverty becomes nearly inevitable as a consequence of poor governance, hostility between groups, and the factor that triggered this cascade in the first place—disease.

(25)   As a rule, it is good to be skeptical of biologists who, like Fincher and Thornhill, propose to explain a whole bunch of things with one simple theory. More so when those biologists are dabbling in questions long reserved for cultural anthropologists, who devote their careers to documenting and understanding differences among cultures and their great richness of particulars. Biologists, and I am no exception, seem to have a willingness—or even need—to see generalities in particulars. Fincher's new theory would offer an example of these desires (and a little hubris) run amok, of biologists seeing the entire history of human culture through

(30)   one narrow lens. It would offer such an example, if it didn't also seem, quite possibly, right.

11. It can be inferred from the passage that the author's main purpose in writing the passage is to

   Ⓐ   argue that disease is often the root cause of cultural diversity.
   Ⓑ   claim that cultural diversity is not unequivocally a positive quality.
   Ⓒ   present a theory from biological research that has cultural implications.
   Ⓓ   emphasize the importance of disease prevention, especially in developing countries.
   Ⓔ   interpret the results of a scientific experiment performed by a team of biologists.

12. According to the author, which of the following cultural phenomena is most similar to *the fleeting popularity of tube socks* as *beyond the realm of explanation*?

   Ⓐ   religion
   Ⓑ   disease
   Ⓒ   sexual customs
   Ⓓ   warfare
   Ⓔ   language

13. According to the passage, if the theory presented is correct, which of the following inferences could logically be made?

   Ⓐ   The primary cause of disease is poverty.
   Ⓑ   The histories of culturally diverse nations are likely more shaped by disease than are the histories of more homogeneous nations.
   Ⓒ   If disease were not a factor in a culture's development, the culture likely would not develop multiple languages.
   Ⓓ   Democratic governments are less likely to exist in nations that have not been significantly affected by disease.
   Ⓔ   If disease were eliminated from xenophobic, divided nations, these nations would become stable and democratic.

14. A poor area of a major city has recently been the site of several random acts of violence from gang initiations. Residents have grown distrustful of their fellow citizens and have restricted their interactions to small groups of trusted members of their community.

   In which way is the situation above most parallel with the theory presented in the third paragraph of the passage?

   Ⓐ   It illustrates how people become rude or mean in their social relations.
   Ⓑ   It is structurally similar to the scientists' theory of how cultural differences arise.
   Ⓒ   It explains how breakdowns in communication can occur in urban neighborhoods.
   Ⓓ   It emphasizes the impact of poverty on the development of distrust within a community.
   Ⓔ   It is an example of how new languages can arise through lack of communication.

15. The European central banks are being <u>criticized not only for their recent actions, they are also being criticized for</u> their questionable ability to intervene meaningfully at all.

   Ⓐ criticized not only for their recent actions, they are also being criticized for
   Ⓑ criticized not only for their recent actions, but they are also being criticized for
   Ⓒ criticized not only for their recent actions but also for
   Ⓓ criticized for their recent actions. Also, for
   Ⓔ criticized not only for their recent actions, and also for

16. *Solar energy lobbyist:* A recent study projected that the cost of both building solar panels and producing and storing solar energy will decrease to a point where solar energy will be cheaper than energy from traditional sources by roughly 2015. If this projection becomes reality, it will represent a monumental landmark in energy technology; since solar power cleanly converts the sun's rays into power, it would be a greener and more efficient option than environmentally damaging, dangerous traditional energy sources such as coal and nuclear power, and would therefore make these power sources obsolete.

If the facts stated in the argument are true, the lobbyist's argument is most vulnerable to which of the following criticisms?

   Ⓐ It is biased because the pro-solar lobbyist is speaking from a subjective point of view.
   Ⓑ It assumes that the projections for a monumental landmark in energy technology will prove correct.
   Ⓒ It fails to consider the cost of construction of new solar power sources.
   Ⓓ It fails to consider that traditional power sources may be needed because of variability in the supply of solar energy.
   Ⓔ It speculates that solar energy will be the norm by 2015.

17. Which of the following most logically completes the argument?

Recently, websites such as iTailor and Indochino have surfaced as a way to give consumers the option to purchase made-to-order clothing at discount prices. By setting up custom factories and providing online interfaces where customers can input their measurements for orders, these websites can offer affordable clothing designed to the customer's exact measurements and specifications. Many domestic, independent tailors have bemoaned the rise in popularity of the concept, claiming that this "outsourcing" of tailoring will drive them out of business. However, these made-to-order websites should benefit independent, domestic tailors, if anything, because _____.

   Ⓐ they promote efficiency in the tailoring industry, which implies greater profit margins in the overall market
   Ⓑ the vast majority of these tailors' business comes from measurements and alterations, rather than designing and creating custom-made clothing
   Ⓒ they provide customers with more tailoring options on the whole and therefore enhance the customer experience
   Ⓓ they give customers who may have previously been unable to afford made-to-order clothes the opportunity to purchase them
   Ⓔ many of these tailors are employed by and receive the majority of their business from these made-to-order websites

18. The HDMI cable, the input cable from the Blu-ray player, and the output cable that runs <u>in the surround sound system connects</u> to the back of the receiver.

   Ⓐ in the surround sound system connects
   Ⓑ to the surround sound system connect
   Ⓒ to the surround sound system connects
   Ⓓ in the surround sound system connect
   Ⓔ to the surround sound system connecting

19. Among the other associates, I sensed a hint of jealousy <u>of the promotions that had been given to Beth and myself</u>.

   Ⓐ   of the promotions that had been given to Beth and myself

   Ⓑ   with reference to the promotions that had been given to Beth and myself

   Ⓒ   of the promotions that Beth and myself received

   Ⓓ   of Beth and me for the promotions we had been given

   Ⓔ   of the promotions that were given to Beth and me

Questions 20–23 refer to the following passage.

With the benefit of hindsight, it seems clear that Sulzberger's first big initiative—to transform *The Times* from a regional paper with national scope to a national paper that happened to be headquartered in the Northeast—was a smart one. In the mid-nineties, *The Times'* print-side balance sheet was in decent shape, and yet Sulzberger, along with a group of editors and executives that included Times Company CEO Janet
(5) Robinson, set about trying to persuade advertisers to fundamentally reconsider their relationship with the paper.

Sulzberger's "national strategy," which involved substantial investments in new printing plants and distribution efforts, coincided with a boom in luxury advertising, and within a couple of years, the plan was working. But even as the ad revenue continued to funnel in, there was a new problem looming on the horizon.
(10) *The Times,* like every other newspaper and magazine in the world, was confronted with the strange, new, virtual world of the Internet. Compared with some of his peers, Sulzberger was an early adopter. By the turn of the century, he had a new mantra: He was "platform-agnostic." In other words, it didn't matter how you consumed your news so long as you were eating from his newspaper's plate. Years before the advent of smartphones or iPads, he told me that one of the company's most pressing goals was to figure out how to
(15) reach all the "people we think have an affinity for *The Times'* news organization who currently don't read *The Times,* either because they can't get access to it or they may not read it because they don't read newspapers and they want to access that information [some other way]."

That type of talk might have sounded good at TED[1] conferences and Sun Valley retreats, but it didn't help relations between the paper's print and online staffs, which had existed as separate entities since the founding
(20) of Times Company Digital, the paper's Internet company, by Martin Nisenholtz in 1995. From early on, *The New York Times* on the Web, as the paper's site was officially called, excelled at creating powerful online content. In 1999, Nisenholtz and his team had put together a database of more than 10 million registered users and had annual revenue of $25 million.

The primacy the company put on its digital operations fueled tension in the newsroom. The subsequent
(25) years felt at the time like a perpetually mutating quagmire: There was the bursting of the dot-com bubble; the eventual merging of the print and digital newsrooms; and the odd, ill-fated TimesSelect plan shut down when the paper realized that whatever revenue was being earned by putting most of its columnists behind a $50-a-year paywall was more than offset by the eyeballs it was losing.

Through it all, Sulzberger plowed money into *The Times'* web operation—and by 2008, *nytimes.com* had
(30) become one of the most impressive news sites on the planet.

[1]TED (Technology, Entertainment and Design) is a global set of conferences owned by the private nonprofit Sapling Foundation, formed to disseminate "Ideas worth spreading."

20. The author's primary purpose of this passage is to

   Ⓐ   provide a history and timeline for Times Company Digital's successful online venture.

   Ⓑ   give an overview of *The Times'* general business from the years 1995 to 2008.

   Ⓒ   tell the story of a visionary executive who overcame obstacles to implement a successful sales strategy.

   Ⓓ   pass on lessons for the online news business using *The Times* as a case study.

   Ⓔ   describe how the dot-com bubble and crash affected *The New York Times.*

21. According to the description in the passage, which of the following situations most closely conforms to Sulzberger's mantra of being *platform-agnostic*?

    Ⓐ A record label that encourages customers to purchase mp3s as well as CDs of their artists' songs and to stream their artists' music videos from YouTube.

    Ⓑ A book publisher that does not allow its authors' books to be sold or read on Kindles or other electronic devices.

    Ⓒ An athlete who builds up a large following on Twitter by promoting his page whenever possible.

    Ⓓ A restaurant chain that provides a limited delivery and takeout menu so that customers may consume its food in the setting of their choice.

    Ⓔ A sporting goods store that also sells nonathletic apparel and merchandise.

22. It can be inferred that the author would most likely agree with which of the following statements?

    Ⓐ While TimesSelect was ultimately shut down, *The New York Times* likely would have reaped the benefits later on had it stuck with the project.

    Ⓑ Sulzberger invested too much money in a flawed business venture and was unwise to do so despite its ultimate growth.

    Ⓒ *The Times* adapted to the digitalization of society faster than many other newspapers did.

    Ⓓ In an ideal world, Sulzberger would prefer that consumers get their news from print papers.

    Ⓔ *The Times* began their push toward digitalization in the early 2000s.

23. The author refers to term *perpetually mutating quagmire* in (line 25) to point out

    Ⓐ the rise and fall of the dot-com bubble during the 1990s and early 2000s.

    Ⓑ *The New York Times'* online presence between 1995 and 1999.

    Ⓒ the newspaper's situation in the years following 1999.

    Ⓓ the speed at which *The Times'* Internet arm grew during Sulzberger's tenure.

    Ⓔ the TimesSelect plan that was ultimately shut down after costing the paper viewers.

24. American patent law is in need of reform. Traditionally, the long-term, thorough procedures and provisions have been necessary for pharmaceutical patents. The development of new drugs and treatments required massive investments in research and development, and companies required significant, lasting insurance to protect their investments. However, the fast-moving, ever-evolving world of technology has made a mess of the system. In nonpharmaceutical arenas, patent litigation lawsuits are associated with far higher costs than actual profits derived from the patents themselves. At least in the technology sector, patent law must be reformed to reduce the term of patents and the potential for frivolous, costly, patent infringement lawsuits.

    Which of the following statements, if true, most weakens the argument above?

    Ⓐ Many lawsuits contributing to high litigation costs are calculated business moves with no basis for infringement.

    Ⓑ Patent law must be uniform across all industries.

    Ⓒ The pharmaceutical industry relies on long-term, powerful patents to support its investments in research and development.

    Ⓓ Studies have shown that the term for most technology patents far exceeds their useful, profit-producing life.

    Ⓔ Profits from technological patents are projected to increase over the coming years.

25. The array of bright lights, beautiful people, <u>and the collection of fancy restaurants were all things that appealed to her</u>.

   Ⓐ   and the collection of fancy restaurants were all things that appealed to her
   Ⓑ   and the collection of fancy restaurants all appealed to her
   Ⓒ   and the collection of fancy restaurants were all appealing things to her
   Ⓓ   and fancy restaurants were all things that appealed to her
   Ⓔ   and fancy restaurants all appealed to her

26. While lockouts occurred in both the NFL and the NBA in 2011, the respective negotiations had very different dynamics. The majority of NBA franchises were losing money at the onset of the lockout; this meant that they had no incentive—other than lost fan interest and loyalty—to end the work stoppage, because any potential missed game simply meant less lost money, rather than lost profits. The majority of NFL franchises, by contrast, were operating at a profit at the onset of the lockout; they were simply operating at *less* of a profit than normal due to poor economic conditions. It is therefore no surprise that the NFL Players' Union held more sway in their respective negotiations than did the NBA Players' Association.

   Which of the following statements can be inferred from the argument above?

   Ⓐ   Most NFL franchises were looking at the prospect of lost profits during each potential missed game.
   Ⓑ   The NBA owners were more reasonable in their demands than was the NBA Players' Association.
   Ⓒ   The NFL Players' Union had more skillful negotiators than did the NBA Players' Association.
   Ⓓ   No NBA franchises were operating at a profit at the onset of the lockout.
   Ⓔ   The NBA lockout lasted longer than the NFL lockout.

27. *Person A:* Immediately following Standard & Poor's downgrade of United States' debt from AAA to AA+, **prices of United States Treasuries *increased* as investors flocked to the government-issued bonds that had just effectively been downgraded.** This is illogical; if investors want a safe investment in an already turbulent market made even more turbulent by the downgrade, they shouldn't be buying securities from the very entity that was downgraded.

   Person B: While it may seem illogical, the fact remains that **United States Treasury bonds are still the safest investments on the market despite the downgrade, and investors tend to seek out safe investments during uncertain conditions.** Besides, the downgrade is largely a technicality and does not imply anything meaningful about the future solvency of the United States.

   In the debate above, the two portions in boldface play which of the following roles?

   Ⓐ   The first describes the situation that is the basis for the debate; the second describes a consequence of this situation.
   Ⓑ   The first describes a seemingly illogical response to an action; the second acknowledges a fact that supports the action that provoked this response.
   Ⓒ   The first describes a counterintuitive event; the second provides a possible explanation for the event.
   Ⓓ   The first presents Person A's main argument; the second presents Person B's main argument.
   Ⓔ   The first provides an example of the phenomenon being debated; the second attempts to discredit this example.

28. After his moment of clarity, <u>the deadline didn't seem as overwhelming to Jason as it previously had before</u>.

   Ⓐ   the deadline didn't seem as overwhelming to Jason as it previously had before
   Ⓑ   the deadline didn't seem as overwhelming to Jason as it had before
   Ⓒ   the deadline didn't seem as overwhelming to Jason as it had
   Ⓓ   Jason no longer felt overwhelmed by the deadline
   Ⓔ   Jason didn't feel as overwhelmed by the deadline as he had before

29. By the time I turn 30, <u>I will make partner at the firm; that is my hope</u>.

    Ⓐ I will make partner at the firm; that is my hope

    Ⓑ I will have made partner at the firm; that is my hope

    Ⓒ I will hopefully make partner at the firm

    Ⓓ I hope I will have made partner at the firm

    Ⓔ hopefully, I will have made partner at the firm

30. The online search engine *EyeLight* indexes Web pages and prioritizes search results by using a complicated algorithm that factors in the number of hits and links to each site, the prominence of the search terms on the site, and the behavior of previous *EyeLight* users after similar searches. Much of *EyeLight*'s revenues come from advertising; however, *EyeLight* also accepts payments from the very websites it claims to objectively index. It is unfortunate that *EyeLight* has decided to accept "bribes" from companies that want to increase their standing in its search index, because this compromises a way of navigating the Internet that is otherwise quite effective and objective.

The conclusion drawn above depends on which of the following assumptions?

    Ⓐ *EyeLight*'s algorithm does not include any additional, subjective factors.

    Ⓑ The payments *EyeLight* accepts from the websites it indexes influence the standing of websites in its index.

    Ⓒ Advertising revenues alone would be sufficient to keep *EyeLight* financially solvent.

    Ⓓ "Bribes" from websites in exchange for better standing in *EyeLight*'s index compromise the effectiveness and objectivity of the search engine.

    Ⓔ *EyeLight* should disclose payments made by companies listed in its index.

31. The corporation in question has been noticeably silent throughout the <u>ordeal, they have never taken</u> an official stance on the matter.

    Ⓐ ordeal, they have never taken

    Ⓑ ordeal, in that they have never taken

    Ⓒ ordeal; they have never taken

    Ⓓ ordeal; it has never taken

    Ⓔ ordeal. They never took

32. The Great Pacific Garbage Patch—or "Trash Island"—is a massive collection of plastics, sludge, and other debris that has gradually formed in the North Pacific Ocean to roughly twice the size of Texas. The accumulation is believed to have slowly grown since the 1950s, as trash has been sucked from shores to a centralized location in the North Pacific Gyre by wind-driven surface currents. In addition to its obvious negative implications—the pollution introduced into the world's oceans and its effects on wildlife—Trash Island also indirectly results in the ingestion of toxins by humans when they consume fish that have consumed toxins originating from the waste. The fact that the United States government has not taken responsibility and taken steps to clean up this mess is appalling and shameful.

Which of the following is the most significant flaw in the author's reasoning?

    Ⓐ It does not identify other countries involved in taking steps to address the issue.

    Ⓑ It assumes that the United States government is responsible for the problem.

    Ⓒ It claims that inaction should be considered "appalling and shameful."

    Ⓓ It confuses causation with correlation.

    Ⓔ It does not consider that the plastics and compounds that make up Trash Island are projected to biodegrade over the coming years.

33. <u>Between the twelve board members, there was</u> a high level of tension.

    Ⓐ   Between the twelve board members, there was
    Ⓑ   Between the twelve board members, there were
    Ⓒ   Among the twelve board members, there was
    Ⓓ   Among the twelve board members, there were
    Ⓔ   Among the board members was

Questions 34–36 are based on the following passage.

       Innovative entrepreneurs grasp the true meaning of "risk." Successful small business leaders tend to treat risk as a two-sided coin: They identify and mitigate threats on one side, while seizing and exploiting opportunities on the other side. Thanks to the rough wake of the global economic crisis, recent technological breakthroughs, better short-term access to specialized skills, and intensifying global competition for skilled
(5)   talent over the long term, there have never been more threats or opportunities confronting U.S. small businesses.

       The 2008–2009 global economic crisis still continues to disrupt businesses, and it's no surprise that "improving access to capital" represents the first, and most frequently mentioned, strategic objective identified in the U.S. Small Business Administration's strategic plan for fiscal years 2011 through 2016. Other
(10) uncertainties, including the nerve-wracking debt-ceiling standoff among federal legislators and major questions about the U.S. tax environment, also pose future risks and complicate medium-range forecasting processes. In addition to inflation, increased regulation and taxes project to be the largest concerns for small business owners.

       The time and resources required to meet regulatory requirements comprise a relatively small percentage of
(15) large companies' expenses. However, compliance costs "can quickly deplete what little profits a startup firm might have," points out Steven Bradley, assistant professor of Management and Entrepreneurship at Baylor University. "The willingness to take risks and introduce new products and services to the market is slowly chocked off by these higher hurdles."

       That's the bad news. The good news is that the opportunities available to small businesses make these
(20) threats worth addressing. One of the leading publishing authorities on small business reports that some of the best startup opportunities exist outside of Silicon Valley this year. This is not because technology and software startups have waned, but because growth is robust in other areas, including education companies, consulting services, and even brick-and-mortar retail. More than half of the companies on the 2009 Fortune 500 list were launched during a recession or bear market, along with nearly half of the firms on the 2008 *Inc.*
(25) list of America's fastest-growing companies.

34. Based on the passage, the author would be most likely to agree with which of the following statements?

    Ⓐ   The potential for opportunity is inherent to the concept of risk.
    Ⓑ   Most small business owners approach risk too conservatively.
    Ⓒ   The ratio of risk to opportunity in the current economic environment is high.
    Ⓓ   Sometimes successful entrepreneurs must ignore risk in order to capitalize on opportunities.
    Ⓔ   Improvements in technology and easier access to skilled workers have helped to reduce risk for business owners.

35. According to the passage, all of the following are concerns of small businesses EXCEPT:

    Ⓐ   The government debate over the debt ceiling
    Ⓑ   Uncertainties regarding domestic taxation policies
    Ⓒ   Potential for market capitalization
    Ⓓ   Ease of attaining funds
    Ⓔ   Inflation

36. Which of the following best describes the author's conclusion about the current climate for small business?

    Ⓐ The abundance of risk in the current economy prevents many small business owners from capitalizing on opportunities.
    Ⓑ Concerns related to legislation and taxation have created a historically risky business environment.
    Ⓒ While threat levels are historically high, the corresponding opportunities provide for a relatively attractive market.
    Ⓓ Despite risky economic conditions, small business owners should spend aggressively in an attempt to grow their businesses.
    Ⓔ Small business owners tend to amplify risks and threats and minimize opportunities and rewards in their projections.

37. One theory claiming that stocks are currently overvalued and due for a correction posits a fundamental shift in the perceived ability of monetary policy to affect the markets and economy. Investors have long held a deeply ingrained belief that the actions of the Federal Reserve were very powerful and that the Fed could always provide a safety net as insurance for investors to prevent complete collapse of the system, which gave stocks extra value. However, there is growing sentiment these days that the Fed no longer has this power and that the market is its own animal, over which the government no longer has ultimate control.

    Based on the information above, the theory presented is most vulnerable to which of the following counterarguments?

    Ⓐ Investors' perceptions of the Fed's abilities were inaccurate in the first place.
    Ⓑ The perceived safety net has historically given stocks additional value that may no longer exist.
    Ⓒ Stock prices may already reflect this shift in perception and need no further correction.
    Ⓓ The Fed has stopgap measures to prevent a collapse of the system that were not available in the past.
    Ⓔ Foreign markets suffer from monetary policies with the same vulnerabilities.

38. <u>I would like guaranteed 5% raise on top of my current salary before we proceed farther, since I believe that I have earned this modest increase in compensation through the work that I do.</u>

    Ⓐ I would like guaranteed 5% raise on top of my current salary before we proceed farther, since I believe that I have earned this modest increase in compensation through the work that I do.
    Ⓑ I would like guaranteed 5% raise on top of my current salary before we proceed further, since I believe that I have earned this modest increase in compensation through the work that I do.
    Ⓒ I would like a guaranteed 5% raise; I believe that my work warrants this modest increase in compensation.
    Ⓓ I would like a guaranteed 5% raise before we proceed further; I believe my work warrants this modest increase in compensation.
    Ⓔ Before we proceed farther, I would like a guaranteed 5% raise; I believe my work warrants this modest increase in compensation.

39. *Congressperson:* While it has only recently entered the public consciousness, the National Debt has long been a ticking time bomb waiting to explode. The United States has consistently borrowed at unsustainable levels, which has put entitlement programs, in particular, on the verge of insolvency. Many of my colleagues have proposed imposing a hard debt ceiling on our borrowing as a solution to this problem; however, many countries that have imposed hard debt ceilings have experienced complete economic collapses in the ensuing years. Therefore, the United States should not impose a hard debt ceiling because it would cause an economic collapse.

    Which of the following represents a flaw in the congressperson's reasoning?

    Ⓐ Assuming that a debt ceiling is the only solution that colleagues have proposed
    Ⓑ Assuming that unsustainable borrowing causes insolvency
    Ⓒ Making a claim without presenting any substantiating evidence
    Ⓓ Conflating the concepts of cause and effect
    Ⓔ Confusing causation with correlation

40. The American Recovery and Reinvestment Act of 2009 (commonly known as "The Stimulus Plan") is currently estimated by the Congressional Budget Office to have saved only between 0.8% and 2.5% of the country's GDP. With the unemployment rate still over 9% and the private sector still struggling, some have called for an additional stimulus plan as a short-term stopgap. However, this is a pandering and irresponsible proposal; the country is already overspent to the point that its credit rating has been downgraded from AAA status, and we cannot continue to throw more money at a problem with no long-term plan for resolution.

All of the following statements, if true, are factors that weaken the above argument EXCEPT:

Ⓐ The "some" calling for an additional stimulus plan are not identified.
Ⓑ The argument implies the only reason for a credit rating downgrade is overspending.
Ⓒ The argument offers key statistics on the financial health of the nation.
Ⓓ The argument uses judgmental negative language, suggesting bias.
Ⓔ The argument offers an unsubstantiated claim that there is no long-term plan for resolution.

41. In retirement terms, the "withdrawal rate" can be defined as the percentage of a retiree's savings that he or she withdraws each year during retirement. (A safe withdrawal rate is considered to be around 3%.) The "savings rate," on the other hand, is the percentage of a worker's yearly income that he or she puts away for retirement each year before retiring. (A safe savings rate is considered to be around 15% over a 30-year period.) The savings rate is certainly important, as it is what defines the "nest egg" that retirees draw upon in retirement. However, the withdrawal rate is the more important metric to consider. The size of the nest egg can be greatly influenced by other factors, such as market conditions, and if a retiree withdraws too high a percentage, he or she risks running out of money before dying.

Which of the following statements, if true, most seriously weakens the above argument?

Ⓐ Given current interest rate projections, most analysts actually consider a safe withdrawal rate to be between 4% and 5%, giving retirees more latitude for spending.
Ⓑ Those who maintain the safe savings rate but retire with a relatively small nest egg during bear markets are generally comfortable during retirement due to eventual market gains.
Ⓒ Many retirees have children or other relatives who can help carry them through short-term withdrawal rate issues.
Ⓓ Many retirees spend less money after retiring than while working.
Ⓔ The process by which a nest egg reaches a certain value is irrelevant, assuming that it reaches the value.

IF YOU FINISH BEFORE TIME IS CALLED, CHECK YOUR WORK ON THIS SECTION ONLY. DO NOT WORK ON ANY OTHER SECTION IN THE TEST.

STOP

Section 4: Integrated Reasoning

Time: 30 minutes

12 Questions

Question 1

The data in the table below show the median home prices for 20 U.S. cities. Prices for March 2007, February 2008, and March 2008 are in thousands of dollars.

City	Mar 07	Feb 08	Mar 08	Mar 07 vs. Mar 08	Feb 08 vs. Mar 08
Atlanta	133.22	125.83	127.61	−4.2%	+1.41%
Boston	168.52	160.31	158.54	−5.9%	−1.10%
Charlotte	130.44	131.22	131.52	+0.8%	+0.23%
Chicago	167.04	153.33	150.35	−10.0%	−1.94%
Cleveland	117.60	106.82	106.42	−9.5%	−0.37%
Dallas	123.10	117.72	119.08	−3.3%	+1.16%
Denver	134.20	127.50	127.43	−5.0%	−0.05%
Detroit	116.44	97.61	95.57	−17.9%	−2.09%
Las Vegas	228.55	177.18	169.31	−25.9%	−4.44%
Los Angeles	264.58	214.83	207.11	−21.7%	−3.59%
Miami	276.89	218.74	208.88	−24.6%	−4.51%
Minneapolis	165.56	145.93	142.24	−14.1%	−2.53%
New York	212.39	198.46	196.58	−7.4%	−0.95%
Phoenix	216.86	172.72	166.97	−23.0%	−3.33%
Portland	181.72	176.24	174.39	−4.0%	−1.05%
San Diego	211.09	190.34	185.44	−12.2%	−2.57%
San Francisco	237.14	174.54	168.38	−29.0%	−3.53%
Seattle	186.44	179.85	178.29	−4.4%	−0.87%
Tampa	226.58	188.59	182.26	−19.6%	−3.36%
Washington, DC	219.67	207.05	202.34	−7.9%	−2.27%

Title row: **U.S. Home Price Comparison by City**

Source: http://bigpicture.typepad.com/comments/2008/05/case-shiller-pr.html.

Directions: Carefully review the table above and read each of the following statements about comparing U.S. home prices. Based on the information in the table, determine whether each statement is *true* or *false* and fill in the corresponding oval. Select *Yes* if the statement is true; select *No* if the statement is false.

Yes	No	
○	○	**1a.** From March 2007 to February 2008, housing prices in Las Vegas decreased by more than 20%.
○	○	**1b.** Exactly four cities showed a reduction in housing prices in excess of 20% between March 2007 and March 2008.
○	○	**1c.** Among the three cities showing the lowest housing prices in February 2008, the mean average price for this month was less than $110,000.

Question 2

The owner of a painting company is planning a large job painting dorm rooms for a college. Altogether, 420 rooms need to be painted. Two crews are available to help with the job. Angela's crew can paint a total of 8 rooms in a day, and Brent's crew can paint a total of 7 rooms in a day. Each crew must be hired independently for a whole number of workweeks, each consisting of 5 days, and the entire job must be completed within 6 weeks. Additionally, the owner intends to paint 3 rooms per day, 5 days a week, for the entire 6 weeks. The rest of the job must be commissioned to Angela's crew and Brent's crew.

Directions: In the table below, identify the necessary number of days for which the owner will need to hire each crew. Make only one selection in each column by filling in the oval in the row that represents the correct answer.

Question 2a Angela's Crew	Question 2b Brent's Crew	Number of Days
○	○	5
○	○	10
○	○	15
○	○	20
○	○	25
○	○	30

Question 3

The bar graph below shows the monthly and average monthly rainfall, in centimeters, for January through June of 2003, 2004, and 2005. Each group of four bars represents one month. Three of the four bars represent a specific year, and one of the four bars represents the average of the three years.

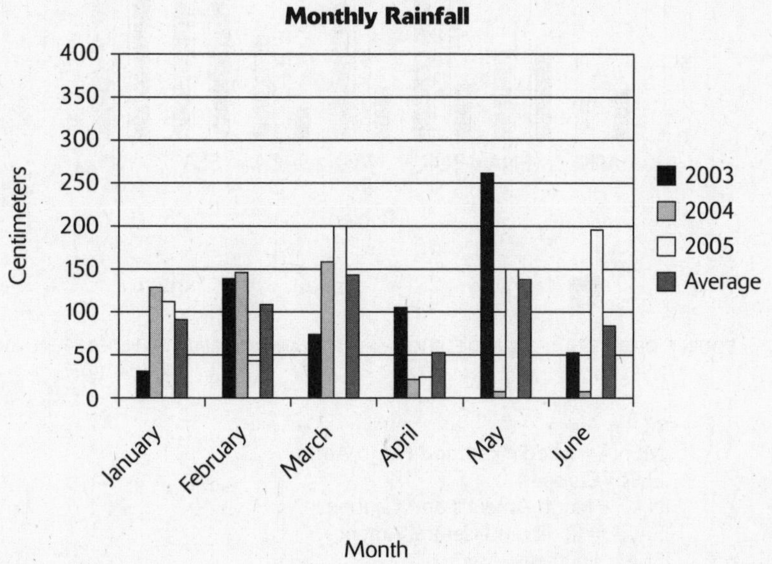

Monthly Rainfall

Directions: In each question you will be presented with a sentence that has one or two blanks indicating that something has been omitted, or left out of the sentence. Use the given data in the graph above to select the best answer that completes the following two statements.

3a. In 2004, the arithmetic mean of monthly rainfall from January through June was _____ (less than 50 cm, between 50 cm and 100 cm, greater than 100 cm).

3b. In January from 2003 to 2004, the range of values for monthly rainfall was approximately _____ (60 cm, 80 cm, 100 cm).

Question 4

The bar graph below shows the number of people with diabetes, by age group, in Africa, the Middle East and North Africa, Europe, North America and the Caribbean, South and Central America, Southeast Asia, and the Western Pacific. The number of people (in millions) is represented on the *y* axis. Each set of three bars represents a specific region, and each bar represents a specific age group.

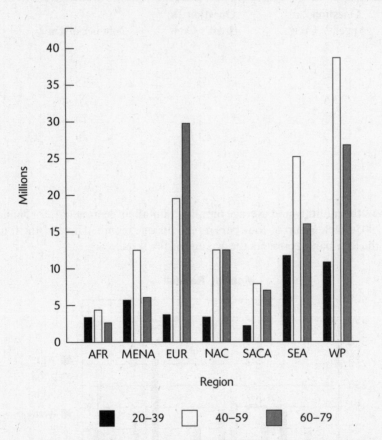

Number of People with Diabetes in Age Groups by Region, 2007

SOURCE: DIABETES ATLAS THIRD EDITION, © INTERNATIONAL DIABETES FEDERATION, 2006

AFR = Africa
MENA = Middle East and North Africa
EUR = Europe
NAC = North America and Caribbean
SACA = South and Central America
SEA = Southeast Asia
WP = Western Pacific

Directions: In each question below you will be presented with a sentence that has one or two blanks, indicating that something has been omitted, or left out of the sentence. Use the given data in the graph above to select the best answer that completes the following statements.

4a. The highest incidence of diabetes among people in the age range from 20 to 39 occurs in the region of _____ (Europe, Southeast Asia, Western Pacific).

4b. Among people in the age range from 60 to 79, the median incidence of diabetes occurs in _____ (Europe, North America and Caribbean, Southeast Asia).

Question 5

Two cable TV companies, CableLife and WorldView, are the only competitors in a city with a current market of 1,200,000 viewers. Currently, CableLife has a 60% market share and WorldView has a 40% share. However, as new customers enter the market, WorldView is growing its customer base faster than CableLife at a constant rate such that WorldView and CableLife are projected to have the same number of customers in 6 years.

Directions: In the table below, identify the necessary number of customers per year by which each company is projected to increase. Make only one selection in each column by filling in the oval in the row that represents the correct answer.

Question 5a CableLife	Question 5b WorldView	Customers per Year
O	O	20,000
O	O	30,000
O	O	50,000
O	O	90,000
O	O	100,000
O	O	120,000

Question 6

The table below shows a variety of tax rate percentages for each of the ten Canadian provinces.

Canadian Tax Rates by Province							
Province	Personal Income Tax – Statutory Range		Comb. Fed/Prov	Corporate Income Tax		Small Business Tax	Sales Tax
	Lowest Rate	Highest Rate	Top Marginal Rate	General	M&P		
Alberta	10.00	10.00	39.00	10.0	10.0	3.0	0.0
British Columbia	5.06	14.70	43.70	10.0	10.0	2.5	7.0
Manitoba	10.80	17.40	46.40	12.0	12.0	0.0	7.0
New Brunswick	9.10	12.70	41.70	10.0	10.0	5.0	8.0
Newfoundland	7.70	13.30	42.30	14.0	5.0	4.0	8.0
Nova Scotia	8.79	21.00	50.00	16.0	16.0	4.5	10.0
Ontario	5.05	11.16	46.41	11.5	10.0	4.5	8.0
Prince Edward Island	9.80	16.70	47.37	16.0	16.0	1.0	10.0
Quebec	16.00	24.00	48.22	11.9	11.9	8.0	8.5
Saskatchewan	11.00	15.00	44.00	12.0	10.0	4.5	5.0

Source: http://www.finance.alberta.ca/calc-script/graphs_all_graphs.htm

Directions: Carefully review the table and read each of the following statements about Canadian tax rates. Based on the information in the table, determine whether each statement is *true* or *false* and fill in the corresponding oval. Select *Yes* if the statement is true; select *No* if the statement is false.

Yes No

○ ○ **6a.** Exactly two of the ten provinces have a combined federal/provincial top marginal tax rate between 41% and 43%.

○ ○ **6b.** The sales tax rate in Nova Scotia is equal to the general corporate income tax rate in exactly three of the ten provinces.

○ ○ **6c.** If a province was selected at random, the probability that it would have a small business tax rate that is less than 4.5% is at least 0.5.

Questions 7–8

Message #1

E-mail from Warren Schaefer to Dr. Penelope Kranz

Dear Professor Kranz,

My name is Warren Schaefer, and I'm a graduate assistant for Professor Lisa McCann. She recommended that I write to you for a bit of clarification.

Briefly, I'm working on a project that contrasts your work with that of Stephen Crawford. Both of you worked with rhesus monkeys and seem to have reached opposite conclusions. You state that in adults, size does not correlate with intelligence; Dr. Crawford seems to conclude that there is, indeed, a positive correlation between the two: larger rhesus monkeys tend to handle a variety of cognitive tasks more quickly and easily.

Can you shed some light on this apparent discrepancy?

Sincerely,
Warren Schaefer

Message #2

E-mail from Dr. Penelope Kranz to Warren Schaefer

Warren,

Thanks for your query. It's a common question, discussed in the three subsequent papers I've attached. Briefly, while objective adult size does correlate with intelligence, as with most findings of this kind, the key to understanding this result lies in a third factor that was neglected in the original studies: in this case, malnutrition.

The issue isn't whether a rhesus monkey is large or small per se, but whether it has grown to roughly its full size given its genetic potential. Stunted growth correlates with malnutrition, and malnutrition correlates negatively with intelligence. And a smaller rhesus monkey is more likely to be small because of stunted growth, which accounts entirely for the discrepancy in measurable intelligence.

My contention is a causal connection: malnutrition causes both stunted growth and stunted intelligence. Concluding causality from correlation is always tricky business; you can decide from the attached papers whether this conclusion is warranted.

Thanks,
Dr. Penelope Kranz

Directions: In each statement below you are presented with a *yes* or *no* question. After considering each statement, determine if the information in the two messages above supports the stated conclusion.

Yes	No	
○	○	**7a.** A larger rhesus monkey is statistically likely to be more intelligent than a smaller one.
○	○	**7b.** According to Dr. Kranz, a small rhesus monkey that has not experienced malnutrition is statistically likely to be as intelligent as a large rhesus monkey.
○	○	**7c.** Dr. Kranz would contend that a causal connection exists linking good nutrition with the intelligence of rhesus monkeys.

8. For which of the following pairs of traits is there a positive correlation?

    Ⓐ   Adult size and intelligence
    Ⓑ   Adult size and stunted growth
    Ⓒ   Adult size and malnutrition
    Ⓓ   Intelligence and malnutrition
    Ⓔ   Intelligence and stunted growth

Question 9

A project to replace a 2,120-foot section of electrical cable that runs under a city park has recently been approved. The Department of Public Works has a crew that can replace 15 feet of cable per hour, and which has already logged 80 hours on the project. Now the Parks Department has added a crew that can replace 10 feet of cable per hour. Both crews are required to work full 8-hour days with no overtime. The project director is trying to decide how to allocate these two crews going forward so that the exact number of feet of cable will be replaced.

Directions: In the table below, identify the necessary number of hours for which the project director will need to hire each crew. Make only one selection in each column by filling in the oval in the row that represents the correct answer.

Question 9a Public Works Crew	Question 9b Parks Crew	Number of Hours
○	○	8
○	○	16
○	○	24
○	○	32
○	○	40
○	○	48

Questions 10–11

Message #1

E-mail sent on Tuesday afternoon from Dorian Henderson, owner of New Day Housekeeping, to Marta Flores, a prospective customer.

Hi Marta:

Thank you for inviting me into your home. After today's walk-through, we are prepared to offer the following cleaning rates:

    Weekly cleaning: $70 per cleaning
    Bi-weekly cleaning: $85 per cleaning

As you requested, this would include every room in the house *except* for the three upstairs bedrooms and the bathroom off the master bedroom. However, if you decide that you would like to add any or all of these rooms, here is how we would calculate them in:

    Additional bedroom: $5 extra
    Additional bathroom: $10 extra

We could begin as early as tomorrow. Please let us know your preferences.

Message #2

E-mail sent on Tuesday evening from Marta Flores to Dorian Henderson

I've discussed this with my husband and we agree that your rates are acceptable. We're also wondering whether our cleaner can come on Friday. We understand that this day is at a premium, and would be willing to pay $20 extra per cleaning for this.

Directions: In each statement below you are presented with a *yes* or *no* question. After considering each statement, determine if the information in the two messages above supports the stated conclusion.

Yes	No	
○	○	**10a.** A bi-weekly cleaning on Friday that includes every room in the house would cost more than $125.
○	○	**10b.** A weekly cleaning on Friday that includes every room in the house *except* the master bathroom would cost more than $115.
○	○	**10c.** A bi-weekly cleaning on a day other than Friday that excludes the three bedrooms but includes all bathrooms would cost less than $100.

11. Which of the following would be the cost of the most expensive option currently on the table?

   Ⓐ $100 per cleaning
   Ⓑ $110 per cleaning
   Ⓒ $115 per cleaning
   Ⓓ $130 per cleaning
   Ⓔ $145 per cleaning

Question 12

The data in the table below give passenger traffic information for the world's busiest airports. For each airport, the table lists the country in which the airport is located, the total number of passengers for the years 2008, 2009, and 2010, and the percent change (plus or minus) from the previous year.

World's Busiest Airports by Passenger Traffic							
Airport Code	Country	2010		2009		2008	
		Passengers	% +/−	Passengers	% +/−	Passengers	% +/−
AMS	Netherlands	45,211,749	+3.8%	43,570,370	−8.1%	47,430,019	−0.8%
ATL	US	89,331,622	+1.5%	88,032,086	−2.2%	90,039,280	+0.7%
CDG	France	58,167,062	+0.4%	57,906,866	−4.9%	60,874,681	+1.6%
CGK	Indonesia	43,981,022	+18.4%	37,143,719	+15.5%	32,172,114	+0.6%
DEN	US	52,211,242	+4.1%	50,167,485	−2.1%	51,245,334	+2.8%
DFW	US	56,905,066	+1.6%	56,030,457	−1.9%	57,093,187	−4.5%
DXB	UAE	47,180,628	+15.4%	40,901,752	+9.2%	37,441,440	+9.0%
FRA	Germany	53,009,221	+4.1%	50,932,840	−4.7%	53,467,450	−1.3%
HKG	China	50,410,819	+10.6%	45,558,807	−4.8%	47,857,746	+1.7%
HND	Japan	64,069,098	+3.4%	61,903,656	−7.2%	66,754,829	−0.2%
JFK	US	46,495,876	+1.3%	45,915,069	−4.0%	47,807,816	+0.2%
LAX	US	58,915,100	+4.2%	56,520,843	−5.0%	59,497,539	−4.7%
LHR	UK	65,884,143	−0.2%	66,037,578	−1.5%	67,056,379	−1.5%
MAD	Spain	49,786,202	+3.2%	48,250,784	−5.1%	50,824,435	−2.4%
ORD	US	66,665,390	+3.9%	64,158,343	−7.5%	69,353,876	−9.0%
PEK	China	73,891,801	+13.0%	65,372,012	+16.9%	55,937,289	+4.4%

Source: Wikipedia

Directions: Carefully review the table and read each of the following statements about passenger travel. Based on the information in the table, determine whether each statement is *true* or *false* and fill-in the corresponding oval. Select *Yes* if the statement is true; select *No* if the statement is false.

Yes	No	
○	○	**12a.** Among the top five busiest airports in 2010, four were also among the top five busiest in 2008.
○	○	**12b.** No airport had more than a 5% increase in passengers all three years.
○	○	**12c.** If one of the U.S. airports in the table was selected at random, the probability that it would have had an increase in passengers between 2007 and 2008 would be greater than 0.3.

IF YOU FINISH BEFORE TIME IS CALLED, CHECK YOUR WORK ON THIS SECTION ONLY. DO NOT WORK ON ANY OTHER SECTION IN THE TEST.

Answer Key

Section 2: Quantitative

1. C	8. C	15. C	22. A	29. E	36. B
2. A	9. B	16. D	23. C	30. E	37. E
3. B	10. B	17. D	24. C	31. A	
4. C	11. A	18. C	25. C	32. A	
5. D	12. C	19. B	26. B	33. A	
6. E	13. C	20. E	27. D	34. E	
7. D	14. D	21. E	28. A	35. B	

Section 3: Verbal

1. B	8. D	15. C	22. C	29. D	36. C
2. C	9. C	16. D	23. C	30. B	37. C
3. C	10. B	17. B	24. B	31. D	38. D
4. D	11. C	18. B	25. E	32. B	39. E
5. C	12. A	19. D	26. A	33. C	40. C
6. A	13. B	20. C	27. C	34. A	41. B
7. B	14. B	21. A	28. E	35. C	

Section 4: Integrated Reasoning

1a. Yes	5a. CableLife: 50,000	9a. Public Works Crew: 40 hours
1b. No	5b. WorldView: 90,000	9b. Parks Crew: 32 hours
1c. Yes	6a. Yes	10a. Yes
2a. Angela's Crew: 15 days	6b. Yes	10b. No
2b. Brent's Crew: 30 days	6c. Yes	10c. Yes
3a. between 50 cm and 100 cm	7a. Yes	11. D
3b. 100 cm	7b. Yes	12a. Yes
4a. Southeast Asia	7c. Yes	12b. No
4b. North America and Caribbean	8. A	12c. Yes

Charting and Analyzing Your Test Results

The first step in analyzing your results is to chart your answers. Use the following charts to identify your strengths and areas of improvement. Complete the process of evaluating your essay and analyzing individual questions in each area for Practice Test 1. Re-evaluate your results as you look for:

- Trends
- Types of errors (frequently repeated errors)
- Low scores in the results of *specific* topic areas.

This assessment and analysis is a tremendous asset to help you maximize your best possible score. The answers and explanations following these charts will provide you clarification to help you solve these types of questions in the future.

Analytical Writing Assessment Worksheet

Analyze your response using the following chart, and refer to the sample "high-scoring strong response" on page 481 as a reference guide. Then estimate your score using the "Analytical Writing Scoring Guide" on page 3 for characteristics of a high-scoring essay to rate your essay. Remember that when you take the actual GMAT, scores are averaged from two separate readers. Since we are trying only for a rough approximation, a strong, average, or weak overall evaluation will give you a general feeling for your score range.

Analysis of an Argument			
Questions	Strong Response Score 6 – Excellent Score 5 – Good	Average Response Score 4 – Competent Score 3 – Limited	Weak Response Score 2 – Weak Score 1 – Poor
1. Does the essay response focus on the specific topic and cover all of the tasks?			
2. Does the essay response identify and analyze important features of the argument?			
3. Does the essay response show cogent reasoning and logical development?			
4. Does the essay response show sufficient supporting and relevant details and/or examples?			
5. Is the essay response well-organized?			
6. Does the essay response show a command of standard written English?			

Analysis Worksheets: Multiple-Choice Questions

One of the most important parts of test preparation is analyzing WHY you missed a question so that you can reduce the number of mistakes. Now that you have taken Practice Test 1 and checked your answers against the answer key on the multiple-choice sections, carefully tally your mistakes by marking them in the proper column.

Reviewing the data below should help you determine WHY you are missing certain questions. Pinpoint the types of errors you have made so that you can focus on avoiding your most common type(s) of errors on the actual exam.

Quantitative Section Worksheet

Types of Questions Missed					
Content Style Topic	Total Possible	Number Correct	Number Incorrect		
			(A) Simple Mistake	(B) Misread Problem	(C) Lack of Knowledge
Arithmetic Problem Solving – Questions 1, 13, 21, 27, 35 Data Sufficiency – Questions 6, 10, 18, 28, 34	10				
Algebra Problem Solving – Questions 23, 37 Data Sufficiency – Questions 2, 12, 22, 30, 36	7				
Geometry Problem Solving – Questions 3, 11, 29 Data Sufficiency – Questions 8, 16, 24	6				
Data Analysis Problem Solving – Questions 17, 25, 33 Data Sufficiency – Questions 4, 14, 20	6				
Word Problems Problem Solving – Questions 5, 7, 9, 15 Data Sufficiency – Questions 26, 32	6				
Data Interpretation Problem Solving – Questions 19, 31	2				
Total Possible Explanations for Incorrect Answers: Columns A, B, and C					
Total Number of Answers Correct and Incorrect	37	Add the total number of correct answers here: _____	Add columns A, B, and C: _____ Total number of incorrect answers		

44

Verbal Section Worksheet

Types of Questions Missed					
			Number Incorrect		
Question Type	Total Possible	Number Correct	(A) Simple Mistake	(B) Misread Problem	(C) Lack of Knowledge
Sentence Correction Questions 1, 6, 8, 9, 15, 18, 19, 25, 28, 29, 31, 33, 38	13				
Reading Comprehension Questions 3, 4, 5, 11, 12, 13, 14, 20, 21, 22, 23, 34, 35, 36	14				
Critical Reasoning Questions 2, 7, 10, 16, 17, 24, 26, 27, 30, 32, 37, 39, 40, 41	14				
Total Possible Explanations for Incorrect Answers: Columns A, B, and C					
Total Number of Answers Correct and Incorrect	41	Add the total number of correct answers here: _____	Add columns A, B, and C: _____ Total number of incorrect answers		

Integrated Reasoning Worksheet

Types of Questions Missed					
			Number Incorrect		
Content Style Topic	Total Possible	Number Correct	(A) Simple Mistake	(B) Misread Problem	(C) Lack of Knowledge
Two-Part Analysis Questions 2, 5, 9	3				
Table Analysis Questions 1, 6, 12	3				
Multi-Source Reasoning Questions 7, 8, 10, 11	4				
Graphics Interpretation Questions 3, 4	2				
Total Possible Explanations for Incorrect Answers: Columns A, B, and C					
Total Number of Answers Correct and Incorrect	12	Add the total number of correct answers here: _____	Add columns A, B, and C: _____ Total number of incorrect answers		

Answers and Explanations

Section 1: Analytical Writing—Analysis of an Argument

Sample student responses are provided below to help you evaluate your essay. Author comments at the end of this section will further help you identify your areas of improvement.

Argument Topic

The following is a memo from the National Binding Company:

> A recent study of workplace behaviors found that employees who regularly eat lunch with their colleagues have higher productivity levels. At our Bridgeton site there are a large number of employees who eat lunch in their offices and at their desks. Over the past two months, total office sales for the Bridgeton office have declined. Therefore, to increase productivity and improve sales, as well as morale, we should make it company policy that employees not eat in their offices or at their desks.

Write a critique of the argument. Your essay should consider its line of reasoning and how well it uses evidence. You should consider what doubtful assumptions undermine the reasoning, and consider what other evidence might support or weaken the argument. Your essay may also consider how the argument could be made more persuasive and its conclusion more convincing.

High-Scoring Strong Response

This well-intentioned policy recommendation has many flaws. Although it may seem appropriate to encourage employees to eat lunch together, there is not enough evidence to suggest a cause and effect relationship between solo lunches and lower sales. There may also be legitimate reasons why employees eat in their offices and at their desks.

The memo singles out the Bridgeton office and makes a connection between the large number of employees eating in their offices or at their desks and the recent lower sales. It also assumes that lower sales are related to low morale, without stating any evidence to back this assumption. It does not address how the Bridgeton office is performing in comparison with the other offices, or whether employees in other offices eat at their desks. The memo is vague about other potential factors, too. What is a large number? Eighty percent? Half? Ten? Is this a widespread phenomenon? Do employees perceive this as a problem? Maybe employees are choosing to eat lunch together at their desks as they work through lunch. Furthermore, there is no evidence to support that people's eating habits are contributing to the lower sales figures. In fact, employees may be working through lunch at their desks because they recognize that sales numbers have dipped and they believe that putting in the extra hour during lunch may make up the difference.

Another flaw is that the data on sales numbers come from only the past two months. There are many other plausible reasons for the decline. There may be seasonal fluctuations in sales. The industry as a whole might be experiencing tough economic conditions. A product cycle may be coming to an end and buyers may be waiting for the new fiscal year to make purchases. In any case, two months are not a long enough period of time to draw conclusions, especially in the absence of other evidence.

A final consideration is that employees are eating lunch at their desks or in their offices for reasons unrelated to sales. Does the Bridgeton office have a place like a lunchroom or conference table where employees can comfortably sit together? If the only location is a dingy area of the office, people may well prefer to eat elsewhere. Have upper managers who eat at their desks set a cultural norm of encouraging employees to eat at their desks, too? If they all eat together, is there someone in upper management who makes a habit of bringing up work-related topics at lunch? Lower ranking employees might find such discussions uncomfortable or even threatening. In the end, the observation that workers at the Bridgeton office are eating at desks and in offices is perhaps a good reason to look into the particular situation in Bridgeton before enacting a policy for all offices.

Although the policy could be a good idea, more information about the survey, the sales numbers, and specifics of the Bridgeton office are needed before making a company-wide recommendation.

Average-Scoring Moderate Response

The memo states that employees are eating at their desks and in their offices and that this is causing a lowering of sales. The problem is that the memo does not consider that people may not want to eat together and that forcing a policy on them may make morale worse.

If employees don't want to eat together they may have good reasons. Some people may be working through their lunch hour so they can leave early to attend a child's soccer practice or pick up their dry cleaning. They are still doing the work but are shifting their time. Forcing them to eat with their co-workers could make them resentful and cuase even worse performance. There may be employees who don't like the topics of conversation at the lunch table, like there are people who gossip and make them uncomfortable. Making a policy about lunch will only make the situation worse.

If the National Binding Company goes ahead with the policy it could make the sales numbers drop even more. The memo points out that the sales have dropped in the past two months. That's not a long period of time but employees know when a company is not doing well. They already feel stressed about the poor performance of their office. Making people eat together at lunch is not going to solve anything. They may even feel more anxious about getting back to work.

In the end, it's bad for companies to get involved with policies like this that try to regulate behavior. The recommendation is a bad one and may in fact make the situation worse.

Low-Scoring Weak Response

The memo has many flaws. It tries to butt into workers' lives and will not solve the problem of lower sales.

First, the company neds to realize that sometimes people need a break from their co-workers. Also, are they going to prevent people from leaving to eat lunch outside the office?

They want to have more sales but don't say how eating lunch makes that happen. Maybe they think that if people have luch at the same time they will talk about making sales and it will improve.

All in all this is a bad idea and shoudl not be implemented.

Comments

The high-scoring sample response examines a variety of flaws in the argument and presents them in well-organized paragraphs. The writer uses evidence from the memo as support and clearly explains the flaws in the memo writer's thinking. Well-chosen words like *phenomenon* and *fluctuations,* along with a variety of sentence types and lengths, lend fluency to the response. The average-scoring essay is also well organized, but focuses on a narrower range of flaws. The writer addresses mainly the issues with morale and only touches on the flawed data on sales figures. The one misspelling is due to a typing error (*cuase*) and does not pose a significant problem, although the following sentence has awkward syntax. The range of vocabulary and sentence structure is also more limited. The low-scoring essay has an organizational plan but is simply too undeveloped in its use of evidence and argumentation to be successful. The number of spelling errors (*neds, luch, shoudl*) in such a short response detracts from any positive aspects.

Section 2: Quantitative

1. **C.** Factor the number 1,500 into the product of primes. Below is one method.

$$1,500 = (2)(750)$$
$$= (2)(2)(375)$$
$$= (2)(2)(3)(125)$$
$$= (2)(2)(3)(5)(25)$$
$$= (2)(2)(3)(5)(5)(5)$$
$$= 2^2 \times 3 \times 5^3$$

Since $1,500 = 2^x 3^y 5^z$ and $x = 2$, $y = 1$, $z = 3$, then $x + z - y = 2 + 3 - 1 = 4$.

2. **A.** Statement (1) ALONE is sufficient, but statement (2) alone is not sufficient.

Step one: First solve the equation in statement (1): $|2x - 5| = 11$.

Either $2x - 5 = 11$ or $2x - 5 = -11$.

$$\text{If } 2x - 5 = 11, \text{ then} \qquad \text{If } 2x - 5 = -11, \text{ then}$$
$$2x = 16 \qquad\qquad 2x = -6$$
$$x = 8 \qquad\qquad\quad x = -3$$

Since $x > 0$, the only value for x is 8. Statement (1) is sufficient.

Step two: Solve the equation in statement (2): $x^2 - 10x + 16 = 0$.

$$x^2 - 10x + 16 = 0 \qquad \text{Solve by factoring.}$$
$$(x - 2)(x - 8) = 0$$
$$x - 2 = 0 \quad \text{or} \quad x - 8 = 0$$
$$x = 2 \qquad\qquad x = 8$$

Since each of the possible values of x is greater than 0, you cannot determine the unique value of x. Therefore, statement (2) is not sufficient.

3. **B.** Because this is a multiple-choice question, you can either solve it using the *elimination strategy* or by *directly* solving the problem.

Elimination method: To solve the problem using the elimination method, first notice that the answer choices include an amount involving π and another amount not involving π. The amount involving π comes from going around the circle portion, and the amount not involving π comes from going around the rhombus portion. Since $ABCD$ is a rhombus (a quadrilateral with sides of equal length) and $BC = 8$, then $CD = 8$ and $AB = 8$.

Since $AE = 4$, then $EB = 4$. Then the portion of the path walked that did not involve the circle, $EB + BC + CD$, has a total distance of $4 + 8 + 8 = 20$. Identifying this helps to eliminate choices D and E as possible answers.

The circumference of a circle (the distance around the circle) is found by multiplying its diameter by π. The diameter is AD and it has the same length as BC, since the quadrilateral is a rhombus. Hence, the distance around the circle is 8π. Since the path involving the circle is more than halfway around circle, but less than all the way around it, that portion of the answer has to be more than 4π but less than 8π. Therefore, only choice B meets these criteria.

Direct method: To solve the problem directly, notice that the rhombus portion of the path is 20 and identify that $\angle DAE = 60°$ to find the exact circle portion. Angle DAE is an inscribed angle and measures half of its intercepted arc. The results show that arc $\overset{\frown}{DE}$ has a measure of 120°. Since a full rotation is 360°, a 120° portion would be one-third of the way around the circle, leaving two-thirds of the circumference as the portion of the path involving the circle. Since the circumference is 8π, as described above, then two-thirds of 8π becomes

$$\frac{2}{3} \times \frac{8\pi}{1} = \frac{16\pi}{3}$$

Hence, the distance traveled would be $20 + \frac{16\pi}{3}$.

4. **C.** BOTH statements TOGETHER are sufficient, but NEITHER statement ALONE is sufficient.

In order to find the probability of randomly selecting a teenager, you would need to know how many people are teenagers and how many people are at the party.

Statement (1) provides how many people are at the party, but does not provide sufficient information to find how many were teenagers. Statement (2) does not provide sufficient information to find either the number of teenagers or how many people were at the party.

Now use the statements together. Let $C = $ # children, $T = $ # teenagers, and $A = $ # adults.

Statement (1): $C + T + A = 20$, $T = 2C$

Statement (2): $T = A$

First take $C + T + A = 20$ and replace A with T.

$$C + T + T = 20$$

Now replace T with $2C$.

$$C + 2C + 2C = 20$$
$$5C = 20$$
$$C = 4$$

Hence, with $C = 4$ and $T = 2C$, you find that $T = 8$. That is, there are 8 teenagers out of the 20 people at the party. The probability can now be calculated as $\frac{8}{20} = \frac{2}{5}$.

Therefore, both statements together are sufficient.

5. **D.** Although the answer choices seem complicated, they are not. First, determine the order of age, from youngest to oldest. Since Juan is older than Brandy, but younger than Julian, Brandy is the youngest and Julian is the oldest. Drawing a quick sketch is helpful to visualize the problem.

(Juan is at least 4 years older than Brandy) (Juan is at least 3 years younger than Julian)

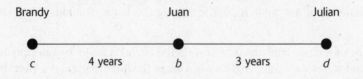

Looking at the sketch, and determining that $c < b < d$, you might conclude that only the first answer choice is correct. But because the answer choices are not comparing the actual age, but a little more or a little less than their ages, a closer look is required. Let us assign some specific ages—ages as close together as possible. Suppose Juan is 20 years old. This would make Brandy at most 16 and Julian at least 23. Substitute these ages in the answer choices and look for contradictions. Using $c = 16$, $b = 20$, and $d = 23$:

$$c+3 < b+1 < d+2 \qquad 16+3 < 20+1 < 23+2 \qquad \text{True}$$
$$19 \;\; < \;\; 21 \;\; < \;\; 25$$

$$b-2 < c-1 < d+1 \qquad 20-2 < 16-1 < 23+1 \qquad \text{Contradiction}$$
$$18 \;\; < \;\; 15 < \;\; 24$$

$$c-1 < d-2 < b+2 \qquad 16-1 < 23-2 < 20+2 \qquad \text{True}$$
$$15 \;\; < \;\; 21 \;\; < \;\; 22$$

Choices I and III are true, therefore, answer choice D is correct.

6. **E.** Statements (1) and (2) TOGETHER are NOT sufficient.

Neither statement alone is sufficient since each statement makes reference to only one of the two variables. Taken together, you find that x can be either 7 or 11, the only prime numbers between 5 and 12, and y can be either 11 or 13, the only prime numbers between 8 and 14. If x is 7 and y is 13, their sum would be 20, making the answer to the question become *no*. But if x is 11, regardless of whether y is 11 or 13, their sum would be greater than 20, making the answer to the question become *yes*.

The answer depends on the replaced values for x and y, and even taken together the statements are not sufficient.

7. **D.** The best method to solve this kind of problem is to use a *tree-diagram*. When initially analyzing this type of problem, you might quickly realize that you have two paths to follow, Plan A or Plan B.

Draw the numbers along each path to indicate the probability of selecting that particular path. After selecting either the Plan A or Plan B path, the next choice you have to make is to determine whether the person is married or not married. In this case, the question only requires the probability values for being married.

The final probability values are the products of the individual probabilities along the chosen path.

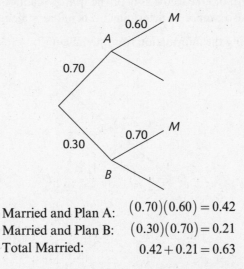

Married and Plan A: $(0.70)(0.60) = 0.42$
Married and Plan B: $(0.30)(0.70) = 0.21$
Total Married: $0.42 + 0.21 = 0.63$

To calculate the probability that a married employee selected at random is in Plan A, divide the Plan A Married probability by the total Married probability (favorable divided by total):

$$\frac{0.42}{0.63} = \frac{2}{3}$$

8. **C.** BOTH statements TOGETHER are sufficient, but NEITHER statement ALONE is sufficient.

In order to find the shaded region, you will first need to find the area of sector AOB and subtract the area of $\triangle AOB$. Locating the area of sector AOB requires knowing the measure of central $\angle AOB$ and the length of the radius $\overline{AO}$. Finding the area of $\triangle AOB$ requires you to identify a base and a height. Once these can be calculated, you can find the shaded area.

This problem also requires the knowledge of 30-60-90 degree right triangles.

Start by redrawing $\triangle AOB$ with an altitude drawn from O to D on segment $\overline{AB}$ together with the information from statement (1).

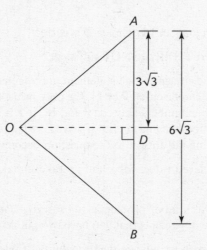

Since $\overline{AO}$ and $\overline{BO}$ are each a radius of the circle, then $AO = BO$ resulting in $\triangle AOB$ as an isosceles triangle. When an altitude is drawn from the vertex where the equal sides in an isosceles triangle meet, it also becomes an angle bisector and a median.

Therefore, $\triangle AOD \cong \triangle BOD$ and $AD = DB$. Since $AB = 6\sqrt{3}$, then $AD = DB = 3\sqrt{3}$. This is not enough information to find the length of $\overline{OD}$, so the area of the triangle cannot be determined. At this point, the measure of central $\angle AOB$ also cannot be determined. Therefore, statement (1) is not sufficient.

Start with a new triangle using the information from statement (2).

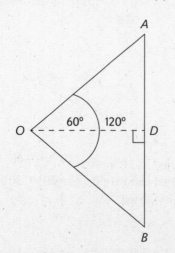

As described previously, $\angle AOD = \angle BOD$ and $AD = DB$. Since $\angle AOB = 120°$, then $\angle AOD = \angle BOD = 60°$. You now have the measure of the central angle, but do not have length measurements. Therefore, statement (2) is not sufficient.

Now look at new triangle that puts the information from both statements together.

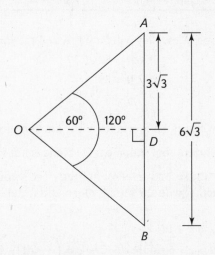

Notice that $\triangle AOD$ is a 30-60-90 right triangle. In any 30-60-90 right triangle, the side opposite the 30-degree angle is the shortest side, the longest side (the hypotenuse) is twice as long as the shortest side, and the side opposite the 60-degree angle is the short side times $\sqrt{3}$.

Knowing the side opposite the 60-degree angle $\left(\overline{AD}\right)$, you can find the radius and the height. With knowledge about the central angle, the radius, and height, the shaded area can be calculated. Thus, together the statements are sufficient.

Remember, that you are not being asked to calculate the area, but to recognize when you have sufficient information to be able to calculate it. To actually calculate the shaded area, you find that $AD = OD\left(\sqrt{3}\right) = 3\sqrt{3}$ then $OD = 3$. Since $AO = 2(OD)$, then $AO = 6$. Then you can perform the following operations:

$$\text{Area of sector } AOB = \left(\frac{\text{central angle}}{360}\right)\left(\pi\left(AO\right)^2\right) = \left(\frac{\overset{1}{\cancel{120}}}{\underset{3}{\cancel{360}}}\right)\left(\pi\left(6\right)^2\right) = \left(\frac{1}{\cancel{3}}\right)\left(\left(\overset{12}{\cancel{36}}\right)\pi\right) = 12\pi$$

$$\text{Area of } \triangle AOB = \frac{1}{2}(AB)(OD) = \frac{1}{\underset{1}{\cancel{2}}}\left(\overset{3}{\cancel{6}}\sqrt{3}\right)(3) = 9\sqrt{3}$$

Shaded region $= 12\pi - 9\sqrt{3}$

9. **B.** This problem can be approached using a *logical perspective* or using a *chart and an algebraic equation.*

Logical perspective: From a logical perspective, when Andrew leaves at 9:00 a.m., Alex has been driving for 45 minutes, or $\frac{3}{4}$ of an hour. Since Alex was driving at 52 miles per hour, he has traveled $\frac{3}{4}$ of that, or 39 miles. Andrew is traveling at 65 miles per hour, which is 13 miles per hour faster than Alex. Each hour Andrew drives, he travels 13 miles farther than Alex. The result of dividing 39 by 13 is 3. Therefore, it takes Andrew 3 hours to narrow the 39-mile gap in driving distance.

Andrew started driving at 9:00 a.m. This means that he will overtake Alex 3 hours later, at 12 noon. Remember to determine how far of a lead the earlier traveler has and determine how much faster the second traveler is going. Dividing the head-start distance by the difference in speeds allows for the overtake time.

Chart and algebraic perspective: From a chart with an algebraic equation perspective, create a *rate × time = distance* chart and insert all of the known information.

Let t = # hours Andrew needs to overtake Alex. Then, $t + \frac{3}{4}$ = # hours Andrew has traveled.

	Rate	Time	Distance
Alex	52 mph	$t+\dfrac{3}{4}$ hr	$52\left(t+\dfrac{3}{4}\right)=52t+39$
Andrew	65 mph	t hr	$65t$

At the time that Andrew overtakes Alex, they will have traveled the same distance.

$$65t = 52t + 39$$
$$13t = 39$$
$$t = 3$$

Therefore, 3 hours after Andrew leaves, he overtakes Alex. Three hours after 9:00 a.m. is 12 noon.

10. B. Statement (2) ALONE is sufficient, but statement (1) alone is not sufficient.

Let a = the smallest integer, b = the second smallest integer, c the second largest integer, and d = the largest integer. Then statement (1), together with the initial information, can be translated into the following system of equations:

$$d = a + 12$$
$$d = c + 6 \rightarrow c = d - 6 \rightarrow c = (a+12) - 6 \rightarrow c = a + 6$$
$$a + b + c + d = 36$$

Replacing d and c with their equivalent values in terms of a into the last equation, you find

$$a + b + (a+6) + (a+12) = 36$$
$$3a + b = 18$$

This last sentence does not have a unique solution; hence, statement (1) is not sufficient.

Statement (2), together with the initial information, can be translated into the following system of equations:

$$d = 4a$$
$$d = b + c \rightarrow (b+c) = 4a$$
$$a + b + c + d = 36$$

Replacing d and $(b + c)$ with their equivalent values in terms of a into the last equation, you find

$$a + (4a) + (4a) = 36$$
$$9a = 36$$
$$a = 4$$

Therefore, the smallest integer is 4, and statement (2) is sufficient.

From statement (2) you can also find that the largest integer is 16 and the sum of the two middle integers is also 16. It is true that this information is not enough to find the exact values of the two middle integers, b and c, but that was not the question.

11. **A.** The described region can be found by finding the area of the triangle and subtracting the three portions of the circles that are within it. The triangle is an equilateral triangle with each side a length of $2x$, since the radius of each circle is given as x.

Because the triangle is equilateral, each central angle has a measure of $60°$ and each portion of a circle is $\frac{60}{360} = \frac{1}{6}$ of a full circle. Thus, the three portions of a circle comprise exactly half of a circle: $3 \times \frac{1}{6} = \frac{1}{2}$.

The area of the equilateral triangle can be found by using the 30-60-90 right triangle side relationships as pictured below.

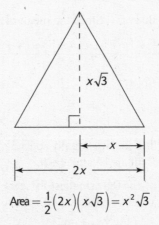

$$\text{Area} = \frac{1}{2}(2x)(x\sqrt{3}) = x^2\sqrt{3}$$

At this point, choices B, D, and E can be eliminated since they do not include exactly $x^2\sqrt{3}$.

If you had started with finding the area of the circle with radius x, you would have realized that half of that area is reduced. That is, $\frac{1}{2}\pi x^2 = \frac{\pi x^2}{2}$ is the amount to be subtracted. With this information, you could eliminate choices C, D, and E. Only choice A shows the correct expression for the described area.

12. **C.** BOTH statements TOGETHER are sufficient, but NEITHER statement ALONE is sufficient.

Statement (1) indicates that the product of x and y is negative. This statement implies that one of the variables is positive and the other one is negative. Since you do not know which one is positive, you cannot answer the question regarding which is greater. Therefore, statement (1) is not sufficient.

Statement (2) indicates that when y is raised to the third power, the result is a positive value. This result only occurs if y is a positive value. However, if the value of x is unknown, statement (2) is not sufficient.

Using the statements together, however, you find that y is positive and x is negative and thus the answer to the questions is *no*. Therefore, together, the statements are sufficient.

Be careful. Just because the answer to the question is *no*, it does not mean that the statements were not sufficient. The fact that the question could be answered indicates the statements were sufficient.

13. **C.** The problem can be solved *algebraically*, but is easier to calculate using straightforward *arithmetic*.

Arithmetic method: Begin with the fraction $\frac{100}{100}$, which is one whole. Decreasing the numerator by 30% causes the new numerator to become 70. Increasing the denominator by 40% causes the new denominator to become 140. The new fraction is $\frac{70}{140} = \frac{1}{2}$. Thus, $\frac{1}{2}$ is 50% of the original one whole you started with.

Algebraic method: Let $\frac{n}{d}$ represent the original fraction. After the numerator has been decreased by 30% and the denominator has been increased by 40%, the new fraction becomes

$$\frac{n - 0.3n}{d + 0.4d} = \frac{0.7n}{1.4d} = \left(\frac{0.7}{1.4}\right)\frac{n}{d} = \left(\frac{1}{2}\right)\frac{n}{d}$$

Therefore, the new fraction is half, or 50% of the original fraction.

14. D. EACH statement ALONE is sufficient.

The seven consecutive odd integers, from least to greatest, can be represented as follows.

$$\underset{\text{1st}}{x}, \underset{\text{2nd}}{x+2}, \underset{\text{3rd}}{x+4}, \underset{\text{4th}}{x+6}, \underset{\text{5th}}{x+8}, \underset{\text{6th}}{x+10}, \underset{\text{7th}}{x+12}$$

Statement (1) states that the mean of these seven integers is 15. With this information, you will eventually find that the value of x (the least integer) is 9, and find that $x + 12$ (the greatest integer) is 21, and find that their sum is 30. Therefore, statement (1) is sufficient.

Below are two methods to find the value of x. Since the mean of the seven integers is 15, then

$$\frac{x+(x+2)+(x+4)+(x+6)+(x+8)+(x+10)+(x+12)}{7}=15$$
$$7x+42=105$$
$$7x=63$$
$$x=9$$

You may have noticed that since the integers are equally spaced apart, the mean and the median are the same. Hence, $x + 6$, the median value, equals 15 and $x = 9$.

Statement (2) states that the median of the four smallest integers is 12. Thus, the average of the second and the third smallest integers is 12. This can be translated into the following equation, and then solved.

$$\frac{(x+2)+(x+4)}{2}=12$$
$$2x+6=24$$
$$2x=18$$
$$x=9$$

As mentioned earlier, both the least and greatest integers can be determined, and therefore, their sums can be found. Hence, statement (2) is sufficient.

15. C. Machine A can do the job in 10 hours; therefore, it completes $\frac{1}{10}$ of the job per hour worked. Working from 9:00 a.m. to 1:00 p.m., Machine A worked for 4 hours and completed $\frac{4}{10} = \frac{2}{5}$ of the job.

Machine B can do the job in 12 hours; therefore, it completes $\frac{1}{12}$ of the job per hour worked. From 9:00 a.m. to 1:00 p.m. Machine B worked for 4 hours and thus completed $\frac{4}{12} = \frac{1}{3}$ of the job. So from 9:00 a.m. to 1:00 p.m., working together, the machines completed $\frac{2}{5} + \frac{1}{3} = \frac{6}{15} + \frac{5}{15} = \frac{11}{15}$ of the job, leaving $\frac{4}{15}$ of the job yet to be completed. Machine B, working at the rate of $\frac{1}{12}$ of the job per hour, can complete the job in $\frac{4}{15} \div \frac{1}{12} = \frac{4}{\overset{5}{\cancel{15}}} \times \frac{\overset{4}{\cancel{12}}}{1} = \frac{16}{5} = 3\frac{1}{5}$ hours, or in 3 hours and 12 minutes, since $\frac{1}{5}$ hr $= \frac{1}{5} \times \frac{60}{1}$ min $= 12$ minutes.

Therefore, Machine B finishes the job at 4:12 p.m.

Solved algebraically, the operations might appear as follows:

Let x = the amount of time Machine B works beyond the first 4 hours.

$$\text{Machine A} \quad + \quad \text{Machine B} \quad = 1 \text{ job}$$

$$\frac{1 \text{ job}}{\overset{}{\underset{5}{\cancel{10}}} \text{ hr}} \left(\overset{2}{\cancel{4}} \text{ hr} \right) + \left(\frac{1 \text{ job}}{12 \text{ hr}} \right) ((x+4) \text{ hr}) = 1 \text{ job}$$

$$\frac{2}{5} \quad + \quad \frac{x+4}{12} \quad = 1$$

$$\frac{24}{60} \quad + \quad \frac{5(x+4)}{60} \quad = 1 \qquad \text{Use 60 as a common denominator.}$$

$$\frac{24}{60} + \frac{5x+20}{60} = 1$$

$$\frac{5x+44}{60} = 1$$

$$\frac{\overset{1}{\cancel{60}}}{1} \cdot \frac{5x+44}{\underset{1}{\cancel{60}}} = 1 \cdot 60 \qquad \text{Multiply each side by 60.}$$

$$5x+44 = 60$$

$$5x = 16$$

$$x = 3\frac{1}{5}$$

16. **D.** EACH statement ALONE is sufficient.

Since $\triangle MIN$ is isosceles, $MN = NI$ and $\angle NMI = \angle I$.

From statement (1), $\angle MNI = 120°$, so you can conclude that $\angle I = 30°$ since the sum of the angles in any triangle is 180°. Since $\angle I = 30°$, $\triangle MTI$ is a 30-60-90 degree right triangle. The side opposite the 30-degree angle is half as long as the hypotenuse.

Because $MI = 12$, then $MT = 6$.

Because $\angle MNI = 120°$, then $\angle TNM = 60°$ since the two angles form a line.

Thus, $\triangle MTN$ is a 30-60-90 degree right triangle.

Since you know the side opposite the 60-degree angle, $MT = 6$, you can divide that by $\sqrt{3}$ $\left(\frac{6}{\sqrt{3}} = 2\sqrt{3} \right)$ to find the length of $\overline{TN}$ and then double that value, $4\sqrt{3}$, to find the length of $\overline{MN}$. Therefore, statement (1) is sufficient. Remember, you don't actually have to find the values, but just know they can be found.

Statement (2) states that $MT = 6$. Use the above discussion from that point to recognize that $\overline{MN}$ can be determined. Hence, statement (2) is sufficient.

17. **D.** "The average (arithmetic mean) of two numbers is y, and one of the numbers is equal to z" is translated into $\frac{x+z}{2} = y$, where x represents the number not yet represented. Solving for x is:

$$\frac{x+z}{2} = y$$

$$\overset{1}{\cancel{2}} \cdot \frac{x+z}{\underset{1}{\cancel{2}}} = y \cdot 2 \qquad \text{Multiply each side by 2.}$$

$$x+z = 2y$$

$$x = 2y - z$$

18. **C.** BOTH statements TOGETHER are sufficient, but NEITHER statement ALONE is sufficient.

Notice that neither statement alone is sufficient because each statement leaves out information about some variable. However, both statements together show that x is odd and either both y and z are even or both are odd since the sum of two even integers is even and the sum of two odd integers is even.

Suppose x, y, and z are each odd. Then xy will be odd since the product of two odd integers is odd and $xy + z$ will be even since the sum of two odd integers is even.

Now suppose that x is odd and both y and z are even. Then xy will be even because the product of an odd integer and an even integer is even, and $xy + z$ will be even since the sum of an even integer and an even integer is an even integer. Thus, in either case, the sum will be even and the answer to the question is *no.* Taken together, the statements are sufficient.

A word of caution: Just because the answer to the question is *no,* it does not mean the statements are not sufficient. The fact that the question could be answered indicates the statements are sufficient.

19. **B.** Salesperson D's total represents 35% of the total for all the salespersons. If x represents the total sales for all salespersons combined, then

$$0.35x = \$28,000$$
$$x = \$80,000$$

In terms of auto sales, Salesperson A had 30% of 30% of the total sales; Salesperson B had 40% of 20% of the total sales; Salesperson C had 20% of 15% of the total sales; and Salesperson D had 40% of 35% of the total sales.

The specific combined total for just auto sales can be computed as follows:

Salesperson	% of Auto Sales	% of Total Sales	Total Auto Sales in $
A	30%	30%	(30%)(30%)($80,000) = (9%)($80,000)
B	40%	20%	(40%)(20%)($80,000) = (8%)($80,000)
C	20%	15%	(20%)(15%)($80,000) = (3%)($80,000)
D	40%	35%	(40%)(35%)($80,000) = (14%)($80,000)

Rather than performing the four multiplications separately and then adding the results, it is faster to write this out as:

$$(9\% + 8\% + 3\% + 14\%)(\$80,000) = (34\%)(\$80,000) = \$27,200$$

20. **E.** Statements (1) and (2) TOGETHER are NOT sufficient.

Statement (1) only states that x is less than y but does not provide sufficient information to find the value of x. Therefore, statement (1) is not sufficient.

Statement (2) states that the middle value of the five values is 3, positioning the 10 and 45 values to the right of 3, and the x and y values to the left of 3 when listed from least to greatest. Therefore, statement (2) is not sufficient to be able to find the value of x.

Even taken together, you only know that x is less than y and they are positioned to the left of 3 when listed in order from least to greatest. This still is not sufficient information to find the value of x.

21. **E.** This is a problem that only requires the *direct replacement* of values to find the answer. Remember that you are finding the replacement that does NOT produce an integer.

x	$\dfrac{12+x}{x}$	Integer?
1	$\dfrac{12+1}{1} = \dfrac{13}{1} = 13$	yes
2	$\dfrac{12+2}{2} = \dfrac{14}{2} = 7$	yes
3	$\dfrac{12+3}{3} = \dfrac{15}{3} = 5$	yes
4	$\dfrac{12+4}{4} = \dfrac{16}{4} = 4$	yes
5	$\dfrac{12+5}{5} = \dfrac{17}{5} = 3\dfrac{2}{5}$	no

22. **A.** Statement (1) ALONE is sufficient, but statement (2) alone is not sufficient.

Using the information from statement (1):

$$5a - 3b = 2a + 7b$$
$$5a - 3b - 2a + 3b = 2a + 7b - 2a + 3b \quad \text{Subtract } 2a \text{ and add } 3b \text{ to each side.}$$
$$3a = 10b$$
$$\frac{\cancel{3}a}{\cancel{3}b} = \frac{10\cancel{b}}{3\cancel{b}} \qquad \text{Divide each side by } 3b.$$
$$\frac{a}{b} = \frac{10}{3}$$

Thus, statement (1) is sufficient to be able to answer the question.

Using the information from statement (2), it is *not possible* to determine an exact value for $\frac{a}{b}$.

However, you can solve $\frac{a}{b} = \frac{b+6}{b}$. Thus, the ratio of a to b depends on the value of b, and statement (2) is not sufficient.

23. **C.** The fastest method to solve this type of problem is to use *direct replacements* of the given values to determine which replacement would end in a true sentence. You can also use an *algebraic method*.

Direct replacements: First notice that x cannot be -1, -2, or -5, since that would create a fraction with zero in the denominator, which is not allowed. Thus, the only replacements to test are -3 and -4 (see the chart below).

x	$\dfrac{1}{x+2} + \dfrac{1}{x+5} = \dfrac{1}{x+1}$	True?
-3	$\dfrac{1}{-3+2} + \dfrac{1}{-3+5} = \dfrac{1}{-3+1}$ $-\dfrac{1}{1} + \dfrac{1}{2} = -\dfrac{1}{2}$ $-\dfrac{1}{2} = -\dfrac{1}{2}$	yes
-4	$\dfrac{1}{-4+2} + \dfrac{1}{-4+5} = \dfrac{1}{-4+1}$ $-\dfrac{1}{2} + \dfrac{1}{1} = -\dfrac{1}{3}$ $\dfrac{1}{2} = -\dfrac{1}{3}$	no

Note that you could have stopped working on the solution to the problem after concluding that –3 resulted in the equation being true.

Algebraic method:

$$\frac{1}{x+2}+\frac{1}{x+5}=\frac{1}{x+1}$$

Multiply each side by $(x+2)(x+5)(x+1)$ to clear the denominators.

$$(x+2)(x+5)(x+1)\left(\frac{1}{x+2}+\frac{1}{x+5}\right)=(x+2)(x+5)(x+1)\left(\frac{1}{x+1}\right)$$

$$(x+5)(x+1)+(x+2)(x+1)=(x+2)(x+5)$$

$$\left(x^2+6x+5\right)+\left(x^2+3x+2\right)=x^2+7x+10$$

$$2x^2+9x+7=x^2+7x+10$$

Subtract $x^2+7x+10$ from each side.

$$x^2+2x-3=0$$

Factor the quadratic.

$$(x+3)(x-1)=0$$

$$x+3=0 \quad \text{or} \quad x-1=0$$

$$x=-3 \quad \text{or} \quad x=1$$

24. **C.** BOTH statements TOGETHER are sufficient, but NEITHER statement ALONE is sufficient.

Given statement (1), $x = 30°$, and identifying the right angle at E, you find that ΔRPE is a 30-60-90 degree right triangle. If you know any one of its sides, you will be able to determine all three sides. However, only knowing $PI = 10$ is not enough information to determine anything about ΔRPE; therefore, statement (1) is not sufficient.

Given statement (2), $\angle I = 60°$, and the right angle at E, you find that $y = 30°$ and that ΔRIE is a 30-60-90 degree right triangle. Again, if you know any one of its sides, you can determine all three sides. If you only identify $PI = 10$, it is not adequate information to determine anything about ΔRIE; therefore, statement (2) is not sufficient.

Taking the statements together, you find that $x = y = 30°$ or that $\angle PRI = 60°$, which makes $\angle P = 60°$ since the sum of the angles in any triangle is 180°. Thus, ΔPRI is an equilateral triangle.

Since $PI = 10$, the perimeter is 30. Therefore, the statements together are sufficient.

25. **C.** Let $x =$ the first number. Then $2x + 1 =$ the second number. And $3(2x + 1) - 4 = 6x + 3 - 4 = 6x - 1 =$ the third number.

Since the mean of the three numbers is 57, then

$$\frac{x+(2x+1)+(6x-1)}{3}=57$$

$$9x=171$$

$$x=19$$

Therefore, the first number is 19, the second number is $2(19) + 1 = 39$, and the third number is $6(19) - 1 = 113$. The *median* of the three numbers is the middle number, or 39. The *mean* is 57. The difference between the mean and the median is $57 - 39 = 18$.

26. **B.** Statement (2) ALONE is sufficient, but statement (1) alone is not sufficient.

Let $j =$ the amount of time Jorge needs do the job alone. Let $t =$ the amount of time Taylor needs do the job alone. Let $g =$ the amount of time Gary needs do the job alone. Since it takes 6 hours for all three working together, then the following equation can be written.

$$\frac{1}{j}+\frac{1}{t}+\frac{1}{g}=\frac{1}{6}$$

In order to find the value of j, you either need to know both Taylor and Gary's individual time necessary to do the job, or how long they will need together to do the job.

Statement (1) only tells you how long Gary needs alone. Therefore, it is not sufficient.

Statement (2) tells you how long Taylor and Gary need to do the job together; therefore, it is sufficient.

Remember, you are not being asked to solve the problem, but just recognize when it is solvable.

Below is the *algebra* that could be used to solve the problem. Since Taylor and Gary would need 18 hours to do the job together, then $\frac{1}{t}+\frac{1}{g}=\frac{1}{18}$.

Replacing $\frac{1}{t}+\frac{1}{g}$ with $\frac{1}{18}$ in the upper equation, you find $\frac{1}{j}+\frac{1}{18}=\frac{1}{6}$.

$$\frac{1}{j}+\frac{1}{18}=\frac{1}{6} \qquad \text{Multiply each side by the LCD, } 18j.$$

$$18j\left(\frac{1}{j}+\frac{1}{18}\right)=18j\left(\frac{1}{6}\right)$$

$$18+j=3j$$

$$18=2j$$

$$9=j$$

It would take Jorge 9 hours to do the job alone.

Remember, you were not asked to find how long it would take Taylor alone, only how long it would take Jorge alone. Statement (2) is sufficient.

27. **D.** Write each ratio as a fraction and then cross-multiply to remove the denominators:

$$\frac{w}{x}=\frac{4}{5} \qquad \frac{x}{y}=\frac{7}{8} \qquad \frac{y}{z}=\frac{3}{2}$$
$$5w=4x \qquad 8x=7y \qquad 2y=3z$$

In order to create a relationship between w and z, multiply both sides of the first equation by 4, the second by 2, and the third by 7 to get the following three equations.

$$4(5w)=4(4x) \qquad 2(8x)=2(7y) \qquad 7(2y)=7(3z)$$
$$20w=16x \qquad 16x=14y \qquad 14y=21z$$

The relationship between w and z can now be seen: $20w=21z$ or $\frac{w}{z}=\frac{21}{20}$. Since $\frac{21}{20}$ expressed in its decimal form is 1.05, the value of q is between 1.0 and 1.25.

28. **A.** Statement (1) ALONE is sufficient, but statement (2) alone is not sufficient.

From statement (1) you can determine that n is divisible by 48, the least common multiple of 16 and 3. If a number is divisible by 48, it is automatically divisible by any number that divides 48. Since 24 divides 48, it will also divide any number that is divisible by 48. Therefore, statement (1) is sufficient.

From statement (2) all that you can determine is that n is divisible by 12, the least common multiple of 12 and 4. Some numbers divisible by 12 are also divisible by 24, and others are not. For example, 12 is divisible by 4 and 12, but is not divisible by 24. However, 24 is divisible by 4 and 12, and is also divisible by 24. Therefore, statement (2) is not sufficient.

29. **E.** Remember, you are looking for integer values. Because the perimeter of the rectangle is 40, the length plus the width of the rectangle is 20. The width and length values of 1 and 19; 2 and 18; 3 and 17; 4 and 16 are all eliminated since the width is less than one-third the length.

A length of 15 and width of 5 is acceptable, because 5 is one-third of 15. A width of 5 and a length of 15 produce an area of 75.

A width of 6 and a length of 14 is acceptable, because 6 is between one-third and two-thirds of 14. A rectangle of width 6 and length 14 has an area of 84.

A length of 13 and width of 7 is acceptable, because 7 is between one-third and two-thirds of 13. A rectangle of width 7 and length 13 has an area of 91.

A length of 12 and a width of 8 is acceptable, because 8 is two-thirds of 12. A rectangle of width 8 and length 12 has an area of 96.

The only value that could not be the area is 64.

If you had recognized at the beginning that a length of 16 and width of 4 are not acceptable dimensions since 4 is one-fourth of 16, you could have also recognized that the rectangle's area of 64 is also not an acceptable area and have finished the problem quicker.

30. E. Statements (1) and (2) TOGETHER are NOT sufficient.

Neither statement alone can be sufficient since each is missing information about one of the variables.

Solve each equation.

$$|x-3| = 2 \qquad\qquad y^2 - 6y + 5 = 0$$
$$x - 3 = 2 \text{ or } x - 3 = -2 \qquad (y-1)(y-5) = 0$$
$$x = 5 \text{ or } \qquad x = 1 \qquad y - 1 = 0 \text{ or } y - 5 = 0$$
$$y = 1 \text{ or } \qquad y = 5$$

Depending on which values are chosen for x and y, you find different responses to the question. For example, if x is 5 and y is 1, the answer becomes *yes*. If x is 1 and y is 5, the answer is *no*. Therefore, even together, the statements are not sufficient.

31. A. Remember that you are looking for the statement that is NOT true.

Let's analyze each choice.

Choice A: Both science and math increased in number. This statement is *not true* since math decreased in number. Hence, A is the correct choice.

Choice B: English increased in number while math decreased in number. That is *true;* hence, it is not the correct choice.

Choice C: Both science and English increased in number. This statement is *true;* hence, it is not the correct choice.

Choice D: The combined number of degrees awarded for science, math, and English increased by more than 1,900 degrees. The combined number of degrees awarded in 2010 for science, math, and English is 800 + 1,400 + 1,200 = 3,400. The combined number of degrees awarded in 2011 for science, math, and English was 1,600 + 1,300 + 2,500 = 5,400. The increase in the number of degrees awarded is 5,400 − 3,400 = 2,000. This is more than 1,900, which makes choice D *true;* hence, it is not correct.

Choice E: The combined *Other* category for these two years had less than double as many degrees awarded than the combined number of degrees awarded for math in these two years. The combined number of degrees for *Other* for these two years is 2,600 + 2,000 = 4,600. The combined number of degrees for math for these two years is 1,400 + 1,300 = 2,700. Since 4,600 is less than double the value of 2,700, that is 4,600 < 5,400, choice E is *true* and hence not the correct answer.

32. A. Statement (1) ALONE is sufficient, but statement (2) alone is not sufficient.

Let A = Anthony's current age. Then $A - 5$ is Anthony's age 5 years ago, and $A + 5$ is Anthony's age 5 years from now.

Let B = Bai's current age. Then $B - 5$ is Bai's age 5 years ago, and $B + 5$ is Bai's age in 5 years.

Now make literal translations of the two pieces of information given in statement (1).

"Five years ago Anthony was 4 years older than Bai" becomes $A - 5 = (B - 5) + 4$.

And "5 years from now he will be 12 years older than half her age" becomes $A + 5 = \frac{1}{2}(B + 5) + 12$.

These two equations can be used to find Anthony's current age. Therefore, statement (1) is sufficient.

Statement (2) is not sufficient since there is no reference to Anthony's age.

Remember, you are not asked to find the actual answer, but to recognize when the answer can be found.

Algebraic method: Rewrite each equation with the A's and B's on one side of the equation with no fractional coefficients.

$$A - 5 = (B - 5) + 4 \qquad\qquad A + 5 = \frac{1}{2}(B + 5) + 12$$
$$A - 5 = B - 1$$
$$A - 5 - B + 5 = B - 1 - B + 5 \qquad 2(A + 5) = 2\left(\frac{1}{2}(B + 5) + 12\right)$$
$$A - B = 4 \qquad\qquad 2A + 10 = B + 5 + 24$$
$$2A - B = 19$$

Now you have the following systems of equations:
$$2A - B = 19$$
$$A - B = 4$$

Subtract the lower equation from the upper equation to get $A = 15$. Therefore, Anthony is currently 15 years old. You can also determine that Bai is currently 11 years old.

33. **A.** Probability is the comparison of the number of favorable outcomes to the number of total possible outcomes. Since A is to be on the left and E is to be on the right, there are only 3 remaining letters to be arranged between them. There will be 3! or $3 \times 2 \times 1 = 6$ ways to arrange the remaining three letters. That is, there are a total of 6 favorable outcomes. The number of total outcomes is 5! or $5 \times 4 \times 3 \times 2 \times 1 = 120$. The probability then is $\frac{6}{120} = \frac{1}{20} = 0.05$. The arithmetic could have been completed more rapidly if you did not multiply out the values in advance, but simply represented the arithmetic and looked for cancelations.

$$\frac{3 \times \cancel{2} \times \cancel{1}^{1}}{5 \times 4 \times \cancel{3} \times \cancel{2} \times \cancel{1}_{1}} = \frac{1}{20}$$

34. **E.** Statements (1) and (2) TOGETHER are NOT sufficient.

Given statement (1), you can determine that J could be 1, 6, 11, 16, 21, or 26 since these are the positive integers that have a remainder of 1 when divided by 5. Thus, statement (1) is not sufficient since you cannot get a unique value for J.

Given statement (2), you can determine that J is 2, 5, 8, 11, 14, 17, 20, 23, 26, or 29 since these are the positive integers that have a remainder of 2 when divided by 3. Thus, statement (2) is not sufficient since you cannot get a unique value for J.

Taking statements (1) and (2) together, you find that J could be 11 or 26 since these are the positive integers that have a remainder of 1 when divided by 5 and a remainder of 2 when divided by 3. Even together the statements are not sufficient since you cannot determine a unique value for J.

35. B. Notice that all of the answer choices are relatively small in size. The best method to solve this type of problem is to make a chart of the positive multiples of 3 and 5 and determine which values can be the sum of two of them. As you work this problem, continue evaluating each choice until four of the five answer choices are eliminated.

Positive Multiples of 3	Positive Multiples of 5
3	5
6	10
9	15
12	20
15	25
18	30
21	35

The value 14 is eliminated since $9 + 5 = 14$.

The value 16 is eliminated since $6 + 10 = 16$.

The value 17 is eliminated since $12 + 5 = 17$.

The value 18 is eliminated since $3 + 15 = 18$.

Thus, the only value not eliminated is 15.

36. B. Statement (2) ALONE is sufficient, but statement (1) alone is not sufficient.

Given statement (1), you can determine that $a = 13$, but that is not sufficient to be able to find the value of c.

Before you dismiss statement (2) as not being sufficient, notice that the original information provided has a "$2a$" and a "$3b$" and statement (2) also has a "$2a$" and a "$3b$." This requires you to look at statement (2) in more detail and compare this to the original information. Rewrite each equation with all the variables, in alphabetical order, on one side of the equation and the constants on the other side of the equation.

$$2a + 5c = 3b \quad \text{becomes} \quad 2a - 3b + 5c = 0$$
$$3b + 25 = 2a \quad \text{becomes} \quad -2a + 3b = -25$$

Now add the equations and to get $5c = -25$, from which you can determine that $c = -5$.

Hence, statement (2) is sufficient.

It is true that you cannot determine the values of either a or b from statement (2) alone, but remember that you were not asked to find either of their values.

37. E. Based on the definition, $\begin{vmatrix} a & b \\ c & d \end{vmatrix} = ad - bc, r = \begin{vmatrix} 2 & 4 \\ 6 & 8 \end{vmatrix} = (2)(8) - (4)(6) = 16 - 24 = -8$. Now replace

r with that value in the next expression and again use the definition to evaluate the new expression.

$$\begin{vmatrix} 10 & 5 \\ 2r & 4 \end{vmatrix} = \begin{vmatrix} 10 & 5 \\ 2(-8) & 4 \end{vmatrix} = \begin{vmatrix} 10 & 5 \\ -16 & 4 \end{vmatrix} = (10)(4) - (5)(-16) = 40 - (-80) = 40 + 80 = 120$$

Section 3: Verbal

1. B. Choice B is the only grammatically correct choice that does not change the meaning. Choice A contains a dangling modifier, as the phrase beginning *Perhaps too eager* . . . mistakenly modifies *debt* rather than *Japan.* Choice C incorrectly uses *to* rather than *too* and arbitrarily adds the adverb *continually;* choice D changes the meaning of the sentence by adding *currently;* and choice E changes the meaning by putting Japan's actions in the past tense.

2. **C.** If *NTIF's business focus quickly shifted to the production of bagged, cubed ice* after the spread of electric refrigeration, and the company's revenues came exclusively from icebox deliveries for the *first several decades* of its existence, then it must logically follow that the spread of electric refrigeration did not occur until several decades after NTIF was founded. Thus, choice C is correct.

Choice A is incorrect because the change in business strategy after the advent of electric ice machines may have been a reflection of new market opportunities rather than a negative effect on business. Choice B is incorrect because it is an inference; the passage does not make this statement in *absolute* terms. Choice D is incorrect because the passage does not say that the icebox ice distributed in the 1920s was cubed. Choice E is a reasonable hypothesis but cannot be concluded because the passage does not give information about the company's finances.

3. **C.** Choice C is the main point of the passage and developed in the second and third paragraphs. Choice A is a supporting detail relating to the rising importance of the subject. Choice B is incorrect because while the passage does warn of drawbacks of cloud computing, it also describes benefits. Choice D is incorrect because the passage defines cloud computing only generally before focusing on its pros and cons and future prospects. Choice E is incorrect because the primary purpose of the passage is not to interpret the research it briefly cites.

4. **D.** The passage suggests the risk of a system outage as a potential *concern* with cloud computing, rather than a benefit. Answer choices A, B, C, and E are all listed as benefits of cloud computing in the second paragraph. Thus, choice D is correct.

5. **C.** Choice C is directly supported by the first two sentences of the passage: *Cloud computing represents a significant shift in how we use information technology. Storage space for digital files, processing power, and services and software are abstracted away from the user's own computing device . . .* The implication is that digital files have traditionally been stored on the user's own computing device.

Choice A is incorrect because while the European market represents a very small proportion of the overall market, we have no way of knowing what percentage the Asian market represents. Choices B and E are incorrect because the author's tone is not so negative as to suggest any disapproval of cloud computing. Choice D is not implied in the passage and may or may not be true.

6. **A.** There are no errors in the original sentence; it is in the past perfect progressive tense, as it is describing an ongoing action in the past in relation to a specific event that occurred during that action. Thus, choice A is correct. Choices B and D introduce verb tense errors, and choices C and E also change the meaning of the sentence by using *until* and *then,* respectively.

7. **B.** The critics' concerns are conditional in that they are worried about the *possibility* of the process leaking out; the passage does not imply that they assume that such a leak is *inevitable.* Thus, choice B is correct. The rest of the answer choices are all assumptions implicit in the stated concerns; that is, choices A, C, D, and E are all necessary to justify the logic of the statement *if information was leaked on the laser process used to enrich uranium, terrorist groups would be able to produce nuclear weapons.*

8. **D.** The original sentence contains two errors: a parallelism error and a verb agreement error. First, *having extravagant parties* is not parallel with the other nouns on the list (*losses, recessions*), which eliminates choices A and B. Second, *goes* does not agree with the plural compound subject; *go* is the correct verb form, which makes choice E also incorrect. By omitting *you would think that,* choice C leaves an awkward, unclear modifier in *from their actions.* Choice D fixes both errors in a straightforward manner.

9. **C.** The original sentence contains an idiomatic error: *less* modifies a general term (e.g., *happiness, space, pressure*), while *fewer* modifies countable terms (e.g., *minutes, apples, followers*). Choice C corrects this error. Choice B introduces a punctuation error by using a semicolon. In choice D, the construction *despite it seeming ridiculous* is ambiguous, as it is unclear what *it* refers to. Choice E is grammatically correct but changes the meaning of the sentence by dropping the phrase *as ridiculous as it may seem.*

10. **B.** The author presents NFL quarterbacks as an example of the *beauty gap*—that more attractive quarterbacks are paid higher salaries than less attractive quarterbacks, despite equal performance—and concludes that this is irrational. However, choice B provides a rational basis for this gap by presenting evidence that a quarterback's value to his employer is based on marketability, rather than simply performance. Thus, choice B is correct.

Choices C and D are incorrect because the author emphasizes that the *beauty gap* exists even when performance is equal. Therefore, the claim that attractiveness and charm may lead to improved performance, even if true, is irrelevant. Choice A is incorrect because it does not contradict the author's claim that the gap is irrational. Choice E is incorrect because the author references scientific studies in which aggregate data were compiled from test subjects' ratings of attractiveness, which provides an objective way to measure attractiveness for the purposes of a study.

11. **C.** The author's primary purpose is to present a theory developed by a team of biologists, choice C. Choices A and B are incorrect because the author does not make or endorse these claims. Choice D is a possible implication of the reported theory but not the author's primary purpose in writing the passage. Choice E is incorrect because the research was not based on a scientific experiment.

12. **A.** The author provides two examples—religion and the fleeting popularity of tube socks—of cultural phenomena that are *simply beyond the realm of explanation*. Thus, choice A is correct. Choice C is presented as an explainable phenomenon, and choice B is presented as the root cause of such phenomena. Choices D and E are not compared to the tube socks example in the passage.

13. **B.** The theory posits that cultural diversity is ultimately a consequence of disease; therefore, it logically follows that culturally diverse nations have been more affected by disease than more homogeneous nations. Thus, choice B is correct. Choice A is incorrect because poverty is presented as both an enabling factor and consequence of disease rather than as a primary cause; choice C is incorrect because the prevalence of disease is not presented as the only cause of multilingualism in societies. Choice D states the opposite of what the theory predicts, and choice E is incorrect because the theory presents disease as a cause of instability and xenophobia historically but not necessarily as a perpetuating factor in present-day societies.

14. **B.** In the third paragraph, the theory of how cultural differences arise is structured as follows: In situations where interactions with strangers are dangerous, people avoid strangers (to the point of being mean) and communicate with a narrower range of people.

The situation presented by the question is structurally similar to this theory, in that it describes a community in which people have started avoiding strangers and sticking to trusted acquaintances due to an increase in perceived danger associated with strangers. Therefore, choice B is correct. Choice A is incorrect because it does not fully describe this parallelism. Choice C is incorrect because it ignores the structural similarities between the situations. Choice D is incorrect because the impact of poverty on the development of distrust is not emphasized in the passage. Choice E is an incorrect characterization of both situations.

15. **C.** The correlative conjunction *not only* should always go with *but,* and preferably *but also,* which makes choices A and E incorrect. Choice B is too wordy, and choice D creates a fragment. Thus, choice C is correct.

16. **D.** The lobbyist claims that solar power would make traditional power sources obsolete, but fails to consider that solar power depends on the sun's rays reaching the panels. Thus, traditional power sources may still be needed. Choice D is correct. Choice A is incorrect because author bias does not affect the logic of the argument; choices B and E are incorrect because the lobbyist qualifies his argument with an *if* and does not claim that the statements are *not* speculative; and choice C is incorrect because it is directly contradicted in the passage (i.e., the first sentence addresses the cost of construction).

17. **B.** In the passage, the author provides some background on made-to-order clothing websites and then explains that the perception of these sites among domestic, independent tailors is that these websites will be bad for business. The correct answer must provide support for the author's claim that the perception is incorrect. Choice B does so by implying that the made-to-order websites would not hurt these tailors' core business, and may even provide a boost to their measurements business. Thus, choice B is correct. Choices A, C, and D are irrelevant to the business concerns of independent, domestic tailors, and choice E is illogical because the passage states that the concerned tailors are independent.

18. **B.** The original underlined portion contains two errors: *in* should be *to,* and *connects* should be *connect* because it is referring to a compound noun, which is plural. Only choice B corrects both of these errors.

19. **D.** The original underlined portion contains two diction errors. First, *me* should be used in place of *myself,* which means choices B and C are also incorrect. In addition, the original sentence implies that the associates were jealous of *the promotions*, rather than of Beth and the speaker for receiving the promotions. *Had been given* (past perfect) is the correct verb choice rather than *were given* (simple past tense), making choice E incorrect. Thus, choice D is correct.

20. **C.** The passage's main focus is on Sulzberger and his successful plan for transforming *The New York Times* into a national, then a digital, presence. Thus, choice C is correct. Choice A is incorrect because it focuses on one publishing unit within *The Times* rather than on Sulzberger and the company. Choice B is incorrect because the passage focuses on specific developments in *The Times'* strategy rather than on the general business. Choice D is incorrect because Sulzberger's story is not presented as a case study to guide other executives, nor does the passage focus on the dot-com crash, choice E.

21. **A.** The passage defines the *platform-agnostic* mantra as indifference to the specific platforms customers use to access one's product: *It didn't matter how you consumed your news so long as you were eating from his newspaper's plate.* Choice A most closely parallels this mind-set, as the record label encourages customers to consume its artists' music via nontraditional channels in addition to CDs. Choice B reflects the opposite of this strategy, and choice C does not refer to multiple channels of access and therefore is not logically consistent with the strategy. Choice D is less similar than choice A, because the restaurant only provides a limited menu of its products to takeout and delivery customers. In addition, the new "platforms" (takeout and delivery) that the restaurant is utilizing are still traditional platforms for consuming food from restaurants, rather than innovative new platforms. Choice E is incorrect because the store does not provide any new platforms for the purchase of its products.

22. **C.** The passage states, The Times, *like every other newspaper and magazine in the world, was confronted with the strange, new, virtual world of the Internet. Compared with some of his peers, Sulzberger was an early adopter.* This implies that *The Times* adapted to the change in the publishing landscape sooner than other newspapers. Thus, choice C is correct. Choice A is incorrect because the passage does not suggest that TimesSelect would have been successful over time; choice B expresses an opposite view of Sulzberger's efforts; choice D contradicts Sulzberger's "platform-agnostic" approach; and choice E is incorrect because the passage states that *The Times* had built a large online customer base by 1999.

23. **C.** The term refers to the *subsequent years* at the newspaper following 1999. Choice C is correct. Choices A and E each represent just one mutation or change that was part of the quagmire, and choice B is incorrect because the *subsequent years* at the newspaper spanned 1999 to 2008. Choice D is incorrect because the positive pace of change overall is not relevant to the negative difficulties the changes presented.

24. **B.** If patent law must apply to all industries, this fact would weaken the author's proposal to reform patent law for the technology sector alone. Uniform reform for all sectors could place some sectors at a disadvantage, such as the pharmaceutical sector, which relies on long-term patents. Thus, choice B is correct.

   Choices A and D are incorrect because they support the argument for patent law reform in the technology sector. Choice C in itself is not relevant unless choice B is also true; reforms in the technology sector alone would not affect the pharmaceutical sector. Choice E is incorrect because increased profits in the future is not a remedy for increased costs of short-term patent infringement litigation, which is the basis of the argument.

25. **E.** The original underlined portion and choices B and C contain a parallelism error. (*Fancy restaurants* is more parallel to *bright lights, beautiful people* than *the collection of fancy restaurants.*) Choices D and E fix this parallelism error, but choice E is the better choice as it is less wordy and awkward.

26. **A.** The passage states that the unprofitable NBA teams were losing money at the start of the lockout, which meant they would lose less for every missed game. It logically follows that the profitable NFL franchises would lose profits for every missed game. Thus, choice A is correct. Choice B is incorrect because many factors could influence how reasonable the respective negotiations were; the fact that NBA franchises were losing money does not mean the players were unreasonable. Choice C is incorrect because the passage does not refer to the skill of negotiators—external circumstances put NFL negotiators in a more favorable strategic position. Choice D is directly contradicted in the passage, and choice E is neither stated nor implied.

27. **C.** Person A uses the first bolded portion to describe a counterintuitive event: the rush to United States Treasuries immediately following the downgrade of United States debt. Person B uses the second bolded portion to provide a possible explanation for this event: investors tend to flock to safe investments during turbulent conditions, and United States Treasury bonds remain the safest investments on the market, despite the downgrade. Thus, choice C is correct. Choices A and B incorrectly characterize the purpose of the second portion in boldface, choice D incorrectly characterizes Person A's main argument, and choice E incorrectly characterizes both boldfaced portions.

28. **E.** The subject of the original sentence is *the deadline,* but the first phrase contains *his,* a modifier that refers to *Jason.* Choices A, B, and C retain this error. Choices D and E correct the error, but choice D changes the meaning by implying that Jason was no longer overwhelmed rather than less overwhelmed than before. Thus, choice E is correct.

29. **D.** The original underlined portion contains a verb tense error and is awkwardly constructed and wordy. The correct verb tense is future perfect—*I will have made*—as in choices B, D, and E (choice C incorrectly uses future tense). Choice B does not correct the wordiness of *that is my hope,* and choice E introduces an error in diction; *hopefully* properly means *I hope.* Thus, choice D is correct.

30. **B.** By claiming *It is unfortunate that EyeLight has decided to accept "bribes" from companies that want to increase their standing in its search index, because this compromises a way of navigating the Internet that is otherwise quite effective and objective,* the author implies an assumption that the payments *do* influence search standing. Thus, choice B is correct. Choice A is incorrect because the author does not claim that the three factors he mentions are the only ones or that the search engine is completely lacking in subjectivity. Choice C is not implied; financial solvency is not the issue. Choice D is explicitly stated, not an unstated assumption, and choice E is a conclusion rather than an assumption and cannot be inferred from the passage. (Another conclusion could be that *EyeLight* should not accept payments.)

31. **D.** There are two issues here: The original sentence is a run-on sentence, and it contains a pronoun error. Two complete, independent clauses cannot be connected by only a comma. In addition, *they* refers to *the corporation* in the first clause; *corporation* is a singular entity, so the correct pronoun is *it.* Therefore, choices B, C, and E are also incorrect. Choice D is the correct answer. It fixes the pronoun error and connects the two clauses with a semicolon, which should be used instead of a period to connect two independent clauses when the clauses are closely related.

32. **B.** The author assigns blame and responsibility for cleanup to the United States government without any evidence or justification. Thus, choice B is correct. Choice A is incorrect because the author does not state or imply that the issue is being addressed, and choice C is incorrect because it states the author's opinion rather than a criticism to which that opinion would be vulnerable. Choice D is irrelevant, and choice E is not stated or implied in the passage and its implication for the author's opinion—that no action is needed—is purely conjectural.

33. **C.** The original sentence contains a diction error; *between* should be used only to refer to two objects. As there are twelve board members, *among* should be used. Thus, choice B is incorrect. Choices C, D, and E correct this diction error, but choice D (as well as choice B) introduces a verb agreement error (using the plural *were* to refer to the singular *level of tension*), and choice E omits key information (the fact that there are twelve board members). Thus, choice C is correct.

34. A. The author posits risk should be viewed as *a two-sided coin,* with the risks on one side corresponding to the opportunities on the other. This implies that opportunity is inherently tied into risk. While the author warns against an excessively conservative approach, choice B is not implied. Choice C is incorrect because the passage implies that the ratio has increased at a consistent rate. Choice D is incorrect because the author advocates identifying and strategically mitigating threats rather than ignoring them. Choice E is incorrect because the two improvements listed have helped to lead to a climate in which there have *never been more threats or opportunities.*

35. C. Market capitalization is never mentioned or implied to be a concern of small business owners by the passage. Choice D is noted as the most prominent concern, while choices A, B, and E are all listed as additional concerns in the second paragraph.

36. C. The author's overall point—and final conclusion—is that *there have never been more threats or opportunities confronting U.S. small businesses,* and that these risks and rewards balance each other out, to an extent, providing for a relatively attractive overall climate. Choices A and E present claims about the majority of small business owners that are never implied by the author, while choice B is only a secondary point of the passage. Choice D is an exaggeration of the author's position.

37. C. The theory calls for a market correction on overvalued stock and would be significantly weakened if it could be shown that a market correction was no longer needed. Thus, choice C is correct. Choice A is incorrect because it would not eliminate the need for a market correction. Choice B supports rather than weakens the author's argument. Choice D is incorrect because it is not supported in the passage. Choice E is not supported in the passage and would not affect the theory regardless.

38. D. The original sentence is wordy and awkward in addition to containing an idiomatic error (*farther* refers to distance, while *further* refers to degree), making choices A and E incorrect. Also, the object *raise* requires an article, *a,* which makes choices A and B incorrect. Choice C omits key information. Only choice D corrects the idiomatic error, adds the article, and reduces excessive wordiness without changing the meaning or omitting key information. Thus, choice D is correct.

39. E. The congressperson assumes that debt ceilings were the cause of the economic collapses in some countries that happen to have imposed debt ceilings, when other factors may have caused the economic collapses. Thus, choice E is correct.

Choice A is incorrect because the argument is specifically against a debt ceiling, so any other proposals would be irrelevant. Choice B is incorrect because nothing suggests that this assumption is unreasonable or flawed; that is, it follows that unsustainable borrowing leads to insolvency. Choice C is incorrect because the congressperson does present evidence to back the claim (albeit limited evidence). Choice D is incorrect because the congressperson does not confuse the concepts of cause and effect.

40. C. The statistics cited in the passage strengthen rather than weaken the author's argument. All the other choices weaken the argument or call into question the impact of the author's bias on the argument. Thus, choice C is correct.

41. B. The passage argues that the withdrawal rate is more important than the savings rate, because the size of the nest egg is influenced by factors such as market conditions (not just the savings rate). However, choice B indicates that due to the self-correcting nature of markets over time, the nominal size of the nest egg at retirement may not be all-important; it implies that if one saves at the safe rate, one will be comfortable during retirement, regardless of market conditions at the time of retirement. Thus, choice B is correct.

Choice A is incorrect because it does not contradict the importance of the withdrawal rate; it just implies that the safe withdrawal rate may be slightly higher than stated in the passage. Choices C and D are irrelevant to the issue at hand—whether the withdrawal rate or the savings rate is fundamentally more important in maintaining a sustainable retirement fund. Choice E is incorrect because it would strengthen rather than weaken the author's point.

Section 4: Integrated Reasoning

Question 1

1a. **Yes** In Las Vegas, the average price of a house was 228.55 in March 2007 and 177.18 in February 2008:

City	Mar 07	Feb 08	Mar 08	Mar 07 vs. Mar 08	Feb 08 vs. Mar 08
Las Vegas	228.55	177.18	169.31	−25.9%	−4.44%

Thus, between March of 2007 and February of 2008, housing prices decreased by 51.37. To calculate the percent decrease, divide this figure by the starting price of 228.55.

$$51.37 \div 228.55 = \text{(approximately) } 0.225 = 22.5\%$$

Therefore, the housing prices in Las Vegas decreased by more than 20% from March 2007 to February 2008.

1b. **No** Sorting by *Mar 07 vs. Mar 08* moves the following five rows to the top of the table:

City	Mar 07	Feb 08	Mar 08	Mar 07 vs. Mar 08	Feb 08 vs. Mar 08
San Francisco	237.14	174.54	168.38	**−29.0%**	−3.53%
Las Vegas	228.55	177.18	169.31	**−25.9%**	−4.44%
Miami	276.89	218.74	208.88	**−24.6%**	−4.51%
Phoenix	216.86	172.72	166.97	**−23.0%**	−3.33%
Los Angeles	264.58	214.83	207.11	**−21.7%**	−3.59%

Therefore, five cities, not four, showed a reduction in housing prices greater than 20%.

1c. **Yes** Sorting the table by *Feb 08* moves the following three rows to the top of the table:

City	Mar 07	Feb 08	Mar 08	Mar 07 vs. Mar 08	Feb 08 vs. Mar 08
Detroit	116.44	**97.61**	95.57	−17.9%	−2.09%
Cleveland	117.60	**106.82**	106.42	−9.5%	−0.37%
Dallas	123.10	**117.72**	119.08	−3.3%	+1.16%

Therefore, Detroit, Cleveland, and Dallas had the three lowest housing prices in February 2008. Calculate the mean average price among these three cities as follows:

$$(97.61 + 106.82 + 117.72) \div 3 = 107.38$$

This amount is less than $110,000.

Question 2

2a. **Angela's Crew: 15 days**

2b. **Brent's Crew: 30 days**

The total job consists of 420 rooms. Of this, the owner will paint 90 rooms (3 rooms a day × 5 days a week × 6 weeks = 90 rooms), so you can calculate the remaining rooms as follows:

$$420 - 90 = 330$$

Thus, 330 total rooms must be accounted for as a combination of work by Angela's crew and Brent's crew, so this is the *target number.*

Angela's crew can paint 8 rooms per day, and Brent's crew can paint 7 rooms per day. The following table shows the number of rooms that each crew can paint in each possible block of 5 days:

Angela's Crew	Brent's Crew	Number of Days
40	35	5
80	70	10
120	105	15
160	140	20
200	175	25
240	210	30

Use the following equation for your calculation:

$$330 - \text{Brent's crew} = \text{Angela's crew}$$

You can limit your calculations by noticing that every number of rooms in the column for Angela's crew is divisible by 10, and the target number is 330, which is also divisible by 10. Thus, the correct number of rooms for Brent's crew must also be divisible by 10. Test these three values in the column for Brent's crew using the equation above:
$$330 - 70 = 260$$
$$330 - 140 = 190$$
$$\mathbf{330 - 210 = 120}$$

Thus, the correct combination is as follows:

15 days of Angela's crew + 30 days of Brent's crew + 30 days of owner

$$= 120 \text{ rooms} + 210 \text{ rooms} + 90 \text{ rooms}$$
$$= 420 \text{ rooms}$$

Question 3

3a. **between 50 cm and 100 cm** The second bar in each group represents rainfall in 2004. Thus, the approximate rainfall in each of the six months was 130 cm, 145 cm, 160 cm, 20 cm, 5 cm, and 5 cm. Calculate the mean as follows:

$$(130 + 145 + 160 + 20 + 5 + 5) = 465 \div 6 = 77.5$$

Therefore, the mean monthly rainfall for January through June was between 50 cm and 100 cm.

3b. **100 cm** In January, from 2003 to 2004, the graph shows a lowest monthly rainfall of approximately 30 cm in 2003 and a highest monthly rainfall of approximately 130 cm in 2004. Thus, the range of values is approximately 100 cm.

Question 4

4a. Southeast Asia The first bar in each set of three represents the incidence of diabetes among people from 20 to 39 years old. The tallest of these is in the set of bars representing the region of Southeast Asia.

4b. North America and Caribbean The third bar in each set of three bars represents the incidence of diabetes among people from 60 to 79 years old. To find the median, place each region in order from approximate lowest to highest.

AFR (2.5), MENA (6), SACA (7), NAC (12.5), SEA (16), WP (26), EUR (30)

The region that is in the middle of the range represents NAC - North America and Caribbean.

Question 5

5a. CableLife: 50,000

5b. WorldView: 90,000

Currently, the market share is as follows:

CableLife:	60% of 1,200,000 = 720,000
WorldView	40% of 1,200,000 = 480,000

Thus, WorldView needs to gain 240,000 (720,000 – 480,000) more customers per year than CableLife over 6 years. Dividing 240,000 by 6 results in 40,000, so WorldView needs to gain 40,000 customers per year.

Use the following equation for your calculation:

$$\text{WorldView} - 40{,}000 = \text{CableLife}$$

Test the values for WorldView using the equation above, starting with the highest value until you find a combination that works:

$$120{,}000 - 40{,}000 = 80{,}000$$
$$100{,}000 - 40{,}000 = 60{,}000$$
$$\mathbf{90{,}000 - 40{,}000 = 50{,}000}$$

The implication is that the market itself is growing, with new customers being taken on by both companies, but at a faster rate by WorldView. Thus, the correct combination is as follows:

$$720{,}000 + 6\left(\mathbf{50{,}000 \text{ CableLife customers}}\right) = 480{,}000 + 6\left(\mathbf{90{,}000 \text{ WorldView customers}}\right)$$
$$720{,}000 + 300{,}000 \text{ CableLife customers} = 480{,}000 + 540{,}000 \text{ WorldView customers}$$
$$1{,}020{,}000 \text{ CableLife customers} = 1{,}020{,}000 \text{ WorldView customers}$$

Question 6

6a. Yes Sorting the table by *Comb. Fed/Prov Top Marginal Rate* moves the following four rows to the top of the table.

Province	Personal Income Tax – Statutory Range		Comb. Fed/Prov	Corporate Income Tax		Small Business Tax	Sales Tax
	Lowest Rate	Highest Rate	Top Marginal Rate	General	M&P		
Alberta	10.00	10.00	39.00	10.0	10.0	3.0	0.0
New Brunswick	9.10	12.70	**41.70**	10.0	10.0	5.0	8.0
Newfoundland	7.70	13.30	**42.30**	14.0	5.0	4.0	8.0
British Columbia	5.06	14.70	43.70	10.0	10.0	2.5	7.0

Therefore, exactly two provinces have a combined federal/provincial top marginal tax rate between 41% and 43%.

6b. Yes Sorting the table by *Corporate Income Tax – General* moves the following four rows to the top of the table:

Province	Personal Income Tax – Statutory Range		Comb. Fed/Prov	Corporate Income Tax		Small Business Tax	Sales Tax
	Lowest Rate	Highest Rate	Top Marginal Rate	General	M&P		
Alberta	10.00	10.00	39.00	**10.0**	10.0	3.0	0.0
British Columbia	5.06	14.70	43.70	**10.0**	10.0	2.5	7.0
New Brunswick	9.10	12.70	41.70	**10.0**	10.0	5.0	8.0
Ontario	5.05	11.16	46.41	11.5	10.0	4.5	8.0

Therefore, exactly three provinces have a general corporate income tax of 10.0%, which equals the sales tax in Nova Scotia.

6c. Yes Sorting the table by *Small Business Tax* moves the following six rows to the top of the table:

Province	Personal Income Tax – Statutory Range		Comb. Fed/Prov	Corporate Income Tax		Small Business Tax	Sales Tax
	Lowest Rate	Highest Rate	Top Marginal Rate	General	M&P		
Manitoba	10.80	17.40	46.40	12.0	12.0	**0.0**	7.0
Prince Edward Island	9.80	16.70	47.37	16.0	16.0	**1.0**	10.0
British Columbia	5.06	14.70	43.70	10.0	10.0	**2.5**	7.0
Alberta	10.00	10.00	39.00	10.0	10.0	**3.0**	0.0
Newfoundland	7.70	13.30	42.30	14.0	5.0	**4.0**	8.0
Nova Scotia	8.79	21.00	50.00	16.0	16.0	4.5	10.0

Therefore, exactly five of the ten provinces have a small business tax rate under 4.5%. Therefore, if one province was picked at random, the probability that it would have a small business tax rate under 4.5% would be 0.5.

Questions 7–8

The first message raises a question as to whether objective adult size correlates with intelligence in rhesus monkeys. The second message confirms that this correlation exists, but brings in malnutrition as an explanatory factor. Malnutrition correlates positively with stunted growth, and both of these correlate negatively with both objective adult size and intelligence.

The following chart captures these relationships:

Positive correlations	**Positive correlations**
Adult size	Stunted growth
← **negative correlations** →	
Intelligence	Malnutrition

7a. **Yes** Adult size correlates positively with intelligence, so a larger rhesus monkey is statistically likely to be more intelligent than a smaller one.

7b. **Yes** Message #2 clarifies that malnutrition "accounts entirely" for the positive correlation between adult size and intelligence. Thus, a small rhesus monkey that has not experienced malnutrition is statistically likely to be as intelligent as a large rhesus monkey.

7c. **Yes** In the last paragraph of Message #2, Dr. Kranz maintains a causal connection between nutrition and intelligence.

8. **A** The chart above shows that adult size correlates positively with intelligence.

Question 9

9a. Public Works Crew: 40 hours

9b. Parks Crew: 32 hours

The total job consists of 2,120 feet of cable. The crew from the Department of Public Works has already logged 80 hours on this job at 15 feet per hour, which accounts for 1,200 feet. Thus, you can calculate the remaining distance as follows:

$$2,120 - 1,200 = 920$$

Thus, 920 feet of cable must be accounted for as a combination of work by both crews, so this is the *target number*.

The Department of Public Works crew can replace 15 feet per hour, and the Parks Department crew can replace 10 feet per hour. The following table shows the amount of cable (in feet) that each crew can replace in the given number of hours:

Public Works Crew	Parks Crew	Number of Hours
120	80	8
240	160	16
360	240	24
480	320	32
600	400	40
720	480	48

Use the following equation for your calculation:

$$920 - \text{Public Works} = \text{Parks}$$

Test the six values in the column for the Public Works crew using the equation above:

$$920 - 120 = 800$$
$$920 - 240 = 680$$
$$920 - 360 = 560$$
$$920 - 480 = 440$$
$$\mathbf{920 - 600 = 320}$$
$$920 - 720 = 200$$

Thus, the correct combination is as follows:

40 Public Works hours + 32 Parks hours + 80 previous Public Works hours

= 600 feet + 320 feet + 1,200 feet

= 2,120 feet

Questions 10–11

Message #1 states that the cost of a cleaning that excludes three bedrooms and a bathroom would cost $70 on a weekly basis and $85 on a bi-weekly basis. In Message #2, an offer is made to add $20 to this cost for a Friday cleaning. Thus, you can chart these base costs as follows:

	Non-Friday	Friday
Weekly cleaning:	$70	$90
Bi-weekly cleaning:	$85	$105

Note that these base costs *exclude* the three bedrooms and the master bathroom. According to Message #2, each additional bedroom costs $5 and the additional bathroom costs $10.

10a. Yes A bi-weekly Friday cleaning has a base cost of $105. Adding in three bedrooms for $15 ($5 each) and a bathroom for $10 brings this total up to $130, which is more than $125.

10b. No The base cost of a weekly Friday cleaning is $90. Adding in three bedrooms at $5 each ($15) brings the cost up to $105, which is less than $115.

10c. Yes A bi-weekly non-Friday cleaning would have a base cost of $85. Adding in the master bathroom for $10 brings the cost up to $95, which is less than $100.

11. D The most expensive option would be a bi-weekly cleaning (base rate of $85) on Friday (plus $20) that includes all three bedrooms ($5 × 3 = $15) and the master bathroom (plus $10):

$$\$85 + \$20 + \$15 + \$10 = \$130$$

Therefore, the correct answer is D.

Question 12

12a. **Yes** Begin by sorting the column *2010 Passengers*:

Airport Code	Country	2010 Passengers	2010 % +/−	2009 Passengers	2009 % +/−	2008 Passengers	2008 % +/−
ATL	US	**89,331,622**	+1.5%	88,032,086	−2.2%	90,039,280	+0.7%
PEK	China	**73,891,801**	+13.0%	65,372,012	+16.9%	55,937,289	+4.4%
ORD	US	**66,665,390**	+3.9%	64,158,343	−7.5%	69,353,876	−9.0%
LHR	UK	**65,884,143**	−0.2%	66,037,578	−1.5%	67,056,379	−1.5%
HND	Japan	**64,069,098**	+3.4%	61,903,656	−7.2%	66,754,829	−0.2%
LAX	US	58,915,100	+4.2%	56,520,843	−5.0%	59,497,539	−4.7%
CDG	France	58,167,062	+0.4%	57,906,866	−4.9%	60,874,681	+1.6%
DFW	US	56,905,066	+1.6%	56,030,457	−1.9%	57,093,187	−4.5%
FRA	Germany	53,009,221	+4.1%	50,932,840	−4.7%	53,467,450	−1.3%
DEN	US	52,211,242	+4.1%	50,167,485	−2.1%	51,245,334	+2.8%
HKG	China	50,410,819	+10.6%	45,558,807	−4.8%	47,857,746	+1.7%
MAD	Spain	49,786,202	+3.2%	48,250,784	−5.1%	50,824,435	−2.4%
DXB	UAE	47,180,628	+15.4%	40,901,752	+9.2%	37,441,440	+9.0%
JFK	US	46,495,876	+1.3%	45,915,069	−4.0%	47,807,816	+0.2%
AMS	Netherlands	45,211,749	+3.8%	43,570,370	−8.1%	47,430,019	−0.8%
CGK	Indonesia	43,981,022	+18.4%	37,143,719	+15.5%	32,172,114	+0.6%

This sort shows that the five busiest airports in 2010 were ATL, PEK, ORD, LHR, and HND. (Strategy hint: Jot down this information before performing the next sort.) Now, sort by the column *2008 Passengers*:

Airport Code	Country	2010 Passengers	2010 % +/−	2009 Passengers	2009 % +/−	2008 Passengers	2008 % +/−
ATL	US	89,331,622	+1.5%	88,032,086	−2.2%	**90,039,280**	+0.7%
ORD	US	66,665,390	+3.9%	64,158,343	−7.5%	**69,353,876**	−9.0%
LHR	UK	65,884,143	−0.2%	66,037,578	−1.5%	**67,056,379**	−1.5%
HND	Japan	64,069,098	+3.4%	61,903,656	−7.2%	**66,754,829**	−0.2%
CDG	France	58,167,062	+0.4%	57,906,866	−4.9%	**60,874,681**	+1.6%
LAX	US	58,915,100	+4.2%	56,520,843	−5.0%	59,497,539	−4.7%
DFW	US	56,905,066	+1.6%	56,030,457	−1.9%	57,093,187	−4.5%
PEK	China	73,891,801	+13.0%	65,372,012	+16.9%	55,937,289	+4.4%
FRA	Germany	53,009,221	+4.1%	50,932,840	−4.7%	53,467,450	−1.3%
DEN	US	52,211,242	+4.1%	50,167,485	−2.1%	51,245,334	+2.8%
MAD	Spain	49,786,202	+3.2%	48,250,784	−5.1%	50,824,435	−2.4%
HKG	China	50,410,819	+10.6%	45,558,807	−4.8%	47,857,746	+1.7%
JFK	US	46,495,876	+1.3%	45,915,069	−4.0%	47,807,816	+0.2%
AMS	Netherlands	45,211,749	+3.8%	43,570,370	−8.1%	47,430,019	−0.8%
DXB	UAE	47,180,628	+15.4%	40,901,752	+9.2%	37,441,440	+9.0%
CGK	Indonesia	43,981,022	+18.4%	37,143,719	+15.5%	32,172,114	+0.6%

This shows that the five busiest airports in 2008 were ATL, ORD, LHR, HND, and CDG. Thus, four airports—ATL, ORD, LHR, and HND—were among the top five busiest in both 2008 and 2010, so the statement is true.

12b. **No** To answer this question efficiently, eyeball the table to look for a year in which there were the fewest positive percentages for (increases in) passenger traffic. Notice that in 2009, only three airports had increased passenger traffic. So, sort the table by the column *2009 % +/–*:

Airport Code	Country	2010		2009		2008	
		Passengers	% +/–	Passengers	% +/–	Passengers	% +/–
PEK	China	73,891,801	+13.0%	65,372,012	+16.9%	55,937,289	+4.4%
CGK	Indonesia	43,981,022	+18.4%	37,143,719	+15.5%	32,172,114	+0.6%
DXB	UAE	47,180,628	**+15.4%**	40,901,752	**+9.2%**	37,441,440	**+9.0%**
LHR	UK	65,884,143	–0.2%	66,037,578	–1.5%	67,056,379	–1.5%
DFW	US	56,905,066	+1.6%	56,030,457	–1.9%	57,093,187	–4.5%
DEN	US	52,211,242	+4.1%	50,167,485	–2.1%	51,245,334	+2.8%
ATL	US	89,331,622	+1.5%	88,032,086	–2.2%	90,039,280	+0.7%
JFK	US	46,495,876	+1.3%	45,915,069	–4.0%	47,807,816	+0.2%
FRA	Germany	53,009,221	+4.1%	50,932,840	–4.7%	53,467,450	–1.3%
HKG	China	50,410,819	+10.6%	45,558,807	–4.8%	47,857,746	+1.7%
CDG	France	58,167,062	+0.4%	57,906,866	–4.9%	60,874,681	+1.6%
MAD	Spain	49,786,202	+3.2%	48,250,784	–5.1%	50,824,435	–2.4%
LAX	US	58,915,100	+4.2%	56,520,843	–5.0%	59,497,539	–4.7%
ORD	US	66,665,390	+3.9%	64,158,343	–7.5%	69,353,876	–9.0%
HND	Japan	64,069,098	+3.4%	61,903,656	–7.2%	66,754,829	–0.2%
AMS	Netherlands	45,211,749	+3.8%	43,570,370	–8.1%	47,430,019	–0.8%

This sort reveals that three airports had increases in passenger traffic that year. Of these three airports, DXB had increases greater than 5% all three years. Therefore, the statement is false.

12c. **Yes** Begin by sorting the column *Country*:

World's Busiest Airports by Passenger Traffic							
Airport Code	Country	2010		2009		2008	
		Passengers	% +/–	Passengers	% +/–	Passengers	% +/–
ATL	US	89,331,622	+1.5%	88,032,086	–2.2%	90,039,280	**+0.7%**
DEN	US	52,211,242	+4.1%	50,167,485	–2.1%	51,245,334	**+2.8%**
DFW	US	56,905,066	+1.6%	56,030,457	–1.9%	57,093,187	–4.5%
JFK	US	46,495,876	+1.3%	45,915,069	–4.0%	47,807,816	**+0.2%**
LAX	US	58,915,100	+4.2%	56,520,843	–5.0%	59,497,539	–4.7%
ORD	US	66,665,390	+3.9%	64,158,343	–7.5%	69,353,876	–9.0%

This brings the six U.S. airports together in the table. Of these, three showed a percent increase in passengers in 2008, which reflects the change from 2007 to 2008. Thus, the probability that a randomly selected U.S. airport would have had an increase in passengers from 2007 to 2008 would be 0.5, which is greater than 0.3.

Final Preparation

One Week Before the Exam

1. **Clear your schedule one week before the exam.** Try to avoid scheduling events during this week so that you can focus on your preparation.

2. **GMAT website.** Visit the GMAT website at www.mba.com for updated exam information. It will help you to know what to expect on the GMAT. Take the time to watch the video on the GMAT website, "What to Expect the Day of the Exam," http://www.mba.com/the-gmat/test-day.aspx.

3. **Review your notes.** Gather together everything that you have studied and review your notes. List topics for each section that require at least one more look. Gauge the priority for each area of review. Make sure that you know the directions and strategies for each question type.

4. **Practice tests.** Allow yourself enough time to review the practice problems you have already completed from this study guide and CD-ROM. Don't forget to time yourself to increase your ability to solve problems within time constraints.

5. **Practice computer skills.** Although you will only need minimal computer skills, computer-simulated practice is integral to your understanding of the exam format. If you haven't taken the online practice test, go to the GMAT website at www.mba.com/gmatprep and download the free software.

6. **Testing center.** Make sure that you are familiar with the driving directions and where the parking facilities are located that are near to the testing center.

7. **List of schools.** This is a good time to make a list of schools where you would like to send your scores. You won't be able to take a list of schools with you into the test center, but it's a good idea to decide which schools you plan to send your scores to ahead of time.

8. **Relax the night before the exam.** The evening before the exam, try to get a good night's sleep. Trying to cram a year's worth of reading and studying into one night can cause you to feel emotionally and physically exhausted. Save your energy for exam day.

Exam Day

9. **Arrive early.** Give yourself plenty of time to arrive on schedule (at least 30 minutes early). Be prepared to wait in line before you check in at the testing center.

10. **Dress appropriately to adapt to any room temperature.** If you dress in layers, you can always adjust clothing to adapt to warmer temperatures.

11. **Identification.** Remember to bring the required identification documents: valid photo-bearing ID and your appointment confirmation letter that was emailed to you.

12. **Electronic devices.** Leave all electronic devices at home or in your car (cell phone, smartphone, PDA, calculator, etc.). You may also be asked to remove your watch during the exam.

13. **Don't get stuck on any one question.** Never spend more than $1\frac{1}{2}$ to 2 minutes on a multiple-choice question.

14. **Guess** if a problem is too difficult or takes too much time.

15. **Use the erasable noteboard as a test-taking advantage.** You will be given five noteboards when you arrive, and can ask for more if needed. Take notes, perform calculations, and redraw diagrams to help you jog your memory to answer questions. You must return all noteboards at the end of the test session.

Sources

Sincere appreciation is extended to the following authors and publishers for allowing the use of excerpts for reading passages.

Barcott, Bruce. "Kermode Bear: Spirit Bear." *National Geographic* (August, 2011) pp. 46–47. (Diagnostic Test)

Carnegie Institute for Science. "Sea Cucumbers: Dissolving coral reefs?" *Carnegie Institute for Science* (Online News Section) December, 2011. (Practice Test 3)

Dunn, Robert. "The Culture of Being Rude: A new biological theory states that cultural behavior is not just a regional quirk, but a defense against the spread of disease." *Smithsonian Institution,* from Smithsonian.com (August 2009). (Practice Test 1)

The Economist. "Falling short: Too much, too young." *The Economist Newspaper Limited.* (April 7, 2011) p. 6 (Chapter 5)

Hawken, Paul, Amory Lovins, and L. Hunter Lovins. *Natural Capitalism: Creating the next industrial revolution.* Little, Brown and Company, 1999. (Chapter 5)

Irion, Robert W. "Something New Under the Sun." *Smithsonian* (April, 2011). (Chapter 5)

Joltes, Richard E. "The Myth of the Empty Continent." *History Magazine,* Aug/Sept 2011. (Diagnostic Test)

Kifayat, Kashif, Madjid Merabti, and Qi Shi. "Future Security Challenges in Cloud Computing." *International Journal of Multimedia Intelligence and Security*, 2010: 1(4). (Practice Test 1)

Krell, Eric. "The State of Small Business: Rolling with the punches and upping the ante." *Baylor Business Review*, 2011: 30 (1). (Practice Test 1)

Lipid, Hadas, et. al. "Scientists Discover an Organizing Principle for our Sense of Smell Based on Pleasantness." This research was carried out by Drs. Hadas Lipid, Sagit Shushan, and Anton Plotkin in the group of Prof. Noam Sobel, together with Dr. Elad Schneidman of the Weizmann Institute's Neurobiology Department, Dr. Yehudah Roth of Wolfson Hospital in Holon, Prof. Hillary Voet of the Hebrew University of Jerusalem, and Prof. Thomas Hummel of Dresden University, Germany. *Weizmann Institute of Science,* September 2011: 10.1038. (Practice Test 4)

Mill, John Stuart. "The Subjection of Women." Longmans, Green and Company, 1869. (Chapter 5)

Mnookin, Seth. "The Kingdom and the Paywall." *New York Magazine,* August 1, 2011. (Practice Test 1)

Montgomery, Sy. "Sharks." *Los Angeles Times,* Feb. 25, 1991. (Practice Test 3)

Reinhardt, Andy. "Ericsson Charts Changing Usage of TV." Retrieved from blog on "Europe Insight" *Bloomberg's Businessweek*, August 25, 2010. (Practice Test 4)

Stamm, James R. *A Short History of Spanish Literature.* New York University Press, 1979. (Chapter 5)

Upton, Albert. *Design for Thinking: A first book in semantics.* Stanford University Press, 1969. (Chapter 5)

Welch, David. "Cadillac and Audi Ham It Up in a Battle of the Hippest." from "The Auto Beat" in *Bloomberg's Businessweek,* January 27, 2011. (Practice Test 4)

Wellness Newsletter. "Brain Push-Ups." *University of California, Berkeley Wellness Letter* (October 2011). (Practice Test 3)

Winograd, Morley and Michael D. Hais. "Millennial Generation Challenges Religion in America." *The Christian Science Monitor,* September 26, 2011. (Practice Test 4)

John Wiley & Sons, Inc.
End-User License Agreement

READ THIS. You should carefully read these terms and conditions before opening the software packet(s) included with this book "Book". This is a license agreement "Agreement" between you and John Wiley & Sons, Inc. "Wiley". By opening the accompanying software packet(s), you acknowledge that you have read and accept the following terms and conditions. If you do not agree and do not want to be bound by such terms and conditions, promptly return the Book and the unopened software packet(s) to the place you obtained them for a full refund.

1. **License Grant.** Wiley grants to you (either an individual or entity) a nonexclusive license to use one copy of the enclosed software program(s) (collectively, the "Software") solely for your own personal or business purposes on a single computer (whether a standard computer or a workstation component of a multi-user network). The Software is in use on a computer when it is loaded into temporary memory (RAM) or installed into permanent memory (hard disk, CD-ROM, or other storage device). Wiley reserves all rights not expressly granted herein.

2. **Ownership.** Wiley is the owner of all right, title, and interest, including copyright, in and to the compilation of the Software recorded on the physical packet included with this Book "Software Media". Copyright to the individual programs recorded on the Software Media is owned by the author or other authorized copyright owner of each program. Ownership of the Software and all proprietary rights relating thereto remain with Wiley and its licensers.

3. **Restrictions on Use and Transfer.**

   (a) You may only (i) make one copy of the Software for backup or archival purposes, or (ii) transfer the Software to a single hard disk, provided that you keep the original for backup or archival purposes. You may not (i) rent or lease the Software, (ii) copy or reproduce the Software through a LAN or other network system or through any computer subscriber system or bulletin-board system, or (iii) modify, adapt, or create derivative works based on the Software.

   (b) You may not reverse engineer, decompile, or disassemble the Software. You may transfer the Software and user documentation on a permanent basis, provided that the transferee agrees to accept the terms and conditions of this Agreement and you retain no copies. If the Software is an update or has been updated, any transfer must include the most recent update and all prior versions.

4. **Restrictions on Use of Individual Programs.** You must follow the individual requirements and restrictions detailed for each individual program on the Software Media. These limitations are also contained in the individual license agreements recorded on the Software Media. These limitations may include a requirement that after using the program for a specified period of time, the user must pay a registration fee or discontinue use. By opening the Software packet(s), you agree to abide by the licenses and restrictions for these individual programs that are detailed on the Software Media. None of the material on this Software Media or listed in this Book may ever be redistributed, in original or modified form, for commercial purposes.

5. **Limited Warranty.**

   (a) Wiley warrants that the Software and Software Media are free from defects in materials and workmanship under normal use for a period of sixty (60) days from the date of purchase of this Book. If Wiley receives notification within the warranty period of defects in materials or workmanship, Wiley will replace the defective Software Media.

   (b) WILEY AND THE AUTHOR(S) OF THE BOOK DISCLAIM ALL OTHER WARRANTIES, EXPRESS OR IMPLIED, INCLUDING WITHOUT LIMITATION IMPLIED WARRANTIES OF MERCHANTABILITY AND FITNESS FOR A PARTICULAR PURPOSE, WITH RESPECT TO THE SOFTWARE, THE PROGRAMS, THE SOURCE CODE CONTAINED THEREIN, AND/OR THE TECHNIQUES DESCRIBED IN THIS BOOK. WILEY DOES NOT WARRANT THAT THE FUNCTIONS CONTAINED IN THE SOFTWARE WILL MEET YOUR REQUIREMENTS OR THAT THE OPERATION OF THE SOFTWARE WILL BE ERROR FREE.

   (c) This limited warranty gives you specific legal rights, and you may have other rights that vary from jurisdiction to jurisdiction.